MAILER

BOOKS BY MARY V. DEARBORN

Pocahontas's Daughters:
Gender and Ethnicity in American Culture

Love in the Promised Land:
The Story of Anzia Yezierska and John Dewey

The Happiest Man Alive:
A Biography of Henry Miller

Queen of Bohemia:
The Life of Louise Bryant

MAILER

A Biography

Mary V. Dearborn

HOUGHTON MIFFLIN COMPANY

BOSTON • NEW YORK

1999

TO ERIC

For information about permission to reproduce selections
from this book, write to Permissions, Houghton Mifflin Company,
215 Park Avenue South, New York, New York 10003.

Library of Congress Cataloging-in-Publication Data
Dearborn, Mary V.
Mailer : a biography / Mary V. Dearborn.
p.   cm.
Includes bibliographical references (p.   ) and index.
ISBN 0-395-73655-2
1. Mailer, Norman.   2. Authors, American — 20th century
Biography.   3. Journalists — United States Biography.   I. Title.
PS3525.A4152Z635   1999
813'.54 — dc21   99-32214 [B] CIP

Printed in the United States of America

QUM 10 9 8 7 6 5 4 3 2 1

The author is grateful for permission to quote from the following
works: *The Armies of the Night,* copyright © 1968 by Norman Mailer,
reprinted by permission of Dutton Signet, a division of Penguin
Putnam Inc. *Advertisements for Myself,* copyright © 1959 by Norman
Mailer; *Cannibals and Christians,* copyright © 1966 by Norman
Mailer; *Deaths for the Ladies (and other disasters),* copyright © 1962 by
Norman Mailer; *Existential Errands,* copyright © 1972 by Norman
Mailer; *Of a Fire on the Moon,* copyright © 1970 by Norman Mailer;
The Presidential Papers, copyright © 1963 by Norman Mailer; and
The Prisoner of Sex, copyright © 1971 by Norman Mailer, all reprinted
by permission of the Wylie Agency, Inc.

Acknowledgments

When I contacted Norman Mailer about this project, he said that he would neither help nor hinder me in my work, borrowing a phrase Samuel Beckett used to biographer Deirdre Bair. He has done neither, though he has been unfailingly gracious throughout. Mine is not an authorized biography; Robert Lucid has long been Mailer's authorized biographer, and Mailer has asked him and Michael Lennon to be his literary executors. As such, they have control of Mailer's unpublished writings and a vast archive of Mailer-related materials. They agreed to let me see some of their holdings, for which I am grateful.

I made a decision very early on that I did not want to invade Mailer's privacy by speaking to his immediate family members, unless they let it be known that they were willing to talk to me. I am very grateful to Beverly Bentley for bravely agreeing to meet with me and review some very painful times. Her comments and recollections have immeasurably improved this book. Similarly, Carole Wagner Mallory took the time to detail the story of her role in Norman Mailer's life, rehearsing an often difficult tale.

Of the many individuals who granted me interviews or otherwise aided me in my five years of work on this book, I would like to thank Lew Allen, David Amram, Bill Ashley, Marvin Barrett, Bowden Broadwater, Phil Davis, the late Ormonde de Kay, Jr., Lina Delano, Susan Dichter, Roger Donald, Ann Douglas, Jason Epstein, Ed Fancher, Dan Fenn, Eileen Finletter, Ivan Fisher, Steve Fishman, Ralph Graves, Morris Gray, Lenny Green, Thomas Griffiths, Michael Hargraves, Ellen Hawkes, Janet Heettner, Daphne Hellman, Fritz Jacobi, Marc Jaffe, Paul Jenkins, Fred Kaplan, Myron Kaufmann, Harrison Kinney, John Klotz, Richard Kostelanetz, Lori LeGendre, Alfred Leslie, Legs McNeil, Thomas Maier, Peter Manso, Thierry Marignac, Charles Michaud, Mark Milburn, Mark Mirsky, Bob Moskin, Keith Nightenhelser, Dave Oates, Carl Oglesby, D. A. Pennebaker, Norman Podhoretz, Ned Polsky, Bern Porter, Nick Proferes, Ellen Ray, George Richardson, Carl Rollyson, Barney Rosset, Rosie Rowbotham, George Scombulis, Richard Stratton,

John Szwed, Jerry Tallmer, Martha Thomases, Amanda Vaill, Nicholas von Hoffman, Bill Ward, Richard Weinberg, Jan Welt, Dennis Wrong, David X. Young, and Harriet Sohmers Zwerdling, as well as several individuals who asked not to be named.

Like every biographer, I am grateful to those who have done earlier work. I am particularly indebted to Hilary Mills's *Mailer: A Biography* (1982), Carl Rollyson's *The Lives of Norman Mailer: A Biography* (1991), and Peter Manso's *Mailer: His Life and Times* (1985). In publishing the interviews that make up his oral biography (including many people now dead or inaccessible to others), Manso, especially, has created a rich mine of information for future biographical scholars and cultural historians and an invaluable source for my own work.

For help with photographs, I am grateful to Debbie Goodsite, who donated her skills as a photo researcher to help me with the initial layout of the photo section of this book. I also received help from Carolyn McMahon at AP/Wide World, Larry Schwartz at Archive, Kathy-Ann Williams and Norman Currie at Corbis-Bettmann, Carrie Chalmers at Magnum, Lauren Rosenblum at *Women's Wear Daily*, Allan Reuben at Culver, and Meryl Delierre at Everett. Thanks are due to Jack Banning, Fred W. McDarrah, Fionn Reilly, and Mark Trottenberg, who supplied photos, and to Jim Wressell, who contributed his design skills. Cassandra McCraw at Special Collections, University of Arkansas at Fayetteville, was extremely helpful to me in my research for this project. I am also grateful to Brian A. Sullivan at the Harvard University Archives; Martin Rosenberg of the National Archives, New York City branch; and Bill Ashley, for providing copies of Mailer's correspondence with Henry Miller.

My agent, Georges Borchardt, lent crucial support and kindly commented on the entire manuscript. At Houghton Mifflin, Janet Silver showed support for this book throughout and provided excellent editorial direction. Margo Shearman was an extremely able and patient manuscript editor. Thanks also to David Eber, Deborah Engel, Heidi Pitlor, and Liz Duvall.

The first pages I wrote for this book were read and commented on by the smart and helpful members of a regrettably now-defunct women biographers' group, which included Dona Munker, Susan Katz, Stacy Schiff, and Julia Van Haaften. The following people kindly read and made comments on versions of the manuscript, for which I thank them: Meryl Altman, Dick and Tommy Dearborn, Jennifer Farbar, David Gratt, Michael C. D. Macdonald, and Dan Rosenblatt (who passed on an interesting piece of history that I was unable to use). I am grateful, as always, to Mary B. Campbell, Jay Gertzman, Martin Hurwitz, Warren Johnson, and Joe Markulin for entering into the spirit of my project. My greatest debt is to my peerless editor and dear companion, Eric Laursen, to whom this book is dedicated. All errors and omissions, of course, are mine.

Contents

PROLOGUE:
COCK OF THE WALK

He was to go on in ten minutes, and the air in the room was charged. Over five hundred people eddied around the Four Seasons, the legendary dining spot on Manhattan's East Fifty-second Street. Near the buffet tables — covered with silver trays of Hungarian goulash, quiche Lorraine, paté with hazelnuts — the jazz harpist Daphne Hellman plucked her instrument, which was nearly inaudible over the party noise. Avant-garde composer and musician David Amram and his quartet played on the mezzanine, and a country and western group called the Foodstamps waited in the wings, to perform after midnight when the guests, it was hoped, would want to dance. At his side stood his assistant, Suzanne Nye, whom the columnists called his "great friend"; Carol Stevens, his mistress and the mother of his youngest child, was elsewhere in the room, as were his current wife, number four, Beverly, and his second wife, Adele, the one he had stabbed and nearly killed fourteen years before. His third wife, Lady Jeanne Campbell, with *Paris Review* editor Frank Crowther, had planned this evening; four of his seven children, and his mother, Fanny, were present. The buzz in the restaurant was tremendous: invitations had promised an announcement of "a subject of national importance (major)." It was Norman Mailer's fiftieth birthday party, and anything might happen.

The suspense had been building for weeks, ever since the five thousand invitations for the February 5, 1973, event, elegantly designed on purple paper, had gone out. The invitation had raised eyebrows: it stipulated an admission fee, to be donated to something called the "Fifth Estate" — what this might be was not specified — of fifty dollars a couple, or thirty dollars per person. As *Washington Post* columnist Sally Quinn later commented, "In Manhattan, nobody who's anybody ever pays to go to a party." In 1973, charity events were staid affairs, drawing mostly established Upper

East Siders, and for the art openings that drew the hippest crowds extra passes were always available. Usually the press simply stayed away from parties that charged admission. Many invited guests elected to boycott Norman's party. But as the date approached, checks flooded in to the suite at the Algonquin Hotel where Lady Jeanne and Crowther were managing the arrangements.

Norman and Carol Stevens had arrived at the Algonquin from their home in the Berkshires around noon, hoping to rest before the party. But calls kept coming in all afternoon. Some were from theater people who had Monday night off and heard there was to be some action at the Four Seasons. The press, undeterred by the admission fee, was clamoring to get in. Calls came from the *New York Times, Newsweek, Women's Wear Daily,* the *Detroit Free Press, Rolling Stone,* the *Village Voice,* and *Oui,* and from French, German, Italian, Canadian, and Japanese publications. The Four Seasons called: columnists Leonard Lyons, Suzy, Earl Wilson, and Eugenia Shepherd refused to come unless the entrance fee was waived. Would Mr. Mailer make an exception in their case? (He would.) Shirley MacLaine called to ask if she could bring Jack Lemmon. Actor Alan Bates and film-maker Bernardo Bertolucci, something of an enfant terrible after the recent release of *Last Tango in Paris,* were in town and wanted invitations. Senator George McGovern had sent in a check but was forced to cancel after learning that his wife had arranged a dinner party for that evening. Gloria Steinem, who had stood by Norman through the contretemps he created with his 1971 contribution to the dialogue on feminism, *The Prisoner of Sex* (and whom Norman had once taken to bed, unsuccessfully), called to send her regrets but added, "Tell Norman it's been a breathless ten years" in the interval since she'd met him.

"This is his answer to Truman Capote's party," a *Women's Wear Daily* writer was overheard to say that evening, referring to Capote's celebrated black-and-white ball at the Plaza Hotel in 1966. (On that occasion Norman had appeared with Beverly and had distinguished himself by asking na-tional security adviser McGeorge Bundy to step outside.) Others were not so sure what this party was all about. A joke circulated that Norman would announce his upcoming vasectomy, to be paid for by the admission fees. Others speculated that the guests' money would fund the writer's consider-able alimony and child support payments. Many, remembering Mailer's run for mayor of New York City in 1969 — an often inspired campaign, with a disappointing finish — speculated that he might announce another elec-tion bid.

Lily Tomlin, making her way past two burly bodyguards borrowed from the Rolling Stones, told a reporter that she supposed she had been invited "out of the telephone book, like everybody else here." This wasn't quite true: a small coterie of Mailer's close friends was present: boxers Jose Torres and Joe Shaw; historian Arthur Schlesinger, Jr., and his statuesque blond wife, Alexandra; writer and editor George Plimpton; former campaign staffers Joe Flaherty and Jack Banning; writer Dotson Rader, escorting Princess Diane von Furstenberg; journalists Pete Hamill, Jack Newfield, and Murray Kempton; and cartoonist Jules Feiffer and his wife, Judy. But few guests knew each other, though many faces seemed familiar. Flashbulbs popped as photographers caught such personages as A&P heir Huntington Hartford, restaurateur Elaine Kaufman, *New York* magazine editor Clay Felker, writers Larry McMurtry and Jessica Mitford, filmmaker Melvin von Peebles, musicians Charles Mingus and Bobby Short, former senator Eugene McCarthy, actor Rod Steiger, *New York Post* publisher Dorothy Schiff, artist Andy Warhol, and Senator Jacob Javits and his wife, Marion.

Those who remembered Mailer's parties of the past might have expected a raucous brawl. There was the party at a Lower East Side loft where Norman was clubbed by invading neighborhood youths; the 1960 affair at which street thugs mingled with celebrities and Norman stabbed Adele; the nonstop party that was the filming of Mailer's *Maidstone* in 1968; and countless parties at his Brooklyn Heights home or his summer place in Provincetown that had ended in fistfights, head butting, and general mayhem. Still, though this seemed to be a sober affair by comparison, expectations ran high. Nobody left before the "announcement."

Near midnight, after an hour or two of milling about, the partygoers drew near a makeshift dais when columnist Jimmy Breslin, who as candidate for comptroller had shared a ticket with Mailer in his run for mayor of New York, appeared with a microphone. Ascending the dais, he called the crowd to order, complaining of the noise: "Hey, what is this? The place sounds like a Reform Democratic club over a Chinese restaurant on Broadway." He introduced Norman as "the one person whose ideas will last" and as "one of the half-dozen original thinkers in this century."

Norman took the dais. Dressed in a blue shirt and tux, his hair in a modest pepper-and-salt "Jewish Afro," he cut a rumpled, paunchy figure. Under a spotlight, waving a fresh bourbon-and-ice in his left hand and pumping his right fist at his side, he immediately put his guests on the defensive. "Can everyone hear? Then I know if I hear people talking, they are simply not interested in what I have to say. All right. Must size up the opposition." He continued, trying to warm to his subject, "I want to say I've discovered tonight why Nixon is president. Tonight I found myself photographed more times than I can count. You see green, you see red, and then you see your own mortality. Now I know why Richard Nixon is president. He has gristle behind the retina."

The remark was met with mild laughter. It hadn't made much sense, but he'd eased a little of the tension in the room. Clearly, however, Mailer was very, very drunk. He soldiered on, and, to the horror of many of his old friends, told one of the most offensive — and often repeated — dirty jokes in his repertoire. The gist of it was this: A man sees his ex-wife in a restaurant with her new, younger husband. He makes his way over to her table and asks her how her new husband is enjoying her "fucked-out cunt." She looks up at him and says sweetly, "Just fine — especially when he gets past the fucked-out part."

A few people in the audience tittered, but the joke was met otherwise by silence, and knots of people started walking out. David Amram, who had heard the joke before, turned to his sax player and said, "You're about to see someone really bomb out big-time." "Christ, he's done it again," Channel 13's Judith Freed was heard to mutter. Sitting at the bar, Joe Flaherty, Norman's campaign manager in 1969, put his head in his hands, groaning, "Oh sweet Jesus, here we go again." Both were remembering Norman's catastrophic, drunken, obscenity-laced performance at the Village Gate during his mayoral campaign, when he'd called his student volunteers "pigs." That time, he'd alienated not only his hardworking campaigners but hundreds of potential voters who read about the incident in the press.

This time, as a broad swath of the crowd started heading for the doors, hoping to avoid witnessing more embarrassment, Norman called out, "Will my agents get the names of the people leaving?" He may have meant the line to be funny, but his choice of words — who were his "agents"? — indicates the paranoid and pugnacious state of mind that had come over him. Gradually people started talking, at first quietly, among themselves: Norman had lost the crowd.

Uncowed, he announced that what he had to communicate was "the best single political idea of my entire life," adding, inexplicably, "It has nothing to do with me." The entity that the party invitation referred to, the Fifth Estate, was to be a tax-free foundation that policed the CIA and the FBI, "a democratic secret police," he said. "I want a people's CIA and a people's FBI to investigate the CIA and the FBI. If we have a democratic secret police to keep tabs on Washington's secret police, we will see how far paranoia is justified."

He rambled on, alluding to J. Edgar Hoover, state-sanctioned electronic eavesdropping, and the Kennedy assassination. His slurred diction and the rising noise level in the room made him bring his comments to an abrupt halt, saying he hoped his guests would "let the idea sink in tonight."

Then, disastrously, he opened the floor to questions, first posing a few of his own: "Is there one plot going on between the scenes in America? Two, are there many plots? Three, is there no plot?" Silence from the audience.

"Won't someone ask a question, a heartfelt question . . . a hostile question?" he asked, repeating, "We must see how far our paranoia is justified." "What *about* paranoia, Norman?" called out one guest. *"What about paranoia?"* Norman shot back cryptically. He tried questioning the audience again: "What one word best sums up the point of this party?" "Love," offered one optimist. "Paranoia," shouted another. "Publicity," muttered a man near enough to the podium for the speaker to hear him. Norman mercifully cut things short, but not before announcing that he would return to the dais in half an hour for "more conversation and questions." There was no applause.

"Mailer looked confused," Pete Hamill later wrote, "exactly like an actor who was being hooted for a performance he thought was brilliant." As Norman walked off, complaining, "There's a lack of humor in these fucking people," a guest, himself quite drunk, approached him, pleading, "I'm with you, Norman, I'm with you . . . But what the hell is it you want?" "I don't know," Norman said dismissively. "I'm too drunk and too stupid." Murray Kempton ushered his friend away to a quiet spot and replenished his bourbon. He tried to comfort him: "Somehow, Norman, somehow out of your embarrassments always seems to come great writing."

The thoroughly antagonized audience headed for the bar to exchange postmortems. *Women's Wear Daily* writer Daphne Davis, who had earlier said she wouldn't miss the party for anything, now called it "a bummer — what can you say about a man whose time has gone?" Jack Lemmon defensively announced to anyone who would listen, "I didn't know a thing about it. I didn't even know it's his birthday. I don't even know him." "Well, there goes one more culture hero down the drain," someone else commented. Carol Stevens wouldn't comment on Norman's performance, simply saying, "You figure it out." Adele was overheard to say, "I think he blew it." Reporters approached Shirley MacLaine as she was leaving. "Norman's party was a disaster," she said.

Norman was now conferring with his advisers, and Crowther talked him out of returning to the dais, which he was very much inclined to do. At that point, he was ready to admit failure, echoing Adele: "I blew it. It was a great party, and I blew it. I have a demon in me." But Sally Quinn, who stuck it out until the party's end, noted that she heard him several times revert to his more characteristic defensive posture, saying, "I don't think it's a matter of whether I succeeded or failed tonight."

The bulk of the guests left shortly after the "announcement," and a small group remained until about 3:30. Norman had elected to get even drunker and forget about his performance. By early morning he was engaged in two of his favorite activities. He butted heads with stockbroker and boxing maven Tom Quinn and boxed with Joe Shaw, a welterweight whose contract he had once co-owned with Quinn. "This time I'll be Frazier and Ali, and you be yourself," Norman challenged. Joe Shaw pulled his punches, Norman was barely able to land one, and no one was hurt.

DAMAGE CONTROL began the next afternoon, when a very hung-over Norman held a press conference at the Algonquin to try to salvage his vision of the Fifth Estate. The "news" was that he intended to form a steering committee composed of the "best literary, scholarly, and detective minds." It was to be a nonprofit organization engaged in objective, scholarly work on such matters as the Warren Commission and the possibility of Republican involvement in the leaking of Senator Thomas Eagleton's history of shock treatments during McGovern's 1972 presidential campaign. "We have to face up to the possibility that the country may be sliding toward totalitarianism. I have an absolute distrust of the American government," he said, adding that he believed in participatory democracy. He compared the Fifth Estate to Nader's Raiders, the ACLU, and Common Cause.

What Norman didn't say was that it wasn't his idea in the first place. An anti-CIA organization already existed in Washington. Called CARIC (Committee for Action/Research in the Intelligence Community), it had been founded in 1972 by veterans of the antiwar movement. Part of its credo was the necessity of publishing the names of CIA operatives, which the group did in its magazine, *CounterSpy*. Tim Butz and Winslow Peck, leaders of the group, had approached Norman in 1972 and asked him to join. Norman explained: "There was an organization in existence already, and I said to them if you call it the Fifth Estate I'll join you." The Fifth Estate would be the fundraising arm of CARIC.

This did not surface at the press conference. The press diligently took notes, but the question period was devoted to his behavior the night before. Norman gave a fairly comprehensive statement:

> The party part went beautifully. Because of the people who planned it. It was the man in whose honor the party was held that failed. My speech never took off. It was not a good speech. It was a fair-to-mediocre speech. I failed because I was a "hint too drunk." That's three words, quote unquote, "hint too drunk." I will have a karmic account to pay. I was furious at myself. Once a philosopher, twice a pervert. I don't trust myself. There's a demon in me.

His statement was a very public postmortem on the gala celebration of a very public writer's personal milestone. And Norman Mailer had played it in characteristic fashion, achieving embarrassment rather than the accolades he might have won and burying his latest intriguing idea with a painful public scene.

The Four Seasons party marked not just Norman's fiftieth birthday, but the quarter-century point in one of the most exhibitionistic careers in literary history. His was a career marked by stunning successes, breakdowns, violence, many social embarrassments, and a body of work that reflected and at times seemed to shape the diverse cultural changes in postwar America.

The story was already well known and well rehearsed by the time Mailer stumbled to the Four Seasons dais that night in 1973, and it now read much like something out of a success-obsessed F. Scott Fitzgerald novel, or the summation of a sometime champion prizefighter's career.

With the publication of *The Naked and the Dead* in 1948, Mailer became an instant celebrity; the public was as charmed by his boyish persona as it was impressed by his talent. Overnight, he became the writer to watch. But his next two books were not well received, and Mailer spent the 1950s obsessed with his position in the public imagination. A feeling of failure gnawed at him, but he exorcised it with the rebellious, attention-getting gesture that was *Advertisements for Myself* (1959), in which he wrote, "I am imprisoned with a perception which will settle for nothing less than making a revolution in the consciousness of our time." He delivered on his promise immediately, including in *Advertisements* the groundbreaking essay "The White Negro," which identified the dangerous, transgressive, underground hipster and his connection to the Zeitgeist. In the 1960s, he turned to journalism, a genre he revolutionized by including himself in his political reportage as an active participant.

On the fiction front, he wrote *An American Dream*, a scandalous tale of an existential hero who murders his wife and gets away with it, a tour de force even if one overlooks the extraordinary fact that it was written on deadlines, serialized in a magazine as Dickens's novels had been. In 1968 he wrote the incomparable *The Armies of the Night*, an account of his participation in the 1968 march on the Pentagon and a moving exploration of the meaning of protest, the workings of the left, and his position in relation to the antiwar movement. This book won the Pulitzer Prize and the National Book Award, and in the same year his *Miami and the Siege of Chicago*, about the violence in Chicago at the time of the 1968 Democratic Convention, was nominated for the National Book Award.

Riding on these successes, Mailer made a run for mayor of New York City, fashioning, with Breslin and others, an innovative and exciting platform whose slogan was the characteristic "No more bullshit." Not surprisingly, he lost. Returning to more familiar territory, he plunged headfirst into the feminist debate with *The Prisoner of Sex*. And, of course, since the early

1960s he had been promising the public his "big one," which by 1973 had assumed the proportions of the Great American Novel, though he had barely begun it.

In the case of Norman Mailer, the man and his life are of equal, often competing stature with his work, and it is for his life as well as his work that he will be remembered. Pete Hamill, Norman's friend, wrote a sad column in the *New York Post* on the fiftieth birthday party, in which he acknowledged this fact. "He is our best writer," Hamill began, "which is not to say our best journalist, or our best moviemaker, but quite simply the best uncategorized writer the country now has. He has lived a life on the edge, a defiant, dangerous life, filled with riot and desert, waste and rebirth."

With his writing, Mailer has achieved literary stature; in his life, he has achieved celebrity. His hero has always been Hemingway, who was not only the most famous writer of Mailer's youth, perhaps, but a legend because of his outsized personality and exploits. Like Hemingway, Mailer is known for heroic drinking, multiple marriages, an affection for bullfighting, a fixation on boxing, and the cultivation of a macho image. He is no stranger to violence. Yet he protested the war in Vietnam in a meaningful way in the 1960s and has produced journalism that, as he had hoped, affected the course of events. In spite of, or perhaps in part because of, his reckless personal style, his determination to tackle any and every issue that seems to bear on the nature of American identity and community has very often resulted in some of the most essential writing on these subjects since World War II.

Yet he so often seems determined to shoot himself in the foot. He alienated almost every one of his literary peers with two essays written in the late 1950s and early 1960s, which dismissed them each in a couple of paragraphs. He has constantly undermined his friendships with other writers, most notably William Styron, James Baldwin, and James Jones. He has earned a reputation for using obscenities colorfully and constantly, in his speech as well as in his work — too often gratuitously. And he seems drawn to attention-getting antics, often with devastating results. The purpose of the 1960 party at which he attacked Adele was to announce his (abortive) candidacy for New York City mayor, and he had invited numerous luminaries and members of the intelligentsia, as well as people off the street. In 1968, just before the march on the Pentagon, he gave a drunken speech about his inability to locate the bathroom, a scene that he describes hilariously in *The Armies of the Night* but that also made the papers and the newsmagazines, which were not amused.

The press has rewarded his behavior, both good and bad, with unrelenting attention. In the years before his personal life seemed to stabilize with his sixth wife, Norris Church, in the late 1970s, reporters had his numerous marriages and his many offspring to comment on. And, over time, they chided him about the long-promised "big one," the major novel he seemed unable to deliver. When Mailer gave such infamous performances as the Four Seasons birthday dinner speech and the Village Gate harangue during his 1969 mayoral campaign, the papers were there to provide lovingly detailed coverage. Certainly by the time of the fiftieth birthday celebration, people had begun to expect him to screw up, especially under pressure: the suspense became not whether he would make a fool of himself, but how, and how badly. His celebrity has often been in ascendancy over his reputation as a writer, and Mailer has not always handled celebrity very well.

"Once a philosopher, twice a pervert." What did Mailer mean in quoting Voltaire at his press conference the day after the birthday party? He has used the quotation often, including it in his fiction, journalism, and countless interviews. He first used it, in the 1950s, in relation to sex. It fit other situations as well, often metaphorically to a man as obsessed with success and failure as Mailer. For him, it has meant that you can fail once at something, but if you fail a second time, you are marked as a failure.

Another favorite saying is "Repetition causes cancer," according to his second wife, Adele. This saying — or its variant, "Repetition kills the soul" — is one that Mailer has used over and over, as recently as December 1998, in a review of Tom Wolfe's novel *A Man in Full,* seemingly unaware that he has been repeating himself ad nauseam. Nevertheless, Mailer clearly has a horror of repeating himself, both in his writing and in his experiences. His life has a certain order that demands regularity and thus a certain amount of repetition. But experience must remain fresh: he has always considered himself an existentialist, and as such he believes that a person who continually makes choices in life will never repeat.

A Freudian analysis of this behavior might conclude that this insistence on avoiding repetition, alongside the repetition of attention-getting bad behavior, illustrates the repetition/compulsion principle. According to that theory, as adults we endlessly repeat the experiences of childhood; only by recovering these experiences in analysis can we free ourselves from the compulsion to do so. Mailer as a child constantly demanded — and received — attention; his attention-getting tactics were rewarded. He seldom acted badly (though in adolescence he relished shocking his mother with four-letter words), but, as he would acknowledge years later, he had a horror of being a "good" Jewish boy from Brooklyn. So, as an adult, he was to make outrageous bids for attention, repeating a practice he had learned in childhood, each act a declaration that he was most emphatically *not* a "good" Jewish boy from Brooklyn.

Mailer would scorn such an analysis: he scorns Freudian explanations and psychological introspection in general. To his thinking, his grand failures, like his fiftieth birthday party, were caused by a "demon" inside him. It is a convenient belief for a man not inclined to self-analysis, and perhaps it is useful as far as it goes. But it seems quite clear that if Norman Mailer were possessed by a demon, the demon was born in his childhood.

Consider Fanny Mailer's experience of her son's fiftieth birthday party. Given a table in the corner, she was joined by several of her grandchildren, Carol Stevens, her daughter, Barbara, and Barbara's husband, and some close family friends. Reporters hovered over her all evening. "I'm always included in everything," she proudly told one who commented on her son's thoughtfulness in inviting her. She was being truthful: she had always been present at every important occasion in her son's life, and at lesser ones like small, at-home dinner parties. A reporter admired her yellow brocade dress and matching jacket, and asked her age; all she would say was, "I'm older than sweet sixteen." Many reporters asked the same question; on another occasion Fan answered flirtatiously that she was fifty-one, one year older than Norman. "It's because my son is such a great man that makes me so young."

She seemed oblivious to the fact that her son had made a fool of himself. About the Fifth Estate, she said, after Norman's drunken remarks, "I didn't know what he was going to announce, but I thoroughly approve." At three in the morning, Fan was still at her corner table with a few friends. She was still beaming, telling Sally Quinn, "I think it's all wonderful." Norman had celebrated many birthdays, she said, but he hadn't changed a bit: "He still has that same wonderful smile." Out of all the parties he'd ever had, she said, "This was the best party for Norman. The second best was his bar mitzvah in 1936." Her son, Fanny Mailer said single-mindedly, was a genius. "Norman was not the ordinary child. Other children always had that sameness about them, but not Norman. He was just different."

Hers was a rather extraordinary statement. Many parents believe their child is special, but few would present this, as Fanny did, as an objective fact. Different her son certainly was, and Fan Mailer's insistence on his difference was a profound force in shaping the psyche of this enormously complicated man.

THE KING

Norman's father, Isaac Barnet Mailer, known to all as Barney, was an immigrant twice. The background of Norman's mother, Fanny Schneider, fit the profile of the typical Jewish immigrant from Russia — intensely religious and steeped in Jewish tradition, fleeing the Pale under threat of pogroms and starvation conditions. Barney's situation, as a South African Jew, was of an entirely different order.

The Schneiders and the family who would become the Mailers were *Landsleit,* or compatriots, both from the town of Anikxt, near Vilna and Kovno, in Lithuania. But the families had very different trajectories. While the Schneiders joined the hundreds of thousands of Jews leaving Eastern Europe and Russia for America, Barney's family was part of a lesser-known wave of immigration to a different continent. Drawn by the booming economy of South Africa, which had been fueled by the discovery of diamond and gold mines in the 1870s and 1880s, Lithuanians and, in smaller numbers, Latvians emigrated to South Africa between 1880 and 1920 by the thousands. By the time Barney's father considered moving there, the new land had a well-established Jewish immigrant community, and stories about the new immigrants' relative prosperity drew more families from Lithuania: they sounded rosier than reports from New York or Philadelphia, where immigrants usually found work in factories or as peddlers. The new community of Lithuanians in South Africa has been characterized as generous and warmhearted, possessed of a strong practical streak, and bearing a great respect for learning as well as a strong sense of Jewish identity — though perhaps more skeptical than other Jews.

Typically, young Lithuanian men would emigrate first, making the long journey to Cape Town by way of London; once there they sent for their wives and children. At first establishing themselves as shopkeepers, farmers, and factory workers and owners, the earliest wave of immigrants had high aspirations for their children, who usually went to universities and joined the professional class.

The result was one of the wealthiest Jewish communities in the world in the first half of the century. South African Jews of Barney's generation were well educated and spoke with British-sounding accents. Barney himself, after college, was licensed and trained as an accountant, a profession he would never embrace with any real enthusiasm. Still bearing his Russian surname, Barney enlisted in the South African military as a supply officer at the outbreak of World War I. By the end of the war he was stationed in England, and when he was released he had the option of returning to Johannesburg or immigrating to the United States. For unknown reasons — perhaps because his sister Anne had married a man who ran a thriving candy business in Brooklyn, New York — he chose to come to America, where he would find a wife and start a family.

Fanny, or Fan, Schneider, the single most important person in Norman's life, told an interviewer in the early 1980s, "Barney was very fond of my family." The Schneiders were more than a family — they were a clan, with a patriarch ruling the roost. "My grandfather . . . that's where all the brains and talent came from," said Fanny's niece Margaret "Osie" Radin. Chaim Yehudah Schneider and his wife, the former Ida Kamrass, along with a brood of six children, found their way to Long Branch, New Jersey, where they eventually opened a grocery store. Chaim Yehudah (to whom Norman bears a distinct physical resemblance) was sent to a yeshiva as a boy in Lithuania and was ordained as a rabbi at the age of sixteen; in the United States he studied all day, reading Talmud, and kept a Torah in the house — unusual in a Jewish American family. He functioned as unofficial rabbi for the small Jewish community in the town of Long Branch and was as such greatly esteemed. On High Holidays a cantor came to the community, while Chaim Yehudah performed the services, never taking money for his contribution. Fanny would reminisce that the children in the family were almost never spanked, because they had no wish to do anything wrong and so displease the old rabbi.

The family-run store, a large grocery passed on to Chaim Yehudah by another Schneider, was run by his wife, Ida, and their four energetic daughters: Rebecca, or Beck, born in 1887; Jenny, born in 1889; Rose, born in 1893; and Fanny, born in 1898. The Schneider women were thought to be very ambitious and were excellent businesswomen; the store thrived, and the daughters, after they came of age, moved into the hotel business all over the New Jersey shore. They were an attractive, vigorous group and would remain fiercely loyal to each other all their lives.

Fanny was twenty-three, still living at home, when she met the thirty-year-old Barney Mailer in the winter of 1921. Since his arrival in the United States, Barney had been staying with his sister and brother-in-law, Anne and Dave Kessler, on President Street in Brooklyn Heights; Dave was enjoying the material success of his candy business, in which the chocolate-covered cherry was the leading moneymaker. Anne was recovering from the flu and needed a place to rest, so the three of them went to Lakewood, New Jersey, a resort town, where they took rooms in a hotel run by the Schneider family. Fan didn't see Barney that weekend, but Anne told her all about him and Fan said she would like to be introduced. Barney eventually visited again, and the courtship began. In 1922, after less than a year, the couple was married in a large ceremony in a Manhattan hotel; they honeymooned in Atlantic City and took up residence with the elder Schneiders in Long Branch. Barney commuted every day to Manhattan, where he had found a job keeping books, and returned every evening for dinner provided by the staff of the family-owned hotel.

The birth of a son on January 31, 1923, at Monmouth Memorial Hospital in Long Branch, was the cause of great celebration. Fanny delivered her child in the early morning, after sending Barney and the doctors home: she would deliver the baby herself, she said, with the help of the nurses. After a difficult twelve-hour labor she resolved to have no more babies, but all that was forgotten when she saw her new son. She chose his Hebrew name first: Nachem (or Norman) Malech ("King"). (Her sister Beck's daughter Osie suggested that Kingsley, not King, appear as the baby's middle name on the birth certificate.) Thus it was established that, within the Mailer clan, Norman was king.

Barney's commute from Long Branch was grueling and expensive, and before long the family moved to Flatbush, where Anne and Dave Kessler also had resettled. Their new home was a flat off Cortelyou Road, in a middle-class Jewish neighborhood. By all accounts, Norman was doted on — not only by his parents but by all the relatives, especially the Kesslers, who had no children of their own. The death of Chaim Yehudah Schneider in 1926, followed not long after by that of his wife, was a deep blow to the family. The patriarch had been a highly learned and even intellectual man; though pious, he was skeptical, and was a great reader of Spinoza. Although Norman had only the vaguest memories of his grandfather, his presence loomed large in the Mailer household. Norman inherited from him a predilection for Jewish mysticism — Chaim Yehudah, as a scholar, would have studied the Cabala — and a fondness for philosophical theism; Norman would never be outwardly religious, but his worldview would be both skeptical and fundamentally informed by a belief in mysticism. What

Norman really gleaned from his grandfather was a manner: Chaim Ye-hudah was a scholar and a patriarch, the veritable king of his clan and community, and Norman picked up that quality very early.

Otherwise, his childhood was a mixture of the secular and the religious, like that of many second-generation American Jews. Fanny stopped keeping kosher after her parents died, as did her sisters, but the hotel at Long Branch remained so. The family was aware of anti-Semitism: Fanny often told stories of having been called "Christ-killer" on the way to school. Norman's parents started out Orthodox, but by 1930 they had joined a Conservative synagogue. Norman later described his Jewishness in somewhat ambivalent terms: "I was a Jew out of loyalty to the underdog. I would never say I was not a Jew, but I took no strength from the fact." He went to Hebrew school and learned Hebrew, but he soon forgot the language. Yiddish, however, he picked up at home, enough so that many years later, in Germany, he was able to ask for directions in the language and be understood.

Another child, Barbara, was born on April 26, 1927, and the family was complete. When Norman was nine, the Mailers moved to Crown Heights, to a two-bedroom apartment in a building at 555 Crown Street, an area even more solidly middle-class and Jewish than Flatbush. The adults put great emphasis on respectability; it wasn't a neighborhood where parents sat on stoops chatting with others. The streets belonged to the children, and there Norman and his friends played football, stickball, and roller-skate hockey. Around the neighborhood, the Mailers were considered to be different from other families, somehow wealthier and of a higher class. This impression came partly from Barney's appearance, for he always left the house attired in an elegant suit and carrying a cane. But it was also apparent in the household itself: Fan kept the house extraordinarily neat, and even the room Barbara and Norman shared was tidy.

Fan treated Norman like the king he was named for. She let his teachers know that he was special, though they needed no such notice, for he distinguished himself at P.S. 161 from a very young age. He could read before he entered school and was always reading. Yet Fanny once had to intervene when Norman received a low mark on his report card. He had frequently been absent from school because family business took Fan and the children to Long Branch, but Fan didn't think the low mark was warranted. She marched down to the school and told the teacher so. "He always had the highest marks," Fan remembered later. "And then this poor card. My only recourse was not to sign." Family legend has it that the grade was changed.

Norman and Barbara were given everything that family resources would allow. Norman took clarinet and saxophone lessons. The Mailers moved within the building several times, and by adolescence Norman had his own room, featuring a chemistry set and a big square desk. Barbara was always neatly turned out in Peter Pan collars, smart dresses, and gleaming patent leather shoes. When Norman was nine, Fan gave him a little notebook and told him to write a chapter in it every morning.

Barbara and Norman — and Fan and Barney, at intervals — spent their summers out in Long Branch. Fan's eldest sister, Beck, had married young, to an ambitious man named Lou Zaremba. In 1923, the year Norman was born, Lou had rebuilt a wonderful old property called the Scarboro Hotel, a grand, two-hundred-room establishment that sat high on a bluff over the Atlantic. This turned out to be a disastrous business decision, for by that time Long Branch, once a glamorous resort patronized by Presidents Grant, Garfield, and Wilson, had an almost entirely Jewish clientele and was far less prosperous. But Long Branch must have seemed to Barbara and Norman like a little empire: other Schneider family members owned other establishments there — one was called Kingsley Court, after Norman — and they, with their cousins, were treated like royalty.

Cy, Beck's oldest son (who would later change his surname to Rembar), was Norman's particular hero. Eight years older than Norman, Cy was, like his younger cousin, adored by his mother, and worshiped by his sister, Osie. But Cy had something Norman didn't: physical grace. Behind the Scarboro was a lawn almost big enough for a softball game, a favorite pastime for the cousins and children of the hotel guests. Norman remembered that Cy almost always delivered a home run when his team needed it: "He was one of the few people I've ever known who had a happy look on his face when he came to bat in the late innings with men on base, his side behind, and the need for a homer prominent in everyone's head. Indeed he had his smile because it was slightly better than even money he was going to hit that homer. In fact, he would." To Norman it was incredible, the regularity with which Cy would come through. Years later, he wrote, "He was very much an older brother all through my childhood and I worshipped him (with enormous funds of love and envy) because he was a hero." Furthermore, Cy represented victory over his surroundings, an alternative way of looking at life: "He was the only figure I encountered in my childhood who seemed to believe it was more natural to win than to lose, and that life was therefore to be enjoyed rather than decried." As Norman grew older, he formed a very clear view of where the power resided in his own household. Barney was keeping the books for another business belonging to his brother-in-law Dave, the Sunshine Oil Company, which sold and delivered heating oil to residents throughout Brooklyn. But Dave's interests were elsewhere — in his candy business, which was eminently more profitable — and Fan eventually took over the oil business, keeping the books herself. When the Depression hit, Barney found that there was little demand for accountants, and his days were given over to looking for work. Norman and Barbara would come home from school every day and ask their father if he had found work yet; the answer was always no. It became eminently clear that Fan ran the household, and Barney seems never to have challenged her authority. Fan was "the motor in the family," Norman later said, "and without her I don't know what would have happened to us. My mother had an iron heart." Like many Jewish mothers, he went on, she had circles of loyalty emanating from her: first, her children; second, her sisters; then, her husband; next, the cousins; and last, the neighbors. "It was a nuclear family," said her son. "And my mother was the center of it and my father was one of the electrons." Still, continued Norman, "I must say he was a most dapper electron."

At another time, Norman said, "My father was a terribly fussy, punctilious man. A marvelous man . . . He had marvelous manners — he came from South Africa, was very English as only a South African can be." The son's impressions of his father emphasize two traits: his strange Englishness and his neatness in dress. According to Norman, his father always wore spats, even when job hunting during the depths of the Depression. His father's English quality made him somehow special in Norman's eyes; indeed, his British accent may have been the source of the vaguely Oxbridge tone Norman's voice would sometimes unaccountably take on when he felt challenged or combative in his adult years.

To outsiders, Barney Mailer seemed prosperous and prepossessing. Norman admired his way with women: "They adored him because he had the gift of speaking to each woman as if she was the most important woman he'd ever spoken to. And he didn't fake it. He adored women." Only within the walls of the Mailer apartment was his ineffectuality apparent. "My father was an elegant, impoverished figure out of Chekhov," Norman later observed. "A dapper gentleman in a bewildering world, a man of such sentimentality that phrases like 'the passing parade' would always bring tears to his eyes."

Barney Mailer, however, did not feel himself a failure, and he certainly did not look it. In fact, he looked the consummate successful and worldly businessman. In all matters other than employment he played the part of one. Though a devoted family man, he adopted the vices of a man about town. He liked to drink, flirt, and, most unfortunately, gamble. Over the years this latter habit would bring the family perilously close to ruin.

Norman, desperately wanting to believe in his father, managed to find something heroic in this. Later, when Norman was in college, Barney gambled himself seriously into debt, finding himself pursued by loan sharks and forced to borrow against Fan's investments. It was a murky matter, and Norman never knew all the details — apparently Fan's sister Beck bailed Barney out — but it transformed his view of his father. Barbara remembers

Norman drawing her aside at the time and telling her, "Our father is an unusual man," confiding in her what details he knew. It was a dramatic, even thrilling moment for him: the father who had seemed powerless in the household, totally under Fan's thumb and with no life outside the family, was actually an independent man with pressing, important concerns, a man who fearlessly took on risks and moved in some of the city's most exciting and dangerous circles. That Barney's behavior seriously endangered his family and their future was not his concern; indeed, that may have been part of what drew him to this new image of his father. Barney's small acts of rebellion mirrored his own desires, and Norman felt heartened that he could escape the fate of the "nice Jewish boy" he had so long feared was to be his.

Growing up in Crown Heights in the 1930s, however, Norman was, in general, comporting himself as a nice Jewish boy indeed. He excelled at P.S. 161; when he graduated from the eighth grade, the principal said before the assembly, "Norman Mailer, IQ of 165, the highest IQ we've ever had at P.S. 161." The neighborhood boys regarded him as shy, obedient to his mother, and somewhat withdrawn. "I was a physical coward as a child," he later wrote. He was not very athletic, though he played stickball and touch football with the neighborhood boys. He had taken up building model airplanes, which would be a passionate interest into his adolescence. One was almost four feet long, and every part of it worked. His aunt Anne and uncle Dave, always thinking of his welfare, began to speak of his becoming an engineer.

Norman's bar mitzvah, in 1936, marked him out as special. He dutifully attended the necessary Hebrew lessons, though he complained to his friend Eppie Epstein, "I hate going through with this." On the day of the ceremony, a heavy snow fell, and Norman wondered aloud whether the guests would get there, especially those legions of relatives making the trek from New Jersey. Fan comforted him, saying that no one in the family would think of missing the event. And come they did. The ceremony was held at the temple of Congregation Sharie Zedek on Eastern Parkway, and Fanny held a catered reception afterward at the Crown Street apartment. Norman went through the ceremony easily, but then delivered a speech designed to shock: he spoke about the philosopher Spinoza, the Portuguese Jew who was expelled from the synagogue because of his unorthodox interpretations of the Scripture. Finally, Norman said he hoped to follow — it was a line slipped in by his Hebrew teacher, a Marxist and, Norman would later realize, probably a Communist — in the footsteps of two distinguished Jews, Karl Marx and the controversial Jewish philosopher Moses Maimonides. Some members of the audience may have been affronted, but to many he must have seemed precocious.

Norman was indeed reading a lot, as well as writing in notebooks his mother provided him. He would later claim that at the age of seven he had written a "novel" called "The Invasion of Mars." It was a science fiction story, tremendously influenced by the Buck Rogers radio serial playing at the time. In his story, the Buck Rogers character and his assistant, Dr. Huer (pronounced the way "whore" was in Brooklyn, he explained later), take a rocketship to Mars. The two notebooks the story was written in, shiny blue, about seven by ten inches, were lovingly preserved by Fan. Later, Norman was struck in looking at them by his strange patterns of hyphenation: if the word *the* appeared at the end of the line, he would hyphenate it *th-e;* similarly, *they* became *the-y.* Presumably, he wanted his writing to look like writing in a book, with justified margins. He knew how a real book looked, and that was what he wanted to produce.

In these early years, before his adolescence, his favorite reading was Edgar Rice Burroughs's Tarzan series, books about a remarkable boy who is regarded as special in every milieu in which he finds himself. In every community he comes across, human or animal, Tarzan is "elected" king. During adolescence, Norman read pulp magazines — *Model Airplane News* and *Spicy Detective* — as well as a good number of comics. But by the age of fourteen he discovered his two favorite writers: Rafael Sabatini and Jeffrey Farnol. Sabatini was the author of *Scaramouche* (1921) and *Captain Blood* (1922), the latter made popular by the 1935 film of the same name starring Errol Flynn, another boyhood hero of Norman's. Sabatini's formulaic swashbucklers owed a lot to the work of Alexandre Dumas, particularly *The Count of Monte Cristo.* The hero is usually an honest man who is cheated or wronged, becomes imprisoned or exiled, and returns to get revenge and right others' wrongs while winning a beautiful woman in the bargain.

Jeffrey Farnol, his other favorite, was a British writer of more than twenty-five novels; the one Norman cited as most important was *The Amateur Gentleman* (1913). It is an interesting choice. The hero of *The Amateur Gentleman* is a country fellow, the son of a pugilist, who has just come into an unexpected fortune; he makes his way to London, getting in fights all the way, and pursues varied amatory interests. The lesson the hero learns is that he must not neglect the duties of a gentleman, like bowing to a lady, or other fine points of etiquette. Even as a gentleman, he does not stop brawling, but he has learned his lesson and, accordingly, wins his loved one.

What is most remarkable about Norman's education, perhaps, is what he did not read. When it was time for him to apply to college, he had to draw up a list of books he'd read, and on it he listed such volumes as *The Rise of Silas Lapham* and *The Americanization of Edward Bok* — none of which he had actually read. There were few books in the Mailer household.

Boys' High, the high school he attended, had its share of students who were thought to be "brains" — Boys' High alumni include Norman Podhoretz, Aaron Copland, and Louis Nizer — but Norman remembered no English or history teacher as particularly influential. It was math and science that interested him; he ignored the high school literary magazine and instead became editor of the student journal *Physical Scientist.* His marks were high enough to get him into Arista, an honor society, and he was president of the Aviation Club.

Everyone felt he was marked out for greatness. Barbara worshiped him, and brother and sister were very close. When Barbara was going through the awkwardness of adolescence, Norman praised her, telling her she was beautiful when she felt clumsy and ugly. He taught Barbara and her best friend, Rhoda, how to blow smoke rings, how to ballroom dance, even how to kiss.

For Norman, in his early teens, was discovering sex. To the other boys, he always seemed just a little more knowledgeable than they were on the subject. He knew four-letter words, taught them to Barbara, and enjoyed teasing his mother by saying them at the table. He was an eager customer at the burlesque theaters — the Star Burlesque on Jay Street in downtown Brooklyn, or the Grady Theater at Times Square in Manhattan. Near graduation he began to turn up with a girl, Phyllis Bradman, who had long black hair and beautiful brown eyes, but he was strictly on handshake terms with her.

Norman would later say, almost wistfully, that he felt he had missed out on things in high school, in much the same way that a student who holds down a full-time job and goes to college at night feels he has missed out on the college experience: "High school went by in a blur of work and doing one's homework as quickly as possible and getting out on the street to play. And there was no high-school life as such. Later I began to realize that for many people high school was the prime experience and all that." He was left with a vague bitterness.

But then his Brooklyn upbringing would never be fully integrated into his experience. He would draw on it when it suited him, relishing painting himself as an outsider, a favorite Brooklynite stance. But most of his life would be given over to negating his childhood, wiping it all out, disavowing it — or trying to. The result was that a sense of never fully acknowledged poverty and loss stayed with him no matter what riches and fame he acquired. "I left what part of me belonged to Brooklyn and the Jews on the streets of Crown Heights," he later wrote. "In college, it came over me like a poor man's rich fever that I had less connection with the past than anyone I knew." He would seek to reinvent himself, forsaking the drab ordinariness of his beginnings. Years later, in *The Armies of the Night,* he would describe how, watching students demonstrating at the Pentagon in 1968, a feeling of modesty came over him.

Referring to himself in the third person, he wrote that "he hated this because modesty was an old family relative, he had been born to a modest family, had been a modest boy, a modest young man, and he hated that, he loved the pride and the arrogance and the confidence and the egocentricity he had acquired over the years, that was his force and his luxury and the iron in his greed, the richest sugar of his pleasure, the strength of his competitive force . . ." He loved the person he had become, not the person he had been born.

In the same book he describes his dismay at seeing himself in a documentary film and seeing not the brawler, the accomplished author, the embattled husband, the philosopher, but instead, "a fatal taint, a last remaining speck of the one personality he found absolutely insupportable — the nice Jewish boy from Brooklyn." All his life he would flee this persona, proclaiming in word and deed that he was most emphatically *not* a nice Jewish boy from Brooklyn.

Yet his past asserted itself at every step. For the greatest legacy of Norman's childhood was the legacy of his mother's absolute, unquestioning love. Nourished by the confidence of such a mother, and surrounded on every side by other adoring females — his aunts, his sister, and his sister's girlfriends — Norman was blessed with the utmost confidence that he could succeed at whatever he put his hand to. The consequent egotism and lack of discrimination were merely the price a son so loved would have to pay. In the 1970s, writing about some student protesters, he would say, "These kids had been raised by mothers who loved them, and taught them their world was theirs to shape — so they had a complacent innocence altogether near to arrogance." He might well have been describing himself. Writing in another context, about the career of another writer so loved by his mother, D. H. Lawrence, Mailer recognized the pitfalls of an upbringing such as Lawrence's — and of his own:

> [Lawrence's] mind was possessed of that intolerable masculine pressure to command which develops in sons outrageously beloved by their mothers — to be the equal of a woman at twelve or six or any early age [—] which reaches equilibrium between the will of the son and the will of the mother, strong love to strong love, is all but to guarantee the making of a future tyrant.

Mailer uses strong language, but it is hard to imagine that he does not know he is talking about himself as well: "Hitlers develop out of [this] and great generals and great novelists (for what is a novelist but a general who sends his troops across fields of paper?)."

Yet emotional tyranny — or the personality traits that go with it, like recklessness, outsize egotism, and indifference to the needs of others — was only a part of what made the man. His father's tenderness, his grandfather's searching intelligence, and the warmth of the Crown Heights neighborhood all left their mark on the man who wished to forget his beginnings. And the love of his mother, however it smothered him, gave him the sense that the simple unfolding of life would be his to command.

HARVARD

Nothing prepared him for Harvard. Not his cousin Cy, who in his self-assured way had blithely noted that it was a good place, once you knew the ropes. Norman had a vague image of himself smoking a pipe and surrounded by girls. That, in fact, informed his choice: the girls in Brooklyn looked blank when he brought up MIT, his second choice, but at the mention of Harvard they perked up. Then too MIT asked that the sixteen-year-old take a year of prep school before enrolling — an impossible condition, given the family's modest means. Harvard did have one unusual requirement: without high school Latin, Norman was eligible only for the B.S. degree, not the B.A. But if there was any significance in this, he did not see it.

The entire Mailer clan treated Norman's passage to Harvard as if it were inevitable, something to which he was entitled. That it would entail considerable financial hardship for his mother and his still-unemployed father seems not to have occurred to him. Tuition was four hundred dollars a year, but room and board brought the yearly tab close to a thousand dollars: the student handbook described that as the bare minimum to get by on. Fanny could not always come up with Norman's pocket money. His uncle Dave pitched in more than once — a fact Fanny would never acknowledge gracefully.

Still, an effort was made to get Norman up in style, and Fanny gave him enough money to buy new clothes suitable for college life. To her consternation, he came back with what she felt was an inappropriate getup: a gold-brown jacket, green and blue striped pants, and saddle shoes — an outfit better suited to a cow college than to Harvard.

His arrival, in September 1939, was less than auspicious. A Boys' High classmate and Brooklyn neighbor, Marty Lubin, had also been accepted as a Harvard freshman, a circumstance that threw Fan Mailer and Eva Lubin together; Norman and Marty also rode up to Cambridge together with Marty's father. Norman had received a mailing from the Phillips Brooks House, a voluntary organization involved in community service, not a Harvard club. The mailing had welcomed incoming freshmen, saying, "When you come to Harvard, come see us first." As soon as they were on campus and Mr. Lubin had driven off, Norman dragged Marty over to the Phillips Brooks House, to find it almost deserted, tended by a tall senior with a pipe. Norman, who liked to tell this story years later at his own expense, realized he had made a mistake, but found it hard to desert the senior, whom he liked. (It proved harder than he let on; Mailer's yearbook lists freshman and sophomore memberships in Phillips Brooks House — a fact inconsistent with the image he was busily constructing.)

Norman's dorm was Grays Hall, an aging veteran of Harvard Yard, not one of its newer, Georgian-style dorms like Wigglesworth. His roommates in Grays 11–12 were Richard Weinberg and Max Kaufer. Richard was a scholarship student from Memphis, where his family had a clothing business; Max was also middle class. Max and Norman shared the larger room, overlooking Massachusetts Avenue and the Hayes-Bickford cafeteria, a popular student hangout.

Both of Norman's roommates were Jews. Jews were routinely assigned rooms together. Just as the notation "A&E" on a student's record meant that he was an Andover or Exeter alumnus, so too were the records of Jewish students marked. Although in 1922 President A. Lawrence Lowell (once a vice president of the Immigration Restriction League) had moved to institute a formal quota for Jews, which had been defeated by the faculty after some scandal, there was still an informal *numerus clausus* of about 10 percent. Jews roomed together and usually, because preppies were also grouped together, socialized together; Norman's best friends were Marty Lubin, Lubin's roommate Harold Katz, and Seymour "Sy" Breslow. Though there were no formal rules, it was understood that there were whole areas of Harvard life barred to Jews. It would have been unthinkable, for instance, for a Jew to be invited to join one of the so-called final clubs like Porcellian, A.D., Fly, or Spee. Students like Norman went their own way, oblivious of these rules without knowing that they were there; some would only learn the rules when they tried to break them.

Growing up in an almost totally Jewish environment, Norman had never encountered anti-Semitism and had no reason to expect it in his first long stint away from home. His family would not have warned him about anti-Semitism; had they given the issue any thought, Fan and Barney would not have doubted that Norman could take his place alongside non-Jewish boys. As a result, perhaps, Norman seemed unconscious of any campus anti-Semitism.

He was not the only one. Few Jews felt singled out at Harvard or discriminated against. Not on the basis of their religion, that is. When classmate Myron Stuart Kaufmann later wrote a novel about campus discrimination, the 1957 bestseller *Remember Me to God*, Mailer said that he now recognized the outlines of anti-Semitism in his college years. But while there he never felt ghettoized.

This is not to say that Norman and his Jewish friends felt totally at home at Harvard. A wide class difference separated them from their prep school classmates. They quickly became aware of the exclusive final clubs. But it was a distinction that, they told themselves, made no difference. Many club members from the "St. Grottlesex" set rarely studied and got gentlemen's Cs, while Norman's set worked hard and valued high marks. The final club types occupied just one corner of a balkanized campus: those dwelling in other corners did not necessarily feel the final clubs' corner was the only arena for competition. As Norman would discover, there were entire areas in which one could become accepted on talent alone. If not the perfect democracy described by some of Norman's classmates, Harvard was a working meritocracy. In time, boys like Norman and his roommate Richard, who recalls arriving at Harvard in equally provincial attire, gradually shed the clothes they brought with them for more understated collegiate wear and, with varying degrees of success, took their places in the Harvard mosaic.

Norman's major, improbably enough, was aeronautical engineering, chosen because of a promise made to his parents, who had noted his enthusiasm for building model planes. Declaring such a major was an interesting move on Norman's part. It suggests that at the outset of his college career, he felt no sense of vocation as a writer or confidence about developing it. It also underscores how badly he misread the social stratifications of Harvard. Engineering was not what one enrolled in at an Ivy League school; to this day, many of Norman's classmates deny that an engineering department existed at the school. Declaring a major like this almost guaranteed being set apart from classmates pursuing studies in the humanities or the sciences. And, because the young engineer had to limit the courses he took in other areas, it deprived Mailer of a well-rounded education. He later acknowledged the gaps in his general knowledge. Within his other main field, there were whole areas of English literature he never read. Outside his field — in history, say, or philosophy — his knowledge was spotty at best. It was typical both of Mailer's iconoclasm and of his sense of filial obligation that he declared his major in engineering and stuck with it.

With one small deviation: along the way he also became a writer.

NORMAN MADE no great impression on his classmates in his freshman year. His roommates remember a slim young man with big ears who talked a big game as far as girls were concerned — and that the wall above his desk was covered with Betty Grable pinups — but had no more real experience than they themselves. The boys gossiped incessantly and vicariously about the stream of girls who passed through the doors of their proctor, law student Caspar Weinberger. Beyond Phyllis Bradman, the girl he had gone with in Brooklyn, Norman did not date. He sent his laundry home to his mother every week. Fan and Eva Lubin would periodically take the night train up to Boston to visit their sons, and Fan and Norman would spend the day largely by themselves, often talking in Norman's room while Fan mended his clothes. Norman would take Fan directly from the train station to his room, ashamed of her full shopping bags, hoping not to run into anyone he knew, and ashamed that he felt ashamed. (He would always view a woman carrying a shopping bag as a detestable, lower-class sight; later, when one of his wives returned to their London hotel bearing such a bag, he was enraged and thoroughly berated her.)

Norman was not accustomed to going unnoticed. He later said that the "bitterest blow" he received at Harvard was going out for the crew team. He trained hard but could not catch the coach's eye, much less make the team. Finally someone took him aside and told him that his arms were too short and that he was throwing the boat off. Norman quit, but the disappointment rankled. "That experience of working one's manful best each day at those oars and never being looked at by the coach" — well, that was not one he would forget.

Academically, the terms had shifted since his days at Boys' High. In Brooklyn, Mailer later explained, you were ashamed of being smart; at Harvard, you were surrounded by smart boys and feared that you were not smart enough. Norman often felt the inadequacy of his previous education. His engineering adviser suggested he take a speech class — the only instance Mailer would remember of possible anti-Semitism. He was required to take English A, which, if not actually remedial, was designed to compensate for the spotty educations of public school boys. You were really only exempt from English A if you went to prep school, recalled Richard Weinberg.

Ironically enough, English A was the turning point in Norman's Harvard career. The course focused on prose technique, the readings including contemporary realists, writers responding to the postwar social flux: James T. Farrell, John Dos Passos, Ernest Hemingway, and John Steinbeck. Mailer would ever after single out Farrell as a particular revelation. The Chicago of Farrell's *Studs Lonigan* trilogy was not so very different from Mailer's Brooklyn, which had never before occurred to Norman as a fit subject for literature. He was drawn by Studs's flounderings in the Irish slums of Chicago's South Side and inevitable succumbing to corruption's lures. Norman hadn't shared the experience, but he recognized the world Farrell described — indeed, he loved it. Farrell also often celebrated the working-class (or worse) lives of his characters, as did Dos Passos and Steinbeck. That too earned Norman's respect.

He later dated the period in which he formed the desire to be a writer to the last two months before he turned seventeen on January 31, 1940. During those sixty days, he said, he read and reread *Studs Lonigan, U.S.A.,* and *The Grapes of Wrath,* saying, "They *were* the novel for me." He started to acquire confidence in his ambition to be a writer. When he received his last assignment for English A in the spring of 1940, he approached his instructor, a man named Simpson, and asked if he might submit a short story instead. The section man agreed, and Mailer received an A+, which stunned him and impressed his friends.

He never really stopped after that. The summer after his freshman year, at the extended family's Scarboro Hotel in Long Branch, he holed up in a cottage lent to him by his aunt Beck, writing through the afternoon and into the night. Later he would say that he had consciously imitated Hemingway, whose prose style was easiest to understand, and whose plots were less elaborate than those of Farrell and Dos Passos. If he was influenced by Hemingway the man, he didn't say so — he wouldn't acknowledge his deep admiration for the most famous writer of the day for some years — but he must have known about Hemingway's exploits. Hemingway was a colorful celebrity, the press giving extensive coverage to his bullfighting, his deep-sea fishing and safaris, his multiple marriages, his boxing, his participation in the Spanish Civil War. Hemingway's was the life of the writer as public spectacle, as performance; his example could not have been lost on Mailer. Being a writer, very early on, meant cultivating an image, an image of a man of action, tough-minded and masculine.

By his sophomore year, Norman had become a bit restless. For reasons that remain unclear — you often didn't get into one of the better houses like Lowell, Eliot, or Kirkland if your grades were low, but Norman's grades were excellent — he, Sy Breslow, and Marty Lubin were not accepted into the houses, so they took a suite in Claverly Hall on Mount Auburn Street, not a very prestigious dorm but with lavish, "Gold Coast" suites and a unique advantage over the houses: a back door through which a woman could be slipped at any hour and no concierge to regulate parietal hours. Again, he was part of a small enclave of studious Jewish boys; again, he seemed not to mind. His uncle Dave had given him an old coupe, whose upkeep he shared with his roommates; it kept them constantly broke. In anticipation of a livelier social life, they installed a mattress in the trunk, which, presumably, could be pulled out at the opportune time and place; for the time being, it just increased the car's carrying capacity, as they piled passengers into the open trunk.

In the fall Norman enrolled in Robert Gorham Davis's writing class, which proved a grueling and toughening experience. Davis, a talented American literature scholar who later became a prominent professor at Smith College, often compared passages from the students' writing to the work of contemporary American novelists — Dos Passos was a favorite. All student work was liable to be read and critiqued aloud. Mailer remembered a story of his being read — a Hemingwayesque exercise about a bellhop, with a particularly bloody ending — and the class's response: they laughed. Later, he learned that Davis had given it an A−, and the professor told him in conference that he would not have read the story aloud had he anticipated the class's response.

But Norman responded well to toughness. He had begun to talk tough and act tough. He went out for a house football team and began to adopt a habit of imposing himself physically. Walking down a hall with a friend, he would jump in front and apply a football block, daring the friend into contact. He aspired to date Cambridge women, known as townies, and bragged of (probably apocryphal) conquests. A classmate remembers him flopping into an armchair in Lowell House, circles beneath his eyes, sighing, "Have you ever been so tired you really didn't want to sleep with a girl?" He chain-smoked now, and tapped his ashes into his upturned trouser cuffs — a gesture that was all part of his new pose. He argued for the importance of describing shit in literature.

It is a somewhat touching picture: the Jewish boy from Brooklyn who had always received immediate praise and gratification from his family, friends, and teachers, reinventing himself in a way that would draw him new attention. Wanting to be different from his classmates, to set himself apart, he found his models in books and in the men who wrote them. If he could write a story that was laughed at in class — well, better affect not to care. Part of the reason he carried off this pose so effectively was that at bottom he retained the complete assurance that was his gift from childhood: he deserved to be admired, to be loved.

It *was* effective. He got noticed. In the spring, he was elected to the board of the *Advocate*, the campus literary magazine. The *Advocate* brought with it admission to the Signet Society, not a final club but a luncheon club, drawing on cultural talent like writers for the *Advocate,* the *Crimson,* and the *Lampoon.* Describing the *Advocate's* dingy offices on Plympton Street, above the Gold Coast Valeteria's dry cleaning shop, Norman later wrote simply, "They were beautiful to me." Overnight, the structure of his days changed. Lunch was at the Signet clubhouse at 46 Dunster Street, following sherry in its pleasant library filled with books by former members. Afternoons and evenings were spent at the *Advocate,* where Norman read manuscripts and engaged in long literary discussions.

He found himself in the center of controversy. There were two camps at the *Advocate* that year. One, led by the genteel, prep school–educated Bowden Broadwater, advocated polished prose; they were considered aesthetes, Oscar Wilde types, and Norman growled that they wrote poems about spring. They preferred fiction and what they called "verse," which was aloof from social problems. The *Crimson* contended that this *Advocate* faction was full of "Freud and frou-frou." The other camp, which formed itself around Norman and included George Washington Goethals, Ernie Roberts, and Bruce Barton, favored raw, realistic prose with proletarian, even political overtones. Thornton Bradshaw, also in this camp but a little older, later said that "the *Advocate* had to be saved from the preciosity of a small group who affected capes and walking sticks and wrote short poems about childhood."

Norman's first story to be published in the *Advocate,* appearing in the spring of 1941, epitomized the tough approach. "The Greatest Thing in the World" relates the experiences of Al Groot, a broke drifter who runs into three men who seem "easy marks" at pool. He beats them handily; then they want to win their money back. Exhilarated by his sudden wealth, Groot tries to escape and is beaten up. Finding himself in a flophouse, his money somehow intact, he reflects on "the greatest moment of [his] life." The story is well plotted and well paced, and the characterization of Al Groot is fine, although Mailer was probably right when he judged that "it reads like the early work of a young man who is going to make a fortune writing first-rate action, western, gangster, and suspense pictures."

Harvard undergraduates were impressed. The *Crimson* even devoted an editorial to it, celebrating the victory of Norman's camp over the aesthetes: "Reaction is the law of life and [Mailer's story] strikes a crumbling blow at the magazine's much-discussed and usually exaggerated 'ivory tower' . . . Though the dialogue sometimes smacks of the Hemingway-Saroyan tradition, Mailer . . . has completely avoided the artificialities and the polished sophistications characteristic of so many *Advocate* short stories and replaced them with conviction, a strongly developed plot, and keen representation of detail."

Even Bowden Broadwater would later describe Norman's *Advocate* contributions as "utterly refreshing." Indeed, it was testament to Mailer's popularity that the magazine's two camps not only coexisted but remained friends despite their aesthetic differences. Almost uniformly, his classmates remember their faith that he would succeed as a writer. "Here's a kid who's going to do something," announced *Advocate* president Marvin Barrett to classmate Fritz Jacobi. Ormonde de Kay remembers Norman sitting at a refectory table in the *Advocate* offices, churning out stories when the magazine needed to fill space. He seemed the consummate professional.

Their confidence was confirmed when "The Greatest Thing in the World" won the *Story* magazine prize for the best story by an undergraduate in the spring of 1941. Robert Gorham Davis had suggested submitting the story to the magazine, an institution under editor Whit Burnett, its competition highly regarded. Norman marked the hundred-dollar prize as a turning point, partly because his family, at best tolerant of his writing ambitions, now accepted that he might become a writer rather than an engineer. The prize was followed by another coup: at an *Advocate* dinner, a *Time* executive, Roy Larsen, complimented Norman on his story. While this was not very impressive — Norman thought little of *Time* — it had an interesting sequel. Larsen recommended Mailer's work to Ted Amussen of Rinehart and Company, who wrote Mailer that he would be happy to see any of his completed work.

That summer, following his sophomore year, Norman decided to put his talent to a test. Back in a cottage his aunt gave him at the Scarboro Hotel, he began a full-length novel, to be called *No Percentage*. (The title derived from a scene in which one character, asked by another why he doesn't cheat and move a card in solitaire, says disgustedly, "No percentage.") It was the first expression of his existentialism. The main character is a rich kid who goes off hitchhiking to see the world; its central drama is whether the kid will have the guts to jump a boxcar. He doesn't, and the novel ends with his failure. Norman thought well enough of it that he sent it on to Amussen, who sent it to John Farrar of Farrar and Rinehart, who found it promising but a youthful effort.

If Norman was disappointed, he didn't let this rejection break his stride. Almost effortlessly, he had established connections with the New York literary world, which he now felt would be waiting for anything new he had to offer. In his junior year, two stories of his appeared in the *Advocate*: "Right Shoe on Left Foot," on a racial theme; and "Maybe Next Year," about a troubled boy's act of violence toward a bum. He now spoke openly about his literary ambitions. Classmate George Richardson remembers Norman holding forth until three in the morning in the Hayes-Bickford — or Hayes-Bick, an eternal haunt of Cambridge bohemia — on his ambition to become the next great American novelist. "You believed him," says

Richardson. "He radiated energy." He had no intention, he told another classmate, of becoming a "literary" writer. In fact, he spoke of himself as a professional, commercial writer, prepared to write Hollywood screenplays if need be. As a result of the *Story* competition, he was invited to try out for the MGM young writers' competition, its prize a seven-year contract; awarded fifty dollars a week at first, the writers by the end of the seven years would earn three hundred dollars a week. MGM was understandably dubious about whether the prize would be of much use to a draft-age writer. Norman tried to convince them, to no avail, that he would not be called up, since "I wanted very much to be one of the six or seven people chosen." It was part of the image he was cultivating to affect disdain for a serious literary career, and to appear congenial to doing any sort of hackwork. Of course he very much did aspire to be considered a serious writer, but it suited his purposes to present himself as merely a skilled worker.

As his confidence as a writer increased, Norman began to explore a new front: girls. During the summer, partly to get material for his novel, and partly because he was uncharacteristically suffering from writer's block, he took time off for a hitchhiking trip down South. At a whorehouse somewhere in Virginia, he lost his virginity, an event he described in detail in a letter to his friend George Washington Goethals. Almost overnight, he developed a new persona: that of an ultra-experienced, cynical, worldly rake. He used four-letter words constantly, cultivating the image of himself as a poor Jew from Brooklyn, often to his friends' exasperation. To the friend to whom he boasted of wanting to write screenplays, he averred that he wanted to sleep with a different starlet every night. But real experience with women continued to elude him. In his junior year, however, that would change.

WAR MIGHT BE impending, and Norman might have been preoccupied with women, but as his junior year began he was consumed by his work on the *Advocate*. One of the few later occasions when he spoke or wrote about Harvard in public was a piece that appeared in *Esquire* in 1977, "Our Man at Harvard." In it, Mailer recalled a strange occasion indeed, involving infighting at the *Advocate* and the perfidy of one of its editors, the so-called Pegasus, or literary editor. The key to the event's significance for Mailer had to do with one player, Bruce Barton, Jr., known to all as Pete.

Pete Barton's name, even today, is spoken by his classmates with a kind of reverence. "He was the quintessential gentleman," remembers Marvin Barrett. Barton was the son of advertising magnate and BBD&O cofounder Bruce Barton, who, as Mailer later said, was as well known as Nicholas Murray Butler, the famous patrician (and sometimes reviled) president of Columbia. Also the author of the influential bestseller *The Man Nobody*

Knows (1926), which described Jesus as the first advertising man and in-spired a new flood of inspirational sales-and-leadership texts, the elder Barton did not get along well with his son. Educated at Deerfield, Pete Barton had exquisite manners but also an ineffable sweetness: he never put on airs. In the *Esquire* piece, Norman cast Pete Barton, the magazine's president, as Billy Budd, Melville's famous innocent, and John Crockett, the magazine's Pegasus, as Claggart, the malevolent first mate who brings about Billy's ruin.

In the fall of 1941, with Barton newly elected president, the *Advocate* staff had high hopes of getting the magazine out of debt; if anyone could effect it, Barton, with his connections and ability to charm the alumni, could. For the first issue, *Advocate* staffers submitted their own work, instead of following the usual practice of soliciting manuscripts from well-known writers and a few Harvard students — a practice that had cost a lot of money. Norman forecast the following turn of events succinctly: "Barton might even have had a benign, well-financed and agreeable administration if not for the new Pegasus, John Crockett, a man as talented as Claggart and equally riven in his soul by detestation of our Billy Budd."

As Pegasus, Crockett took the job off to the printer, asserting he had found a cheaper one in Vermont. Weeks passed with no sign of the issue. What finally appeared was the old, profligate *Advocate* with a vengeance, a fat volume with contributions from the likes of Marianne Moore, Wallace Stevens, William Carlos Williams — and one poem by John Crockett. The issue cost three times what Barton had budgeted. Despite fine notices in the Boston papers, the *Advocate* plunged even more deeply into debt.

The next step was the truly tragic one, according to Norman. Barton, who "had been agitated for weeks at the long wait on our first issue," wrote Norman,

> finally demonstrated his father's blood. He called an emergency meeting where he calumniated himself for his dereliction of atten-tion, took the full blame for the financial disaster of the issue . . . and — Billy Budd to the last, absent even to intimations of a fur-ther notion of evil — stated that he would not ask for Crockett's resignation if he could expect his cooperation in future projects.

It speaks to Barton's character that he apologized so profusely for what was clearly Crockett's fault.

Crockett probably had never intended to resign; in fact, he responded with the momentous news that W. Somerset Maugham had accepted an invitation to an *Advocate* party. It sounded to the *Advocate* staff as if they were about to pull off a terrific coup. "Nothing in four years at Harvard, not Dunkirk, Pearl Harbor or the blitz," wrote Mailer, somewhat taste-lessly, "could have lit Harvard up more." Invitations were greedily sought. On the night of the party more than four hundred people jammed the magazine's small offices.

Maugham never showed up. Confronted the next day, Crockett admitted that several weeks before, Maugham had telegraphed his response to the invitation. "Certainly not," it had read. Because of the war and accelerated graduation, new officers were elected immediately. There was never even time to ask for Crockett's resignation; he got off scot-free.

Why did Norman find this college dustup so compelling? Certainly he was absorbed in the *Advocate*'s fortunes; he credited the club, in part, with his becoming a writer. Moreover, he was an accepted member of the group and felt a certain loyalty to it. Part of what fascinated him about the incident must have been its Manichaean quality: good, in the person of Pete Barton, pitted against the forces of evil in the Claggart-like Crockett. Manichaeism was already and would remain the fundamental underpinning of his philosophical outlook. But he seems also to have been drawn to the story of Pete Barton, which he relates in a postscript to his *Esquire* piece: Barton became a navy officer and ship commander, and then went to work in a modest position at *Time* (a publication Mailer detested, seeing it as the bastion of the company man) until he died tragically before the age of forty. Crockett had gone on to a dashing career in the State Department, including, it seems, espionage, an area that would come to fascinate the novelist. The article ends, "Rest in peace, Pete Barton."

Finally, the episode could not be read in purely Manichaean terms. Barton was good and attractive, but he failed, while the flawed Crockett triumphed. It was a fundamental injustice, but things would never be that simple in Norman's experience. By the time Mailer wrote "Our Man at Harvard," he knew that in his career he had danced between two poles, and that, if anything, he had moved more easily in the ambiguous, shadowy sphere of a man like Crockett, who, in the end, was more compelling to him. While Barton represented innocence and purity, his life was one of opportunities missed, of risks not taken. He had been a true gentleman, however, without snobbery or pretension, and Norman saluted his memory for that.

Norman's junior year was punctuated by the outbreak of World War II. Until this point, politics had simply not interested him. In 1939, in Norman's first week at Harvard, immediately after Germany invaded Poland, the poet Archibald MacLeish gave a speech warning the students of impending war and predicting that few of those before him would graduate without seeing battle. Norman had disagreed violently. He held no particular position on the merits of U.S. intervention, but he simply did not believe war was imminent. Over the next two years his attitude more closely resembled cool indifference. The Harvard student body was, in those early years, for the most part noninterventionist. But by the autumn of 1941 and Hitler's invasion of Russia there was increasing talk of war, with many students arguing passionately for intervention. After the Pearl Harbor attack galvanized the campus and the nation, Norman still insisted that U.S. entry into the war was of little moment to him. This remains a mystery, given the involvement of some of his favorite writers in political and anti-Fascist causes like the Spanish Civil War. But there is simply no evidence that Mailer had any coherent political view at this time. It is possible that he was simply ill-informed and chose to remain so.

Things were changing all around him. The "biddies," or "nannies" — the women who cleaned the students' rooms — were leaving to serve in war-related industries, and meals were now served cafeteria-style. Many of the older boys graduated early in order to sign up, and many clubs simply went on hiatus. Norman wouldn't even serve on the editorial board of the *Advocate* his senior year. And the engineering department was completely retooled to serve the war effort.

Yet Norman remembered his experience with the *Advocate*, not the outbreak of war, as the defining feature of his junior year. It was as if he finally felt he belonged at Harvard and wanted to enjoy every minute of it. That fall he had been admitted to Dunster, a real house, and he fully participated in its social life. It wasn't an intellectual house like Adams, Eliot, or Lowell — its inhabitants were known as the Dunster Funsters — and Norman may well have enjoyed the respite. He played house football. He took advanced composition with Ted Morrison, something of a teaching legend on campus, and wrote furiously. And, by spring 1942, he had a girl.

Bea Silverman, a Boston University music major from Chelsea, Massachusetts, the daughter of a local butcher, had met Norman in December at a Boston Symphony concert. No great music lover, Norman was accompanying a friend, Larry Weiss, who knew Bea through his roommate. When Bea realized that Norman had no interest in music, she proposed that they skip the concert, and they went back and spent the afternoon talking in his Dunster room.

Bea, ten months Norman's senior, was an extremely attractive woman, with dark hair and a wide mouth, amply endowed. Perhaps her greatest attraction, however, was her open-minded attitude toward sex. She freely went to bed with Norman — he acquired quite a reputation for "shacking up" with her for several days at Dunster House. What is more, she talked about it. Norman willingly joined in, and the two became quite a team, discussing sex loudly in Boston coffeehouses, larding their speech with four-letter words. On the Harvard campus they were even less restrained. Classmate Myron Kaufmann remembers being with them at the dining room table in Dunster with a couple of other women. Bea turned to the women and asked, "Do you girls fuck?" To cover the embarrassed silence, classmate Ed Horowitz muttered, "Only on Tuesdays and Thursdays." If Bea set the tone, Norman quickly became the ringleader, and many of his friends felt that Bea was going along with the act just to please him. They were inseparable, their performances indistinguishable.

Bea also introduced a measure of politics. If not an outright Marxist, she had marked radical views on social and, increasingly, international issues, and held forth on them freely. This was all new to Norman. While reared in the kind of urban, working-class Jewish neighborhood that often produced radicals, he had no political interests. Early on, Bea was a vigorous proponent of U.S. entry in the war; she had participated in the Bundles for Britain program and cheered Roosevelt's support for British resistance to Germany. As a Jew, she fully felt the dangers of Hitler's rise. She held her beliefs so strongly that it is inconceivable that she did not play an essential part in Norman's awakening to political consciousness, if not at this troubled time, then certainly later, as disillusionment with the war set in.

While many of his classmates received accelerated degrees and enlisted early, Norman, for reasons never explained, did not enlist and would not be drafted until almost a year after graduation, when, at last, his lottery number came up. He knew he would eventually serve, but he was also happy at Harvard, secure in what was clearly a fulfilling sexual and romantic relationship with Bea, and totally dedicated to his career.

Aware from the start that Norman intended to be an important writer, Bea supported him completely. In his senior year Mailer took Robert Hillyer's Advanced English 5A, holding himself to an allotted number of words per day. He continued to shock. A young John Simon, the future critic, witnessed a performance in Hillyer's class when Norman read a long prose poem about a woman giving birth — "to a bastard, of course," remembers Simon — in which there was recurrent tree imagery. "Hillyer, somnolent behind his desk, nodded approvingly each time this bucolic trope was invoked. But he nearly fell out of his chair when, at the very end, the woman (in Mailer's voice) identified this thing that only God can make as 'John's tree,' the penis of the bastard's father."

More and more often Norman spoke of the war as a possible mine for writing material, but for the time being, he looked for material wherever he could. In the summer of 1942 he heard a rumor that there were jobs to be had at Mattapan State Hospital, a mental institution in Boston, and with Doug Wolf, another aspiring Harvard writer, he applied. It was a brutal, dehumanizing job, mostly emptying bedpans, and Wolf left after a day or two. The schedule was grueling, thirteen hours a day, five days a week, and the pay was low, nineteen dollars a week; worse yet, the job required the workers to board on the premises, so there was no respite from the oppressive atmosphere. Norman was shocked by the way the aides treated the violent inmates. One day a black patient went berserk, and Norman, standing nearby, was the one who caught him; he felt terribly guilty when the guards afterward administered a terrible beating to the patient. He complained, and his superiors moved him to the senior ward, where he mostly changed more bedpans and listened to the inmates rave. The experience made a great impression on him, resurfacing later in his life when he was confronted with the threat of forced hospitalization. He spent the rest of the summer trying to write a play about the experience, which he called *The Naked and the Dead.* He later transformed the play into a novel, *A Transit to Narcissus,* which he would work on for the next two years, until he joined the army.

In the fall of Norman's senior year, a fire broke out at the Coconut Grove nightclub in downtown Boston, and it took the lives of 492 victims, many of whom had been crushed trying to get out of locked exit doors. Harvard officials awakened the students and told them to call their parents and reassure them that they weren't among the dead. Hearing that the bodies had been laid out for public identification and sensing that he might never see anything comparable, Norman called a couple of classmates and asked them to go down with him to see the scene. He found the sight of the charred, shrunken bodies mesmerizing. Some of the victims hadn't died of burns so much as from having been clawed and ripped at the exit doors. Although it was a horrifying sight, he looked for several hours, registering it all. Just months later he would write about the scene, transforming it into a wartime experience:

> He remembered the burnt body of a man that he had looked at for quite a time. It had seemed a terrible degradation, as if the man in burning to death had reverted to a prehistoric type. He had been blackened all over, his flesh in shriveling had given the appearance of black fur, and his features, almost burnt off, had been snubbed and shrunken, so that the man's face in death had only registered a black circle of mouth with the teeth grimacing whitely and out of place in the blackness of the ape.

The instincts of the writer triumphed over the instincts of the man. War loomed, but he would see no casualties worse than those sustained at a nightclub fire — and he would record them with the same critical eye.

THREE

THE ARMY

After his graduation in June 1943 — a decidedly sober ceremony, given the war and the diminished class size — Norman was at loose ends, sure he would be drafted any day. He was anxious to begin his literary career, having just received what must have seemed warm encouragement from the New York literary world, which he viewed, he later wrote, with something like the reverence of Thomas Wolfe. This had come in the form of acceptance of a short story he had completed the previous winter, "A Calculus at Heaven," by *Cross Section*, a literary annual dedicated to young writers, edited by Edwin Seaver. He later dismissed the long story, about a soldier fighting in the Pacific, as influenced by war propaganda, evidence of "a young, fairly good mind throwing off large gobs of that intellectual muck at the same instant that it is creating its own special variety of the muck." Certainly the story reveals the first inklings that Norman wanted to be known not only as a stylist but as a thinker. The hero is writing an autobiography in which he elaborates on Malraux:

> Malraux says that all that men are willing to die for tends to justify their fate by giving it a foundation in dignity. Perhaps, everywhere, this is felt. But in America, men live, work and die without even the rudest conception of a dignity. At their death . . . well then they wonder what the odds are on a heaven, and perhaps they make futile desperate bets at it, adding up their crude moral calculus, so that if the big team, heaven, comes through, and wins, and therefore exists, they will be able to calculate their bets that evening.

Norman was preoccupied with the issue of a human being's dignity and his or her dignity at death, perhaps as an intimation of his own mortality, a live issue because of the war. He met *Cross Section* editor Seaver briefly, toward the end of 1943, and told him that in writing the piece he had been greatly influenced by *Man's Fate*. "I'd like to be another Malraux," he blurted.

Indeed, he was deeply attracted to the French thinker who had witnessed both the Long March in China and the Spanish Civil War. Malraux was France's answer to Ernest Hemingway, the very essence of the artist *engagé*, a mover in world affairs. Moreover, Malraux was not only a major writer but a philosopher and a political activist; *Man's Fate*, set during the Chinese Revolution of 1927, was a meditation on revolution and its relation to the meaning of life. Malraux represented to the young Mailer the principle that the writer must do nothing less, as Norman would later famously write, than to effect a change of consciousness in the affairs of our time. Thus, while his admiration for Malraux may have seemed incongruous at the time, in this young man who had seen so very little of the world, it spoke volumes as to his ambition and expectations.

It was a strange time. Though Bea would not graduate until January 1944, and he was reluctant to part from her, Norman decided to use this interim to work on his craft. Evidently, he did not consider volunteering for the armed forces, the course some of his classmates took. He later admitted that he felt guilty about this: "I was a little frightened of going to war, and a great deal ashamed of not going to war." The fact that his draft notice took so long to come evidently disturbed him as well. He later speculated on the reason: "The only explanation I can find for such a delay is that my draft card must have fallen into the back of the file." The delay added to the vague guilt he already felt over not enlisting. So he was in a strange state as he waited for the draft to find him.

For the time being, he moved in with his parents at their Brooklyn Heights apartment. For a place to write, he took a cheap studio by the old Fulton Ferry terminal under the Brooklyn Bridge, near the old Navy Yard; he would be drawn for studio space to this semideserted warehouse district over the years. With great diligence, he began what would become a seven-hundred-page novel called *A Transit to Narcissus*. Drawn from his experience on the mental ward at Mattapan State Hospital and the play he had attempted to write about it, the novel follows the progress of Paul Scarr as he is at once drawn into and repelled by the corruption and brutality of the asylum system. The hero fears violence, has "an almost mystic fear of bodily contact," but finds himself attracted to the power and domination in beating inmates.

There is a lot of Norman in Paul Scarr, which at first seems puzzling. Nothing in Norman's childhood would have compelled an interest in violence and authority; at Harvard he rather liked his professors, and any bullying he suffered was nothing more than minor schoolboy ragging. (Though he could, of course, seem something of the swaggering bully himself.) It might be most fair to say that Norman perceived that there was a world out there where power and authority ruled, and that his was a culturally born preoccupation. *A Transit to Narcissus* details the beginnings of Norman's fascination with the workings of power. The moral drama of the novel's sprawling, Manichaean world prefigures Mailer's profound ambivalence toward violence and power, which would motivate the most successful conflicts of *The Naked and the Dead,* and which in turn reflected certain deeply seated conflicts in his own life.

When he finished it, in February 1944, nine months after he had begun, *A Transit to Narcissus* went as a matter of course to Ted Amussen at Rinehart, who rejected it just as he had Norman's earlier effort, *No Percentage.* Norman managed to interest an agent, Berta Kaslow at William Morris, and she sent it on to some twenty other publishers, all of whom would eventually turn it down; Norman asked to be released from the agency after he learned Kaslow left it. The warmest reception his novel received was at Random House, where Robert Linscott, a respected editor who Norman later said was equal in stature in his day to Maxwell Perkins, tried in vain to convince his colleagues to take it on. (The novel was not printed until 1978, when it appeared in a facsimile edition, as a collectible.) Norman seldom spoke of this rejection. He would not excerpt the novel in *Advertisements for Myself,* the 1959 collection in which most of his other early work appeared. Perhaps he knew that it was patently an apprentice work, a warming up. Equally likely, however, it simply got lost in the tumult of the times, for by the time he wrote the last pages he had received his draft notice. Norman Mailer's war was on.

WITHOUT MUCH ADO, he eloped with Bea. Theirs was a civil ceremony in Yonkers in January 1944; Bea wore a dime store wedding ring, and they didn't tell their parents. Neither family would approve, Bea's because Norman's future looked too uncertain to their middle-class, respectable eyes, and Norman's because Fan would not have approved of any young woman he presented, especially at his young age. She had particular qualms about Bea, sensing that she would not be content unless, in Fan's later words, she could be "top banana." But the couple presented their marriage to their families as a fait accompli, and as a concession they staged a religious ceremony at Bea's family home in Chelsea in March.

"Getting married was the one thing I never regretted in my life," Norman wrote a Harvard friend some months later. Certainly the short time the newlyweds had together was happy; their intense sexual attraction continued, and their intellectual companionship was still very strong. But Bea was eager to join the war effort, and around the time Norman's draft number came up, she enlisted in the recently formed WAVES, or Women Accepted for Volunteer Emergency Services. She would not see action — WAVES were reservists, though they were sometimes called overseas — and would end up spending most of the war at a base in Vermont. She enrolled as an officer, a lieutenant. This bothered Norman, who was determined to enlist as a private. Indeed, he made a joke, which he repeated ad nauseam, about having to salute his wife before "putting it in" (surely a well-worn joke in families with officer wives). But this man, so finely attuned to differences in rank and power, was genuinely upset that his wife technically held a position of authority over him. It is likely that he was not entirely comfortable even with the relatively new phenomenon of women in the military. War was a man's activity, he may well have felt. Even though he knew Bea could hardly be a stay-at-home wife, particularly when the war against fascism was so important to her, he was always slightly uncomfortable with her wartime service, and for the first time something turned a little sour in their relationship.

April found Norman at Fort Bragg in North Carolina; basic training would last until August 5, 1944. From the start it was an entirely new experience, and he was a quick study in negotiating the terrain. He had deliberately enlisted as a private, when the option of Officers' Training School was the more obvious route for a Harvard graduate. (Most of his classmates became officers as a matter of course.) Part of his motivation may well have been his reluctance to put himself in any position in which he would be resented; from earliest childhood he had been accepted and admired, and he suspected — and knew from war novels — that officers were often deeply resented. Publicly he said that as a private he would see more action, and he wanted experience to transmute into fiction. Indeed, he began writing about every detail of army life in letters to Bea, instructing her to save the letters for future use or, in a darker mood, so that they might be cobbled into a narrative if he died.

The issue of rank nagged at him from his earliest days at Fort Bragg, and it would fester into an obsession by the time he left the war. One of the unit's sergeants, Sergeant Mann, a relatively good sort, didn't abuse his authority, but the other, a career army man named Ernest Aud, was a bully. Norman's unit, officially the Fourth Platoon, Able Battery, Twelfth Battalion, Fourth Regiment, was an instrument and survey battalion, and as such the men were generally better educated than most enlisted men. It was thought that Aud resented this. Norman got into trouble very quickly. He was not good about inspection, and his platoon, promptly after his arrival, lost a weekend pass over the state of his bunk. After that, they saw to it that his bunk area was shipshape.

He found friends among the men. The New Yorkers in the unit — mostly

Jews — gravitated together, and Norman was often heard talking about jazz. He played a lot of chess. He also continually questioned the men about their sex lives; only in hindsight did any of them realize he was taking notes, as it were. Later many saw themselves or those around them recreated with eerie faithfulness in *The Naked and the Dead:* there was Joe Heiman in the tall, blond Buddy Wyman, there was Rappaport in Goldstein. "Here they are, dammit," one of them later said. "Those are the guys from basic."

At the end of basic training, thirteen of the men were told to report to Fort Ord in California in ten days because they would be going to the Pacific. Norman and another private, Clifford Maskovsky, made the trip together, first stopping in Brooklyn, where Norman introduced Clifford to Bea. After reporting late to Fort Ord (it was Norman's idea; he wanted to see a little of San Francisco, and their lateness went unnoticed), where they were supposed to remain for just nine days, they found that the army seemed to have no idea what to do with them. Intelligence and survey men with specialized training were so valuable that the army simply couldn't decide where they would be most useful, so the nine days stretched into three months. Understandably, Norman grew restless. Three times a week the men were ordered to make a twenty-five-mile, all-night hike around Ord reservation — a pointless exercise, it seemed, after it had been done once or twice. Norman convinced Clifford to split off from the hikers a couple miles out, get a good night's sleep, and rejoin the men after they'd circled back toward morning.

The near future remained uncertain. At one point the men were fitted out with winter clothing and equipment, and it looked as if they were headed for Europe. Norman would later say, on many occasions, that he had always hoped to go to the Pacific, that the weight of generations of culture in Europe would have been too heavy for him to construct his novel. He wanted a fresh slate, unfamiliar surroundings. But of course, in the tide of events, he had absolutely no control over his fate. It was not until late November, when he and his buddies found themselves on a small troopship called the *Sea Barb* and were issued sunglasses and suntan oil, that they understood they were going to the Pacific.

They were headed for the Philippines. Lost to the United States in the winter of 1941–42 in the famous campaign that ended with General Douglas MacArthur vowing, "I shall return," the Philippines were again in the military eye in 1944. There was a U.S. victory in the Battle of the Philippine Sea, which took place in the stretch of ocean between the Philippines and the Marianas and was sardonically known, for the ease with which the Japanese were shot out of the sky, as "the Great Marianas Turkey Shoot"; following this battle, the naval command wanted Admiral Chester Nimitz to move toward Japan. But Roosevelt intervened and ordered the combined forces to join MacArthur in an attempt to retake the islands. In the Battle of Leyte Gulf in late October 1944, the Japanese failed to repel the landing Americans, and a long struggle to recapture Leyte ensued. When the Allies finally secured the Gulf, they began a similar operation on the island of Luzon in early January 1945; it was to this conflict that Norman and his friends sailed.

After about two weeks Norman and a few of the others from Fort Ord were ordered to join the 112th Cavalry, which had begun as a horse cavalry out of San Antonio, Texas. Because of heavy losses to their fleet, the men had been forced to leave most of their horses on the way, in New Caledonia. They had seen a lot of action, and the core that remained was tough-talking and hard-bitten — rough men, no strangers to bullying. Many of them had risen to become sergeants of some kind as well, while the new recruits were privates. It seems certain that this was an uncomfortable situation for a Harvard-educated Jew from Brooklyn; he told an army buddy that the Southerners aroused in him nothing less than "muted terror." Yet the Texans also seem to have held a fascination for him. It was at this time that he learned to mimic a Deep South accent, a Texas drawl that he would affect at moments of crisis or great excitement. In later years it grew to be a sort of defensive affectation, which would surface at odd moments even in his well-known public speeches — for instance, at the Village Gate during his run for mayor of New York. While some people found his "Southern sheriff" persona either faintly ridiculous or downright embarrassing, Norman couldn't seem to resist it. It was one of the biggest changes his friends would note on his return from the war.

While in the 112th, Norman formed his closest friendship of the war years, with a Southerner, Francis "Fig" Irby Gwaltney, who would remain a very close friend until Gwaltney's death in 1980. Fig, who joined the regiment as a radio operator, was an aspiring writer from Charleston, Arkansas. Though he had lost his father at a young age and was forced to go to work early in life, he had the manners of a Southern gentleman — very much in contrast to the redneck Texans. Fig was an earnest and gentle man, and he entertained Norman with stories about fishing and hunting — a side of male life that Brooklyn-born Norman knew nothing about. In turn, Norman acquainted Fig with what he knew about the literary establishment and urged him to read Thomas Wolfe. The very idea of a Southerner who wanted to write without having read Wolfe was absurd, he sniffed.

His friendship with Fig was one of the few pleasures of these months. Norman did not fit in well otherwise. At first, he served as a telephone lineman; later, after falling out with his superior, he peeled potatoes in the kitchen. When even that did not work out, he became a rifleman. Conditions on Leyte were awful. The men slept in hastily constructed bivouacs.

The ground underfoot turned to dust in the blazing sunshine of the day, and torrential rains turned everything to mud; just as quickly, the sun dried out their gear again, leaving it salty and stiff. The Japanese had supposedly been beaten back, but intelligence was not very good, and Japanese soldiers were sometimes found near the camps. The threat of a Japanese counterattack — however weak — was real. The hot jungle climate, bad food, and stress were taking their toll on Norman, and the end of February 1945 found him stricken with jaundice in a military hospital outside Manila. From the suburbs around the city he could hear exploding shells.

He had always wanted to go on a patrol — in fact, he was forming an idea for a short novel written about a long patrol — and eventually found himself assigned to a reconnaissance unit. Even then, a lot of the work was dreary. He would later remember endless drills on the nomenclature of the machine gun. He had to stifle his own intelligence: the only man of his rank, he later said, who could read a map properly, he had to sit through endless drills on map reading; in one such session, the instructor pointed to a spot on the map and asked Norman the coordinates. Startled, he gave them exactly, down to the correct decimals, which won him no points among his peers.

But he did get to go out on patrol, and one particular expedition, along the Agno River, stuck with him. Thirty men went out to locate and destroy one hundred Japanese who had infiltrated the American lines. Their leader was a man Norman detested; indeed, writing of him in a letter to a Harvard classmate, he portrayed him as a homosexual: "a hermaphrodite who frequents the Village and speaks of the necessity of living unconditionally in an airy voice." The idea of a patrol appealed to Norman — perhaps because it reminded him of the exploits of his childhood hero Captain Blood, he later said — but the reality was crushing:

> Going out on patrol every day in the Philippine sun, carrying a heavy pack on your back, that kind of ever present fatigue and diarrhea and just feeling generally awful, broke down any desire I had for action and adventure. And also the feeling that you're going to be killed — I was emotionally convinced of it, and I didn't care any more what happened.

They never located the Japanese, but along the way they climbed an enormous hill with a "mean, slimy trail" — surely the model for Mount Anaka in *The Naked and the Dead,* if on a smaller scale. There an incident occurred that would make its way into the novel's pages. One of the men kicked over a hornets' nest, and the insects attacked in swarms. Half the platoon fled up the hill, while the machine gun squad escaped into the valley. The patrol was completely dispersed, and all the men slunk back into bivouac the next day separately. It was a quintessential army experience: a futile mission, the men defeated by something other than the expected enemy, decidedly anticlimactic. Yet it struck Mailer the writer in another way as well: the men were ready to lose their lives in battle, but they didn't want to be stung by hornets. There was a kind of elusive nobility in the incident that moved the novelist.

But Norman saw little real action. It is not known whether he ever killed a man — though if he had, he probably would have said so. He did see a lot of dead men, and the impact of the war experience hit him hard in other respects. His deep dislike for authority developed into a kind of philosophy that would later express itself brilliantly in the characters of General Cummings and Sergeant Croft in *The Naked and the Dead*. The abuses of power and authority he found in the relations between officers and men he came to see as but one manifestation of the fascism the Allies were allegedly fighting. It was all one colossal struggle for power, and the war was a colossal waste. Many men would be disillusioned — the word is perhaps not strong enough — by World War II, but Norman was so profoundly affected that the result would be the ringing indictment of *The Naked and the Dead*.

As the months passed, patrols became fewer and fewer. The war in the Philippines wound down. The battle for Luzon ended on March 4, 1945, and mopping up was all that remained. American forces cleared Manila in early summer. With the Philippines retaken, Japan's supply lines were cut. Then word reached the American forces of the atomic bombs dropped on Hiroshima and Nagasaki, on August 6 and August 9 respectively. By the end of the month Norman was on a ship headed for Japan, arriving in Tokyo Bay on September 2, 1945; two ships away was the USS *Missouri*, and through binoculars Norman and the other soldiers watched Japanese representatives signing the document of surrender handed to them by MacArthur.

Because Norman had been drafted so late in the war, he was not sent home immediately, and was instead assigned to occupation duty in Japan. He was given a job as cook — a job he strangely liked, if one is to judge from a description he later wrote of Carter, another wartime cook, in a 1951 story, "The Language of Men":

> This was the happiest period of Carter's life in the army . . . The kitchen became his property, it became his domain, and since it was a warm room, filled with sunlight, he came to take pleasure in the very sight of it. Before long his good humor expanded into a series of efforts to improve the food . . . He baked like a housewife satisfying her young husband; at lunch and dinner there was pie or cake, and often both . . . He taught the K.P.s to make the toast

come out right. He traded excess food for spices in Japanese stores. He rubbed paprika and garlic on the chickens. He even made pastries to cover such staples as corn beef hash and meat and vegetable stew.

When the men don't appreciate Carter's improvements, he loses interest in his work, and the same may have been true of Norman. (Fig Gwaltney remembered Norman as a terrible cook, who couldn't separate the whites of eggs from the yolks.)

Perhaps during the period in which he liked his work, Private Mailer was promoted to sergeant technician fourth grade, T4, a first cook. But, given his ambivalence about rank, this brought him little satisfaction. In a report to his Harvard class more than twenty years later, he chose to report the promotion as an embarrassment because it was so distinctly ignoble: "The occupation inspired me with shame, however, Harvard snobbery being subtler than one expects." So, he continued, he "picked a contretemps one day, and was busted. Left the Army a private." This was a compressed version of the incident. In reality, Norman picked a fight with a superior and then "crawfished" — an army term meaning that one retreated or, more precisely, groveled — and was given back his stripes. Finding his debasement so intolerable, he went back the next day and resigned his stripes, becoming a private again.

The incident was to become a memorable vignette in *The Naked and the Dead*, in which Lieutenant Hearn is forced to "crawfish" before the fascistic General Cummings. A power struggle has been going on between the men for some time, the general trying to force Hearn to confront and embrace his own desire for power and love for authority, and Hearn has now subtly shifted the scales in an act of defiance, after grinding out a cigarette butt on the floor of Cummings's tent. In a confrontation, Cummings insists that Hearn pick up the butt; Hearn, realizing that he means it, does so. After Hearn's exit, Cummings is elated — and Hearn is in agony: "For almost an hour he lay face down on his cot, burning with shame and self-disgust and an impossible impotent anger. He was suffering an excruciating humiliation which mocked him in its very intensity . . . 'I never thought I would crawfish to him.' That was the shock, that was the thing so awful to realize."

In the novel, the incident works beautifully, for Hearn is engaged in an internal struggle with his own tendencies toward exercising power in a fashion fully as brutal as Cummings's behavior, and his defeat before the general mirrors his defeat before his own impulses. Mailer masterfully turns an incident in his own experience into a neat and upsetting parable about the misuse of power. But if we bear in mind its basis in fact, his response seems outsized. It is a measure of the toll that daily contact with authority took on him that he experienced actual agony when he capitulated to an officer. That he could transmute this into art is essential to understanding his creative processes.

So it was as a private that Norman served out his time, and his resentment only grew, bordering on obsession. His old friend from basic training, Clifford Maskovsky, showed up in Japan. Clifford had risen to the rank of battalion sergeant major — but had also been missing in action for a short time. When he saw his friend, Clifford expected a warm greeting, perhaps an expression of pleasure that he had survived. But Norman walked up to him and demanded combatively, "Whose ass did you kiss to get those stripes?" Maskovsky was not only taken aback but deeply hurt.

At last it was over. On May 2, 1946 — "a magic day" — Norman was discharged, and he boarded the USS *Grant* for the journey to the West Coast. From there he took a troop train back east. The cars were filled with jubilant soldiers. By June he was reunited with Bea and his family. Very soon the couple decamped for Cape Cod, and Norman began writing *The Naked and the Dead*.

Norman would later confide to his second wife that his discharge papers had carried the notation "This man does not know how to take orders," he himself adding, "Fuck this guy." It was his way of putting paid to an almost intolerable situation.

PROVINCETOWN EXERTED a special pull on Norman, and would continue to do so for decades. The tiny town, three miles long and two streets wide, had been discovered by bohemians at the turn of the century and had a flourishing artistic community. The setting is dramatic: nestled around a bay in the curl at the tip of Cape Cod, the town is surrounded by towering dunes and, beyond them, the surf. The quality of light on the bay side is fantastic: in the evenings, everything is lit by an ethereal golden glow that infuses colors with dramatic intensity. Once a whaling community, Provincetown used to be populated entirely by Portuguese fishermen; in the summers, tourists, many of them gay, fill its narrow streets.

Bea and Norman rented a cottage on the outskirts of Provincetown, one of the Crow's Nest cottages at Beach Point, on the bay side of the town. Later the area would become a tacky strip of motels and cottages; then it offered quiet and solitude. When the walls got too close, they had only to walk into town to have a cheap Portuguese meal and drinks in one of the many bars. And for the time at least, money was not a problem; they had saved up about two thousand dollars from Norman's allotments and Bea's pay.

However romantic the setting may have been, Norman went about the business of writing his novel in thoroughly professional, even obsessive fashion. He went carefully through his wartime letters to Bea, cataloguing on three-by-five cards events and characters he planned to include. One of the great strengths of the embryonic novel was characterization; Mailer kept a veritable dossier on each figure, including the character's previous girlfriends, his parents, the foods he liked, any idiosyncrasies whatsoever. Many — perhaps half — of these characters were based on men he had served with, Fig Gwaltney observed, though Mailer felt free to shape them fictionally.

He structured the novel around the invasion of a fictional island called Anopopei in the Philippines, a mop-up operation to rout any last Japanese, and the novel's minor characters, lovingly resurrected from their three-by-five cards, were a kind of galaxy of ordinary enlisted men. To each he devoted, intermittently throughout the novel, a lengthy flashback describing his life before the war. Heavily influenced by Dos Passos's "time machine" flashbacks in *U.S.A.*, these devices were the novel's only real technical innovation. As such, they would ultimately compromise the otherwise hyperrealistic tone of the book, but they are undeniably effective in bringing this small group of otherwise unremarkable men to vivid life.

More conventionally rendered are the novel's three central characters, all figures of authority who reflect the author's decided ambivalence toward that concept. The most chilling of these is the deeply reactionary General Cummings, the leader of the campaign, who believes that war is the proper state of humankind and that men can be ruled only by fear: "To make an Army work you have to have every man in it fitted into a fear ladder. Men in prison camps, deserters, or men in replacement camps are in the backwaters of the Army and the discipline has to be proportionately more powerful. The Army functions best when you're frightened of the man above you, and contemptuous of your subordinates." In his personal life, Cummings is a deeply complex man, a closeted homosexual, given to humiliation and secrecy in his loveless marriage. Cummings voices not Mailer's beliefs but what he seems to fear are the beliefs of those in power.

Cummings takes as his aide-de-camp the Harvard-educated Lieutenant Hearn, the novel's most sympathetic central character. Hearn, though he understands the demands of rank, feels he must buck certain long-standing army modes of behavior — challenging, for instance, a fellow officer at mess on his racist views. Cummings is determined to draw Hearn in and convert him to his fascist views, and he knows his man well, for Hearn, though fundamentally decent, is himself fascinated by power and, beyond that, the ideology of power and, by extension, fascism. He struggles to understand the workings of power and his own place on the "fear ladder."

He muses about his relationship with Cummings after displeasing him in a minor way:

> He had been the pet, the dog, to the master, coddled and curried, thrown sweetmeats until he had the presumption to bite the master once. And since then he had been tormented with the particular absorbed sadism that most men could generate only toward an animal. He was a diversion for the General, and he resented it deeply with a cold speechless anger that came to some extent from the knowledge that he had acquiesced in the dog-role, had even had the dog's dreams, carefully submerged, of someday equaling the master.

It is Hearn who, in the ultimate drama of power and authority, "crawfishes" before the general.

When Hearn is killed by enemy fire as he starts out on patrol with a platoon of men, it falls to Staff Sergeant Sam Croft, the third major character in the novel, to lead the men up the formidable Mount Anaka. A Texan, Croft is zealously committed and sadistic; he is a fearless soldier who is indifferent to the loss of his men's lives. Each of them will imagine killing him before the patrol is over.

Mailer's depiction of the characters of Hearn, Cummings, and Croft was representative of a certain method that would characterize much of his later writing, especially his second novel, *Barbary Shore* — and not always with good result. They are not stereotypes at all, though it is tempting to see them as such. Rather they are walking embodiments of ideas and as such are fraught with enormous weight. Cummings represents fascism and power (the novelist hates the former and is ambivalent about the latter); Hearn, power (because of his rank) and the lack of it (again, because of his rank), as well as morality and psychological strength (both compromised at various points, most memorably when he "crawfishes"); and Croft, corrupt power and sadism. This tendency to make characters embody ideas can be seen in the much later, very bad film version of *The Naked and the Dead* (1958), directed by Raoul Walsh: the actions of the lower-ranked men seem universally boring, while scenes among Hearn, Cummings, and Croft are the only ones that hold the viewer's interest. It is a quality that Mailer's writing shares with that of a man who would become a great influence in his life, Jean-Paul Sartre, whose memorable (and not-so-memorable, in the case of, for instance, Jean Genet and Gustave Flaubert) characters are similar embodiments of ideas, albeit in different ways. In Mailer's case, characters like Steven Rojack in *An American Dream* (1964), Sergius O'Shaugnessy in *The Deer Park* (1955) and elsewhere, all the characters in *Barbary Shore*

(1951), and even Gary Gilmore in *The Executioner's Song* (1979) are representatives of Mailer's ideas, though often, as in *The Naked and the Dead*, with results that are great successes for the narrative.

As part of an exercise in control, Cummings sends Hearn on an impossible intelligence and recon patrol over the towering Mount Anaka. The platoon is made up of beautifully delineated minor characters — Red Valsen, Martinez, Wilson, Gallagher, and Goldstein — and is led by Croft. The sergeant is not a man of Cummings's intelligence, but he is consumed by a similar lust for power. He bridles at serving under Hearn, and especially despises the lieutenant's easy ways with the men. As the patrol makes its grueling way, Croft's brutish nature emerges starkly. The gentlest of his men befriends a tiny bird; Croft demands to hold it, and wavering between "compassion for the bird and the thick lusting tension in his throat," he crushes it. Croft leads the men in a clearly futile assault on Mount Anaka; two men die. The men are forced down the mountain when they run into a hornets' nest and flee pell-mell, all observance and rank scattered to the winds. The patrol, even if it had been successful, was hardly necessary: the Japanese had been routed while the men were absent, and headquarters had simply forgotten about the men on patrol.

What was emerging was a deeply pessimistic novel. Although it would not be received as an antiwar book, it is in fact antiwar in its very fiber. The idiocies of the army, the waste of human time and finally of human life, the petty indignities of daily existence — all are part of Mailer's indictment of what was still considered, in 1945, an exalted sphere, and the epitome of normative masculine experience. The war may have been fought to combat fascism and spread democracy, but the army was so endemically authoritarian and undemocratic, in Mailer's view, that the whole endeavor was futile, a joke. Overcome as he was by the daily experience of war and the army's power structure, and with the war itself winding down, he was coming to see the whole war machine and the entire armed forces as an exercise in fascism.

Back in Brooklyn that fall, and over the next year Mailer spent writing the book, world events shaped his view of war and the postwar future. Just a month after his release from the army, Winston Churchill announced, "From Stettin to the Baltic to the Trieste in the Adriatic, an Iron Curtain has descended across the continent." The Potsdam Conference, held the summer that Bea and Norman spent in Provincetown, raised new fears about Soviet demands in Eastern Europe and the Mediterranean. President Truman began to speak in increasingly belligerent tones about the Soviets. Like many Americans, Norman and Bea were horrified by these developments; they wanted better relations with the Soviet Union, not an escalation of tensions between the East and West. Much of this anxiety made its way into

Mailer's portrayal of General Cummings, who in this sense seems positively prescient. Cummings says,

> For the past century the entire historical process has been working toward greater and greater consolidation of power. Physical power for this century, an extension of our universe, and a political power, a political organization to make it possible. Your men of power in America . . . are becoming conscious of their real aims for the first time in our history. Watch. After the war our foreign policy is going to be far more naked, far less hypocritical than it has ever been. We're no longer going to cover our eyes with our left hand while our right is extending an imperialist paw.

In short, Mailer was writing his great war novel at the dawn of a war that would be quite different from the conflict he was describing: the Cold War. As he worked, combining his memories with new perceptions of the world that was emerging, his outlook was bleak indeed.

FOUR

PARIS

By the end of the summer Norman had written two hundred pages. Four books were lined up on his writing table that summer — Tolstoy's *Anna Karenina*, Wolfe's *Of Time and the River*, Dos Passos's *U.S.A.*, and Farrell's *Studs Lonigan* — but he couldn't even think of his book in comparison to them. Elements of them showed up as traces, he later observed, a bit cryptically: the "atmosphere" from Tolstoy, the "rococo" out of Dos Passos, the "basic style" from Farrell, and the occasional rich descriptions from Wolfe. He felt himself distinctly untalented compared with each of these writers. The characters who gave him the most trouble, he said, were the officers, particularly Cummings and Hearn. Originally, Hearn, the Harvard graduate, had been a weak, mean, lifeless character; later Norman thought he had been basing the character too much on himself, wondering what he would have been like as an officer. When he shifted his focus and made Hearn physically strong and handsome, the character began to come together. Still, he was beset by doubts, and even with two hundred pages under his belt, he knew he had a long way to go.

But he already had an avid reader, and one advantageously placed: Adeline Lubell, a Radcliffe roommate of his sister Barbara's, who had taken a job as a junior editor at Little, Brown. Barbara had told Adeline about her brother and had kept her informed about the book's progress, and Adeline had written to Norman twice asking to see the manuscript. Norman must not have felt he had enough to show her, for he didn't respond until the end of summer. The two exchanged letters, and Adeline arranged for Norman to drop off his pages at the Little, Brown offices in Boston while he and Bea were in the Boston suburbs visiting Bea's family on the way back to Brooklyn.

Adeline was terrifically impressed, and fired off a brief, forceful memo arguing that *this* was the most important novel to come out of World War II and that Little, Brown must publish it. She diligently filled out what the press called a Blue Card — recommendations for print run, pricing, and the like — which editors did only when they were serious about a book. And she sent a carbon to Norman, which Barney Mailer would save and carry in his wallet for years, pulling it out to show to strangers as he told his son's success story.

But the book's fate was not at all assured. The language was very strong, given the usual subject matter and verbal style of GIs. Norman was aware of this very early on. Almost every other word would have to be *fuck* if he wanted to reproduce the soldiers' speech accurately. Yet if he used such words, the published novel might be banned from the mails and the author and publisher prosecuted. Early on Norman hit upon the solution: he would substitute the word *fug*. (His cousin Cy still insists that this was his suggestion; it's fair to say they probably discussed it together.) It was a felicitous choice, for in the gerundive form, *fugging* is a phonetically better spelling for the pronunciation (though *fug you* doesn't roll off the tongue quite as happily).

This did not placate the editors at Little, Brown. The editor-in-chief, Angus Cameron, backed Lubell, but the rest of the editorial board either opposed publication or insisted that Norman clean up the language before they could accept the manuscript. Finally they agreed to stand by the decision of an outside authority and sent the manuscript to the noted critic Bernard DeVoto. This choice left Adeline hopeful, as she had heard good things about DeVoto — not least that he had one of the foulest mouths in town — but DeVoto returned a report that stated right at the outset that the book, because of its language, was "barely publishable."

It was Adeline's sad task to write to Norman asking him to clean up the language and offering him a three-hundred-dollar advance and an option contract — which meant that even on delivery Little, Brown reserved the option not to publish it. Norman put the letter aside, so disgusted he did not even answer it, despite his warm feelings for Lubell. He grimly went on writing.

By this time nearly two months had passed, and Norman and Bea were back in Brooklyn, having taken a two-room apartment at 49 Remsen Street, just around the corner from Norman's parents. The place was extremely small; the tiny kitchen took up the apartment's entryway.

Fan had found the apartment for the couple — at just seventy-five dollars a month. Though one wonders about Bea, it seems that Norman took for granted that proximity to his parents was a plus. Apparently he never considered living in a different area — another city, perhaps, or even, less radically, Manhattan. His strong feelings about the area might have played a large part in this, but it still seems curious that Norman would want to set up housekeeping only a stone's throw from his mother's house.

He did love Brooklyn, however, and part of his willingness to live near his parents was due to his instinctive feeling that his roots were in Brooklyn and that he could do his best writing there. If he was to remain in Brooklyn, the Heights was the most congenial area. Brooklyn Heights is a beautiful neighborhood of stately brownstones and peaceful, tree-lined streets; the sweeping Promenade looks out over lower Manhattan and the Roeblings' magnificent Brooklyn Bridge. And the Heights had drawn writers since the country's beginnings. Walt Whitman and Hart Crane had made it their home. More recently — and perhaps more important to Norman — John Dos Passos had lived on Columbia Heights in the 1920s, as had Thomas Wolfe in the early 1930s, when he was finishing *Of Time and the River* (1935). A writer who would become very important to Norman, Henry Miller, had lived on Remsen Street with his wife, June, in the days before *Tropic of Cancer* (1934). Another Miller, the playwright Arthur, actually rented an apartment in the elder Mailers' building on Pierrepont Street. Norman knew Miller was a writer and often encountered him at the mailboxes, but the playwright wasn't known yet, and Norman was not impressed.

Another Heights writer, however, was to become an important friend. Bea had met Norman Rosten first — which aroused some suspicion in her husband. When he learned of Rosten's accomplishments and met the man himself, however, Mailer was quite impressed. Rosten, about ten years his senior, had recently had a book published in the Yale Younger Poets series — a considerable honor — and made a living writing radio plays. In memory, Mailer would inflate these achievements. What was important was that Rosten was the first published writer he knew. Robert Gorham Davis at Harvard had been published, to be sure, but he was a professor. Rosten actually made a living by his pen, a goal Mailer, ever the businessman when it came to his writing career, shared. Moreover, Rosten knew of Mailer's work: he had had a poem in the same issue of *Cross Section* in which Mailer's "A Calculus at Heaven" appeared.

Most immediately, Rosten was instrumental in finding Mailer a place to write. He had an attic studio at 20 Remsen Street that he was vacating for several months, and asked Mailer if he wanted to rent it. (Mailer would later use this incident in *Barbary Shore*.) The rent was just a few dollars a week, which was important to Norman and Bea, for their savings were running out. Like most veterans, they were members of the 52-20 club, which paid out $20 a week for a year (52 weeks; thus the name), but that didn't go very far, even in 1946.

Mailer began to question the wisdom of letting Little, Brown's offer of an option contract languish, fearing it might be his only chance at publication. Running into Rosten on the street, he confided his worries to the older man. Rosten immediately volunteered to take Mailer to his publisher — who turned out to be Ted Amussen at Rinehart, the same editor who had been interested in Mailer's early Harvard writing. The two men visited Amussen's offices together, and Mailer left his manuscript.

Later, Mailer would be struck by the stark difference in how he was treated by the two houses. Amussen gave him an answer in two days, compared with the two to three months Little, Brown had taken. Like Angus Cameron, Amussen said he was worried about the book's language, but, unlike Cameron, he agreed to publish the book no matter what — in other words, he offered a "straight" contract rather than an option contract. Mailer viewed this as the gentlemanly thing to do; the option contact had made him feel terribly anxious, which was certainly understandable in a young writer. Furthermore, Amussen was offering a handsome advance, $1,250. Norman took it. He couldn't resist writing a little note to Adeline Lubell at Little, Brown, putting particular emphasis on the fact that Rinehart had taken just a few days to return an answer. (Mailer did not know that his manuscript had run into trouble at Rinehart as well, saved only by Amussen's decided enthusiasm. Amussen's editor-in-chief, John Selby, insisted that they reject the book, but Amussen went over his head, bounding into the office of Stanley Rinehart himself, president and cofounder of the company. He persuaded Rinehart to read the manuscript, saying it would be a grave mistake to let such a property go, and Rinehart was convinced.)

Bea and Norman were elated, of course: a contract was a major hurdle. But the manuscript was unfinished, and he knew it needed a lot of work. He signed the contract in November, but he'd need at least six months more just to finish, so work began in earnest. He was at the studio from ten in the morning until late afternoon; he later estimated that he wrote at least twenty-five pages a week. At night, he read his work to Bea. She had begun a novel as well, which she would in turn read to him. Every few days they would bring their manuscripts to Barney and Fan and read them there. Fan would moan, "Oh Norman, the language!" but generally his parents were an uncritical audience.

Mailer showed the manuscript to anyone who would agree to look at it. In this way he made another important friend: another neighbor in the rooming house at 20 Remsen Street, Charlie Devlin. Devlin was what is known as a "black Irishman," a slightly eccentric, small, thin man who never had enough money. He always remained something of an enigma to Mailer and others who knew him. Here is the way Mailer introduces Devlin's fictional counterpart in his second novel:

> In everything he did there were elements of such order, demanding, monastic. He was unyielding and sometimes forbidding. Dressed in the anonymous clothing of a man who buys his garments as cheaply as possible, there were nonetheless two creases always to be found in a vertical parallel upon his buttocks. The straight black hair was always combed, he never needed a shave. And his room, clean as any cell . . . described an unending campaign against the ceiling which sweated water and the floor which collected dust.

Himself a writer, Devlin was unable to find a publisher for his work, which was strongly influenced by James Farrell. Devlin was very serious about writing and was, his friends believed, an outstanding critic. He could be mean, but he was always right.

Rosten introduced Devlin to Mailer — again, the meeting would appear transmuted into fiction in *Barbary Shore* — and there is the impression that Devlin almost immediately started to make changes in Mailer's manuscript, mostly by cutting. Before long the arrangement was formalized, with Mailer paying Charlie for fifty-hour weeks. The editing took about a month. Mailer adapted to it very quickly, once he learned how Charlie's mind worked.

But Charlie Devlin was more than a brilliant editor. He was a philosopher manqué, although the nature of his philosophy was difficult to pin down. A lapsed Catholic, Devlin was drawn to leftist causes. A strong and powerful kinship formed between the two men. Devlin was never a success as a writer himself, but for years he carried with him his tattered, signed copy of *The Naked and the Dead*. A friend saw a certain nobility in his promotion of Mailer's career over his own. For his part, Mailer would make 20 Remsen Street the setting for *Barbary Shore* and Devlin the model for the mysterious McLeod, his relationship with Devlin reflected in the hero Lovett's strange fascination with McLeod, the enigmatic ex–Party member. Sadly, however, he lost touch with Devlin not long after.

With Devlin's help, the manuscript finally took shape, and in August 1947, Mailer turned it in to Rinehart. He dedicated it to Bea and his mother, and added an acknowledgments page on which he thanked Amussen and Amussen's successor, William Raney, as well as Charlie Devlin.

THROUGH THE LONG ordeal of writing and revising *The Naked and the Dead*, Norman was in constant touch, by letter, with his army buddy Fig

Gwaltney, now back in Arkansas, attending college on the GI Bill, and courting the woman he would marry in 1949, Emma Clara ("Ecey"). Like Norman, he was embarking on a literary career — he would eventually write eleven novels, some optioned to Hollywood — and many of their letters contained long, no-holds-barred critiques of each other's work. (Their friendship would suffer a major break in the 1950s over their writing; Norman was often terribly hard on Fig, who was understandably somewhat resentful at what he saw sometimes as condescension.) They discussed domestic details and planned Norman's frequent trips to Arkansas, when Fig would take him off into the Ozarks to fish. Openly affectionate, Norman's letters often closed, "I love you, you son of a bitch"; after Fig married Ecey, they invariably closed "Love to Ecey." Fig was affectionately called "old eagle nose" and "you white-haired baboon" (his hair was so blond as to appear white), and Norman derided Fig's "illiteracy," especially his atrocious spelling. Much was made of the North/South divide, as Norman continued his love/hate affair with all things Southern. In 1947 Fig served as a sounding board for his terrible doubts, and tentative hopes, for his war novel.

For *The Naked and the Dead* was out of Norman's hands. He was so unsure of its reception that he could not even contemplate beginning another book. If *Naked* (as he and Fig referred to it) were taken simply as a historical novel, he would be condemned to write potboilers for the rest of his career. If it received the reception he half hoped it deserved, his would be the career of a serious literary man. Either way, it was hard to know how to proceed: what kind of novel would the public expect of him? Moreover, he felt he had no immediate wellspring of experience on which to draw. This was to be a continuing problem. For now, he felt suspended, in limbo until the book came out and he had some idea of its reception. Like many other intellectuals after the Second World War, Norman and Bea decided to take advantage of the GI Bill and go to France. They sailed in October 1947 on the RMS *Queen Elizabeth*.

On board, Norman wrote Fig a long letter outlining his anxieties about the book. He said the book was a nearly poisonous antiwar novel and feared that he would be called terrible names because of it, *Communist* and *Red* the milder ones. He also confided that he'd become quite a bit more left-wing lately, believing that most of the world simply wanted to return to war, and also that the Soviet Union was not the villain it was made out to be. The radicalization of Norman Mailer was well under way.

In France, the GI Bill paid tuition and living expenses (about $150 a month) for any veteran who had served for ninety days and was honorably discharged. The exchange rate — 226 francs on the dollar in the black market — would allow them to live well and even to save money. Norman and Bea both enrolled at the Sorbonne, in a year-long survey called Cours de Civilisation Française. The course was seemingly designed for Americans on the GI Bill; the work wasn't very demanding and the lectures not terribly interesting, and sooner or later just about everyone dropped out, including Norman.

He complained to Fig Gwaltney that he and Bea were "lonesome" in Paris, able to meet only other Americans. Paris had been hit hard by shortages, which was a little depressing. Electricity was being conserved, and in the evenings it looked as if a brownout was taking place, thanks to the dimmed lights. Gradually, Norman and Bea bonded with a circle of Harvard graduates attending the Sorbonne course. Mark Linenthal, a fellow *Advocate* staffer, lived in the Place d'Italie on the Left Bank with his then wife, the smart Southerner Alice Adams, herself to become a major writer. Adams remembers that they met almost every day, having coffee at the Mailers' small apartment in the rue Brea or at the Café de Flore. Stanley Geist, another Harvard man a few years older than Norman, lived on the Avenue Gabriel with his wife, Eileen; gradually they too became part of the Mailers' circle.

It was an exciting time to be in Paris. Memories of the heyday of the Lost Generation were still fresh, and a new generation of expatriates was flocking to the city. The *Paris Review* was not yet born, but already some of its glamorous founders were making their mark in the city. Gay Talese has described how members of the new generation all seemed to be eternally twenty-six years old, singling out a crop of them who made a pilgrimage to postwar Paris:

> But they were not Sad Young Men, nor were they Lost; they were witty, irreverent sons of a conquering nation and, though they came mostly from wealthy parents and had been graduated from Harvard or Yale, they seemed endlessly delighted in posing as paupers and dodging the bill collectors . . . they lived in happy squalor on the Left Bank for two or three years amid the whores, jazz musicians and pederast poets, and became involved with people both tragic and mad, including a passionate Spanish painter who one day cut open a vein in his leg and finished his final portrait with his own blood. In July they drove down to Pamplona to run from the bulls, and when they returned they played tennis . . . at Saint-Cloud on a magnificent court overlooking Paris — and when they tossed up the ball to serve, there, sprawled out before them, was the whole city: the Eiffel Tower, Sacre-Coeur, the Opera, the spires of Notre Dame in the distance.

The man who best represented this generation, observed Talese, was George Plimpton, who would later become an important friend of Norman's. The more famous of the postwar expatriates — William and Rose Styron, Jim and Gloria Jones, Peter and Patsy Matthiessen, Terry Southern, and Harold Humes — had not arrived yet; nor had Alexander Trocchi and the colorful cast of characters associated with the literary magazine *Merlin*. But as Talese has pointed out, the atmosphere was ripe for such an invasion, even in the year the Mailers were there: he chalked it up to a search for Hemingway, and there may well have been elements of that. At any rate, a small but earnest group of expatriates found themselves, like their forebears, sitting on Paris *terrasses* and discussing literature and politics as the saucers piled up before them.

The expatriates were interested not only in each other, but in the lively French intellectual scene as well. Malraux's star was still in the ascendancy. Jean-Paul Sartre and Simone de Beauvoir were the talk of all the cafés — indeed, if you were very lucky, you might see them there, conversing under a cloud of blue smoke. Sartre's *Being and Nothingness*, published in 1946, set forth the then radical philosophy of existentialism: that human consciousness is engaged in a perpetual, and futile, flight from the anguish of realizing our own absolute freedom. Though Sartre did declare that "man is a useless passion," the existentialist point of view was not on the face of it as nihilistic or futile as many of its followers believed, mainly because of its emphasis on human freedom.

Mailer was immediately drawn to the concept of the existential hero: the man living outside the law, free from social roles, entirely his own. (Sartre would probably have disagreed, seeing Mailer's interpretation as yet another mystification and a form of bad faith.) He would later declare his next novel, *Barbary Shore,* which may well have been gestating by this time, "the first existential American novel." But it was never really clear what he meant by this. He seems to have been inclined, not entirely wrongly, to view it in rather seamless combination with the ideas of an earlier hero, Malraux: that the existential hero could be and must be politically committed. Sartre's life, in this light, was a testimony to this concept as much as was Malraux's.

Other aspects of Sartre's life and ideas drew Mailer to existentialism and to an ongoing comparison of his life with Sartre's. Both thinkers, for instance, were fascinated by the edge, especially the criminal edge: Sartre's fascination with Jean Genet, the criminal and writer, as expressed in his long, somewhat obsessive *Saint Genet* (1952; English translation, 1963), in many ways prefigures Mailer's deep and tragic involvement with prisoner Jack Henry Abbott in 1981. Although it was Gide who invented the concept of the *acte gratuit,* Sartre found the concept very useful and gave it new currency; his conception of the *acte gratuit* was arguably central to Mailer's worldview. Both men believed — and their beliefs shaped their work in this period — that, throughout the forties and fifties, the world was changing radically at every moment, and both wanted to *be there* in some way; both asked all the right questions during these years in their work and in their lives. Both believed — it was a fundamental truth in Sartre's philosophy — that the writer must be *engagé*, and this conviction came from romantic strains in the makeup of each writer, though Sartre probably would not admit to this.

There were also striking biographical parallels between them: each was, though neither admitted it, at bottom a mama's boy, both deeply tied to their mothers throughout their lives and shaped by their early childhood relationships with their mothers. Each, though again neither would admit it, wanted to be on the cusp of what was happening, to write from the edge, yet each was peculiarly bourgeois. Sartre, except in early childhood and during the war, lived in comfortable surroundings; in spite of his general disdain for possessions, there's a wonderful scene in Ronald Hayman's 1987 biography in which Sartre shows off his beloved collection of Pléiade editions of the classics (while living in an apartment with his mother). Norman would live most of his life in a comfortable brownstone in Brooklyn Heights a few blocks from his parents, with whom he would have dinner almost every Friday night.

More important is the fact that each would come to define the age in a meaningful way, Sartre as a public intellectual whose influence was almost immeasurable, both as a symbol and as a participant and prime mover on the political scene, and Mailer as a writer whose work demanded to be taken seriously and as, like Sartre, a recorder and participant in the important political and cultural events of his time. It is impossible to imagine this century without either man.

Finally, each was in many ways a product of modernity. Existentialism as Sartre defined it grew organically out of the fact of World War II, the ensuing Cold War, and the enormous concomitant psychological, cultural, and ontological changes in those who had lived through them; similarly, Mailer would be driven to alternative literary forms to express this phenomenon, and at the same time he felt an ongoing need to define and articulate the changes modernity wrought.

But it is hard to know in what form Norman was imbibing Sartre's ideas. Most likely he found them in the press, for Sartre and de Beauvoir were constantly in the newspapers, and of course had their own magazine, *Les Temps Modernes*. In 1948, *Being and Nothingness* was available only in French — it wouldn't be translated into English until 1956 — and Norman's French was, though fairly accomplished, not really good enough to handle complex philosophical abstractions. The philosophy had been popularized, of course — in Sartre's novel *Nausea* (though that too would not be translated until 1949) and in de Beauvoir's three published novels. Most likely, Norman knew Sartre's work through an extremely popular paperback, William Barrett's *What Is Existentialism?* (1947), published by Grove Press, a publisher known to be up-to-the-minute. It is also likely that Norman would have been exposed to Sartre's ideas through the 1946 Broadway production, directed by John Huston, of *No Exit,* and in the popular American press. But it was Sartre's image that influenced him and led him to follow Sartre's career and later read many of his writings: Sartre represented the philosopher hero, the public intellectual who altered the course of events through his work and through his actions. Many of Mailer's works show the influence of Sartre's ideas (as Mailer understood them), and he, in effect, felt himself to be no less than his country's Sartre.

The Mailers and their expatriate friends were exploring other potential arenas for political and intellectual expression. Somehow they fell in with a group of Spaniards, refugees from the Franco regime. Following the end of the Civil War in 1939, Spain had remained neutral in World War II, but when the Cold War succeeded it, Franco began to pressure the Spanish left, many of whom left the country for centers like Paris, where they sought out members of the Resistance and other antifascists. Norman wrote enthusiastically to Fig on May 21, 1949, that he and Bea had spent April in Spain and that the people in the Underground were remarkable. He was especially impressed, he said, by the stark difference between black and white that he encountered in Spain; since the war he had thought grayness would prevail in every country.

These Spaniards were deeply committed to political action. They enlisted the Mailers and the Linenthals to provide material aid and even, it seems, to help arrange prison escapes for their comrades back in Spain. Mark Linenthal has told the Mailer biographer Peter Manso how he, his wife, and the Mailers made a trip to Barcelona to arrange one such escape. Norman and Mark changed their francs into pesetas in Geneva. They rolled the pesetas into tight wads, put them into condoms, and inserted the condoms into toiletry tubes and jars. They stuffed propaganda in the spare tire of Norman's Citroën, making their way across the technically closed border between France and Spain, where they found their contacts, and then returned, feeling quite adventurous.

Undeniably, Norman and his expatriate friends were doing good deeds, and their commitment ran deep, but the politics behind this commitment were relatively straightforward. Norman was an antifascist, and because the fascists opposed the left, he identified himself as a man of the left. Beyond that, he seems to have devoted little thought to where he stood on the spectrum of left politics. Just as he believed himself an existentialist without reading Sartre, so he believed himself a Marxist sympathizer without reading Marx. In reality, although it was a concept that would horrify him within a very short period of time, he was a left-leaning liberal. All this, however, was about to change.

At a party given by Harold Kaplan, the Paris correspondent for the *Partisan Review* (who paid the bills by working at UNESCO), Norman and Bea met the remarkable Jean Malaquais, the man who would become Norman's political mentor and lifelong friend. The forty-year-old Malaquais, according to Eileen Finletter (she and her husband, Stanley Geist, were perhaps Malaquais's closest friends), was a short, romantic figure, a Polish Jew who had worked his way to Paris on a boat à la Joseph Conrad (though without Conrad's social background). He'd taken his name from the quai Malaquais. For a time secretary to André Gide, he was a novelist in his own right, though barely known in the United States, and was the winner of the Prix Renaudot for his second novel, *Men from Nowhere* (1943). In left politics, he was "a figure to be reckoned with . . . He was a Trotskyite — but so far out he couldn't be called that," says Finletter.

Malaquais had traveled to the United States a couple of months before, and when they met in Paris he and Norman almost immediately began talking about American foreign policy. Malaquais would later recollect how utterly unsophisticated and uninformed he found Mailer: he complained that Norman knew nothing of the Russian Revolution, nothing of the history of radicalism. He went right to the heart of things when he said, "In Western Europe all students are political animals, but in America a writer is a writer is a writer. Mailer grew up without political orientation and didn't have the curiosity." Perhaps he voiced this opinion to Norman; if he did, it must have cemented their friendship. For Norman had long felt that the writer must be a man *engagé;* that was why he admired Hemingway, and that was why he said he hoped to be another Malraux. Of course, Norman was making a grave error: to effect political change it is necessary to put one's ego aside, for politics is a collective, not a solitary, endeavor. But Norman preferred the more romantic view. This contradiction would bedevil him in the years to come, compromising some of his best thinking and his best work.

Malaquais saw that Norman's politics were naively romantic. What he and Norman argued about most heatedly was Norman's belief in American electoral politics — and, more specifically, Norman's support of a Henry Wallace candidacy. Wallace, a former New Dealer and vice president during FDR's third term, had been fired from his post as secretary of commerce under Truman in 1946 for criticizing the Democrats' hard-line stand against the USSR. In 1948, he was running for president as the candidate of the newly formed Progressive Party, advocating sweeping social reform and friendship with the Soviet Union. The Progressives won the support of the U.S. Communist Party, which would prove to be a dubious victory indeed. Yet, like many Americans frightened by the specter of the Cold War, Norman and Bea and most of their friends found Wallace the only alternative, the best hope for the future.

To Malaquais, this was utter nonsense. The electoral system he found infinitely corrupt, as far from democracy as fascism. Norman would never see eye to eye with him on this point. But Malaquais's other objections would come to trouble Norman deeply over the years. With painstaking erudition, Malaquais explained to Norman that one couldn't be sentimentally "for" Russia. As a Trotskyite, Malaquais was deeply opposed to Stalin's regime, and he hammered away at Norman with talk of Siberian labor camps, repression, and purges. Though Norman would never become an anti-Stalinist first and foremost, this line of argument was not without effect. Malaquais had a larger, more complicated worldview that deeply transfixed Norman, though he could never quite puzzle it out to his satisfaction. Malaquais believed that capitalism was as great an evil as fascism, and that the West had as great a capacity for tyranny as the Soviet Union. Both the United States and the USSR were essentially systems of state capitalism, and thus inherently fascist. It was not a view that left any clear line of action open, and thus it was not entirely attractive to Norman. But Malaquais's view was intellectually compelling and had the philosophical complexity he was coming to admire, and the argument took hold in his mind over many months and years.

For the time being, Norman remained a Wallace supporter, and rather enjoyed his quarrels with Malaquais. The men became fast friends. Jean's wife, Galy, was an artist, and got Bea, as well as Norman (who told Fig in a February 1949 letter that he'd taken it up), interested in painting. The Malaquaises loved the theater, and the Mailers went often with them. On one memorable occasion they went to the Ringling Brothers circus and discussed politics so heatedly that they missed all the action in the rings below.

If it seems odd that this older French intellectual should have taken up a young American studying at the Sorbonne on the GI Bill, it must be remembered that word was out that Norman's first novel was going to be a major sensation, and that the author might well become a prominent literary figure. Then too Norman radiated a certain glow on this account. Rinehart had mounted an impressive publicity campaign, and sent Norman mockups of the ads, which slightly embarrassed him. He received many sets of bound galleys — Rinehart printed many more than was their custom — and Norman circulated them among his friends. They all thought the book was brilliant. Alice Adams and Mark Linenthal remember a trip the two couples made to Normandy, where, on the rocks by the sea, they reenacted scenes from *The Naked and the Dead*, with Norman playing Croft, strutting about and shouting in a Southern accent.

Stanley Karnow, in his 1997 memoir, *Paris in the Fifties*, recalls that Norman was not really a part of the social scene in Paris — until the publicity machine for *The Naked and the Dead* began operating at full speed. Then Bea and Norman threw a party at which, as Karnow remembers it, "*le tout* Manhattan" was in attendance. It was merry enough, but when a German made a pass at Claude, Karnow's companion, the party "degenerated into a brawl." In hindsight, such an event seems almost an omen of what was to come. But Norman and Bea were new to partying, and a rocky evening served to round out their enjoyment of Norman's day in the sun.

For Norman, no idyll would be complete without his family there to share it with him. It was the Mailer family way, and everybody around him seemed to accept that. So Fan sailed over with Barbara in April 1948; Barney, who had been working as an accountant for a Jewish relief agency in Poland, joined them in Paris, where they took an apartment near the Trocadero. The situation, Norman told Fig, wasn't perfect; he cited family dinners as an example. He was, however, looking forward to a planned trip to Italy on which Barbara and Fanny would come along.

It must have been odd for Norman to learn that his book was sparking interest from a continent away, like distant thunder. In June, Barbara and her mother accompanied Norman down to Rome, meeting the recent family friend Barbara Probst at the Hotel Hassler. From there Fan went back to Paris, and the three young people drove to Capri. At Nice, Norman called for his mail at American Express. He came out with a whole stack of it, and got into the hot, stuffy car to read it. Cables, reviews, letters. Norman looked up and said, "Gee, I'm number one on the bestseller list."

THOUGH HE HAD sensed that a "big" war novel would be a good trying ground for his talent, Mailer underestimated how deep was the country's need for literary attention to the recent trauma. The public was still in the grip of war fever, eager for books and movies about their most recent experience.

The novel remained at the top of the bestseller list for two months, and nearly two hundred thousand copies would be sold in the next year. *The Naked and the Dead* was indisputably "a good read," devoured by ex-GIs and booklovers alike. Its flaws — an occasional turgidity in style and an overreliance on Dos Passos — were not those likely to affect the book-buying public. Reviews generally both assessed the book correctly and understood the response to it: it was a great war book, and it addressed the public's need to make sense of the war experience. Quibbles concerned the book's length, its repetitiousness, and, of course, its language, though most lauded the latter's accuracy. The *New York Herald Tribune Book Review* wrote: "With this astonishing book, [Mailer] joins the ranks of major American novelists. This reviewer has no hesitation in calling *The Naked and the Dead* a great war novel. Do you want to know how American combat soldiers of the second World War ate, slept, swore? Read *The Naked and the Dead*." David Dempsey, reviewing for the *New York Times,* was more tempered in his praise, though he started out strong: "Undoubtedly the most ambitious novel to be written about the recent conflict, it is also the most ruthlessly honest and in scope and integrity compares favorably with the best that followed World War I." But he faulted the book's excesses in obscenity and attention to sexual matters, closing by saying, "*The Naked and the Dead* is not a great book, but indisputably it bears witness to a new and significant talent among American novelists."

Somewhat numbed, back in Paris Norman celebrated, taking the Linenthals to the Tour d'Argent. Excitement gave way, of course, to doubts. "I must have done something wrong," he fretted. "They shouldn't have liked it." He was absolutely serious: he viewed the book as a serious literary venture and as a strong antiwar statement; it wasn't supposed to be a bestseller. He had never seen it as a commercial book, and commercial success seemed to demand that he change his view of his career, though how he didn't know. Moreover, even mediocre reviews hailed him as a "major" new writer, a talent to be reckoned with and from whom great things were expected; this, of course, was exactly what he had hoped for and worked for, but he was bewildered once it came to pass. He had a sense that he was going off into unknown territory, and brave as he was, he was worried. Finally, he really didn't know if the book was that good. It might all have been just incredible luck.

FIVE

POLITICS AND HOLLYWOOD

The success of *The Naked and the Dead* and its effects on Mailer would continue to reverberate throughout the rest of his life. But in the summer of 1948, when he and Bea returned from Europe, he seemed to family and friends remarkably well adjusted to it. When visiting family at the resort in Deal, New Jersey, in July, he impressed his cousin Cy as seeming to have everything pretty much in perspective. He had minor quibbles — now that he had access to American publications, many reviews seemed to him to have missed the point — yet he seemed generally content. He had started a second novel in Paris, but he wasn't especially eager to get back to that.

The immediate reason Norman and Bea had returned home was to attend Bea's sister's wedding in Boston, but Norman also had a pressing professional reason for returning home, which was a little curious: Lillian Hellman, the playwright who had won esteem and fame for *The Children's Hour* in 1934 and in 1939 for *The Little Foxes,* had seen *The Naked and the Dead* in galleys and wanted to take out an option to produce it as a play. Cy conveyed her offer to Norman, and he and Bea immediately made plans to return so that he could confer with Hellman. This wasn't particularly unusual. Like many middle-class intellectuals of the time, he and Bea venerated the theater. At Harvard, Norman had tried to produce scripts for the Drama Society and had also been involved with a Boston experimental theater, painting scenery and performing any necessary function short of acting. Hellman's plays were big popular successes that took risks, conventional though often didactic stories that attacked social injustices and hypocrisies in ways that would appeal to Norman. Her 1941 *Watch on the Rhine,* for example, was a powerful drama about the incipient dangers of fascism. But a little over a month later Hellman gave up, feeling that she could not do justice to the book's complex narrative structure. Moreover, the financial incentive was almost ludicrous: Hellman offered the standard option fee of five hundred dollars.

On the other hand, finances hardly mattered. Sudden wealth of the kind that came to the Mailers in 1949 is probably best understood by the example of lottery winners. Norman likes to tell a story about receiving his first real check from Rinehart, in the amount of forty thousand dollars. He took it to the Brooklyn Heights branch of Bankers Trust to deposit it, where the clerk, eyeing his combat jacket and T-shirt, asked him where he usually banked. Norman finally remembered the Manhattan branch and the name of a bank clerk who could identify him. The Brooklyn clerk called Manhattan, and Norman heard him emitting a long "Ohh" of recognition. He got off the phone and congratulated Norman on his book's vault to the bestseller list.

Norman told Lillian Ross, who wrote a brief profile of him for *The New Yorker,* that he had received a royalty check for the year for thirty thousand dollars, after taxes, and that he intended to bank it and live on it for five years. In this, more plausible account, Norman failed to address, and perhaps did not foresee, the longevity of his book's success — for he had produced what every writer and publisher dreams of, a book that comes close to being a perennial seller.

Norman was, not unexpectedly, immediately bewildered by the money. He called in his cousin Cy, now a lawyer, to manage his affairs. Perhaps because his relationship with his cousin acquainted him with censorship and publishing issues, Cy would become an expert in publishing law and a pioneering censorship lawyer. There were those who questioned Norman's dependence on Cy, and many found the lawyer's elegant, crisp demeanor faintly off-putting. But Cy was blessed with sound financial sense, and Norman would remain loyal to him over the years. In a sense, the idealization of Cy on Fanny's side of the family during Norman's childhood never abated.

Perhaps he feared that too much change would disrupt his life to an even greater degree. In any event, he and Bea did not even take an apartment — he told Lillian Ross he distrusted apartments — and instead, after Bea's sister's wedding in July, a few days' vacation in Maine, and a visit to Arkansas to see Fig and Ecey Gwaltney, they rented a furnished room in the boardinghouse at 20 Remsen Street where Norman had kept a writing studio before their trip to France. The rent was thirty dollars a month. It had no cooking facilities, and Bea and Norman usually took their meals with Fanny and Barney on Pierrepont Street.

The press was eager for news about the young best-selling writer. The jacket copy had helped to fuel the publicity machine; the caption under the author photo read, in part, "Brooklyn, Harvard, Leyte, Japan, soda-jerk, usher, flat painter, rifleman; Story magazine, Cross Section, first novel — Mr. Mailer's literary itinerary reads like the traditional background for the novelist." But Norman was reluctant to provide the personal interest type of material the press sought. He had already embarrassed himself by showing up at a Rinehart reception wearing a T-shirt and baseball cap. He later said that it had been a hot day and he hadn't expected anyone to dress up, yet rumors that he acted and looked like a truck driver persisted. When Lillian Ross profiled him she expressed great surprise when he showed up in a gray suit and nice tie. All the attention was somewhat mystifying, though Bea noted in a letter to the Gwaltneys that Norman had become a real local hero in Brooklyn. Mothers no longer wanted their sons to grow up to be doctors and lawyers, she said. "'Go to your room, Sonny,' they tell their offspring, 'and write a book like Norman Mailer did.'"

Yet Norman seemed without direction, which was uncomfortable for him. It is not possible to overestimate the extraordinary pressures he was under at the time. His success had opened up any number of avenues to him. It ensured that whatever he had to say, people would listen, thus in a sense recapitulating his childhood, when Fanny's love made him feel he was the center of the universe. At this juncture, he may well have sensed what would become obvious over the course of his career: that his would be a life of moment, a life in the public eye, a life with consequences. He had prepared himself for this, he wanted it, he was eager to set forth. But he was only twenty-five years old.

THE DIRECTION he chose to take was one he had been hinting at for some time. Through Rinehart, he issued a press release stating that he did not think it was possible for a writer *not* to be political in this age. More tellingly, in an August interview with Louise Levitas for the *New York Star*, he very pointedly turned the conversation repeatedly to politics. He was, he told her, suspending work on his next novel to immerse himself in the Henry Wallace campaign. He had been a member of the Progressive Citizens of America, he told his interviewer, even before he left for Europe — and what he had seen over there only increased his sense of urgency. His leftist leanings were clear, as in these remarks about Italy and the effects of the Marshall Plan:

> Italy is pretty bad right now, a pretty ugly country. The Marshall Plan is keeping in power the smartest, dirtiest, old-time politicians, the broken-down aristocracy that would normally have been

kicked out. Italy would be better off under communism than under the kind of very bad capitalism they have there. You don't have to be a Communist to see that.

Norman couldn't have known that he was jumping into the middle of the very last truly "progressive" presidential campaign the United States would see for twenty years, until "Clean Gene" McCarthy ran on an antiwar ticket in 1968. The Wallace ticket represented the last mainstream effort to carry forward the New Deal program in its original spirit before the urgency of the Cold War and the red-baiting hysterics of Joe McCarthy made any such effort impossible. Between 1946 and 1948, the Taft-Hartley Act had taken the wind out of the union movement's sails, Truman's national health care bill had been narrowly defeated in Congress, and Representative Richard Nixon (R-California) had initiated a new era of Communist paranoia with the revelation of the Hiss papers. The progressive hopefulness of the postwar years would end abruptly with Wallace's resounding defeat and Stalin's invasion of Czechoslovakia, events occurring within months of each other. Thereafter, it would be difficult if not impossible for a politically left artist or writer to make a living in the United States for well over a decade. But Norman couldn't have known this when he signed on to the Wallace campaign in 1948.

For the time being, he and Bea threw themselves into the campaign, Bea canvassing by telephone from campaign headquarters on Fifth Avenue, and Norman making speeches. The two speeches best remembered were at Columbia University and the Ninety-second Street Y; Norman was not particularly effective in either, yet he was greatly in demand as the young author of *The Naked and the Dead,* and he was eager to oblige the Progressive Party. Its goals — sweeping social reforms, disarmament, and a less hostile stance toward the Soviet Union — made sense to Norman; like many progressives, he understood and perhaps feared that the permanent state of emergency created by the Cold War could ultimately dampen if not suppress any efforts to pursue a progressive social and economic agenda internationally, and possibly domestically as well.

Still, he was not very clear about the relation of Communism to Wallace's progressivism, just as he was uncomfortable that his celebrity made his political stance seem so weighty. At a Wallace rally in Yankee Stadium, which he attended with two friends from Paris, Stanley Karnow and his French wife, Claude, a spotlight played over the crowd, focusing on celebrities. Norman said to his friends, "When it reaches me, I'm going to declare that tomorrow I'm joining the Communist Party." When the spotlight was trained on him, however, he merely stood up, gripping his hands over his head like a boxing champion.

In October Norman made a two-week trip to Hollywood to campaign for Wallace. He was warmly welcomed by the left-leaning segment of the industry, especially the actor Gene Kelly and his even more progressive wife, Betsy Blair. Kelly and friends John Huston, Fredric March, and Humphrey Bogart welcomed Norman at a fundraising party given by the Kellys. According to actress Shelley Winters, who met him on this occasion, he made a considerably better impression than he seems to have made in his earlier speaking appearances, and the Hollywood crowd was much taken by him, urging him to leave the East Coast and write for the movies. Another occasion at which Norman spoke was a huge Wallace rally sponsored by the Independent Citizens' Committee of the Arts, Sciences, and Professions Committee. Here, according to Winters, Norman briefly met Marilyn Monroe, who was working as an usher, though he would later make a famous case about never having met her. (It's most likely that she made no impression.)

Not everyone was impressed by Norman's impassioned activity on the part of Henry Wallace. Many felt he was essentially naive, especially concerning the role of Communists in the Progressive Party. Irwin Shaw, something of a rival because of his own war novel, *The Young Lions* (1948), met Mailer in Hollywood and tried to convince him he was following the wrong course, offering traditional arguments about the dangers of a third-party candidate dividing the vote. Novelist Calder Willingham approached him more directly, confronting him with traditional anti-Stalinist arguments about the Moscow trials. Norman, he felt, simply hadn't heard of such things.

After Wallace's resounding defeat in November, Norman was left without an organized political cause. But this in no way lessened his activism. He must have seen it as providential when word reached him that his political mentor, Jean Malaquais, was now in New York, having accepted a job teaching at the New School for Social Research. Norman located him through the writer Dan Wolf, a friend who was Malaquais's student at the New School. Bertram Wolfe, the ex-Communist author of *Three Who Made a Revolution* (1948), had found Malaquais a room in his own building on Montgomery Street in Brooklyn. Norman and Malaquais struck up their old friendship, though the terms had shifted significantly. Because the immediate challenge of the Wallace campaign was over, Malaquais no longer felt the need to convert Norman from his belief in democracy and electoral politics; he now set out to start from the beginning, educating Norman in the true politics of socialism.

Through the fall and winter of 1948–49, Norman and Malaquais thrashed out the major terms of their argument. Through long evenings in their Brooklyn rooms, Malaquais gave Norman extensive reading lists.

When Norman brought Charlie Devlin, his other political mentor, around to meet Malaquais, the Frenchman dismissed Devlin as a Party hack, which must have both wounded and impressed Norman. Mailer's attitude toward Malaquais was one of near-total devotion. Malaquais was translating *The Naked and the Dead* into French, and took great pains to show Mailer just how bad his writing was, in this sense replacing Devlin as his mentor. Mailer later acknowledged that Malaquais had been a tremendous influence on him stylistically, but at the time it must have been a humbling and even humiliating experience. That he sat there and took it shows how deep his respect for and dependence on the Frenchman was.

There were those who watched Norman's growing thralldom with dismay. Fanny Mailer was deeply suspicious of her son's friend, though in this case she seems wisely to have kept her own counsel. Bea and friends like Mickey Knox, an actor Norman had met in Hollywood, questioned the Frenchman's relentless critiquing of Norman's writing. Those on the left who knew Malaquais, and who were watching Norman's progress with interest, generally found Malaquais dangerous or, at the very least, a phony. Lillian Hellman, among others, worried about Malaquais's influence on Norman; Irving Howe, from a different position on the left, credited Malaquais with educating Norman about Stalin. Furthermore, there was the sense that Malaquais and his wife, Galy, were just too close to the Mailers; Bea and Norman rented a house in the winter of 1949 in Jamaica, Vermont, and the French couple were almost constant guests. Harvard acquaintance Mark Linenthal found it odd that because of Malaquais's criticisms of his style, Mailer kept a copy of *The Oxford Book of English Verse* on his bedside table.

Matters came to a head at the end of March 1949, at the so-called Waldorf Conference, or the Cultural and Scientific Conference for World Peace, sponsored by the National Council of Arts, Sciences, and Professions. Though many anti-Stalinists were in attendance, and though the State Department had anticipated a Communist powwow and thus limited foreign involvement in the conference, the meetings were still largely pro-Stalinist and pro–Soviet Union. (The actual Communist Party kept an extremely low profile due to the Soviets' recent invasion of Czechoslovakia.) In attendance were such New York intellectuals as Irving Howe, Dwight Macdonald, Mary McCarthy, and Lillian Hellman, whose role, as they saw it, was to infiltrate and speak from the floor. Mailer was scheduled to speak on March 26 at a panel on writing and publishing; his fellow panelists were Howard Fast, Harvard professor F. O. Matthiessen, and Russian writer A. A. Fayadev; Louis Untermeyer would moderate.

Expectations ran high that the boy wonder and ardent Wallace supporter would either deliver a rousing speech denouncing the United States and praising the Soviets or condemn the whole conference as Stalinist and reactionary. Calls for Mailer to speak punctuated the other panelists' presentations.

But Mailer instead stood up and denounced the very idea of a peace conference, declaring that the expansive foreign policies of both superpowers absolutely precluded any peace efforts. "I have come here as a Trojan horse. I don't believe in peace conferences. They won't do any good. So long as there is capitalism, there is going to be war," he said. Then he moved on to his main theme: "I am going to make myself even more unpopular. I am afraid both the United States and the Soviet Union are moving toward state capitalism . . . The two systems approach each other more clearly." As for his own position, he added, "All a writer can do is tell the truth as he sees it, and to keep on writing. It is bad, perhaps, to inject this pessimism here, but it is the only way I can talk honestly."

He was roundly booed. Anti-Stalinists like Irving Howe and Norman Podhoretz were relieved that Mailer was no longer a "fellow traveler." But it was difficult to understand exactly what Mailer was putting forth as his political program, if indeed he had any. No one is on record as having wondered why the young author had strayed so far from writing novels, or why he bothered to participate in a conference in whose very premise he did not believe. Mailer's career as a public persona, a walking controversy, was effectively launched.

POLITICAL ACTIVISM had failed to give Norman any immediately clear sense of direction. As his and Bea's temporary move to Vermont indicates, they weren't even sure where they wanted to live. They thought of locating in the Midwest — Norman envisioned a novel about a small Midwestern town — but when it came down to it this notion had little appeal to these seasoned urbanites. On visits to the Gwaltneys in Arkansas they toyed with the idea of the South as a subject and a place to live, but rejected it for the same reason.

Mailer had no clear idea of what he wanted to write next, either. He thought of writing a novel about a labor union but realized that he knew as much about labor unions as he did about life in Midwestern towns. He felt tremendous pressure to produce a second novel that would be as successful as his first: "It has to be just perfect," he wrote to the Gwaltneys. The subject matter was crucial: what could compete with the war? More than that, what would best further the image of himself he wished to project? With his crash course in public relations, Mailer knew full well that his career required intense management. The problem was that he wasn't sure how to go about it, and he wasn't mature enough to have any real sense of what subjects could engage his attention.

What he would write, Mailer consciously decided, would be a book about revolutionary socialism, a book about the dangers of state capitalism: in short, a book whose subject matter might have been announced by Jean Malaquais. In the spring of 1949, he turned to the manuscript he had begun in Paris. *Barbary Shore* had always been projected as a political novel; now he set about to make it more so. Set in a Brooklyn boardinghouse modeled almost exactly on the one in which Mailer had written *The Naked and the Dead*, the novel has as its hero Michael Lovett, a young writer suffering from amnesia who suspects he had been a war hero in his forgotten past. Lovett's encounters with an ex-Communist named McLeod, loosely modeled on Charlie Devlin (though that would change as the book took shape and McLeod came more and more to sound like Malaquais), give him an education in revolutionary socialism. An FBI agent named Hollingworth is in pursuit of a "little object" — never named, but obviously significant as something McLeod has salvaged from his Party days. Completing the political allegory is another boarder, Lannie Madison, an informer and Trotskyite driven crazy by Trotsky's death.

Mailer would later say that he was interrupted in the writing of *Barbary Shore,* and critics have agreed that the second half is the book's downfall. The manuscript, as Mailer took it up in 1949, opened with great promise, with a lively depiction of daily life in the boardinghouse. The landlady is a brilliantly drawn, lusty creature called Guinevere (Norman Rosten said to biographer Peter Manso she was based down to the smallest detail on their actual landlady in the Remsen Street house), whom Lovett ambivalently pursues. She is a mysterious figure; her young daughter is strangely precocious, haunting her like a shadow, and her husband's identity is a mystery (only later do we learn he is McLeod). Lovett is an attractive character; his struggles with writing are vivid, and his attempts to recover his past are touching. In the first half of the book, Mailer's touch is deft, and the reader is drawn inexorably into the drama of the Brooklyn boardinghouse.

But the novel would not be finished for another year and a half. Mailer was, as he would later tell the critic John Leonard, interrupted, and the results, for the novel, were disastrous.

IN THE SUMMER of 1949 Norman and Bea found themselves in Hollywood. It seems unlikely that Norman was seduced by the promise of fame, fortune, and glamour, all of which were readily available on the East Coast. The writers whom he had most admired — Dos Passos, Hemingway, and Farrell — had not been among those who, like Fitzgerald and Faulkner, were lured to the movie world. Rather, his move seems to have been born out of a sense of rootlessness and lack of direction. After his Waldorf

Conference appearance, he was something of an anomaly in New York intellectual circles; he didn't seem to fit in, politically speaking.

The prospect of Hollywood was compelling on many fronts. Mailer very much wanted to see *The Naked and the Dead* turned into a movie; indeed, he had approached the actor Burt Lancaster in New York City to see whether he could interest him in playing the part of Hearn. He also found the Hollywood people whom he had met on his brief visit in the fall of 1949 unpretentious and congenial. Politically sympathetic, they had welcomed him with no great ado, and *not* to be lionized was becoming something of a relief. The writer in him was always alert to the possibility of getting new material. After contemplating novels about things he knew nothing about, such as labor unions, the idea of finding more suitable grist for his mill must have been deeply appealing.

In May 1949 Norman set out by car, driving first through the South to visit the Gwaltneys. For some reason the couple felt that Bea, in an advanced state of pregnancy, should not make the long trip by car, so she took the train to meet Norman in Chicago, where they visited with his sister, Barbara, and Adeline Lubell, Norman's old champion at Little, Brown. They made their separate ways to Hollywood from there. Once they arrived, they took a small, unpretentious house above Laurel Canyon on Marley Drive, and Norman unpacked the manuscript of *Barbary Shore*.

But his immediate priority was selling *The Naked and the Dead*. He wanted to write the screenplay himself, and that severely limited his options. He still had Burt Lancaster in mind for the role of Hearn. It was the actor Mickey Knox, with whom Norman quickly resumed his friendship (they began lifting weights together at a gym in Santa Monica), who brought the project to Lancaster's agent, Harold Hecht. Hecht was an ambitious, interesting man, and Norman admired him from the start. He and Lancaster hoped to get into producing, beginning with this film; he formed a company called Norma Productions, as Norman wrote Fig in September 1949. Hecht and Lancaster were impressed by the book and even more by its author. But almost immediately problems arose. The most insurmountable — if not the most ludicrous — was the difficulty in negotiating with the army on the use of equipment such as tanks and artillery. Later, when the negotiations collapsed, Norman asked Hecht and Lancaster for the rights back to the film, though they still owed him twenty thousand dollars. Eventually the project passed out of his hands. It would not be made into a movie until 1958, when Raoul Walsh would direct.

Taking care of *The Naked and the Dead* was a reasonable course of action, but Norman did something else promptly upon his arrival in Hollywood. He sent for Jean Malaquais and his wife, inviting his friend to collaborate on a screenplay with him for Sam Goldwyn. Malaquais had some experience in the movies, having worked as an assistant director and scriptwriter in France and Mexico, but his general cynicism and antipathy to the capitalist ethic made him an unlikely candidate for a screenwriting career. Norman's invitation speaks, of course, to his tremendous dependence on Malaquais — the French couple even moved in with the Mailers for a couple of months — but Malaquais's acceptance suggests that the relationship was not entirely one-sided. Norman's coattails were capacious indeed, and Malaquais was as susceptible as anyone else to the lure of celebrity and money.

Their collaboration makes for a bizarre story. As each tells it, the principal buffoon was the legendary producer himself, from start to finish. Goldwyn met them at his mansion in a bathrobe, in a room lined with fake books; his shifting false teeth made him lisp. Later the two men would imitate the lisp mercilessly. A contract was agreed upon, with the collaborators getting $50,000 for an original screenplay — $5,000 for the first draft, $15,000 for each revision. Another feature Jean and Norman found amusing was that they were offered a passel of secretaries and told to specify whether they should be Spanish, French, or Italian: it was almost as if a whorehouse madam were offering them their choice of bedmates.

The script they were writing (which Malaquais always claimed was mostly his own invention) was the truly bizarre element of the story. It was loosely based on Nathanael West's *Miss Lonelyhearts* — they would come to refer to the script by that name — but with strange elements. The protagonist, whose sponsor was a coffin manufacturer, was a radio announcer who gave advice to the lovelorn and then secretly spied on them; eventually he denounced his whole operation as a hoax, at which point the audience stormed the radio station — thus grafting elements of *The Day of the Locust* onto *Miss Lonelyhearts,* perhaps to make the story more politically left or populist. They had Montgomery Clift in mind to play the lead. Norman had formed a particularly close bond to the young actor, partly because Monty had intellectual aspirations, but mostly because he and Monty shared a deep distrust of the studio system.

In another exchange that Malaquais and Mailer found absolutely ludicrous, they presented the partially completed script to Goldwyn, who didn't like it at all. There was nothing morally uplifting about the story, he lisped: it was un-American, the bad guy went unpunished, it was outrageous! But, according to Malaquais, he wanted the script anyway, willing to let the writers have the five thousand dollars promised for the first draft. The two men refused, fearing their brainchild would end up in the hands of hack writers. *Variety* reported the news of the broken contract the next day, and it was the beginning of the end for Malaquais and Mailer in Hollywood.

(Clift would play the lead in a fairly faithful, if uninspired, version of *Lonelyhearts* some years later.)

Norman was disgusted by the experience. But his reputation was not greatly affected by it. He was genuinely well liked in Hollywood. Shelley Winters, who became a good friend, was particularly impressed by his lack of pretension, and by the way he paid as much attention to a lesser actor (which she then was) as to a big star. He maintained his friendships with those left-leaning figures he had met during his two-week trip promoting Wallace in 1948: Gene Kelly and Betsy Blair, John Garfield, Montgomery Clift, Kevin McCarthy. The Mailers gave one memorable party, which Malaquais nearly ruined. It was so well attended that guests later joked the Mailers had simply invited everyone out of the *Players' Directory*, the Screen Directors and the Producers Guild Book, and the *Writers' Almanac;* the joke later became a serious point of debate. Montgomery Clift escorted the young Elizabeth Taylor, and a reluctant Marlon Brando, who agreed to go only because he wanted to meet Charlie Chaplin, took Shelley Winters; Cecil B. De Mille and John Ford were among the guests, beyond the regulars. Brando, wearing a suit several sizes too small, at one point pretended to be a waiter; when he left, he confronted Norman, saying, "What the fuck are you doing here, Mailer? You're not a screenwriter. Why aren't you in Vermont writing your next book?" For his part, Malaquais was disgusted by the presence of what he called "crypto-Communists": Albert Maltz, Howard Fast, and Chaplin himself. Chaplin interrupted one of Malaquais's anti-Stalinist diatribes with a mild remark about letting the Russians be, and Malaquais turned on him. The evening ended badly.

Though his unhappiness in Hollywood wasn't readily apparent to those around him, Norman would later speak of it as a very bad period, one that changed his personality somehow. This was due in part to his failure to make any real progress with *Barbary Shore;* he was unhappy with it, plagued by his own insistence that it be "perfect."

A lot of his unhappiness had to do with Bea, and the progression of troubles besetting their marriage. On their arrival in Hollywood Bea had been hugely pregnant, with the usual complaints about her condition: she was as big as a barrel, she said. Norman wasn't exactly sympathetic, describing her to the Gwaltneys as "my pore flabby wife." Daughter Susan was born in late August, and Norman's paternal tendencies were not immediately aroused. Bea's behavior after the birth of the child deepened the rift between them. Up nearly all night every night, pushed to the limit by the demands of the newborn, she annoyed Norman, who saw her as "castrating," playing the role of the long-suffering martyr. He felt guilty all the time, he complained to the Gwaltneys.

This was, of course, not an uncommon pattern in bourgeois postwar marriages, before men were expected to sympathize fully and participate in the events surrounding childbirth. In the Mailer marriage, it exacerbated other, more endemic tensions. Bea was having trouble adjusting to Norman's celebrity. They had flown back to the States from Paris to avoid reporters at the docks, but even so Bea was horrified by the press at the airport. While she didn't exactly resist the adulation he was achieving, she grew jealous of it. Characteristically, she too began a novel while Norman was finishing *The Naked and the Dead*. Norman remembered it years later as "a book which in effect would have been a precursor of Women's Liberation." Bea, he explained, "was tremendously taken with the ideas of Simone de Beauvoir." Unfortunately, since the book sounds promising, no publisher showed any interest, and she gave it up: writing was too hard, she concluded. Yet she was a woman of great energy and resources, and she was frustrated at her inability to find an appropriate outlet; as she had in Paris, she turned in Hollywood to painting, but again without much luck. The marriage had begun as a union of equals — with Bea, if anything, taking a slight lead. She had enjoyed working as a WAVE, but now she had nothing to do but wait for her husband to finish writing every day. And it was simply not in her nature to bask in the light of Norman's reflected fame. Though at first she liked meeting the Hollywood set socially, later, especially after Susie's birth, she refused to take part. Fan Mailer, who came out for a visit after the baby was born, warned Bea that this was not wise, but Bea was beyond listening to her mother-in-law.

The air between Norman and Bea had always been highly charged, partly because of their continued sexual attraction, and their fights were florid, marked by shouted obscenities. This too seemed to escalate in their year in Hollywood; Jean and Galy Malaquais moved out of the Mailer residence partly because they found these fights a little frightening. Love had not totally flown, and Norman gradually found his paternal instincts awakening (he thought Susie, though cute, looked a little bit like him), but life from day to day was not very pleasant. Though they had a long lease on the Hollywood Hills house, they broke it in May and made the trip back east.

ENTER ADELE

As if he were running from something, Mailer plunged back into *Barbary Shore* on his return from the West Coast. He and Bea rented the Hawthorne House on Miller Hill Road in Provincetown. They were beginning to feel as if the fishing village were their second home, and Norman, in rare respites from the novel, eased his way into the community. He served on a panel at the Art Association, and he and Bea made friends with several artists. Despite Provincetown's history as a haven for such writers as John Dos Passos and Eugene O'Neill, in the 1950s it was better known as home to painters and sculptors — someone in the art world called it "Greenwich Village with clam sauce" — an atmosphere that eased some of Bea's feelings of isolation.

By the end of the summer of 1950, Mailer had finished a second draft of the novel, though he felt it needed several months' work yet. Still without a permanent place to live, he and Bea, seemingly without much thought, bought an eleven-room house in Putney, Vermont. It is tempting to think that he had internalized Brando's taunt that he should be in Vermont writing books, but it is equally likely that he felt he needed quiet in order to write, especially in light of the temptations the city offered with his new fame. Norman would search for rural retreats again and again, a compulsion his friends never really understood. Perhaps he instinctively knew that his public persona would overcome him in an urban setting, often with disastrous results. But the isolation of country living would never serve him well. To friends, Norman said he simply wanted to be near the ski slopes; he was by this time an avid, if amateurish, skier, and his letters to Fig Gwaltney were punctuated by constant taunts that the Southerner would miss out on this exhilarating sport.

Though Putney had something of a literary and artistic community, Bea's discontent grew, and Norman was plagued continually by worries about his novel. Bea's frustration at the lack of an outlet for her talents touched Norman; one day he brought home a little supermarket book on careers and told Bea she had all the makings of a good doctor. (She would later, in fact, become a psychiatrist.) But in the isolation of Vermont no course of action presented itself to her. She could not even entertain the idea of divorce, though it was clear that things were worsening between her and Norman, despite their pleasure in Susie and the new house. They even bought a puppy, a black French poodle who came with the name Thibault — soon Americanized into Tibo.

Mailer's fears about his novel revolved around not only its quality but also its content. After the "interruption" of Hollywood, the book had changed shape entirely. Significantly, its earlier working title, *Mrs. Guinevere,* had reflected the lively, picaresque tone of the first half of the book. But as he worked on the second half, the suspense and interest generated by the first largely evaporated as the book devolved into little more than a political tract. Several chapters are virtually given over to McLeod's speechifying against state capitalism, which came across as half-digested chunks of revisionist leftism. A representative passage reads:

> Witness the problem the bureaucrats of state capitalism must face. If they are to retain their power and privilege, there is a limit beyond which they cannot depress the standard of living or they are left only with slave labor and the complete deterioration of their economy. Yet the working class can be neither coerced nor driven to begin to match the productivity of monopoly. Their morale is too low. Only the adrenaline of the last war could solve that problem temporarily. Therefore, no matter how they suffered in that war, no matter how the mass may want peace, peace is impossible.

It's not that the thinking here is bad, necessarily; Norman had digested Malaquais's lessons fairly thoroughly and could reason them through deftly. But the voice here is the problem: it's not McLeod's, it's not Mailer's, it's not even Malaquais's. It's that of a tedious pamphleteer. The plot line of the novel, once promising, sinks under the weight of this rhetoric and never recovers.

Norman anticipated that the ideas he advanced in the novel might be unpopular, but he did not anticipate that its literary qualities would be questioned. And he would always maintain a special fondness for *Barbary Shore*. It was the most autobiographical of his works, he would often say later. His statement is quite true, and not just in the sense that Lovett's experiences in the teeming Brooklyn boardinghouse closely mirrored his own. *Barbary Shore* maps Mailer's intellectual preoccupations in the period after *The Naked and the Dead:* his conversion to a new kind of maverick leftism at the hands of a McLeod type of mentor (Malaquais), his determination to ascribe every political problem to the phenomenon of state capitalism, even the public birth of his political self in the Wallace campaign and, more significantly, at the Waldorf Conference.

When the manuscript of *Barbary Shore* arrived at the Rinehart offices in late 1950, everyone, from the editors to the sales force, was disappointed. It was immediately clear that this was not a book to follow *The Naked and the Dead* successfully, and Rinehart lowered the first print run as well as the promotional budget. In retrospect, it seems surprising that they did not reject the book; the probable explanation is that they believed Mailer still had promise and wanted to keep him on their list.

The reviews, coming in late May and June 1951, were a disaster. *The New Yorker* didn't leave any room for his fans to argue that he was being attacked only for his political views: "The truth is that it has a monolithic, flawless badness, like Mussolini's play about Napoleon, that lifts it clear out of the political arena." The *New York Herald Tribune* commented, "Dull, in execution if not conception, it wraps itself in a billowy atmosphere of dreamlike unreality." And the *New York Times* reviewer wrote, "At best, the result is not unlike a good modern painting, a yellow mist through which the reader sees only the essential shape and line, and in which a guilt similar to that informing *The Trial*, is felt. At worst, Mailer can be very dull, and in his insistence on the lost purity and nobility of the Communist Left, sentimental and untrue."

Mailer's first response was to rationalize, and he would be rationalizing a decade later, in *Advertisements for Myself.* It was impossible for a book about socialism to be accepted when the Chinese had just entered the Korean War, he began to think. He would not give up on the novel, maintaining that after one hundred years' time it might be considered his best. What he had done in *Barbary Shore*, he suggested hopefully, was to get under his readers' skin in a profound way:

> I suppose I might have learned to take my return ticket to the minor leagues without weeping too much into my beer, except I was plagued by an odd intuition: what I sensed (to my deep depression) was that I was working my way toward saying something unforgivable, enough so that most readers were already agitated — or what is worse — bored, by their quick uneasy sense that my vision — what little I had of it — was leading toward the violent and the

orgiastic. I do not mean that I was clear about where I was going, it was rather that I had a dumb dull set of intimations that the things I was drawn to write about were taboo.

This is a typical Mailer statement: remarkably insightful, yet strangely awry. What he was saying about his future as a writer — that he would move into the realm of the orgiastic, the taboo — was indeed true, and the process would begin soon after he took up writing again after the failure of the second novel. But there is nothing in *Barbary Shore* to indicate this: socialism, to most of his readers, was not taboo, nor were the goings-on at the boardinghouse. He suggested that readers had been agitated, or worse, bored, in reading the novel; only the latter was true.

Yet there are moments in this remarkable passage that are tantalizing indeed: Mailer's reference to his "return to the minor leagues" and to his deep depression. The fact was that the reception of *Barbary Shore* pushed him into one of the deepest crises of his life; in fact, *that,* rather than anything in the novel itself, more likely propelled him into the realm of the orgiastic, the taboo.

An old obsession reared its head: the question of his success. He found success even more difficult than failure, he wrote to Fig Gwaltney about this time. It was a subject he knew well. A rather charming vignette from Norman's Hollywood days told by Shelley Winters indicates how thoroughly fascinated he was by the vagaries of success and failure. Over dinner at a Mexican restaurant in Hollywood in 1949, Winters complained loudly to her boyfriend, Burt Lancaster, and to Norman, about her career. All she was getting were dumb blonde roles, and the role she really wanted was that of the demure, ill-fated Roberta in George Stevens's film of Dreiser's big novel, *An American Tragedy.*

Burt was bored and excused himself, but Norman went back to Winters's apartment and stayed up all night with her, convincing her she could get the role. (As Winters tells it, in spite of her leopard-skin couch, her attraction to Norman's "great, piercing blue eyes," and the fact that "Lancaster was being unfaithful" to her with his wife, they just talked.) Scarcely able to contain his enthusiasm, Norman explained *An American Tragedy* to her: Clyde Griffiths's enormous drive for success, his involvement with the factory girl Roberta, and his desperate need to shed her in his upward climb, his tragic cowardice when she falls — or he pushes her — from a rowboat and drowns. The story was as much about success as it was about tragedy, he argued. In fact, it was a success story — *the* American success story, which is why Stevens's title, *A Place in the Sun,* was so fitting. When Clyde Griffiths found himself alone in the boat with Roberta, denied his place in the sun with his society girl, he was trapped: such was the harsh reality of

American success, the dark side of the American dream. Winters got the role — her first break as a serious actress — and she never forgot the faith Norman had placed in her.

Norman was not a particular fan of Theodore Dreiser's. But with the unparalleled success of his first novel, the Brooklyn kid with a Harvard degree was living out his own version of the great American success story. An overnight sensation, nurtured on the ideal of literary celebrity that marked the lives of the preceding generation of American novelists — the "lost generation" of Hemingway, Fitzgerald, and Dos Passos — at twenty-six he found himself sitting up all night in a Hollywood actress's apartment, explaining why poor Clyde Griffiths's life was a tragic version of the American dream. The moment prefigured what was to be a classic drama of American success and tragedy. At the very beginning of a bumpy road through the heartland of literary and cultural celebrity, Mailer had already hit upon one of his biggest subjects. But he didn't understand that yet.

On the contrary, in the winter of 1950–51 failure was his abiding preoccupation. When the reviews of *Barbary Shore* began to pour in, he experienced a variety of disbelief that bordered on dissociation. The effect was not unlike a one-two punch: he did not seem to realize how great a success *The Naked and the Dead* had been until he was finishing his second novel and waiting for reviews — only to be knocked off the pedestal. He seemed to have lost all sense of perspective. Seemingly overnight, as he saw it, he had completely lost the respect of his reading public and his peers. Public fickleness was a factor he had never considered. He had expected to be taken seriously with his new book, no matter how controversial it might be, and instead he felt himself totally dismissed as both a writer and a person. For a man who on one level wanted desperately to be liked and admired, and on another wanted to be no less than America's greatest postwar writer, this was a devastating blow indeed.

MAJOR UPHEAVALS followed this catastrophic disappointment. Norman began spending more and more time in New York City, leaving Bea alone in Putney; Susie spent a lot of time with her grandparents in Brooklyn. The Mailers' marriage was rapidly becoming unglued. While Norman and Bea were not fundamentally incompatible, they were unhappy individually and accustomed to taking out their unhappiness on each other. Years later, Norman would tell an interviewer: "[Bea] was a very strong woman. She profoundly resented the female role into which my success had thrust her. You see, when we married she was, if anything, stronger than me . . . Then what happened? I become successful so suddenly I got much more macho." Norman began to suggest that they open up their marriage and see other people, and Bea was angry enough to agree. Very swiftly, they paired off with others. But the swiftness did not make the process any less miserable. Norman's friend Dan Wolf, a writer who had been a student of Malaquais's at the New School, was the not-so-unwitting ambassador, introducing both Mailers to their new partners. Bea was drawn to a large, good-looking Mexican man, Steve Sanchez. Volatile in temperament, and with an arresting physical presence, Sanchez was a committed radical, which had to appeal to Bea. Their mutual attraction was tremendous. Bea began making her own trips to New York to see Sanchez, eventually spending most of her time there with him. Norman wrote Fig that it was really all for the best; the marriage had been a good one for a long time, but now they were bringing out the worst in each other, and it was best this way. Later he would remark that he and Bea simply split up the money they had, about forty thousand dollars, and went their separate ways.

One night in the spring of 1951 Norman was drinking with Dan Wolf in a borrowed apartment at 224 East Sixty-fourth Street when the talk turned to women. Dan insisted that Norman meet his friend Adele, whom he described in detail, and on impulse telephoned her and asked her to come up. Adele protested — it was two o'clock in the morning — but Dan put Norman on the phone. Norman offered to pay for her cab fare and begged her to come; she was won over when he quoted a line from Fitzgerald "about adventure and getting up and going out into the night." Adele relented, was charmed by Norman's talk and his blue eyes. The next morning found Norman and Adele in the kitchen, still talking, very happy after a night in bed together.

Adele Morales, the woman who was to become Norman's second wife, seemed to him distinctly exotic. Her mother was from Spain and her father a Peruvian Indian; Adele was born in Cuba in 1925 as the couple made their way to the United States. Al Morales was a tough, imposing presence; once a boxer, he now worked as a typesetter for the *Daily News*. Adele, who had majored in art at Washington Irving High School, was a serious painter. Eschewing college, she studied at the prestigious Hans Hofmann School of Fine Arts, founded in 1932 by the German-born Abstract Expressionist. She made her living in a fashion well known to aspiring artists: designing department store windows, a seventy-dollar-a-week job she continued to hold well into her relationship with Norman. Her specialty was papier-mâché.

She was also an inveterate learner, and frequently took courses at the New School, where she had met Dan Wolf and his friend Ed Fancher, who was studying psychology. Fancher began courting Adele in traditional fashion, calling on her at her parents' apartment in Bensonhurst. But Manhattan beckoned, and Adele soon prevailed on Ed to find her an apartment, a sixteen-dollar-a-month cold-water flat in the building next to his on East

Sixteenth Street; they visited each other by way of rooftops and fire escapes. She would be involved with Ed for the next three or four years, though they were primarily friends by the time she met Norman.

Adele thrived in the city. She frequented the Village bars, especially those, like the San Remo and the Cedar Tavern, favored by artists and writers, and she dressed in fantastic, gypsylike outfits. By all accounts, she had extraordinary physical presence. With striking dark good looks and a beautiful body, she seemed to exude sexuality. (It was widely known that her lingerie was ordered from Frederick's of Hollywood.) Her relationship with Ed was never exclusive. Among Adele's boyfriends was the young writer Jack Kerouac, who was working on an early version of his novel *On the Road*. She saw him infrequently; she would later attribute this to his career as a merchant seaman, but his days on board ship were over by this stage in his life; more likely, his frequent absences were due to the peripatetic experiences that would make their way into *On the Road* (1957). It was not a particularly important relationship, but it would later interest Norman greatly, when he came to see Jack as a potential literary rival.

Following their middle-of-the-night introduction, Norman and Adele quickly established themselves as a couple, moving into adjoining flats, with a combined rent of sixteen dollars a month, on the sixth floor of Dan Wolf's walk-up building at 41 First Avenue near Second Street, overlooking the lugubrious New York Marble Cemetery. Soon Norman was breaking down the wall between their flats and plunging into a flurry of renovation, redoing the wiring and plumbing. Dan, Adele, and Norman constituted a kind of tight little family; for a few months, they were seldom seen apart.

Though Bea would leave with Steve and Susie by spring to get a Mexican divorce, there was a brief, uneasy period when the two newly formed couples were traveling in the same New York circles. Dan Wolf's future wife, Rhoda — a good friend of Barbara Mailer's — remembers a party that Bea and Steve and Norman and Adele all attended. There was no public scene, but things were tense. Norman was reluctant to let his parents know what was going on, and Bea stayed with them for a time, Norman's absence going unexplained. This pattern persisted for a fairly long time, until Norman eventually married Adele, on April 19, 1954. At a holiday gathering at the elder Mailers' home in 1953, Norman later informed Fig and Ecey, Bea got drunk and shocked the assemblage with a stream of four-letter words.

The Gwaltneys chose this unpropitious time to make a visit, and they stayed with Bea in Barney and Fan's apartment while the older couple took Susie to visit relatives in New Jersey. The Gwaltneys remember Bea as being particularly angry, and their account suggests that sexual competition had come into play. Bea complained that the sexual relationship had fallen off since the birth of the baby — and now Norman had found a woman known for her sexuality.

"I don't need this Adele who has fifteen orgasms at one time," Bea complained to the Gwaltneys. Of course, it would have been Norman who told Bea about Adele's orgasmic capabilities, which suggests he rather encouraged the competitiveness, or that he was simply acting vindictively and even sadistically — not uncommon behavior, of course, in the breakup of a marriage. The Gwaltneys themselves thought he was enjoying the drama.

But Bea left for Mexico shortly thereafter, and in any case Norman was thoroughly absorbed in his new relationship. Things were electric between him and Adele. He enjoyed the attention she got, the way heads would turn when she came into the room. She changed his life in other ways as well. He knew Brooklyn, he knew Harvard, he knew the army, and he knew Hollywood, but Greenwich Village was entirely new territory, and Adele was his guide. He took up the bohemian way of life with gusto. From First Avenue they moved to a huge, 2,500-square-foot loft on Monroe Street, on the Lower East Side beneath the Manhattan Bridge. Adele ordered deli from Katz's and a vast quantity of liquor, and they invited a number of their friends, including Montgomery Clift, for a two-day painting party; the walls thereafter were a streaky, slightly greasy white. Norman once again proceeded with the other renovations entirely on his own. With all the money he had made on *The Naked and the Dead,* of course, he could have afforded much more respectable digs — and he certainly could have hired a contractor — but he seemed to have set out purposefully to live on the fringes.

NORMAN'S FRIEND Shelley Winters recalled in her memoirs the time in the early 1950s that she spent in New York:

> It was the postwar world, and everybody was getting rich and giving parties: café society parties out on Long Island, musicians' parties in Greenwich Village, Old Money parties on Park Avenue, parties at El Morocco, parties at the Village Vanguard, ritzy parties at the Sherry Netherland, bohemian theater parties at the Hotel Chelsea.

Cultural and social boundaries were in flux, with people crossing and re-crossing them in every kind of permutation in search of a good time. They were heady days indeed. Norman and Adele hit the party circuit with a vengeance. Adele dutifully ran out to buy a whole new wardrobe — Norman was financially quite generous — which consisted largely of black velvet gowns. She remembers that they turned down few invitations. She recalls, also, that though previously she had drunk little alcohol, her drinking now escalated, to the point where she could almost match Norman drink for drink. Many of the parties were sexually charged, and Adele responded in kind. She was willing to experiment, and during a time when Norman was briefly out of town, found herself in a threesome with a married couple. Though Norman responded to that behavior by spitting at her, more often he encouraged her sexual adventurousness. At one rather dull gathering where Norman was holding forth to a group of literary and intellectual types about the psychology of the orgy, Adele impatiently shucked off her clothes — if he wanted an orgy, here was the real thing. When the partygoers did not respond, a chastened Adele quickly dressed again. But Norman was looking on, beaming with pride.

The Monroe Street loft was ideal for party-giving, except for the dangers associated with getting there, and Norman and Adele hosted numerous and legendary large gatherings. Norman knew most of the actors who passed through New York. Through Montgomery Clift and Marlon Brando he came to know actors associated with the influential and then quite controversial Actors Studio, founded in 1947 and headed by Lee Strasberg, a proponent of Stanislavsky's method acting. In fact, this period marked the beginnings of flirtations with careers in the theater for both Norman and Adele.

Other guests at the Monroe Street loft included painters whom Norman knew largely through Adele. The so-called New York School was thriving; 1950 was a banner year that brought all its major practitioners to the city at the same time, nearly every one of whom had a one-man show. Adele knew best the downtowners, Cedar Street Tavern denizens Franz Kline, Willem de Kooning, Jackson Pollock, and their disciples, but uptowners like Mark Rothko, Adolph Gottlieb, and Barnett Newman sometimes made their way downtown as well. Norman numbered among his acquaintances Kline, Hans Hofmann, Robert Motherwell, William Baziotes, Larry Rivers, and Helen Frankenthaler. A few artists, like Weldon Kees, also a poet and critic, were trading in their Village garrets for lofts like the Mailers' in areas farther downtown; Kees had a loft on Stanton Street not far from Norman's. Though this was a tremendously variegated group, one common denominator was that nearly all lived intensely and often self-destructively while at the same time taking their art extremely seriously, despite the new element of play many found in their work.

And Norman was getting acquainted with the New York writing community. Instrumental in this was the young critic John Aldridge, just a year older than Norman. He had written an influential book, *After the Lost Generation* (1951), about the postwar American novelists, focusing on Mailer, Robert Lowry (*Find Me in Fire*, 1948; *The Big Cage*, 1949), Vance

Bourjaily (*The End of My Life,* 1947), Alfred Hayes (*All Thy Conquests,* 1946), Merle Miller (author of three novels, best known for *That Winter,* 1948), John Horne Burns (*The Gallery,* 1947), Gore Vidal (author of five books, the then best known being the war novel *Williwaw,* 1946, and *The City and the Pillar,* 1948), Truman Capote (*Other Voices, Other Rooms,* 1948), Irwin Shaw (*The Young Lions,* 1948), and Frederick Buechner (*A Long Day's Dying,* 1949). Aldridge was generally critical of the lot, his book a highly ambitious attempt to size up the literary scene at the middle of the century and to see what it said about the Zeitgeist. His theory in essence was that the novelists writing after World War I were driven by a profound disillusionment that set their works apart and distinctly marked them as a literary generation. An illusion can't be lost twice, he wrote, and the post–World War II writers were generally too slick or journalistic. Writing was no longer a struggle for them — they could and often did support themselves with jobs in advertising or teaching, which made them materially comfortable. Their only major innovations had been to introduce racial conflict and homosexuality to the novel — a shortcoming he found understandable, as he believed that "the basic social changes brought about by the rise of modern America in the first three decades of the century have been largely completed. The social patterns have been set."

Aldridge's book was reviewed on the front page of the *New York Times Book Review* on May 27, 1951, the same day Mailer's *Barbary Shore* was given a negative review on page five. Aldridge, in fact, had had more good things to say than bad about *The Naked and the Dead;* although he criticized its style for being facile and derivative (by this time, Mailer, influenced by Malaquais, would have agreed), he compared it to *The Red Badge of Courage* and *War and Peace* in its descriptions of combat and military life. Aldridge focused the attention of the reading public on the idea of a new generation of American writers, the successor to the famous lost generation.

At the time, no one read Aldridge's book more avidly than the novelists themselves, and it drew them together in a way that previously had not been possible. Vance Bourjaily was inspired by it to write Mailer after the reviews of *Barbary Shore* came out; he was having tremendous difficulties with his own second novel. And it was Bourjaily who brought Aldridge and Mailer together at his Grove Street apartment that summer. The two would become good friends, and Aldridge would come to function as a sort of "official" Mailer critic, whose pronouncements on the writer's publications were often awaited as definitive.

There were serious oversights in Aldridge's book, and three of them were to become good friends of Norman's, as well as fierce rivals: Calder Willingham, whose 1947 *End as a Man* had established him as a preeminent postwar novelist; William Styron, whose *Lie Down in Darkness* had appeared in 1951; and, perhaps most important, James Jones, the author of the "other" big war novel, *From Here to Eternity*, which had also just been published.

Mailer later wrote Jones of his reaction to *From Here to Eternity*:

> I remember when I read Eternity. I was sick with the grippe at the time and I just got sicker. Because deep inside me I knew that no matter how I didn't want to like it, and how I leaped with pleasure at its faults, it was still just too fucking good, and I remember the still artist's voice in me saying, "Get off your ass, Norman, there's big competition around." But what the hell, I don't have to explain it to you. I think in a way, Styron, you and me, are like a family. We're competitive with each other, and yet let one of the outsiders start to criticize and we go wild. And there's a reason for it, too. I think our books clear ground for one another.

It was Bourjaily who introduced Jones to Mailer, inviting them to dinner at his apartment. They hit it off immediately. Though the thirty-year-old Midwesterner had a distinctly macho side, he was not the tough guy Norman expected: he found the writer "completely without front, very plain mid-western with good manners. With his blond hair, blue eyes, and good coloring, he looked like a farm hand. I had known such people in the Army, but here was one who could write." Soon they were hitting Village bars together. Jones might show up at the loft and propose, "Let's go and knock over some garbage cans!" Over drinks, often with Mickey Knox, they played a kind of liar's poker in which you would make up your hand according to the serial numbers on dollar bills.

Over the years the relationship between the two men would grow strained to the point of rupture, but for the time being his friendship with Jones excited Norman. He felt Jones was his equal — if not his superior — and he thrived on the challenge. Styron effortlessly became a member of the group. Mickey Knox has described an evening when the three writers burst forth from a bar; Styron, the tallest, threw his arms over the shoulders of the other two and crowed, "Here we are, the three best writers of our generation, and we're all together!"

It was clear that the makings were there for some kind of artistic community. Most of the current crop of writers were very aware of the sense of fellowship that had nourished their forebears, the 1920s writers and especially the Paris expatriates. Aldridge had perhaps been right in questioning the future of the novel in a time when social change was slowing down. As the war gave way to the Cold War and the seeming sterility of the Eisenhower decade, the direction of the novel was very much in question. Sensing that isolation was not a viable option for the writer, some of the celebrated younger novelists sought to form some sort of literary alliance. Bourjaily and Aldridge started a literary magazine called *Discovery,* and Mailer was among its biggest supporters. Mailer himself — though some say it was Bourjaily — tried to get a salon going on Sunday afternoons at the White Horse Tavern on Hudson Street in the Village.

The White Horse afternoons were successful in that they lasted several months — almost a year — but they lacked a clear focus. Members came and went, and they were a disparate lot: it's hard to imagine what Upper East Side novelist of manners Louis Auchincloss had to say to downtowner Dan Wolf, for instance. Norman recalls the group as including Calder Willingham, Aldridge, John Clellon Holmes, and Herman Wouk, as well as a woman writer said to be a wrestler, Rosalind Drexler. Hortense Calisher, in her memoirs, described the first meeting:

> Word had been passed around to writers who often met at Vance and Tina Bourjaily's . . . that "Norman" wanted us to meet of a Sunday and get some needed café discussion started, the bar chosen being The White Horse on Hudson Street — which is how it came to be known as a place where writers went, by the time Dylan Thomas was taken there. The day we first go, in a group of about ten, of which I recall for sure only Mailer, the Bourjailys and [novelist] Frederic Morton, the bar and its usual patrons, mostly the remainders of the indigenous Greenwich Village Irish, are no more unhandy with us — don't we *know* whether we want a glass or a stein — than we are with ourselves. The White Horse doesn't yet know it is going to be a literary pub. And we have the sad sense, or I do, that stuff like this is hard going in America. At one point Mailer takes out a dollar bill, and pleads for somebody to start an argument going with him, "on anything." Nobody much takes him up on it . . . Nothing memorable having been said by anybody, we leave, unsure that we have consecrated the place.

It's an awkward, uncomfortable scenario to contemplate. The confusion as to whether Bourjaily or Mailer initiated the meetings seems to be clarified by Calisher's account. It was Norman's idea, but he delegated Vance to carry it out, whether out of self-effacement — unlikely — or, more likely, a desire to *have* a salon without the embarrassing business of assembling it himself, which smacked of literary vanity and self-promotion. It marks as well a rather strange moment in literary history, for the White Horse would indeed become infamous over the years as the place where Dylan Thomas drank out his last days; it is forgotten today that the bar was home to an important segment of New York writers prior to the Welsh poet's arrival on the scene. Apparently, Thomas got wind of the fact that the White Horse was a place where writers congregated, but it never occurred to him that they might meet during the daytime rather than in the evening, and thus his path never crossed that of Mailer and the others.

Mailer's halfhearted attempts to form a literary community seem to have been born out of a desire to maintain his primacy of place in that world after the devastating reception of *Barbary Shore*. If he had hopes that his contemporaries would reinvigorate his own writing, he was sorely disappointed. Stymied in his attempts to begin a third novel, he had gone back to writing short stories for magazines — an activity that would occupy him into the spring of 1952, with results at best indifferent.

His depression intensified. His relationship with Adele was solid, but two such volatile people were bound to fight, and sometimes the fights got ugly. Adele lived from moment to moment, at dizzying heights. She later compared herself to the title character in *Carmen,* the opera she had first seen at the Brooklyn Academy of Music at thirteen:

> I decided I was going to be that beautiful temptress who ate men alive, flossed her teeth, and spit out the bones, wearing an endless supply of costumes by Fredricks [*sic*] of Hollywood . . . To me, a relationship was like that opera. You lived from crisis to crisis, sang love duets, and had screaming fights.

Adele believed that in Norman she had found a lover "whose need for drama equaled my own." Norman egged her on in her displays, to be sure, but the edges of their relationship were beginning to show wear. Jealousy carried things along at a fever pitch: a typical gambit was for Adele, when arriving at a party, to tell Norman that she had slept with one of the men there and refuse to say which one: it would drive Norman wild.

The setting did not feel right: Adele was not really happy with loft living, at least in such a dangerous area. Norman had to meet her at the subway, often carrying a rolled-up newspaper wrapped around a tire iron. He had made an uneasy truce with some of the black and Hispanic young men in the neighborhood, but tensions remained.

Things culminated at one of the Mailers' more infamous parties, this one in 1955. Oddly enough — one wouldn't usually be inclined to travel to Monroe Street in evening wear — it was a black-tie affair, one of several early indications that Norman, in spite of his protestations to the contrary, sought acceptance by the moneyed elite such as he had known at Harvard and in Hollywood. Among the fifty or more guests were representatives from Hollywood, the literary world, and the New York art scene. Brando came with Rita Moreno; Montgomery Clift sat brooding in a corner. Calder

Willingham and Vance Bourjaily talked literature with Louis Auchincloss and Lillian Hellman. A lot of drinking went on, and with it flirtation and arguments.

At about two in the morning, when the party was in full swing, thundering knocks at the door stopped all conversation. There had been an altercation between one of the arriving guests and some thugs on the street: Ruth Goldenberg, walking with Esther Leslie and another painter friend, was the target of some obscene comments, and she retaliated by swinging at the kids; they chased her to the door of Mailer's building. Early that morning, their anger roused to a pitch, the thugs somehow got into the building and burst through the door of the loft, looking for Goldenberg. Jean Malaquais stepped in and asked them to leave, but a fight broke out, and in the ensuing pandemonium Norman was hit on the head with a hammer six or seven times. Incredibly, he was still standing, blood streaming down his face. The kids were scared away, and the party broke up rather quickly. Norman wore a bandage for the next week or two, which inconvenienced him only when he had to see his mother. (He told her he had been in a taxicab accident.) The party guests did not quickly forget the incident. Violence was coming to hold a certain pride of place in the Mailer universe, it seemed.

THE DEER PARK

The parties and socializing merely masked the fact that Mailer spent what he would later call "the deadest winter of the dead years 1951–1952" entirely blocked in his efforts to begin a new novel. For relief, he turned again to his short stories, stories that he would either finish in a day or abandon. "I had been looking for therapy rather than for art," Mailer commented. "I was working up my nerve to write . . . the quick disappearance of *Barbary Shore* was, in a quiet way, as bad perhaps as any time I ever had." The results were uneven; he produced three war stories, "The Paper House," "The Language of Men," and "The Dead Gook," as well as a very short piece called "The Notebook," a rather odd vignette describing a fight between a writer and his girlfriend, revolving around her accusation that he is just an observer in life and love, always looking to write every experience down in his notebook. The war stories hark back to the naturalism of *The Naked and the Dead*, but with overtones of professional slickness. Cy, who was acting as Mailer's agent, was able to place them only after a lot of effort. (Two appeared in small literary reviews, one in *Esquire*, and one in Bourjaily's *Discovery*; only *Esquire* could pay him.) As Mailer later acknowledged, he had made the mistake of writing them without a specific magazine in mind. A meeting between Mailer and an editor of a women's fashion magazine who was thinking of publishing "The Paper House" ended flatly, convincing Mailer that he could not even find a place in the slicks. Eventually, he would understand that he was just not cut out for this kind of publication. "The Paper House" was about a romance between a geisha girl and a GI, and "one would have to win the Nobel Prize before a fashion magazine would like a heroine who was a whorehouse whore."

The stories were marked, Norman thought, by "a sadness in the prose. My mood of those poor days was usually tied to the feeling that I had nothing important left to write about, that maybe I was not really a writer — I thought often of becoming a psychoanalyst." He even thought of going into business to get material — he had no desire to continue making the war his subject — or getting a job working with his hands, as Theodore Dreiser had done during a particularly bad period.

That he was thinking of psychoanalysis is hardly surprising. It was something of a fad in postwar New York, albeit a fad Mailer's circle took very seriously. He struck up a close friendship with psychiatrist Robert Lindner during this period, very likely after reading his 1944 book *Rebel Without a Cause: The Hypnoanalysis of a Criminal Psychopath* (the Hollywood studio that produced the 1955 film was to buy the title from Lindner). Already the notion of the underground hero, dwelling on the edges of society and violating its most essential norms, seems to have drawn Mailer. The genesis of his later insights on the hipster might be traced to this point — as well as the connection between hip and violence.

During this time Lindner, who was almost ten years older than Mailer, was working in Baltimore, often in institutional settings: army hospitals and psychiatric facilities. He was gathering material for a popular collection of case studies to be called *The Fifty-Minute Hour,* which appeared in 1955. Mailer was soon making regular trips to Baltimore, ostensibly to work with Lindner on his manuscript. He would always vigorously deny being analyzed or otherwise treated psychiatrically; there seems to be no evidence that anything therapeutic took place in the Baltimore meetings. While some of the most striking features of Mailer's psyche — his preternaturally close relationship to his mother, his ambivalent attitudes toward women, his paranoiac grandiosity, and his obsessive competitiveness — would become more apparent as the decade wore on, nothing suggests that during this period he felt any urgent need to understand or come to terms with them.

It is clear, however, that Norman gained a great deal from what were probably purely intellectual discussions with Lindner: most notably, his insights into the relationship between alienation and violence and the necessity for rebellion in the conformist climate of 1950s America. Just as he was less interested in applying psychological concepts to himself than he was in intellectualizing about them, so too was he more interested in the psychosocial rather than the psychological motivations behind alienation and aggression. He wanted to know how society produced the psychopath more than he wanted to understand the psychological roots of the psychopath's behavior. Lindner also helped him shed his preconceived notions about psychoanalysis, though Mailer would resist treatment, turning instead to self-analysis, albeit of the most idiosyncratic and curiously detached sort.

All-out rebellion was what Norman sought at this time. In a fall 1951 letter to the Gwaltneys, he described speaking at a forum in Provincetown and being asked whether a writer shouldn't affirm values. He had shouted back, he said, that everyone, all authority figures, affirmed values, and that it was precisely the writer's place to question and overturn them. He had nearly asked the crowd to join with him in staging a revolution.

All this was not just talk. Norman was testing out some of his new ideas about the alienated individual and the *necessity* of alienation for the artist and intellectual. In the spring of 1952, *Partisan Review* asked him to participate in a famous symposium entitled "Our Country and Our Culture." *Partisan Review* had been founded in 1934 by Philip Rahv and William Phillips as a Communist Party magazine devoted to proletarian literature and culture. It died during the Moscow purge trials of 1936, after which Rahv and Phillips revived it as an anti-Stalinist and promodernist magazine in 1937. The magazine was backed in the 1950s by the American Committee for Cultural Freedom, a group that ran the anti-Communist gamut from liberals like Arthur Schlesinger, Jr., and Richard Rovere to former radicals who had moved right, like Sidney Hook. Much later, in the 1960s, it turned out that the ACCF was funded by the CIA to engage on Cold War intellectual and cultural fronts.

But in the 1950s, *Partisan Review* was often the most active locus for intellectual debate on American culture and politics, and what Lionel Trilling called "the bloody crossroads," the place where the two realms intersected. Literary critics Irving Howe, Alfred Kazin, and both Diana and Lionel Trilling appeared in its pages. So did sociologists Daniel Bell and Nathan Glazer; art critics Clement Greenberg and Harold Rosenberg; intellectual theorists and journalists Irving Kristol, Dwight Macdonald, and Norman Podhoretz; and literary figures like Mary McCarthy, Saul Bellow, and Delmore Schwartz.

Today, the intellectual community represented by *Partisan Review* may seem inbred and self-absorbed. Its writers were sometimes obsessed with the Cold War to the point of losing track of the realities of American life. At the time, however, *Partisan Review*'s project was impressive and exciting. Its members were generalists, not specialists (though some were academics), who took as their subject all of culture and society. At once observers and participants, they were engaged in ongoing political and cultural debate. The cultural critic of this era was not detached or superficially judgmental; his or her mandate was to evaluate and even to shape the course of culture and society.

One corollary of this passionate seriousness was that the New York intellectuals were, by many accounts, given to pettiness, backbiting, and the passing of personal judgments on unworthy peers. What did they make of Norman Mailer? He *seemed* to be one of them: he had the almost requisite lower-middle-class Jewish background, he had educated himself into an entirely different class, and he was strongly, if idiosyncratically, politically committed. It was precisely his politics, however, that puzzled the intellectuals. Even his speech at the Waldorf Conference had placed him off the political map as they understood it. He couldn't be counted on to toe the anti-Communist line; distinctions among Stalinism, Trotskyism, and anti-Communism didn't interest him. Not by accident, he would become most intellectually sympathetic to Irving Howe, who, while an anti-Stalinist, held on to his radicalism more tenaciously than most, and to Dwight Macdonald, who had himself moved from Trotskyism to a kind of anarchism. Furthermore, while to the *Partisan Review* group Jewishness was a vital, ongoing issue, a political and cultural phenomenon demanding commentary and debate, Mailer didn't seem particularly interested in Jewish issues. At a time when Jewish self-identification and solidarity seemed mandatory, he did not assert his Jewishness. One of the few comments Norman Podhoretz could bring himself to make about Mailer in later years was that he had never (according to Podhoretz) circumcised his sons and never been to Israel.

Another strike against Mailer was subtler. Though the *Partisan Review* group's origins were partly based on championing "proletarian" culture, they rarely considered mass or popular culture a worthy subject. In the 1940s and 1950s, the group came to view high modernism and the avant-garde as the only worthwhile moral and political forms of expression, with mass culture suspect. As the critic Leslie Fiedler commented, "We grew up, the readers and writers of my generation, at the end of a desperate attempt to redeem the novel from success and the bourgeoisie." As a result, the *Partisan Review* group suspected work that enjoyed popular success, considering its political and moral view essentially irrelevant. *The Naked and the Dead,* an immensely popular book, was dismissed as a naturalistic, nonmodernist project by some of the *Partisan Review* crowd. More broadly, its author was deemed too successful, thus too mainstream. *Barbary Shore,* despite its explicitly political content and its distinct lack of success, did little to change the initial impression. To some, Mailer seemed too middlebrow to be relevant.

Yet by some mysterious consensus, they sought Mailer out; he was too big a fish to be thrown back. The subject of the symposium that the *Partisan Review* was planning in the spring of 1952 — the individual's relation to the American community — was sufficiently broad to include even someone nominally outside the *Partisan Review* community. Moreover, the editors wanted contributors to address this issue not just from a political or cultural point of view, but from a literary one as well. Besides Mailer, invitations went out to Lionel Trilling, Schwartz, Hook, William Barrett, and Jacques Barzun, among others. The call for papers was a moral broadside in the Cold War, an assertion that since Communism was no longer an alternative, individual Americans could no longer hold themselves aloof from the American community.

At a time when many progressive Americans were alienated by the sterile conformity of the Eisenhower years, *Partisan Review* editors showed themselves out of step with the times by advancing the idea that alienation was not an alternative. The call for papers read, in part,

> Until little more than a decade ago, America was commonly thought to be hostile to art and culture. Since then, however, the tide has begun to turn, and many writers and intellectuals now feel closer to their country and its culture . . . The American artist and intellectual no longer feels "disinherited" as Henry James did, or "astray" as Ezra Pound did in 1913 . . . More and more writers have ceased to think of themselves as rebels and exiles. They now believe that their values, if they are to be realized at all, must be realized in America and in relation to the actuality of American life.

Mailer's response was an elaborate version of an obvious response to the above: "Says who?" No doubt he was flattered to be asked to add his voice to the symposium; as his attempt to set up a literary salon indicates, he was underneath it all wistful for the idea of community. But, as his earlier tirade to Fig Gwaltney suggests, he bristled at the idea that an artist must feel part of the American community, at one with the culture rather than in opposition to it. "I think I ought to declare straightaway that I am in almost total disagreement with the assumptions of this symposium," he began. He agreed with the basic idea that much of the culture had been mainstreamed, that writers he'd admired at Harvard, like Dos Passos, Farrell, and Hemingway, were now part of the American way. But he disagreed with the assumption that being part of any larger American cultural project was desirable:

> Everywhere the American writer is being dunned to become healthy, to grow up, to accept the American reality, to integrate himself, to eschew disease, to revalue institutions. Is there nothing to remind us that the writer does not need to be integrated into his society, and often works best in opposition to it? I would propose that the artist feels most alienated when he loses the sharp sense of what he is alienated from.

Citing Joyce, he advanced the notion that the next truly great writer to come along would work in "silence, exile, and cunning," rather than manifesting "a strapping participation in the vigors of American life."

Mailer ended his paper with a ringing cry to the free world: "It is worth something to remind ourselves that the great artists . . . are almost always in

opposition to their society, and that integration, acceptance, non-alienation
. . . have been more conducive to propaganda than art." Responses to the
call for papers had appeared in three issues of *Partisan Review* in 1952.
While most writers accepted the terms of the debate, some mildly fretted,
while others, like Delmore Schwartz, had demurred gracefully. Two respon-
dents (William Barrett and Arthur Schlesinger, Jr.) actually suggested the
need to reclaim the fictional Babbitt as an American hero. A representative
response was that of Sidney Hook, who wrote irritably, "I cannot understand why American intellectuals should be apologetic for the fact that they
are limited in their effective historical choice between endorsing a system of
total terror and *critically* supporting our own imperfectly democratic culture with all its promises and changes." In this sea of affirmation, only
Mailer, Irving Howe, and C. Wright Mills questioned the terms of *Partisan
Review*'s call to arms.

Mailer's statement was an act of performance born out of his own alienation, and it sounds accordingly bitter. Yet the hope it held out was that an
alienated artist would be best able to articulate whatever — if anything —
there is to say about American culture. That he intended to be the writer to
do that is clear. His statement would inaugurate almost a decade-long study
and exercise in alienation — with all its attendant costs. In answer to an
invitation from the literary elite of postwar America, Mailer had made his
declaration of alienated independence.

THOUGH NORMAN was not yet talking about writing "the big novel," the
idea that he was due for one was never far from his — or his public's —
mind. *The Naked and the Dead,* while of requisite length and depth, had
been written in a naturalistic, accessible style that broke no new artistic
ground. With *Barbary Shore,* his attempt to write a novel of ideas within a
conventional narrative framework had failed. He felt constrained by the
demands of the traditional novel; more than that, he felt that to be perceived as a truly major writer he needed to write an innovative tour de force
on the order of Proust, Joyce, or Mann.

For a man as depressed as he was in the wake of *Barbary Shore*'s reception, this was a tall order. Yet Mailer was resilient and ambitious, always
relishing a challenge. So, when he woke one morning and effortlessly turned
out a story he rather liked, he decided it would be the prologue to an
eight-volume work whose subject was nothing less than Time itself and that
would along the way cover the issues of homosexuality, race, pleasure,
business, church, the working class, crime, and mysticism.

The eight parts of the novel were to correspond to eight stages of a dream
of Sam Slovoda, the protagonist of the book's "prologue," "The Man Who
Studied Yoga." Read on its own, the prologue is a moving story. Sam

Slovoda, an old leftist who makes a living writing for comic strips while aspiring to write a novel, lives with his wife, Eleanor, in a Queens housing project. A major and upsetting diversion in their static lives comes in the form of a pornographic movie, brought to Sam's apartment by some friends, other old leftists who have slipped into the petty concerns of the middle class. Like the Slovodas, Sam's friends look for answers everywhere: in religion, in mainstream politics, in mysticism, and especially in psychoanalysis. But the narrative makes clear that what they are really looking for are the sexual possibilities suggested by the pornographic movie, which they all view together and which Sam later watches with Eleanor while making love. Because they are only voyeurs, however, the viewing of the movie leaves them further disconnected. Sam's depression is paralyzing; he will never write his novel. The story ends with Sam drifting off to sleep, thinking, "What a dreary compromise is life!"

"At least I was out of my depression," Norman wrote later, "and I spent the best of days for many a month, fired with notes and more notes for my characters and my eight novels." The few people to whom he showed "The Man Who Studied Yoga" — Lillian Ross, his sister, Barbara (now married to Larry Alson), Dan Wolf, and Adele — were enthusiastic about it, and he was convinced he was on the right track. Gradually the idea for *The Deer Park* took shape, the novel he projected as the first of the series. It would be a long and bumpy road, with results almost as personally disastrous as those of *Barbary Shore*.

The narrator of *The Deer Park*, as he emerged in the first draft, is a veteran air force pilot named Sergius O'Shaugnessy, raised in an orphanage and given an invented Irish name. Sergius is a war hero, now haunted by memories of strafing villages with chemicals and the image of burning flesh; the experience has made him, in Hemingwayesque fashion, impotent. Living off the winnings of a single poker game, he has drifted to the town of Desert D'Or, a desert community modeled on Palm Springs, a hundred miles south of the "capital," or Hollywood.

The novel's other protagonist is Charles Eitel, a director who has been blacklisted for failing to supply the names of his Communist friends before an investigative body that is clearly the House Un-American Activities Committee; Eitel's blacklisting and his eventual decision to testify bracket the novel. (His name, a homonym for "I tell," is particularly apt.) Eitel, whom Sergius nearly idolizes, has taken up with a strange woman named Elena, a beautiful if shopworn dancer, innately intelligent but uneducated, with a troubled past. She will do anything to please Eitel, and their relationship is volatile and often mutually sadistic.

A bizarre cross section of hangers-on, outright criminals, and refugees from the film industry inhabit Desert D'Or. Perhaps the most memorable (though he did not appear in this draft) is the pimp Marion Faye, the proto-type of the existential hipster/hero who would come to fascinate Mailer. Sergius, who both admires and detests Faye, becomes caught up in the community and eventually starts an affair with Lulu Meyers, a self-centered actress who reawakens him sexually. In fact, in the novel, despite Eitel's dilemma, Mailer is far less interested in politics and power than he is in sex and power; at the novel's cryptic close, Sergius wonders whether sex is where philosophy begins. (Looking forward to the larger eight-volume project, which is to be about time, Mailer's narrator even more cryptically concludes that he would "rather think of sex as Time, and Time as the connection of new circuits.") The novel is prefaced with a quote from a French text about the infamous Deer Park at Fontainebleau, which a suc-cession of French kings, most notably Louis XV, used as a place of assigna-tion. The text describes it as "that gorge of innocence and virtue in which were engulfed so many victims who when they returned to society brought with them depravity, debauchery and all the vices they naturally acquired from the infamous officials of such a place."

In "The Man Who Studied Yoga," Sam Slovoda thinks of Deer Park while watching the pornographic film, and imagines it as a place where there

> were brought the most beautiful maidens of France, and there they stayed, dressed in fabulous silks, perfumed and wigged, the mole drawn upon their cheek, ladies of pleasure awaiting the pleasure of the king. So Louis had stripped an empire, bankrupt a treasury, prepared a deluge, while in his garden on summer evenings the maidens performed their pageants, eighteenth-century tableau of the evil act, beauteous instruments of one man's desire, lewd trans-lation of a king's power.

No longer content to introduce graphic sexual scenes — and *The Deer Park* was to get him into considerable trouble on that score — or to use sex as the engine of his plot, Mailer in *The Deer Park* set out to make sex not just his subject but the linchpin of a new philosophy; he was moving toward the concept of the orgy as existential act, the only locus of meaning in a mean-ingless world.

BY THE END of the summer of 1952, Norman was able to write the Gwaltneys that he was 140 pages into a novel so he guessed it would stick. He had spent the summer in Provincetown, and it was an eventful time.

In those summers after the war, much of Greenwich Village migrated to Provincetown, Truro, and Wellfleet for the season. Provincetown in 1952 was a kind of bellwether, anticipating changes in society at large, and ushering in an age not just of artistic fervor but of heavy partygoing, drug use, drinking, and sexual exploration — behavior that pushed the limits of all taboos. It was an atmosphere that Norman and Adele embraced and even helped create.

Adele, many felt, held the limelight. It was she, not Norman, who knew the painters and sculptors flocking to the Cape. Hans Hofmann moved his Village art school up to Provincetown for the season, and his students followed. Larry Rivers, a disciple of de Kooning's and a student of Hofmann's, spent the summers there in the 1950s. So did Franz Kline, Jan Muller and his wife, Dodie, Bob Beauchamp, and Robert Frank and his wife, Mary. Everyone worked hard in the mornings, headed for the beach around one, and threw lively, flirtatious parties in the evenings, where Adele was admired as an uninhibited and frankly sexual exotic. Norman and Adele had recently discovered marijuana, and the Provincetowners partied amid clouds of its acrid smoke. Norman, however, began to use it increasingly during the day, while writing.

He also often drove down to Wellfleet, the summer home to a more settled cultural scene, including many members of the New York intellectual set. Dwight Macdonald and his wife, Nancy, were prominent among them, Macdonald organizing weekly Saturday softball games and picnics for the community. Norman and Cy Rembar, a dedicated second-base man and shortstop respectively, made the trip down from Provincetown each Saturday morning to play softball; often, they returned that evening with their wives for the picnics. Mary McCarthy and her then husband, Bowden Broadwater, Norman's friendly *Advocate* nemesis, lived in Wellfleet, as did her former husband, Edmund Wilson; all three figure prominently in her Wellfleet novel, *A Charmed Life* (1954). Over the next few years, Arthur Schlesinger, Jr., and Richard Hofstadter would settle in Wellfleet, while Irving Howe bought a home in nearby Truro. Many others, like Robert Gorham Davis, Alfred Kazin, and Jason and Barbara Epstein, would rent in Wellfleet for several summers.

It was in Wellfleet, then, that Norman got to know members of the New York intellectual community, the group he had distanced himself from the previous winter. They were at times an insular group, like any group of people fond of their own gossip and bickerings; for some eager to join them, that was part of their appeal. Norman Podhoretz, not one of the Wellfleet crowd, would later describe how badly he'd wanted to be part of the "family" in the late 1950s:

> There was nothing I loved better than to sit around . . . and listen
> . . . to tales of the patriarchal past: how "Mary" had left "Philip"

> to marry Edmund Wilson . . . how "Dwight" had once organized
> nude swimming parties on the Cape, how "William" really felt
> about "Delmore," and how "Isaac" really felt about "Saul." Oh to
> be granted the right to say "William" and "Philip" and "Dwight"
> as I could already say "Bob" and "Clem" and "Nat."

With his increasing sense of alienation, Mailer was not eager to be part of any such community. But he respected and admired certain individuals, and craved their respect and admiration.

After Mailer, Dwight Macdonald and Irving Howe had emerged as the most disaffected, the most unwilling to accept the premises of liberal anti-Communism absolutely. Mailer was most drawn to these two figures. Howe, an anti-Communist and strong social democrat, would later invite Mailer to join the editorial board of *Dissent,* a socialist journal opposed to Cold War liberalism. But it was Macdonald who formed a special bond with Mailer in the summer of 1952. Born in 1906, Macdonald came from a background sharply different from that of most of the intellectuals. Educated at Exeter and Yale, he had been a *Fortune* writer during the early 1930s, before editing *Partisan Review* and then his own independent radical magazine, *politics;* in 1952, he had just joined *The New Yorker*'s staff. Known for his moral integrity, he strongly opposed both Stalinism *and* McCarthyism, and grounded his radical politics in a kind of socialist anarchism. He was the most open and engaging of the group, and his writing was also accessible and lively. By 1952, Macdonald was devoting some of his energies to criticizing popular culture. He would later coin the influential terms *masscult* and *midcult* while writing for a wider audience in *The New Yorker.*

Most of Mailer's liaisons with the intellectuals would be volatile, marked by perceived betrayals and political squabbles. But his friendship with Macdonald was relatively untroubled and continued for several decades. That summer, they played softball and tennis and talked far into the night about politics and literature. Macdonald, who never swore and was essentially a family man, saw in Norman a kind of Peck's Bad Boy, according to his son Michael; it was oddly liberating for Dwight to be around Norman. By aligning himself with Macdonald, and to a lesser extent Howe, Mailer maintained a close tie to the intellectuals without being drawn too closely into their quarrels and debates, which would have blurred his focus in writing *The Deer Park.*

Back in New York that fall, Mailer struggled to turn the pages he had accumulated into a rough draft. He was smoking pot frequently. Never a recreational user of the drug, he regarded it as an instrument to reach a higher consciousness. Every time he lit up he expected some kind of mystical insight; given the intensity with which he focused on the experience, it was not uncommon for him to achieve one. More and more, he was looking to sex — unbridled sexual expression — as at once a guide and a goal in his quasi-mystical quest to find meaning, to break through convention and realize larger truths. Marijuana helped him on his quest: "Mary-Jane, at least for me, in that first life of smoking it, was the door back to sex, which had become again all I had and all I wanted," he later wrote. The connections he was making were tenuous at best; in any event, he was living intensely.

But the book was not taking coherent shape. By December Mailer had a draft to turn in to Rinehart; it was still prefaced by "The Man Who Studied Yoga" and still designed as the first part in a series. The editors at Rinehart were not impressed; the draft was rambling, at times obscure, and the narrative line was weak.

Mailer demanded that Rinehart show the draft to an outside reader, one of his choosing: his friend John Aldridge. Accepting the assignment, Aldridge informed the publisher he was a friend of Mailer's and wanted his report to be considered an in-house document, not to be shown to Norman. Aldridge wrote summarily that he thought the manuscript as it stood was a failure, that it single-mindedly courted the obscene without ever discovering it (he may have been prejudiced by the manuscript's crossed-out subtitle, "A Search for the Obscene"). The result, wrote Aldridge, was a monotonous, flat work. He concluded that Mailer should never have submitted the manuscript; that in doing so he revealed that he felt that the novel was weak, and was turning to the judgment of others rather than going back to the drawing board.

Rinehart, against Aldridge's wishes, showed the report to Mailer. The result was an angry exchange of letters in the early months of 1953. Mailer acknowledged that the manuscript was only a draft, but defended his decision to seek outside opinions on how to revise it. Eventually the two men patched up their misunderstanding. But the salient fact remained: Rinehart had effectively rejected the book, obliging Mailer to do a complete rewrite.

He devoted his energies to this task for the next year. He dropped the prologue and the whole idea of a series of novels, enabling him to concentrate on giving the book a stronger internal narrative. Most important, Mailer added the pivotal character of Marion Faye. Apparently based on Mickey Jelke, a rich, overweight oleomargarine heir indicted for running a Manhattan call girl operation, Marion Faye, pimp and pothead, gives the book an amoral center, a mystical locus for Mailer's growing fascination with the hipster hero, sex, and the struggle between good and evil. Through drugs and his own off-kilter personality, Faye also indulges in a quasi-religious search for the relation between God and the devil. Although a thoroughly evil character, it is Faye who advises Eitel not to name names before the committee, and who functions as a kind of redemptive figure to Sergius.

"Most of the time," Mailer later wrote, "I worked on *The Deer Park* in a low mood; my liver, which had gone bad in the Philippines, exacted a hard price for forcing the effort against the tide of a long depression, and matters were not improved when nobody at Rinehart & Co. liked the first draft of the novel." By May 1954, feeling he had a final draft, he resubmitted the novel to Rinehart. Norman and Adele were eager to spend a long vacation in Mexico, where he hoped to visit Susie, rest, and rehabilitate his liver. They had finally married in a ceremony at City Hall on April 19, and looked on the trip as a kind of honeymoon. A pattern had been established: Susie would come up during the winter months, when Mexican schools had vacation, and Norman would try to get to Mexico in the summers.

Rinehart asked for a week to evaluate the work and decide whether they wanted to publish it. They really had little choice, under their contract with Mailer, for if they rejected it they would sacrifice his sizable advance. In fact, they hoped that their lawyers would find it obscene, which would release them from the contract. Reluctantly, Stanley Rinehart agreed to publish the book in late 1954. Hedging his bets, he asked Norman to wait until publication to receive the second half of the advance, actually due him on delivery of the manuscript. It is not clear what rationale Rinehart might have given for this request. Strangely, Norman agreed, saying he'd done it "to cheer [Rinehart] a bit."

He and Adele left for a much-needed rest in Mexico. Yet Norman was strangely unsatisfied with the book. Its future was not at all assured, and before it saw the light of day, Norman would have to wrestle with inner demons he had never previously known.

SIX MONTHS in Mexico healed Norman's liver — he cut down on his drinking — but it did little for his psyche. The trip began auspiciously, with Norman and Adele setting out in their new, sleek Studebaker to visit the Gwaltneys in Arkansas. There they rented a little house for two weeks and Norman made a few stabs at writing; he was working on the idea for a novel about a concentration camp. (He never described it further, unfortunately, so we can only guess at the nature of this, the only project he seems to have considered that focused on Jewishness.)

In Mexico City Norman enjoyed a reunion with Susie, who would stay with him while he was in Mexico and come north with the couple afterward. His sister, Barbara, and her husband, Larry, joined them in Mexico City, and the two couples rented a suburban modern villa, with a living room featuring a semicircular wall of glass, at a place called the Turf Club, for fifty-five dollars a month. They were elated to see how low prices were there, as Norman wrote Fig: a bottle of Canadian Club cost $2.50, and a bottle of tequila could be had for the price of two quarts of ginger ale. They also took long drives into the lush countryside, Norman enjoying the treacherous mountain roads.

After Barbara and Larry left, the Mailers rented a three-hundred-year-old villa in San Angel near Vance Bourjaily and his wife, Tina. Norman and Vance's mutual friend Lewis Allen, a theater producer, came down with his girlfriend, Bette Ford, who was, to Norman's delight, an actual bullfighter.

Following in the footsteps of Hemingway, author of *Death in the Afternoon* and "The Undefeated," Norman had immediately investigated the bullfighting world upon his arrival in Mexico. He did not care for the first fights he saw; "the formality of the ritual bored me." But by the third or fourth time, "I got religion." He became a particular fan of El Loco, a *novillero,* or one who fights beginning bulls, and yearned to try the sport himself. With Bourjaily and another American, Hank Lopez, Norman began taking bullfighting lessons from Ford, and the three dreamed of renting a ring and holding a contest. The dream never materialized, though after Norman's departure Bourjaily and Lopez did manage to get into a ring testing cows as suitable mates for bulls. Norman was livid when they phoned him in New York and told him they'd had the experience without him.

More and more, Norman was smoking marijuana. He later wrote that he found it liberating: "In Mexico . . . pot gave me a sense of something new about the time I was convinced I had seen it all." But it was also bringing out a destructive, even violent side to his nature. Friends have recalled some ugly scenes in Mexico and hinted at sexual adventures that pressed the limits of convention as well as sanity. In her memoir, Adele describes a particularly unpleasant evening that started out as a wife swap and ended in a threesome, with Norman excluded. At another Mailer party, Norman met an ex-con who had gone to jail for killing his wife and spent the evening questioning the man about how it had felt at the time.

And the fate of *The Deer Park* loomed over him. He felt sure that something would go wrong with its publication. "Keeping half busy I mended a bit, but it was a time of dull drifting," he later wrote. Galleys came in, and he marked them dutifully and sent them back.

The first real sign of trouble with the book came when he returned to New York in October. The novel was already in page proofs, and ads were appearing in the trade magazines, when Stanley Rinehart called to tell him that six lines of the book had to come out because of potential obscenity problems. The scene in question depicted the aged producer Herman Teppis taking a call girl, Bobby, into his lap, letting her slip between his legs to perform fellatio.

Something in Mailer balked. He made some small changes, but called back to say he wanted the passage to remain. His refusal made it possible for Rinehart to turn down the book. Further, Stanley Rinehart would not give him the agreed-upon balance of his advance. It took Mailer many months and the services of Cy Rembar to extract the money from Rinehart, the experience deepening Norman's sense of crisis. He had long thought of publishing as the last preserve of gentlemen, but that belief was smashed: "I realized in some bottom of myself that for years I had been the sort of comic figure I would have cooked to a turn in one of my books, a radical who had the nineteenth-century naïveté to believe that people with whom he did business were 1) gentlemen, 2) fond of him, and 3) respectful of his ideas even if in disagreement with them." As these remarks indicate, he knew this realization was naive enough to border on the comic: "If the years since the war had not been brave or noble in the history of the country, which I certainly thought and do think, why then did it come as [a] surprise that people in publishing were not as good as they used to be, that the day of Maxwell Perkins was a day which was gone, really gone, gone as Greta Garbo and Scott Fitzgerald?"

In fact, of course, his ego was so strong and his sense of self-importance so long unchallenged — the response to *Barbary Shore* was as nothing to this — that this revelation, when it came, was a complete and devastating surprise.

Matters only got worse as Mailer showed the novel to other publishers. On learning that Rinehart had rejected it, he called William Styron, who had written to Mailer after reading the book in manuscript that "I don't like *The Deer Park,* but I admire sheer hell out of it." He asked for an introduction to Hiram Haydn, Styron's editor at Random House, whom he had heard of from friends at the New School, where Haydn had taught a legendary novel seminar. The meeting that followed was dismaying on one level — Haydn confessed that the book had never really come alive for him and that he had recommended rejection — but Mailer admired the editor's honesty.

The ten weeks that followed were terrible, as the novel was summarily turned down by Knopf, Simon and Schuster, Harper's, Scribner's, and Harcourt Brace. Perversely, this energized Norman. He went into overdrive promoting his manuscript: "I had never had any sense for practical affairs, but in those days, carrying *The Deer Park* from house to house, I stayed as close to it as a stage-struck mother pushing her child forward at every producer's office. I was amateur agent for it, messenger boy, editorial consultant, Macchiavelli of the luncheon table, fool of the five o'clock drinks, and I made a hundred mistakes and paid for each one by wasting a new bout of energy."

Just as Mailer was about to approach Viking with the manuscript, Peter Israel, an assistant editor at G. P. Putnam's, heard that it was making the rounds and passed the news to Walter Minton, the son of the firm's chairman, who would head the house the next year. Minton immediately contacted Cy Rembar, who said the book was on its way to Viking. Minton said he was ready to publish the book sight unseen, promising an official offer within three days.

Much later, Minton would say that he believed the controversy surrounding *The Deer Park* alone would propel sales. Many were under the impression that the book was rejected all over because of its obscenity, and the book was the subject of considerable gossip — always a good sign for sales. (In fact, while some publishers had worried over the book's explicitness, most were simply lukewarm about the novel.) He felt sure that Mailer's name alone would sell copies. As an admirer of *The Naked and the Dead,* he also thought Mailer had another such book in him — if not *The Deer Park,* then another one soon.

The book proceeded through the editorial process, and page proofs were duly sent to Mailer in February 1955. But once again matters hit a snag. Mailer wanted to make a few changes, he said. Minton objected strenuously, for he felt the public wanted to see nothing less than the exact manuscript Rinehart had rejected. But Mailer insisted, and put himself through a grueling total revision, a process so traumatic that he would devote ten pages to describing it in *Advertisements for Myself.*

Something seemed fundamentally wrong to him about the writing itself: "I could at last admit that the style was wrong, that it had been wrong from the time I started, that I had been strangling the life of my novel in a poetic prose which was too self-consciously attractive and formal, false to the life of my characters, especially false to the life of my narrator who was the voice of my novel and so gave the story its air." He chipped away at it, word by word and sentence by sentence, feeling at times like Flaubert searching for the *mot juste.* Judging from the before-and-after excerpts he later included in *Advertisements for Myself,* he toughened up his style, making it leaner, more direct, more clearly the idiosyncratic voice of Sergius O'Shaugnessy. But the psychological cost was great.

With this compulsive behavior came unbidden compulsive thoughts: worried about censorship, Mailer made changes he once would not have considered. He worried obsessively about the reviews, mentally ticking off the critics he could count on to be sympathetic and those who would pan whatever he wrote. He took stock of his entire career, coming to believe that it all rode on the success of *The Deer Park;* if it was not a success, he feared, he would lose not only his career and reputation but perhaps his mind.

Norman came, in fact, dangerously close to the edge of insanity during this orgy of revision. He was subsisting on pot and two packs of cigarettes a day; now he added Seconal and Benzedrine to the mix. As he later wrote,

> I was forced to drive myself, and so more and more I worked by tricks, taking marijuana the night before and then drugging myself into sleep with an overload of seconal. In the morning I would be lithe with new perception, could read new words into the words I had already, and so could go on in the pace of my work, the most scrupulous part of my brain too sluggish to interfere. My powers of logic became weaker every day . . . What I wanted and what the drugs gave me was the quick flash of associations, and there I was often oversensitive, could discover new experience in the lines of my text like a hermit savoring the revelation of Scripture.

Mailer's revisions forced numerous delays in publication, but finally Putnam's announced an October date, giving him an August 1 deadline. As the summer wore on, he was reduced to working only one hour a day, the rest of the time sitting in his chair watching daytime TV, venturing out only once a day for a sandwich and malted at the drugstore, in the evening exhausted but unable to sleep without a double or triple dose of Seconal. After he turned in his revisions, he and Adele went off to Provincetown, where Norman weaned himself from sleeping pills and read Thomas Mann's *The Magic Mountain,* which, he later said, somewhat cryptically, restored his perspective. On his return he took some mescaline, then wrote the book's final sentence.

As the publication date neared, Mailer's fantastic energy and compulsiveness fell away. His obsession with reviews recalled King Mithridates' practice of adding a little poison to his meals, immunizing himself against potential poisoners. Mailer so expected bad reviews for *The Deer Park* that when they materialized, they seemed not to bother him. For every seven good reviews there were eleven bad ones, he estimated; the out-of-town papers weighed in against it by roughly three to one. Reviewers felt strongly either way. Malcolm Cowley in the *New York Herald Tribune* wrote, "In this book Mailer has made a real advance over *The Naked and the Dead* . . . The book leaves us with the feeling that Norman Mailer, though not a finished novelist, is one of the two or three most talented writers of his generation." John Brooks in the *New York Times* thought it inferior to Mailer's first novel, but far superior to *Barbary Shore:* "It is studded with brilliant and illuminating passages and, by and large, it is good reading." The reviewer for the *San Francisco Chronicle* sounded a typical sour note: "Norman Mailer has established a new par for the modern writing course: he has succeeded in making sex dull."

While negative reviews are always painful, Mailer was at least amused when he found bad reviews that misquoted his work or got key parts of the plot wrong. His reaction to sales also indicated how far he had come from the days of his obsessive revisions: in those feverish months, he had decided that the novel had to sell over a hundred thousand copies or be counted a failure. But when *The Deer Park* sold over fifty thousand copies and reached sixth place on the *New York Times* bestseller list, he counted himself lucky. The book had been "a draw," he thought.

Though his worries about the novel may have expressed themselves in extreme ways, Mailer was fairly accurate in his judgment of what was at stake and the quality of the work. He envisioned a masterpiece, a "big" novel in the tradition of the major modernists, powered by a complex philosophy that linked sex with time itself. He did not achieve that; the novel's philosophical claims are meager. But *The Deer Park* is a hugely enjoyable and provocative book, the writing stylistically Mailer's strongest to date. Its characters are unforgettable, the milieu of Desert d'Or as richly evocative as any Deer Park in France. He had written a first-rate book, but, typically, because he had aimed for greatness, he felt he had fallen short.

A great deal of damage had been done along the way. As he later put it in *Advertisements for Myself,* "something broke in me" during the years he spent on *The Deer Park*. His grave disillusionment with the publishing establishment, the literary life, and his place in both had made "something shift to murder in me." With the help of marijuana, he had reached some new place in himself, a place he hadn't known existed, and it would lead to nothing less than a revolution in his thinking and disaster in his personal life: "All I felt then was that I was an outlaw, a psychic outlaw, and I liked it, I liked it a good night better than trying to be a gentleman." From alienation he moved to a life beyond the law.

EIGHT

HIP

On their return from a trip to visit Susie in Mexico in the summer of 1954, Norman and Adele rented a duplex apartment, with two rooms up and two down, at 320 East Fifty-fifth Street. Sleekly modern, with stark white walls, the apartment was distinctly not bohemian. Adele redecorated the place completely, outfitting it with Danish modern furniture on the advice of an architect friend and laying wall-to-wall white carpeting. For the beloved poodle Tibo, they bought a brown mate, Zsa Zsa, and watched their new carpeting systematically destroyed. The furniture took almost two months to be delivered, and Norman complained to Fig and Ecey about eating off packing boxes while sitting on folding chairs. He bought an expensive hi-fi system, which he would listen to while lying on the floor with his head against one of the speakers. It was as if Norman, at age thirty-one, was trying to put as much distance as possible between his life now and his life back in the loft, slaving over *The Deer Park*. Midtown was respectable, more the province of ironic and self-assured *New Yorker* writers than it was a congenial place for the alienated existential hero Norman was aspiring to be.

But his surroundings belied his state of mind, for the time to come was to be among the most turbulent of his life, harrowingly and amply chronicled in *Advertisements for Myself*, the collection of fugitive and confessional pieces that would cap this period. He began what amounted to a course in self-analysis, seeking illumination through such avenues as jazz, Harlem, heavy drug use, experimental sex, Reichian thought, and, increasingly, violent behavior. Friends grew genuinely worried as they watched Norman's personality undergo transformation upon transformation, each more bewildering than the last. He began to drop friends, with brutal snubs and ugly fights, and among those closest to him, worry in many cases gave way to disgust. Some friendships would not be patched up for years; others never were. Adele accompanied him in his downward spiral, but no netherworld camaraderie existed between them; their marriage became severely strained, often hellish. Adele remembers going to several parties a night, the two and their friends swigging from a bottle of Jack Daniel's between stops in their taxi. Norman flirted outrageously, as did Adele; often they simply went their separate ways at the end of an evening, meeting again in the morning, exhausted and furious with each other.

Friends noticed that Norman was adopting accents even more markedly than before. He had at least five: a British, upper-crust one (no doubt picked up from his father), a black jazz player's, a kind of gangster one, an Irish brogue, and, most notably, his Texas voice. He'd often use one accent at one party and then, moving on to another venue, adopt a different one. Dwight Macdonald asked him about it once, and Norman told him pretty frankly that he lived in a kind of perpetual stagefright, going to so many parties and functions, and that he consciously assumed the accents as a kind of mask. But drinking, which over the years was becoming involuntary, had a lot to do with the habit as well.

The Deer Park's reception, while not so bad as Norman had feared, grew to rankle him. He sent Mickey Knox on scouting expeditions to bookstores to see how it was displayed and to sound out booksellers for their reactions. And, in a stunning gesture that starkly reveals his perversely combative state of mind, he decided that he must have the reaction of his old idol, Ernest Hemingway. It wasn't odd in itself that he should send the novel to his acknowledged master, but the note he sent with it was distinctly so. The inscription declared that Mailer wanted to know "after all these years" what Hemingway thinks of "this" — "but if you do not answer, or if you answer with the kind of crap you use to answer unprofessional writers, sycophants, brown-nosers, etc., then fuck you, and I will never attempt to communicate with you again."

When the book was returned in its original wrappings with foreign markings saying RETURN TO SENDER, Norman mulled over the various possibilities — from the logical (incorrect address) to the wildly improbable (Hemingway had read the book and/or the inscription and had employed elaborate devices to return the package seemingly unopened). In the wake of this act, as he later described it, he sent off almost twenty copies to writers, including Graham Greene and Cyril Connolly; only Alberto Moravia replied. Norman's hunger for approval was sending him close to the brink, he would write a few years later: "It occurs to me now that I must have carried the memory as a silent shame which helped push me further and deeper into the next half year of bold assertions, half-done work, unbalanced heroics, and an odd notoriety of my own choice." He added, honestly and accurately, "I was on the edge of many things and I had more than a bit of violence in me."

He couldn't write in any sustained fashion, yet he was restless with energy. If he was, as he saw it, a failure as a novelist, he nonetheless wanted to be a man of letters, a cultural figure, someone to be reckoned with. His many statements at this time indicate that he saw himself as a figure who would be an outlaw, the spokesman and leader of a transgressive and antiauthoritarian movement. While he had yet to explore the meanings of the term, he wanted to be the embodiment and interpreter of the world of the Hip.

"At heart, I wanted a war, and the Village was already glimpsed as a field for battle," Norman would later write. He funneled his energies into what at first seemed a promising venture: the founding of the alternative newspaper the *Village Voice*. During the year Norman was revising *The Deer Park*, Dan Wolf and Ed Fancher had begun discussing the idea of a weekly avant-garde newspaper that would speak for the bohemian Village more directly than the existing, staid *Villager*. In the spring of 1955 they approached Norman, who immediately agreed to invest five thousand dollars to match Fancher's investment. (Wolf would contribute sweat equity.) Wolf was to edit, Fancher to be the publisher; the three men had 30 percent stakes in the company, with Cy Rembar holding a 10 percent share. Later they brought in a fourth investor, Howard Bennett, whom Fancher had met at the New School; he invested fifteen thousand dollars, and Norman and Ed each invested another ten. Bennett got Cy's 10 percent share and each of the others contributed 5 percent, so the four owned the paper equally with twenty-five shares each.

Fancher and Wolf spent the summer of 1955 planning the paper and hiring staff: Joel Slocum as business manager, John Wilcock as news editor, Nell Blaine as art director, and Jerry Tallmer as associate editor and film and drama critic. A name was chosen — Fancher, Tallmer, and Mailer each believed he had thought of it — and the first issue hit the stands on October 26, just as *The Deer Park* was coming out.

Norman had almost nothing to do with the paper's earliest days beyond investing his money; he was too engaged in the publication of *The Deer Park*. In fact, his first appearance in the paper, in November, took the form of a half-page ad that he bought the space for and designed himself: "All over America, *The Deer Park* is getting nothing but RAVES," it began — and then went on to quote the most negative, damning reviews. Essentially a performance, the ad was Norman's statement to the world that he was going deliberately against the grain, thumbing his nose at the literary establishment and all it stood for.

By the end of the fall Norman saw that the paper was floundering in sheerly practical ways: Ed and Dan knew almost nothing about publishing; they relied very heavily on the skills of Jerry Tallmer, who had edited the student paper at Dartmouth and served as an assistant editor at *The Nation*. Newly at loose ends, Norman took to hanging around the offices, helping out with routine tasks. He volunteered to become circulation manager. Convinced their distributor was doing a poor job of getting the paper on the stands, Norman took on the job himself. This entailed getting up in the wee hours every Wednesday morning and driving all over downtown delivering papers — at best a questionable use of his time and talents.

Yet it was not long before Norman decided to take an active role in the *Voice*. Now an institution, the paper began as a radical, alternative "voice" for the disenfranchised, the down-and-out, the disaffected, the rebels. As such, it was defiantly distinct from other publications of the time. Aside from the *Villager*, whose masthead read REFLECTING THE TREASURED TRADITIONS OF THIS CHERISHED COMMUNITY and which featured announcements of cake sales, births, deaths, and marriages, business news, and a column written by a cat, the Village had not had its own publication since the flourishing years of the teens and twenties; the folding of the last Village newspapers, *Quill's Weekly* and *Bruno's Bohemia*, marked the end of the era. Most recently, two New York–based radical journals, the *New Masses* and the afternoon daily *PM*, had published their last issues. The *Voice* — its masthead read THE NEWSPAPER DESIGNED TO BE READ — was more or less the first of its kind, the alternative weekly, and thus a publishing milestone that would spawn imitations in college towns and cities across the country and usher in a new brand of iconoclastic, highly personal journalism covering radical politics and alternative culture.

Though Norman never pointed it out explicitly, it is hard to miss the irony that he chose to align himself not with the organs of the New York intellectuals (though he did serve in a mostly honorary position on the editorial board of Irving Howe's *Dissent*), but with a publication decidedly *counter*cultural. Political infighting didn't matter, Norman seemed to be saying: what mattered was an oppositional stance to all institutions, an exploration of the fringes of culture, inherently more important than what the intellectuals called culture.

It was a riveting cultural moment, in short, and Mailer helped to define it. But he wanted to push it further: he wanted the paper to become more radical, to give more coverage to sex and drugs. "I had the feeling of an underground revolution on its way," Norman wrote, and he wanted the newspaper to anticipate that revolution, to articulate it, even to make it happen. Fancher and Wolf were less enthusiastic; they wanted to build a solid readership with cultural event listings, community news, and useful reviews: "They wanted [the paper] to be successful," Norman explained. "I wanted it to be outrageous." All three agreed that their goals could be accommodated if Norman became a regular columnist for the paper. Fancher and Wolf thought his name would help sell papers, but Norman had other ideas: "What they did not know was that the column began as the declaration of my private war on American journalism, mass communications, and the totalitarianism of totally pleasant personality."

The secret weapon in this war, Norman would confide to his readers in *Advertisements for Myself,* was marijuana. Pot fueled the rage that animated his columns, pot generated some of his most outrageous — whether good or bad — ideas, pot strengthened his vision of himself as a literary outlaw. Pot also was responsible for some of the worst writing Mailer has ever done, for his columns, at best provocative, were at worst pompous and dull, obscure and even nonsensical. Norman was able to see this later, and to connect it with his drug use:

> With marijuana for analyst, there were weeks when the need of the psyche must have been to free itself of habits of style which had bedded themselves in the mind like geological strata. The drug had acted as an explosive charge — the debris of mediocre ore seemed to have collected at every exit of the brain, and there was little to do but mine it out.

He never gave the reader a chance. In his first column ("Quickly: A Column for Slow Readers" was the ornery title he gave the piece) he said defiantly that he was writing it out of sheer egotism. Straightaway he fired off an insult to his readers, saying the Village was a bitter province of snobs and critics "frustrated in your ambitions, and undernourished in your pleasures." His second column was meant to be philosophical, so he prefaced it with a statement that his "lazy" audience should read it more slowly and carefully than usual.

Letters poured in; the response from *Voice* readers was predictably critical. The editors' favorite respondent was one Kenneth J. Schmitt, who signed his letters "Normal Failure." The protests made almost as good copy as the columns. Readers attacked Mailer's narcissism, noted his condescension, and complained that his novels weren't any good either. Yet Norman continued in the same combative, provoking fashion; it was as if he was determined to engage his readers, if not with his arguments then through his sheer hostility.

With the untimely death of Robert Lindner on his mind, he took up the subject of psychoanalysis, daring an analyst to come forward and engage him in debate. Though he acknowledged that most of his readers were sympathetic to psychoanalytic thought, he made it clear that he had no use for it. He liked Lindner, he said, for his attention to the psychopath and for his view that it was healthy to be a rebel, and that analysis should not stifle that impulse. Fundamentally, he asserted, "The artist [is] a rebel concerned with Becoming, the analyst a regulator concerned with Being." When an analyst did respond, Norman took the letter apart line by line and then diagnosed its writer's neurosis, not very charitably. In another combative column, in which he seriously proposed Ernest Hemingway as a candidate for president, he acknowledged that he was a "Village villain," arguing that the advantage of being one "is that one is always certain of influencing events by arguing the opposite of what one really wants."

A striking feature of Mailer's *Voice* columns is his increasing use of the third person to describe himself. Very early on, in responding to a letter to the editor about his second column, he referred to himself as "Mailer." As time went on, he called himself "the General" (whose chief weapon is pot) and the "Village villain." He may in part have been responding to a reader who wrote in tallying the number of times Norman used the words *I* and *me* in one column. But he obviously enjoyed the device, for it would mark his journalism for years to come. Perhaps he felt it made his writing more dramatic, or that it blurred the line between his journalism and his fiction. More likely, it fit his sense of himself as a public persona, a kind of anti-exemplar whose actions were as important as his words.

At this point, however, the effect was that Norman's voice seemed pompous and aloof where he wanted to appear provocative and engaged. His stance served only to distance him further from his readers. In fact, Norman was never really sure who his readers were. Were they like him, living on the cutting edge, interested in social change and revolutionary new ideas? Or were they parochial observers, too timid to follow where he led them? Norman realized that they shared many of his interests — psychoanalysis, for instance — but he ridiculed them for it, rather than taking them seriously and engaging in real dialogue.

Only with his sixteenth column, "The Hip and the Square," did he feel he had hit his stride. The concept of Hip had, of course, been around for some time, defining any alternative, transgressive movement that challenged the status quo or otherwise defined itself in defiance of the dominant culture. As the concept developed in the 1950s, it was coming to define those who challenged the concepts of the Silent Generation and the Organization Man by living on the edges of conventional society or rejecting it altogether. Articulated in the lives of jazz musicians, street hustlers, the writers who were coming to define themselves as Beat, Hip was an attitude; it was also a way of life. It was a subject that had preoccupied Norman for some time, and he would spend the next two years trying to define and explore it. With "The Hip and the Square," Mailer began his attempt to understand the topic.

He opened the column with a subject calculated to offend: rape. To the Square, he said, rape is rape, all rapes the same, all rapes to be punished and forgotten about. But to the Hip, there are rapes and there are rapes, some with more "artistry" than others, "the act of rape . . . a part of life too." Hip, he elaborated, is about the self rather than about society, based on "a mysticism of the flesh," a kind of American existentialism. "Its origins can be traced back into all the undercurrents and underworlds of American life, back into the instinctive apprehension and appreciation of existence which one finds in the Negro and the soldier, in the criminal psychopath and the dope addict and jazz musician, in the prostitute, in the actor, in the — if one can visualize such a possibility — in the marriage of the call-girl and the psychoanalyst."

"The Hip and the Square," often deeply offensive, conveys Mailer's message incompletely — the reader understands only obliquely what he means by Hip, for Mailer was not really able to define it. Yet the essay represented an important new direction in Norman's thought. "Hip" was gradually coming to represent for him an approach to life he had been seeking for some time: at once rebellious and affirmative. To introduce his thinking on the subject with a deliberately provocative thesis about rape may seem repugnant, but it was central to his emerging view. Sexual expression, the more transgressive the better, was at the heart of Hip, he believed; so too was violence, which had implicit energy and even a kind of bravery. What Mailer had been trying to do with his philosophy of sex and the figure of Marion Faye in *The Deer Park* was coming into focus in "The Hip and the Square": only outside the law, where our darkest instincts hold sway, he began to believe, is there real vitality. The thought process was sometimes ugly, but at the time Norman seemed able to find inspiration and stimulation only in the ugly and the raw.

He later wrote that his sojourn with the *Voice* gave him "a fine novelistic education in such subjects as ambition, failure, office politics, the economics of small business, loss, disorder, and how it feels to be a club fighter in an off-year." From first to last, his experience with the paper was an odd, thwarted affair, and not just in his relationship with his readers. He found himself at odds with his old friends Wolf and Fancher, which forced him into a strange alliance with Howard Bennett. And he became involved in a protracted feud over typos with the editor Jerry Tallmer, who proofread every inch of the paper, including the ads. He behaved like a petty tyrant around the office, prompting Wolf to remonstrate, "Norman, you're acting like the worst capitalist in a *Daily Worker* cartoon." He had little sympathy for the staff, who spent many a sleepless night getting out the paper. It was a dispute about typos, absurdly enough, that spelled the end to his contributions: an overworked Tallmer read the phrase "the nuances of growth" as "the nuisances of growth." Norman called Dan Wolf and raised hell, and Dan told him to fuck off.

Mailer wrote just one more column, a piece that was representative in its sheer perversity. Its subject was Samuel Beckett's *Waiting for Godot*, recently opened on Broadway and enjoying a great vogue, particularly among downtowners. Mailer hadn't read or seen the play, but denounced it roundly anyway in his column, relying on what other people said about the play to conclude that it was about impotence and as such appealed only to the impotent. (Tallmer, who as theater critic had reviewed the play favorably for the *Voice*, took this as a personal affront.) Mailer devoted the rest of the column to his quarrels with the paper, and then, as if to show that he could be as obscure as Beckett, signed off by including "The Drunk's Bebop and Chowder," a poem written in Joycean wordplay that had appeared in *The Deer Park* as an invention of Sergius O'Shaugnessy.

At this point Norman, seeking to formalize his new position with the paper, called in his cousin Cy to reorganize its finances. Ed Fancher and Dan Wolf each invested more money and each in turn received another 10 percent of the *Voice*, so that they held a 60 percent stake while Norman and Howard Bennett had 40 percent. In addition, Cy imposed a new fiscal discipline on the paper that would protect his cousin: management agreed to keep a certain amount of assets liquid, and that if they fell below a certain point, control of the paper would pass to Mailer and Bennett. (Norman would hold on to his shares in the *Voice* until the late 1960s and would later call the paper "actually the most successful investment I ever made.")

There was one loose end to tie up. Two days later, on May 4, 1956, Norman and Adele went to see *Waiting for Godot* on Broadway. On the way home, as Norman was realizing what a mistake he had made in his "review" of the play, Adele murmured, "Baby, you fucked up." There was nothing for it but to buy a full-page ad in the *Voice*, where he gave the play a proper assessment.

AS HE CONTINUED to explore the world of alienation and Hip, Norman was alienating friends right and left. He would not speak to Dan Wolf or Ed Fancher for some time. Dan's wife, Rhoda, still saw Norman but was becoming extremely worried about him. He was using drugs — mostly pot, but also Seconal and Benzedrine — too often, she felt, and it was affecting his personality. He dressed like a worker or artist in flannel shirts and jeans, with the shadow of a beard on his face constantly. Soon he would grow a goatee. Rhoda recalled evenings at the Fifty-fifth Street apartment when he would play certain jazz records over and over, telling those in the room what they were supposed to be hearing. Or he would play tape recordings of himself talking; his favorites were those in which he used his Texas accent.

Strange incidents suggested to his friends that all was not well. One evening Norman took Tibo and Zsa Zsa, the poodles, both clipped stylishly, on a walk. When he didn't return for over an hour, Adele called family friend Jack Begner, a doctor. By the time Begner arrived, Norman was home, with one eye nearly popped out in a fight and a strange story to tell. He'd run into two sailors, he said, and one of them had called one of his dogs a queer. At that, Norman turned over the leashes to one of the two men and proceeded to fight the other. When asked why he hadn't kept walking, he said, "Nobody's gonna call my dog a queer." Of course, what more likely happened was that the sailors called Norman a queer on account of his poodles, but he either could not or would not say that.

To his worried friends Norman would explain that he was undergoing a course in self-analysis. He had come to admire the ideas of the psychoanalyst Wilhelm Reich, and particularly his theory of orgiastic potency, which held that the surrender to love and pleasure in the sexual act was the basis of mental health. He built a structure in his apartment, a carpet-lined box big enough to stand in, which may have been meant to be an orgone box — a device that Reich believed accumulated "orgone" energies and released them to the person using it. Reich was, in fact, currently in prison for defying an injunction not to produce this device, a fact that contributed greatly to his standing as a cult figure in the late 1950s. Norman used the box as a place to scream in, some years before the concept of primal screaming had surfaced.

Norman had long been a patron of New York bars; now his nightlife gathered new steam. Like many other New Yorkers, he was discovering jazz — bringing to the medium a rare intensity, despite a distinctly nonmusical ear. On nearby Fifty-second Street, he visited such clubs as Birdland and the Three Deuces; increasingly, though, the scene was downtown, at clubs like the Village Vanguard and the Open Door. It was bebop that drew him: fast, complex tunes that featured virtuoso solos. A favorite was the pianist Thelonious Monk, the so-called mad genius, who influenced a whole generation of listeners and musicians with angular, original compositions like the ballad "Ruby, My Dear" and the uptempo "Off Minor." As Norman drew up mental categories of the Hip and the Square, the pieces began to fall into place. Dave Brubeck, the white pianist whose more accessible work was a favorite of college boys, was Square. Monk was Hip.

Mental lists of the Hip and the Square: Norman was clearly making a study of the Hip world. Characteristically, his was a personal quest; he was seeking to expand his consciousness in listening to jazz, as well as to make meaningful cultural connections. Nowhere is this clearer than in his interest in trumpeter Miles Davis, a proponent of the new, "cool" jazz, sparer than bebop, less focused on complexity for complexity's sake. Later, Davis would play entire sets with his back to the audience, a phenomenon that bespoke detachment and an intense dedication to the music — as well as contempt for his white fans. He was self-obsessed to the point of absolute aloofness; not surprisingly, Norman was captivated.

Abundant evidence in his later life indicates that Norman was not particularly musical. It's obvious that he viewed these jazz greats as highly symbolic figures. Thus, for Norman, Miles Davis was very much about race: he was the avatar of Hip, and, with his lean, chiseled good looks and his ultracool manner he was distinctly a sex symbol as well, appealing to white women as well as black; rumor had it that he was omnivorously sexual. Norman was beginning to see blackness as the ultimate in Hip — a connection he would make powerfully, and often objectionably, over the next few years — and to place a premium on black male sexuality, which, as many whites did, he held to be formidable. He seems to have had no idea that he was engaging in racist stereotyping, and probably wouldn't have cared had he known.

Mailer would begin to put some of these pieces together as he hammered out his thoughts for "The White Negro"; he would also make extraordinary use of the figure of Miles Davis in creating the character of Shago Martin in his 1964 *An American Dream*. Shago, like Miles, is a black musician, a previous lover of the narrator's girlfriend, Cherry. "I mean, Shago's a *stud*," says the singer Cherry to the hero, who hears the word as "a blow to the soft heart of my belly." The switchblade-wielding, marijuana-smoking Shago becomes a measure by which the narrator evaluates his own manhood.

However ridiculous Mailer's extrapolation of issues about masculinity from a musical movement might seem, his exploration of the jazz world shows his creative process at work. He found in this culture themes that obsessed him personally: in this case, an apprehension approaching paranoia about black male sexuality and his own ability to measure up, as it were. He brought this concern before the public in extremes, daring to seem at once partly silly and partly crazy — and yet this is where the energy of some of his best work resides. He simply did not care whether he was thinking stereotypically about race, gender, or sexuality: he *wanted* to break taboos and root out stereotypes. His personal investment in the process guaranteed that this kind of thinking and artistic creation would be risky business.

Thus Mailer was staking out some highly charged territory in his forays into jazz. He was leading a life on the edge in other ways as well. He and Adele were guests at rent parties in Harlem given by friends of their Jamaican maid, Hetty. Norman viewed this as sociological research. Adele and he were experimenting sexually: he encouraged lesbian impulses he thought he saw in his wife, and, basically, liked to watch — especially if he could goad Adele into physical fights with her female partner. And Norman was seeing other women openly, enjoying Adele's compliance, whether willing or not. The realm of Hip that Norman sought was fraught with danger as well as promise; the edge that he was looking for was sharp indeed.

AMONG THOSE who distinctly disapproved of this turn in Norman's life was James Jones. The two writers had corresponded since their meeting in 1952, and Norman and Adele had paid Jones a visit in Marshall, Illinois. Jones's circumstances in the mid- to late 1950s were peculiar indeed. He was the lover of a married older woman named Lowney Handy and was living at a writers' colony in Marshall that Handy essentially ran, which had strange, cultlike rules and regulations. Members spent most of their days copying excerpts from great books and had to follow strict dietary directives. Norman tactfully never questioned his friend's circumstances, but Jones was defensive, anticipating criticism and worse: that his New York friends might hatch some kind of plot to win him away from Handy. He also had involved Norman in the publishing efforts of several colony members and did not always like the results. In the context of the old competitiveness between the two men, these differences rankled.

Jones had written to another friend, with his characteristic lack of punctuation, that he thought *The Deer Park* "opens up new sexual ground," adding, "Someday hes going to explode on the world like a nova, with a classic," but he also felt the novel "lacks something." To Norman he was blunter: "As far as I'm concerned, its not a good book, and in fact isnt as good by far as *Barbary*, which I liked very much — when read as an allegory, and not as a novel which of course it is not." This remark must have galled Norman and, most likely, puzzled him. (How was *Barbary Shore* an allegory but "of course" not a novel?) *The Deer Park* was his assay at greatness, and to hear it unfavorably compared to his failed second novel was not pleasant.

Though his remarks were harsh, Jones seems to have felt genuine concern for Norman. He wrote, in the same letter,

I still believe there are great books in you. *Great* books. If you can ever get them out. But I certainly doubt very much if youll ever do it while writing a fucking column for the *Village Voice*. Thats another serious mistake in judgment youve made I feel. Certainly, I know that my own ego-vanity could never survive such an operation, and in spite of what you say Im positive yours is at present ballooning — both from the admiration you get and from the dislike you get.

Later in the letter, he again defended his own approach, which was to work in relative isolation, concentrating on his craft: "I want to be a novelist, not a political and moral essayist. Sorry. A dig. But you got it coming."

Jones's opinion meant a lot to Mailer, and his criticism of Mailer's writing cultural commentary must have stung. He was partly right, of course, in seeing Mailer's columns as an exercise in vanity. Jones was at the time completing his second novel about servicemen, *Some Came Running*. His strategy was to stay with a successful topic — exactly the opposite of his friend's. Jones did not understand that in seeking the cultural edge, as Norman was doing in his writing and his extracurricular activities, he was working toward a new voice, one that would take him for the time being beyond fiction, into uncharted waters.

IN THE WAKE of the *Voice* column, with no new writing project clearly presenting itself, Norman sailed with Adele for Paris. On his arrival, he had once again to wean himself from Seconal and Benzedrine, this time for the last time. But it wasn't easy. Norman and Adele stayed at the Hôtel Palais Royale on the quai Voltaire, where Norman's sleeplessness often drove him out into the streets in the early morning, just as the sun was coming up.

They reestablished contact with old friends like Eileen Finletter, who found that Norman talked a lot about pot and was aggressive in advancing his ideas, but did not realize the extent of the changes he had been going through until she read "The White Negro" a year later. Norman and Adele ran into Provincetowner Harriet Sohmers in a café, and they paid a short visit to the writer Maria Irene Fornes, a friend from the Dan Wolf and Ed Fancher days, in Ibiza. Friends thought the couple seemed happy, and in their relative isolation the rifts that New York City life had brought to their marriage were indeed healing over. Adele was pregnant, and both were looking forward to the baby's birth. It was also her first trip to Europe, and Norman enjoyed showing her around. In the three months of their stay, they made side trips to Rome, where they joined Mickey Knox, and to Germany, where Norman, heart in his mouth, toured Buchenwald.

They spent a good deal of time with Jean and Galy Malaquais, who had long since returned to France. Malaquais hadn't liked *The Deer Park* much; it was too mystical for his tastes, and he wished his friend had continued in the vein of *Barbary Shore*. Significantly, he had little to say about the book's style — the style that Norman had worked on so compulsively.

At the Malaquais apartment Norman and Adele met the writer James Baldwin, who was to become a key figure in Norman's life over the years — not exactly as a friend, but not quite as an enemy either. Baldwin's *Notes of a Native Son* had come out in 1955 to much acclaim, and he was considered, after Richard Wright, to be perhaps the foremost black American writer. Norman engaged with him first as a fellow writer and competitor. But other issues both drew them together and created confusion between them.

James Baldwin was openly homosexual, though he was not without conflicts about his sexuality. He had just finished *Giovanni's Room* (1956), a novel about a gay relationship in Paris, and was still uneasy about the wisdom of gay portrayals in fiction. (Norman would kindly give the novel a blurb.) As might be expected, Norman's responses to a homosexual like Baldwin were fairly complicated, though perhaps little more so than those of the average heterosexual male of the time. Earlier in the decade, *One*, a magazine devoted to homosexual topics, had solicited an article from Norman on the subject; though he had little desire to write such an article, something in him compelled him to do so. It wasn't a very good piece — he thought later it was one of the worst articles he'd ever written — but the same kind of compulsion, perhaps, led him to include the piece in *Advertisements for Myself*. "The Homosexual Villain" was at least a fair and honest statement of his own prejudice and ignorance and his attempt to overcome them. He had always been bothered, he wrote, by the easy equation he made between homosexuality and evil, as represented by the characters of General Cummings in *The Naked and the Dead* and the movie star Teddy Pope in *The Deer Park*. He admitted he had a lot to learn. As a libertarian socialist, he wrote, he believed every individual had the right to express himself however he chose, and that included sexual expression. He acknowledged the possibility that his feelings had masked latent homosexuality in himself, but he felt that he had gotten past that now.

Generally speaking, Norman suffered from few conflicts about outright homosexuality, despite his fascination with male sexuality and so-called manly behavior. Later he would tell Selden Rodman, "My answer to my Women's Lib critics is: *Of course* I'm a latent homosexual. But I choose, as Sartre puts it, to be heterosexual." He seems to have been, on the whole, fairly comfortable with homosexuals, and would, much later on, in his 1983 novel *Ancient Evenings*, explore the world of homosexuality in an-

Above: Norman's father, Barney (standing, center), with his parents and extended family in South Africa. (*Courtesy of Beverly Bentley*)

Left: Norman in short pants, ca. 1930. (*Culver Pictures*)

Below: Norman's mother, the redoubtable Fanny Mailer. (*Courtesy of Beverly Bentley*)

NORMAN KINGSLEY MAILER

Born January 31, 1923, in Long Branch, New Jersey. Prepared at Boys' High. Home address: 555 Crown Street, Brooklyn, New York. Dunster House. *Advocate*, literary board (2, 3); *Red Book*, editorial board; Phillips Brooks House, social work (1, 2); Engineering Society (1). House football (2, 3). Signet Society. Field of concentration: Engineering Sciences.

BEATRICE SILVERMAN

25 Cary Ave., Chelsea
Chelsea High School
A.B.   Psychology
   Dean's List 3, 4; Psychology Club 4; Sociological Society 3, 4; *The Beacon* 4, Book Editor; University Chorus 1, 2, 3; Varsity Debating 1, 2; Post-War Planning Committee 4.

Top: From the Harvard College Class of 1943 album. Norman dropped the Engineering Society and joined the literary magazine, *The Advocate*.
(*Copyright © Harvard University Archives*)

Middle: From the class of 1943 Boston University yearbook, *The Hub*. Bea's activities are those of a politically committed intellectual.
(*Courtesy of Boston University*)

Left: The newlyweds in a happy interval before each signed up for service in the war.
(*Culver Pictures*)

Right: The serious young author, just after publication of *The Naked and the Dead*.
(*Archive Photos*)

Below: Mailer and Dan Wolf in the office of the *Village Voice* which they launched in 1955.
(*Copyright © Fred W. McDarrah*)

Above: Mailer as hipster, with his second wife, Adele.
(*AP/Wide World Photos*)

Below: Holding his second daughter, Danielle, born to Adele in 1957.
(*Courtesy of Dan Rosenblatt*)

Mailer used this photo on the cover of *Advertisements for Myself*, despite his publisher's objections; perhaps he thought it made him look handsome. (*Archive Photos*)

Above: In a paddywagon on
November 22, 1960, three days
after he stabbed his wife.
(*UPI/Corbis-Bettmann*)

Left: Adele and Norman after
hearing that the case had been
postponed until January 12, 1961.
Adele did not press charges, and
they tried again to make a go of
their marriage. (*UPI/Corbis-
Bettmann*)

Above: Lady Jeanne Campbell, shortly before becoming Norman's third wife, in 1962. A good sport, she could hold her own with him. (*AP/Wide World Photos*)

Right: Beverly Bentley in a publicity shot for *The Heroine*, which closed on Broadway the night before she met Norman, in March 1963. (*Copyright © Sam Siegel, courtesy of Beverly Bentley*)

Mailer with his imaginary city built entirely of Lego blocks. The structure still stands in his Brooklyn Heights living room.
(*Copyright © Fred W. McDarrah*)

cient Egypt in tolerant and even erotic fashion. Yet Norman was also intensely competitive, and one level on which he waged his battles was that of sexuality. He took the sexual measure of every man he met. With gay men, the process often left him bewildered — and sometimes combative.

These problems with homosexuality shed light on Norman's friendship with James Baldwin. The issue was compounded by Baldwin's blackness, for Norman was deep in the grip of his obsession with black male sexuality. Baldwin immediately picked up on this. He saw every issue through the filter of race; that was his style, and that was his subject as a writer. In discussing race with Norman, and sizing up his ideas on the matter, Baldwin was struck by how often Norman reduced the racial question to black sexuality. Later, in 1961, he would write about his relations with Norman, and especially their initial encounter in Paris, for *Esquire* in an article called "The Black Boy Looks at the White Boy," in which he objected to Norman's reductive vision. Norman was having a romance with blackness, he felt, and his views would do more harm than good for race relations. At the same time, Norman's sexual competitiveness had awakened his own, and he acknowledged the fundamental edge the black man has in matters of sex, and how captive Norman was to that notion: "It is still true, alas, that to be an American Negro male is also to be a kind of walking phallic symbol: which means that one pays, in one's own personality, for the sexual insecurity of others. The relationship, therefore, of a black boy to a white boy is a very complex thing." Their meeting created, he wrote, a situation in which "the toughest kid on the block was meeting the toughest kid on the block."

He also got in a few digs at Norman's distinct *lack* of hipness. He took the Mailers around to Paris nightspots but found, he wrote, that "Negro jazz musicians, among whom we sometimes found ourselves, who really liked Norman, did not for an instant consider him remotely 'hip' and Norman did not know this and I could not tell him . . . They thought he was a real sweet ofay cat, but a little frantic." Not, that is, appropriately "cool."

Yet Baldwin called the piece "a love story," and there is no question the two men were drawn to each other. Baldwin described Norman as "confident, boastful, exuberant, and loving — striding through the soft Paris nights like a gladiator." Baldwin was coming off a very bad love affair, and was wandering the streets at night, often finding himself in trouble with the police; he and Norman may have recognized each other's precarious state. And Adele, who by no means approved of all her husband's friends, took an immediate liking to Jimmy.

Given the circumstances, then, it is no wonder that this was an important relationship. Given also the volatility of the issues involved, and the personal characteristics of the two men — especially their powerful competitiveness — it was equally inevitable that it would be a relationship of considerable intensity. Jimmy Baldwin and his friendship fueled "The White Negro," the essay that Norman was writing even at this point in his head, and that was to preoccupy him over the next year. It would mark a significant shift in his career and reputation.

"THE WHITE NEGRO"

When Norman and Adele returned from Paris at the end of the summer of 1956, Norman later wrote, "the city was not alive for me. I was on edge. My wife was pregnant. It seemed abruptly too punishing to live at the pace we had been going for several years." They began to look for a place in the country, preferably relatively close to the city and in an area frequented by other writers.

One September weekend they visited the producer Lew Allen — whom Norman knew through Vance Bourjaily — and his screenwriter wife, Jay Presson, at their house in Washington, Connecticut. Washington was a charming location: a small New England town surrounded by miles of lush farmland and rolling hills. Most houses in the area dated back to Revolutionary days and offered almost total seclusion. It was only about a hundred miles from Manhattan, and residents could make a short drive to Danbury to catch a train to the city.

A literary and artistic community was beginning to form in the area, and that drew the Mailers as well. Arthur Miller had lived with his wife, Marilyn Monroe, in nearby Roxbury; when they left for London for Monroe to film *The Prince and the Showgirl*, critic John Aldridge and his wife, Leslie, moved in; Aldridge had taken a one-year job at Sarah Lawrence College, within commuting distance. Gallery owner Julien Levy lived nearby, which ensured a steady stream of artist visitors. Also in Roxbury were William Styron and his wife, Rose.

Norman and Adele began house-hunting immediately, and found a sprawling white saltbox farmhouse in Bridgewater, roughly equidistant between Roxbury and Washington. They had Susie with them for the fall, and they took up bucolic family life with great enthusiasm. With some bitterness, however, Adele noted that, following their customary slipshod housekeeping arrangements, they never furnished the house with the antiques it cried out for. Instead, they installed their old Danish modern furniture, and their house looked like the beatnik pad so many of their quarters resembled. Still, they were trying.

A two-pack-a-day smoker for many years, Norman, in a sudden passion for clean living, gave up the habit. His weight ballooned to 175 pounds, a lot to carry for a five-foot nine-inch man, but he felt much healthier. He built a studio in the attic for Adele's painting, punching out some dormers for light. Adele at first took to the countryside and enjoyed living in a house rather than an apartment. She was beautiful in her pregnancy. The baby, a girl named Danielle, called Dandy, was delivered in March 1957; Norman was present at the delivery, which was somewhat uncommon for the time. Norman handled his wife's labor and delivery a little strangely, insisting that his wife's pubic area not be shaved for the delivery, a standard procedure. Unused to this kind of participation, the doctors insisted, and Norman had to give in. (Later, when Norman resisted having Danielle — and all his children — immunized, because immunization was "plastic" or "corporate," Adele and his other wives all overrode him or went behind his back.)

For himself, Norman installed a workbench in the barn and bought a complete array of power tools. He busied himself with a number of woodworking projects, some quite accomplished. One friend remembered some beautifully crafted large wooden eggs; Norman had converted one to an orgone box by installing a hinge on its lid so the user could climb in and be gently rocked by a friend.

He also hung a punching bag from the middle of the ceiling, installed some weights, and made a ring-sized space for boxing. He had always been drawn to the sport, and now he took it up with a vengeance. In the early months in Bridgewater his favorite sparring partner was Adele's father, Al Morales. Al had been a promising featherweight before his wife made him give it up as a career, and he was a formidable opponent. Norman credited his regular sparring sessions with Al for keeping him off cigarettes. Most visitors to the house, male and female, were invited to box with him; most declined. Chandler Brossard, who had trained with George Brown, who had in turn trained Hemingway, explained to Norman that he would probably hurt him badly if they put on the gloves; Norman argued, but eventually Brossard prevailed.

Norman had other, stranger habits: he was inventing things, like the egg-shaped orgone box. He built a large ring-shaped structure that a person could stand akimbo in, with feet and hands strapped to the ring, presumably to be rolled down a hill; a more dangerous device is hard to imagine. Another such invention was a modified Bongo board. A fad in the 1950s, a

Bongo board was essentially a plank that sat atop a small, rolling barrel; the idea was to stand on the plank and try to balance it. The stunt seemed easy to do but in practice was fairly challenging. Norman had made it nearly impossible by adding footboards and rollers so the device could be turned and rotated; perhaps the idea was to use it to work on his footwork for boxing. One night Lew Allen watched as Norman spun off the board into the air and took a bad fall, bloodying his nose. As he reeled back to the house with Allen, Norman convinced Allen to say that they had had a fight in which Allen knocked him out, a story he evidently thought much more impressive than taking a fall from a Rube Goldberg–like children's toy.

Winters were long in the country, and the evenings closed in quickly. As his dedication to boxing and inventions indicates, Norman was rather desperate for amusement. The critic Nat Halper, whom Norman knew from Provincetown, remembers Norman working for a long time with him — Halper was good at games — making up a board game based on the concept of success. Players made career moves, took risks, all in the quest for success. It was, of course, a natural subject for Norman, but he brought to the venture an unusual intensity, believing he could make money with it. That, in fact, may have been a real concern, for although the investments Cy had made for him were doing nicely, he was seeing little income from his writing.

His favorite diversion, however, was drinking. Mailer held his liquor well, but over the course of a long evening, fueled by bourbon, his combativeness often got the better of him. Leslie Aldridge remembers that after a minor quarrel with Adele, Norman tried to get the two women to fight each other physically. Chandler Brossard witnessed a constant low-level hostility between Norman and Adele, which got worse when they drank. Frequently the Mailers would assemble a carload of people to drive down to the city, driving home early in the morning perilously drunk.

Not surprisingly, Norman had almost completely stopped writing. Ideas were still percolating for the piece he wanted to write on Hip, but his complete inability to put anything on paper worried him terribly. As he wrote in *Advertisements for Myself*, "At times it would come over me that I could not keep away from writing much longer, and I began to live with the conviction that I had burned out my talent." He attributed the block partly to his withdrawal from nicotine; he couldn't write without a cigarette, he thought.

The one exception was a curious piece of prose he wrote at the instigation of publisher Lyle Stuart, up for a weekend visit. Stuart was a novelist and controversial journalist whose exposés of columnist Walter Winchell had resulted in a libel suit, which Stuart won. A great believer in free speech, Stuart published everything from celebrity biographies to books containing frank discussions of sexual behavior, which often drew lawsuits. Mailer and Stuart stayed up late talking about freedom of speech and the media. Stuart threw down the gauntlet, saying that there was nothing he would not publish in the *Independent,* a small monthly newspaper he ran. Mailer replied that if he were to write four paragraphs on school integration in the South, the *Independent* might print it but no large newspaper would pick it up. Stuart thought it would be an excellent experiment. That very night, Norman wrote his piece, feeling punch-drunk to be writing again.

What he wrote was decidedly strange. It reflected his old belief in black male supersexuality. The argument ran thus: "Everybody . . . knows" the white man fears the black man's sexuality, and the black in turn hates the white because whites have possessed black women for two centuries. "The comedy is that the white loathes the idea of the Negro attaining equality in the classroom because the white feels the Negro already enjoys sensual superiority." The arrangement was considered fair by blacks and whites alike, he wrote, though he conceded that a reversal of the situation "ought to be nourishing to both races."

Stuart thought there was a good bet that the news services would pick this up, but first he sent the piece to William Faulkner for comment. Faulkner wrote back rather mildly that he had heard this notion before, though never from a man, only from middle-aged Northern or Midwestern women — a fact he wondered whether a psychiatrist would understand. Mailer responded with a furious letter to Faulkner, calling him a timid man. He had never heard the notion advanced by middle-aged ladies, he bragged, but by a pimp, a black carwasher in Queens, and a Harlem woman who had once been a madam of a South Carolina brothel. He was stung, no doubt, by having his idea said to be one held by bourgeois women and was asserting his own authentic street credentials in reply. He also totally misunderstood Faulkner's reference to a psychiatrist, closing his letter by writing, "I'm a bit surprised that William Faulkner should think a psychiatrist could ever understand a writer." Faulkner had not wondered what a psychiatrist would make of Mailer, but what a psychiatrist would make of what he believed to be the fact that middle-aged non-Southern ladies held this belief; Norman was clearly on the defensive about the state of his own psyche.

Stuart sent the whole package — Norman's piece and the Faulkner exchange — around to such notables as W. E. B. Du Bois and Murray Kempton. Mailer's favorite response was from Eleanor Roosevelt: "I think Mr. Mailer's statement is horrible and unnecessary." Mailer wondered if this was the first time she had felt compelled to use the word *horrible* in print. Stuart did send the piece and its responses to a number of newspapers, but nothing much came of it.

Of course, Mailer had shown extraordinarily poor judgment in writing the piece. It was merely outrageous — not constructive, not even very interesting. He realized this later, calling it "incendiary but unilluminating." He would have to do better, he knew. That he had involved Faulkner in the whole affair particularly pained him. "Like a latent image in the mirror of my ego," he would later write, "was the other character Faulkner must have seen: a noisy pushy middling ape who had been tolerated too long by his literary betters."

On the other hand, it could be said that Mailer was trying to participate, however clumsily, in an ongoing dialogue among major American writers about black male sexuality. Involving Faulkner was very much to the point: *Light in August* (1932) is, among other things, about white men's fear of black men's sexuality. The issue had been addressed by black writers as well — notably Richard Wright in *Black Boy* (1945) and Ralph Ellison in *Invisible Man* (1952). Even Lillian Smith, a pioneering Southern woman, took on the theme in her 1944 novel *Strange Fruit* and promoted a bizarre Freudian theory about sex and race in her call for integration, *Killers of the Dream* (1949). The subject drew a variety of writers, and Mailer was only the latest. His approach was unfortunate but would soon yield more interesting results.

In the wake of this humbling experience, he took a week off, traveling to Mexico to return Susie to Bea. Somewhere along the way, his scattered thoughts about race jelled, and he returned strengthened in his resolve. He immediately took up smoking again: he would need cigarettes for the all-out attack he had planned. He began "The White Negro," the essay that would change the course of his career.

THE ESSAY Mailer wrote in the spring of 1957 is a difficult piece and is not marked by the clarity of its writing. Yet it demands close, careful reading. It was to be one of the most influential writings of his long career.

Mailer begins by setting forth the postwar situation: nothing is the same after the death camps and the atomic bomb, phenomena that have made us insignificant, part of a mass rather than individuals. From this arid soil sprang the American existentialist, the hipster.

The hipster knows we can die instantly by the bomb or by the state, or slowly by conformity. The only way to live with death is to go outside society, to go wherever the self leads. Otherwise one is doomed to live with "other people's habits, other people's defeats, boredom, quiet desperation, and muted icy self-destroying rage." The choice is clear: one is Hip — a rebel — or one is Square — a conformist.

Clearly, Norman was developing some ideas that had germinated in the pages of *The Naked and the Dead,* namely the connection between power and totalitarianism. Totalitarian society constricts the human mind, he wrote, and being in opposition to it requires considerable bravery. The Negro, who has lived between totalitarianism and democracy since coming to these shores, is thus the source of Hip. Hip announced its presence through the largely Negro medium of jazz, which had an enormous influence on Mailer's entire generation. But Hip, he added, had its intellectual roots in the writings of Henry Miller, D. H. Lawrence, and Wilhelm Reich, and also in Hemingway, who saw, quite simply, that in a thoroughly bad society the one necessary virtue is courage. What made Hemingway feel good he took to be the Good, which Mailer saw as entirely consistent with the hipster, whose focus is the self rather than society.

In bohemian quarters in certain cities, that part of a generation that understood these concepts instinctively was drawn to what the Negro offered. In the Village, for example, a ménage à trois, joined in holy alliance by a wedding ring of marijuana, bonded together the bohemian, the juvenile delinquent, and the Negro, a union that created the hipster. The Negro brought to the occasion certain essential elements: he knew what it meant to choose between living with danger and living with humility. The attraction of this approach to life was clear: in a state of psychic and cultural war one must live in the present — rage, joy, orgasm, and again, jazz.

"So there was a new breed of adventurers, urban adventurers who drifted out at night looking for action with a black man's code to fit their facts," Mailer wrote. "The hipster had absorbed the existentialist synapses of the Negro, and for all practical purposes could be considered a white Negro."

The hipster, whom Mailer believed to be a genuine mystic, has chosen to live with death, and thus his private vision is all-important. The hipster, he continues, is a philosophical psychopath but is not psychotic, though he is often taken to be so. Mailer quotes Robert Lindner: The psychopath is a rebel without a cause (though we have become so familiar with the James Dean movie title that we need to pause and consider this concept carefully). He must have immediate gratification, is egotistical and must satisfy his ambitions by performing in transgressive, often violent ways. The psychopath, Mailer argues, may be the precursor of a new personality. He is everywhere.

In the most controversial passage of the essay, Mailer wrote that violence and even murder on the part of the psychopath require courage. No matter how brutal the act, the psychopath is daring the unknown. The passage, which most readers objected to, parenthetically describes a hypothetical situation in which two hipsters beat up and murder a fifty-year-old shopkeeper. Because it was so controversial, it should be quoted at length. Mailer defends the notion that the psychopath murders to purge himself of violence and hatred, for without ridding himself of his hatred he cannot love, and consequently must hate himself for his cowardice:

> (It can of course be suggested that it takes little courage for two strong eighteen-year-old hoodlums, let us say, to beat in the brains of a candy-store keeper, and indeed the act — even by the logic of the psychopath — is not likely to prove very therapeutic, for the victim is not an immediate equal. Still, courage of a sort is necessary, for one murders not only a weak fifty-year-old man but an institution as well, one violates private property, one enters into a new relation with the police and introduces a dangerous element into one's life. The hoodlum is therefore daring the unknown, and so no matter how brutal the act, it is not altogether cowardly.)

This is vintage Mailer: determined to shock, not thinking things entirely through. The most obnoxious part of his argument is that killing a candy store owner is not "therapeutic" because he is not an equal to the thugs — yet Mailer acknowledges that he is using the psychopath's logic in reasoning thus. What Mailer says about the bravery behind the act — however specious it might seem at first — is not without some truth. It is hard to imagine a criminal mind that is not frightened in committing a murder; in doing so, the killer is, as Mailer says, pitching himself into another realm. In that sense the hipster does overcome cowardice in his mind.

At this point Mailer turns to the orgasm. The psychopath seeks love — not in terms of a mate but for an apocalyptic Orgasm. He is aware of the liberating potential of the good orgasm and at the same time of the deadening possibilities of the bad one (Mailer does not explain the difference between the two). But this is often an elusive quest, for if the hipster/psychopath is always purging the hatred in himself, there is always more to take its place — both from without and from within. Nevertheless, it remains a goal.

He returns to the Negro; the Negro is a natural psychopath because, living in a white society, he's hated and hates himself, and thus he explores the moral wildernesses of civilized life that Squares condemn as evil, immature, self-destructive, and so forth. Mailer addresses the question of Hip language. It is ambiguous, he argues, for the Negro learned to speak from oppression. Hip language can't be taught. And there is competition here. Hipsters, like children, fight for the sweet — the one with the most energy gets it.

Mailer moves into the final phases of his argument. Hip, with its emphasis on complexity, has no definition of moral responsibility. Humans are not simply good or bad but, obviously, both. Character changes constantly in different contexts. Thus, he writes, "the only Hip morality . . . is to do what one feels whenever and wherever it is possible and — this is how the war of the Hip and the Square begins — to be engaged in one primal battle: to open the limits of the possible for oneself, for oneself alone, because that is one's need." The Hip "ethic" is immoderation, childlike approval of the present. Every social restraint should be removed.

As the essay closes, Mailer looks to the future, returning to the condition of the black — not white — Negro. If the black emerges and becomes equal, it will shake every white to his roots. Hip may erupt as psychically armed rebellion. There might be then a time of violence, hysteria, rebellion, but liberals will try to envelop Hip as merely a colorful element in society. But if the black really succeeds, all politics will be turned upside down and the liberals will be powerless to gloss things over. Events will force liberals to acknowledge some political "truths": that the issue at hand is not desegregation but, as "radicals" like Mailer "know," miscegenation. Liberals can't bear to admit the hatred the Negro feels, preferring to imagine a sunny future where blacks and whites can coexist, blacks even becoming good liberals themselves. Mailer "knows," he writes, that a worse world will come before a better one does.

MUCH OF "The White Negro," of course, is off the wall, and it could be argued that Mailer's whole argument is based on a bedrock of racism, and sexism to boot. Certainly his assumptions about "blacks" and "the Negro" are indefensible. Many readers understandably cannot get past this. But many others would find the essay profound and prophetic. Certainly he was mining a rich vein. Mailer felt a fine measure of confidence after he finished it, first privately publishing the essay as a pamphlet and showing it around to Connecticut friends and then mailing it off to Irving Howe at *Dissent,* which would publish it that summer.

Mailer had taken the pulse of 1950s society and found that though outwardly it seemed reassuringly measured, wild irregularities were surfacing. Not only was the hipster a real, new phenomenon, but, more important, the conditions that helped to create him were affecting a whole generation of American youth. Increasingly alienated, choosing rebellion for its own sake, more and more bohemians were inhabiting the fringes of the culture, their goals to express themselves creatively, sexually, and through drugs. It is obvious that Mailer saw the 1960s coming, not only in terms of the "youth generation" or hippies, but also in his prediction of the widespread social and cultural upheavals when black power followed on civil rights.

Mailer's equation between the hipster, the psychopath, and the black was more complex — and would cause bitter disagreement — but nonetheless compelling. Alternative culture was without question heavily influenced by black culture. Mailer's citation of the enormous influence of jazz was only one case in point. Never before — not even in the 1920s, when the Harlem Renaissance was at its height — had the black man been a figure for white men to admire and emulate. His manner of speaking and walking (of course Mailer was generalizing here) transfixed many white observers, as did his aloofness. Hardly a natural quality, this aloofness, this "cool," was in itself, as Mailer hinted, a result of living in a hostile environment. Mailer neglected to recognize the overly romanticized aspect of this view — and the pernicious implications of a belief in black supersexuality — but he correctly recognized the pivotal role the black hipster was playing in the cultural imagination of 1950s youth.

Most problematic is his glorification of violence. In his hypothetical description of the shopkeeper and the hoodlums, the connection Mailer makes between violence and bravery is relatively clear, if highly debatable. What is strange, however, and what may have upset many readers, is how highly Mailer values this "bravery." It was a quality that always held for him outsize importance, in almost any context. However offensive it is that the shopkeeper is simply swept away so that we can imagine the hoodlums' actions and their consequences, it was part of Mailer's rhetorical strategy: the bravery that comes from transgressing societal norms was what interested him, not the form such transgression took. In many senses his argument was morally indefensible — and that would be one of the objections to it held by, for instance, the Beats, who felt violence had nothing to do with Hip — but it made enormous sense to Norman, who was increasingly coming to see violence as a locus for vitality and even bravery. It should be noted as well that his essay was not prescriptive (though it may have had that effect) but descriptive; violence happens, he was saying. What does it mean? What is at work here? What is its role in the alienation of the hipster?

Many readers of "The White Negro" did not understand it at first, coming to appreciate it only when events made them see how prophetic Mailer had been. Others, however, reacted very negatively at the outset. Irving Howe, for example, found the piece terribly exciting — and of course his journalistic instincts told him it would be a great moment for *Dissent* — but he said in retrospect that he wished he had had Mailer cut the part about the hoodlums and the candy store keeper. Norman Podhoretz, in his 1958 attack on the Beats, "The Know-Nothing Bohemians," wrote about the same passage that it was "one of the most morally gruesome ideas I have ever come across, and [one] which indicates where the ideology of hipsterism can lead." Dwight Macdonald, who had rented a summer place in nearby New Milford, confronted Norman directly, using a stock phrase of his: "You must be crazy!" He thought Norman was temporarily deranged, according to his son Michael, and he and Norman had a long argument on the subject.

Malaquais weighed in with his response, which was typically avuncular — or paternalistic. He wrote to Mailer directly, but Mailer turned the letter over to *Dissent*. Malaquais objected to Mailer's naiveté: hipsters were everywhere — all over Europe, for instance — and there was hardly a black among them. He felt Mailer was romanticizing blacks, bestowing on them a "Messianic mission." Using Marxian analysis, Malaquais insisted that hipsters were really part of the lumpen class and as such wanted to conform and eventually would.

A different criticism, subtly more appreciative, came from a group very similar to those he was describing: the Beats. Though Norman had met few of them, with the exception of poet Allen Ginsberg, his essay circulated among them and caused a great deal of thought. They recognized Mailer as, if not a kindred soul, certainly a sympathetic one, and though they never said so, they may well have welcomed a mainstream essay on the idea of the Hip. But they defined themselves in fundamentally different terms. Though there is much argument over the coining of the term *beat* — many took it to mean "beaten down" — Kerouac always insisted that he had invented the word as a derivation of *beatific*. Therein lay the world of difference between Beat and Hip. The beatnik (the patronizing suffix was added by the Sputnik-obsessed media) valued peace and tenderheartedness, not violence. Some of the Beats had gone through their own flirtations with violence and psychopathology in the 1940s, hanging around Times Square with junkies like Herbert Huncke and William Burroughs; Burroughs had even killed his wife in a game of William Tell. They had had enough of that world and sought to cultivate warmth and openness rather than the cool, spare qualities of the hipster.

Kerouac in particular was angry with Mailer for making the whole Beat scene seem violent. Others thought Mailer quaint and naive. Ginsberg felt that Mailer had it all wrong but had shown courage and perspicacity in publishing the piece; it especially touched him that Mailer gave the piece to poet Lawrence Ferlinghetti to publish in his City Lights series.

Indeed, the example of the Beats raises a key point: the wisdom of "The White Negro" as a career move. Mailer had, of course, not given up on the novel as a form, but it was coming to frustrate him more and more. The more conventional novelists of the 1950s in general feared their era was passing as the Beats became the new literary game in town, darlings (or devils) of the media in a way that the likes of Calder Willingham and Vance Bourjaily had never been. Mailer saw a new sensibility on the horizon and wisely aligned himself with it, by writing, in fact, its first polemic. It was a bold move indeed. He was forsaking his Harvard beginnings, origins that would have granted him a role as a literary gentleman. With the disappointments of *Barbary Shore* and *The Deer Park,* he came to see how outmoded such a role really was. The place for a writer in the late 1950s was on the edge, and with "The White Negro" Mailer situated himself there.

Despite (or perhaps because of) all the controversy the essay aroused, the gamble paid off. Almost immediately, it brought him renewed attention from the New York intellectuals, who, to their credit, realized that Mailer was a cultural critic to be reckoned with. After its publication, he began to move in their social circles; he met Lionel and Diana Trilling, for example, at a party given by Lillian Hellman. Norman was gentlemanly and gracious — but he wasn't pulling any punches. Seated between Diana Trilling and another woman at dinner, he paid due attention to the other woman and then turned to Diana, saying, "Now what about you, smart cunt?" Rather than being shocked, Diana, taken completely off guard, was charmed. A genuine friendship sprang up between the two. With Lionel, who was respectable to the point of being intimidating, Norman kept his distance, but he maintained a lively, flirtatious manner with Diana, and she responded warmly.

At the same party Mailer met Norman Podhoretz, who was for a time to be another important friend, and would function as a kind of Greek chorus in his life for many years. Seven years younger than Mailer, Podhoretz, Brooklyn-born and trained at Columbia and Cambridge, was a Trilling acolyte. Still socialist in the late 1950s, Podhoretz, while more culturally conservative than Mailer (although who in the group was not?), had an excellent grasp of what Mailer was trying to do. In the summer of 1959 he would publish a piece on Mailer in the *Partisan Review,* over the objections of Philip Rahv and William Phillips, who still thought Mailer too "middlebrow," and in any case didn't like to publish articles that were as laudatory as Podhoretz's. Perhaps it was the similarity in their backgrounds, but for the next couple of years the two Normans saw each other a great deal, taking long walks together, talking endlessly. Podhoretz was considered a comer on the intellectual scene, and he spent a good deal of energy convincing other members of the group that Mailer's was an exciting new voice.

Still, others hung back, and it wasn't until the publication of *Advertisements for Myself* in 1959 that Mailer would be fully accepted, even lionized. For one thing, he and Adele were still languishing in Connecticut. The scene there was getting claustrophobic, the air increasingly thick with animosity. The writer Dawn Powell, after a visit with the Mailers, remarked in her diary that "Norman Mailer (in Bridgewater) wants to move as all that green makes him sick."

Ominous tensions arose between the Mailers and the Styrons, for example. Bill and Rose Styron, well established in the area, had been the social arbiters of the community until Norman and Adele arrived, stealing some of their thunder. Styron was a likable, boyish man from a middle-class Southern background, though his aristocratic manner and pretensions suggested otherwise. Rose, darkly handsome and Jewish, was the heir to a Baltimore department store fortune. Styron, then working on *Set This House on Fire,* was a notoriously slow writer, and Rose's money supported them. They had quite a lavish spread, with a large house, lots of land, and a smaller house that Styron converted to a studio. They were great entertainers, and every weekend brought several houseguests.

Jim Jones and his new wife, Gloria — a show-stopping, dramatic beauty with a magnetic personality — were frequent visitors at the Styrons' and the Mailers'. Though the three couples had numerous good times, tensions surfaced. Adele and Rose Styron did not get along. And in such a setting Norman found himself unable to resist stirring up a little competitive sport, especially because Jones and Styron had formed a close alliance that he felt might exclude him. Jones wasn't immune to the competition between the three, often asking Mailer whether Styron was really in "our" class. And Styron hosted an evening in which he read excerpts from Jones's new book, *Some Came Running,* making fun of what he thought was Jones's bad writing. Mailer felt a little uncomfortable but joined in nonetheless.

But Norman was developing a personal animosity toward Styron. There was a general feeling that Styron was too much of a literary politician; most of his houseguests were people with real clout in the literary and publishing worlds. And the personal antagonism between the Styrons and Adele really got in the way. The friendship effectively ended in March 1958, when Mailer wrote Styron a furious letter calling him to terms for spreading rumors that Adele was a lesbian. He had it from "a reliable source," Norman wrote, that Styron had spread such a rumor. He closed the letter with a veiled threat: "So I tell you this, Billy-boy. You have got to learn to keep your mouth shut about my wife, for if you do not, and I hear of it again, I will invite you to a fight in which I expect to stomp out of you a fat amount of your yellow and treacherous shit."

As it happened, Jim and Gloria Jones were visiting the Styrons at the time, and after much discussion of the letter the four decided that their friendships with Mailer had come to a natural close. It was a sad moment for the three men who had once stumbled through the Village streets proclaiming themselves the greatest writers in the country.

AS THE DECADE wound down, Norman was busying himself with other projects, in the wake of "The White Negro." He was still trying to "save" *The Deer Park* by writing fragments about its characters. He also turned it into a play; in fact, his interest in it as a play would persist for over a decade.

Mailer's interest in this project grew out of his growing involvement with the Actors Studio in New York City. In 1957 a group of writers, including Molly Kazan and Sol Stein, formed a playwrights' group within the Studio; the idea was to have Studio actors and directors stage their works, with the writers remaining involved in the production. Mailer was not an official member of the group, but he came frequently to its meetings.

Mailer's friends Montgomery Clift and Marlon Brando had been involved with the Studio since the forties, and Norman had been interested in its work since then. Mickey Knox was also associated with the Studio, and through him Norman met other actors who would become close friends, most notably Rip Torn and Kevin McCarthy, the novelist Mary's younger brother. It was Knox who brought the script of *The Deer Park* to the attention of director Frank Corsaro, and they put up some semistaged readings, with Anne Bancroft playing Elena, McCarthy Eitel, and Knox playing first Marion Faye and later Collie Munshin, the son-in-law of the producer Herman Teppis. In this version of the play, the action is set in hell. Marion Faye is given a more central role, and both Charles Eitel and Faye have served prison sentences.

Progress on the production would proceed in fits and starts over the next couple of years until it was finally staged in 1960. Corsaro had Mailer put the script through several rewrites. There were other hitches: Norman had first loved Anne Bancroft in the part (and even made a pass at her offstage) but then had become dissatisfied, insulting her royally. Adele had begun taking acting lessons from Corsaro, commuting from Bridgewater once a week, and Norman got the idea that she should play Elena. Corsaro worked with her closely, and he felt she had promise.

For the most part, however, the play adaptation was frustrating work. The prose fragments that Mailer was spinning out of the novel were more ambitious and more promising. "Advertisements for Myself on the Way Out," which appeared in *Partisan Review* in the fall of 1958 and later in *Advertisements for Myself*, delves deeply into the world of Marion Faye. Set partly in Provincetown, the story tells of a murder and a suicide, and includes what is meant to be a profound conversation between a black ex–call girl and a physicist; there is a lot of theorizing about time and sex.

The other piece, "The Time of Her Time," which would first appear in *Advertisements for Myself*, is far more successful as a story, though the ideas behind it would generate considerable controversy. It is the story's odd premise — no doubt based on a passing fantasy of Norman's own — that Sergius O'Shaugnessy has moved to a loft on the Lower East Side of New York, where he teaches bullfighting. A great seducer, he becomes involved with a Jewish student, Denise, and sets out to conquer her with his "avenger" and bring her to orgasm for the first time. Eventually, after much sadomasochistic back-and-forth, he succeeds in doing so, whispering in her ear, "You dirty little Jew" as she reaches climax. She has the last word, calling him a homosexual as she exits, and Mailer makes Sergius's response ambiguous. It is a difficult story, but one element is obvious: the narrator's absolute contempt for women. Simply to call one's penis an "avenger" bespeaks a terrible misogyny. But another element in the story is equally compelling: the redemptive, almost holy value of the orgasm. The value of the orgasm seems to increase, strangely, in direct proportion to how much contempt he feels for his female partner. Given its absolute primacy for him, it is not difficult to understand why sex, and the relationship between the sexes, had become such a battleground for Norman.

TEN

LITERARY POLITICIAN

Disenchanted with country life, and particularly with the feuding in the local literary community, the Mailers moved back to New York in the fall of 1958, taking an apartment this time in the Village, at 73 Perry Street. Their social life was making new demands on them, and both were involved in the dramatic production of *The Deer Park*. Adele thought the new apartment gloomy, but it had the advantage of a small outdoor garden; in planning an early party, they hired a gardener who, for eight hundred dollars, landscaped it completely, adding a lawn, flowerbeds, and a birdhouse. But the partygoers, many women in high heels, completely undid their work, and the garden eventually became a dog run for Tibo and Zsa Zsa.

Their circle of friends was growing, and it included people from vastly different walks of life. Norman and Adele could change like chameleons according to the social setting. So, for example, the Trillings and Norman Podhoretz, as well as Podhoretz's wife, Midge Decter, were frequent guests for staid dinner parties at the Perry Street apartment. Irving Howe remembers that Norman always wore a three-piece suit and tie to meet him, either, Howe thought, as a jab at Howe's square respectability or simply as a sign of respect and affection. "He had a certain gallantry," wrote Howe, "that made you respect him no matter what he said . . . I also suspected that within the noisy public Norman there was a reflective private Norman, who kept a skeptical eye on the former's recklessness of speech and wondered whether there might be a speck of truth in the cautions of his liberal and socialist friends." As Howe's comments indicate, the intellectuals had a special fondness for Norman, and his craziness was no small part of it. Yet Norman, at thirty-five, needed this world as much as it needed him. "The White Negro" had launched him on a new phase in which he sought to become a public persona, to put himself on the social and intellectual map.

He was consciously shaping a new career as a literary politician — a role he had once accused Styron of playing.

Suddenly Norman Mailer was seen all over town. Once again he was accepting every invitation he received; Adele, a little tired from mothering, often stayed home, a circumstance that led to harrowing 4:00 A.M. fights, as Adele sat home brooding about Norman's probable infidelities. But the party scene was too exciting for Norman to pass up. Tall, handsome, and talented George Plimpton, the editor of the *Paris Review* and perhaps the city's most sought-after bachelor, hosted regular parties at his East River apartment, peopled with tall, beautiful models, writers like Bruce Jay Friedman, Philip Roth, and John Marquand, and such editors as Jason Epstein and Bob Silvers. Norman held court there, a glass of bourbon in his hand: people gravitated toward him, and he was often at the center of a large knot of people. Plimpton remembers several of Norman's pastimes at parties, which he seemingly never tired of. One was thumb wrestling; after a bout with Norman, your thumb would be so sore you couldn't pick up a fork at breakfast the next day. Another was engaging a fellow guest — usually a woman — in a staring match: "At cocktail parties it was not an uncommon tableau to see his somewhat chunky figure, legs slightly akimbo, a drink in one hand, swaying slightly as he engaged in this sort of ocular showdown with the girl opposite."

But Norman was navigating other literary terrains as well. One night Jack Kerouac, whose *On the Road* had appeared the year before, showed up at the apartment on Perry Street with Allen Ginsberg in tow. To Ginsberg's recollection, Kerouac was shy and a bit standoffish — he still mistrusted Norman for placing violence at the heart of the alternative scene — but Norman was genuinely affectionate and respectful of Kerouac's achievement. He caught a certain innocence in Kerouac, who, though celebrated, was essentially a private writer, unconcerned about his public — the very antithesis of Mailer. In years to come he would be extremely protective of Kerouac, after his fashion. Once, when Norman was driving down the Taconic Parkway with Gore Vidal, Vidal revealed that he had had anal sex with the bisexual Kerouac. Norman nearly drove the car off the road, and would for years to come irrationally blame Vidal for "ruining" Kerouac's life, even, in effect, causing his decline and death from alcoholism.

Mailer never formally joined forces with the Beats — his relationship with Kerouac, for example, was never a real dialogue — but he sensed, as did some of them, that he was running on a distinctly parallel course. Like the Beats, who were experimenting with setting their words to jazz, he found jazz a liberating art form that provided a road map for a new way of being. Ginsberg was excoriating 1950s America in his poetry, and Mailer saw himself similarly situated on the fringes of American life, self-appointed to be its most biting critic. Both he and the Beats felt and expressed dread about the future of the country. When he wasn't entertaining Irving Howe in a suit and tie, Norman wore the Beat uniform — plaid flannel shirts and blue jeans. Out in Connecticut, he had sported a goatee. It is even tempting to compare Jack Kerouac's lifelong devotion to his mother to Norman's feelings about Fan.

To be sure, however, Norman was coming from a distinctly different direction. Though the Beats were famously alienated, they also sought and welcomed ways in which they could feel whole or at one with the world, most notably through Buddhism. Norman sought comfort solely in the orgasm. The alienation of the Beats extended into the literary realm, as many of them rejected conventional literary forms in favor of extremely free verse or, in Kerouac's case, spontaneous "bop" prose. Mailer remained a traditional novelist, though he was beginning to see the limitations of that form.

Some of the Beats, especially Michael McClure and Ginsberg, were suspicious of Mailer, noting the ocean of difference that separated the Hip from the Beat. Mailer's hipster hero was jaded, cool, and detached. The Beats, however critical they were of the dominant culture, sought to be accepting to the point of passivity. The signal point of departure between Mailer's project and that of the Beats was that Mailer's hipster embraced violence and found meaning in it. The Beats had had their flirtation with violence earlier in the decade, but that was an era they had put behind them. They were determinedly peaceful.

Ginsberg was very aware of these differences, and would have held Norman at arm's length had he not been constitutionally incapable of doing so. He admitted to admiring Norman tremendously for his courage in undertaking the project behind "The White Negro": investigating the edges of culture, prophesying the tremendous social upheavals that were just around the corner. Ginsberg, of course, took his own kinds of risks, and not just in being openly homosexual. His reading of the epic poem "Howl" at the Six Gallery in San Francisco in 1955 had been, by all accounts, one of the defining moments for the Beats and for modern poetry. It was a naked, confessional work, and the poet who stood in front of that crowd came across as the essence of bravery, which Norman admired.

His personal affection for some of the Beats aside, Mailer the literary tactician remained impressed with the splash they were making. A *Life* cover story in 1959, called "The Only Revolution in Town," treated the Beats as glorified juvenile delinquents, making them feel that the Luce empire was out to demonize them — if not lock them up — and that the rest of straight America would soon follow. Norman no doubt noted the publicity and was impressed by it. At the same time he was sympathetic enough to the goals of the Beats that he realized their chagrin at such coverage. The only rational response when the media has created a monstrous sensation is to destroy it, and Norman was instrumental in organizing a 1959 theme party in the Village, dubbed "The End of the Beats" or "The Funeral of Hip." A big slice of the literary world was there, from Village poet Tuli Kupferberg to uptown essayist Susan Sontag, and Mailer and Jimmy Baldwin staged a mock debate, with Norman getting most of the attention.

But Norman missed one social occasion that would have meant more to him than any of these: a meeting with Hemingway. The older writer kept an apartment at Sixty-second Street and Fifth Avenue, and one evening George Plimpton and a date joined him at a gathering there; among those present were Hemingway's biographer, A. E. Hotchner, the bullfighter Antonio Ordonez, and one of the Hearsts. Plimpton asked Hemingway if Mailer could join them and Hemingway said yes. Plimpton then phoned Mailer, telling him to wait for confirmation of the evening's plans. In the meantime, however, A. E. Hotchner, mindful that Mailer was not just another writer but an outsize literary ego who idolized Hemingway, said he didn't think it was a very good idea, and Hemingway acquiesced. Plimpton never did call Mailer back. He later realized that Mailer had probably sat waiting by the phone all evening.

Mailer might have been gratified to know that Hemingway had shown interest that evening when Plimpton described some of his combative hobbies: staring contests, thumb wrestling, and a new sport Norman had taken up — headbutting. This game was played by two males, who stood about five feet apart and then bowed heads and went for each other, the crowns of their skulls colliding with a sickening hollow sound. After one participant got knocked down, he would simply get up and start again.

Of course, Norman wasn't practicing his new sport with Lionel Trilling or Irving Howe. For sport like this he turned to the younger men who surrounded him everywhere he went, a virtual entourage. Many, like the aspiring actor Mickey Knox, were genuine friends, but others were hangers-on who basked in Norman's reflected glory, hoped to pick up any stray women who wandered into his orbit, or wanted to be part of the show. Provincetowners like Bill Walker, an ex-welterweight from Washington, D.C., who often worked as a bouncer, were willing to arm-wrestle or headbutt at the slightest instigation. Those who had known Norman a long time — old friends like the Gwaltneys — were dismayed by this new development; Norman seemed to be surrounding himself with a court of the most frivolous kind. It seemed to them that he was demeaning himself by accepting such feckless followers. They hadn't seen anything yet.

It is hardly surprising, given his interest in combative games, that Norman would dedicate himself seriously to boxing. His interest was whetted one evening in 1958 at a private party in an East Side bar when Roger Donoghue, who had been a world middleweight contender from 1946 to 1952, introduced himself to Norman and Mickey Knox. Donoghue agreed to give Norman lessons and act as his sparring partner, even taking Norman to a New Jersey training camp where he sparred with Ralph "Tiger" Jones and Yama Bahama. Norman didn't do too badly, Donoghue felt. His short stature and arms meant that he had to be very aggressive as a fighter, punching from underneath and risking blows from above. This style, imposed by physical necessity, meant that boxing was risky business for Norman, especially because he sought accomplished partners.

On the other hand, it is unlikely that Norman ever faced real danger in the ring, given his sparring partners' considerable professionalism. A boxer like Donoghue could have killed him with one punch; Chandler Brossard knew this when he refused to box with Norman in Connecticut. Rather, these semiprofessional and professional boxers humored Norman, literally pulling their punches. It wouldn't have been onerous for them; they got a nice workout and taught him a few moves. As time went on and his admiring entourage grew, Norman would have no shortage of sparring partners. Boxing gave his combativeness an outlet, and the encouragement he received from Donoghue and other pros gratified his ego.

OUT OF SHEER egotism, as well as a masterly instinct for career direction, Norman was growing into a public figure. His writing reflected this. In 1958 he was working on the project that would become *Advertisements for Myself*, which would be seen, on its publication in the fall of 1959, as a major book and an important cultural moment. A collection of miscellaneous writings — his earliest stories, excerpts from his novels (including what he announced would be his "big one"), his *Voice* columns, political essays, and "The White Negro" — *Advertisements* was held together by the author's running commentary set in italics. The commentary contains some of Mailer's finest and most revealing autobiographical writing. He threw all caution — and modesty — to the winds, baring his naked ambitions and his fears of failure and encapsulating the emotional and professional rollercoaster ride that began with the success of *The Naked and the Dead*. The book is an unsparing look at a literary career: Mailer describes in detail his drug use, his bouts with depression, his directionlessness, his spates of bad writing. Of course, for all its honesty, there is much that the book doesn't reveal, most notably his relations with women and with his family. But it is the career of the *writer* Mailer wants to illuminate, not the life of a man.

The book marks an inspired leap in that career. At this juncture, Mailer was expected to produce another traditional novel — as his primary rivals, Styron and Jones, were doing. But with *Advertisements* he announced another move, upping the ante both on himself and on those still caught up in novel-making. It was an unprecedented move: no other writer had produced something so open about his or her career, something that acknowledged and celebrated the career of the writer as much as the work he or she produced.

With *Advertisements,* Mailer announces his presence as a major writer. The major writer, he explains by the examples of "The White Negro" and "The Time of Her Time," confronts the taboo, looks into the heart of darkness. But in a larger sense, he argues that the major writer is a public figure, an outsized character who has the potential to change the entire current of the culture. He ambitiously, if grandiosely, puts himself forward as the best candidate for that office.

The book's title catches the tone exactly: Norman, taking his cue from the Madison Avenue mentality that so dominated American life in the 1950s, states what he is trying to do. "The way to save your work and reach more readers is to advertise yourself," he writes bluntly and unapologetically. In the opening paragraph of the first commentary in the book, he announces that he had been doing nothing less than running for president in his own head for the past ten years, and admits he hasn't been winning. The failure has made him bitter and angry, he says, and thus brutal. He knows he will sound arrogant, he says, but

> it cannot be helped. The sour truth is that I am imprisoned with a perception which will settle for nothing less than making a revolution in the consciousness of our time. Whether rightly or wrongly, it is then obvious that I would go so far as to think it is my present and future work which will have the deepest influence of any work being done by an American novelist in these years. I could be wrong, and if I am, then I'm the fool who will pay the bill, but I think we can all agree it would cheat this collection of its true interest to present myself as more modest than I am.

It's an interesting strategy. He establishes an intimate connection with the reader ("I think we can all agree") while at the same time throwing down a gauntlet. You be the judge, he seems to be saying — but he clearly intends to mount a mighty argument in his favor.

He proceeds to do so, invoking with outright bravado the specter of Hemingway in his opening pages. Hemingway might not have written much that was very good lately, he argues, but "he knew in advance, with a fine sense of timing, that the best tactic to hide the lockjaw of his shrinking genius was to become the personality of our time. And here he succeeded." Mailer's commentary explores exactly how the writer can accomplish such a task. For his part, he writes, he cannot reach his public "as a lover." He has to engage his readers head on, rough them up a little bit: "I started as a generous and very spoiled boy, and I seem to have turned into a slightly punch-drunk and ugly club fighter who can fight clean and fight dirty, but likes to fight."

The collection, then, is a call to arms. It is also a declaration of who he is as a writer, and he holds back nothing. He includes juvenile short stories that he admits have little merit, political essays he describes as containing his worst writing, and his windiest *Voice* columns. Yet in his running commentary he explains what he had been trying to do and why in this or that instance he has failed. His perceptions are very sure and the reader is disarmed, won over by his candor. Though he by no means asks for sympathy, he wins it by his sheer effort. He laboriously reproduces passages from early drafts of *The Deer Park,* along with their tortuous revisions; he invites the reader to understand how mighty has been his task. About his stronger pieces he says little, recognizing that they speak for themselves.

The commentary is more than the glue that holds this rather uneven collection together; it is a performance in itself, one that succeeds remarkably well in presenting Norman as a personality, not just a writer. He might well have quoted one of his favorite writers, Henry Miller: "My book is the man that I am." Those pieces that do not work are carried along by those that do: the novel excerpts, the scenes from the play of *The Deer Park,* and, most especially, "The White Negro." The book, to be sure, contains a lot of detritus: unremarkable poems, fragments of a play, a letter to the *New York Post,* a mediocre essay on Picasso reprinted from a Provincetown journal. Also thrown in are a couple of interviews, a literary setting in which Mailer would never shine. One would expect that a man who so valued performance and the nourishment of a public persona would excel at the personal interview, but all too often Mailer waxes bombastically philosophical and remains elusive about his private feelings, and his interviews are in the end unrevealing. But in the running commentary in *Advertisements,* performing for the reader rather than face to face with an interviewer, he is keenly introspective.

As if to prove that he was serious in his stated goals to take on his public like a fighter and to establish the primacy of his place in literature, Mailer wrote one essay especially for the book, which was destined to explode like a bomb in the literary community. "Evaluations: Quick and Expensive Comments on the Talent in the Room" is a ruthless, no-holds-barred look at his fiction-writing contemporaries. He discusses, in this order, James Jones, William Styron, Truman Capote, Jack Kerouac, Saul Bellow, Nelson Algren, J. D. Salinger, Paul Bowles, Vance Bourjaily, Chandler Brossard, Gore Vidal, Anatole Broyard, Myron S. Kaufmann (a Harvard classmate and friend), Calder Willingham, Ralph Ellison, James Baldwin, Herbert Gold, William Burroughs, and, in a last, dismissive footnote, "the talented women who write today" (he names Mary McCarthy, Jean Stafford, and Carson McCullers). The only writers for whom he offers unqualified praise are Broyard, who gets two sentences ("I've read two stories by Anatole Broyard. They are each first-rate, and I would buy a novel by him the day it appeared"), and Burroughs, whom he discusses in a footnote. Though every other writer discussed gets his due, he is ultimately dismissed, sometimes with faint praise (Capote, Algren, Kerouac, and Willingham), sometimes with outright scorn. The calculus by which Mailer judges these writers is curious: his only criterion is whether or not they are "major" or have the potential to be. In other words, he is making no pretensions about being a literary critic, or even a reviewer: he is simply sizing up the competition, in an impressionistic and idiosyncratic way.

His assessment of James Baldwin is a representative case in point. Mailer announces straight out that Baldwin is "too charming a writer to be major." He admires the "moral nuances" of *Notes of a Native Son* (1955), but finds its paragraphs "sprayed with perfume." Baldwin is incapable of saying "Fuck you" to the reader (whatever that means), but he feels Baldwin is not without courage, as can be seen in *Giovanni's Room* (1956), "a bad book but mostly a brave one." Baldwin is too detached, writes Mailer: "One itches at times to . . . smash the perfumed domes of his ego." But he issues Baldwin a challenge, as he does to all of the writers discussed in the piece: "If he ever climbs the mountain, and really tells it, we will have a testament, and not a noble toilet water." (The references to perfume and toilet water seem to be coded references to Baldwin's sexuality.) Until then, he concludes summarily, after this not very illuminating critique, Baldwin "is doomed to be minor." To Mailer, this is all that matters.

Clearly, Mailer did not intend a detached overview of his contemporaries but rather a set of deliberate provocations. Baldwin was his friend, for example, and these remarks, however much they were intended to spur greater creative effort, were also destined to offend. The essay begins with an extended reading of the work of another friend, James Jones, and the first two lines indicate just how personal Mailer's assessments were intended to be: "The only one of my contemporaries who I felt had more talent than myself was James Jones. And he has also been the only writer of my time for whom I felt any love." He proclaims *From Here to Eternity* (1951) the best American novel about the war. But he cannot resist adding that "it is ridden with faults, ignorances, and a smudge of the sentimental." And he goes on to accuse Jones of selling out, damning the two novels that followed, *Some Came Running* (1957) and *The Pistol* (1958). Jones is too preoccupied with fame and with making money, Mailer believes, too much the literary hack. (Of course, this could be read as a simple projection on Mailer's part.)

Styron comes in for similar treatment, with *Lie Down in Darkness* (1951) dismissed backhandedly as "the prettiest novel of our generation." Styron's case clearly worries Mailer, who knows Styron is a first-rate literary stylist, and he suggests that his friend's work-in-progress, *Set This House on Fire* (1960), might be a literary tour de force that will be welcomed as a great novel. But, unless Styron has the "moral courage" to write a book "able to turn the consciousness of our time" — Mailer's own stated goal — he will never be truly major, for that achievement is, Mailer says in a provocative locker-room metaphor, "the primary measure of a writer's size."

The reaction among his contemporaries to this piece when *Advertisements* appeared in November 1959 was as might be expected. The storm center was the Paris home of Jim and Gloria Jones, an apartment on the Île St.-Louis that was a legendary meeting place for visiting Americans. Baldwin recalled the first time they read the piece together — he, Styron, and Jones. They read it aloud in the Joneses' apartment "in a kind of drunken, masochistic fashion." After the shock of the attack, rank bitterness set in. Jones could not leave it alone. He kept a copy of *Advertisements* behind the huge altar that served as a bar in the apartment, and brought it out for visiting writers to see, inviting them to write comments in the margins. Later, trying to sort out his friend's betrayal, he wrote to Styron that he didn't mind Norman's honesty about their work; what disturbed him was the fact that he had given "the authority of print to statements of ordinary gossiping talk. There is a considerable difference to me between saying these things during a drunken evening of discussion and putting them in a book which will be printed and sold with the dignity of literature." Jones's distinction was apt, but it was probably wrong to assume that Mailer's words would be taken as authoritative simply because they appeared in print; most discerning readers could recognize the piece for what it was: a gossipy performance.

The essay effectively marked the end to Norman's friendships with Styron and Jones. Baldwin, however, was locked into a kind of love-hate relationship with Norman, which the piece only made stormier and more intense. Baldwin's first reaction, on reading that he lacked the courage to say "Fuck you" to his readers, was to send a wire saying "Fuck you" to Norman, but he thought better of it. When he saw Norman next, at a production of *The Deer Park* (Baldwin deliberately arrived too late to see it, for he feared that he would instinctively denounce it), the two repaired to a bar, Baldwin saying calmly, "We've got something to talk about." Norman was waiting for this, and sat tensed, his shoulders hunched, Baldwin thought, like a boxer. Why had he done such a thing? Baldwin asked. Affecting the Texas drawl he often adopted when in fighting mode, Norman said, "I sort of figured you had it coming to you." Baldwin objected that Norman should have criticized him to his face rather than in a public forum, and Norman answered, evasively, "Well, I figured that if this was going to break up our friendship, something else would come along to break it up just as fast." But he had a special fondness for Jimmy, and he backed down a little, saying, "You're the only one I regret hitting so hard. I think I — probably — wouldn't say it quite that way now."

Norman was lucky the response wasn't more heated. He was criticizing writers, after all, and writers could retaliate with their pens. On the other hand, he seems to have found nothing untoward in this mode of attack: he was simply declaring a contest, daring his competitors to take him on. So he praised them for their strengths and came down hard on them for their weaknesses. It was an odd exercise, to be sure: why not a reasoned assessment of the contemporary literary scene, rather than all this reckoning of "size"? Yet it is consistent with the combative tone of *Advertisements for Myself*, whose author is not a literary gentleman but a public force.

As it happened, *Advertisements* received a greeting from the critics far different from what his last two efforts might have led him and Putnam's to expect. This time, many, if not most, would *not* "understand [him] too quickly," but rather would consider seriously the kind of literary performance he was trying to put over. One of those he criticized in "Evaluations," Gore Vidal, caught Mailer's purpose exactly. Vidal, two years younger than Mailer, was perhaps the most seasoned writer of the lot. The mixed reception of his early novels had led him to turn his hand, successfully, to writing television dramas; he was also a skilled essayist. As such, he was less invested than writers like Styron or Jones in being considered a "major" writer, or, as Mailer was, in writing "the big one." Though his personality was marked by an undeniable strain of narcissism, professionally Vidal was strangely free from the literary egotism of many of his contemporaries. Moreover, he liked Norman, whom he had first met at a party in 1954 and pegged right away as "a born party-orator." He reviewed *Advertisements* for *The Nation* in January 1960. Though he dismissed many of the pieces in the book, he admired a couple of stories and "The White Negro" a great deal. But he correctly assessed the book as a whole as a kind of public statement:

> Mailer is forever shouting at us that he is about to tell us something we must know or has just told us something revelatory . . . He is a public writer, not a private artist; he wants to influence those who are alive at this time, but they will not notice him even when he is

good. So each time he speaks he must become more bold, more loud, put on brighter motley and shake more foolish bells.

This is an apt assessment, but evidently Vidal felt he was giving the reader the wrong impression of where *he* thought Mailer stood among his peers, for he added, "Yet of all my contemporaries I retain the greatest affection for Mailer as a force and an artist. He is a man whose faults, though many, add to rather than subtract from the sum of his natural achievements."

Mailer could not have hoped for a more understanding response. Because of the running commentary, *Advertisements* was the most personal book he had written, yet he was oddly less invested in its reception than he had been with his novels. It was as if it was just something he had to do. He later said, simply, "I wanted to declare myself, put myself on stage firmly and forever." He'd assumed sales would not be impressive. His publisher, Walter Minton, shared this view, advancing Mailer just ten thousand dollars. Minton thought Mailer was wasting his time putting together a collection rather than writing a novel, and he objected to certain small things in the book, scenes from the play *The Deer Park,* for instance, but by and large Putnam's humored Mailer. Minton thought the photograph Mailer wanted for the cover — of him in a yachting cap — was a little silly, but Mailer thought it made him look handsome, and he argued Minton down.

Vidal was not the only critic who seemed to understand what Mailer was trying to do. Although *Time,* which had never been kind to Mailer, wrote that he had produced "a record of an artistic crackup," and Granville Hicks, writing not altogether unsympathetically in the *Saturday Review of Literature,* complained that he was "frittering away his time," other reviewers spotted something fresh, even daring. Charles Rolo in the *Atlantic,* citing Mailer's "considerable literary talent," admired "the rowdiness of his polemics" and wrote, in a comment Norman would have liked, "Mailer has chosen to be a literary terrorist." The reviewer for the *New York Times* had reservations but wrote that "Norman Mailer shows once again that he is the most versatile if not the most significant talent of his generation."

Modest sales, and a modest critical reception. Yet *Advertisements for Myself* was to have a huge impact in two senses. It affected a whole generation of readers, remaining even today a favorite of many of Mailer's followers. The Beats and their supporters, whatever their differences with Norman, circulated it among themselves, many of them admiring its bravery. The New York intellectuals sat up and took note again, though many of them, like Diana Trilling, did not weigh in immediately with written critical responses. *Advertisements for Myself* worked like an open letter announcing to the world that Norman Mailer was down but most definitely not out, that, in fact, his was a voice that demanded to be heard.

The effect of *Advertisements* would resonate in the coming decade, a time dominated by the politics of celebrity, manifest in such diverse figures as John F. Kennedy and Andy Warhol. Among other things, Mailer was mapping the coming cultural scene. He was also mapping his own literary future, for he would produce several similar collections in the 1960s, and he had refined a persona that would serve him well as he moved into other genres. It was also his first manifesto about writing or not writing "the big one": having failed to follow up *The Naked and the Dead* with another blockbuster, he was raising the stakes rather than staging a strategic retreat. And he was outlining the themes that would be his coming fictional concerns, even though he didn't have much of a project in the works yet: sex, politics, masculinity, death, and celebrity.

In terms of his career, *Advertisements* was also an incredibly shrewd move. Though the excerpts from the "big novel," of which *The Deer Park* was only a small part, drew little attention, "The White Negro" and the cultural and political pronouncements strewn through the commentary put the public on notice that here was an innovative thinker, a keen observer of contemporary life, as well as someone who was himself making a difference on the cultural scene. Attention was deflected from Mailer's fictional prowess and redirected toward his skills at essay writing and even reportage. The way was paved for his evolution as a journalist.

The editors at *Esquire* were among the first to take notice. Founded in 1933, the magazine had an interesting history. Editor Arnold Gingrich referred to the 1930s as the "Hemingway and Fitzgerald years," and indeed in that period the likes of Dashiell Hammett, John Dos Passos, Langston Hughes, Knut Hamsun, Theodore Dreiser, and John O'Hara graced its pages with their work. With World War II, the magazine underwent a transformation, running stylized pinups by artists George Petty and Alberto Vargas, though as often as not text by a writer like Thomas Mann ran alongside them. After the war, the magazine struggled to find its identity and to distinguish itself from the newly founded *Playboy*. By the late 1950s — following the magazine's twentieth anniversary, when it really hit its stride — *Esquire* had evolved into a magazine for the new urban male, offering advice on fashion and other so-called lifestyle matters, but also running fiction by the likes of Philip Roth, Arthur Miller, James Baldwin, Gore Vidal, and William Burroughs. The magazine recognized in the late 1950s that a cultural sea change was imminent, and the editors wanted to be part of it. They were looking to locate the magazine on the cutting edge journalistically as well, seeking fresh new voices who could write about politics and culture.

One young editor, Harold Hayes, read "The White Negro" when it appeared in *Dissent* and saw Norman Mailer as just the sort of talent

Esquire was looking for. He bought first serial rights to *Advertisements for Myself,* and gave Mailer free rein as to what would be excerpted and how it would be titled. Hayes thought Mailer's selection — from the commentary that described his difficulties with *The Deer Park* — and the title he chose for it — "The Mind of the Outlaw" — were inspired, and the piece ran in November 1959, the month *Advertisements* appeared. Arnold Gingrich, who mistrusted Mailer, later wrote, "Mailer's earnestness about the . . . significance of hip and hipsterism was pretty prophetic. Though the terminology now seems dated, nevertheless the phenomenon to which he clearly pointed has since grown to worldwide proportions, except that its exponents became known as hippies rather than hipsters." Thus began a long, sometimes rocky, but extremely productive relationship between Mailer and *Esquire.* Within its parameters, Norman was able to test out a wide variety of literary approaches, to hone his skills as a journalist, to experiment with writing a serial novel; perhaps most important, he was given a public stage for his most immediate responses to events around him. As time went by, and *Esquire* evolved into "the hottest magazine of the 1960s," according to *Esquire* historian Hugh Merrill, "Mailer was to *Esquire* . . . what Hemingway was in the 1930s — the hairy literary chest."

Though Hayes's instinct was sure, the next stage in Mailer's association with the magazine came about almost accidentally. Editor Clay Felker was visiting the Five Spot one night when the headwaiter, an acquaintance, assumed Norman and Felker knew each other and seated Felker at a table with Norman, Adele, Mickey Knox, and Adele's sister, Joanne, soon to marry Knox. Adele was drunk and angry that night, baiting Norman about something, eventually demanding the car keys and storming out of the club. An embarrassed Felker, looking for something to say, asked Norman if he'd ever thought about writing about politics. Norman said yes. Felker then suggested he go to Los Angeles and cover the 1960 Democratic National Convention. Though Norman expressed reservations — he had no political connections, he said, no entree to that world — a deal was quickly struck, and finalized the next week, with Felker agreeing to pay $3,500 for the piece. Felker said he would accompany Norman to Los Angeles and introduce him around.

Mailer flew out to Los Angeles in mid-July; when he picked Felker up at the airport he confided that he had no idea how he was going to approach his subject. At first the convention, held at the Biltmore Hotel, seemed like just so much old-style, backroom politics. Introduced around by writer and editor Max Lerner, Mailer met and conferred with other journalists covering the event: Ted Morgan, an Adlai Stevenson man also writing for *Esquire* (his piece would not appear); Richard Rovere, writing for *The New Yorker;* Gore Vidal; John Kenneth Galbraith; James Reston; and Arthur Schlesinger,

Jr. Though Felker helped, Norman found he easily gained entree to the back rooms at the convention. He met with Eleanor Roosevelt, who was determined that two-time loser Stevenson beat Senator John F. Kennedy of Massachusetts at all costs. Norman's old Hollywood connections served him well too. Shelley Winters, an ardent Stevenson supporter, arranged for him to be at the best parties. The Democrats responded warmly to him, and he had free access to many important meetings and events, introductions to all the movers and shakers.

One day he told Felker he had at last figured out how he was going to write the piece. He had an epiphany when, standing on an outdoor balcony at the Biltmore, he saw Kennedy arrive in a motorcade. He was struck by the candidate's sheer presence: "the deep orange-brown suntan of a ski instructor," his dazzling white teeth. It was an apparition of a movie star. With that moment, the convention "came into focus for me . . . The Democrats were going to nominate a man who, no matter how serious his political dedication might be, was indisputably and willy-nilly going to be seen as a great box-office actor, and the consequences of that were staggering and not at all easy to calculate."

In other words, this was not going to be, as the saying goes, politics as usual. Norman had his reservations about Kennedy, in particular the political machine that had created him. But he sensed that Kennedy was a force who could ignite America, making possible real changes and real protest. His youth, his good looks, his beautiful wife "were not trifling accidental details but new political facts." If he were elected, it would be an "existential event." He saw the ghosts of men like MacArthur and Eisenhower, Nixon's talismans, being laid to rest in a new spirit of adventurousness. It was indeed an epiphany to Norman: he had introduced the new culture of celebrity with *Advertisements for Myself,* and now he was witnessing the birth of the new politics of celebrity.

Back in Provincetown, Mailer wrote the convention piece with ease. The Kennedy people were aware that he was writing what might be, for their purposes, a very important story, and someone — either Jacques Lowe, a Provincetowner who was Kennedy's photographer, or Pierre Salinger, who was Kennedy's press secretary and who had met Norman in Los Angeles — arranged a meeting at the Kennedy compound in Hyannisport. For what would be the first of two interviews, Norman prepared himself in a highly unusual way. He clipped out a quote from a man who had responded to a *Village Voice* poll asking him how he was going to vote: "Well," the man was quoted as saying, "as between Kennedy and Nixon, Kennedy is a zero and Nixon is a minus, so I'll vote for Kennedy." The other was an ad he'd saved, a Republican answer to the Democrats' famous campaign poster that featured a swarthy Nixon and the tag line, "Would you buy a used car from this man?" This parody ad went on, "However, if you bought the car from Jack Kennedy, you would trust him and you would buy the car, and then after you'd bought the car, he'd drop by to pay a visit and see how it was working, and then he'd seduce your wife."

Kennedy politely looked the two pieces over and commented, "The first one's kind of absurd, you know. After all the difference between a zero and a minus — I really don't think of myself as a zero, and I'm sure Richard Nixon doesn't see himself as a minus." About the second piece, the ad, he said, "I really don't know what that means."

On the way out, Kennedy guessed what kind of car Norman drove, and he guessed wrong, picking a Volkswagen. Norman corrected him, "No, it's a Triumph TR-3." At this point, Norman supposed, "I had him twice." But he blew it, he thought, when Kennedy asked him to come back the next day and bring a guest. Norman chose to take Adele, which he later came to believe was a mistake. Kennedy would know Norman was trying to impress his wife, whereas "if I'd brought Arthur Schlesinger or someone of that ilk he would have known he was dealing with somebody formidable." It is difficult to see how impressing the president was more important than showing the simple good manners of inviting his wife, but Norman had invested this meeting with considerable meaning.

For this second meeting, Adele and Norman speeded down the Cape, Norman late and angry because Adele couldn't provide him with a clean shirt. The Kennedys met them with their usual charm; Jackie admired Adele's sweater and Jack gave her a tour of the house, showing her Jackie's paintings and asking about her own artwork. Somebody had obviously briefed them about the Mailers, for in his private meeting with Kennedy, Norman was most impressed that Kennedy named not *The Naked and the Dead* but *The Deer Park* as the work he'd read and admired. It confirmed Norman's impression: only a true "existential hero," as he called Kennedy in his piece, would appreciate this existential novel about sex and time.

The essay Mailer was writing, "Superman Comes to the Supermarket," represented a radical departure from traditional journalism. While he sticks to the basic elements of classic reportage, describing, for example, the city of Los Angeles, the appearance of each candidate's delegates, and the nominating speeches, he also stops to ruminate on the meaning of each of these phenomena, often in idiosyncratic and impressionistic fashion — as when, for instance, he digresses on the aptness of JFK's middle name, his resemblance to the glamorous writer. He is first-rate on details — describing, for example, the "life of bad banquet dinners, cigar smoke, camp chairs, foul breath, and excruciatingly dull jargon" that is politics — and the essay accordingly moves along at a pleasantly frenetic pace. But the overarching thesis is what makes "Superman Comes to the Supermarket" inspired.

Norman sensed that the country had come to a moment when "the life of politics and the life of myth had diverged too far, and the energies of the people one knew everywhere had slowed down." Though Americans had always in their rootlessness been inclined toward homogenization, "yet America was also the country in which the dynamic myth of the Renaissance — that every man was potentially extraordinary — knew its most passionate persistence. Simply, America was the land where people still believed in heroes." Much over time had altered that, nothing more than eight years of Eisenhower, "the triumph of the corporation." The result has been "a tasteless, sexless, odorless sanctity in architecture, manners, modes, styles." A profound alienation dominates the land, and America's need is "to take an existential turn, to walk into the nightmare, to face into that terrible logic of history which demanded that the country and its people become more extraordinary and adventurous, or else perish." Mailer does not propose what we might next expect, that Kennedy is the hero the country needs. His argument is not linear, and he has enough doubts about Kennedy that he cannot simply write as a booster. Yet he senses possibility in Kennedy, possibility the country desperately needs: he cites the country's need to "recover its imagination, its pioneer lust for the unexpected and incalculable." With a man like Kennedy as president, he continues, "the myth of the nation would again be engaged." Thus the essay is not simply an endorsement of Kennedy but an exploration of the national psyche, a clarion call to arms demanding that the American people be brave enough to embrace change. "Superman Comes to the Supermarket" transcends the genre of convention coverage to become a cultural statement and rallying cry.

In mid-August Felker flew up to Provincetown to see how the piece was coming along. He needed it immediately if it was to make the November issue, which would be on the newsstands on October 15, in time to beat the election. What he read excited him, and he took the manuscript directly down to New York. Not everyone at *Esquire* was as enthusiastic, however. Harold Hayes didn't like it — but then, he usually took sides against Felker. Arnold Gingrich raised more serious reservations. "This isn't writing," he complained. "It's just smearing anything on the page that comes into his head." He insisted the piece run without any mention of it on the cover, and, most unforgivably as far as Norman was concerned, changed the title from Norman's euphonious "Superman Comes to the Supermarket" to what *he* thought was the more euphonious "Superman Comes to the Supermart." Mailer wrote a furious letter to the editor that appeared in the January 1961 issue, complaining about the title change, the type the piece was set in, and the out-of-date photograph of him that appeared in the contributors' column. There followed a bitter, if temporary, rift between him and *Esquire.*

But "Superman Comes to the Supermarket" — Mailer would reclaim his title when he published it in a collection — had a tremendous effect. Norman covered the Democratic convention in a highly personal, idiosyncratic style, making no bones about the fact that he was a participant in the events he described, and in so doing he changed the face of American journalism. Pete Hamill, then a reporter at the *New York Post,* commented on the essay's impact:

> It went through journalism like a wave. Something changed. Everybody said, "Uh oh. Here's another way to do it." Mailer had altered the form, and you said, "Okay. It's not the same, and you've got to deal with that." Everybody in the business, guys my age, were talking about it. Norman took political journalism beyond what the best guys — Mencken, Teddy White, Richard Rovere — had done. Rather than just a political sense there was a moral sense that came out of the piece.

Mailer himself acknowledged that "Superman" "had more effect than any other single work of mine," but he wasn't speaking of the piece's effect on a generation of journalists. He firmly believed that he personally had gotten Kennedy elected: "My piece . . . added the one ingredient Kennedy had not been able to find for the stew — it made him seem exciting, it made the election appear important." Perhaps he hadn't delivered a certain bloc of votes, as politicians typically claim, "but a million people might have read my piece and some of them talked to other people." He believed that he had given Stevenson supporters a reason to get behind Kennedy, and that his piece had brought volunteers to the Kennedy campaign.

"At bottom I had the feeling that if there were a power which made presidents, a power which might be termed Wall Street or The Establishment, a Mind or Collective Mind of some Spirit, some Master, or indeed *the* Master, no less, that then perhaps my article had turned that intelligence a fine hair in my circuits." Writing in 1962, he continued, "This was what I thought. Right or wrong, I thought it, [and] still do."

This is fair enough, on a rational level. Certainly Mailer's piece may have won many votes for Kennedy, though it is equally fair to say that if the brilliance of "Superman" lay in Mailer's bringing to light Kennedy's outsize personality, and the way that personality was itself a political force, the personality remained Kennedy's own. What is more to the point is that the article's effect confirmed Norman's growing sense of his own importance, which was based both in reality and in a projection derived from what was becoming clinical grandiosity. Earlier, in *Advertisements for Myself,* he had talked of running for president — in his own mind. Now he began to take the idea a step closer to reality: he began toying with the idea of running for mayor of New York City. If Kennedy, who could win an election not because of his politics, which Norman thought rather humdrum and traditionally liberal, but because of his personality, then Norman, no less a personality in his own eyes and, increasingly, those of others, himself had a fair shot at elected office.

ELEVEN

BEYOND THE LAW

In the summer of 1959, Norman drove his wife, his two children, and the two poodles up from New York City to Provincetown with him in his forest-green Triumph. Adele had negotiated for a station wagon, but that option he held, like immunization, to be "plastic" and "corporate" — thus the overstuffed sports car. His fame followed him to the Cape, where he became the central figure in an increasingly wild scene in the summer of 1959 and especially 1960. To the mix of painters and writers in the summer colony were added a number of what Village writer Seymour Krim characterized as "a gang of post-Beat kicks-oriented writer-fighters and wild-assed gallants from Washington, D.C., P-town and the East Village." The Mailers rented Hawthorne House on Miller Hill Road, a place very large by Provincetown standards and something of a landmark. It was to be the scene of countless parties — and countless fights.

Participants remember the vast quantities of alcohol and marijuana that fueled them in those summers. Revelers would meet almost nightly at bars along Commercial Street: the Old Colony was a favorite, but they also frequented the Surf Club, the Ace of Spades, and the A-House, where you could hear musicians Eartha Kitt, Gerry Mulligan, and Mose Allison. After Norman, the most infamous party givers were photographer Rick Carrier and his wife, Barbara; they rented a place at the waterfront owned by Eldred and Mary Mowery, who had previously rented to the Mailers. Eldred Mowery's sister, Fay, was visiting in the summer of 1960 and met Roger Donoghue, whom she would soon marry, thus cementing the bonds between the Mailers and the permanent Provincetowners.

Norman had many playmates. The D.C. contingent — Bill Walker, one of Norman's sparring partners, the aspiring poet Lester Blackiston, and *Washington Post Weekly* writer Dick Dabney — were always ready to indulge him in his physical high jinks. Bill Ward, editor of the newly founded literary journal *Provincetown Review,* began an affair with the Mailers' old friend Harriet Sohmers. The Cape tradition of Saturday morning softball games, led by Dwight Macdonald in Wellfleet, continued, with sons (sometimes daughters) joining in. Dwight, with a handkerchief with the corners knotted on his head, teased the children, and a shirtless Arthur Schlesinger, Jr., manned first base, sometimes lending that position to Edwin O'Connor.

Rumors flew, many of them wildly improbable but with some basis in fact. One was that the Macdonalds regularly threw nude parties on Phillips Beach near their cottage in Wellfleet's back woods; Adele remembers such an occasion, an almost surreally sedate affair. Dwight Macdonald's son Michael has an indelible impression of Adele in a leopardskin bikini bottom. Harriet Sohmers called Norman a homosexual at the Old Colony one evening, provoking a fight. Norman was said to have been beaten up by three blacks on another night on Shank Painter Road. At a party at John Frank's house on Atkins Mayo Road, Adele got into a hair-pulling fight with Sohmers, with Norman urging them on.

Norman was fighting anyone who would take him on. Roger Donoghue was willing, of course. Another partner was an Irishman named Tom Curran, a good boxer who, unfortunately, did not pull his punches as consistently as others did; Norman came away from one fight with a bloodied nose.

In the summer of 1960, in the middle of this chaos, Jimmy Baldwin came for a visit, and barely knew what to make of the scene. Adele was then dancing in a production called *The Pirates of Provincetown,* and Baldwin attended the opening, praising her performance afterward, though she had no lines beyond one scream, which she delivered with gusto in high "method" style. While Adele had a special fondness for Baldwin, except for one big fight about "The White Negro," Norman left him to his own devices. At about the same time, in an unfortunate incident involving HCE, Nat Halper's art gallery, Norman revealed his new highhandedness, the flip side to his party antics. Halper had agreed to include a painting of Adele's in an upcoming show. He hung it in what he thought was a nice spot, between a Robert Motherwell and a Marsden Hartley. But when Norman saw that it was located in a smaller room off the main gallery, he demanded that the painting be returned to him. Apparently he expected not only lively companionship from the Provincetowners but also respect.

All these events played out in a peculiarly tense atmosphere. As in many summer colonies, the natives — in this case a mix of old WASPs and Portuguese fishermen — were wary of the influx of summering out-of-towners, even though the visitors supplied a good part of their living. The police force felt that it was their job to protect the locals, especially when the summer visitors showed a flagrant disregard for convention. They were known to close down gallery shows that contained nudes or other "offensive" material, and they were thought to be overzealous in policing the outsiders, giving them citations at the slightest provocation and even manhandling them in the process. Homosexuals especially were singled out for harassment. For their part, the summer visitors were already distrustful of authority, inclined to see the police as the enemy. One policeman, specially assigned to the summer force, earned particular enmity; though his name was William Sylvia, he was nicknamed, ominously, Cobra.

Inevitably, Norman came into confrontation with the Provincetown police. On June 9, after the bars closed, he and Adele were walking back to Miller Hill Road when a police cruiser came by. Norman called out, "Taxi! Taxi!" As Adele tried to quiet him, the cruiser crawled by and then turned around and came back. The officers — one of them Cobra himself — asked if Norman thought the car looked like a taxi. "Well, you know — that little thing on top," Norman responded. At this, the police laid hold of him and pushed him into the car, Norman crying out to Adele to witness that he had not resisted arrest. After a stonily silent ride to the station house, the police helped Norman out and began to escort him inside. But Norman didn't want their help, and squirmed out of their hands. He didn't hit them (though later he thought he might have been "yellow" not to), but he was clubbed on the back of the head with a nightstick. In his cell, the officer approached him and told him the cut on his head — which would require thirteen stitches — happened when Norman hit his head on the car bumper. Norman belligerently asked if the cop was Catholic and then told him he would go to hell for lying.

Eventually Adele arrived with the fifty-dollar bail. Norman had told her on the phone that he had been clubbed, but she became incensed when she saw his bandaged head. "You'll wish you'd never begun this!" she shouted, letting the police know they had tangled with no ordinary victim. Norman was released two hours later, with a drunk-and-disorderly charge on his sheet.

At the trial on July 23 — his run-in with the police bracketed his coverage of the Democratic Convention, suggesting the extremes of his world at this time — Norman elected to represent himself. He carried it off fairly well, putting Adele on the stand to establish that he had had only four drinks and thus could not have been *that* drunk. In questioning the police officer, he lapsed into his Texas drawl, and kept referring to Patrolman Sylvia as Cobra, though the judge repeatedly admonished him not to. Allowed a certain latitude by the judge because he was not a lawyer, Norman tried to introduce a psychiatric line of testimony to establish a pattern of brutality in the police force's behavior, but the judge kept him from pursuing that line of argument before long. In his summary, Norman said, "A middle ground may apply here. A man has a few drinks and is sassy, but I question whether this is a cause for arrest . . . I don't want to be flowery. I've been coming here ten times in the last fifteen years. I like Provincetown, and there's no reason it can't have a police force that is as good as the rest of the town."

After a short recess, the judge delivered his opinion. The defendant, he said, had "had enough to drink to act like a fool." But the police had been too "thin-skinned." He found Mailer guilty of drunkenness, though no verdict would be filed, which meant there would be no fine or sentence, and nothing on his record unless it happened again. He found Mailer not guilty of disorderly conduct, and advised him to be more polite to the police in the future.

And so the summer of 1960 played itself out. That fall, his public and his friends in New York read "Superman Comes to the Supermarket" and marveled at Mailer's impressive journalistic debut. At the same time, however, they could read in the pages of *The New Yorker* a lively account of his not very dignified brush with the law in Provincetown — for Dwight Macdonald had covered the trial for that magazine as one of its "far-flung correspondents." They were interesting spectacles to reconcile.

"NINETEEN FIFTY-NINE–SIXTY was a great year to fall apart," observed Beat poet Michael McClure. He had his own reasons: too many drugs, growing paranoia over the public response to the Beat movement, and the intrusion of the media into his life and the lives of other heretofore anonymous people. But McClure was not alone. Norman, for example, shared many of McClure's complaints. He was still smoking pot and drinking very heavily; he was thrust into a peculiar position in the public eye for his championship of the hipster; and he was cultivating what would be a long love/hate relationship with the media.

Yet being in the public eye was proving to be a mixed blessing for Norman and other "fringe" cultural figures. While they had circulated largely underground in the 1950s, they were now enjoying a new notoriety, recognized as public figures. But the cultural conservatism of the 1950s hadn't really relaxed enough to welcome them with wide-open arms. Unsettled by Castro's Cuban revolution and in the grip of a recession, the country was scrambling to gain a technological edge in the space race and unwilling to embrace the marginal. The police, for example, were on their cases. There was generally a tense suspicion of Norman, the Beats, and jazz musicians, though middle America was beginning to buy their records and books.

New York City that year reflected the craziness of the time. The cabaret-club scandal was shaking up the entire jazz community, seeming evidence to those involved of a police conspiracy to silence, literally, those whom the authorities did not approve of. New York had a long tradition of denying cabaret card licenses — essentially police ID cards — to musicians with a police record or those suspected of drug use; Billie Holiday, Stan Getz, and Gerry Mulligan, among others, had been denied cards. Blacks and Hispanics seemed to be singled out. Getting the card back was hard too; you either had to pay someone off or get a lawyer to fix things somehow. Thelonious Monk was said to have had to pay ten thousand dollars to get his card back. When, in the fall of 1960, Lord Buckley was denied a cabaret card, a group of club owners, musicians, and sympathizers formed the Citizens' Emergency Committee, in an effort to stop the practice of fingerprinting musicians who wanted to play in cabarets. Mailer, Podhoretz, and Village Gate owner Art D'Lugoff were among those who demanded an audience with Mayor Robert Wagner, and they circulated a petition to be sent to Governor Nelson Rockefeller.

Members of the Emergency Committee focused their attention on November 15, when they planned a confrontation at the license bureau. But the evening before, Norman had another confrontation with the police. After a few drinks at the jazz club Birdland, he tried to pay his $7.60 bill with a credit card. During an altercation with the manager, who claimed Norman used "profane language," the police were called in. Recognizing Norman as one of the cabaret-card agitators, they arrested him on charges of disorderly conduct. The charges were later dropped, but Norman had made the papers again, and whatever suspicion he may have had that the law was not on his side had been substantially reinforced.

The chairman of the Citizens' Emergency Committee was the novelist H. L. "Doc" Humes, a man temperamentally inclined to view the scene — and Mailer's arrest — in the most paranoid light. Doc Humes had written a sprawling, experimental novel called *The Underground City* and had then had a nervous breakdown. Now mostly recovered, he was still in a strange state of mind. Kennedy's election had convinced him that great changes were about to take place in society. Though he and others like him admired Kennedy, they were afraid that the Establishment might view things differently and exert a reactionary and repressive counterforce to the enlightened administration; bad times might lie ahead.

Norman was spending a good deal of time with Doc Humes in these days. When Norman and Adele needed a new apartment because the Perry Street place was no longer big enough for them and their two daughters (Betsy Ann had been born in September 1959), it was Doc Humes who found them one — a sublet right above his apartment in a building on the southwest corner of West Ninety-fourth Street and Broadway. Things were tense for the couple and had been since the summer, when Norman told Adele he was seeing another woman.

Norman spent his time in the new apartment and in Doc Humes's apartment below laying plans for his mayoral candidacy, an idea that had resurfaced with urgency. Humes was to be his campaign manager, said Norman, though Humes believed Norman should run largely as a symbolic gesture, sensing, quite correctly, that he could never win. Norman, in contrast, treated the idea of running with deadly seriousness. Yet every preparation he made for the campaign indicated just how little sense of political reality lay behind his thinking. His constituency, as he saw it, was New York's disenfranchised: the criminals, the junkies, the prostitutes, the runaways, the hipsters; he hoped to build a coalition between them and the artists, writers, and intellectuals of his own set. That this approach overlooked the vast middle range of New Yorkers — including the working poor and their families — seemingly did not occur to him, or did not interest him.

Norman was, as usual, onto something: the city was ripe for a political upheaval and would indeed undergo one in Wagner's third term, with the complete fall of Carmine De Sapio, the beginning of the decline of the influence of Robert Moses, and John Lindsay's eventual mayoral victory. But Norman was at this juncture more interested in the politics of style and personality than in actual issues. He organized no petition drives and sought no endorsements. He developed few positions.

Norman's major position paper for the impending 1961 mayoral race, in fact, was a strange document indeed. He planned to read his "open letter" to Fidel Castro — who had taken power as Cuba's revolutionary dictator in early 1959 and was very much in the forefront of American consciousness at the time — on the day he set for a formal announcement of his candidacy, Tuesday, November 22, 1960. Mailer praised Castro (who, in fairness, had not yet taken Cuba into the Soviet bloc) "for sending the wind of new rebellion to our lungs," but he seemed more interested in outlining just how bad the "tyranny" in America was. Ominously, he praised the open violence of the Cuban revolution, which he saw as being in sharp contrast to the covert atmosphere of repression and hostility in the United States: "In Cuba, hatred runs over into the love of blood; in America all too few blows are struck into flesh. We kill the spirit here, we are experts at that. We use psychic bullets and kill each other cell by cell." The letter rambles in disturbing fashion; it is a sign that Mailer has strayed far indeed from any potential mayoral concerns when he suggests that Castro write an open letter to Hemingway asking him to return to Cuba. Mailer signed the letter, "Still your brother."

Norman would later admit that he wrote the letter "in a state of huge excitement," usually late at night when drunk (though he worked it over in the sober light of day). He was, to those around him, obviously in emotional distress and showing it physically. Adele noticed that he had adopted strange new mannerisms. Doc Humes noticed textbook signs: "paranoid ideation" and "self-referential thinking." Norman seemed to think everything was about him. Even his appearance changed, thought Humes: he slunk around with his shoulders hunched over, as if in anticipation of being struck, and he was using his Texas sheriff accent almost all the time.

Taboos were being violated. One afternoon his adored sister, Barbara, brought over some campaign-related typing she'd done for him; Norman goaded her into an argument and abruptly hit her across the face, breaking her glasses. A horrified Barbara and Adele secretly discussed committing him — things were that bad. If Norman's elaborate family support system — of which Barbara was a linchpin — was breaking down, that meant he was in terrible trouble indeed.

In mid-November, at a lecture at Brown University, Mailer appeared drunk and hostile; when a student asked that he read a scene about a chow line from *The Naked and the Dead,* Norman stepped away from the lectern, made an obscene gesture, and said, "Eat this." He adjourned to a downtown bar, leaving students and faculty shaken. "Clearly, we all agreed, Norman was finished, over the hill, done in from mixing drugs and alcohol," remembers one of those present. Professor John Hawkes, a fellow writer, "attempted to put some perspective on Mailer's garbled rambling, pointing out the dangers of premature glory for the artist, the impact of World War II on Mailer's psyche, and Mailer's battleground metaphor for life." But the students were not convinced; the most ominous aspect of his appearance was that he kept mumbling something about knives being symbols of manhood.

Yet nobody intervened. Many of his friends were simply bewildered and had no idea how to help him. But it is a curious phenomenon of celebrity that people will watch in grim fascination when a certain kind of public figure seems to be running amok. Norman had lived much of the previous decade on the edge, often successfully; perhaps he was breaking new ground. It was Norman's style, after all, to be extreme, and perhaps his behavior left his friends anticipating exciting new directions. He also may well have given everyone a reason to be glad if he fell; he was a mean drunk, not a happy one, after all, and if he fell, it promised to be messy.

Nowhere was the potential for violence more evident than in the events leading up to the party on Saturday, November 19, at which Norman stabbed his wife. It was to be a joint party held in the Ninety-fourth Street apartment, he announced: a birthday party for Roger Donoghue and an unofficial kickoff for his mayoral campaign, only three days before he was supposed to declare his candidacy officially. Because Norman had decided that the disenfranchised were his constituency, he made sure that they would be present, even to the extent of collecting strangers and homeless people off the street. But as he saw it, the disenfranchised had to be convinced that he had clout, or connections to what he called the "power structure." To this end, he enlisted his well-connected friends to summon any representatives of the "power structure" they could find to the party. George Plimpton remembers spending the day calling names off a somewhat mystifying list Norman had given him: the fire commissioner, the police commissioner, David Rockefeller, Brendan Behan, Sadruddin Aga Khan. By the time the party rolled around, Plimpton did not much want to go. He had always had trouble, however, saying no to Norman.

When Plimpton arrived at the party with society bandleader Peter Duchin, they saw immediately that a disaster was in the making. The disenfranchised were out in force, but looking uncharacteristically cowed because they feared they'd been lured into a police snare. One man was swathed in bandages, said to be a victim of police brutality. Grove Press publisher Barney Rosset, picking up bad vibrations, believed there actually were cops in the apartment — the atmosphere was that hostile. The eminent sociologist C. Wright Mills sat on a sofa looking on. Allen Ginsberg got into a fight with Norman Podhoretz over Podhoretz's insulting article about the Beats, "The Know-Nothing Bohemians," and the two had to be separated — in Ginsberg's recollection, unnecessarily. Poet and critic Delmore Schwartz was also in attendance, as was the actor Anthony Franciosa; *New York Post* columnist Leonard Lyons would write the party up the next day, commenting, "It's been quite apparent, for more than a year, that the gifted writer needed psychiatric help."

Plimpton was unable to find Norman in the commotion and so went downstairs with Duchin. There they found Norman, wearing a gaudy bullfighter's shirt, wandering on the street, obviously extremely drunk. He struck Plimpton with a rolled-up paper, demanding to know where the "power structure" was. A brief scuffle ensued. Two police officers in a cruiser looked on. Plimpton remembers wishing the cops had stopped it, or that Roger Donoghue had intervened and taken Norman out for the evening with a good punch.

Guests were leaving at a steady rate, genuinely frightened by what was going on. Barbara Probst Solomon's husband told her he didn't like the look of things and took her home. Barney Rosset's girlfriend grew so agitated that they had to leave. But new guests kept arriving, some straight off the street. Things were getting surreal. Adele was holed up for a long time in the bathroom with Harriet Sohmers, according to Sohmers, crying about her marriage — a situation that made those who noticed tense. Norman tried to box with editor Jason Epstein; he was so drunk that when Epstein held up his hand to gesture his refusal, Norman fell to the ground. When his old Connecticut friends, Lew Allen and his wife, Jay, decided to leave, Norman took them down in the elevator, having somehow acquired a bloody nose. By three in the morning, when the party had thinned down to about twenty people, Norman staged a curious drama in the kitchen, demanding that his guests divide themselves into two lines, those who were for him and those who were against him. When nobody made a move, he separated them himself, putting Adele and most of those present in the ranks of those against him. Among the few he allowed in the line of supporters was the Jamaican maid, Hetty, who, he muttered, had never betrayed him. Minutes later he was reeling back down to the street. He seemed to be seeking some kind of confrontation outside, some transformative event that would bring the party to a head; when he did not find it, he created his own trouble upstairs, in the apartment.

At about 4:30 in the morning, Norman reappeared in the apartment, with a black eye and a ripped shirt. Accounts differ about what happened next. Adele remembers that she shouted, "*Aja toro, aja!* Come on, you little faggot, where's your *cojones,* did your ugly whore of a mistress cut them off, you son of a bitch!" Before any of the few lingering guests could react, Norman stabbed her in the belly and back with a two-and-a-half-inch-long knife, narrowly missing her heart.

Nobody was very clear about events after that. In her memoir about her years with Norman, Adele gives a plausible version of what happened, which she says she remembers with perfect clarity — clarity that seems unlikely given the shock of the stabbing and the extent of her drinking that evening. In her version and in those of others, it is clear that certain guests were being protected — or were distancing themselves — from a potentially criminal situation. Only by examining the plausibility of various accounts does a coherent narrative emerge. What seems to have happened is this: Doc Humes's wife helped Adele make her way down to the Humes apartment, Adele clearly in shock. Doc took her in, pulled a mattress from a guest room, and had her lie down on it while he called a Village doctor he knew, Conrad Rosenberg. The Humeses managed to keep Adele very still, which was fortunate, for it turned out that one of the knife thrusts had penetrated her cardiac sac. Adele remained conscious and kept voicing her concern that the matter be kept out of the papers. When Rosenberg arrived with an ambulance to take her to University Hospital at Second Avenue and Twentieth Street, she told him — as she would tell the admitting physicians — that she had fallen on some glass. Not until Monday afternoon, when she was recovering from emergency surgery, did she tell a detective that her husband had stabbed her.

NORMAN'S BEHAVIOR after the stabbing raises more questions than it answers. His family and friends drew around him, supporting him unquestioningly. The only real issues were how to keep him out of jail and whether he needed immediate psychiatric supervision. For his part, Norman was determined to evade the authorities until he had some kind of game plan together. But his priorities the next couple of days were strange indeed: he was scheduled to appear on the Mike Wallace television show Monday morning, and he was determined not to miss it, still intent on launching his mayoral campaign.

After Adele went downstairs to the Humeses' and was seen off in the ambulance, Doc Humes went upstairs to check on Norman. He was lying down, passed out, and when Doc Humes roused him, Norman blearily told him to go away. Alarmed to find Betsy Ann and Dandy back in their bedroom, watched over by Hetty, Humes went downstairs and, at about 5:30, called Barbara and her husband, asking them to come over. By the time they arrived, Norman was missing. He later told Norman Podhoretz, who lived with his wife on nearby West 106th Street, that he had gone to their building and shouted up at their windows but was unable to awaken them.

In the meantime, Barbara and her husband, Larry Alson, had phoned Fan and Barney, as well as Cy and his wife, for a family summit meeting at the Ninety-fourth Street apartment. They telephoned all Norman's friends they could think of, trying to locate him. Cy, meanwhile, who was not a criminal lawyer, arranged for Joseph Brill to represent Norman. Barbara and Larry, believing that the situation was at least under some kind of control, left for the hospital around nine Sunday morning to check on Adele. They were surprised to find Norman there, seemingly sober and in relative control of the situation. Adele was being prepared for surgery, and Norman was rather officiously telling the surgeon the extent of what he would find when he opened her up. Brother and sister, with Larry, sat in the waiting room grimly until the operation was over. Presumably it was only because of the expediency of emergency surgery that Norman was not arrested at this time.

Afterward, the three returned to the Ninety-fourth Street apartment, where Roger Donoghue and a friend of his, a retired detective, joined the general summit meeting. The ex-detective advised Norman to leave the city and register at a hotel under an assumed name until the whole thing blew over, a suggestion Norman wisely did not take. Seemingly frightened by the implications of this advice — it suggested the extreme seriousness of his situation — Norman slipped out of the room and dressed in a dark suit, one that he could wear on the Wallace show, and went over to the Donoghues'. Fay offered to put him up for the night, while warning him that appearing on the Wallace show, given Wallace's aggressive style of interviewing, might be the very worst thing for him psychologically. It might also, she warned, make it appear as if he were running from the law, as by then the police were looking for him.

Sometime in the midst of this confusion, on Sunday night, Norman slipped into Adele's hospital room and asked her not to tell the police what had happened. Frightened, she agreed, and after he left she asked that she be moved to another room and that better procedures be put in place to check any would-be visitors.

Amazingly enough, Norman appeared on the Wallace show as planned. Wallace, who had no idea what had happened two nights before, was not particularly hard on him, though he listened skeptically as Norman announced his plans to run for mayor and elaborated on one of his more far-fetched schemes: that juvenile delinquency could be alleviated if jousts were held in Central Park, in which miscreants could blow off steam by charging at each other in armor and on horseback. He made — in the context — some strange remarks about the importance of the knife to the juvenile delinquent, echoing the remarks he had made at his Brown University appearance days before the stabbing — "You see, the sword's his word, his manhood." He explained his black eye by saying he had been in "quite a scrape" on Saturday night, but otherwise he seemed outwardly sane, if quintessentially Norman.

After the taping, Norman went to Larry and Barbara's apartment on Bleecker Street. Barbara insisted that he see a psychiatrist she knew, and finally Norman agreed. He disappeared after meeting with the doctor, who called the Alsons with his findings: Norman's defenses were so great that he was virtually untreatable.

Norman continued roaming the city, calling on Mickey Knox, who drove him around for a few hours. Norman was insistent that he had to retrieve his open letter to Castro, though Knox couldn't quite understand why. Knox also asked whether Norman was still carrying the knife. Norman said yes but refused to give it to Mickey. He didn't intend to use it, he said, but he needed it "for personal reasons." Perhaps it had become the symbol of manhood he had said it was for juvenile delinquents; certainly his very identity felt tenuous enough at that point, not to mention his manhood. Toward evening Norman stopped to make a call to Podhoretz, who agreed to meet him at University Hospital. At about 9:00 P.M. they showed up outside Adele's room. Adele once again told the nurses she didn't want to see her husband, and one of them called the authorities. Podhoretz was with

Norman when he was arrested in the hospital corridor and taken to the precinct on West 100th Street, where he was held overnight. Conrad Rosenberg, the doctor who had attended Adele, was called in to examine him and submitted his report, recommending admission to Bellevue: "In my opinion Mr. Norman Mailer is having an acute paranoid breakdown with delusional thinking and is both homicidal and suicidal."

Rosenberg, sympathetic to Norman's cause, was following the line of attack agreed upon by the Mailer camp. Norman must avoid jail at any cost. Norman agreed wholeheartedly with that, but he was equally adamant that he not be sent to a mental hospital. At his arraignment before Magistrate Reuben Levy in Felony Court on Tuesday, November 22, he made this statement:

> Naturally I have been a little upset but I have never been out of my mental faculties. I only saw Dr. Rosenberg for thirty seconds or a minute.
>
> It's important for me not to be sent to a mental hospital, because my work in the future will be considered that of a disordered mind. My pride is that I can explore areas of experience that other men are afraid of. I insist I am sane.

Magistrate Levy, in response, said that it appeared Mailer could not distinguish fiction from reality, and that "in your interest and the public interest" he had to commit him. Beat writer Seymour Krim, present at the arraignment with another of Mailer's Provincetown entourage, Lester Blackiston, remembers Mailer adding, "If you put me in Bellevue, it will be an indictment of my work as the work of a crazy man." While his worries about his career were perhaps a sign of sanity in view of his constant obsession with the subject, Mailer seems to have had no conception that he might in fact be in need of treatment. Or, for that matter, that he had any culpability or even responsibility in the whole affair. He never said anything in public about remorse.

He spent seventeen days in Bellevue. Little record of his stay there is available. If he had expected a repeat of what he had seen when he worked as an aide at Mattapan State Hospital during his Harvard years, he was happily disappointed. Indeed, as he later said, "The awful thing was that Bellevue wasn't awful. The horrors weren't that horrible." But he confided to Gore Vidal later that the experience *had* been "horrible." He had feared that he might never get out: "I was really in danger of being put away as insane, because the doctors there were all Jewish, and I'm a Jewish writer, and Jews just don't do this sort of thing unless they are really crazy."

The entire aftermath of the stabbing is colored by the sense that Mailer was operating under a lucky star — or, more prosaically, with the fierce support of a group of family members, friends, and sympathetic judges. On December 9 he was declared legally sane and released from Bellevue. At the request of his lawyer, Irving Mendelson (who had replaced Joseph Brill), and with the consent of the district attorney's office, General Sessions Judge Mitchell Schweitzer set bail at $2,500. Norman later told his old *Village Voice* colleague Jerry Tallmer that Judge Schweitzer had said to him, "I gamble on human beings and I intend to gamble on you."

Adjudged sane, Norman was ordered to appear before the Felony Court on December 21 to answer the felonious assault charges against him. Again, however, Norman seemed to be leading a charmed life — at least as far as the law went. Adele had been unequivocal two days after the stabbing when she finally withdrew her story about falling on some glass and told a detective that her husband had done it: "He came at me with a funny look in his eye. He didn't say a word. There was no reason. He just looked at me, and then he stabbed me." But on December 22, the *New York Times* reported that Adele had refused to sign a complaint against Norman: "I have no complaint to make against anyone," she stated. When Mailer was called before a grand jury in early January, she again refused to sign a complaint, stating that she and her husband were "perfectly happy together." She had been drunk at the time of the stabbing and didn't remember what happened, she said; nor did she remember telling a detective that Norman stabbed her. She had never seen the knife, she claimed. (Later, Adele would say that she acted in the best interests of the children.)

Mailer's case wound its way through the courts with no further surprises. He was indicted by a grand jury on January 30, 1961. After various continuances, he finally pleaded guilty to the stabbing on March 9; on May 10 he was put on probation, and on November 13 he received a suspended sentence and was put on probation for a period not to exceed three years. His lawyer at that time, Joseph Brill, argued successfully that his client was working on a new book "and could make a contribution to society." Judge Schweitzer noted that the probation officer had reported that Mailer had reduced his drinking to a minimum and that Mrs. Mailer had requested that leniency be shown in the sentencing. The case was closed.

NORMAN MAILER was fond of recalling how his friends and family commonly spoke of the stabbing as "the Trouble." Not that the disaster wasn't discussed. Debate raged in the literary community as to whether Norman had been insane or whether the stabbing was simply a natural extension of his long flirtation with violence. Diana Trilling, for example, believed he had had some kind of psychotic break and needed psychiatric treatment, while her husband, Lionel, asserted that Norman had been experimenting, committing some kind of Dostoyevskian existential act. Whatever the analysis — and scores of them were put forward — it was clear to all that Norman was a victim.

It was Adele's fault, was the conclusion of many. Fan was probably the most outrageously outspoken of these, complaining, "Why does Norman keep marrying these women who make him do these terrible things?" The general consensus was that Adele had it coming to her, with her provocative behavior, her distinctly unwifely demeanor, and her open anger at her husband. When Norman sent a note from Bellevue to the Gwaltneys, Fig filed it away after noting on the envelope, "Letter written in psycho ward after he finally did to Adele what should have been done years earlier." The first reaction of Eileen Finletter, on hearing the news in Paris, was "What a tragedy! What did she do to provoke it?" More specifically, many pointed to Adele's behavior on the night of the party, when, by locking herself in the bathroom with another woman and generally making disparaging remarks about Norman's masculinity, she was thought to have undermined his already shaky sense of identity and manhood. Of course, Norman was probably downstairs on the street when the Sohmers incident occurred, but he had long encouraged his friends to see Adele as a manipulative, castrating woman, one given to sexual and emotional blackmail. Friends were familiar with her behavior, behavior Norman encouraged. He rather enjoyed the fact that she had developed a reputation for the outrageous. Perhaps he knew it might serve his purposes one day.

It was as if Norman's fragile state of mind had been forgotten overnight. Those who had noted his growing dissociation and paranoia, his increased drinking and use of drugs, and his grandiose ambitions now seemingly forgot them in their rush to blame Adele and help Norman forget the Trouble. Twenty-two years later, Norman would still be incredulous at how quickly his friends rallied round him. "A week or two after I got out of the coop," he told a reporter from *New York* magazine, "Norman Podhoretz and Midge Decter took me to a party and everybody was shocked that they would take me there, but still they all closed ranks behind me." He had expected a reaction, he said, but he was surprised at how small it was: "Five degrees less warmth than I was accustomed to. Not fifteen degrees less — five."

Even more remarkable is the refusal of those around him — including the New York intellectuals, with their finely honed moral distinctions — to hold Norman in any way culpable. This is especially notable in light of Mailer's complete abdication of responsibility in the days after the stabbing. Fay Donoghue, for instance, thought Mailer's appearance on a television talk show was not *wise* — yet she did not question the cowardice of his going into hiding so as not to miss the taping of the show. Doc Humes was concerned about Norman being alone in the apartment with the Mailers' children after the stabbing — yet no one had questioned the propriety of throwing a raucous party with young children present, or the wisdom of not removing them when it showed signs of escalating out of control. Similarly, few questioned Adele's initial explanation that she had fallen on a piece of glass, or Norman's willingness to go along with that story, or her eventual refusal to bring charges against him. Many, in fact, applauded Adele's astonishing retraction as a sign of respect for her husband's genius and proof that she was indeed "a lady" after all.

Finally, nobody at all seemed to question whether Norman should be punished for his actions. Norman clearly hoped to evade any such consequences. It was unthinkable that he go to jail; in that notion he was reinforced by his lawyers, family, and friends. Jail would finish his career, his supporters said, and he was in too fragile an emotional state for the experience. Norman does not seem even to have entertained the idea of prison as a kind of enriching, existential experience that would fuel his writing; in a single stroke he revealed that he was far more conventional than his public image implied. Of course, only a rare person would welcome the idea of jail, but the very *impossibility* of it in Norman's case suggests just how deeply entrenched he was in the bourgeois, privileged circle of his supporters.

Yet Norman absolutely refused the alternative, entering a plea of insanity; to do so would cause potential injury to his future career, he said. An intermediate line of defense — that he had been temporarily insane, his faculties diminished by enormous quantities of alcohol — seems never to have been considered. He simply wanted the incident to go away.

His comments about the stabbing suggest just how detached he was. In the most florid phase of his dissociation, he remarked to his brother-in-law, Larry, that he had stabbed Adele to "relieve her of cancer," suggesting that his actions had a certain nobility. In the shattered months that followed, when all he could produce were scraps of poetry, one piece scandalized many who read it or heard him recite it at an infamous poetry reading in early 1961 at the Ninety-second Street Y, when the curtain was rung down on Mailer because of the obscenity of what he was reading:

> So long
> as
> you
> use
> a knife
> there's
> some
> love
> left.

Much later, he would tell interviewer Charles Ruas that the stabbing had not in any way ruined his life, and that in fact his recovery from it gave him optimism about his resiliency. He feared most for the legacy he was leaving his children: if they lost their temper, they might be forced to ask themselves, "Do I have a truly dangerous temper?" Again, his logic is somewhat curious. Such a burden might well be part of the stabbing's legacy, but surely there were other, more immediate burdens his action carried with it: Was it safe for him to be around Adele? Or, for that matter, might he stab somebody else? Could he trust himself around *any* other people, including his children?

In yet another take on the subject, he described later efforts that he and Adele made to reconcile: "The man wasn't good enough. The woman wasn't good enough. A set of psychic stabbings took place." While he was fair enough in taking his share of the blame for failing to resurrect the marriage, his attempt to make a metaphor out of the stabbing suggests an effort to shift some of the blame for the actual stabbing to Adele.

With nineteen years' distance, Norman would treat the stabbing as just another marker in his life, an event that, much like a celebrated *Esquire* piece or a well-received novel, signaled a shift in his fortunes. "A decade's anger made me do it," he told James Atlas of the *New York Times Magazine*. "After that, I felt better." The remark is reminiscent of the self-referential thinking that characterized his behavior before the stabbing. It was all about him. Adele, the victim, was forgotten.

TWELVE

THE NEW JOURNALIST

Incredibly, Norman and Adele tried to make a go of their marriage in the months after the stabbing. Norman, shaken and unsteady, most likely hoped he could regain some stability by continuing to live with Adele. In the wake of the violence, the hostility between them seemed to decrease. Norman was grateful to Adele for refusing to press charges. Adele temporized: "I told myself that if he were still dangerous, he would still be in the hospital . . . Whatever else had happened, I knew in my heart that Norman would never physically harm [the girls]. As for me, what more could he do that he hadn't done?"

Adele was also, as always, heavily invested in the idea of being the wife of a genius; it was in her interest to get him back on track. Both wanted to heal any trauma suffered by their daughters. Gore Vidal, then living at Edgewater, his estate on the Hudson River, invited the couple up for a weekend. He seems to have been the only Mailer friend who debated whether it was morally right to entertain someone who had committed such an action, but his innate goodheartedness won out. Over the weekend he noted that Adele and Norman seemed subdued. Among the others who visited Vidal during the Mailers' visit were neighbors Saul Bellow, Ralph Ellison, Mary McCarthy, F. W. Dupee, and Richard Rovere; Norman must have felt reassured to be among these illuminati so soon after the debacle.

Yet he was by no means whole in the early months of 1961. He feared that, while he had not been declared insane, the taint of insanity clung to him, and that the reading public might not take him seriously. The most he could do was write poems; later, he wrote about the time, "It was . . . a period in which I wrote very little, and so these poems . . . were my lonely connection to [writing,] the one act which gave a sense of self-importance." Apparently his family and friends, unwilling or unable to intervene before the stabbing, continued to feel powerless about his behavior. He continued to drink heavily, he wrote, and usually went to bed "with all the vats loaded," waking every morning with a bad hangover. What saved him from turning to drink in the mornings, he said, was the scraps of poetry he found on pieces of paper in his pockets from the night before; he spent the days rewriting those he could make sense of and working them over. "Since I wasn't doing anything else very well in those days," he wrote, "I worked the poems over every chance I had." By the summer of 1961 he could tell an interviewer that he'd written four hundred poems in the last six months. These would be collected in *Deaths for the Ladies* — a provocative title. It appeared in April 1962 and was almost universally ignored. (Norman would later describe himself as "the world's worst printed poet.")

Norman was obviously treading water. The stabbing, marking as it did the end of a decade, seemed to signal a new direction for him. For one thing, it was soon clear that he and Adele could not continue together. Also, Norman continued to see the woman he had been seeing before the stabbing, a woman whose existence Adele had been aware of since the summer. More than that, however, too much had passed between the couple for anything to be "normal" again. They spent much of their time apart, and in March 1961 they separated for good. In April 1962 they got a "quickie" divorce in Juárez. Over Christmas 1961, Norman had met yet another woman, and while she was not in New York that spring, she stayed on his mind.

AT GORE VIDAL'S Christmas party, Jacob Javits's wife, Marion, introduced Norman to the woman who would become (briefly) his third wife. Lady Jeanne Campbell had a formidable pedigree. The granddaughter of financier Lord Beaverbrook, a newspaper magnate and former member of Churchill's war cabinet, Jeanne was raised primarily on her grandfather's estate at Cherkley. A colorful figure, deeply conservative yet irreverent about titles and fortunes, Lord Beaverbrook did not find his daughter and her husband fit parents for Jeanne and her brother, William; "For all the awful things I've done in my life," he once said, "I am paid back by my children's behavior." He once introduced his daughter, Janet, by saying, "This is m' daughter. She der-rinks." Janet's husband, Ian Campbell, the duke of Argyll, was a drinker, womanizer, and gambler; Lord Beaverbrook temporarily put him in charge of one of his three newspapers, the *Evening Standard*. The couple separated and remarried when Jeanne was only three, and Lord Beaverbrook, disapproving of their antics and believing Jeanne needed a stable household, took their children in.

Lady Jeanne, born in 1930, grew up independent and iconoclastic. Educated at boarding school, she briefly studied acting at the Old Vic before moving home to be her grandfather's companion in 1949. She enjoyed his busy social life and showed herself early on as a defier of convention, even having a brief affair with Sir Oswald Mosley, the much older and thoroughly out-of-favor former Fascist leader. In 1956, while in France on a two-week holiday with her grandfather, she met Harry Luce, the redoubtable *Time* publisher. (By coincidence, Jeanne was then a researcher at *Time*.) She began an affair with the married Luce that would last several years. In 1960, when it was winding down, she gave up the research job he had secured her at *Life* for a position as a reporter on her grandfather's *Evening Standard*.

Norman found all this tremendously appealing. The greatest frisson may have been Jeanne's status as a Luce mistress. Norman always took great interest in his wives' boyfriends and lovers; it was as if sharing the same woman brought him into contact with them, and if they were famous or, like Kerouac, masculine icons, so much the better. With Jeanne, he was not merely inheriting the mistress of one of the most powerful men in publishing. He was also getting revenge. Norman hated Harry Luce, attributing all the evils of mid-century America to him and to the *Time* empire and its bland, homogenized view of the world, reflected in its Orwellian language, Time-ese. Luce was the Establishment personified. As Norman would later write,

> There had been a period in his life when *Time* solemnly took him out in the backyard every few weeks to give him a going-over — in return he had never been able to strike back with more than a little iniquity until the mighty occasion when he captured the mistress of a Potentate of *Time*. That lady, in the final phase of an extended liaison [with Luce], had most certainly been on the lookout for the particular sweet fellow who would most outrage her Boss.

Jeanne's aristocratic lineage was just as attractive to him, perhaps because of the lingering snobbishness he had somewhat uneasily observed and absorbed at Harvard. For all his bohemianism, Norman had always craved respectability — throwing elaborate black-tie parties even when he occupied the most rundown of digs, whether on Monroe Street or on the Upper West Side. His exposure to Kennedy and his circle had impressed on him the glamour of the very rich, a separate universe into which he sought entrée as any man with the curiosity of a good novelist might. Yet the world of the rich appealed to him on a visceral level as well. While he favored a Texas sheriff accent and a recently invented Irish brogue, he also commonly trotted out a sniffily British accent. The role of an aristocratic gentleman was one he liked to imagine and try out; with Lady Jeanne he could aspire to live it.

She was also a woman of enormous charm. Though she was taller than he and large-boned, and though her hair often rose in a frizzy brown bush around her head (much like Norman's), she was physically charismatic; there was something sexy about her. She had a loud and ready laugh and was fond of practical jokes; she could drink alongside Norman without drifting off into hysterics or tearful scenes, as Adele so often had. In short, she was a highly likable woman, what men would call "a good sport." Long-time Provincetown resident Bill Ward said of Lady Jeanne, "She wouldn't take shit from anybody." She was "good people," he added. Moreover, Norman found her highly interesting as he got to know her better. He later described this "dear pudding of a lady" as "a remarkable girl, almost as interesting, complex, Machiavellian, and spiritual as himself," referring to himself in the third person.

Norman didn't really catch up with her until June 1961, in Provincetown, when she showed up to interview him for the *Evening Standard*. She was newly back from the Soviet Union, where she had interviewed the cosmonaut Yuri Gagarin, with whom she was rumored to have had an affair. While Jeanne took an apartment of her own above Eldred and Mary Mowery on the wharves, soon she and Norman were seen together at the usual Provincetown parties. Though the parties were as wild as ever, and though Jeanne's sense of fun assured that they joined in as heartily as Norman and Adele had, some were amused to see that Norman often showed up in a suit, as if announcing his new status.

In July Norman left for Mexico to get a divorce from Adele, and Jeanne went with him. There the news reached him that Ernest Hemingway had shot himself on July 2, 1961. He was assailed by shock and then grief. Hemingway had been many things to him: a prose stylist whose writing had heavily influenced his own; a model of masculinity, in his at once stoical and lusty approach to life and his passion for fishing, hunting, brawling, and multiple marriages; and the consummate celebrity, comporting himself as America's greatest living writer as if he held the world heavyweight crown. Why else would Norman nominate him for president, and in the same volume in which he announced that he himself had been running for president for years in his own mind? Norman felt intimately connected to Hemingway, as his long discussions of the writer in *Advertisements for Myself* make clear. And he had turned to or invoked Hemingway in moments of crisis as well; his doubts about *The Deer Park*'s success, for example, had prompted him to send off a copy of the book to his idol.

Most recently, he had written two poems dedicated to Hemingway. One, "A Wandering in Prose: For Hemingway, November, 1960," describes a visit by his mother to Bellevue thirty-six hours after the stabbing. He had wanted to hit Fan but hadn't, he wrote — perhaps the strongest statement he ever made about her. A cancer was now growing in him as a consequence of that unleashed violence. The message seemed to be that Hemingway knew that violence contains an "ecstasy" or energy that when renounced leads to inner revolt. Another, "A Wandering in Prose: For Hemingway, Summer, 1956," was written in March 1961 and looked back to his 1956 visit to Paris with Adele, when he was kicking his Seconal habit. He blames Adele for wearing face powder that smells like "the corporation" and that reminds him sharply of that summer, when they could find "little joy" in each other. The connection to Hemingway seems to lurk in the notion of bravery and the impossibility of it in the face of a "castrating bitch":

> I have been brave a little but not nearly
> brave enough for you, greedy bitch,
> Spanish lady, with your murderous
> Indian blood and your crazy purity
> hung on courage in men as if it were
> your queen's own royal balls

Writing in the third person eight years later, Norman confessed, "Hemingway's suicide left him wedded to horror."

By the early 1960s, Hemingway seemed a bit like a relic of an earlier age, and no tributes were forthcoming from writers like Kerouac, Jones, or Styron, for instance. Though Norman too was moving into new realms having little to do with Hemingway in his thinking on subjects like the hipster, blacks, and the politics of style, he had found nothing so romantic as the Hemingway code of manhood, and he mourned him as his first influence, evocative of a kind of lost innocence. For Norman, the death of the iconic Lost Generation writer marked the end of an era, and he saw only horrors ahead: "Hemingway constituted the walls of the fort: Hemingway had given the power to believe you could still shout down the corridor of the hospital, live next to the breath of the beast, accept your portion of death each day. Now the greatest living romantic was dead. Dread was loose." He would return to the subject many times over the years.

IN THE MEANTIME, life with Jeanne was good. She was introducing Mailer to a whole other world, the social set of Londoners and Europeans living in New York, and he was taking it in with the novelist's constitutional curiosity — and a good deal of personal pleasure. In the fall of 1961 Jeanne's mother came for a visit, and Norman and Jeanne threw a party for her in Jeanne's apartment on Ninety-fourth Street between Madison and Fifth, where the couple were then living. Fan seems to have been uncharacteristically intimidated by the situation; she visited the apartment once to cook for Jeanne's mother but found that Lady Argyll kept her distance.

Around Christmastime Jeanne discovered she was pregnant. Norman, writing to Fig, wondered whether after three girls he might be due for a boy. She and Norman were secretly married a few months later. Before the stabbing, Norman had formed a corporation called Colhites (for Columbia Heights), with his mother, to buy a large brownstone at 142 Columbia Heights in Brooklyn, overlooking the famous Promenade, the harbor and the Brooklyn Bridge, and the lower Manhattan skyline. The stabbing and divorce intervened, and he and Adele never moved in. Now Norman and Jeanne began renovations, carving the building into five floor-through apartments.

First, however, they went to Europe on a honeymoon — and to surprise Jeanne's grandfather with a visit to tell him about the marriage and the coming child. The honeymoon was lovely, but the visit to La Capponcina, the Beaverbrook villa in Villefranche, outside Nice, did not go well. Jeanne thought her grandfather treated Norman horribly, playing the part of the outraged old-fashioned father whose daughter has conceived out of wedlock. Norman later described the visit to two Beaverbrook biographers:

> As I was saying good-bye to Beaverbrook . . . I said to him in parting, "Well, sir, under the circumstances, you've been gracious," at which point the, I suspect, famous gleam came into his eyes and he repeated in an evaluative voice, half statement, half question, "Under the circumstances." I would like to think it amused him but I can't bet on it.

Lord Beaverbrook was not amused, however. Lady Jeanne was, for the time, disinherited, a loss of some $10 million.

Lady Jeanne brought back with her from Europe her old black maid Sadie, who was too infirm to do much heavy work but who could help in small ways with the coming baby. Norman's fourth daughter, Kate, was born on August 18, 1962. The family lived downstairs in the garden apartment of the new house while the top floor was being renovated, Betsy and Danielle joining them on weekends. And an ambitious renovation it was: the roof was raised, making the living room two stories high, with large windows commanding a view of the New York skyline. Norman's carpenter friend Ray Brock transformed the place, building a loft up near the roof that would serve as Norman's office. It was reached by way of a crow's nest that led to a catwalk and then to a rope ladder. Simply going to work each morning would become a physical challenge. Norman enjoyed pointing this out to guests, who were suitably awed, and he often dared them to make the climb themselves. (He evidently tired of this arrangement, moving his office to a spare room carved out of the apartment directly below.)

Though Norman had been preoccupied with personal matters for the last two years — the stabbing, recovering his sanity in the aftermath, beginning a new life with Lady Jeanne — his reputation had been growing, an engine of its own. Perhaps the stabbing, ironically, helped — according to Adele, letters poured in afterward, nearly all protesting that this great talent be protected. The makings of a literary reputation are elusive indeed. But the result was that the impact of essays like the Kennedy piece and the earlier *Advertisements for Myself* was spreading like ripples in a pond, and Mailer's was becoming a household name. Finally he was doing some serious writing again, easing back into it slowly, writing seemingly off-the-cuff observations on contemporary affairs, but gradually growing into an important new role as cultural commentator.

In terms of publishing, he was considered a difficult writer and a significant risk, but one with a big potential payoff. *Esquire,* Norman's major employer in these years, was a case in point. *Esquire* editors Harold Hayes and Rust Hills had quarreled over taking Mailer back after his snit over the "Superman" piece. Hayes contended the magazine was more important than just one writer, while Hills retorted that "the magazine should kiss Mailer's ass in Macy's window if that's what it takes to make amends." Hills prevailed, and apologized effusively to Mailer, making an "absolutely firm, personal guarantee" that the magazine would not in future change a word of anything he submitted. It was agreed that Mailer's first assignment would be a piece on Jackie Kennedy.

Norman had a little problem with that. In the fall of 1960 he had received a gracious note from the first lady complimenting him on "Superman Comes to the Supermarket" and remarking how nice it had been to meet him and Adele the previous summer. She wondered, she wrote politely, if the "impressionistic" method he had used to write about the convention could be applied to events in the past. Norman, in the throes of the paranoid state that would culminate in the stabbing — a state in which sex and violence were inextricably linked in his psyche — wrote back that he did hope someday to write a biography of the Marquis de Sade that would bring out the "odd strange honor of the man." Vaguely he thought that Jackie, with her well-known interest in the eighteenth century and France, might find the subject appealing. Though he would later see that he "had smashed the limits of letter-writing," he thought the odds were pretty fair that he would get a reply.

He not only did not get a reply, he was denied an interview when he accepted the *Esquire* assignment. So the Jackie piece had to be written even more impressionistically than the piece on Jack. In his article "An Evening with Jackie Kennedy, or the Wild Witch of the East," Norman describes his meeting with her and the Marquis de Sade debacle, and directs a few observations toward the White House about the manner in which its much-vaunted receptiveness to the arts was expressing itself. Norman found the administration culturally timid. Richard Wilbur, he thought, would be welcome at the White House long before Allen Ginsberg, and Salinger and Bellow before Burroughs and Mailer. His only strategy beyond this was to cover a televised tour of the White House the first lady gave in February. His impressions were biting, accurate — and catty. He found Jackie lackluster and wooden. Because he had invested so much in the dreams the Kennedy White House offered, he could not forgive her for being bland: "What we needed and what she could offer us was much more complex than this public image of a pompadour, a tea-dance dress, and a Colonial window welded together in committee. Would the Kennedys be no more intelligent than the near past, had they not learned America was not to be saved by Madison Avenue, that no method could work which induced nausea faster than the pills we push to carry it away." She was a royal phony, he concluded. It was clear, in short, that she no longer turned him on, as she had once done with some urgency.

Many Americans were in the throes of a veritable love affair with the Kennedys and the New Frontier, feeling that the country, under the leadership of the young, charismatic JFK, had turned a corner and embarked on a course of rebirth. His aggressive anti-Communism was tied with a vision of America as a world leader, capable of presenting an alternative to the Soviet Union that was positive and open to progressive change, unlike the buttoned-up McCarthy-tinged Republican leadership of the Eisenhower years. Norman had been bewitched by this vision, but the scales were falling from his eyes. As his impression of a new, sexy, and open administration receptive to the arts gave way to a suspicion that Kennedy, far from being a symbol for change and possibility, was simply a creation of politics-as-usual, his enthusiasm gave way to crankiness. Though he continued to write and publish "open letters" to the president, he more often gave vent to pet obsessions, some more trivial than serious. He had strong views on modern American architecture (too bland and faceless), fluoridation (intrusive, perhaps a plot), television (a force for homogenization), antibiotics (overused, leading to the outbreak of new diseases), education (encouraged being "right" rather than thinking), and cancer (his overall metaphor for what was happening to America). By June 1962, when he participated in a symposium on "The Womanization of America," to be published in *Playboy*, he was developing one of his favorite obsessions: that contraception was evil, that sex without the possibility of procreation was unnatural, approaching onanism. Masturbation, he told Paul Krassner in an October 1962 interview for the *Realist,* was the ultimate evil: "The ultimate direction of masturbation always has to be insanity." He even took a strong position on the Twist ("I hated the Twist"): it mimicked sex but without any meaning.

Holding strong views on a variety of subjects, he now felt ready, some years after his unsuccessful *Voice* columns, to interpret America for itself, offering *Esquire* a monthly column. Culturally, his thoughts were moving from liberalism to what would later be called libertarianism. Today, he sounds a little like the Camille Paglia of his times. Like her, he wanted to preserve a degree of danger and transgressiveness in the culture, even at the cost of a society that continued to be repressive; he valued the frisson of danger that would elevate certain activities, like sex or violence, beyond the everyday. Middle-class culture seemed too "safe," and sex and violence were being drained of their meaning. Again, Mailer was arguing for a life lived on the edge, but now he was extending his criticisms beyond the realm of the personal and into cultural and social arenas. Modern architecture, in all its blandness, was not only ugly but even evil, in his ethos, because, in breeding homogenization and dullness, it killed the soul. It was imperative to innovate and transgress.

While the editors at *Esquire* almost certainly did not share these particular views, Mailer's iconoclasm was just what they were after. The magazine and Mailer shared one particular goal as the 1950s gave way to the 1960s, as Harold Hayes wrote in an introduction to an anthology of *Esquire* pieces from the 1960s. The magazine's identity emerged "out of a reaction to the banality of the Fifties," wrote Hayes. "From the raspberry to the hoax," he continued, "in words and/or pictures . . . and occasionally with some loss of dignity, the idea was to suggest alternate possibilities to a monolithic view." Moving beyond its traditional coverage of fashion, leisure, entertainment, and literature "onto the more forbidding grounds of politics, sociology, science, and even, occasionally, religion," the magazine welcomed any point of view "as long as the writer was sufficiently skillful to carry it off." The new writers the magazine took up — Gay Talese, Tom Wolfe, Garry Wills, Terry Southern, Richard Rovere, Gore Vidal, and Tom Wicker, among many talented others — proved themselves more than equal to the challenge, and under shrewd editorial guidance transformed the magazine from just another magazine for men to required reading for the educated, engaged, and up-to-the minute male. *Esquire* had become a magazine with attitude, satire and irony its hallmarks but excellence in reportage and fiction its foundation.

Esquire accepted Mailer's offer to write regularly for the magazine, and the first column, in a series called "The Big Bite," appeared in November 1962. He would continue to contribute until December 1963. The editors had their doubts about allowing him so much space, feeling that it was "so much of one man's voice in the magazine" and that the sum tied up in his fee — seven hundred dollars a column — would prevent them from signing other writers they wanted. But on the whole they felt it was better to have Mailer in their pages than not. The first column addressed the deaths of Marilyn Monroe and Hemingway; the second took a more extended look at Hemingway's suicide, which Mailer thought might have been accidental; the third addressed the evils of taped television; the fourth, the Cuban missile crisis. Mailer had learned the first lesson of the journalistic commentator since the days of the *Village Voice:* he would try to engage, not alienate, his readers. Though he was deliberately provocative, his goal was not to offend but to make converts. The strategy was enormously effective, and *Esquire*'s circulation soared; the magazine's editors realized that there were those who bought the magazine only for Mailer's column. *Esquire*'s Carol Polsgrove explained:

> He had the audacity to address the President of the United States directly from our pages, thus we acquired the audacity. He spoke out boldly on politics, sex, architecture, literature, civil rights, cancer, anything that challenged his imagination. Most of the time, when he shouted people listened; and to hear him, they had to read *Esquire.*

Esquire had begun 1962 by awarding its first Dubious Achievement Awards — which perhaps best encapsulated the magazine's irreverence and timeliness — and had named Norman Mailer "White Man of the Year"; by the end of the year, he was one of the magazine's greatest assets.

The summer of 1962 found Norman speaking on an international stage, though in expectedly idiosyncratic fashion. A historic challenge to long-standing censorship laws governing book publishing was under way in the early 1960s, as Barney Rosset's Grove Press finally brought out Henry Miller's long-banned *Tropic of Cancer* in 1961, with the legal help of, among others, Norman's cousin Cy Rembar. Rosset's next project was William Burroughs's *Naked Lunch,* but in the spring of 1962 he was still too caught up in legal battles over *Cancer* and Miller's other books to attempt publication yet. John Calder, roughly his British counterpart, thought of the month-long arts festival scheduled for Edinburgh in August and September as a forum for discussion of the topic, and planned and announced a writers' conference, to be held August 20–25. Over seventy writers would be in attendance (and the paying crowd was estimated to be around 2,500); the American contingent chosen consisted of Henry Miller, William Burroughs, Mary McCarthy, and Norman Mailer.

The conference, the first in an ongoing successful August series in Edinburgh, was a free-for-all. Stephen Spender, the self-appointed voice of literary tradition, chaired, and the overarching argument was between tradition and innovation, with censorship and nationalism emerging as equally energetic special issues. Such figures as Alex Trocchi (author of the controversial 1960 novel *Cain's Book*) and William Burroughs kept jumping to their feet to proclaim the virtues of heroin addiction and homosexuality; Hugh MacDiarmid, resplendent in Scottish garb, pleaded for Scottish literary separatism, prompting a number of Eastern European writers to make similar demands. Mary McCarthy complained in a letter to Hannah Arendt about "the number of lunatics both on the platform and in the public." Though Mailer spoke up several times in the first three days, usually to support Burroughs, it was not until Thursday, August 23, that he took the floor in earnest. The panel that day was on censorship, and Burroughs opened, as might be expected, by ringingly denouncing it. Mailer, according to Burroughs's biographer, warmed to the subject by playing the devil's advocate, arguing that the absence of censorship weakened the young, making them less warlike.

Perhaps carried away by the international setting, or perhaps because the Cold War was constantly on his mind in these years, he suggested that the forces who controlled the United States might decide that too much sexual freedom would make Americans weaker than their Russian adversaries. Mary McCarthy returned the conversation to its proper terms: she could see why the Catholic Church would want to ban heretical works, and Communist regimes insurgent ones, but why would a capitalist state ban overtly sexual works? Mailer reverted to his original argument, pointing to Stalin's repressive laws and his desire to build a warlike nation: "When people are effectively repressed they tend to be more warlike. The proof of it is that it is considered sacrilege for a boxer even to have a woman when he is in training." Clearly under pressure, Norman was falling back on some of his strangely conservative sexual beliefs to hold up his end of the discussion.

Yet Mailer was brought up short when the elderly Henry Miller, who everyone thought was asleep, rose to make an eloquent plea, calling for freedom of action as well as of expression. We all have impure desires, he said: "We should have the pure and impure, they exist together. Good and evil belong together, you can't separate them." Mailer greatly admired Miller, both his work ("his influence has been profound on a good half of American writers") and his personality, which Norman found "is all of a piece, all composed, the way a fine cabinetmaker or a big-game hunter or a tightrope artist has a personality which is true to himself all the way through." Miller's comments brought him to his senses, and he concluded the session by saying, "One has to enter this terrible borderland of sex, sadism, obscenity, horror, and anything else because somehow the conscience of Western man has become altogether muddy in refusing to enter it . . . We have got to get further into it, that is why I salute Mr. Burroughs's work, because he has gone further into it than any other Western writer today."

Mailer chaired the conference on the last day, which was given over largely to Burroughs's work and Burroughs's defense of his use of the "cutup" method, a collage-like approach to making literature that Mailer did not much like. Another point of contention was Burroughs's suggestion that the future of fiction belonged with Space; Norman, obviously thinking of his big novel, the extension of *The Deer Park,* believed it belonged with Time. Still, it was a sign of Mailer's genuine respect for Burroughs and the general tenor of the conference that he remained dignified and respectful.

Norman had a minor quarrel with Mary McCarthy during the conference, one that may have influenced his vitriolic review of her novel *The Group* the following year. The BBC, perhaps hoping for a literary battle of the sexes, offered each writer a thousand dollars to participate in a televised debate. Mailer, eager for publicity and always ready for public confrontation, liked the idea of such a forum. Ever since he had seen the enormous effect on audiences of the performer Lenny Bruce, he had been attracted to the idea of public performance. Having seen the impact of the new medium on JFK's career, he was drawn to television as an outlet for his views; it was, simply put, a great way to reach huge numbers of people. He accepted the BBC's offer eagerly and enthusiastically tried to convince McCarthy by granting her the choice of subject. She rejected the whole offer, leaving Norman deeply disappointed. "You're the regent of American writers," McCarthy remembers him saying to her, "but you're a weak regent."

Another, more ominous incident suggests underlying hostility on Norman's part. The festival had unleashed a chaotic mood in Edinburgh, and gangs roamed the streets, often beating up visitors. Burroughs's biographer describes what happened: Mailer was at a party one evening when an unnamed writer came into the room complaining that he had been beaten up downstairs. Something about the man bothered Norman. He was reminded of a joke, he later said: A man complains to God about his constant ill treatment and asks God why He is so unfair. God answers, "Because you bug me." That was the way Norman felt, and he said some nasty things to the writer and, telling him that after such abuse, he might as well "have some more," pushed him down the stairs. Mailer was, he said, horrified by his own action, which he tried to rationalize as expressing his need to explore his dark side — which, after all, was precisely what Miller and others had been arguing for at the conference. Such a rationalization is not, finally, convincing: he had been gratuitously cruel toward someone who revealed weakness. Cruelty, not compassion, carried the day.

IN LATE AUGUST, Norman flew to Chicago for a couple of rounds of combat. *Esquire* was paying the bill, apparently no longer believing there was any such thing as too much Mailer in its pages. The editors wanted him to cover the Sonny Liston–Floyd Patterson fight on September 2; he would do so in high fashion, creating his own fracas along the way.

First, however, he accepted a challenge issued by the *National Review* to debate the conservative *National Review* editor, William F. Buckley, Jr. The subject was announced to be "What Is the Real Nature of the Right in America?" and the contest was billed by the organizers as a debate "between a conservative and a hipster." Mailer had been preparing his speech for some time, and he felt he had a clear advantage over Buckley, who was due to fly into Chicago only that day with an unfinished speech. "I had honed myself like a club fighter getting ready for the champions," Norman later said, indicating his pugilistic state of mind. The sportswriters for the Liston-Patterson fight got into the act, giving Mailer odds of two and a half to one.

The debate took place at the Medinah Temple, a grand auditorium designed on the lines of an opera palace. More than 3,600 people showed up, and the event grossed $8,000. (Mailer and Buckley each got $1,250 to speak.) Buckley delivered his speech first. Looking tall and lean, the former Yale debater pointed an outstretched index finger straight out at the audience. He attacked the pro-Cuban left and spoke of his opponent's "swinishness." When Mailer's turn came, he acquitted himself famously. Making short, jabbing motions at the crowd, he positively barked his speech. The right wing, he said, was most susceptible to the plague sweeping the country, a plague whose symptoms were the decline of architecture, nature, language, philosophy, and education. He made short work of the rising conservative senator Barry Goldwater; the huge defense budget would mean cuts in welfare and social programs, a problem any conservative government would face. His solution was simple: end the Cold War. Presciently, he said simply, "Let Communism come to those countries it will come to," a position that would surface very soon as the conflict in Southeast Asia escalated. Americans should instead spend their money to better themselves as a nation, he said. The real war was not the war without — Communism against capitalism — but the war within — the conservative against the rebel. Let's have it out, he concluded.

The exchange that followed, reported in the *New York Times,* was inconsequential, mostly a trading of insults. Buckley asked Mailer if he really thought the right wing wanted to end the Cold War; Mailer said no, the right wing's real goal was to blow up the world. The reason, Mailer said, was that the right would rather be dead than Red. Buckley asked if it was not better to be alive and free; Mailer said it was, but that the way to achieve this was to end the Cold War. At another point, Mailer interrupted one of Buckley's lengthier statements. "Mister Buckley," he said, "do you want me to lie down on the railroad tracks, tie my hands to the rails, and wait until the engine of your logic gets around to riding over me?" His remark drew a big laugh from the audience.

The *New York Times* observed that the audience in the hall was mostly right-leaning; that may have led them to declare the debate a draw. But Mailer was infuriated by the reporting of the newspaper of record; he believed he had won, and, after he left the auditorium, everyone he drank with told him he had. The whole affair left him in an angry mood, and by his own admission, he stayed drunk until after the Liston-Patterson fight.

The boxing match — "one of the last great boxing scenes," according to Pete Hamill, then a reporter for the *New York Post* — was one giant testosterone fest; publicity agent Harold Conrad, who would become an important friend of Mailer's, arranged to have the reporters put up at Hugh Hefner's Playboy Mansion. The press was there in full force, as well as a number of novelists: A. J. Liebling, Nelson Algren, Budd Schulberg, Ben Hecht, James Baldwin, and Red Smith. Conrad set up a press room in the enormous Grand Ballroom at the Sheraton Hotel. Before and after the fight, rowdy if strangely sexless parties percolated at the Mansion; women were mostly absent, and Hefner was rarely seen, emerging only late at night, in his bathrobe, to fetch peanut butter sandwiches.

Jimmy Baldwin, representing *Nugget,* another men's magazine, and decidedly uncomfortable with the whole spectacle — a black man fighting another black man — made friendly overtures to Norman and wound up in a near-brawl, arguing about the sexual prowess of the black man. Norman described the confrontation the next day as "a pretty definitive fight with someone with whom I had hoped to be friends." Reporters who heard of the argument speculated that the Baldwin-Mailer argument was the real brawl out in Chicago. They were wrong, however; Norman and Jimmy would make up when they totaled their losses on the Patterson fight. Norman lost twenty-eight dollars, Jimmy seven hundred and fifty.

Though he was not the only one excited by the fight, Norman whipped himself into a rather extraordinary frenzy in anticipation of the main event. The contest was by all estimates fraught with tension, and as in so many great fights, the press and the public invested a great deal of emotional and sociopolitical capital on each side. Floyd Patterson, the defending champion, was cast as the good guy. A good Catholic, he trained at a boys' camp in Elgin, a small town northwest of Chicago, nourishing his wholesome image. Sonny Liston, on the other hand, with a jail record and what seemed to be Mafia backing, was perceived as a thug. Norman couldn't find a single black who favored Liston, and whites overwhelmingly supported Patterson. Competitively, the boxers were thought to be well matched: Patterson was perhaps a better fighter, but Liston was bigger.

For his part, Norman was a Patterson man, though he was interested in Liston, as one would expect. Liston, he believed, had made a pact with the devil: "Liston was Faust. Liston was the light of every racetrack tout who dug a number on the way to work. He was the hero of every man who would war with destiny for so long as he had his gimmick: the cigarette smoker, the lush, the junkie, the tea-head, the fixer, the bitch, the faggot, the switchblade, the gun, the corporation executive. Anyone who was fixed on power." If Liston represented evil, it was imperative that Patterson, "a churchgoer . . . a liberal's liberal" (however boring that might make him, in Norman's eyes), win. The fight became a sort of moral showdown in his eyes, and nights of little sleep and much alcohol had brought him to a kind of psychic edge. He admitted, in "Ten Thousand Words a Minute," his essay about the fight, that "I had noticed, whenever I was overtired, a sensitivity to the magical would come over me." The slightest circumstance, the smallest detail, was loaded, even the choice of what cab to climb into on his way to Comiskey Park, the location of the fight. At times such as these Mailer did indeed lapse into magical thinking, believing that he had the power to affect the outcome of a match. "All of one's small actions became significant," he wrote, describing his mood before the fight. Taking the wrong cab, he wrote, "One had the psychology of a ghost choosing the hearse he would ride to a funeral, or of a general, brain livid after days of combat, so identifying himself with his army that he decides to attack first with the corps on his left because it is his left foot which has stepped first into the command car. It is not madness exactly." Norman might have comforted himself with the fact that Dostoyevsky, when the gambling fever was upon him, was every bit as serious a magical thinker.

Magical thinking may have been an indication that something more was going on. He was feeling particularly paranoid on this occasion, believing that the rooms at the Playboy Mansion were bugged and that cameras were trained on everyone — the fighters and the writers. He described how he felt to the writer Natalie Robins: "At one moment, I did get this incredible feeling I was being photographed, and I froze." He seemed to realize that this sounded irrational, and added, "There was a lot of subtle stuff, but I could never swear to it in a court of law." Real or not, his sense of being watched colored his responses and actions, many of them not entirely rational.

Drinking at the Playboy Club before the fight with Gene Courtney of the *Philadelphia Inquirer*, Hamill and Mailer bet that Patterson would knock out Liston in the sixth round, while Courtney bet on Liston in the fifth. To act it out, they played a game with a black Playboy lighter with a bunny's white face on it: they spun the lighter so that each spin represented a single round, and the outcome of the spin was determined by which way the bunny's ears pointed. The game came out as Mailer and Hamill hoped: Patterson in six.

The actual fight played out quite differently. Two minutes and six seconds into the first round, Liston knocked out Patterson; Patterson didn't even land a solid punch. Jimmy Baldwin, two seats away from Norman, was heard to say, "What happened?"

What indeed had happened? Most agreed that Patterson, at 189 pounds, was not heavy enough for Liston at 214. But Norman was still fired up, unable to rid himself of the adrenaline that had built up in him so ferociously. At a six-hundred-strong party at the Playboy Mansion that evening, Norman began boasting that if people would leave things to him, he would see to it that Patterson would fight Liston again and win — and that he could arrange a $2 million gate in New York City that would beat the $200,000 gate in Miami that Patterson seemed bound for.

His reasoning? Patterson had been beaten by the Evil Eye. Norman thought it was his own fault, and at the same time the fault of liberal America, who "had rooted for Floyd in the same idle, detached fashion as myself, wanting him to win but finding Liston secretly more interesting, in fact, and, indeed, demanding of Patterson that he win only because he was good for liberal ideology." More directly, it was the Mafia's fault, for they had put the Evil Eye on Patterson, and Patterson, who had distanced himself from his manager, Cus D'Amato, the master of such things as Evil Eyes, had left himself vulnerable. In a rematch, Mailer could sort all this out and ensure a fair fight.

This seemingly absurd theory had some basis in reality, and in fact demonstrated Mailer's instinctive understanding of the boxing world. D'Amato, Patterson's manager since 1953, was known as a stubborn man who had absolutely no truck with the Mafia, and was forced in consequence to sleep in a back room at his gym with a German shepherd by his side. He allowed no Mob-run boxer to fight Patterson, a policy that earned him accusations of coddling an untested fighter. But in a series of fights between Patterson and the Swedish heavyweight Ingemar Johansson, D'Amato indirectly accepted promotion money from "Fat Tony" Salerno, a man with Mob connections. D'Amato thereby had his New York State license revoked, which was the reason the Patterson-Liston fight was held in the much less lucrative venue of Chicago. In the aftermath of the Johansson debacle, Patterson *had,* as in Mailer's fantasy, distanced himself from D'Amato. D'Amato got the third due to him as manager, but Patterson otherwise held him at arm's length in order to prove he was not driven by the Mob. Norman thought that he had only to patch things up between Patterson and his manager by alerting Patterson to the need for protection from the Evil Eye, and he could easily beat Liston in a rematch.

Norman found his insight so compelling that he called a press conference for the next morning, scheduling it before Liston's so that reporters wouldn't rush away to file their stories before they heard him speak. The Playboy Mansion party lasted until five in the morning, and Norman decided to stay up until his scheduled hour rather than sleeping, engaging the housekeeper in spirited conversation. But when he went to the floor where his conference was to take place, he learned that Liston was scheduled for the same hour. So off he went to the press room, where he went up on the dais and sat in what turned out to be Liston's chair. Harold Conrad, seeing that his planned press conference was headed for disaster, wanted Norman ejected. He didn't want a fight, however, so he instructed two guards to lift Norman bodily in his chair and carry the chair out to the hall. Newspaper photos caught a grinning Mailer being carried from the ballroom.

But he was back in the press room soon after, in the crowd of reporters. While Liston spoke, Norman kept trying to advance his theory, saying that he had been right in predicting that Patterson would win in six — forces had just prevented that from happening. Cries of "You're still drunk" and "Shut the bum up" rang out in the room, and Liston continued with his replay of the fight. When he said something about newspaper writers, Norman again jumped to his feet, saying, "I'm not a newspaper writer!" Liston shot back, "You're worse than a newspaper writer," to general laughter. But when cries of "Throw the bum out" surfaced again, Liston, evidently amused and complacent after his win, welcomed Norman as a fellow bum, shaking hands with him.

The incident was not without consequence. Red Smith mentioned Norman's behavior at the press conference in the *Times,* echoed by A. J. Liebling in *The New Yorker.* The gossip columnists got hold of the story, Dorothy Kilgallen scrambling it by saying Mailer had tried to fight veteran boxer Archie Moore. This would not have bothered Norman overly but that it provoked a call from the probation officer assigned to him after the stabbing, who extended his probation period.

The piece he wrote for *Esquire* represented Mailer at his best. Because of the magazine's three-month lead time, it had to be more than reportage; Patterson's loss would be old news by the time the magazine hit the stands. Accordingly, the essay is a sustained meditation on the boxing world: on the fighters, the men behind them, and, above all, the men who write about them. Mailer begins the essay with a long look at the press, which he collectively calls the Goat, dwelling in particular on the odor of press headquarters. He captures the dread of deadlines and the haze of cigarette smoke as well as the adrenaline of the free ride: The odor of a press room, he writes,

> is like the odor in small left-wing meeting halls, except it is worse, far worse, for there is no poverty to put a guilt-free iron in the nose; on the contrary, everybody is getting free drinks, free sandwiches, free news releases. Yet there is the unavoidable smell of flesh burning quietly and slowly in the service of a machine . . . All the trash, all the garbage, all the slop and a little of the wealth go out each day and night into the belly of that old American goat, our newspapers.

It is in fact the atmosphere of the big fight that he evokes so masterfully in "Ten Thousand Words a Minute," an atmosphere in which magical thinking and mystically significant drinking games do not seem at all out of place. Cus D'Amato was particularly impressed that Norman caught so thoroughly the complexities of the boxing world and its links to the Mafia: only Mailer's essay and *Sports Illustrated* ever really got that right, he said. The International Boxing Club controlled not only boxing itself but all of the inside fight media, and the mainstream media simply wasn't able to unravel all the connections. Not so Norman.

If he was back at the top of his writing form, however, Norman was still psychologically fragile. Recovering from his week in Chicago must alone have been exhausting. Back in New York, Rhoda Wolf, Dan Wolf's wife, thought Norman was in worse shape than he had been in before the stabbing. Roger Donoghue, who had his eye on Norman during his time in Chicago, telephoned Jeanne from there to warn her that her husband was in deep trouble again. He gave her the name of a psychiatrist to call, which, quite typically, caused a rift in his friendship with Norman. And Norman's relationship with Jeanne was unraveling as well.

THIRTEEN

CHANGING PARTNERS

Though the physical attraction between Norman and Jeanne was strong, and their fondness for parties and drinking made them temperamentally well suited, they brought entirely different agendas to the marriage, and strains were evident from the beginning, showing in small but telling ways. Norman was fond of informing friends that Jeanne may have given up $10 million for him, but she refused to make him breakfast — and indeed, beginning in the fall of 1963, when he hired a secretary and general assistant named Anne Barry, the job of making meals and walking the remaining poodle, Tibo, fell to her. For her part, Jeanne used to complain that she had thought she was marrying an eminent and distinguished novelist and instead found herself attached to a dutiful Jewish son who insisted they spend Friday evenings at his mother's house eating a traditional Sabbath meal of pot roast, potato pancakes, and apple pie.

Though Jeanne was like Adele in her volatile moods, the two women could not have been more different in their approaches to being Mrs. Norman Mailer. Deeply invested in her role as the wife of an important man, Adele had been prepared to play the traditional wife to the hilt. Despite the pot smoking, wife swapping, and drinking, she had aspired to a life of bourgeois respectability. In the face of marital chaos, she cooked, planned elaborate parties, and efficiently managed the constant stream of maids provided by the Miss Baltimore Agency, a domestic help firm run by Fan Mailer. In her memoir about her husband, Adele recounts in detail the elaborate menus she planned and executed in their entertaining. She accepted Norman's closeness to his parents as part of the territory. Being a wife of a successful, even famous man was so important to her that she hung on to her marriage even after the great calamity of the stabbing.

But for Jeanne, far less was at stake. She was an important figure in her own right, with a career as a journalist and a social life of her own. To her, Friday nights at the elder Mailers' were nothing but a waste of time, and cooking — well, she had always left that to others and had no intention of changing. A few years earlier, perhaps, this would not have been a problem. But Norman's view of sex roles was becoming more conservative, so this became a source of conflict. He may well have internalized his mother's immediate response to Jeanne: she was simply unacceptable as a wife. Fan wanted Norman to have a traditional wife who would support her husband's career and remain in the background; furthermore, she undoubtedly found Jeanne entirely too high and mighty for her tastes.

Fights began to erupt in the Brooklyn Heights brownstone. Norman was ever a contentious husband, telling an interviewer a few years later, "I like to marry women whom I can beat once in a while, and who fight back." Jeanne was a strong-minded woman and could give as good as she got, though her style in marital quarrels was not hysterical, as Adele's had been, but imperious. She could be withering. Before long, Norman and Jeanne were living virtually separate lives, and Norman returned to his philandering habits. Fall 1962, domestically speaking, had been hectic. Jeanne and Norman still nominally occupied the crowded garden apartment while renovations proceeded above; Norman often slept upstairs or elsewhere. Quarters became even more cramped when his eldest daughter, Susie, came to live with them. Bea had decided that she would take the child for the summers in Mexico but that Susie needed American schooling; Norman enrolled her at the Elisabeth Irwin School in the Village.

Norman wrote the Gwaltneys that the collapse of the marriage to Jeanne was a mess, a series of separations and reconciliations. Anne Barry wrote in her diary that Jeanne departed for good on January 27, 1963, leaving her old black maid Sadie behind. Five days later was Norman's fortieth birthday. His children, probably because they were not apprised of it by their mothers, seem not to have noticed. At any rate, that evening Norman found himself alone, and he called up Gloria Steinem, then a twenty-nine-year-old *Esquire* writer, and asked her to dinner. After a pleasant enough evening — Steinem, a strikingly beautiful and clever woman, was an excellent dinner companion — Norman walked her back to her apartment building. He then asked her how much cash she had on her. She took out her wallet and told him she had about twenty dollars. "Great," Norman said, "I've got the same. If we pool it we can get a hotel room." Steinem declined, though she and Norman would go on to become friends.

After Lady Jeanne's departure a lively bohemianism ruled in the Mailer household. Barely a month later, a woman in her early twenties named Jeanne Johnson appeared on the doorstep. Norman had engineered her release from Bellevue, where he had met her the year before. She had run away from home when she was seventeen, getting a job with a book publisher after lying about her age. At twenty, she'd left a party and run howling into the street, which promptly landed her in Bellevue. After Norman gained her release, he became her legal guardian.

A waiflike charmer in a miniskirt, Jeanne brought great merriment to the ménage, playing practical jokes on Norman, striking up an alliance with Anne Barry. She engineered a grand plan to get the domestically useless Sadie on welfare. The nature of her relationship with Norman is not clear. They may have had some relatively inconsequential couplings. Essentially, however, Norman cast himself as a father figure. Lately he had taken up Paul Krassner, the young, iconoclastic editor of the prototypical counterculture magazine the *Realist*, even granting Krassner a lengthy, no-holds-barred interview. With obvious enjoyment, he arranged a match between Paul and Jeanne, even hosting their wedding in his apartment — a wedding that may or may not have been legal. As a present, Norman gave the couple a pair of marmoset monkeys, whom they named Idiot and Delight.

Though Norman's personal life was chaotic, he was working steadily and even entering into what were for him professionally uncharted waters. His secretary, Anne Barry, remembers typing the manuscript of *The Presidential Papers* — a collection of pieces, mostly from *Esquire*, ostensibly addressed to President Kennedy and strung together by lively and revealing commentary reminiscent of *Advertisements for Myself*. He also continued to turn out his *Esquire* column.

In December 1962 he took a different tack, approaching Norman Podhoretz with the idea of writing a monthly column for *Commentary*. He had become fascinated by mystical Judaism, and wanted to write his column around the ideas of Martin Buber's *Tales of the Hasidim*. As Podhoretz understood it, Mailer saw in Buber an exploration of one of his favorite subjects, the relationship of God to the devil.

On another level Norman seems simply to have been fascinated by the Hasidim, who were then arriving in the United States from Eastern Europe in large numbers. He had no strong sense of Jewish identity. While Fan, like many Jewish mothers, had left him a childhood legacy of unconditional love and supreme self-confidence, she was unlike many Jewish mothers in that she did not temper this with a strong sense of the ideas and values of Jewish tradition — beyond, of course, feeding him pot roast on Fridays. He never had a strong, reassuring sense of cultural "belonging," as many people from stable traditional cultures tend to have. While this made him more prototypically "American," less likely to be cast as a Jewish writer like Jewish contemporaries such as Saul Bellow, Bernard Malamud, and Philip Roth, it also meant that he was really on his own during periods when he felt adrift.

So it was almost as a non-Jew that he approached the idea of the Hasidim. It was not likely that he would be drawn to the more legalistic Orthodox Judaism; rather, the mystical sect of the Hasidim attracted him. Here was an alien culture — much like that of Texas sheriffs or brogue-speaking Irishmen? — to which he could authentically claim kinship, and which attracted him because in the Hasidim's mystical spiritualism he found philosophical concerns that mirrored his own.

He pestered Podhoretz to take him to a Hasidic Yom Kippur service, and Podhoretz nervously agreed, begging Mailer to dress respectably and wear a hat. They met on Eastern Parkway in Crown Heights — not far from where Mailer had grown up — and made their way to a Lubavitcher Hasidic synagogue, an unprepossessing basement room. As they awaited the rebbe, the Hasidim, oblivious to the strangers in their midst, smoked cigarettes and shouted back and forth, grinding their butts out on the floor. When the rebbe arrived with his entourage, the congregation made room in the packed synagogue by moving a wooden bench and shrinking back among themselves.

Though Mailer told Podhoretz he'd had enough partway through, the experience left a serious impression. He liked their unruly behavior before the rebbe's appearance; he liked the crude setting; he liked the very extremism of the Jews' reverence for the rebbe. Those Jews, he said with a genuine admiration, were "a bunch of crazy motherfuckers, hard core and mean and tough."

But it was all too foreign for him to assimilate in any meaningful way; as much as he admired the Lubavitchers, he wasn't exactly going to try to emulate them. The trappings of Judaism — even those of a "mean and tough" sect — would never interest him. He returned instead to Buber and mystical Judaism, convincing Podhoretz to let him write three bimonthly columns for *Commentary* on the subject. The columns were curious pieces, often running far afield from any Judaic grounding. One, reproduced in *The Presidential Papers,* invented a character with a compulsion neurosis, involving touching a doorknob, and an analyst to go with it. Though the character's neurosis, like many compulsion neuroses, is quasi-mystical in nature, any point Mailer tries to make about God and the devil, much less Martin Buber and the Hasidim, is elusive at best. It seems, in retrospect, a strange episode in his writing career, though it indicates again his intellectual curiosity and his willingness to take cultural risks. In his quest for publicity, he'd outgrown the readership of a magazine like *Commentary,* in any case.

THE FOURTH Mrs. Norman Mailer first read her future husband's work in an issue of *Esquire,* where her eye was caught by a piece about the Benny

Paret fight. She had watched on television as Emile Griffith landed eighteen punches that sent the Cuban fighter into a coma from which he would not recover: his soul seemed to breathe out of him as she watched. She had been amused to see Norman on a talk show, being bleeped. He was a rebel, and that's what drew Beverly, a rebel herself, to him. On the evening of March 10, 1963, sitting at the bar at the New York restaurant P. J. Clarke's with the painter Charlotte Gilbertson and a male actor friend, Beverly noticed Norman at the end of the bar talking to her friend Roger Donoghue. When Donoghue brought Norman over to be introduced, the boxer Jake LaMotta trailing behind, the beautiful, fresh-faced, and green-eyed honey blonde let Norman know that while she was impressed by his writing, she wasn't at all impressed by his celebrity. Before the night was over, she and Norman had discovered a major mutual attraction; when LaMotta excused himself at one point, Norman gave her a kiss, and when the boxer returned, Beverly informed him that she was Norman's date, thus heading off an altercation between the men. Beverly came on like the strong-minded, independent woman that she was — a stance that masked her corresponding vulnerability — and Norman was entranced.

Born in Atlanta into a large Southern family, Beverly Bentley, née Rentz, had dreams of becoming an actress, even as a child. Her mother, of Swedish and Cherokee ancestry, married a Georgian from the prosperous Rentz and Kendrick family, postbellum land granters, divorced her husband during World War II, and married an Army Air Force man, who moved the family to Sarasota, Florida. After the move, Beverly was quite shy in school, and teachers steered her into school productions and later acting classes, where she overcame her reticence. "I dreamed of New York City, acting on the stage," says Beverly. She moved to live with her father in her early teens, then with a sister in Kentucky at sixteen, and at nineteen to Pensacola. There, through a friend of her mother's, Beverly met and auditioned for the radio and television personality Arthur Godfrey. He said he would help her when she came to New York; at age twenty, she moved there and got a job as a "Toni Twin" on his television variety show, advertising Toni hair care products in commercials. Soon he promoted her to become a "little Godfrey," dancing, singing, and acting in skits and receiving many fan letters. Her career progressed steadily from there. To make a living, she acted in TV commercials and worked as a weather girl and a hostess on quiz shows. Her wages — she was making between twenty and thirty thousand dollars a year when she met Norman — served to pay for classes in acting in the classics with a teacher recommended to her by Bess Myerson, Alice B. Young, who corrected Myerson's Bronx accent and Beverly's Southern drawl. She studied voice and dancing and took classes in method acting as well.

She was performing in some prestigious off-Broadway and Broadway productions, as well as in some quality television dramas. Her acting debut was in Clifford Odets's *The Big Knife,* in which she played the part of Connie Bliss, and her Broadway debut was in George S. Kaufman's 1956 *Romanoff & Juliet.* Other credits included *Eurydice,* with William Shatner, and Jean Giraudoux's *Tiger at the Gate,* in which she played Helen of Troy. The night before she met Norman, she closed the last performance in a leading role in the Philip Rose Broadway production *The Heroine.* She appeared in several movies, debuting in Elia Kazan's 1957 *A Face in the Crowd.* Most recently she had starred in Mike Todd, Jr.'s *The Scent of Mystery,* with Peter Lorre and Denholm Elliot. Her reviews indicated that her future as an actress was promising indeed. Major movie studios tried to sign her, but Beverly turned them down, finding their seven-year contracts too confining. By the time she met Norman, she had a twelve-year career as an actress and was understandably upset when she later learned that Norman had described her in a letter to Fig as someone who made a fair living through commercials.

Along the way she had dated a number of remarkable men, and this would be a pivotal factor in Norman's attraction to her. Moreover, during the filming of *The Scent of Mystery* in Spain in 1959, Beverly enjoyed a good friendship with none other than Ernest Hemingway, there to write a series of articles later collected as *The Dangerous Summer.* Mary Hemingway, who also became a friend, in her memoir included Beverly on the extensive guest list of those who attended Ernest's sixtieth birthday party in the village of Churriana. But Beverly's connection to his idol was a tremendous draw to Norman, though he would come to be not exactly jealous but resentful of it — as if Beverly had cheated him of his own connection to "Papa."

A very recent boyfriend of Beverly's was equally formidable: jazz trumpeter Miles Davis, who had long impressed Norman as a symbol of black male supersexuality. Davis was also an enthusiastic amateur boxer. Beverly's connection to Miles Davis was significant in other ways. When in Spain, after hearing a traditional lament, or *saeta,* at a Holy Week observance, she found a flamenco music anthology and gave it to Davis on her return. It influenced his *Sketches of Spain* album (1961), for which he recorded adaptations of Holy Week hymns, most notably the *saeta* and the stately *solea.*

Miles was a compelling presence in Beverly and Norman's relationship, a part of her life that was seldom far from Norman's mind. As with Adele and Jack Kerouac, Norman found in Beverly's connection to Miles a way that he himself could connect to a man he saw as a powerful embodiment of masculinity. More prosaically, the image of his predecessor perhaps at once heightened his valuation of Beverly's desirability and fed his anxieties about being able to compete.

Very early in the relationship Beverly set about putting Norman's domestic affairs in order. She seemed supercharged with energy, giving elaborate parties, paying compulsive attention to every household detail. She had very high standards, and there was a rapid turnover of household help in the Heights brownstone and in Provincetown. Though her career, and her suspension of it, would later surface as a sore point in the relationship, for the time she devoted herself to her new family. After Jeanne, Norman was delighted to have found a beautiful woman who actively wanted to assume a traditional role in his life. But it was not always easy. The first time Beverly tried to make salmon croquettes, a favorite of Norman's, the maid, Hetty, took her aside and said, "You should make those just like his mother does," using onions to garnish the dish rather than including them in the cakes. Beverly went out of her way to learn to make dishes exactly as Fan did, right down to Norman's eggs in the morning. Even Fan liked Beverly, finding her open and generous. Fan celebrated a birthday shortly after Beverly came on the scene; Beverly made Fan a birthday cake, and Fan wept, admitting that no one had ever made a birthday cake for her before. Beverly would never think of letting a family member's birthday pass unnoticed, and she enjoyed mounting productions for other holidays as well; New Year's Day, for example, called for the meal Southerners deemed essential for a prosperous year to come: black-eyed peas, collard greens, and ham.

In the summer, Norman took Beverly — with Tibo in tow — on a cross-country trip, first swinging through the South to visit the Gwaltneys in Arkansas. While at the Gwaltneys' Beverly and Norman asked a doctor friend of theirs who owned a lab if he could run a pregnancy test for them. Norman did not believe in birth control and had made this very clear, so pregnancy was a real possibility.

Norman and Beverly were on their way to Las Vegas to join his friend Hal Conrad and his wife, Mara Lynn, for the Liston-Patterson rematch. Norman was not covering the match — though Conrad did arrange for him to comment on it afterward for local television — but emotions about the fight ran high. In the wake of the match, which Liston lost, Norman, who was still on probation and was supposed to avoid such scenes, narrowly avoided some brawling fights in the hotel casino.

Meanwhile, Beverly had noticed the first signs of trouble in their relationship. Along the road, in Santa Fe, Norman began to harp on something in her past: her name change eleven years before, while working on the Godfrey show, from Rentz to Bentley. At first she thought he was jealous over Godfrey — which he certainly was. But he seemed most incensed about the name change, which he believed Godfrey had his hand in. A mystified Beverly could not make sense of his objection at the time, but would later attribute it to his need to control those closest to him: "Because I changed my own name, that meant to him I was not entirely his own creation — and worse, to his mind, maybe that of another man. I see now that it was the fact that I was my own creation that really got to him."

Things were still uncomfortable after they arrived in Las Vegas, even more so when a telegram reached them at their hotel saying that Beverly's Arkansas pregnancy test was positive. She expected Norman to be delighted, but noticed that he became inexplicably abusive, harassing her over the slightest matter. On top of the fight about her name change, this abusiveness hurt her terribly. The last night there she left the hotel when one of the casino fights was raging, at about five in the morning, and walked out into the desert alone, planning to end the relationship and return to New York.

The disagreement chastened them, and they resolved not to let it happen again. Norman suggested they press on to San Francisco. Their friends there found Norman and Beverly very sober and determined to make a go of their relationship; Alice Adams remembers the meticulous care with which Beverly ironed Norman's shirts. Felix Rosenthal, a close friend of Adams and her husband, Mark Linenthal, took the two couples on a picnic in Napa Valley, where they enjoyed wine and cheese in a meadow under a bay tree. Things seemed idyllic in Norman's new relationship.

Adams noticed a change, however, when she visited New York in the fall. Norman was behaving unpredictably, often boorishly. Though Beverly had brought new stability to his life, or at least a resolve to conduct himself more reasonably, he was still on shaky ground emotionally, still compelled to act out publicly, still intellectually committed to living life on the edge.

He brought a certain grim humorlessness to his public escapades, as became clear in a Carnegie Hall appearance in May 1963. He hired the hall and billed his appearance as a benefit for himself. Unfortunately, it was scheduled for the day after Memorial Day, and the hall was nearly half empty. Those attending might have expected a wild bohemian, but instead they were met with the spectacle of Norman in a wrinkled dark blue suit, intoning about cancer and other social ills. When asked about homosexuality, Norman responded not with what his questioner might have expected, some remark about the value of sexual freedom, but rather with a lengthy and pompous explanation of his belief that homosexuality was a vice that people mistakenly and deliberately chose. But he had promised the audience an "existential caper," and he delivered, closing his show by reading a paragraph from his contract with the hall stipulating that he use no four-letter words. He then read a poem containing obscene language and took his bows.

Those present remember it as an embarrassing, even painful evening, but clearly Mailer had some higher purpose in mind. Paul Krassner had recently been making public appearances where he delivered impromptu monologues, performances that were well received if, to some, shocking, and he believes Mailer was influenced by his work. But Norman had been fascinated with public performance for years. Adele believes he was greatly influenced by the comedian Lenny Bruce, who shocked and outraged his audiences to a point beyond laughter. She recalls at least two Lenny Bruce performances in the late fifties at the Village Vanguard that she and Norman saw together, evenings where Bruce was hassled by the police. At one performance Bruce traversed political and sexual ground and then moved onto the subject of snot, which left the audience shaken and silent. Norman, it seems, was greatly impressed by the power of the comic's irreverence and use of obscenity: Lenny Bruce could, by shaking them up, move his audiences, leave an indelible impression on their lives, perhaps even, indirectly, effect social change. These were, as Norman saw it, noble goals, and he instinctively liked the idea that the comic achieved them by shock, by the obscene, by the transgressive. Yet whenever he tried to work the same sort of routine he made a fool of himself: he had, of course, no comic skills, no timing, and, perhaps most important, no sense of fun on these occasions. Lenny Bruce, as a comedian, wanted to shake his listeners up, but he also — at least at this stage of his career — wanted to entertain. Norman took the enterprise of public performance with unmodulated deadly seriousness, and invariably alienated or even disgusted his audiences. He had done much the same before, at his poetry reading at the Ninety-second Street Y just after Adele's stabbing, and he would do so again.

He continued to be combative in his writing for *Esquire*. In the May 1963 issue he recounted a conversation he had had with Gore Vidal about the general frustrations of the writing life. At one point Norman laughed and said, "Gore, admit it. The novel is like the Great Bitch in one's life. We think we're rid of her, we go on to other women, we take our pulse and decide that finally we're enjoying ourselves, we're free of her power, we'll never suffer her depredations again, and then we turn a corner on a street, and there's the Bitch smiling at us, and we're trapped. We're still trapped. We know the Bitch has got us." Gore laughed; the novel was, he agreed, the Great Bitch. Taking this curious point of departure — characterizing the novel as a bitch does not yield much in the way of insight — Norman then announced that in a future essay he would return to the ground he had covered in *Advertisements* in "Evaluations" and survey the state of current fiction, assessing ten authors who he felt had wrestled with the "Bitch."

In "Some Children of the Goddess," which appeared in the July issue of *Esquire*, Norman once again skewers his contemporaries, delivering impressionistic pronouncements about the size of their talents and the specific odor of their writing (Baldwin, in "Evaluations," reeks of perfume; Updike's style, in "Some Children," smells like "stale garlic"). As in his essay in *Advertisements*, he proffers not useful literary criticism but insults, faint praise, and jeremiads about conquering the Bitch. Burroughs, Heller, and Bellow are the only writers of whom he remotely approves. He damns Baldwin's *Another Country* (1962), finds J. D. Salinger beneath contempt, and rather nervously writes off John Updike. With Styron and Jones he settles some personal scores — letting Jones know, for instance, of the winter nights in Connecticut when he and Styron had read *Some Came Running* (1957) aloud and laughed at its badness. But he grudgingly admires *The Thin Red Line* (1962), his only criticism being that he wishes Jones relied less on his technical knowledge of warfare (which Mailer actually admired very much) than on "the mystical side of his talents." (Of course, this was, as he well knew, asking that Jones become a writer he could not and did not want to be.)

But he reserved his real venom for Styron, who he felt was ruined by lack of widespread recognition, which made Styron furious and overly competitive. The example he gives is the readings of Jones's book, at which Mailer of course participated. What Styron has produced with *Set This House on Fire*, the big novel, almost a decade in the writing, that followed *Lie Down in Darkness* (1951), Mailer tells us, is "a bad novel. A bad maggoty novel . . . the magnum opus of a fat spoiled rich boy." Finally, he blamed the failure of *Some Came Running* and *Set This House on Fire* for his own inability to write the "big one" he had promised in *Advertisements for Myself*:

> I knew [Styron's] failure was making me complacent again, and so delaying once more the day when I would have to pay my respects to the lady. And indeed I lost something by the failure of *Some Came Running* and *Set This House on Fire*. I never did get going too far on my novel. I wrote a four-hour play and essays and articles, two hundred thousand words accumulated over the years since *Advertisements for Myself*, and I showed a talent for getting into stunts, and worse, much worse. Years went by.

Here he offers his justification for the essay: "I did not feel sure I could do what I had now settled for doing, and to my surprise I was curious what others were up to. If I couldn't bring off the work by myself, it might be just as well if someone else could give a sign of being ready to make the attempt."

Perhaps because it lacks the context of the openly egotistical *Advertisements,* "Some Children of the Goddess" reads more unpleasantly than the earlier "Evaluations." Besides, to try the exercise of voicing one's true feelings about the work of one's colleagues may be transgressive the first time, but to do so regularly indicates merely an excess of ill will or an obsession with grades unbecoming to a grown man, especially a successful one. The essay contains nothing constructive: it is a juvenile exercise in sizing up the competition and settling old scores. And because Mailer had not weighed in with fiction for some time, it seems even more gratuitous. Who is he to talk? a typical reader might have thought.

One contemporary whom he neglected altogether decided to call him on it: Calder Willingham. Willingham had drawn Mailer's wrath in the *Advertisements* essay; his exclusion in the recent piece situated him to answer. "The Way It Isn't Done: Notes on the Distress of Norman Mailer" appeared in the December 1963 *Esquire;* Willingham anticipates Mailer's transformation into something other than a "mere" novelist — a literary personality. The example of Mailer's exercise, he writes, is a perfect example of "how not to be a writer."

But this was something Mailer already knew. He was not a traditional novelist any longer, though he considered himself very much a writer. It was hard to describe what it was he wrote, hard even to distinguish between his writing and his public antics. His journalism was not simply reportage; indeed, the scrapes he got into covering an event were often integral to the story. He wrote poems that didn't pretend to be "serious" poetry; he wrote on topics like mystical Judaism without ever getting to the announced topic.

This lack of predictability, this refusal to be categorized, was part of what riveted his readers. They read, it seemed, almost as if they wanted to see what would happen next. The critics, quite understandably, did not know quite what to make of Mailer's new direction, as he discovered in the fall of 1963, when reviews of his collection *The Presidential Papers* began to appear.

The Presidential Papers announced itself boldly, like *Advertisements for Myself,* as an exercise in audacity. Even the dedication was flamboyant: the book was dedicated, Mailer wrote, to "some ladies who have aided and impeded the author in his composition." First, he named the two who had been his companions during the process: "Beverly Rentz Sugarfoot Bentley" and "Jeanne Louise Slugger Campbell." Next he named his four daughters, and then "my adopted daughter, Jeanne H. W. The Invaluable Johnson," his secretary, "Anne Morse Towel-Boy Barry," his sister, and finally "Sadie

[Lady Jeanne's maid], Hetty Diggs [the long-time Mailer maid], and Every-Mae [unidentified, possibly Everywoman]." The title of the collection was misleading only in the sense that, with the exception of one or two pieces, including "A Program for the Nation" and his open letters to the president and Castro, the essays were not position papers addressed to JFK, although Mailer in his preface announces himself "a court wit, an amateur advisor." As he goes on to explain, "The President suffers from one intellectual malady — intellectual malnutrition." A few pages on, Mailer grades Kennedy, giving him high marks for arithmetic (meaning how he used statistics), mediocre ones for passion and rhetoric, and zero for his imagination. Accordingly, *The Presidential Papers* contains papers "about all the topics a President ought to consider and rarely does, and some of the topics he considers every day, but rarely in a fashion which is fresh." He provides a list of these topics, which includes capital punishment, censorship, the Negro emergence, the nature of the Jews, the press, the Mafia, scatology, witchcraft, the end of the Cold War, cannibalism, architecture, and totalitarianism.

The resulting collection is a compendium of Mailer's thinking, mostly on matters political and social — though an interview with Paul Krassner touches on the mystical — which is offered to the president as an example of creative ways to approach problems. "She Thought the Russians Was Coming," a piece on juvenile delinquency, is representative. Based on the premise that "juvenile delinquents have a need of danger," Mailer paints a portrait of a Brooklyn gang. He then revives the idea he had conceived earlier, during the psychotic period in which he contemplated running for mayor, of introducing jousting contests in Central Park for delinquent youth. But because the idea is presented here as a radically new and imaginative way the president (or Mailer's readers) might approach the problem of juvenile delinquency, the idea takes on new freshness. Mailer describes his approach, which he characterizes as "existential politics": if human nature contains a strong streak — here, the need for a means of expression for violent tendencies — why not encourage it, "find an art into which it can grow"? The Peace Corps is all well and good, continues Mailer, but why not an Adventurers' Corps, in which the young can enroll to fight alligators, ski, or learn to hang-glide? While the concrete suggestions may seem bizarre, Mailer is calling for extremes in addressing social problems. The entire collection is no less than a demand that the president — and the citizenry — use some imagination. Norman wanted to turn politics into a creative activity in the artistic sense, where character, imagination, style, and largeness of spirit were encouraged and given full rein. He could claim to have anticipated the Yippies, formed a few years later, for they too advocated the injection of imagination into political life.

The Presidential Papers presents Mailer's approach to life as exemplary, and is no less an advertisement for the author than his earlier collection. It also throws down an audacious gauntlet, both to the president and the reading public: here's how Norman Mailer approaches issues like capital punishment and the black bourgeoisie. Who is the more imaginative, the bolder, the more visionary? Pieces like "Ten Thousand Words a Minute," on the Liston-Patterson fight, seem out of place only until one realizes that it is necessary to his argument that Mailer indulge in some pyrotechnics, present an example of how a truly radical-thinking journalist will cover a prizefight. He is not afraid to offend; "An Evening with Jackie Kennedy, or The Wild Witch of the East" is a rallying cry addressed to the first lady — and, by extension, to his readers — pointing out how large her potential for true elegance and greatness is and how far she is from realizing it.

So *The Presidential Papers,* while ostensibly a collection of essays, or taken by many to be a collection of assays into the new genre that would later be called the New Journalism, is in its totality quite another beast. In the first place, like *Advertisements for Myself,* it is not simply a collection of essays but an interlocking whole, each piece to be seen as a move in a game. Second, its intention is quite clear, and it is an unprecedented one. It is a personal and open dialogue with the president, a didactic project in illustration, and an invitation to the citizenry to think more creatively and expect more from their leaders. It defies genre classification, creating quandaries for those faced with the task of reviewing it. The most important review, appearing in the Sunday *New York Times,* addressed exactly this problem. John Kenneth Galbraith liked the premise of the book — writing papers for the president — and thought the collection an advance in Mailer's career. But writing as a historian, he simply couldn't manage a straight review, explaining, "I have dealt with this book of Mr. Mailer's as a work of fiction. Out of consideration for the author," he continued, "I hope that other reviewers and critics will do likewise. But it should be noted that some perverse instinct causes him to insist that it is serious history." Mailer, on the contrary, never insisted that his work be taken as serious history, but he expected it to be taken *seriously;* the genre he chose — or his refusal to choose a genre — made it possible for critics like Galbraith to dismiss him.

Other reviews were similarly mixed. The *Saturday Review* vacillated, writing, "Half the time the premise (of writing for the President) is justified . . . But half the time the premise is a bad joke . . . Norman Mailer is a writer one must read for the flashes that come when he is paying attention to his better angel." Richard Kluger at *Book Week* was one of the few who understood Mailer's direction: "What Norman Mailer is doing, and doing more provocatively and occasionally more preposterously than any other literary figure we have, is to tell us what life is like now in America."

Norman recorded no response to these reviews. If he was still sensitive to the opinion of the critical establishment — and he seems to have become less so — he also understood the value of negative criticism, especially given his view of himself as a literary outlaw. But as "Some Children of the Goddess" and Calder Willingham's reply to it made painfully clear, whatever he had been writing for the past few years — poetry, journalism, manifestos — he had not been writing fiction. In setting up a nice conceit of the novel as a Great Bitch, Norman, a superstitious and competitive person, confirmed that he was ready for another round with Her.

FOURTEEN

A GAMBLE AND
A NEW DIRECTION

In the fall of 1963, Norman was financially strapped, and everyone knew it. The few checks that came in went to Barney, who handled the cash flow; Norman amassed huge bills for food and liquor every month. He was paying alimony to Adele and child support for four children, and soon he would have a fifth, Beverly's first child; he and Beverly would marry in December. Cy had handled Norman's investments over the years, but there simply was not sufficient income. He was still receiving substantial royalties from *The Naked and the Dead* every year, and smaller amounts for *Advertisements for Myself*, but with the exception of the latter his collections would never sell very well; thus his real income came from magazines, which at the time didn't pay munificently, even to Norman Mailer. The only way to raise a large amount of cash was to write a novel, and to do it in the shortest possible time.

Slowly, an idea took shape. Mailer approached the editors at *Esquire* with an unexpected proposal: he wanted to write a novel in serial form, in eight parts, each part about ten thousand words, to be published in the magazine. Only under this kind of pressure, he thought, could he write a novel quickly enough. In making his pitch, he compared himself to Dickens and Dostoyevsky, two great serializers of the last century.

It was a wager, and the stakes were high. When *Esquire* approved the idea — not without some hesitation, knowing the risks — Norman put in a call to Scott Meredith, a literary agent known for savvy deal-making; not since very early in his career had he used an agent, Cy being designated to negotiate his contracts. Meredith proved his mettle immediately by placing a few small Mailer pieces; then, in October 1963, he swung into action trying to sell the serialized novel. Although Minton at G. P. Putnam's had Mailer under contract for his projected "big book," Meredith convinced him this was something entirely different from the "big book," assuring the firm that it would get Mailer's "big one" when he delivered it.

The proposed book wound up at Dell. Some confusion exists over whether it was sold to Don Fine at Dell and then given to Dick Baron, head of Dial Press, Dell's new division, or whether Baron himself made the deal. The amount Mailer received is also unclear: either $100,000 or $125,000. Minton had a chance to match this offer but couldn't, and instead waited for the "big" novel promised him. Baron, thrilled to have Mailer in his stable, assigned the book to editor E. L. Doctorow, and became fast friends with his new celebrity author; he would take a house next door to the Mailers in Provincetown the following summer.

All this happened very quickly, and Norman was off and running, after so much dodging, on his first major work of fiction in eight years. He compared the process in a letter to Fig Gwaltney to playing ten-second, or "speed," chess — he had to make quick decisions as to the direction of the plot and then work with them. He was a novelist who in the past had produced three and sometimes four drafts, and now he would not have the luxury of polishing even his first drafts. The project demanded concentrated energy, and he thrived on the discipline: it was an enforced time-out from his busy and often destructive social life.

In writing *An American Dream*, he made his boldest move in the first installment, which ends with the hero, Steven Rojack, killing his wife. It was a bold move in two senses. First, murder stories that identify the murderer up front demand innovative ways of creating suspense. Second, Mailer had cooked up an audacious, even outrageous premise for this piece of work, given his own recent past, as his hero commits a crime that his inventor once came close to committing. Although many readers would denounce *An American Dream* because of this, Mailer's decision to fictionalize his experience made a certain amount of sense. Desperately seeking some kind of peg to hang a work of fiction on, to get him going, he chose the one event in his recent life about which one could truly say, "You can't make this stuff up." Whether Norman had ever thought seriously about what he had done since his brief stay in Bellevue is not known, but it seems doubtful. Now, with the express purpose of making money, he would take up the task of self-examination.

Steven Rojack, in fact, is the quintessential Mailer hero: he is a lot of things Norman would have liked to have been. A war hero, awarded a Distinguished Service Cross, Rojack returned from the war, was lionized, and ran successfully for Congress at a young age. He left office after running for reelection on the Progressive ticket in the year of Wallace's defeat, and when the story begins, he is a professor of "existential psychology" at New York University with his own popular television program. He has written a successful book on international methods of execution called *The Psychology of the Hangman.*

He is unhappily married to — currently separated from — the redoubtable Deborah, the daughter of Barney Oswald Kelly, a multimillionaire — in short, a formidable shiksa princess, the kind of person Mailer/Rojack is bound to have ambivalent feelings about. Deborah bears a distinct resemblance to Jeanne Campbell. She is large and rich, and has multiple lovers. Significantly, Rojack initially met her on a double date with Jack Kennedy; he had been a year behind Kennedy at Harvard, though he hadn't met the future president there but rather in Congress.

In killing his wife, Rojack feels himself cured of cancer — a feeling Norman had shared after stabbing Adele. Indeed, he is off on a strange, mostly nighttime odyssey that will include a love affair with a sultry singer named Cherry, closely modeled on Beverly (and on Carol Stevens, a singer with whom Norman had been having an off-and-on affair since March 1962), an encounter with Cherry's black pimp, the singer Shago Martin, and a final confrontation with Kelly, the consummate picture of evil, in which Rojack forces himself to walk the parapet of a skyscraper. In the end, he loses Cherry and is last seen in a phone booth in the desert outside Las Vegas. He is heading for Mexico, a common conceit in art of the time, as in the film *Vera Cruz* (1954) and Kerouac's *On the Road* (1956); Mexico symbolized anarchy, cruel but somewhat elemental distinctions between good and evil, a place where a man could be a hero in an unambiguous way. Throughout, Rojack plays a cat-and-mouse game with the police, who are convinced of his guilt; ultimately he evades justice — a point that would further alienate some of Mailer's readers.

After the killing, Rojack's odyssey begins, most infamously with a scene in which Rojack, immediately after stabbing Deborah, has sex with her German maid, Ruta, in which he alternates between anal and vaginal intercourse, the former representing the Devil, the latter God. When this installment — the second — reached the *Esquire* offices, editor-in-chief Arnold Gingrich wanted the whole serialization called off. Never one of Mailer's big supporters, Gingrich found this scene simply too much. When Rust Hills and Harold Hayes told Gingrich that they couldn't just cancel the series, he insisted they could. Finally Hills, pondering the problem, decided that the intercourse scene could be made more metaphorical, with the emphasis on the alternation between good and evil. For the sake of continuing the series, Norman made some changes, and Gingrich let him continue.

If serialization had the benefit of forcing Mailer to produce, it had its disadvantages as well. By the fifth installment he felt he had barely gotten started — and yet he was limited to eight. There were problems with continuity: at one point Anne Barry pointed out that his hero had gone for nearly two days without eating, and Norman promptly had Cherry fix Rojack a meal of scrambled eggs, spaghetti, and steak. At another point he sent Barry off to research dependent lividity — marks on a corpse that indicate how long it has lain in a certain position. Barry's results didn't tally with the facts of the murder case Mailer was unfolding — so he simply worked around the problem, making dependent lividity the sticking point on which the cops try to nail Rojack. The last installment, quite understandably, went far beyond the allotted word count, so *Esquire* just set it in smaller type. For the most part, however, the serialization was a huge success; it gathered momentum properly, and Norman knew how to write cliffhanger endings. Any unevenness could be smoothed out when the series was revised for book publication.

Dick Baron at Dial urged Mailer to take some time and develop the series into a longer novel, one that explored metaphysical themes the series only hinted at. But Norman rightly insisted that such revision would create an entirely different novel. He had made the story fly with only intimations of Rojack's deeper mysticism, and he resisted the idea of such significant change. He also felt he had weighted down Rojack with exactly enough freight. Indeed, the character of Rojack carries the whole story, for he is the one constant in an otherwise jagged narrative, and because he is a remarkable figure, perhaps Mailer's best so far, precisely because he's not a construct built on an idea; rather, he's a strange fictionalization of the author. *Flawed* is not even the word for Rojack; he's unlikable, and Mailer doesn't seem to care. He has constructed a hero who embodies the kind of on-the-edge, risk-taking persona onto whom he had projected himself so well, most notably as Sergius O'Shaugnessy of *The Deer Park* and "The Time of Her Time." But the fundamentally sympathetic Sergius misses the mark slightly; he is somehow too callow. And, in *An American Dream,* Mailer imagines a perfect setting for his hero, one that suggests a Hollywood thriller (dangerous women, dodging the police, fights, a final escape). It is important that Rojack doesn't "deal with" the murder of his wife. He goes through a kind of purgatory following it, but there's no hint he will pay for it in any way. The result is a sort of amoral, hipster version of a film noir, with the hero, or antihero, getting away in the end. It is an interesting missile to launch at the idealistic America of the civil rights movement and the Great Society, a book whose hero is guilty but has no conscience and deals in bad faith, but at the same time a book that exposes America's guilty conscience about its actions.

His instincts were sure. *Barbary Shore* had nearly sunk under the weight of political/philosophical baggage, and *The Deer Park* had been marred by a theoretical underpinning concerning the connection of sex and time. With *An American Dream,* Mailer returns to the novelistic terrain of *The Naked and the Dead* and the better parts of *The Deer Park:* it is first and foremost a good *story,* and the allusions to more mystical concerns embellish the story without distracting the reader.

An American Dream provides many clues to the thought and feelings of its author, particularly his state of mind after stabbing Adele. Rojack's agonies — his nausea, his prodigious drinking — all characterize Norman at around the time of the incident; unquestionably he drew on his own experiences in creating Rojack's psychology. Most important in this connection, however, is Rojack's obsession with magical thinking. In the first installment, Rojack worries that his thoughts are so powerful that they will force him to jump from a terrace when he is determined not to do so. After killing Deborah, Rojack believes his shirt has magical powers; Cherry points out that he looks "like he'd been painted by a touch of magic." Watching Cherry sing in a nightclub, Rojack sends mental darts all over the place. He causes a heckler to stop laughing and then makes his foot hurt; the evidence that his mind has power is that the man rubs the toe of the shoe against his calf. He makes a detective get hiccups, and an Irish politician weep. Finally, he shoots "one needle of an arrow into the center of Cherry's womb," an action that makes Cherry look deathlike and brings on enormous nausea for Rojack.

We learn from Kelly that Rojack's "philosophy" — what he expounds in his books and on his television show — is that the root of neurosis is not, as Freud would have it, Oedipus, but rather bravery. If one defies magical thinking by acting bravely — by, in Rojack's case, walking the parapet of Kelly's terrace — one overcomes neurosis, according to Rojack's (and Mailer's) logic.

What Mailer fails to see is that Rojack's magical thinking is not a sign of some connection he has to the moon or to positive magic, but rather the logical state of mind for the severe narcissist who is drawn to magical thinking in the first place. Both Rojack and Mailer, in thinking their thoughts have the power to affect events, are assuming their own superimportance. As egotists, they feel an urgent need to be connected with the world and to have some control over events; they believe they are important enough that they can influence events through what goes on in their heads. Just as Norman felt that he, as potential mayor of New York City, had an urgent connection with Fidel Castro, so Rojack believes that his thoughts can actually harm audience members at a nightclub. Of course, Norman was not connected to anything magical when he stabbed his wife; nor does the reader really believe Rojack is mystically endowed. The egotist's conviction is persuasive only to himself. *An American Dream* provides a glimpse of a fascinating psychological state, severe narcissism that has tipped over into life without consequences.

Rojack's psychology reflects other aspects of his creator's psychology. He believes, with Norman, that conception is the ideal goal of intercourse. Because Cherry and Rojack enjoy great sex, it follows immediately that she is sure, after their second mating, that she has conceived, and readers are subsequently meant to take this as a fact — that is, when Cherry dies, Rojack's baby dies too. More important, Rojack shares Norman's hatred of contraception, his view that it is technological, plastic, cancerous; Rojack removes "that corporate rubbery obstruction I detested so much" from Cherry's vagina and then they ("our wills now met") begin really to fuck. That Mailer manages to create a hero with many of his own bizarre beliefs and views without making him ridiculous is an extraordinary feat indeed. It speaks to the power of his narrative, his skill at storytelling, that the reader is carried along with the unlikable, obsessive, egocentric Stephen Rojack.

The serialization of *An American Dream* was over in August 1964, and Dial would not publish it in book form until March 1965. Because he had decided against major revisions, Norman was freed up to take on other assignments. In July *Esquire* sent him to San Francisco to cover the Republican Convention. The article that resulted is not one of Mailer's most memorable — the occasion brings him to such a pitch of emotion that his sentences, never simple to begin with, become impossibly convoluted — but it is one of the best expressions of his evolving political consciousness. In it one can find the origins of his maddening insistence, going on four decades now, that he is a "left conservative."

The moment, as he saw it, was without a doubt apocalyptic; indeed, he introduced his piece with a quotation from *The Day of the Locust* about the grand destruction of a California city. There was little suspense in the events he described in the first two thirds of the article: it was apparent to all that William Scranton, the governor of Pennsylvania and, as Mailer believed, the choice of the Eastern Establishment, had hardly a hope to snatch the nomination from the new-style, Western, extreme rightist, Arizona senator Barry Goldwater.

In fixing on this moment, Mailer showed himself an acute observer, uncannily prescient, of the political scene. Goldwater's nomination was a historic moment: the first indication of the rise of the West that would gradually take over the GOP in the next decade and a half, and would culminate in the election of Ronald Reagan and George Bush in 1980. Just as the New Deal tradition was being reinvigorated by LBJ, something very new and very threatening was surfacing. Goldwater's chances of actually winning were small — Mailer got that wrong — but the important point was that a new political force was in the ascendancy.

Goldwater's climb was the first visible sign of something that had been building since the thirties: the rise of new Western money (from Texas oil, mainly, but also from natural resources, forestry, gambling, and the accumulation of wealth in the Sunbelt). Though this new force was built on government subsidies of one sort or another, it was fiercely antigovernment in its politics and was prepared to use its money at least as ruthlessly as the Eastern Establishment. C. Wright Mills, among others, had been warning his readers of the potential power of this new force in American society at least since *The Power Elite* (1956). Now Mailer was apprehending this new force, and he caught its methods and moods with precision.

In "In the Red Light," Mailer took the opportunity to muse on the battle in the Republican Party for power; it was a struggle, he suggested, between new money and old, between the West and the Midwest on the one hand and the East on the other, between Main Street and Wall Street. He analyzed Scranton's failure to win Eisenhower's support and the feeble efforts of Henry Cabot Lodge to convince Goldwater delegates to switch their votes. (He barely mentioned Nelson Rockefeller, whose candidacy most other journalists, who were comfortable with the Eastern Establishment, were focusing on.) Mailer hated Goldwater, that's clear; Goldwater had recently voted against the Civil Rights Act. But his admiration grew for the might Goldwater commanded, culminating on the last day of the convention, after Goldwater had indeed won the convention. "One thing was certain: he could win." Indeed, Mailer continued, "I knew Goldwater could win because something in me leaped at the thought; a part of me, a devil, wished to take that choice. For if Goldwater were President, a new opposition would form, an underground — the time for secret armies might be near again." In other words, the time might be right for the kind of dialectic Mailer had believed, since the fifties, the country needed.

This led him to a strange-seeming digression, for he remembered that blacks would fare very badly under Goldwater. This in turn led him to a blind fury at the failure of the left in this country, and ultimately the failure of traditional Establishment liberalism — a remarkably prophetic response, for few were saying anything of the sort at that time, and wouldn't be until the late 1970s. But first Mailer remembered, with fury, watching Jimmy Baldwin taking phone calls on a late-night TV talk show. A white liberal called and asked how he might help the civil rights movement. "Don't ask me, baby," responded Baldwin, "ask yourself." The caller persisted: he was informed on the subject, but confused. He needed help, he said. "That's *your* problem," said Baldwin with finality. The memory of it made Norman seethe, and he thought of calling Baldwin and hissing, "You get *this,* baby. There's a shit storm coming like nothing you ever knew." He repeated this refrain two pages later, after reviewing the "disease" affecting the country. Separatism between blacks and whites, or a politics of resentment, he seems to be saying, would get the country absolutely nowhere.

A great sense of urgency seemed to be affecting him. At one point he asked a young delegate if he'd ever considered the possibility that Castro might be a braver man than Goldwater and was told yes, "but Castro has a criminal mentality"; Mailer had to cut off the argument, he was so angry. Overwhelmed and disgusted, he realized that under a Goldwater administration the United States would almost certainly invade and destroy Cuba, a country one-hundredth its size. At this point Goldwater made his famous declaration, "Extremism in defense of liberty is no vice . . . Moderation in the pursuit of justice is no virtue." Mailer wrote it in his notebook, reflecting bitterly, "Dad, you're too much. You're really too much. You're too hip, baby. I have spent my life seeking to get four-letter words into U.S. magazines, and now you are ready to help me." The extremism Mailer built his life around, that he found so urgently needed for the American character, surfaced in the unlikeliest, indeed the most repellent, of places.

MARRIED IN DECEMBER 1963 in his brownstone home, Norman spent the summer of 1964 in Provincetown with Beverly and their new child, Michael, born that March 17. Norman was unabashedly proud of having a son after four daughters; later, he would boast to a *Life* interviewer about butting heads with Michael. He would crow in years to come about the birth of his boys, saying, "I had gone around for ten years shaking hands with people and saying I, sir, am a buttonhole maker." More seriously, the event prompted him once again to give up smoking, this time successfully. Beverly was happy to have a healthy baby and touched that Norman was so proud of having a son. She had a lot to handle that summer at Provincetown. Norman's daughters were there for the season, as usual. Dick Baron and his wife rented a house nearby and were frequent visitors, and Barbara, now divorced from Larry Alson, visited with her son, Peter. The usual suspects, like Bill Walker and Eddie Bonetti, hung around the house. For Beverly, it was like running a small hotel — with a good-sized restaurant attached — but she really did not mind, at least under most circumstances. She had begun to detect an alarming pattern in her husband: he could be the sweetest and most charming of men, but when he got drunk his personality changed, and he grew abusive.

Norman had recently made two important new friends who visited the Mailers that summer. One was Bernard "Buzz" Farbar, an editor at the *Saturday Evening Post* whom Norman had met at *Esquire*'s 1963 Christmas party. An extremely handsome, charismatic figure, Buzz was an athletically inclined Jew from Brooklyn, who'd won a football scholarship to

Dartmouth as a teenager. "Everyone admired him for his physique and athletic prowess. He was just magnetic," said his good friend Nick Proferes. Married, with two small daughters and soon a third, Buzz shared Norman's passions for hard drinking, women, fighting, and other macho pursuits, but according to Proferes, he had a very middle-class, family-oriented side as well. Buzz wanted to do more — perhaps to write — and Norman encouraged him, but Buzz simply didn't have much staying power. In the meantime, they took enormous delight in each other, sharing enthusiasms, going out on the town (Buzz drew the women in), and devising complicated schemes, both literary and business-related, bouncing ideas off each other.

Perhaps because of jealousy — no one but Beverly had Norman's ear as completely — there were those who were suspicious of Buzz. But everyone was fond of José Torres. Torres, a Puerto Rican light-heavyweight contender, had become acquainted with journalist Pete Hamill, who gave him a crash course in liberal politics and the literary life; Hamill also introduced him to Norman. For the time being, Torres was simply an up-and-coming boxer — he would go for the championship in March 1965 — but over time, under the tutelage of Hamill and Mailer, he would try his hand at writing. Torres was spontaneous, likable, and unimpressed by celebrity; he genuinely liked Norman, who in turn took him quite seriously and encouraged him to write.

Despite these distractions, that August Norman was writing his piece on Goldwater and the Republican Convention. At the convention, he sensed he could not go so far as to vote for Goldwater; now he was sure. But he thoroughly disliked the alternative of voting for LBJ. He outlined the nature of his distrust in a review of Johnson's book, *My Hope for America,* which set forth the president's vision of the Great Society. Norman's discussion was based on intuition and feeling rather than on specifics; he applauded, for instance, most of the tenets of the Great Society. But he found LBJ's prose to be "totalitarian" (by which he usually meant that the "vision" so named by LBJ was too easily based on a panacea), shameless in its sentimentality, which in turn he considered the "emotional promiscuity of those who have no sentiment."

But his main objection to Johnson grew from what he feared was America's imminent involvement in Vietnam. The United States was becoming ever more deeply committed, militarily and financially, to propping up the Saigon regime; a rationale was taking shape in policy-making circles that, if South Vietnam were to fall to Communism, other Asian states would soon follow. In early August two American destroyers in the Gulf of Tonkin were reported (or rumored) to have been attacked by North Vietnamese torpedo boats. Johnson responded by asking Congress to pass the Tonkin Gulf Resolution, which would open the way for massive American intervention in the war. On August 7, both houses passed the bill, and Johnson began to mobilize U.S. troops; by 1965 massive bombing and harbor mining were under way, and by the end of the year more than 150,000 American troops had arrived in Vietnam. When Johnson won the election in November 1964, it was already clear to many that Vietnam would become a national preoccupation over the coming years. America's worldwide opposition to Communism had at last crystallized into an all-out war over a specific country — albeit a small and remote one.

Though college campuses would, of course, become a hotbed of antiwar activism, it is important to remember that opposition to the "police action" in Vietnam manifested itself in many quarters of society, including even some of Johnson's aides. Norman disagreed with much that the student youth movement stood for — he was no longer a great believer in drugs, for example — and he felt it was not appropriate for him to join in most of its protests. When he did so, he would wear a jacket and tie. But he also knew that he could play an important role by showing support for student antiwar protesters, and by raising his voice as a public intellectual. Carl Oglesby, then president of the strongest radical antiwar force in the country, Students for a Democratic Society (SDS), believes that Norman was instrumental in convincing the New York intellectuals — many of them — that opposition to the war was a moral imperative.

Mailer's first experience with the antiwar movement was a positive one; indeed, it was his first wholly successful public performance, and it was, by all accounts, extremely effective. The University of California at Berkeley was one of the first campuses to be rocked by student unrest. When, in early 1964, the administration banned the dissemination of political materials on campus, the Berkeley Free Speech Movement of 1964–65 was born, a locus for antiwar and other radical activity. In the spring of 1965 student activists planned two days of nonstop protest against the rapidly escalating war in Vietnam. One of the organizers, Jerry Rubin, had been following Mailer's coverage of the Republican Convention and had heard that the writer was very much against the war. He asked Norman to come speak, and within a couple of days Norman agreed.

Norman's speech was apparently quite extraordinary. He was speaking to a crowd of about fifteen thousand, and surely this energized him. Nobody had really attacked Johnson head on before, much less made fun of him, which is what Norman did. Perhaps his old fury at the Texans who had bullied him during the war fueled his words. As printed in *Cannibals and Christians,* the speech clearly shows why the students responded so avidly. Though to a reader it feels a bit long-winded, it is obvious where the students would have applauded — as when he says that "our present situation is so irrational that any attempt to deal with it rationally is irrational," or "The great fear that lies on America is not that Lyndon Johnson is privately close to insanity so much as that he is the expression of the near insanity of most of us." His argument is masterful and shrewd: he traces the history of the Cold War, concluding, "The greatest danger to Communism lies in its growth. Attack from capitalism is Communism's transfusion of blood. So our war against Communism, most particularly our war against Communism in Asia, is the death of our future." But it is in his ability to bring the argument back to the Vietnam War and the causes for student outrage that he is at his best. Echoing statements he had made during the Kennedy administration, he urged the protesters to bring a little imagination to their work. The time for rational discussion is over, he asserts; it's time to go a little crazy. He closes with a radically new suggestion for a bit of guerrilla theater. He addresses this to Lyndon Johnson, telling him he has gone too far this time, and that there are young people who will persecute him in a multitude of ways:

> For listen, this is only one of the thousand things they will do. They will print up little pictures of you, Lyndon Johnson, the size of postcards, the size of stamps, and some will glue these pictures to walls and posters and telephone booths and billboards . . . These pictures will be sent everywhere. These pictures will be sent everywhere, upside down . . .
>
> You, Lyndon Johnson, will see these pictures up everywhere upside down, four inches high and forty feet high; you, Lyndon Baines Johnson, will be coming up for air everywhere upside down. Everywhere, upside down. Everywhere. Everywhere.
>
> And those little pictures will tell the world what we think of you and your war in Vietnam. Everywhere, upside down. Everywhere, everywhere.

The applause when he stepped down from the podium was deafening, building in crescendo. Emcee Paul Krassner waited and waited for the tumult to die down before he could continue with the rally, and the next scheduled speaker, Dick Gregory, refused to go on, saying no one could follow that act. As Norman came offstage, Krassner pulled him aside and asked if he could print the speech in the *Realist*; Norman, aware that his speech marked an important moment, agreed.

NORMAN'S BERKELEY appearance came in the middle of a busy month. Torres's match against light-heavyweight champion Willie Pastrano was scheduled for May 30, and Norman had become very involved in his training, even at one point volunteering to put up some money when one of José's backers pulled out (it didn't turn out to be necessary). Norman and knowledgeable friends like Buzz Farbar and Roger Donoghue were betting heavily on Torres to win. Norman even scheduled a party for the night of the bout, inviting, besides the usual suspects, Archie Moore, Peter Falk, and Jimmy Baldwin; David Amram and his quartet would play jazz. Torres won the bout with a knockout in the ninth round and headed for the party, where he promptly, and uncharacteristically, got drunk. He went home and slept, and returned the next morning to find the party still in full swing.

There were other parties that month, including a bash at the Village Vanguard to celebrate the publication of *An American Dream*. Jim and Gloria Jones were there, putting aside their differences with Norman. Inexplicably, Miles Davis was also there. Norman, evidently believing that Miles was there to see Beverly (Beverly does not remember that Miles was even at the party), issued a challenge. The two men engaged in a staring match for half a minute — an act of considerable bravery on Norman's part, for Miles had one of the greatest "game faces" of all time and an underground reputation for violence. Then Miles turned on his heel and left.

Gloria Jones later said she and Jim had come partly because Jim felt the reviewers were roughing up *An American Dream*. The novel was receiving wildly mixed notices. Perhaps Norman had expected as much, insisting that Dial use an author photo of him with a black eye. He also had considerable input on the cover, which displayed the American flag in red, black, and blue and had an inset photo of Beverly.

Some of the reviews were indeed devastating. Granville Hicks, writing for the *Saturday Review*, wondered if *An American Dream* was intended as a hoax, and went on to say, "If one believes that Mailer intended *An American Dream* to be taken seriously, one has to conclude that he has gone to pieces as a writer . . . The absurdity of the book is not limited to the plot . . . The writing is the sloppiest Mailer has ever done." A trade publication flatly dismissed it while acknowledging it would be widely read, asserting, "Mailer wanted to make money with this book. Hollywood should go for it. It should make the Best Seller lists. But it is a book calculated to leave all America holding its nose." Tom Wolfe, writing for the *New York Herald Tribune*, compared Mailer — unfavorably — with James M. Cain. And Philip Rahv wrote, quite seriously, that Norman was guilty of "false consciousness."

Yet for every negative review, Mailer's first novel in nearly a decade incited a thoughtful and often insightful response. The book seemed to invite comparison. Joan Didion, writing for the *National Review*, compared Mailer with Fitzgerald. The academic Richard Poirier, already emerging as one of Mailer's most understanding critics, compared him with Robert Lowell; the two writers, he wrote in his review in *Commentary*, were "alone . . . in having created the style of contemporary introspection, at once violent, educated, and cool. Their language substantially extends the literary resources of English, and people will later turn to them in any effort to determine the shapes our consciousness has been taking." Even *Time*, seldom kind to Mailer, liked his latest: "This sounds like a ride on a hobbyhorse. But because Mailer is a born writer, it is a heady ride — a bit absurd but, like all of the latter-day Mailer, somehow disarming because it has been attempted by a man who knows all along that the bystanders may laugh."

The writing of *An American Dream* had been an exhibitionistic gamble, akin to Molière's accepting a challenge and writing *Le Bourgeois Gentilhomme* in two weeks. It diverted attention from the "big one" so long awaited by the critics and Mailer's readers, to be sure. But it showed his remarkable range, and it did not fail to shock. Negative reviews notwithstanding, it brought Mailer a great deal of attention, which he had always craved. And he had enjoyed himself hugely.

FIFTEEN

PROJECTS

Sandy Charlebois, who took over from Anne Barry as Norman's secretary in 1966, has said that her employer tried repeatedly to explain himself to her by describing himself as an "Edwardian" — his term. It's an interesting word to choose — ridiculous, on the face of it, but strangely apt. Norman was a man given to excess, but for all that he was cultivated; a man of large appetites, he saw sixties America laid out as a groaning board, a huge, toothsome feast of the senses. Yet like an Edwardian, Norman would consume it with fine manners, even prim ones. This outsized, greedy, but oddly refined approach — this "Edwardian" stance — to the world marked Mailer's involvement in the decade, particularly the "mature" second half of the sixties, when the antiwar movement and the counterculture were in full swing. The cultural rifts barely discernible earlier in the decade now appeared as veritable canyons, dividing, for instance, the Old and the New Left, the old-line Democrats and Republicans and the insurgent conservatives of the West. Mailer would, indeed, strive most mightily toward his long-held goal: to make a revolution in the consciousness of our time. In these years, he would test the limits in both his prose and his personal conduct, exploring far-reaching and even wildly improbable ideas, arcing out into new genres.

In the background, literally, was a project Mailer began in the fall of 1965, ongoing for the rest of the year and still in residence in the living room of his Brooklyn Heights brownstone: a model for an imaginary city, made entirely out of Lego blocks.

In many ways this was a typically Mailerian project. He announced it in advance in the pages of the *New York Times Magazine* and, to underline his seriousness, in *Architectural Forum*. The prose city he outlined would change the face not only of public architecture but of society itself. He had long blamed architecture for many of the woes of contemporary society, and now he applied himself to setting forth his plans in pronouncements and, beginning in the fall of 1965, the creation of an actual model city, immense in scale and meticulously planned.

The building of an elaborate model out of children's blocks may seem frivolous, but Mailer was very earnest about addressing social ills through architecture. In reviewing Lyndon Johnson's book *My Hope for America* (1964), he was struck by Johnson's claim that in fifty years there would be 400 million Americans, four-fifths of them in urban areas, and that it was necessary to "rebuild the entire urban United States." In response to this, Mailer decried blandly institutional modern architecture, especially flat-topped skyscrapers, devoid of ornament. He thought that to "spare the countryside," maintain small towns and exclusive suburbs, and keep the old urban neighborhoods, especially those with character, cities must be built upward. As he wrote in *Architectural Forum,* "We must be able to live in houses one hundred stories tall, two hundred stories high, far above the height of buildings as we know them. New cities with great towers must rise in the plain, cities higher than mountains, cities with room for 400,000,000 to live." Those who didn't wish to live in these cities, he added graciously, might live in small towns or suburbs, or the old neighborhoods of the "old" cities. It's quite clear that he would choose to live in the new, vibrant, mile-high cities.

This new obsession was not so odd. Norman had trained at Harvard as an engineer; he loved building, enjoyed making things, and was reasonably proficient at it, always inventive. He decided to build a model of a city that could be populated by 4 million people, and to build it in his own living room. He conceived it as a monument to his sweeping utopian vision.

At the quotidian level, Norman acted as the brains behind the project, soon discovering that he didn't like the sound of the plastic Lego pieces snapping together; it struck him as vaguely obscene. He delegated the task to Beverly's stepbrother, Charlie Brown, who worked as a kind of handyman for him, and to Eldred Mowery, a friend from Provincetown now in the city. The two men drove Norman's 1961 blue convertible Falcon out to the Lego plant in New Jersey and returned with cases of the colored blocks. Then Norman directed them, instructing them to create hanging bridges, buildings with trapdoors, and four-foot-high towers, all constructed on an aluminum-covered piece of plywood on a four-by-eight-foot sheet of plywood supported by five-foot legs.

Construction proceeded apace, and Norman never really did call a halt to it. But someone from the Museum of Modern Art came out to Brooklyn to take photographs of the model, hoping to display it at the museum. At that point Mailer and his helpers found that the "city" could not be taken out of the apartment; though they consulted movers with cranes and took measurements of the glass in the front windows, they soon saw that it couldn't be removed without being disassembled first. Here Norman drew the line. He told Mowery to build a fence around it and leave it where it was. There it still sits, occupying a third of the living room's floor space. Beverly, who contributed a scale model of the United Nations to indicate the overall scale of the city, professes that she loved it, but concedes, "It was a bitch to dust."

In the foreground that fall, however, Norman was immersing himself in a new calling — the antiwar movement. His opposition to the war crystallized after his speech at Berkeley. His initial conclusion was logically, and typically, Mailerian: he must convert his influential New York friends to the cause, however reluctant they might be to support a movement that would take them into direct opposition to official U.S. policy. He undertook this task at a most uncomfortable time for the people he sought to proselytize. Most members of the New York intellectual community were tenaciously liberal, yet constitutionally incapable of taking any radical stance. Vietnam raised particular problems for them, because the New Yorkers traced their roots to the Old Left, and were anxious that support for civil rights and liberal democracy not be mistaken for support for Communist liberation. They were very uncomfortable about opposing U.S. policy anywhere, particularly in an area threatened by Communism.

Matters came to a head when Norman was sent a draft of an open letter to appear in the fall 1965 issue of *Partisan Review* (was it sent to anyone in government, or did it reach only *PR* readers?), signed with the names of Eleanor Clark, Martin Duberman, Irving Howe, Alfred Kazin, Bernard Malamud, Steven Marcus, William Phillips, Norman Podhoretz, Richard Poirier, and Richard Schlatter, all major figures in the New York scene. The letter is very lukewarm, though no doubt its signers considered it a bold and brave statement. They begin by saying, "We do not think that the present or past policies of the United States are good ones," and they lament the U.S. military involvement. However, they "have not heard of any alternative policy" that would lead to peace in Southeast Asia and help those who live there. Free societies must be able to exist in the world, write the signers, and U.S. policy has strayed dangerously far from its democratic principles in working to that end. The letter's closing statement is bland indeed: "Obviously, the time has come for some new thinking. And some of it has to be about what's happening in different parts of the world, regardless of what the United States does or fails to do." Let the bombs drop as they may, the letter writers seem to be saying, the intellectuals will still sit around thinking about distant regions of the world.

Norman responded in the same issue, "Three cheers, lads. Your words read like they were written in milk of magnesia." To the letter writers' statement that they did not know any "alternative policy" to the present U.S. one, Norman impatiently offered an idea: "The editors ask for a counterpolicy. I offer it. It is to get out of Asia."

He marshaled his facts impressively, urging the letter writers to reconsider some shibboleths about the importance of ridding the world of Communism. If World War II was best explained by *Catch-22*, this war's work of art would be *Naked Lunch*, Norman wrote. Caught up in the absurdity of it all, Norman suggested — and it is clear that he was speaking only partly in jest — that instead the country should buy an immense tract of land in South America, and let fighting men from all over the world join in, with real war games and live television coverage and phone-in audience participation. (Like radicals Rubin and Hoffman, he understood well the power of the media and the possibilities of presenting opposition to the war as public spectacle; indeed, many of his pronouncements anticipate the guerrilla theater of the Yippies' movement.) He concluded his reply, a bit more soberly, but still reveling in the obscene absurdity of the country's mood:

> Unless Vietnam is the happening. Could that be? Could that really be? Little old Vietnam just a happening? Cause if it is, Daddy Warbucks, couldn't we have that happening just with the Marines and skip all that indiscriminate roast tit and naked lunch, all those bombed-out civilian ovaries, Mr. J., Mr. L.B.J., Boss Man of Show Biz — I salute you in your White House Oval: I mean America will shoot all over the shithouse wall if this jazz goes on, Jim.

With this statement, Norman served warning to the New York intellectuals that he was breaking ranks.

IN THE FALL and winter of 1965–66, while his public life was becoming more contentious, in private Norman was trying to settle into domesticity. He had finally bought property in Provincetown the preceding summer — a gray shingled house on the bay side of Commercial Street in the town's East End. It had a deck over the water and was the immediate neighbor of the John Dos Passos home and Mary Heaton's legendary wharf, the birthplace of modern American drama, where Eugene O'Neill's first play, *Bound East for Cardiff*, was staged in 1916; its history was important to his actress wife. For the first time the family had a refuge to go to whenever they liked, and Beverly had her first home. She was pregnant again, and a second son, Stephen, would be born on March 10, 1966. The girls were getting older; Susie, the oldest, was now fifteen. Norman and Beverly were enjoying, as usual, a somewhat frantic social life, and the strain of juggling this with running a household sometimes showed. Keeping up with Norman and his entourage took a great deal of effort. Norman, primed by before-dinner drinks, liked nothing more than a good fight at the dinner table — Beverly had observed that this extended to lunches and dinners with his mother — and he often insulted Beverly mercilessly. Beverly, nothing if not spirited, tried gamely to parry his meaner remarks. Over time, however, Norman's determined abuse was wearing her down. Yet she also wanted to be an impeccable wife, housekeeper, and mother, and these conflicting goals sometimes stretched her thin indeed.

In the summer of 1965, Beverly and some friends from New York talked about setting up a theater production company in Provincetown; the following summer Act IV, a company that would specialize in one-act plays by emerging playwrights, was born. That first summer Leroi Jones's *The Dutchman* was mounted, with Beverly playing the lead, for which she received considerable attention. It was the first time Norman had seen her act, and Beverly felt he was threatened by the attention she was getting. In response, he staged a three-act play from *The Deer Park,* the script of which he had been working on for nearly a decade. The dry run was successful enough that he decided to stage a full version of the play off-Broadway the following winter.

Mailer decided that since the play was about Hollywood, he should write it like a screenplay. He thought this meant that he should have as many scenes as there would be camera shots in a comparable film. There would be eighty-eight scenes in all — Mailer called them "changes" — each one announced with a blackout, a number on a lighted scoreboard, and the ringing of a bell, for an effect something like that of a boxing match. The cast included Beverly as Lulu (though the part she wanted was that of Elena), Rip Torn as the pimp Marion Faye, Mailer's friend Mickey Knox as the producer Munshin, and a white-suited Buzz Farbar as the wife swapper Don Beda.

The show was scheduled to open at the Theatre de Lys on Christopher Street in the Village on January 24, 1967, but the date was pushed back to January 31 because of a physical production problem with the scene breaks. While Buzz Farbar got some positive reviews for his largely cameo role, earning him the nickname "Buzz Cameo," the reviewers were not kind to the play, the general consensus being that there were too many scenes. The *Village Voice* reviewer found it "pretentious." The play "doesn't have the depth Mailer claims for it." Edith Oliver of *The New Yorker* wrote, "Mr. Mailer may have adapted his novel but he has not dramatized it, and he has drowned it in words, even filling the chinks between scenes with narration, so that very little registers — and the busy, fuzzy production is no help at all

. . . There is a good deal of talk about truth and reality and guilt; at times the air is filled with guff."

Reviews notwithstanding, the play would run for nearly 150 perform-ances, and Rip Torn, known for his magnetic stage presence, would win an Obie Award for his performance. "We were a hit," Mailer wrote. "Not a smash hit, but a hit." The play remained a favorite of Norman's, and he would attempt to revive it several times, once in 1984 as a film. Norman loved *The Deer Park* and he loved putting it on stage. By the time it went up, he wrote in his introduction, he'd lived with the themes and characters for eighteen years. He'd worked on the play for ten years, rewriting it four times. "It was by now perhaps the dearest work of all my work. There were times when I thought I even cared for it more than the novel from which it was delivered," he said. "It was certainly different from the novel, nar-rower, more harrowing, funnier I hoped, sadder, certainly more tragic."

The play was, for him, another creation — his novel had spawned a play! — and it's understandable that he showed poor judgment in prefer-ring it to its original. Yet the novel *The Deer Park* is far more successful than the play *The Deer Park*. In the novel Mailer's ideas have room to "breathe," as it were; he has the space to expand on them, and the complicated sen-tences are much more easily read than heard. Moreover, a long novel can accommodate many complicated characters, but a play with thirteen such characters and eighty-eight scenes is unwieldy.

While Mailer had his doubts during the run of the play — at one point he ran out and saw ten Broadway shows and a handful of off-Broadway plays just to figure out how his fared in comparison — he enjoyed the experience overall and considered his play a success. As a result, he would try to make plays of many of his works over the years.

A play, after all, is a performance, and Norman was by nature a per-former. He was drawn to genres previously unfamiliar to him and he of-ten achieved small — though sometimes large — successes with them. The modest success of his play was due to an aspect of his character that he would just as soon others didn't see: beneath the cultivated persona of the rebellious, existential individual given over to the *acte gratuit,* he was an immensely likable person, and this came through in his play and, later, in his films. Furthermore, everything he touched became *interesting,* whether in a meaningful way or not. Partly it was the challenge of his writing, but mostly it was his far-reaching, ambitious intelligence.

FOR BEVERLY, however, *The Deer Park* was a disturbing experience. It nearly overwhelmed her, and struck a serious blow to her marriage. Nor-man could be abusive to her in front of the cast. As a professional actress, she felt he had no particular talent as a director, and had told him so when he tried to direct her in *Dutchman,* saying, "I don't tell you how to write; I don't expect you to tell me how to act." Offstage he was even worse, constantly belittling her talent and seriously undermining her confidence. In one particularly ugly incident, Beverly, driving to rehearsal, was hit by a car that had run a stop sign. Her head smashed the window, and she was dazed. She called the stage manager at the Theatre de Lys, who immediately came over and escorted her to the emergency room at St. Vincent's. As she was waiting to see a doctor and be x-rayed, Norman, clearly very drunk, appeared suddenly at her side and grabbed her arm. "You're a professional," he hissed. "You're going to come with me and go on." And he dragged her off to the theater; she fell several times along the way, her head still spinning.

Beverly attributes such gratuitous, inexplicable cruelty to Norman's profound ambivalence about her career. "My acting was something I had that he didn't have," she says. It's not that Norman wanted to be an actor, exactly, but he was jealous of anything Beverly had for herself — just as he had been enraged that she changed her own name herself. In such a climate, Beverly nearly broke down, sometimes fearing for her own sanity. It was one thing to be the object of Norman's daily ridicule in the domestic realm, but quite another when he extended his abuse to her career. "I don't feel like a person any more," Beverly wrote in her diary during the run of *The Deer Park*. The experience was dehumanizing.

Yet she had to keep up a good show, domestically speaking. The problem was that her husband, though he seemed to share this goal, felt conflict over the nature of his proper role. The summer that *Deer Park* was running at Act IV, Norman outfitted the Provincetown house's porches with tightropes, and the quest was on for the ideal tightrope-walking shoes. Guests included Midge Decter and Norman Podhoretz — Decter remembers how drunk they all were — Beverly's mother and "Brownie," her stepfather, who interested Norman because he'd been in the army and was a Southerner; José and Ramona Torres; and Rip Torn and his wife, Geraldine Page. Norman tried to get the Gwaltney family, which now included two children, to visit, describing to them his wonderfully challenging — even, he hinted, dangerous — Sailfish, which he had put together from a kit, but Fig couldn't make it this time.

In a familiar pattern, Norman played the role of a somewhat patrician, benevolent head of the household, but he showed no understanding of the pressures Beverly was under. Hetty came often, but Beverly still needed extra help. Fan would send baby nurses from her Miss Baltimore Agency, but Beverly found that they resented being asked to do any cooking or cleaning. Those she hired herself were usually more competent. Still, conflicts inevitably arose, and visitors that summer recalled many unpleasant scenes.

Guests and neighbors remember an oddly manners-conscious Mailer emerging in the late 1960s. Since his time at Harvard, he had admired the social customs of the very rich, and he had, of course, been born into a rather proper middle-class family. Like many newly rich people, he was grimly fascinated by propriety. Beverly's stepbrother has spoken of an incident when a local fisherman came around for a drink. The fisherman put his feet on the coffee table, and Norman delivered an angry tirade about boors and proper behavior.

Still, this was only one side of him. The other would drink and shout and beat up strangers, as often as not ending an argument by challenging the other man to a boxing match, much like a gentleman demanding a duel. This confused apprehension of what was proper for a man seems to have been bound up with the whole fascinating question of his own masculinity. How does one go about being a man? Sometimes by being a gentleman, the proprietor of a well-managed household; at other times, by being a macho daredevil.

The summer of 1966 saw many fights between Norman and his men friends, and in one Norman suffered a whopping black eye. His doctor friend Jack Begner had to close the surrounding cuts with butterfly stitches. Begner took a picture of Norman, one that he would proudly display on the cover of his next novel, *Why Are We in Vietnam?*

At one of the most curious events of the mid-century, Truman Capote's black-and-white ball of November 28, 1966, each side of Norman — the gentleman and the brawler — showed itself flagrantly. The black-and-white-attired guests, most wearing fantastically ornate masks, viewed the event with wonder; Capote had drawn four hundred guests to the Plaza's ballroom, all of them well known, many of them celebrities, and many of them from the ranks of the very rich. Others found the spectacle decadent in the extreme, especially given the ongoing war in Vietnam; later, recalling the scene, some spoke of "tumbrels rolling," as they had in the French Revolution.

Norman received an award for the worst-dressed man at the ball from *Women's Wear Daily*, for his "dirty gabardine raincoat with [his] black tie." He considered the ball "one of the best parties I ever went to . . . It certainly was [Truman's] greatest coup. For some, and I might be one of them, that party was even greater than one of his books." Yet he couldn't stay out of trouble. "I was dissolute and very drunk," he recalled years later. Norman Podhoretz, Lillian Hellman, and McGeorge Bundy, Johnson's special assistant for national security affairs and a key adviser on Vietnam, were assembled in a group talking when Mailer strode up and joined in. He challenged

Bundy about the war, declaring, somewhat cryptically, "I paid you too much respect." Bundy put his hand gently on Mailer's arm, saying, "Well, of course, you don't really know much about it," at which Mailer, inflamed anew — "I'd have killed him that night" — invited him to step outside. Lillian Hellman intervened, telling Mailer to get lost, and they in turn had a shouting match, sounding for all the world, according to Mailer, like a big sister and her kid brother. Nor did this scene satisfy him: he challenged others to fight during the course of the evening, including his old adversary William F. Buckley. His first real excursion into high society — aside from the few encounters he'd had in the company of Lady Jeanne Campbell — seemed to bring out the worst in him, while he clearly remained in awe of higher social circles. (His main objection to Hellman's harangue, in fact, was that she'd made it "right in front of McGeorge Bundy," the man he'd just asked to step outside.)

IN THE SUMMER OF 1966, Norman assembled his last couple of years of reviews, articles, and transcripts of his speeches for a collection to be published by Dial. He named it *Cannibals and Christians,* the meaning of which he offered in his introduction: Cannibals were those on the right, from Republicans to Nazis, who feast on the flesh of their own species — but not on that of their own families. Christians are liberals, moderates, and radicals, Christians and Jews, and Communists, from Lyndon Johnson to Ho Chi Minh, who have good intentions and high hopes. The sixties have been the age of the absurd, he argues; their time "contains happenings, Pop art, camp, a theater of the absurd, a homosexual genius who spent thirty years as a thief." Things have lost their meanings. Writing the introduction at Provincetown that summer, he describes how a friend had brought him a seven-foot Gulf Oil sign she had rescued from the dump. At first Norman was greatly excited, imagining a coffee table that would inspire poets to meditate on the name Gulf and musicians to explore the sound of a cocktail glass striking its metal surface. But he rejected the idea, because he was not sure that its meaning would be clear: "Some might decide that putting a huge gasoline company's totem into one's private space helped to mock civilization and its hired man, the corporation; others would be certain the final victory of the corporation was near when we felt affection for the device by which a corporation advertises itself." (He ended up leaving the sign to rust on the beach — environmentalism was one movement he did not anticipate.)

The collection, published in August 1966, is suitably absurd — and absurdly uneven. His pieces are interspersed with scraps of poetry, seldom felicitously. The last fifty pages are given over to interviews, both actual ones and ones he makes up himself. The interview was a genre that he would always be curious about, but it was never good to him. The interview form allowed his egotism full rein, allowed him to ponder a subject like time or the Devil or sex over a number of pages, with hair-splitting precision but, in the end, very little insight.

He also included such ephemera as a couple of letters documenting a feud with the book review editor at the *New York Times,* letters that are amusing diversions but do not stand the test of time. He includes a couple of book reviews, one savaging Mary McCarthy's *The Group,* a book he obviously enjoyed hugely but that afterward made him feel manipulated. His essays about the imaginary city are here, and pieces about Bobby Kennedy and John Lindsay, both of whom he would support in their coming races for president and mayor, respectively. "Some Children of the Goddess," his second quick "survey of the talent in the room," is also included.

It is the political pieces that carry the book: his essay about Goldwater and the Republican Convention, his review of LBJ's book, and his wonderful rant to the editors of *Partisan Review* about Vietnam. Mailer had always been considered "political," but with *Cannibals and Christians* he put the country on notice that he was ready to join the students in protest against what had for twenty years been official U.S. foreign policy. When even LBJ is a Christian, Mailer wants no part of it; he wants to go on beyond cannibals and Christians to a new utopia.

As he writes in his introduction, two kinds of writers bring out collections of their work: those who write about ladies' fashion and professional football each in the same way, and those who try to mix it up a little, to see what ladies' fashion has to "say" to professional football. He clearly belongs to the latter camp. What he has produced is an interrogation of everything, a journal of discovery, an organic, if absurd, whole. (He mentions that D. H. Lawrence, Henry Miller, and Ernest Hemingway, his personal heroes, are also members of the latter group of writers; he coyly does not say he is among them.)

The reviewers liked it. With this somewhat loopy, unpredictable collection, Mailer had finally become respectable again, almost twenty years after *The Naked and the Dead.* But they also seemed to understand what he was driving at. Many critics seemed to be writing against some perception of Mailer as a has-been, another sign that the highly personal style of cultural and political commentary he had been refining over the years was finally making its point with the reviewers. John Aldridge, always an astute Mailer critic, said in *Commentary* that

> there are sure to be readers of *Cannibals and Christians* who will consider its angry polemic, irreverent speeches, obscene poems, and endless interviews to be simply another collection of rubble

from a bombed-out talent. But it is becoming more and more evident as the years go by and the rubble continues to pile up that Mailer's talent is above all for being bombed out, and for registering in a manner nearly miraculous the impact of psychic and public catastrophe on a man who is at once its most eager victim and its most articulate analyst.

Even the reviewer at *Newsweek* seemed to get it, which probably horrified Norman: "It takes a strong stomach and iron nerves to cheer Norman Mailer — much less to warm to him. But the strong talent that is often reflected in his free-form, intensely charged, prophetic prose deserves an audience."

Norman Mailer, known for having prefaced *The Deer Park* with a quote from Gide, "Do not understand me too quickly," was in grave danger of being understood. He would have to do some fancy footwork to escape from this danger.

EARLIER DURING that summer, Mailer was called to Boston to testify before the Superior Court of Massachusetts in favor of William S. Burroughs's novel, *Naked Lunch*, which had been banned in the state. Testifying with Allen Ginsberg and John Ciardi, among others, Mailer offered compelling testimony on the importance of Burroughs's book to him, to other writers, and to society in general. In the course of the trial, which ended with the book's being declared not obscene, Mailer found himself reading *Naked Lunch* very closely. The writing was extraordinary, he thought, and he wondered if Burroughs had produced another modernist masterpiece on the level of Joyce's *Ulysses*, but finally concluded that it didn't have the structure to be found in a work of that caliber. Nevertheless, "[*Naked Lunch*] has great importance to me as a writer," Mailer testified.

Burroughs's lesson was not lost on him. If *Naked Lunch* was deemed not obscene, the road was cleared for stronger language in fiction. *Naked Lunch* had also suggested some things that might be helpful in his next novel: finding hidden conspiracies and extravagances in everyday events, and how to use a different voice — indeed, a different language — to bring out the deeper implications of the story.

Experimental fiction had always intrigued Mailer, and he began a project, the short novel *Why Are We in Vietnam?*, which would take him only four months to write, and which represents his own sampling of that genre. He succeeded handsomely, even startling himself a little. Interviewing himself in the pages of the *New York Times Book Review* a year later, when *Why Are We in Vietnam?* was about to appear, he would admit that he had moments when he considered it one of the ten funniest books written since

Huckleberry Finn: "Sometimes I think it's the best 200 pages I've yet done. The most American, certainly the 200 pages least alienated from genius."

He had intended to write a book about two rich boys who commit meaningless murders in Provincetown, but one of his central preoccupations — Vietnam — got in the way. Instead he wrote about two young men, D. J. (for Dr. Jekyll, and for Disk Jockey) and Tex (Hyde), who go on a bear hunt in Alaska with D. J.'s father, Rusty, the manufacturer of a cigarette filter that causes cancer, a couple of other corporate types (M.A.s, or Medium Assholes), and some half-demented guides, who outfit their "guests" with heavy artillery and helicopters (Cop Turds). The action is "broadcast" by D. J., the narrator, in hallucinatory (or hallucinogenic) rants, with the action set forth in "Chaps" (or chapters) interspersed with "Intro Beeps," containing station identification and other pertinent material.

The book is a testament to testosterone, a chronicle of an obsession with violence, blood, hunting, fucking, and, Mailer insists, anality — all, to Mailer, the preoccupations of American manhood. By making his protagonists Texans, Mailer signals that they represent the ultimate, the most, of everything: that they are, in this case, the ultimate in masculinity. Tex and D. J., bound together in the most male way, receive a telepathic message in which God tells them, "Go out and kill — fulfill my will, go and kill." Vietnam is not mentioned in the book until the last page, when we learn that D. J. and Tex are bound for Vietnam, and D. J. closes his narrative with the words "Vietnam, hot dam." We are in Vietnam, the book says, because of this testosterone orgy.

Mailer's message is a mixed one. He genuinely hates the war in Vietnam, and blames this imperialistic and sadistic exercise on a deep pathology related to masculinity. American troops committing hideous acts in a small Asian country: it's the ultimate perversion of the masculine. But Mailer brings great ambivalence to the subject of manhood. After all, he is a man, cherishes macho pursuits like boxing (interestingly, there's no indication that he ever hunted), and sees the Southern redneck as the quintessence of testosterone. Yet, just as some part of him hates the very Texans whose accent he loves to mimic, some part of him cannot reject the notion of machismo. *Why Are We in Vietnam?* thoroughly explores his own interest in, and ambivalence about, his own masculinity.

But the book is more than that. It is delightful to read, a no-holds-barred document of Mailer's love for language. Consider this sample from the opening pages of D. J.'s "rant":

> By gum, man, bite on D. J.'s Texas dick — America, this is your own wandering troubadour brought right up to date, here to sell America its new handbook on how to live, how to live in this

Electrox Edison world, all programmed out, Prononzo! (this last being the name King Alonso gave to the Spanish royal condom). Well, Huckleberry Finn is here to set you straight, and his asshole ain't itching, right? So listen to my words, One World, it's here for adolescents and overthirties — you'll know what it's all about when you and me are done, like the asshole belonged to Egypt, man, and the penis was the slave of the Hebes and the Brews, for they got it girdled with a ring of blood fire, and the nose was the Negroes, for they split it. Now remember? Think of cunt and ass — so it's all clear.

Why Are We in Vietnam? displays, in almost every sentence, an outright affection for obscene words, reflecting another aspect of Mailer's feelings about language. In his next book, he would explain why he loved what obscenity spoke for in the American people, the kind of obscenity he heard in the army: it expressed the humanity of America, as expressed in its humor. Speaking of himself in the third person, he wrote, "He had kicked goodbye in . . . *Why Are We in Vietnam?* to the old literary corset of good taste, letting his language play on obscenity as freely as it wished, so discovering that everything he knew about the American language . . . went flying in and out in the line of his prose with the happiest beating of wings — it was the first time his style seemed at once very American to him and very literary in the best way."

Like *An American Dream, Why Are We in Vietnam?* is a bit of a stunt. But it wasn't written to make money. Mailer was very serious in his concentrated effort to make testosterone, for lack of a better word, visible, palpable: it's the force that propels the protagonists in directions that the government has told us are prudent and based on policy. How does this happen? he asks. Once again, writing quickly (something he had done only with *An American Dream;* books like *Barbary Shore* and *The Deer Park* took great amounts of time), he produced something extraordinary. Readers looking for an explanation of where the macho impulse comes from would be disappointed. Mailer's more limited purpose is to bring it out into the open, to make it palpable.

On the other hand, *Why Are We in Vietnam?* is a relatively uncomplicated book, nothing as complex as Joyce's *Ulysses* (Mailer invokes Joyce twice in the narrative) or even Burroughs's *Naked Lunch*. There are no grand schemes, and the structure is fairly simple. But on the sentence level, Mailer works wonders: the best of the rather mediocre poet and the lover of wordplay (like "The Drunk's Bebop and Chowder" in *The Deer Park*) comes to the fore here.

The critical reception was, for the most part, positive, though many complained about the language (Mailer's only real rival in obscenity, at that time, was Henry Miller). Mailer attributed it to the "crankiness" sweeping the country, for readers who had defended obscenity in *The Naked and the Dead* condemned its use in this novel. Eliot Fremont-Smith, writing for the daily *New York Times,* concluded that Mailer, "as American as cherry pie . . . [is] America's most courageous writer, and . . . one of its most serious, penetrating and responsible interpreters of itself to its haunted self." Many reviewers noted the cover of *Why Are We in Vietnam?,* which had two photographs of Mailer, one with a black eye, and one of him in a suit. "Will the real Norman Mailer stand up?" asked the caption. Mailer, always involved in the design and promotion of his books, was hereby insisting that he was both — and he would bring both personae, the street hooligan and the literary man-about-town, to the task of chronicling and shaping the second half of the sixties.

THE ARMIES OF THE NIGHT

With *Why Are We in Vietnam?* Mailer made a change in his writing life, among other things. He was still under contract to Putnam's to write the "big one," now understood to be about a Jewish family from ancient times down to the present. Editors around town picked up hints that the novel might be set in Egypt. Mailer tried to present *Why Are We in Vietnam?* to Walter Minton at Putnam's as the so-called big one, but Minton balked. This was not the book he had contracted for, and apparently he didn't think much of it. Given the ambitious-sounding teasers, the piece of fiction Norman had just completed must indeed have seemed slight. Still, Minton was bound contractually — albeit for a thousand-dollar advance to the author, a sum Scott Meredith was able to raise to twenty-five thousand when an agreement was made with a new publisher, New American Library (NAL), to publish *Why Are We in Vietnam?* in March 1967.

Mailer, on the other hand, was ready to change publishers again. Publishing was moving into a big-money phase, contemporaries like Jones and Irwin Shaw were commanding huge advances, and Mailer wanted a million-dollar advance for his big novel. Scott Meredith went to Dick Baron at Dell, who, with Ed Doctorow, tried to convince Helen Meyer, then running Dell, that the house should give him a million for a specific number of words of fiction, Baron thought for five hundred thousand words. But in the end the Dial people felt they did not have adequate confidence that Mailer would produce the big book, and the deal fell through.

Nobody was getting million-dollar advances, and if Mailer thought he would be the first, he was disappointed. The million-dollar contract was not to be, this time at least. Scott Meredith told Norman that New American Library was willing to advance a still impressive $450,000 for what was understood to be the big novel, and Norman agreed. For the time being, he and his big book were with a new publishing house.

WHILE *Why Are We in Vietnam?* was in production, Mailer was exploring an area in which he had an intense interest: filmmaking, which would in fact become a second career for him for the next several years. During the run of *The Deer Park* in the spring of 1967, the cast and those involved in the production would usually head to a bar and restaurant on West Tenth Street called Casey's. In the early morning hours, Norman, Buzz Farbar, and Mickey Knox began to develop an amusing act: they played at being Mafiosi. They traded insults, experimenting with Irish, Italian, and black accents, and they thought the result hilariously funny. In fact, they thought their routine would make a great movie. They began referring to themselves as the "Maf Boys," their answer to Andy Warhol's recently released *Chelsea Girls,* saying, "Jesus, isn't it a shame we can't film it?" Norman thought they could, and began developing a plan to make a movie. All they needed was a camera and sound equipment, he thought, having observed the contemporary film scene and particularly the work of Andy Warhol. By the end of March he had contacted noted documentary filmmaker Donn Pennebaker, and the venture took off.

Norman's interest in filmmaking began in the early sixties, when he began going to the movies in earnest, usually at the Charles Theater at Twelfth Street and Avenue B. The introduction of lightweight, 16mm cameras and sound equipment in the late fifties and early sixties had made it possible for anyone to make a film. Thus were born two extremely important developments in filmmaking: cinema verité and underground films.

In cinema verité, filmmakers took advantage of the new lightweight camera to make documentaries that registered the close involvement of the camera with the subject, creating films that were forceful and engaging — a revolutionary change in moviemaking. In the United States, Donn Pennebaker, Ricky Leacock, and Al Maysles broke ground with their 1960 film *Primary,* about the Kennedy-Humphrey contest in Wisconsin; Jean-Luc Godard had also used the team in the filming of the verité-influenced *One American Movie,* which boosted their reputations. Pennebaker, Maysles, and those who followed them were professional, accomplished filmmakers.

Many underground filmmakers, on the other hand, were usually complete amateurs, drawn to the new technology not just because it was lightweight and portable but because anyone could use it. This movement attracted talent from many different fields, and it's not surprising that Mailer was drawn to it. The Charles moviehouse, and later the Cinema Bibliotheque, drew an audience from those who would be on the cutting edge of the arts in the years to come: filmmakers Jonas Mekas, Ron Rice, and Kenneth Anger; the eccentric creator of shadowboxes, Joseph Cornell; singer and writer Patti Smith; Allen Ginsberg, Michael McClure, and other members of the Beat poetry scene. Even Salvador Dali was there, together with a startlingly beautiful woman, Ultra Violet, and artists Christo, Robert Rauschenberg, and Jasper Johns. Perhaps the avatar was Andy Warhol, the pop artist who turned to experimental film with such deceptively deadpan works as *Sleep, Eat,* and *Kiss,* which evoked new ideas about time and repetition by showing one person performing the titular activities. Norman was hugely impressed by Warhol's technique — the minimal editing, the slow-moving style of his films, and the artfully "raw" look of his performances. While Norman would never produce anything as radically stripped down in style as the Warhol films, he did learn from Warhol "that an uncut piece of film was beautiful." And he would follow Warhol in using his friends and acquaintances in his films. He may well have envied Warhol his "Factory," his fascinating, exhibitionistic court. But the macho earthiness of Norman's own circle — Knox, Farbar, Donoghue, Torres, and the like — captured his imagination. In fact, the subject of Norman's early films would be men; he wanted to record and define the macho impulse.

Norman turned to Pennebaker for a number of reasons. First, Pennebaker's partner, Ricky Leacock, had been in Norman's class at Harvard, and Norman had always liked him (he would become an important friend). Second, he'd been greatly impressed by Pennebaker's *Don't Look Back* (1967), a documentary film about Bob Dylan's 1965 United Kingdom tour, which had just opened successfully and was actually making money. Later, remembers Pennebaker, Norman was most impressed by footage of the 1967 Monterey Pop Festival, which Pennebaker, Al Maysles, Nick Proferes, and Leacock had just finished shooting (it would be released as *Monterey Pop* in 1969). "He thought [the films] represented some kind of new age in publishing, in getting your material out," says Pennebaker. "He thought films were a new artistic medium." Norman knew that he didn't have the technique to produce a movie himself, so he hired Pennebaker and Leacock for two thousand dollars.

And Norman, as a nonprofessional, would encounter constraints on every side. The film was to be shot on 16mm film with a magnetic sound tape; because film at the time was so expensive — raw stock cost about thirty cents a foot, or ten dollars a minute — Norman and his production partner, again Buzz Farbar of Supreme Mix, could only spend $1,500 on film, which would net them two and a half hours of raw footage. The location would be a storeroom behind Pennebaker's offices on West Forty-fifth Street, a location that, Norman complained, lacked the ambience of Casey's.

The film was to be called *Wild 90,* which Norman believed was Mafia-speak for "we're in big trouble now" or "the shit's hitting the fan." There was no script, but as it emerged — it was shot, with no retakes, over two days and nights in late March 1967 — it was "about" three hoods in trouble who were holed up in a hiding place for twenty-one days. Norman emerged as the ringleader, called the Prince, and Farbar and Knox were Buzz Cameo and Twenty Years, respectively. Beverly played the Prince's Gun Moll, and in one memorable scene, which ends in a kiss, she confronts him; when it was shown at the Actors Studio, the women in the audience applauded loudly. A German shepherd was on hand, and in one scene Norman outbarked the dog.

Wild 90 was ruined by its soundtrack. A technical problem caused a loss of 20 to 30 percent of the sound, and as a result the dialogue — the film's single point — is impossible to understand. Pennebaker despaired when he heard the soundtrack, and he told Norman not to try for a theatrical release. But somehow Norman convinced a theater on Forty-second Street to run it. Predictably, viewers complained about the sound. Later, Norman would joke about it. "You got three guys talking in a room and you can't hear what they're saying," he said. "It sounds as if *everybody* is talking through a jockstrap." (In reality, Norman's words were those that could not be understood, because he barked and grunted his dialogue so loudly.) The movie was also criticized for its pace, which was glacial. Norman might have been most encouraged by this, for it was the criticism most often leveled at Warhol.

Despite the financial loss — Norman would lose the fifty thousand dollars he had sunk into it, money earned, ironically enough, from selling *An American Dream* to the movies — and *Wild 90*'s mixed reception, Norman had caught the bug, and hardly six months had passed before he tried filmmaking again, this time with slightly better results. He put a little more time into the planning, expanded his cast, made his "plot" more complicated, and worked with two filmmakers, Jan Welt and Lana Jokel, on the editing — thus the modest success of *Beyond the Law.*

This film, which was to be feature-length, was shot over the course of four nights and resulted in eleven hours of film to be edited down to 105 minutes. It is an improvisation, the premise being that Norman, who plays an Irish police lieutenant named Pope, and his henchmen, Buzz Farbar, Mickey Knox, Harold Conrad, and others, work over the criminals who wander in and out of the precinct, among them prostitutes, gamblers, pimps, a wife-murderer, and some others who have been wrongly arrested. Rip Torn and Michael McClure played Hell's Angels, and George Plimpton played Mayor Lindsay, who comes to the precinct investigating charges of police brutality. Some unidentified women showed up and Norman staged some sex scenes; later these would be included in a so-called blue version, which circulated privately. The film was shot by Jan Welt, Pennebaker, and Nick Proferes, using three cameras and thus producing footage more complex than had been the case with *Wild 90*. For the editing, Norman relied on Welt and Jokel, two professionals; Norman never actually worked at the editing table but instead told his editors what he wanted in the way of cuts and emphasis.

Beyond the Law was shown at the New York Film Festival in September, and it then opened at the Art Theater on October 23. Eventually Norman sold the distribution rights to Barney Rosset for fifteen thousand dollars. Rosset didn't have much luck finding theaters to take *Beyond the Law* and gave Norman the rights back. The high production costs had taken their toll; Mailer eventually lost eighty thousand dollars on the film.

Still, the film was well received. One reviewer for the *New York Times* found it "so much better than Norman Mailer's last movie . . . that it is possible to like it a lot"; he singled out Norman's facial expressions as "real acting after all," though he found the camera work "abominable," perhaps, he said, because of Norman's direction. Vincent Canby, writing for the *Times*, was somewhat snide — referring to "the self-styled Prince of Bourbon, Normal Norman" — but commented that the film "dramatizes the existential relationship between cop and crook." He noted that Norman, dressed throughout in a three-piece suit and hat, was always sweating and sounded a lot like Senator Joe McCarthy, but he said that the film "is so good and tough and entertaining so much of the time that you have to simply forgive those moments when the actors suddenly smirk self-consciously . . . and when it becomes unintelligible."

But Norman was encouraged. And Pennebaker, for one, believes the film had a considerable effect on those who had seen it. Many writers of television cop shows have seen the film, he says, and it was "a real course in filmmaking for Hollywood." *Beyond the Law* "really said something about the police, how they are sort of a counterpart to the crooks. Both sides are both good and bad."

Pennebaker is right in identifying the film's focus: Mailer's insistence on the interchangeability of the cops and the crooks, and his fascination with both sides. In fact, *Wild 90* and *Beyond the Law* have a lot in common and together speak to a pattern in Mailer's writing life. He was avoiding writing his big novel by turning to narratives about crime, violence, the outlaw, and masculinity; the happy results were *An American Dream* and *Why Are We in Vietnam?* The films represent the same impulse: when Norman sought some quick, improvisatory drama, this is the territory he headed for.

Again, as in *Why Are We in Vietnam?*, the subject of the two films is men. Again he wanted to see what happens when men are thrown together in a pressure-cooker situation. What happens? Anything? What boundaries are tested or transgressed? The advantage of film over writing, he found, was that he could address these issues without an intrusive literary "voice." He wasn't hampered by a voice that gives away what he thinks of the men involved. The logical way to address issues like machismo, violence, and the outlaw was just to show these qualities in action. Norman would call this process existential, for the men thrown together on a single suggestion — you're a cop, for instance — improvised and tangled with one another, creating their roles as they went along.

With the release of *Beyond the Law*, Mailer put filmmaking aside for a time. But he fully intended to go back to it. He told an interviewer in 1970 that the freshness of filmmaking attracted him, reminding him of the freshness he had last felt when he was beginning as a writer at the age of eighteen or nineteen. Writing was still his first love, though it was by now a lot of hard work. "But making a film," he said, "is a cross between a circus, a military campaign, a nightmare, an orgy, and a high." And even his two earliest films have their admirers; as filmmakers Jonas Mekas and Donn Pennebaker have observed, anything Mailer touches has a certain energy and a certain intelligence and, above all, a certain *interest*. The foray into filmmaking was, for Norman, invigorating, refreshing, and challenging. Besides, it was inevitable that he, as a public figure, would be drawn to films: he was a performer, and his public would lose interest if he did not perform.

FILMMAKING FED Mailer's energies instead of draining them. For it was while making *Wild 90* that he produced what would be his most celebrated book since *The Naked and the Dead, The Armies of the Night*.

It wasn't clear just what Mailer was up to in writing *Armies*. *Harper's*, which published the first half of the book, "The Steps of the Pentagon," in its March 1968 issue, and *Commentary*, which published its companion piece, "The Battle of the Pentagon," in its April issue (*Harper's* had rejected it as too dry), seem to have realized they were publishing important work. But it was not until May 1968 — May 8, the twentieth anniversary of the publication of *The Naked and the Dead* — when NAL brought out *The Armies of the Night*, and when skeptical readers began reading it, that it became clear that a masterpiece had evolved. Mailer put subtitles beneath the titles of the two articles, the first "The Novel as History," the second "History as a Novel"; at the very least, he had invented a new genre, a form of narrative that questioned the boundaries between fiction and history, between the self and the observer, the observer and events. Even those who disagreed with Mailer's politics — Jerry Rubin on the one hand, Irving Howe on the other — recognized the book's unique achievement. Mailer, not an activist himself (though, with the book, he arguably became one), had written what would be one of the most lasting testaments to the activism of the sixties, an insightful analysis of the politics of the New Left and the mentality of the police and the military. The book is a vivid personal account of the conflicts he encountered and the epiphanies he experienced in the four days in October that culminated in the 1967 march on the Pentagon and his arrest, imprisonment, and eventual release. It is also, in a very small and charming way, a record of his flirtation and jockeying for place with the venerable East Coast poet Robert Lowell, whom he admires but feels the need to vanquish. (Lowell didn't, finally, get arrested, but when Norman saw him next, he'd already written eight hundred lines of his poem about the event — which Norman invites us to compare with his finished book.)

Though there was no leader of the March on the Pentagon (and that was in itself significant; one participant said, "There was no leadership, that was what was so beautiful"), one man was behind it: Dave Dellinger, an activist and the editor of the anarchist-pacifist journal *Liberation*. He had, in the spring of 1967, organized a massive peace march in New York City. The size of the march was unprecedented, but the war continued to escalate, so the National Mobilization Committee — a group of representatives from religion, academia, many moderate peace groups, SNCC, SDS, and various socialist parties — met in New York in May to plan a rally in Washington that they hoped would draw a million demonstrators. The date was set for October 21.

In early September, Dellinger called in Jerry Rubin to act as project director for the march. Rubin had organized Vietnam Day in Berkeley in 1965, when Mailer gave his famous LBJ speech; had served several jail sentences; had run for mayor of Berkeley (getting an impressive 22 percent of the vote); and had appeared before the House Un-American Activities Committee in a Revolutionary War uniform. Rubin, who had great clout with the students and the hippies, had pioneered a new method of resistance with the blocking of troop trains in Berkeley, and Dellinger's inclusion of him in planning for the march was summed up in the march's slogan, "From protest to resistance." Dave Dellinger put it differently: the march would bring together "Gandhi and Guerrilla." In other words, there would be acts of disruption at the event, and challenges made to all authority. It might get violent.

Dellinger envisioned a march past the White House down Pennsylvania Avenue to the Capitol, which the marchers might or might not take over in order to create a People's Congress. But Rubin didn't like the symbolism — the Congress was not really the source of power. Instead, he suggested a march on the Pentagon, which the marchers might or might not try to take over. After the organizers carefully reviewed the site, they settled on an approach to the massive Defense Department headquarters. Then the Mobilization Committee turned to the task of organizing the march, negotiating with the many disparate groups that were joining it, negotiating with the government over what routes the march would take, and getting roundly denounced by the press and Congress for undertaking such an action. (Congress even passed a bill the day before the march protecting the Capitol from men bearing arms.) Government assembled its powers, enlisting city police, Washington National Guardsmen, White House and capital police, U.S. marshals, and six thousand troops from the 82nd Airborne Division. Everybody was prepared, but it is safe to say that not one person knew exactly what they were prepared for.

For Mailer, the sequence of events began in September 1967, when fellow writer Mitch Goodman, the author of a World War II novel, *The End of It* (1961), which Norman had written a blurb for but whose title he could not now remember, called to tell him about the march, describing it as an attempt to enter the Pentagon and disrupt its operations. Goodman asked him to join in a demonstration in support of some young men who would be turning in their draft cards the day before. Norman remembered Mitch and his wife, the poet Denise Levertov, from the late forties in Paris, and, recalling his youthful idealism, agreed. A week later a young woman asked him to appear with Dwight Macdonald, Robert Lowell, and Paul Goodman at Washington's Ambassador Hotel before a young audience to raise bail money for those who might be arrested at the march two days later. Again, not quite sure what he was getting into, he agreed.

On a Thursday afternoon, on October 19, Norman stepped off a plane in Washington and was met by Ed DeGrazia, the lawyer he had worked with on the *Naked Lunch* trial, who was to emcee the event at the Ambassador and, Norman later learned, to organize lawyers to defend those who might be arrested at the march. (At this early point, Norman did not fully comprehend the possibility of violence and arrests, although he was sure of the march's importance.) Later that evening, at a dinner party given by Suzanne Fields and her husband, a liberal academic couple of a sort Norman distrusted, he got drunk with Robert "Cal" Lowell, who had angered him in 1962 by praising his book of poems, *Deaths for the Ladies,* but not giving it a blurb. Lowell was fond of telling Norman that he and his wife, the writer Elizabeth Hardwick, thought Norman was the best journalist in America. At the party, Norman one-upped him by saying, "Well, Cal, there are days when I think I'm the greatest writer in America." They went on to the hotel, Norman clutching a mug full of bourbon. Once there (all this is described in his book), he needed to use the men's room. When he couldn't find the light switch, he proceeded to miss the urinal. Drink still in hand, he mounted the stage, finding DeGrazia acting as emcee. Without too much trouble, he got DeGrazia to sit down, introduced Goodman and Macdonald and let them speak, and then opened his speech using his Texas sheriff accent. He attacked LBJ by presenting himself as his "dwarf alter ego," and then described his own debacle in the bathroom, an event he tied in to the "shit" that was going on in the world at large, which in turn made his obscenity, he thought, appropriate.

Strangely enough, he carried the evening. Macdonald and Goodman were not entirely effective, and Lowell, who looked drunk and tired, read from his poetry to a standing ovation, but Mailer gave the memorable performance. His old enemy *Time* ran an account of the evening that centered on his drinking, his obscenity, and his reference to missing the urinal. (Norman would preface his account with the clipping, getting in the last word by saying, "Now we may leave *Time* in order to find out what happened.")

The next day, when protesters were turning in their draft cards with their elders offering counsel, Norman was racked with doubts. He had real problems with joining in demonstrations, believing himself more effective as a kind of elder statesman, symbolized by his dressing for the event in a three-piece English-made suit and a regimental tie with a Windsor knot. Aside from having sworn not to pay a 10 percent increase in income tax, the bill before Congress that, if passed, would represent LBJ's surcharge for the war effort, he had always managed to duck actual involvement in the Vietnam controversy, as he later wrote: "He had piped up every variety of the extraordinarily sound argument that his work was the real answer to Vietnam, and these mass demonstrations, sideshows, and bloody income tax protests just took energy and *money* away from the real thing — getting the work out." He found himself challenged by urgent questions: Can writing be a form of activism? What kind of activism is it? Is Mailer an activist?

Norman was more subdued the day after his drunken performance, and gave a "modest" speech at the draft card demonstration. The quarrel between him and Lowell had reached the level of détente, and each man repeatedly complimented the other on his words of the night before, but Norman remained resentful about Lowell's reputation. Watching Lowell talking to a fellow protester on the way to the demonstration, it struck Norman that they looked like two Harvard deans walking together and conversing, and this awakened some old class resentments. "No dean at Harvard had ever talked to *him* that way," he wrote later, referring to himself. But the match between Norman and Cal was again an uneasy draw, as both men admitted that they were eager to get back to New York early enough the next evening, the day of the march; each had a very promising party to attend.

On the eve of the march, Norman again ruminated on what was happening. He tried to analyze what the New Left meant by revolution, and he was impressed. Their revolution was most like the Cuban revolution: it grew from the people, from disparate causes, rather than from an ideology. It was a kind of organic revolution, the students having added to their core resistance to the war their mass support for civil rights and an end to poverty, among many other goals.

Norman was too primed, too nervous, to eat; he turned down even a bite of a candy bar, and when he finally took some water, later in the day, he considered it a highly charged act. His writing conveys his sense that every action he takes is somehow numinous — the reader is not expected to agree with this judgment but is meant to register Norman's belief. The march began with a rally at the Lincoln Memorial, and then the protesters began to march across the Arlington National Bridge into Virginia (the location of the Pentagon would prove to be extremely significant), Mailer in the front line with Macdonald, Lowell, Dave Dellinger, and Jerry Rubin. There was some panic on the bridge as the huge group was funneled across, but eventually they ended up in a Pentagon parking lot, their agreed-upon meeting place. Norman was glad to be in the front lines; if his was a symbolic role, he might as well be on television, he reasoned. By this time he wanted only to get arrested and to get back to New York in time for that party. He was diverted, however, by watching a performance by the Fugs (a band named in tribute to his euphemism for *fuck* in *The Naked and the Dead*), and by a piece of theater designed by Abbie Hoffman, an attempt to levitate the Pentagon and then exorcise it, accompanied by chants of "Out, demons, out!"

It seemed the march could go no further. Things were getting chaotic, and it seemed that occupation of the Pentagon was no longer on the agenda. Mailer, Macdonald, and Lowell wanted to get arrested now. Finally they walked up to some MPs behind a rope. Norman stepped over the rope, saying, "If you don't arrest me, I'm going on to the Pentagon." In due time, after some confusion, he was arrested, and said first that he was guilty of "transgressing" a police line; in retellings of the arrest, he was precise in his rather odd choice of verb.

The events following the arrest were confused, but Norman retained some lasting impressions: of a confrontation, for example, with "a Nazi" in a police van, a young man, also in custody, calling Norman a "dirty Jew with kinky hair." All along there had been something military about the whole affair, something that reminded him of his army days, which was certainly appropriate, since he was at the Pentagon protesting a war. Norman was very civil to the MPs and cops, remembering both the army and Beverly's military brothers and stepfather — memories that reminded him of the soldiers' humanity. Yet what had impressed him most about the student movement was the protesters' resolution to challenge authority, a challenge that went to the heart of his long-held anxieties about authority and power. (He'd just made *Beyond the Law,* remember, exploring the workings of power in the police mind, and had played an Irish cop.) It's just this kind of identification and empathy that marked all of Norman's apprehension of the events playing out around him, and this is what would make his account so powerful: the sense that the writer is constantly measuring his beliefs, his personal conduct, and his attitudes against those of the people he sees participating in this extraordinary event.

Those arrested were taken first to the Alexandria post office, where Norman was allowed to call Beverly; he then got lost in a reverie about the state of his marriage and his children. The processing of prisoners began, and it was a long, boring affair. Norman had two hundred dollars on him, fifty of which he meant to keep for himself. But he doled out the rest to young men who needed to pay fines. Some he had to convince to take the money. One of these was a kid who had been arrested in spectacular fashion, and he gave Norman an incisive critique of the staging of *The Deer Park* which the writer enjoyed very much.

After a long day, the prisoners were bused to Occoquan, a minimum security prison twenty miles down the road. There Norman found a bunk and settled in, pleased that he recognized several friends: the architect Bob Nichols, Tuli Kupferberg of the Fugs, and Teague, a man who had been arrested with him, who was now holding forth on Leninism to a group of rapt listeners. Norman's bunk was next to Noam Chomsky's; Chomsky, the vocal antiwar linguist, was someone he had always wanted to meet, but now they just exchanged news of the day. Reviewing the arguments for and against the war in Vietnam, Norman finally slept, attending his New York party obviously a lost cause.

In the morning, he found that his suit was much the worse for wear; he went in his shirtsleeves for his meager breakfast. Back in the cell, Teague was holding forth again, and everyone was waiting for the lawyers to show up. Most of the protesters were pleading nolo contendere and getting off with fines, but Norman wanted to plead guilty. A problem emerged: was he getting special treatment or not? Other protesters remember that Norman was treated especially badly, that he was detained until Monday, his case heard only after most of the protesters had been freed. Ed DeGrazia, frustrated by all these notables' thinking he was their lawyer rather than an organizer of lawyers, advised Norman not to plead guilty lest his be perceived as a special case. Before the commissioner, DeGrazia asked if filing a guilty plea would prejudice Norman's case; not surprisingly, the judge replied that it might, so Norman changed his plea to a nolo.

As it turned out, DeGrazia's request itself turned out to prejudice the case, and the commissioner let Norman off only after DeGrazia called in a Virginia lawyer, Phil Hirschkop, who argued the commissioner into changing his initial ruling — that Norman be fined five hundred dollars and serve thirty days in jail, twenty-five of them as a suspended sentence, which meant, effectively, five days in jail — to letting Norman out on five-hundred-dollar bond pending an appeal.

When he emerged from the prison on bond, Norman made a speech before an assembled group of reporters. It began, rather strangely, with an invocation of Jesus Christ: "Today is Sunday, and while I am not a Christian, I happen to be married to one. And there are times when I think the loveliest thing about my dear wife is her unspoken love for Jesus Christ." He knew Beverly would think he was crazy, he said, but he meant it: there was something in her that was deeply, if nonspecifically, religious, and he felt he was right to make this claim. He also knew that he had hit upon a metaphor that would resonate with a religious nation. He went on to explain why the protesters were arrested — "in order to make symbolic protest of the war in Vietnam" — and he stated that while most of them had taken short sentences, the war's opponents might have to be prepared to sacrifice much more in the future if the war was to be stopped: "You see, dear fellow Americans, it is Sunday, and we are burning the body and blood of Christ in Vietnam. Yes, we are burning him there, and as we do, we destroy the foundation of this Republic, which is its love and trust in Christ."

Upon being released, Norman had felt a keen euphoria, a sense that "there was a sweet clean edge to the core of the substance of things" and "a liberation from the unending disciplines of that ladder whose rungs he had counted" — that is, freedom from all the doubts, the moral reckonings, that had plagued him throughout the march. He felt that the good he had done outweighed the things he had omitted to do, and he felt happy. He wanted his speech to be "salient," and he thought it appropriate to use the language of a nearby clergyman, John Boyle from Yale, in order to reach his audience. It was by a kind of shorthand, then, that he spoke of Christ. He was brought up short later, however, when he read the *Washington Post*'s report of his speech. The report quoted his remarks about Christ, and then tersely closed the account with the illuminating statement "Mailer is a Jew." Norman commented wryly, "It was obvious the good novelist Norman Mailer had much to learn about newspapers, reporters, and salience."

After his speech, Norman immediately took a shuttle to New York. He met Beverly at P. J. Clarke's (the scene of their first meeting four years before), where an old girlfriend tapped him on the hair, provoking an argument with Beverly, whom he had come to see, over the last four days, as the embodiment of America.

WITHIN A WEEK of his return from Washington, Mailer was talking to *Harper's* editor Willie Morris about an article on the march. Scott Meredith stepped in, and a deal was hammered out: Mailer would produce a twenty-thousand-word piece for ten thousand dollars. As he began writing, the number of words inevitably shot up, and Meredith turned to NAL, which agreed to publish it as a book for twenty-five thousand dollars; *Harper's* would have to make more space for the article.

Meanwhile, as Mailer began writing, he sensed that he could produce something more than an article: a book that would anatomize the march as a study in the politics of the New Left. He would need a lot more information, however. It became clear that he needed to understand the political moment in detail: how Black Power fed into the New Left, how the Six-Day War in the Mideast in June 1967 had altered many alliances and political realities. He needed to explore the formation of the march, the differing agendas of Dellinger and Rubin, the groups involved, the costs, even the physical details of what it looked like inside the walls of the Pentagon — the decor, the hunting pictures hung in the corridors of power, which Norman and his fellow protesters never got to see, but which the organizers had seen in the course of planning the march. For this kind of background, he had his secretary, Sandy Charlebois, find Jerry Rubin and interview him several times, and then he asked Rubin to come to the Heights brownstone. There, Norman himself interviewed the Yippie leader for hours, taking notes in longhand on a yellow pad.

Willie Morris and Midge Decter of *Harper's* flew up to Provincetown to edit the piece over Christmas and New Year's. They were tremendously excited by what they read, sometimes hovering over Sandy's typewriter and pulling out pages as she finished them. It was a terrible Christmas; Sandy caught the flu, and then the rest of them came down with it. But by mid-January the essay was at *Harper's*, and Mailer had turned his attention to the second half of the book, "History as a Novel," in which he would step back from his participatory role to analyze how the events of October fit into the larger historical scheme of the sixties. By May the entire manuscript was at NAL.

Norman chose the book's title, *The Armies of the Night,* from Matthew Arnold's poem "Dover Beach," evoking the futility of war, the absence of religious faith, and the elusive promise of love and camaraderie. The first section, "The Novel as History: The Steps of the Pentagon," emerged as a dramatic narrative of the events of the four days Norman had spent in Washington that past October. It is dramatic storytelling on Mailer's part: the events provided their own climaxes and eddies that helped the writer along. Interspersed are insights about the nature of war, the failures and successes of the New Left, the mood and direction of the country. But perhaps the most impressive creation is Mailer's comical and quirky rendering of himself as a character, as "the Novelist," "the Ruminant," "the Historian," "the General," and his use of the third person to describe himself.

Far from distancing himself from the reader, however, Mailer in *The Armies of the Night* presents himself far more nakedly than he had ever done before, even in *Advertisements for Myself*. We learn, for example, that he eats the same breakfast every day of the year except perhaps ten: scrambled eggs prepared according to a special recipe. That he wears a three-piece, English-made pinstriped suit and that he worries about his clothes getting mussed. He is self-deprecating, especially in the beginning, describing his drunken appearance at the Ambassador; he came very close to making a fool of himself there, he seems to know — although he gets in some potshots at *Time* for its glib, dismissive coverage of his speech. He is very candid about "his habit of living with his image"; he has two hundred dollars with him in jail and gives it out to those who've been fined, so as to give the (untrue, he admits) impression of not carrying any money. He is extremely revealing on the subject of his marriage and his feelings for his children (the girls, he feels, being girls, will always forgive him, but as for the boys — a lot is at stake there). His four-year marriage to Beverly, he believes, is still strong, perhaps because he has married a truly American girl (his first wife was a Jew, he explains, his second a Latin, his third an Englishwoman). But he worries that he and his wife are still strangers and is infuriated because he cannot decide whether Beverly's "final nature" is good or evil. He has hoped his wife could somehow be magical, yet he fears she might be human; it was all so fraught, because if she were human,

> why then he would finally lose some part of his love affair with America, he would have to, because there were too many times when thinking of his country and some new one of the unspeakable barbarities it invented with every corporation day, he would decide that no it could not be an altogether awful country because otherwise how would his wife, a Southerner and an Army brat, have come out so subtle, so supple, so mysterious, so fine-skinned, so tender and wise.

At such moments, *The Armies of the Night* becomes a conflicted love story of sorts, about Norman and his country.

Throughout this section and, in lesser part, the next, "History as a Novel: The Battle of the Pentagon," Norman is candid about his misgivings about and his fundamental sympathies for the student protesters. He doesn't hate America, he seems to be saying, but he hates the ruthless imperial power it is becoming, and the ways it has formed the protesters too, perhaps without their knowing it. "They would never have looked to blow their minds and destroy some part of the past if the authority had not brainwashed the mood of the present until it smelled like deodorant. (To cover the odor of burning flesh in Vietnam?)" The mood of the book is distinct, constant ambivalence.

In a sense, however, *The Armies of the Night* recapitulates his first book, *The Naked and the Dead*. *The Armies of the Night*, like his war novel, is about confrontation with and the reaction to authority. The writer is interested in the way others approach authority: the hippies, Lowell, Teague, Kupferberg, DeGrazia, and the organizers. He is ambivalent about the organizers and seasoned activists, people like William Sloane Coffin, Dave Dellinger, and Noam Chomsky, finding them practical but missing the point, mostly too earnest, too dedicated to doing a job and not enough to "transgressing." They were committed to making the march a moral gesture rather than a personal form of expression or protest as Norman hoped to do. They were exemplars rather than artists or individuals, and Norman is per se uneasy about them. He is especially cautious about Teague, the Leninist who holds forth in the jail dormitory, who seems to know the ropes a bit too well. Though Norman succeeded in creating a personal form of protest, he could not recognize that not everyone can do this: that politics requires in fact submission of the ego to the collective process. That kind of politics — represented by Teague and Noam Chomsky, among others — did not much interest him, perhaps because he recognized that it was not for him.

But it is finally his own apprehension of authority that interests Norman, authority designated as the Pentagon, which remains inscrutable. His insistence on using the verb *transgress* to describe his actions suggests that the march represented for him an existentialist experience. To approach the march in an individualist and existential mode was the best way, he found, to help Americans understand the event; he treats it not as a stirring mass movement toward a common goal, as the Leninist Teague tended to do, but instead as a tricky logistical gamble in which a group of people moved collectively to a certain point and then acted collectively — or, in Norman's case, individually.

The Armies of the Night is also the first work of Mailer's, after years of political journalism, in which he admits he has a political philosophy of his own: he is a "left conservative," he says. This isn't as meaningful as he seems to think, although Norman's political philosophy, entwined as it was with existentialism and a streak of idealism, was complex indeed. Put simply, he believed in many of the basic propositions of U.S. democracy — he cites Edmund Burke — but he found that these values are better supported by the antiwar dissidents than by the government, the military, and the corporate state. This isn't an unreasonable view; in fact, it may be a fairly liberal, responsible one.

But political participation remained a problem for Mailer. He had stayed out of politics since his participation in the 1948 Henry Wallace campaign. In Berkeley in 1965 he was given the opportunity to speak to thousands; his speech, urging the students to turn LBJ images everywhere "upside down," was, according to his views, an existentialist performance. Again, during the march on the Pentagon and also while writing about it, politics provided him with the occasion for another episode in his own existential drama. It was not a pleasant experience, mostly because he constantly tested himself, questioning himself and his motives.

In the dormitory jail Norman put himself through numerous tests, but one of the most difficult for him was a talk with Tuli Kupferberg. The Fugs' lead vocalist told Norman that he had told the authorities he would not agree to stay away from the Pentagon for six months, and therefore was to serve out his five-day sentence. This created a quandary for Norman, for he very much wanted to get out of jail and at the same time to do the right thing, to put it simply. He uneasily tolerated becoming "enmeshed in these unmanageable connections between politics and personal morality." He invoked Sartre in describing a "moral ladder" that could best be understood in terms of prisoners: each time you climbed a step, there would be another rung to reach — much, much harder than the one you had just achieved; eventually, you had to take a step down, and "the first step down always presented the same kind of moral nausea." This is why Norman could not stay in prison; he reasoned finally that he could promise to stay away from the Pentagon and then break that promise — lying would be better than confronting the "nausea" of the moral ladder.

After Norman was released from jail, he "felt a liberation from the unending disciplines of that moral ladder whose rungs he had counted while listening to Kupferberg, no, all effort was not the same, and to eject oneself from guilt might yet be worth it, for the nausea on return to guilt could conceivably prove less." He is freed from the moral ladder, and he finds he feels compassion for all — though not quite, not for the commissioner who heard his case or for the U.S. attorneys, but a "sense of nice expectation and shining conception of his wife, and regrets for the guards, and pride in the prisoners, too much, too much."

Norman's personal triumph — and the triumph of the book — is that as a middle-aged man who wears a suit and has an established literary career at stake, he has nonetheless found a way to be *engagé,* to be part of the protest in a meaningful way. For his arrest did mean something, it did count, and he was right to ask whether the book he wrote could be compared to the eight hundred lines of poetry Robert Lowell had to show from the same event. For the book had a profound effect. The second half provided an anatomy of the New Left and the mechanics of mounting a mobilization; young leftists found it an astute analysis and were impressed by the passion Mailer brought to the work. Across the political spectrum, readers who watched the student movement with varying degrees of approval or censure were made to understand that what was going on in the streets and on college campuses — and in the capital itself — was a real phenomenon that had to be taken extremely seriously; the country's future, no less, was at stake. By inserting himself in the narrative and making himself so fundamentally likable, with all his foibles, Mailer created a character who was believable and trustworthy. He demanded to be heard but in the most beguiling way possible. If what he had to say was unpalatable to many, he reminded his readers of his fundamental love of and concern for his country, and asked that everyone come together in this dark hour, when "ignorant armies clash by night."

1968

T*he Armies of the Night* represented, for Mailer, a new pinnacle. Readers — and reviewers — were stunned by the book. It was a grand
performance, magnificently documented. As a "nonfiction novel" (so he
labeled it), it was a very new beast.

The critical response was resounding. Nobody expected such a book.
After *An American Dream* and *Why Are We in Vietnam?*, the experimental
movies and the idiosyncratic political reportage, critics were not sure what
to make of Mailer. But reviewers were almost unanimous in acclaiming *The
Armies of the Night*. Alfred Kazin set the tone, on the front page of the *New
York Times Book Review*. Crediting Mailer with a new form, he compared
The Armies of the Night to Walt Whitman's *Specimen Days* and *Democratic Vistas* in the public breadth of its very personal story: "I believe that it
is a work of personal and political reportage that brings to the inner and
developing crises of the United States at this moment admirable sensibili-
ties, candid intelligence, the most moving concern for America itself." In the
Nation, Alan Trachtenberg, a leading critic of American culture, found
The Armies of the Night "a permanent contribution to our literature — a
unique testimony to literary responsiveness and responsibility."

Many critics appreciated the book as autobiography, combined innova-
tively with performance art. "Mr. Mailer's autobiography — in which we
hope 'The Steps of the Pentagon' is but a chapter — will constitute the
Confessions of the Last American," wrote Conor Cruise O'Brien in the
New York Review of Books. Richard Gilman, in the *New Republic,* recognized the book's achievement. The entire public was in Mailer's debt, he
declared, and considerations of whether he is the best writer, the best novelist, the best journalist, all fall away; in other words, Mailer's achievement in
participating, intervening, observing, and recording in a breathtaking new

way makes him more than a writer: he has at once entered, defined, and changed American culture.

It was a golden time for Norman. The good reviews kept coming, and other accolades followed. In December, *Time* magazine, his old nemesis, put him on the cover, running a profile by Raymond Sokolov. *The Armies of the Night* was nominated for a National Book Award and won in the category of arts and letters, the most prestigious of the awards. Norman was somewhat embarrassed, telling the *New York Times,* "There's something obscene about a middle-aged man who wins an award," a statement he retracted at the awards ceremony. In due time he received the Pulitzer, which led him, inevitably, to hope for the Nobel.

WHILE MAILER and his work were being celebrated, his friend Norman Podhoretz had recently finished a project of his own, an intellectual autobiography called *Making It,* to be published by Random House. The galleys — and an incipient scandal — arrived in Provincetown with Podhoretz and his wife in the fall of 1966. *Making It* tells the story of Podhoretz's rise from a poor Jewish background in Brooklyn to Columbia University, then to Cambridge, and finally to his position as editor of *Commentary.* The book's thesis was that success — power, fame, and money — had replaced sex as the "dirty little secret" of our time. Much of Podhoretz's story is charming, like his account of a high school teacher and mentor who had snobbish ambitions for her pupil. But a good deal of it turns on his relationship to "the family," Podhoretz's term for the New York intellectuals. He describes every member uncritically, even confessing that he had long dreamed of the day when he could call them by their first names — Diana, Dwight, Mary, Philip, et al. It was this aspect of the book that attracted the most attention and made the publication of *Making It* a sensation within the intellectual community. It was an airing of dirty laundry, and the community would not forgive Podhoretz easily.

Making It is a modest book that makes distinctly immodest claims. Podhoretz confesses at its close that he had long thought of writing a book about Norman Mailer and success but had decided not to hide behind another writer. Instead, he would simply produce "a frank, Mailer-like bid for literary distinction, fame, and money, all in one package." In closing, he writes, "I just have."

When the work was still in manuscript, friends who knew of it felt Podhoretz had stumbled. It was not that he had identified success as the new "dirty little secret" of American life — the phrase was originally D. H. Lawrence's and referred to sex — though reviewers would raise questions about his taste in doing so. The problem was, rather, that he had written about "the family," had named their names — indeed, had confessed his slavish admiration for their very names. Lionel and Diana Trilling, Philip Rahv, Daniel Bell, and others decidedly did not care to have their names vulgarly bruited about; it was a betrayal of what they stood for, or felt they stood for: an intellectual integrity that was free from undue personal ambition. Their objections were so strong that Roger Straus, the book's initial publisher, was forced to reject the book, though he had already advanced Podhoretz twenty-five thousand dollars.

At this point, Mailer seems to have tried to intervene in his friend's favor, arranging to review it for *Partisan Review*. At first he liked what he read in the galleys and told Podhoretz so. Podhoretz was weathering the trials of publication well, but he was pleased that Mailer — an honorary member of the family, or at least someone they listened to — was going to speak out on his behalf, especially in the pages of a family journal.

But four months later, as Podhoretz's magazine, *Commentary,* was running "The Battle of the Pentagon" in its spring 1968 issue, Podhoretz was appalled to read his friend's review of *Making It* in the galleys of the April *Partisan Review,* the "other" family journal. Titled "Up the Family Tree," Mailer's review began with an overview of critical responses to the book, not all of them negative. He discussed the writing in the book, some of which he liked very much. Then he stepped back and reviewed its publication history, enabling him to get to the meat of his essay: Podhoretz had been naive to believe the family would approve of such a book. Moreover, what Podhoretz misunderstood was the family's attitude toward success — though Mailer's better, if somewhat grand, term for them was the Establishment, or the Quality Lucifer Lit Biz Clan.

The Establishment, he said, had begun "as a put-on," a bunch of timid souls with earnest opinions about art and culture, who found themselves taken as authorities. Once established as authorities, however, they took themselves and their position with deadly seriousness. Now, in the sixties, they saw a great gulf opening between themselves and the rest of America, particularly between themselves and new youthful literary pretenders and the youth culture in general; they saw frightening forces massing on a distant shore. Although accustomed to roughing up one another, they were not amused to find betrayal in their ranks.

Mailer's review managed at once to defend the other Norman and to undermine him, calling into question the continued existence of the family that spawned him. It's irrelevant that the intellectuals may have influenced Mailer to "change his mind" (as Podhoretz remembers it) about *Making It;* the point, for Mailer, was not about the book or the other Norman, but the very existence of the Establishment.

Of course, a lot of other things went into Mailer's review of *Making It*. Podhoretz, though still against the Vietnam War, was beginning his slow drift rightward; as he now maintains, the break between him and Mailer would have happened anyway. Mailer, however, was being disingenuous in slighting Podhoretz's premise in the book, that success had replaced sex as the object of desire: Podhoretz had, after all, used Mailer's career as a bouncing-off point for his thoughts on success; like Podhoretz, Mailer was a Jewish boy from Brooklyn by way of the Ivy League who had won the trappings of success — celebrity, money, and widespread influence. In this sense, Mailer's review was a rebuke to Podhoretz for putting himself in the same category as Mailer — another, obviously more successful, writer. More meaningfully, the review was a rebuke — indeed, a thundering denunciation — of the whole lot of them, Podhoretz and his "family," whose success Mailer considered to be just so much ash in a world in a state of grim moral emergency. At the moment that Mailer was achieving such acclaim for *Armies* and its follow-up, *Miami and the Siege of Chicago*, he evidently cared little about material success or the kind of moral success the family prized. Rather, his political identity was in the ascendancy, and he cared most about the concrete effect of his actions and words.

At the same time, the whole brouhaha may have referred to something pettier, as Mailer indicated to biographer Peter Manso in 1985. Podhoretz had given a dinner party for Jacqueline Kennedy Onassis in 1969, and she accepted on the condition that Mailer not be invited. Podhoretz had not only caved in but added insult to injury by inviting Bill Styron ("then my dire rival," wrote Norman) to the party.

Of course, he was being facetious in tracing his quarrel with Podhoretz to a social slight. But it's hard to believe, with all these not-so-distant echoes of thunder and with Mailer's review of Podhoretz's raison d'être appearing in the same season, in another Establishment magazine, as his blistering piece on the March on the Pentagon in Podhoretz's own journal, that a power struggle of some sort was not going on here. With Norman P. attempting to claim pride of place with the family, Norman M. had to set him straight about who the family's real darling was, while undermining the whole idea of the family. In this high-flown version of a Brooklyn street fight, Mailer set his principles aside.

THE SUMMER OF 1968 opened with the assassination of Robert Kennedy on June 5 and ended with the Democratic presidential convention in Chicago at the end of August, the so-called siege of Chicago. Yet Mailer's attentions were elsewhere; he was making a movie, *Maidstone*, his most ambitious filmmaking attempt to date. It would be a near disaster.

Convinced that the reason for the failure of *Wild 90* and *Beyond the Law* to reach wide audiences was lack of funds, Norman decided to pour as much cash as he could into this new venture. To this end, he arranged to sell a part of his stake in the *Village Voice,* which netted him about a hundred thousand dollars. He wanted his film to be in color and feature-length, and he once again hired Donn Pennebaker, Ricky Leacock, Nick Proferes, and others to do the camera work. He would produce (with Buzz Farbar, as "Supreme Mix"), direct, and star. It was strictly a Norman Mailer production. Indeed, the film would be shot without a script, with a mix of professional and amateur actors; Norman's role would be more that of a host giving a very large party.

Maidstone was conceived, Norman later said, in the days following the assassination of Bobby Kennedy, an event that left him, like many others, feeling rudderless. Following the assassination of Martin Luther King, Jr., that April, it seemed the country was in dire straits. Norman's response to this tragic confluence of events was, curiously, to imagine a film about a movie director, Norman T. Kingsley, contemplating a run for president. According to the film's premise, Kingsley has a half-brother, Raoul Rey O'Houlihan (played by Rip Torn), who may or may not be planning an assassination attempt on Kingsley. Aiding O'Houlihan — or perhaps Kingsley — was the Cash Box, a loose band of comrades, a sort of Praetorian Guard, modeled on, and in some cases played by, members of Norman's coterie, with Raoul Rey as its ringleader. Some of the action would take place in a male brothel, and there would be a large party scene, later called the Assassination Ball, at which, Norman let on, an attempt would be made on Kingsley's life. Norman had no idea how the film would end.

The experience was, in the words of poet and participant Michael McClure, "some kind of psychotic pigout." Nobody involved has any good memories of the filming, though some participants would later praise the film itself. The filming, Norman's version of a sixties happening, took place over five days in mid-July on the grounds of five different estates in the Hamptons: the fantastical mansion shared by artist and art collector Alphonso Ossorio and his lover, Ted Dragon; the grounds, and especially the bathhouse, of Grove Press publisher Barney Rosset; the home of Robert David Lyon Gardiner, who played the head of an intelligence group; the grounds of Gardiner's Island; and a Tudor mansion owned by tax accountant David Brockman and his wife. Indoor and outdoor swimming pools were deployed, and vast quantities of liquor were supplied. More informally, marijuana was brought in.

Three of Norman's wives — Beverly, Jeanne Campbell, and Adele — were on hand, with their children; also on the premises was Norman's longtime girlfriend, nightclub singer Carol Stevens, who would star in a so-called blue loop filmed at Barney Rosset's bathhouse. Buzz Farbar, wearing a white suit, played the producer; also appearing were Mailer cronies Eddie Bonetti, Harold Conrad, Mailer's official biographer Robert Lucid,

Peter Rosoff and his wife, Bianca, Leo Garen (the director of *The Deer Park*), Warhol star Ultra Violet (who would be filmed having sex with a black man), longtime friend Adeline Naiman, and José Torres. Journalists were there in force, James Toback writing for *Esquire* and Sally Beauman for *New York*.

Over the course of the filming a number of disgusted or frightened "cast members" and filmmakers dropped out. Tom Quinn, an ex-boxer and stockbroker, took off with his upset and pregnant wife (she'd been knocked down by an aggrieved townie). By the second day, Michael McClure wanted no more filmmaking, though he hung around to drink. The last day of shooting was to be at Gardiner's Island, where Norman would wrap up the film with a talk to his cast and Pennebaker and Proferes would shoot a little film — home movies of the children, they thought. Rosset and McClure refused to go.

By this time Rip Torn, one of the few professional actors, felt let down and insulted by the amateurish filming. There had been no real action, only hints of a conspiracy; a climactic "Assassination Ball" had failed to produce a spontaneous dramatic resolution. The film was a monument to ego, Norman's ego. The glorious grounds, the magnificent dunes, the weather, the beautiful women, the near-famous actors, all that food and drink — and expensive color film — all were going to waste. Torn decided to provide the needed denouement.

As Norman was strolling through a meadow on Gardiner's Island with Beverly, his children nearby, Rip went for him with a hammer, shouting that he must assassinate Norman T. Kingsley. Norman Mailer turned on him and in the ensuing scuffle bit off a piece of Torn's ear. A macho exchange followed, with Norman, blood running down his face, telling Rip he was going to cut the scene out of the film — as Pennebaker's cameras took it all in. Torn, his ear badly swollen, insisted he had made the "attempt" in order to save the film; according to the film's logic, his character, Raoul Rey O'Houlihan, had to attempt to assassinate Kingsley. The scene was, in the end, grotesquely comic, with Rip/Rey shouting, "You're supposed to die, Mr. Kingsley. You must die — not Mailer, I don't want to kill Mailer, but I must kill Kingsley in the picture," and Norman, all hurt pride, countering with "I'm taking the scene out of the movie."

As it turned out, Torn was right, though Norman wouldn't come to see this for nearly a year. Writing after the film was recut to include the attack, Norman characterized the exchange as "a fight to give him a whole new conception of the movie." Pennebaker agrees: "[The film] was just going nowhere until the thing with Rip happened. Norman underestimated Rip." Pennebaker got to know Torn well later, and the actor explained to him that he "saw a bullshit film and wanted to fix it." Torn chose a hammer because it was "the best way to fake killing someone and not hurt them or look wrong. A gun that shoots blanks doesn't work; a knife is too dangerous."

Some sort of final scene was certainly needed to give some cohesiveness to *Maidstone*. But even a year of editing couldn't mask the film's flaws, the most prominent of them the repellent character played by Mailer. Norman T. Kingsley is sexist and brusque, openly irritated with his cast, mean to his wife, and a bore. The film contains some beautiful scenes: the shots at Gardiner's Island are truly pastoral, and the theme music, with Carol Stevens singing an elusive little tune, very evocative; the opening, with the camera moving around the estate at dusk, musing over classical statuary lining the driveway, gets the film off to a promising start. Yet nobody liked the film while it was being shot — except perhaps Norman. Cameraman Nick Proferes remembers the gratuitous scene in which Ultra Violet makes love with a black man; the actor "obliged, but treated it as a job." The scene was emblematic of the movie as a whole: a supposedly festive scene belied a grim determination. Pennebaker was unimpressed by the bathhouse scene, especially the so-called blue scenes of Carol Stevens taking on all comers. "The whole old boy atmosphere turned me off," he said. Free love, in the movie, seemed an oxymoron; it was more like hard work. With so little real action, the players kicked back, indulging in pot and liquor and putting on disinterested little sexual performances. Norman obviously had in mind a Buñuelian sensuous excess, but the film radiates just excess: outlandish behavior, nastiness, paranoia, fatigue.

What really happened was simple: the only point of the film was Mailer's ego. What had Norman intended? He knew he wanted his film to be a spontaneous happening. He wanted his good friends and his family — and his mistress — to be in it, along with some well-known people, and as many beautiful women as possible. It needed to be shot in a beautiful area and in stately, opulent houses. Beyond that, he was in the dark. So he simply showcased his fantasies. He would be the director of a film, and in the film he would be a movie director and a presidential candidate.

Running for president was, of course, something Mailer had been doing for many, many years, as he had long ago observed in *Advertisements for Myself*. But the Norman T. Kingsley of the film has no discernible political views. Perhaps Mailer, fondly recalling the existential drama of the Pentagon march, hoped to recreate it. But he had no subject and no political content. Norman Kingsley the candidate had no mission; nor did Norman Mailer the filmmaker. Only ego remained.

AFTER THE FILMING of *Maidstone* was over, Norman began editing the film with Lana Jokel and Jan Welt. But before long he was flying off to Miami to cover the Republican Convention, and then, a few days later, to

Chicago to report on the Democratic Convention. Once again he was working for *Esquire* and on a very tight deadline; the pieces had to appear before the November election. This simple journalistic stricture, the deadline, was to play an important part in the essay that became "The Siege of Chicago."

The book in which this piece eventually appeared, *Miami and the Siege of Chicago,* is an interesting counterstatement on the Movement to his own *Armies of the Night.* What he saw at Miami surprised him: he found he didn't hate Richard Nixon as much as he had thought he would. The arrival of a baby elephant, a gift to Nixon from the people of Anaheim, California, put Norman in a good mood; the ceremony of the elephant's arrival — complete with handlers, photographers, and "Nixonettes" — and its kneeling trick seemed auspicious. "The air had been better than one might have thought. So it was a warning to one's perspective and proportion: the Nixon forces and the Nixon people were going to be in command of small subtleties he had not anticipated. It was his first clue to the notion that there was a new Nixon." In fact, he had to revise his old opinion of the man, which dated back to 1952 and the Checkers speech, because "in his previous conception of Richard Nixon there had been no room for a comeback."

But Mailer never found out whether there was a new Nixon. Indeed, he closed his piece, "Nixon in Miami," by saying that he couldn't decide whether he was ready to like or detest him. Speaking modestly of himself as "the reporter," Mailer wrote, "He had no idea at all if God was in the land or the Devil played the tune . . . He felt like an observer deprived of the privilege to witness or hold a chair." Finally, Norman did not *engage* with the convention, and his coverage of the Republicans falls short of his reporting on the 1968 Democrats.

Though Norman had known for some months that the Yippies were planning an action in Chicago during the convention, he was taken unawares when he flew into Chicago (which he called "the great American city") on August 24. The convention was to mark a personal watershed, as Norman grappled with the questions he had answered before in his actions at the Pentagon: was he an observer or a participant, or both? What was the price of participating? Of not participating?

As the police and, later, the National Guard bore down repeatedly on the youths gathered in Lincoln Park, lobbing tear gas grenades and stink bombs, Norman watched from his hotel room on the nineteenth floor. Later he busied himself by taking notes in the convention hall, worrying about McCarthy, interested in McGovern, intensely disliking Humphrey. Eventually he made his way to Lincoln Park, arriving after eleven at night, when the protesters had been ordered to leave. Accompanied by José Torres, who was covering the convention for *El Diario,* he vacillated about whether to leave. Since he didn't intend to stay, why not leave now? He was ultimately fortified by José's presence, somehow believing that Torres could "take out" several policemen if they harassed him.

This was only the first moment in which Norman was wracked by doubts. As he cogitated over New York journalist Murray Kempton's statement that "politics is property" — that everything is turf, everything negotiable — finding it strikingly true, he wrestled with other demons. He saw that "the Yippies might yet disrupt the land — or worse, since they would not really have the power to do that, might serve as a pretext to bring in totalitarian phalanxes of law and order." He found himself overcome by fear, a fear he identified as "conservative": he sensed Mayor Daley's enormous power in the city and the brutality of the police. He worried that he might get badly beaten if he participated in the action, which would deprive him of the chance to use every possible moment up until his deadline to write his report. He saw that he would have to make similar choices at many different moments in the coming years, that he could not conceivably choose the "dangerous alternative" every time. Finally, he wrote, he was afraid of losing "even the America he had, that insane warmongering technology land with its smog, its superhighways, its experts and its profound dishonesty. Yet, it had allowed him to write — it had not even deprived him entirely of honors, certainly not of an income." Reflecting on his age — forty-five — he asked, "Where was his true engagement?" He had even told Dave Dellinger that he would not speak, and Dellinger had understood. He had made himself very clear right from the start.

But he wound up speaking anyway, asking Dellinger if he could take the podium after Allen Ginsberg led a chant of "Om" and Burroughs and Genet spoke. He even explained his fears to the audience, and *they* understood, admonishing him to "write good, baby." He didn't go on the planned march to the Amphitheater, where the convention was held, but in an extraordinary moment later that night, he "had an impulse" to confront the National Guard troops surrounding Grant Park. Looking "like an inspecting officer," he walked past the troops, his face only a foot away from the soldiers', seeing them tense "agreeably" under his gaze. He then took a microphone from the young people and used it, first to address the troops (though he realized that these soldiers were in the Guard precisely because they did not want to fight in Vietnam) and then, turning 180 degrees, to address the protesters. He reviewed his fears, and the crowd assured him that to "do the writing" was the important thing. But he nonetheless announced a march that he would lead the following day, rounding up three hundred delegates to march with him from the park to the Amphitheater (a figure he lowered to two hundred on the advice of some delegates in the crowd).

Despite the bourbons he had consumed over the course of the evening, he was unable to sleep that night, and the result was a "total failure." He never got to talk to McCarthy or McGovern, was frustrated by the absence of a secretary or a walkie-talkie or a functioning phone; he could not, as he wrote, "deliver the vote."

The march he promised never happened. After hearing speeches by Humphrey and Muskie the last night of the convention, as well as seeing a movie about Bobby Kennedy that the Daley people had supplied, Norman was still feeling responsibility for the protesting young people: "Perhaps he was too old for orgies on the green. Still, these white children were his troops." He had gone through some complicated thinking about blacks. In Miami, he had confessed to being tired of hearing about black people's problems. In Chicago, he recognized that it was a lot more complicated than that, concluding that if the white children were his troops, left-wing blacks were his "polemical associates." Unable to leave the subject alone, he remained profoundly confused about race.

On the last night of the convention, after drinking in a bar with friends, including Torres, Pete Hamill, journalist Douglas Kiker, Kennedy speechwriter Dick Goodwin, and Murray Kempton, Norman was in a strange mood. While they talked of such gambits as putting LSD in the city's water supply and burning money, or, more seriously, of building a multiparty political system, he had a staring match with a man he identified as a "petty Mafia" type at the next table, his magical thinking, under stress, coming to the fore. When the bar closed at 4:00 A.M., the others wanted to go to the Playboy Mansion. Instead, Norman, with Hamill and Kiker, took a last look at the phalanx of National Guardsmen on Michigan Avenue. Hamill and Kiker went along with Norman as he inspected the troops. He stopped before a Jeep fitted out with a tangle of barbed wire on its front bumper and hood. He began to take notes.

At last, the confrontation with authority — although not the cataclysm the whole ugly Chicago scene had led him to expect — was at hand. Three or four soldiers seized Norman as his drinking companions protested that he was a journalist. The soldiers took him before a policeman in the Hilton's lobby. The cop released him with a warning. But another fracas arose in the hotel lobby, with a delegate who called the protesters "cocksuckers." The delegate punched Norman, there was a scuffle, and Norman found himself again before the same cop, Tom Lyons. This time a phone call from friends upstairs established Norman's identity, and Lyons, who recognized his name, again let him off. After his own "curious double-bust," he went on with Hamill and Kiker to the Playboy Mansion.

Norman's conclusion about the whole affair, while writing his piece, was that he would not vote — unless it was for Eldridge Cleaver, the Black

Panthers leader: "Eldridge at least was there to know that the barricades were building across the street from the camps of barbed wire where the conscience of the world might yet be canned. Poor all of us. The fat is in the fire, and the corn is being popped." Norman saw the extremism of the Black Panthers as a legitimate response to contemporary events, though he hoped that domestic peace would prevail.

Miami and the Siege of Chicago, the book documenting the Republican and Democratic conventions, appeared in November 1968. Many critics thoroughly misunderstood it, believing Norman had recorded his ambivalence about the Movement but "[did] not seek any resolution." Conservative critics hailed it. Writing in *Commentary,* Peter Shaw described it as "a far more thoughtful book than [his] last, [*The Armies of the Night*]." These critics felt that Mailer had given Nixon the benefit of the doubt, and were cheered that he did not wholeheartedly endorse the Chicago protesters. Misreading his ambivalence toward the protesters as a new maturity, they claimed him for the conservative cause.

Wilfrid Sheed, in the *New York Times Book Review,* was one of the few who saw what Mailer was up to: "[Mailer] was out there by himself, without his name or his reputation or last year's ideas, feeling what was out there to be felt, willing to make himself a blood offering to the New Left or anyone else, in order to bring back the evidence." Whatever the critics concluded, it was a surprise to none of them when the book was nominated for the National Book Award in the category of biography and history; 1968 was Mailer's year for awards.

Sheed was right to have concentrated on Mailer's role in covering the events at Chicago in 1968. In fact, it is difficult to understand how conservative critics could have liked the book. Norman's reportage describes a grim passion play, with the protesters arrayed against a frightening force: Chicago cops and the National Guardsmen brought in to help them. Compared with the MPs in the March on the Pentagon, these authority figures were often menacing; many visibly enjoyed wielding power over the protesters. They were backed, moreover, by Mayor Daley and his machine, which Mailer presents as somewhat fascistic. While ambivalent about his own involvement with the protest, Mailer highlights the sinister quality of these authorities.

Miami and the Siege of Chicago can be seen as a kind of bookend to *The Armies of the Night,* with Norman's filming of *Maidstone* sandwiched in between. The earlier book takes the pulse of the sixties and pronounces the moment of the March on the Pentagon a defining one. *Maidstone* represents the worst of the sixties: excess, drug use, meaningless and grim sexual couplings, waste of resources, chaos and confusion. Though Norman had hoped for a great, memorable happening on film, things simply got out of hand, and it was largely his fault.

The months bracketed by *The Armies of the Night* and *Miami and the Siege of Chicago* were among the most turbulent of the always turbulent sixties. April had begun with the assassination of Martin Luther King, Jr., followed by anguished riots in over a hundred cities; it ended with the student uprising that closed Columbia University for two months. Then came the May days of the student revolt in Paris, leading to a series of strikes paralyzing France for several weeks. June began with Robert Kennedy's murder; August would end with the chaos in Chicago's streets.

Miami and the Siege of Chicago shows Mailer taking a more sober view of the decade and the Movement. He thought his participation in the Chicago action of dubious value, but it turned out he was wrong. So he participated anyway — but to no real effect. He remained sympathetic to the Movement, even more convinced of its necessity, but he had seen the forces against it — from Nixon to Mayor Daley and the police. He realized that a bloody battle might well lie ahead, and that 1968 had been, indeed, a near-apocalyptic year.

THE CANDIDATE

The last year of the decade opened auspiciously for Norman. Formal ceremonies awarding him the National Book Award and the Pulitzer Prize took place in March; at the National Book Award event, his citation noted that *Armies of the Night* was "something of an American epic." A few months before, in reviewing *Miami and the Siege of Chicago,* his old nemesis, *Time,* had remarked how in synch with the times the writer was: "Mailer — Eastern seaboard exotic, alienated artist, New York practitioner of improvisational cinema — is strangely in touch with heartland America . . . His own surprisingly shifting views of civil rights and Negroes, of WASPs and Nixon, seem to reflect the national mood."

Norman would have applauded that statement. Certainly he never felt more in tune with his times than in early 1969. He had spent the sixties examining, anatomizing, and to a certain extent participating in American politics. With his filmmaking, his brief forays into architectural criticism, and his interest in the counterculture, he had situated himself in the middle of the major cultural currents of the decade. It was not altogether surprising that he should begin to think about running for elective office again. The relative success of the presidential run of Eugene McCarthy, a Washington outsider, may have suggested to him that the time was right for a candidate like himself. On the West Coast, Timothy Leary was mounting a campaign for governor of California; this encouraged Mailer to believe he could succeed on the East Coast.

His earliest thoughts in this direction, however, were checked by memories of his disastrous run for mayor almost a decade before. Then too he had felt himself in tune with the Zeitgeist, in the forefront of Hip. In fact, the difference between 1960 and 1969, for Mailer, was that in 1960 he had been in the grip of paranoia and perhaps mental derangement, his mayoral bid a reflection of just how outsized and wrong his vision was. His marriage was turning ugly; he was drinking heavily and using drugs, and yet he felt that New York voters would throw themselves behind his candidacy. In short, in 1960 he was close to crazy.

In 1969 he was, on balance, not.

MAILER'S SECOND mayoral bid is best considered as a major statement, the culmination of over a decade of observing, reporting on, and participating in American politics. The positions he took and the speeches he made can thus be read as his treatise on government, both as it was and as it could be. Ever the individualist, Mailer wanted not to sign on with anyone else's political movement but rather to start his own. And instead of writing a book about how things could be changed, he took a more existentialist route, choosing to act — to run for office.

Not that his candidacy began that simply. The idea of running Norman Mailer for mayor first surfaced at the end of winter, after the disastrous snowstorms that made the possibility of upsetting Mayor John Lindsay a real one, when a party was held at Mailer's apartment to discuss the possibility of the candidacy of Herman Badillo, the young Bronx borough president, who was emerging as a liberal favorite. Those present included Jason and Barbara Epstein, Bob Silvers, George Plimpton, McCarthy campaign veteran Michael C. D. Macdonald, and two representatives from either side of the recent United Federation of Teachers strike, Michael Harrington and Norman Podhoretz, as well as two representatives from the newly formed and already influential *New York* magazine, editor Clay Felker and columnist Gloria Steinem. They weren't able to muster much enthusiasm, however, for the professionally comported Badillo; Macdonald, driving back to Manhattan with Felker and Steinem, heard them dismiss Badillo as lacking in charisma.

In the wake of this meeting, according to Joe Flaherty, a longshoreman-turned-journalist who would become Mailer's campaign manager, the real impetus for a Mailer candidacy came from two slightly surprising sources: on the one hand, Jack Newfield, a somewhat left-wing writer for the *Village Voice,* and on the other, Noel Parmentel, a conservative writer for the *National Review.* Mailer later characterized this alliance as the "Hitler/Stalin pact," but at the time he announced, "The hope is that a few sparks from the fires on the right and left will fly up and form this coalition." It was a question not so much of Mailer's agreeing to run as of forming a coalition of people who felt they could support — and win support for — a Mailer candidacy. On March 31 a summit meeting was held in the Mailer brownstone on Columbia Heights. In attendance were, among others, Flaherty, *New York* writers Steinem and Peter Maas, journalist Pete Hamill, Parmentel and Newfield, black lawyer Flo Kennedy, Jerry Rubin and his girlfriend, Mailer buddies José Torres and Buzz Farbar, and McCarthy campaign veterans Paul Gorman, John Scanlon, and Paul O'Dwyer. Jimmy Breslin, columnist and veteran New Yorker, perched on a stool in the back of the room; several of those present wanted him to run on the Mailer ticket, for president of the city council. Breslin was thought to have a feel for New York's white working class and the man in the street (or at the bar), and running an Irishman — especially one as aggressively Irish as Breslin — on the same ticket as a Jew was always a good bet in New York City.

After an hour or two of serious drinking, Norman asked those present for an opinion of his and Breslin's candidacies. Bedlam ensued, with some suggesting that Breslin should be dumped. Hamill thought a Mailer candidacy would be a betrayal of Herman Badillo. Flo Kennedy urged Norman to step aside so that U.S. representative Adam Clayton Powell could run, and Jerry Rubin wanted to run a Black Panther. It was moved that Gloria Steinem join the ticket as a candidate for comptroller, but she declined. Norman tried to quiet the crowd. "Camp and college-boy pranks are repulsive to me," he said, reminding listeners of the dire straits the city was in; New York was beset by air and noise pollution, inadequate transportation, an unwieldy welfare system, miserable conditions for the working poor, racial division, burgeoning crime, needless bureaucratic excesses, and devastatingly low morale — a kind of spiritual malaise. To the assembled supporters, Norman proposed a "hip coalition of left and right," which provoked more arguments and jokes, but the evening ended with an understanding that he and Breslin were going to run.

The next evening, a smaller and soberer group — fewer dissenters and more followers — convened at Norman's apartment and adjourned to Foffé's restaurant on Montague Street. Norman and Beverly, Newfield, Flaherty, Gorman, Torres, Jimmy Breslin and his wife, Rosemary, and Scanlon were joined by Joe Ferris, an Irish organizer from Park Slope, to discuss the field of candidates. The Democratic Party in the city was in a shambles, all agreed, controller Mario Procaccino a worse than useless contender. Liberal Bronx congressman James Scheuer was a threat, as was ex-mayor Robert F. Wagner.

Badillo they identified as the real competition, but in fact the Badillo camp saw it differently. Many of them felt that Lindsay and his supporters were encouraging a Mailer candidacy — even to the point of aiding him in his campaign — in order to siphon off liberal votes from Badillo. From Badillo's campaign, Michael Macdonald assembled a delegation consisting of his father, Dwight Macdonald, Norman Podhoretz, Michael Harrington, and Irving Howe, to cross the East River and "reason with Achilles in his tent." But no such delegation ever approached Norman, and he indeed drew off votes, volunteers, press, and financial backing from Badillo, who appeared to be the more conventional of the two candidates. In fact, according to Macdonald, Lindsay campaigners Arnold Segarra and Geoffrey Stokes helped the comparative amateurs in the Mailer camp collect valid petition signatures correctly — an involved and intricate process. Without them, says Macdonald, Mailer would never have made the ballot — and his presence there was much desired by the Lindsay people.

At the meeting at Foffé's, Norman listened most closely to Ferris, whose ideas about neighborhood control he found intriguing. Why not give power to individual neighborhoods, and let them determine their own character and their own policies? Why not declare Malcolm X Day in the Bronx? he wondered. Or John Birch Day in Staten Island?

This was clearly not going to be politics as usual. As it evolved, the Mailer-Breslin platform would rest on several key issues. The first, and the most controversial, was a proposal that the city seek statehood. The way Norman and his aides figured it, this was "not an option but a necessity" if the city's ills were to be cured. As Norman wrote in a *New York Times Magazine* piece that would appear in mid-May, "New York City is today a legislative pail of dismembered organs strewn from Washington to Albany. We are without a comprehensive function or a skin. We cannot begin until we find a function which will become our skin. It is simple: Our city must become a state." The city-state, in Mailer's plan, would become eligible for federal funds directly, sparing both the federal and state administrations time and money. The potential benefits to the city-state were enormous.

The new state's charter could rewrite the means by which neighborhoods constituted themselves: townships, hamlets, sub-boroughs, even small cities could form themselves out of the old city, each funded directly and each running its own municipal services and even schools. The fifty-first-state plan led Mailer to some of his more imaginative, even utopian proposals. It was not fully grounded in reality: the mechanisms for seeking statehood were complicated, and success was not guaranteed. Also, the ticket overlooked or chose not to see the financial shakiness of the proposal (what bank would float a bond for the new city-state?). But the idea of statehood for the city suggests the imaginative force of the Mailer-Breslin candidacy.

Other proposals followed this one naturally. Some were good, some not; many have surfaced again in the years that followed 1969. The banning of private automobiles in Manhattan, for example, was a new, somewhat crackpot idea when Mailer proposed it, but it has come up again and again as the city's traffic problems and their effect on the quality of life continue to concern New Yorkers. Similarly, the Mailer-Breslin ticket's pledges to legalize gambling, provide free bicycles in city parks, control pollution, institute day care centers and nurseries, rebuild dilapidated waterfront areas, provide methadone to addicts, and encourage police to live in the areas in which they work were remarkably prescient, reflecting the cutting edge of urban and social planning in the decades to come. Some were more fanciful but unlikely to hurt anyone seriously: to build "Vegas East" at Coney Island, hold a yearly Grand Prix in Central Park, have a central-city farmers' market with ethnic foods for sale, build a zoo in every neighborhood, return national baseball teams to Brooklyn and Manhattan, grow ivy on housing projects (was Norman picturing Harvard Yard?), provide craftsmanship training in gardening, and use stained glass windows in public buildings and parks. One of the ticket's more innovative and controversial proposals was dubbed "Sweet Sunday" — one Sunday a month when all traffic, including incoming and outgoing ships and airplanes, was to be banned and all power, except generators in hospitals, shut off. Norman did acknowledge that "on the first hot day," when they found themselves without air conditioning, "the populace would impeach me."

This was the kind of platform Norman had called for during the Kennedy administration: an existential politics, as it were, with a touch of the Yippie. He had called on Kennedy, for example, to create an Adventurers' Corps along with the Peace Corps to curb juvenile delinquency: the young could joust in Central Park, form an amateur army, fight alligators in the Everglades, or ski the snowfields of the West. Everyone, even street hoodlums, has an urge to act, even must act, he reasoned, and society should provide people with a means to do so. This distinctly Mailerian thinking informed his own campaign at the end of the decade.

The worst possible course for a politician, as Norman saw it at the outset of his campaign, was to follow business as usual; the best, to introduce imaginative measures that would allow citizens to act and express themselves fully. From such beliefs Norman's campaign derived. In tying his ideas together for an intrigued but puzzled press, Norman described himself as a "left conservative," representing, as he had said, a Hip coalition of the left and right that would combine liberal measures with a sprinkling of what would later be termed libertarian proposals. He seems to have meant simply that certain ideals held by the left — a belief in government as a benign democratic institution and in the necessity and value of social services — were more meaningful when understood in the light of certain ideals praised by the right — individualism, for example. According to Norman and his aides, liberalism was too often responsible for the sterility and totalitarianism of the social bureaucracy, as symbolized by Norman's longtime bugaboo, the public housing project. In practical terms, this meant Norman was running as a candidate of neither the left wing nor the right wing; rather, he could appeal to voters of either inclination, or those whose instincts placed them somewhere in between.

This can be illustrated by one of his platform's key issues: power to the neighborhoods. To those on the left, this might echo the radical slogan "Power to the people," implying the grassroots progressivism that had come to characterize thinking about social problems in the last decade. To more conservative voters — such as future policemen at the John Jay College of Criminal Justice, whom Mailer and Breslin addressed early in the campaign — Mailer insisted on the fundamental conservatism of the issue, saying, "You conservatives are right about one terribly important matter: that a man has the right to control over his own life." A city run by Albany and Washington, he argued, is one in which the individual sacrifices this goal; if power were returned to the neighborhoods, self-determination might again rule. Nominally a Democrat, Norman would stand out — so went his logic — in a field of party candidates of both liberal and conservative stripes.

But the main problem with this highly original campaign was its style. Both Mailer and Breslin were great personalities, capable of drawing and engaging audiences. But they were also individualistic, even eccentric men with a sense of irony and a sense of humor. Their personae threatened to obscure their message. Emblematic of this problem was their first and only mention in the *New York Times*'s editorial column. The two-paragraph item mentioned Mailer's stand on parks, punning on the title of his book *The Deer Park,* made a sly reference to Breslin's taking a stand on a beer keg, and finally gave the candidates some backhanded praise that suggested the lack of seriousness with which journalists took the whole endeavor: "At least the novelist and ex-columnist honestly tell their college audiences, 'I'm no good and I can prove it!' They may be curious, but not yellow. We hope their campaign rhetoric continues to be more naked than dead."

The campaign was built on frankness; Mailer and Breslin's slogan was "No more bullshit." Naturally, it could not be quoted in family newspapers or uttered on TV; a button bearing the slogan would bar the wearer — whether candidate or supporter — from being photographed. This aspect of the campaign rendered it almost a joke. The single most common response to the idea of a Mailer-Breslin candidacy was, in fact, that it must be a joke. These candidates couldn't be serious. Of course, they were, but they were unable to convince the voters. As the campaign wore on, this became a substantive issue. In a May 6 press conference, Norman said, "I think I've finally become a serious man, and I submit to you that in your heart of hearts you know that nobody like Breslin or myself could run unless we were serious. I will say that anybody who thinks we're running in fun has got a perverted notion of fun."

After the Brooklyn Heights meetings, Norman retired to Provincetown for two weeks to think over his candidacy. In his absence, Flaherty and the others ran a full-page ad in the *Voice* asking for donations and volunteers. Scores responded. As one volunteer said, "Their platform made real sense. This was a new kind of thinking — not liberal, not conservative, but some of both. Mailer and Breslin promised something new."

On another front, Gloria Steinem tried to drum up support among the Upper East Side crowd. Both efforts were encouraging — though attempts like Steinem's to raise funds among the wealthy would never be very successful — and when Wagner declared his candidacy, Flaherty called Mailer on the Cape and urged him to come back and declare. Steinem found office space for the campaign at 989 Eighth Avenue, on Columbus Circle, the former site of the McCarthy-for-president headquarters. On April 15, a rested Norman began a grueling round of speeches before Democratic clubs and at universities to test the waters, and Breslin joined him on the campaign trail on April 22.

Troubles abounded, even in the early days of the campaign. Breslin, uncomfortable with being in the public eye, threatened to withdraw. Media coverage was inadequate at best when not frankly derisive; on May 6, when holding a press conference, ostensibly on having won the Pulitzer Prize, Norman took the occasion to blast the press. As Flaherty pointed out later, the conservative *Daily News* took the candidacy as a huge joke, while the *Times* (apart from its derisive editorial) and the *Post* took it more seriously, warning that Mailer and Breslin could split the liberal vote, clearing the way for a conservative candidate to win.

Norman was particularly offended by a column by former *Post* editor James Wechsler, headlined "An Odd Couple," partly because, as Flaherty remembered it, he didn't like the association with the 1968 Lemmon-Matthau film comedy, taking it as an assault on his manhood. But Wechsler's point also hit home: he couldn't believe Norman was taking himself so seriously. He described the candidate's recent appearance on the *Tonight Show*: "Mailer took the stage. But this was not the Mailer of local folklore, garrulous, disheveled, rambling, and profane. This was The Candidate, his demeanor sedately and sedatively reminiscent of Robert F. Wagner . . . His voice had the ancient sound of a cautious politico awaiting the results of a secret Lou Harris poll." It seemed that the candidate was damned if he did and damned if he didn't.

Other problems dogged the campaign. One trait of Norman's in particular got in the way: his penchant for surrounding himself with hard-core street types: angry young men, usually black, often street or club fighters. In his memoir *Managing Mailer*, Flaherty would characterize them as "young, obscene, brazenly sexual, laced with physical daring," and added, "If someone had been part of an experience foreign to his own (being Black, a convict, a prizefighter), Mailer found in him occult powers bestowed only on the children of the gutters . . . This enchantment had to do with Mailer's high sense of intrigue and his romantic notion of the streets."

At the disastrous party to launch his first mayoral bid nine years earlier, Norman had invited all sorts of street people who frightened his other guests and contributed to the general paranoia of the evening. His thinking this time was decidedly less feverish, but he still believed the disenfranchised were an integral part of his constituency and that they injected vigor into his campaign. The problem was that these outsiders had little to contribute to a serious campaign beyond lending it a mood of anarchic menace. Then, too, many questioned the way Norman surrounded himself with his admirers and friends, most of them inactive in the campaign, some of them simply clueless when it came to politics.

It seemed the candidate was leading a kind of double life: on the one hand, he was deadly serious and "on" throughout his sixteen-hour days (during what he called "the hottest May and June he could ever recall") and genuinely enjoyed getting in touch with the people. This did not square with the popular image of him as a talkative and profane brawler, which bothered critics like Wechsler. On the other hand, his irrepressible bad boy side threatened to assert itself. He drank steadily and heavily throughout the campaign, as did most of his advisers, and drinking brought out his combative, often nasty side. Though he seldom showed this facet of himself to potential voters, campaign insiders saw it daily, sometimes with disastrous results.

On May 7, Norman was scheduled to hold a fundraiser at the Village Gate. The volunteers had the evening off to attend; for many, this would be the first time they met their candidate. Rock and roll pulsated through the nightclub as 11:00 P.M. neared, when Norman was scheduled to speak. Flaherty noted with dismay that the volunteers had been herded to tables on the fringe and served no drinks, while Norman, Beverly, Farbar, Norman's Provincetown friend Bill Walker, and Parmentel were drinking convivially at a ringside table. Newfield, Breslin, and Flaherty spoke, and then the event was disrupted by a black woman who appeared on stage, visibly drunk, rambling about the small number of blacks in the room and a personal grievance against an employer. At this, Norman mounted the stage and talked her off, addressing her and the audience, saying, "Now let me talk, because it's my evening, and you know it." Flaherty noted a stunning transformation as the candidate began his speech: he "performed a Stanislavskian miracle — he grew fat and sweaty before our eyes! He also launched into his much-heralded Southern accent."

After some rambling introductory comments, punctuated by shouts of "Fuck you" to hecklers, Norman got to his point: "Now look, look, let's be sensible for a while. You're just nothing but a bunch of spoiled pigs . . .

You've been sitting around jerkin' off, havin' your jokes . . . Yeah! And more than that — more than that. You all want to work for us? You get in there, and you do your discipline, and you do your devotion . . . Don't come in there and help us because 'we're gonna give Norm a little help.' Fuck you!"

Many volunteers listened to the abuse in shock and horror, while others shouted "Fuck you" right back. Some attempted to steer Mailer back on course, shouting, "Norman, talk about the fifty-first state, you're among friends," to which Mailer responded, "Hey, I'll tell you something. Shut up. You're not my friend if you interrupt me when I'm talking 'cause it just breaks into the mood in my mind. So fuck you, too."

Though he did eventually run through the themes of the campaign, he punctuated his words with abusive taunts to hecklers and challenges to the campaign workers to "get over your silly little ego-tired trips." He ended strongly if cryptically, asserting that the "profound notion" on which he was running was "Free Huey Newton, end fluoridation." In closing, he said, "What we are running on is one basic, simple notion — which is that till people see where their ideas lead they know nothing; and that, my fine friends, is why I am running. I want to see where my own ideas lead."

"The next day everything was coming apart at the seams," commented Flaherty. "The kids walked around headquarters dazed, looking like they had been slapped in the face." "I walked out of the Gate just crushed, absolutely crushed. The guy's a maniac, I thought," said volunteer Dave Oates. The campaign faltered at this point and never really recovered. The candidates and staffers hoped the press had overlooked the event, but Sidney Zion reported it in the *New York Times* the next day.

Norman blamed the Zion article for the damage, evading admission of his own responsibility. The candidate also had some odd ideas about campaign politics. He believed that his name and reputation as an eminent writer spoke for themselves, but in reality the average New Yorker either knew about such things only vaguely or was not impressed. A poll in mid-May revealed that 60 percent of canvassed voters had never heard of Norman Mailer. In an appearance at Aqueduct racetrack, Norman circulated a tout sheet giving the odds on the candidates (he modestly gave himself odds of twenty to one). A reporter noted that his hair was disheveled and that Breslin was wearing a shocking pink shirt with a florid tie. Two old men looked on. One said, "What's his name?" and the other replied, "Norman Miller." The event was an emblematic epilogue to the debacle at the Village Gate.

Yet Norman was earnest about the race and really believed he could win. Those around him saw this as a problem; they believed that his bid should be symbolic, that he could breathe some fresh air into the Democratic Party and the left. Instead of doggedly campaigning for an impossible victory, they thought, Norman should be making brilliant speeches, courting the press, throwing out ideas. They were surprised and dismayed by the serious, sober-sided candidate as much as they were horrified by the Mailer of the Village Gate. A *New York Times* reporter commented on his "relentless — almost inexhaustible — energy," noting that it "surprises his supporters and possibly even the candidate."

Some events in his writing life intruded in May, when Mailer signed a contract with *Life* and Little, Brown to write about the Apollo 11 moon shot, scheduled for that July. Scott Meredith announced the deal to the press in mid-May, and somewhere in the exchange the figure became inflated to $1 million. The *Post* even claimed he might receive as much as $1.5 million. Mailer quickly denied the story, asserting that he would in fact receive much less than the quoted figures, in the neighborhood of $450,000. But the damage was done. The press rode the issue hard, creating the impression that Mailer was now rich, which in turn may have influenced would-be donors. The public may have reacted as well, as many voters might have been reluctant to vote for a millionaire or a candidate with other preoccupations. Again Norman denied there was a problem, asserting, "I'm devoting all my time to my candidacy for mayor. The only writing I'm doing at this time has to do with the campaign." But a hint of doubt was planted. Despite the hours he was logging on the campaign trail, how serious was Mailer? Was he a writer first or a politician? These were valid questions, and their presence was a serious handicap to Mailer's candidacy.

Norman lost one of his first supporters early on, when Gloria Steinem defected, largely because she wanted to devote her time to Cesar Chavez's farm workers' movement. But Norman had already jeopardized his friendship with her by insistently hitting on her — so aggressively that she eventually gave in and went to bed with him. "Their attempt was unsuccessful," according to Steinem biographer Sydney Stern. "The thing was," Steinem told Stern, "he was so focused on it, it mattered so much to him. And he's so vulnerable, in a weird way. And we were working together all the time, and I think some part of me thought it would make the tension go away." It had the opposite effect, however, and Norman found himself without Steinem's services as an organizer and fundraiser.

In fact, Norman was beginning to feel besieged. Further tensions surfaced among his aides, with the result that his camp was split in two by the time of the primary. Norman surrounded himself with three men who stayed by his side at the Brooklyn Heights apartment — he almost never appeared at the Columbus Circle headquarters anymore. Peter Manso was an English professor at Rutgers and a longtime Provincetown friend who was writing a book about Norman; as short as the candidate, over the course of the campaign Manso came to mimic him physically. Bill Walker, another Provincetowner, and Luke Breit, a poet and the son of the writer Harvey Breit, rounded out the trio. The divide began when Norman demanded "loyalty" from his staff — and defined it as the men's willingness to cut their hair and shave their beards. Advance man Jack Banning, a radio announcer and former State Department employee, shaved his beard and mustache, and Norman held him up as the paragon of loyalty; he named him co-campaign manager, telling the still-bearded Flaherty that he was to stay invisible for the rest of the campaign. (The loyalty issue backfired with Banning, as he was disgusted to find himself held up as an exemplar and tried to distance himself from the candidate.) The two sides couldn't even talk to each other; when Flaherty and others phoned the Brooklyn Heights apartment, Bill Walker would tell them that Norman was asleep.

Of course, loyalty really was an issue, for Norman began to feel cornered and beaten toward the end of the race, and mild paranoia had set in. Though seemingly ridiculous, the demand about beards and long hair also was about a real issue: Norman did not want to be seen as surrounded by hippies. Staff cars were too often embellished with psychedelic symbols and hand-lettered signs. But the tone Norman and his inner circle took toward this issue seems exaggerated: he took to growling about the "fucking beards and leftists" among his staff.

In spite of these setbacks, Mailer and Breslin soldiered on into June. They spoke at St. John's University in Queens (where Mailer took a back seat to Breslin, who knew the audience better), Columbia University, New York University (where both men were hung over), Brooklyn College, and Sarah Lawrence College (where they sought volunteers, not voters, given the school's Westchester location, and where both ran afoul of feminists for using condescending endearments). They made appearances at street rallies, block festivals, and sporting events; they rode the Staten Island ferry and campaigned at subway stops; they made appearances at Upper East Side fundraisers (Mailer more often than Breslin). Toward the end of the campaign Mailer made a whirlwind tour of Jewish centers and temples in Queens and the Bronx, though he was not an automatic success with the Jewish audience — too many wives, too much involvement with non-Jewish activities, and his insistence on neighborhood control. All this was at odds with Jewish support for Albert Shanker and the United Federation of Teachers. Each ran into trouble at unlikely places: Breslin at a Gaelic Park curling match in the Bronx, where he ran into a pocket of Irish-bashing Irishmen, Mailer at a Greenwich Village Neighbors for Peace meeting, where a group called the Crazies stormed the podium with Vietcong flags, shouting that liberals like Mailer were responsible for Richard Nixon. Flaherty observed that a division of labor between the two came about naturally: "There was a subtle class distinction: Jimmy would handle the cops and crooks; Norman, being too well bred and too well educated to know about such things, would combat the cosmos."

Norman genuinely connected with many of his audiences, and Breslin helped a great deal, reaching out to the working-class and white ethnic communities, leavening the campaign with his beery, down-to-earth presence. Norman hammered away at one major point: the decline of New York City. He asserted that the city's problems were not economic or political but spiritual. In one amusing and telling incident, he revealed to campaign staff his dismay over the city's decline: standing atop a clocktower at Queens College, surveying the infamous sprawl of homogeneous Queens, he asked wonderingly, under his breath, "Who did this?"

He made a truly impressive appearance on June 3, speaking to the staff of *Time* and *Life* magazines. Perhaps because he had entered what was enemy territory to him, the Luce camp, he spoke with exceptional force and integrity. He outlined clearly the central tenets of his campaign — statehood and neighborhood control — and then closed ambitiously, trying to situate his campaign metaphysically. His closing words:

> The notion that we're running on, then, is that until we begin to know a little more about each other — not through the old-fashioned New Deal governmental methods of tolerance — but through the quality of human experience in societies, small societies and somewhat larger societies founded upon various principles — philosophical, spiritual, economic, geographical, territorial, historical, or whatever — we know nothing at all.
>
> And that's why I feel a certain optimism about this candidacy. Because I think it offers to all the people of the city of New York a chance to turn this city around and make it what it once was — the leader of the world.

Mailer and Breslin lost badly. In the primary on June 17, Mailer came in fourth, with 39,209 votes, just ahead of Scheuer. Badillo came in far ahead of him, winning 203,317 votes, and Wagner finished second with 208,936. Procaccino won handily with 233,486 votes. The Mailer campaign had rented a suite in the Plaza, and Mailer took the loss graciously, watching the results on TV beside Breslin, who had slung a beefy arm around Norman's shoulders. At eleven o'clock Norman conceded, tenaciously holding on to his vision: "If I'm right about this city being on the edge of doom, then heaven help this city, because there's not much to look forward to with the men they elected today."

After the primary, there was a lot of second-guessing in the Mailer camp, and another round of the same after John Lindsay, running this time as a

Liberal Party and Independent candidate, defeated the Republican John Marchi and the Democrat Procaccino. Mailer had split the liberal vote, leaving the remaining Democrats with a conservative Tammany Hall nominee in Procaccino. But he could also claim that he had pointed out the need for the Democrats to embrace a new kind of politics if they were to have any hope of finding a new direction for New York City.

What was the point of the campaign, and why had it failed? Mailer advanced some truly sound new ideas; after his election, Lindsay requested the Mailer-Breslin position papers. In the end, however, the campaign's two leading ideas, statehood and neighborhood control, lacked universal appeal; they seemed too difficult to implement, too threatening, too wacky. But behind these two positions was a commitment to change and a conviction that New Yorkers wanted more control over their city.

Mailer had committed a great deal to the campaign, personally and financially, perhaps more than he expected. For two months he had not slept more than three or four hours a night. He brought immense dedication to his task: for all of his staffing blunders toward the end of the campaign, he had assembled a team of people who were committed and capable and who helped him assemble the facts and figures necessary to buttress his most high-flown proposals. The process by which New York City would become a state, for example, he had outlined to the smallest detail.

In the Mailer-Breslin camp there was, naturally, a tremendous letdown when they lost, particularly because Norman had not wavered in his belief that he could win. However, he felt some sense of relief, for he had realized that if he became mayor the likelihood was that he would never write again. With characteristic hubris, he had felt that if he became mayor he would be a politician for life, and he had always thought of himself as primarily a writer. As he wrote months later, referring to himself in the third person, "Norman was lazy, and politics would make him work hard for sixteen hours a day for the rest of his life. He was so guilty a man that he thought he would be elected as a fit and proper punishment for his sins. Still, he also wanted to win. He would never write again if he were Mayor (the job would doubtless strain his talent to extinction) but he would have his hand on the rump of History, and Norman was not without such lust."

On the other hand, the experience was immensely invigorating. At forty-seven, Norman fervently believed that the city he loved was dying, and that his vision could save it. For many people, to lose such a venture would have been devastating; instead, Norman seemed to take it rather philosophically. New York City wasn't ready for him.

IN THE WAKE of the campaign, a vague depression came over Norman, which would not lift for more than a year. Writing in the third person, he commented, "He had in fact been left with a huge boredom about himself. He was weary of his own voice, own face, person, persona, will, ideas, speeches, and general sense of importance . . . He had burned something in his soul those eight weeks of campaigning."

Another factor contributed to his dampened spirits: his marriage was in real trouble. Beverly had felt the strains of the campaign: she saw Norman by himself only rarely, though she campaigned with him enthusiastically. She was with him at one campaign stop in Bedford-Stuyvesant when aides introduced her to a young black girl, around Betsy's age, in the crowd. Beverly befriended the girl, whose name was Emily Jones, and convinced her mother to let Emily spend the summer with the Mailer family in Province-town. Emily came up, had a great time with Dandy and Betsy, and even, inspired by Norman, wrote some stories.

Beverly was devoting herself to running the (at times enormous) Mailer household. Norman's children from his previous marriages came and went, and there were always staffers and Norman's friends underfoot, waiting to be fed.

In fact, as Norman later wrote, it was the raising of a family that was "the point on which his last marriage began to wallow, then had sunk: his fourth wife, an actress, had seen her career drown in the rigors of managing so large a home." (Beverly would not agree with this interpretation.) Norman wrote as if he fully understood Beverly's ambitions and how thwarted she felt at having to put them on hold: "She was an actress who now did not work. An actress who does not work is a maddened beast." He claimed he had tried to help her maintain her career by staging *The Deer Park,* but he criticized her acting and her ambitions so much that, as Beverly says, "I began to believe I had no career."

They were still half in love with each other, and their two sons bound them together. But both had volatile temperaments and were given to shout-ing matches. Then too, Norman was seeing other women, as Beverly was well aware. His infidelities became an issue early in the marriage; on one of the first nights after she came home with baby Michael, Beverly recalls, Norman was out all night with another woman, prompting Beverly to throw her wedding ring dramatically out the window. When Stephen was born, he was having an affair with an airline stewardess, says Beverly.

Depressed, deflated, his marriage crumbling, Norman was about to take on one of the most disastrous projects of his writing life, and one that would consume an entire year: covering the first trip to the moon.

THE MOON

I f Norman began his 1969 mayoral campaign feeling completely attuned to his culture, he ended it feeling completely alienated. Setting out to write the *Life* piece and the book he had contracted for in June, he wondered if it was appropriate to call himself "Aquarius": "Born January 31, he is entitled to the name, but he thinks it a fine irony that we now enter the Age of Aquarius since he has never had less sense of possessing the age." He had a sense that something was coming to an end: "Aquarius was in a depression which would not lift for the rest of the summer, a curious depression full of fevers, forebodings, and a general sense that the century was done — it had ended in the summer of 1969." The supposedly imminent Age of Aquarius may have heralded great things astrologically, but in fact it ushered in the seventies — a distinct comedown. It was a vantage point that filled Norman with dread. He had been something of a prophet in the sixties, he admitted, having known ahead of time that marijuana was coming, and Hip, and a time of unrest, and loss of belief. "Now they asked him what he thought of the Seventies. He did not know. He thought of the Seventies and a blank . . . came over his vision. When he conducted interviews with himself on the subject, it was not despair he felt, or fear — it was anesthesia."

Part of the reason for Norman's dull mood was that he was reduced to writing for money. He had gone into debt with the making of *Wild 90, Beyond the Law,* and *Maidstone,* and then into further debt to his agent, the IRS, and various other sources. He needed a tremendous amount of money to maintain his Brooklyn and Provincetown houses, his children, Adele, and his mistress, and to keep himself and Beverly living well. Royalties from his past books were declining, and were in some cases nonexistent.

But he was not thinking of money when Willie Morris of *Harper's* first broached the idea of an article on the Apollo 11 moon landing. Despite the cautions of his cousin Cy Rembar — who instinctively thought it would be a very bad project to take on and told him so — Norman said he liked the idea, liked it so much, in fact, that he suggested that he participate in the moon landing itself, since what he wrote, apart from novels, was participatory journalism.

Nothing came of this idea, and nothing came of Mailer's tentative agreement with Morris. Instead, he called Morris to inform him that *Life* had offered him so much money that he had decided to write for that magazine. *Life* had covered the astronauts since the space program began, but editor Thomas Griffith was looking for a writer with a distinctive voice; the magazine had a good relationship with the astronauts, which gave any journalist an edge. He had assigned stories about the space program to science fiction writer Arthur C. Clarke and to the poet James Dickey, and he envisioned Mailer doing a piece about the scruffy lives of those who worked around the space center. "We were doing too many 'Jack Armstrong, All-American Boy' stories, and I thought Mailer could bring a new slant to it," says Griffith.

If Norman had any qualms about going to work for Time, Inc., his longtime enemy, he did not voice them publicly. *Life* magazine's relationship to its parent, in fact, made it necessary for him in effect to change publishers, because Time had just bought Little, Brown, and it made sense for Little, Brown to publish the hardcover book Mailer would fashion out of his *Life* coverage. (NAL, which still had first rights to anything Mailer wrote, would get paperback rights for the book.) The entire deal, with foreign rights thrown in, netted Norman over four hundred thousand dollars — not the million the papers had announced. It was enough, after the repayment of debts and taxes, to allow Norman to live and think for a year. "Not so bad," he wrote. "He had only to write a book about the moon shot. Small matter."

But it was not a particularly promising project, either, nor did it come at an auspicious time. Worn out from the mayoral race, Norman arrived in Houston on the first of July; he spent ten days there and then went on to Cape Kennedy in Florida. He returned to Provincetown on July 23, in time to see the splashdown on television on the twenty-fourth. Then he had to settle in to write the book, which would take him into the following spring. A difficult year indeed — especially as it saw as well the end of his marriage.

Furthermore, it was an unlikely assignment for a man so opposed to technology. He would try to suspend his judgment and then to moderate the unrelenting technological tone of his subject by writing about such matters as "the psychology of machines," but in the end he had to immerse himself in technical manuals and science texts to write the second part of the book,

"Apollo," which takes up fully half of the published volume. As he said on reaching the NASA Manned Spacecraft Center in Houston, "The first and most unhappy truth was that there were no smells coming out of NASA," adding, "It was hardly the terrain for Aquarius." Philosophically speaking, the subject was not congenial. Questions about the real value of the space mission dogged him throughout the year: "Was the voyage of the Apollo 11 the noblest expression of a technological age, or the best evidence of its utter insanity?" He could not accept that the reality probably lay somewhere in between, and totally missed its political importance, as a further expression of U.S. imperialism and a Cold War chess piece. The moon was too wonderful a symbol, pregnant with meaning; he believed the mission had to "mean" in an equivalent way.

But covering the Apollo mission wore him down thoroughly. He disliked Houston and, after that, Florida. He was not used to being part of a huge, international press corps; as opposed to political conventions or prizefights, the moon shot attracted few reporters with whom he had an affinity. Many of these reporters wanted to interview him, which he declined: "He who had once thought he had only to get on all the radio and television available and he would be able to change the world, now wished only to flee this room with its hundreds of journalists, some so bored and aimless they even wished to interview him, he who now had nothing to say." It was a cruel irony.

Moreover, finding something worthwhile to say about the mission was very difficult for him. Compared with what he was used to reporting on, the moon shot seemed so removed, connected at no point with his usual triggers and obsessions. He often was so overcome with perceptions about the events, the places, and the people that he could write volumes. People — indeed, personalities — usually shaped the events he wrote about. "But in NASA-land," he wrote, "the only thing open was the technology — the participants were so overcome by the magnitude of their venture they seemed to consider personal motivation as somewhat obscene." He wondered if he might not just as well go back home and watch the moon shot on television.

Also, in covering Apollo he could not even get near those most closely involved: the astronauts. According to Tom Griffith, *Life* was unable to get Norman access to them, so leery had the astronauts' lawyers been of what Mailer might write. Time Inc. had enjoyed almost total access to the space program throughout the sixties, and its magazines had in turn enjoyed increased circulation because of this relationship, but this was beginning to change. With the war in Vietnam, the government, and governmental bodies like NASA, had become far less friendly toward outsiders — even conservative writers like those at Time Inc. One can imagine the chagrin of

NASA officials and the astronauts' lawyers — who were in turn supplied by NASA — on being told that an independent writer would be covering the moon shot for *Life* — and especially an independent writer like Norman Mailer, who had made his antiwar and leftist sympathies well known. *Life*'s assigning the story to someone like Mailer was the very sort of action for which the government and the military-industrial complex distrusted the media.

In this case, they need not have worried. Mailer barely got to know the astronauts. He usually called them "WASPs" in his reportage, but this was as far as it went. Only Pete Conrad, who was not even on the Apollo 11 mission, spent any time with him. Mailer met the wives of Buzz Aldrin, Neil Armstrong, and Michael Collins, but he complained that they talked like the wives of corporation executives. His major complaint was that the astronauts were not sufficiently flamboyant as heroes (he invokes Ernest Hemingway, Joe Namath, Cassius Clay, and Jimmy Dean) — "it was as if the astronauts were there to demonstrate that heroism's previous relation to romance had been highly improper." Technology and the absence of emotion "were the only fit mates for the brave," he wrote.

Furthermore, he was in no sense a participant in the event and so could not write the participatory journalism he was best at. He made himself a character in the story, Aquarius, but that character was almost completely passive. His participation in the March on the Pentagon had been central to *Armies of the Night*, as had his political participation to *Miami and the Siege of Chicago*, but in *Of a Fire on the Moon*, the Mailer character watches closed-circuit television and regular television, attends press conferences, and reads technical journals. This was not his fault, of course, but it suited the mood of the man who confessed that by this time, in the summer of 1969, he found his own thoughts boring. Moreover, covering the astronauts without ever really seeing them was "like covering an assignment by watching television."

The liftoff of the Apollo on July 16 moved Norman, and he wrote an excellent description of that. But news of the Chappaquiddick tragedy, which reached the reporters while Apollo 11 was in space, threatened to eclipse the space mission in general interest. Norman watched the moon landing from the Manned Space Center in Houston, but then flew back to Provincetown to watch the splashdown on television. He was working under a deadline, and needed to get written the first of what would be three articles for *Life* for publication on August 29. (The others would appear on November 14, 1969, and January 9, 1970.)

Life editor Ralph Graves, who had only recently become managing editor, had just given a speech to his staff in which he said, "There's too much text in this magazine. There are to be no more long pieces. This is, after all, a picture book." But then the first of Mailer's lengthy articles came in. Mailer, nervous about working with an unfamiliar editor, made it a condition that his text was not to be cut without his consent. Graves was obliged to publish the text as it stood, though he made some suggestions for cuts, some of which Mailer agreed to.

"To write was to judge," Norman wrote in *Of a Fire on the Moon,* "and Aquarius may never have tried a subject which tormented him so." The moon shot was not a subject that could engage him, finally. He did his best, writing through the summer and fall of 1969 and on into the spring and summer of 1970. He made several trips back to Houston for the "Apollo" half of the book, the section in which he explains the scientific and technological aspects of Apollo 11. The section never really takes off; Mailer cannot animate the machines. Perhaps because of his Harvard training, he can understand how a rocket works and such issues as gravity and orbiting. But he communicates no enthusiasm for what he describes. He seems to know that, and expresses several times his own doubt about what he is attempting. In fact, these asides, and the author's occasional references to his personal life, provide the book's few sparks of life. Overall, however, a grimness reigns, and Mailer confides his dismay:

> In this hour they landed on the moon, America was applauding Armstrong and Aldrin, and the world would cheer America for a day, but something was lacking, some joy, some outrageous sense of adventure. Strong men did not weep in the streets nor ladies copulate with strangers . . . It was almost as if a sense of woe sat in the center of the heart. For the shot to the moon was a mirror to our condition — most terrifying mirror; one looked into it and saw intimations of a final disease.

When Little, Brown published the book in late 1970, Mailer was glad to be through with it. He'd earned his money — indeed, had likely spent it over the course of the year. Mailer was not happy with the book. He recognized that his presence was problematic — that he had written the book very much as a reporter who acted as if he were present but was not really. "I liked the book in a lot of ways, but I didn't like my own person in it — I felt I was highly unnecessary," he said in an interview a decade later.

The summer of 1969, the summer that saw the book's beginning, was an awful one for Mailer. He returned home from Houston, he wrote in *Of a Fire on the Moon,* to find the Provincetown house "sour." It smelled as if the milk had curdled, he explained. What he meant, of course, was that his marriage had soured. There had been tension between husband and wife since he began his coverage of the moon shot. "His wife and he were getting on abominably," he wrote. "They had had hideous phone calls these last weeks while he was away. Several times, one or the other had hung up in the middle of a quarrel. It was impossible to believe, but they both knew — they were coming to an end." But the summer seemed as if it would go on forever. Beverly had taken up with a young Frenchman named Philippe; it was her first infidelity. Though Philippe was younger than she, the two really connected; the affair repaired Beverly's shattered confidence and helped her begin to recover from Norman's abuse. Norman was still seeing Carol Stevens; she would join him at 565 Commercial Street, however, when Beverly decamped with Philippe. Meanwhile, there was another girl he kept somewhere in Provincetown. "He had women stashed everywhere," says Beverly.

Provincetown had acquired a new edge by the late sixties. In the summers, hordes of tourists and visiting bohemians honed this edge until it was dangerous, transforming the fishing town into, as Mailer wrote, "the Wild West of the East." "It took forty-five minutes in the middle of August," he continued, "to drive a car half a mile down the one-lane main street." Marijuana was everywhere; it seemed as if the majority of people one talked to were stoned. Mailer observed that the drinking parties held by those who preferred booze began at five in the evening and ended at five in the morning. "Stoned out of the very head of sensation," he wrote, "the summer populace was still groping and pondering the way down the gray and lavender beach in the red-ball dawn, sun coming over the water in one long shot of fire — Provincetown was the only place in the East he knew where the land spiraled so far around that you could see the sun rise out of the dunes in the east and set in water to the west."

In 1969, however, Norman "hated his beloved Provincetown this summer above all." He saw a kind of objective correlative at work: Provincetown seemed to go a little crazy as if in answer to the craziness of the Mailer household. Other marriages were breaking up, he observed. He counted at least five, when most summers would see one or maybe two. And the unlikeliest couples were parting — couples who had been locked in unhappy marriages for twenty years, so long it seemed incredible that they would bother to break up now.

In another kind of objective correlative, strangely enough, as if playing out a drama about ambivalence toward technology — the subject on which Norman was hard at work — artists in the town seemed to be fixated on machinery. Several "happenings" involved machines made into sculptures or otherwise transformed. Jack Kearney, a local sculptor, staged one of the first when he invited guests to watch as he bulldozed Beverly's "delphinium blue" Citroën into a pancake. He then cut it into pieces and gave it away to friends. Before he crushed the car he took off the fenders to make a caricature of de Gaulle, which he mounted on the Mailers' porch, adding ball bearings to make it spin like a weathervane (it still adorns Beverly's Provincetown deck).

Mailer said in *Of a Fire on the Moon* that his friends in Provincetown would take a lawnmower apart to make a salad. When Norman and Beverly's friends the Bankos discovered that the car they had bought at the beginning of the summer had died long before Labor Day, they decided to make a happening around burying it. Jack Kearney presided over the ceremony, and local poets gathered to read lines over the half-buried car. The Bankos circulated bearing beer, and children enthusiastically joined in, making paintings on the car's exterior. Kearney dubbed the sculpture "Metamorphosis." The message of the burial was not lost on Norman, who described the sculpture as "a massive Yorick of half a Ford standing twelve feet high, first machine to die with burial in the land of the Pilgrims and the cod."

Beverly left the house on Commercial Street with Philippe on Labor Day, September 2, leaving the boys in the care of Bobbie Swafford, a housekeeper she fully trusted. Norman did not ask her to stay, which saddened her but strengthened her resolve. She and Philippe traveled from New York to Mexico and back, and Philippe left for Paris on October 10, their affair sadly over. For the next year, she would stay at 142 Columbia Heights and return with the boys for holidays in Provincetown, where she would live in the old house. Later she moved to Provincetown so the boys could be near their father. Relations with Norman were a little strained but cordial; the possibility remained that they would get back together.

THE WINTER OF 1969–70 Norman spent finishing up several projects: getting *Of a Fire on the Moon* ready for book publication, putting the last touches on the editing of *Maidstone,* and watching his marriage finally come apart. During this period, Carol Stevens came to the fore in Norman's life, frequently staying with him in the Brooklyn brownstone. A dark-haired Jewish beauty from Philadelphia, Carol, at forty — the same age as Beverly — was deeply in love with Norman. He had first met her in March 1962, when she was singing at Small's Paradise in Harlem, and the affair had continued intermittently. Her voice was low and tremulous, and she often sang without lyrics. An entire side of her LP, *That Satin Doll,* was given over to scat singing. In 1957, the same year her album was released, *Time* magazine, noting her "wicked black sheaths and vampira makeup," called her "visually and musically the most striking of the new girl singers." Many considered her the warmest of Norman's women; a friend's daughter remembered her as being "like a typical earth mother." As a singer, she had superb stage presence; off the stage, she had a similar talent for putting people at ease. She was probably the first of Norman's women with whom he did not fight, though many observers felt he didn't treat her very well, leaving her at home while he partied and pursued other women.

Norman took a break from his domestic upheavals in January, when he flew to Chicago to appear as a witness for the defense in the Chicago conspiracy trial. The so-called Chicago Eight — Bobby Seale, Abbie Hoffman, Tom Hayden, Rennie Davis, Dave Dellinger, Jerry Rubin, John Froines, and Lee Weiner — were charged with conspiracy and crossing state lines to "incite, organize, promote and encourage" riots in Chicago at the 1968 Democratic Convention, the event Mailer had covered so incisively in *Miami and the Siege of Chicago*.

At the outset of the trial, Abbie Hoffman announced that it promised to be "a combination of the Scopes trial, revolution in the streets, the Woodstock festival and People's Park all rolled into one." And indeed the trial was, by all accounts, a circus, with Judge Julius Hoffman maintaining only the most tenuous control of the courtroom. The defendants and other observers, responding to what they felt was clear bias on the part of the judge and the prosecuting attorneys, indulged in extreme guerrilla tactics meant to highlight what seemed a travesty of justice; the tone was perhaps set when, at the outset of the trial, Bobby Seale was brought into the courtroom gagged and tied to his chair. Norman Mailer was one of a series of countercultural heroes brought in by defense attorneys William Kunstler and Leonard Weinglass as "state of mind" witnesses: since the charge in part alleged a "state of mind" or "intent" to incite riots in Chicago that summer, witnesses such as Allen Ginsberg, Timothy Leary, Judy Collins, and Pete Seeger all sought to establish the defendants' "state of mind" regarding racism, the war in Vietnam, poverty, and other social ills as the "youth culture" saw them.

Whatever reputation he had earned for recklessness or roistering, in this context Mailer was present to lend an air of sobriety and authority to the Yippies' cause. When he first took the stand and his accomplishments and literary awards were enumerated, "Norman Mailer absolutely magnetized the courtroom," according to one reporter. Mailer was, of course, fully aware of the circus the trial was proving to be.

The prosecution hoped to establish that Rubin and perhaps Hoffman had informed Mailer in advance of an action to take place at the Chicago convention, and in fact Mailer did know that Rubin, for one, had anticipated the events of the summer of 1968. But Mailer's testimony was crucial

Above: Norman and his fourth wife, Beverly, look down at their newborn son in March 1964.
(*Courtesy of Beverly Bentley*)

Below: The novelist at forty-two, on the roof of his Brooklyn Heights brownstone, overlooking the East River.
(*Copyright © Inge Morath/Magnum Photos*)

Above: Arm wrestling with Muhammad Ali in 1965. Some of Mailer's finest writing is about Ali's fights.
(*AP/Wide World Photos*)

Below: Walking a tightrope across the deck of his new house in Provincetown in the summer of 1966, while Kate, Norman's daughter with Jeanne, looks nervously on.
(*Copyright © Daniel Kramer, courtesy of Beverly Bentley*)

Arriving at Truman Capote's famous black-and-white ball on November 28, 1966. *Women's Wear Daily* named Mailer the worst-dressed man of the evening. (*Women's Wear Daily*)

Above: Mailer (center) at the March on the Pentagon, October 1967, the subject of his Pulitzer Prize–winning *The Armies of the Night*. Robert Lowell is on his left, Noam Chomsky on his right.
(*Copyright © Fred W. McDarrah*)

Left: Sometimes at odds, Mailer and the Beat poet Allen Ginsberg found common ground in protest against the Vietnam War.
(*Copyright © Fred W. McDarrah*)

Right: Barney Mailer in the mid-1960s.
(*Courtesy of Beverly Bentley*)

Below: Fanny Mailer with her grandson Michael.
(*Courtesy of Beverly Bentley*)

Above: Fig Gwaltney, Mailer's friend and longtime correspondent, pictured in the University of Arkansas *Razorback*, 1940s. (*University of Arkansas, Fayetteville*)

Left: Mailer's protégé Richard Stratton, 1990s. (*Copyright © Fionn Reilly*)

Below: Mailer on the set of *Wild 90* with Buzz Farbar, perhaps his closest friend. The gun is a prop. (*Courtesy of Beverly Bentley*)

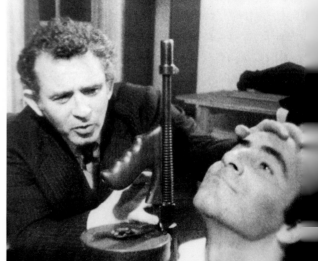

Mailer installed a series of catwalks and aeries in his Brooklyn brownstone. He reached his office by way of a catwalk and ladders.
(*AP/Wide World Photos*)

Above: Directing the 1968 movie *Maidstone*, which Mailer also "wrote" and starred in, playing the part of a film director who runs for president.
(*Copyright © Elliott Erwitt/Magnum Photos*)

Left: Three of Norman's wives — Beverly, Jeanne, and Adele — participated in the making of *Maidstone*, as did his mistress Carol Stevens.
(*Copyright © Daniel Kramer*)

in establishing that Rubin had no intent to start a riot, merely to hold a music festival. It was a fine point, because Rubin knew full well that any gathering of young people in Chicago at that time might lead to trouble, but Mailer's point was precisely that the Yippies would not be the inciters of any violence.

Mailer testified that he had met with Rubin in December 1967, when he was doing background research for *The Armies of the Night,* and that Rubin had indicated he and others were planning a "youth festival" for the following summer in Chicago. "It was his idea that the presence of a hundred thousand young people in Chicago at a festival with rock bands would so intimidate and terrify the Establishment that Lyndon Johnson would have to be nominated under armed guard." Norman's response at the time, he said, was "Wow."

Prosecutor Richard Schulz returned to this point, seizing it as evidence that Rubin and other organizers sought to "intimidate" the Chicago police into violence. No, replied Norman, *intimidate* was a word that he — not Rubin — would use, "because possibly since I am a bully by nature, I tend to speak in terms of intimidation, but I don't think Mr. Rubin does." Rubin had, in fact, said that that was the whole beauty of it: "We won't do a thing. We are just going to be there and they won't be able to take it. They will smash the city themselves. They will provoke all the violence." Mailer explained that Rubin thought "in terms of cataclysm, of having people reveal their own guilt, their own evil." The presence of the young people, as Mailer understood it, was to drive the Establishment "out of their bird" — an expression that rocked the courtroom with laughter.

The defense lawyers and Mailer wanted to establish that the students' and young people's actions were in direct response to greater evils: an unjust war, an unjust society, unjust racial conditions. As Mailer said, "[Rubin's] whole notion was that the innocent presence of one hundred thousand people in Chicago would be intolerable for a man as guilt-ridden as Lyndon Johnson."

Mailer's testimony probably did little to help the defense, however. He may have set it back a bit even, by mentioning that he'd seen some of the same faces at the March on the Pentagon as he had in Chicago, thereby establishing a link that might suggest conspiracy. But his presence had enormous symbolic weight. The Chicago Eight trial was to many the nadir of 1960s radicalism, a show of Yippie excess at its worst, but it was guerrilla theater of the kind Mailer the existentialist valued most highly, and the principles at stake were ones he held closely to his heart. Then too he could explain in detail precisely why his involvement in the Chicago action had been limited, as he told the story again about fearing to join the fray because he wished to make his deadline. Indeed, to J. Anthony Lukas, covering the story for the *New York Times,* "It was plain that Mailer had come back to exorcise a nagging sense of guilt about his own role that week in Chicago."

In a sense, his appearance at the trial was one of Mailer's last actively political moments. As the turmoil of the 1960s died down on one front and escalated on another, with the New Left dissolving into violent underground factions, Mailer the political activist retreated. He would reappear, however, when the bells of the sex wars seemed to toll, he thought, directly for him.

TWENTY

THE PRISONER OF SEX

Throughout the late 1950s and the 1960s, Mailer had distinguished himself by anticipating and identifying many of the sweeping social and cultural shifts that defined his time, among them the rise of the counterculture; the emergence of Black Power; the Westernization and growing conservatism of the Republican Party; a new generation of innovative urban planners and the primacy of neighborhood control in their thinking; threatening contradictions in the New Left; and the sterility and alienation induced by much of modern technology.

But the growing dissatisfaction of American women, culminating in the birth of the feminist movement in the 1960s and the rise of radical feminism as well as the more widely accepted principles of mainstream women's liberation, completely eluded him. Mailer did not see it happening, and when he finally did see it, he did not know why it had happened and did not know how to respond. He did not understand its goals and made only token attempts to do so, and even then, only under the burden of a publishing contract. Still largely in a state of ignorance, he wrote a major magazine piece on the topic, republished it as a book, and made himself available for a debate on women's rights (as if, as many observed, such rights were a matter for debate). Far from contributing enlightenment on the subject — which was perhaps inevitable, since he was so clearly unenlightened — he only muddied the waters, along the way insulting many feminist leaders and their followers and establishing himself, rightly or wrongly, as one of American culture's outstanding male chauvinists. The case can be made that Mailer is not, in fact, a run-of-the-mill sexist — as a nonconformist who above all wanted to see something approaching social revolution, he had much in common with the feminist movement. But the evidence for the case is not to be found in his 1971 statement on relations between the sexes, *The Prisoner of Sex.*

BETTY FRIEDAN recognized and named the growing dissatisfaction of the typical 1950s housewife in her groundbreaking *The Feminine Mystique* (1963): domestic ideology of the postwar years tried to keep women in their "proper" place, ignoring such modern realities as the fact that many middle- and upper-class women were college-educated and had smaller families than the women of the previous generation, and that technological improvements to a variety of appliances had cut down on the physical labor and time that housework required. The specter of the bored and isolated housewife, which Friedan delineated so brilliantly, became the object of media attention in the early 1960s, and a women's movement was born, recognized by President Kennedy with the Presidential Commission on Women, attested to by the passage of Title VII of the Civil Rights Act, and formally represented by the formation of the National Organization for Women (NOW) in 1965. In the second half of the 1960s, the professional organizers and activists who had brought NOW into being were joined by many grassroots women's rights activists. Sometimes as a result of their participation in the civil rights movement in the South and radical antiwar student groups in the North, women came to question routine male dominance in protest movements and the inability of the male left to extend its understanding of "oppression" to include the women who staffed their offices, ran their mimeograph machines, and made their coffee.

By 1970, women of all political persuasions had identified themselves with the movement in many different ways. Consciousness raising, which helped women talk with other women in intense and personal sessions to see the many ways in which they were oppressed in the home and the workplace, represented one type of activity. Many women concentrated on the campaign for equal pay for equal work. Some attempted to modify the sexual revolution to allow for women's needs: the notion of the vaginal orgasm was attacked, and masturbation was encouraged. Others worked for an equal rights amendment. Still others questioned the system in more radical ways: joining separatist movements, becoming or coming out as lesbians, working for ways to bypass the reproductive process, fighting for abortion rights, and performing guerrilla theater (most infamously in the protests at the Miss America pageant in Atlantic City in 1968, at which bras were said to have been burned). The dominant theme, or perhaps the most succinct statement, of the new movement was "The personal is political": the division of labor in the home was political, relations with men were political, the actions women undertook in their daily lives were political. Most relevantly, in considering Norman Mailer's response to the movement, feminists were developing impressive political theory, reexamining and rewriting history to reclaim women's place in it, recovering previously dismissed works by women, and writing often brilliant polemics and manifestos. It was, in other words, and among other things, an important intellectual movement, a revolution in ideas, a new "scene" in American culture. Strangely, Mailer did not play any part in this intellectual movement, missed out on participating in this particular revolution, and remained aloof, for a time, from the scene. When he finally did enter the fray, the result was, among other things, a major intellectual blunder.

IN *The Prisoner of Sex,* Mailer describes how his involvement with feminism began. As was usual, he had custody of the children (except for twenty-year-old Susan, who was in Europe) for the summer, which he elected to spend in a rented house on Soames Sound on Mount Desert Island in Maine — perhaps to find a vacation spot alternative to Provincetown. What was not usual was that he had no wife to see to their needs. He hired "a good Maine woman" to do the cleaning and laundry, and enlisted his daughters — Dandy, thirteen; Betsy, ten; Kate, eight — to help with the shopping, cooking, and care of the boys — Michael, six; and Stephen, four. His sister visited for two weeks and helped out, as did Carol Stevens. In fact, Carol was such a help that he invited her up for the rest of the summer.

Even with the help of all these females — six, all told, though of course at different times — Norman found his six weeks on the Maine coast "mindless," filled with menus, packing lunches, outings, and other details associated with running a large household. By the end of the summer he decided that he could run a household for the rest of his days if need be — but also that he would never get any writing done under those circumstances.

While in Maine, *The Prisoner of Sex* goes on to relate, a telephone call came from the editor of *Time,* asking Norman if the magazine could send a reporter up to get his views on women's liberation for a cover story. Norman misunderstood the offer, overlooking the part about the women's movement — he thought only of how a cover might help his struggling movie, *Maidstone,* now in search of a distributor. He declined, not wishing his children's privacy to be invaded. The editor told him that *Time* was not interested in his home life or his children, that the subject was his reaction to women's liberation — and how, the editor informed him, many women had targeted him as the enemy. Norman was surprised, and again tempted, but he realized he would get no money for such a venture, only exposure, and declined again.

How could Mailer not know he was a favorite target for feminists? He had been directly provoking them for years with such statements as, in *The*

Presidential Papers, "Most men who understand women at all feel hostility toward them. At their worst, women are low, sloppy beasts." In a conversation he had had with Orson Bean on TV as recently as July, he stated that he didn't hate women but merely thought "they should be kept in cages." He was a sexual conservative, and many of his views on matters relating to sex were offensive to women (and to many men). For example: "The fact of the matter is that the prime responsibility of a woman is to be on earth long enough to find the best mate possible for herself, and conceive children who will improve the species" — as he said in interview after interview. His reputation as a womanizer — even, or perhaps mostly, for it seemed emblematic in these times, as one who had stabbed his second wife — was sure proof of his misogyny, many feminists believed. Yet Mailer was seemingly unaware of any of this. To make cavalier statements about keeping women in cages was at best tactless, at worst downright provocative. But he seemed oblivious to the climate — or he simply ignored it.

Yet after returning from Maine, free of the children and the burdens of running a household, he mulled over the idea of writing about feminism. What Norman doesn't say in describing this summer, but what is clearly implied, is that he felt it gave him a new understanding of what "women's work" entailed, and how oppressive it could be. But this explanation leaves all kinds of threads untied. He understands the oppressiveness of domestic details, yet he contrives to rely on women completely for help, even enlisting his daughters to assist in the care of their brothers, from whom nothing is expected. If women's work is so boring, what is the solution? He doesn't offer one.

Still, the subject of women's liberation drew him; also, though he does not say this, he could not resist an opportunity for combat. Moreover, "the themes of his life" were attached to feminism, as he understood it: "Revolution, tradition, sex and the homosexual, the orgasm, the family, the child and the political shape of the future, technology and human conception, waste and abortion, the ethics of the critic and the male mystique, black rights and new thoughts on women's rights" — all these were his abiding preoccupations.

And yet he wavered. There were many arguments against weighing in on the subject. Among other things, his vanity could not sustain losing the affection of women, who he presumed were not fans of his writing but who, he thought, admired his persona. He had a bit of a reputation as a stud, and he was not sure how to manage that reputation in writing about the women's movement. Furthermore, he recognized, at least, that it was a progressive movement, and his fundamentally progressive side cautioned him against taking on such a topic too critically.

But the subject kept coming up. A publisher sent him a copy of Mary

Ellman's *Thinking about Women,* noting that it had more references to him in the index than to any other living writer and asking him to comment. Ellman's was a tough-minded and very witty critique, but Norman viewed it "as a lady kicking him in the nuts." He also read an article by Kate Millett in *New American Review* that was critical of *An American Dream.* Then, six months after he refused to cooperate for a *Time* cover story about him and his views on the women's movement, the same magazine came out with a cover story on Kate Millett, of all people, whose groundbreaking study, *Sexual Politics,* had just appeared. A good part of *Sexual Politics* was given over to a critical appraisal of D. H. Lawrence, Henry Miller, Jean Genet, and Norman Mailer. Mailer felt he had no choice but to respond.

Millett's book is remembered today for its scathing assessment of misogyny in the four male writers' works. She selects passages of what to her seem the most egregious examples of sexism from their prose, and dissects them cleverly and insightfully. Her particular argument against Mailer's work is that he always sees sex in terms of power and violence. To Mailer, she argues, sexuality is in effect a game of power. In Lawrence and Miller she sees similar instances of sexual relations as political, about power.

It was certainly the section in which she criticized male writers that bothered Mailer the most, and he would devote much of his essay to slicing and dicing Millett. Having done his reading, which included, besides *Sexual Politics,* Germaine Greer's *The Female Eunuch,* Ti-Grace Atkinson's essays, and Valerie Solanis's "SCUM (Society for Cutting Up Men) Manifesto," he began writing his response.

As he does in most of his nonfiction writing, Mailer invents and names a persona for himself. At the outset, he is the Prizewinner, or PW (which he notes in an aside could also be read as Prisoner of Wedlock). This refers in part to a recent experience: rumor had it that he was to be awarded the Nobel Prize, and this prompted him, in the many hours that passed before he learned the rumor was false, to think about his place among the world's writers and to ruminate about the consequences of fame. It is a curious and even spurious beginning for an essay on the women's movement. Mailer then describes the process by which he came to write about feminism and what he did to prepare.

"The Acolyte" describes his reaction to the feminists' writings. He admits that he admires the toughness of what he read, which clearly surprised him — but somehow his praise manages to hit a sour note: "Some of the writers were writing like very tough faggots." He has assembled a somewhat idiosyncratic but generally sound reading list for his study of the women's movement. Yet he singles out the most extreme case to establish his argument: the "SCUM Manifesto," by an unbalanced young writer who later shot Andy Warhol. The "SCUM Manifesto" states the most threatening version of women's revolutionary thought: men are unnecessary for reproduction, and are themselves biological accidents who ought to be phased out of existence. To Mailer, for whom reproduction was a locus of mystery and wonder, this seemed to topple a fundamental human structure. As a man, he responds to Solanis's willing men out of existence as a clear and present danger. Mailer's anxieties about the phenomenological issues the "SCUM Manifesto" raised inform his arguments throughout the essay. Along the way, and very typically, Mailer fails to notice that he has found another provocateur, and answers overseriously an essay that many read as incisively Swiftian.

Mailer grants the unequal economic position of women, agreeing that it must be righted. He also understands that economic equality cannot be achieved without a cultural revolution and a sexual revolution. At the latter he stops short, and this will be the subject of the essay: men and women cannot be equal, because they are different. The position Mailer takes here is biological essentialism, the belief that women and men have fundamental biological natures different from one another. Such a position precludes equality. Mailer trots out some old "proofs": during and just before menstruation, women get into car accidents more than half the time, are committed to mental institutions, and commit more crimes. Women's biology handicaps them, ties them down, makes them different — and thus rightly subject to being treated as not equal, he claims.

From this point Mailer turns to the insistence of many feminists, including Solanis, that women be freed from the burden of reproduction. He cites Ti-Grace Atkinson's assertion that women cannot go forward until a means of extrauterine reproduction is devised. Mailer interprets this as a vile technological intrusion into what he sees as the most sacred of mysteries, reproduction.

In hindsight, it is easy to dismiss arguments like Atkinson's as fantastical, as Mailer does. But to do so is to misunderstand one of the most important aspects of the women's project. The hypothesis went as follows: To become equal with men, women had to be freed of those biological functions that made them different from men. It is easier to understand if one puts specifics like extrauterine reproduction aside and views arguments like Atkinson's as metaphorical: to achieve equality with men, and to understand and thus improve female sexuality, it is necessary somehow to negate or bypass (even if only imaginatively) the biological burdens that differentiate women from men.

Mailer could not comprehend this line of reasoning, so strongly held was his belief in the special biological differences between women and men. According to Mailer, one can "speak of women and men as the poles of the universe, the universal Yang and Yin, offer views of the Creation in such abstract lands as seed and womb, vision and firmament, fire up a skyworks of sermon and poem to the incontestable mystery that women are flesh of the Mystery more than men." Not only are men and women biologically different, but it is "incontestable" that woman, being endowed with a womb, is thus a link to life's mysteries. When Mailer invests the biological difference between men and women with such romantic and metaphysical significance, he marks himself as someone who will never see past his own atavistic impulses and comprehend the feminist project.

From here, Mailer takes on issues relating to female sexuality. He heads right to the orgasm, taking as a personal attack the idea that vaginal orgasms do not exist. He is especially insulted by the idea that the particular women with whom he has had conventional intercourse might not have had orgasms; in fact, he dismisses that possibility — *his* women have had vaginal orgasms. But the evidence for the clitoral orgasm is compelling, and he temporarily cedes the point. Not, however, without a taunt: he threatens to "treat these ladies to a bit of male irony on the relative comparison of the clitoris to penis, yea, as a pea, as a curled anchovy, as a shrimp to a cucumber." Girls may have clitorises, in other words, but penises are bigger. Finally, though, he rejects the evidence: "So the vaginal orgasm was safe."

In the second section of the essay, "The Advocate," Mailer takes on Kate Millett directly, and mounts an impressive attack based on her use of quotations. Using the case of Henry Miller — long one of his favorite writers — he shows how Millett quotes Miller out of context, how she leaves out crucial sentences in her selections, and along the way constructs a convincing argument in favor of Miller and frank expressions of sexuality in literature.

It is a powerful argument and the strongest part of the essay, but it is damaged and rendered unconvincing by the writer's tone. Mailer taunts and mocks Millett throughout, calling her things like "Kate-baby," "laboratory assistant Kate," and "literary technologist." She is a prude, he says, with no sense of nuance: "Millett hates every evidence of the dialectic. She has a mind like a flatiron, which is to say a totally masculine mind. A hard-hat has more curves in his head."

The tone renders this section of the essay an exercise in mean-spiritedness. It's emblematic that he calls Millett by her first name throughout; it is a personal attack on a woman he has never met. He treats her like a naughty child; the whole argument gives the distasteful impression that he means to put this bitch in her place.

Having disposed of his chief critic, Mailer returns to the issues surrounding sexuality that he thinks lie at the heart of the women's movement. In the closing section, "The Prisoner," Mailer approaches the metaphysical definition of sex by way of masturbation, a practice he condemns almost in biblical fashion: sex should always involve the sacred mysteries of reproduction. There follow the ruminations of a true sexual conservative and romantic: a woman's periods have the resonance of a loss; sexual encounters either "succeed" or "fail" at conception; a man grieves for his lost sperm. Pondering the mysteries of conception leads him, in a logic-defying turn, to pick up a paperback called *Your Baby's Sex: Now You Can Choose,* and to meditate on X and Y chromosomes. Contemplation of the women's movement has brought him to a critical pass, confronting the very question of male and female identity: manhood, and nothing less, is at stake.

In concluding "The Prisoner" (If one "give[s] meaning to sex, one becomes the prisoner of sex"), Mailer returns again to his earlier statement that woman's first responsibility is to find the best mate she can and to conceive children to improve the species. He endorses this idea, but, anxious to affirm his commitment to human freedom even here, he allows that women must be "liberated" in order to search freely for a mate:

> So let woman be what she would, and what she could. Let her
> cohabit with elephants if she had to, and fuck with Borzoi hounds,
> let her bed with eight pricks and a whistle, yes, give her freedom
> and let her burn it, or blow it, or build it to triumph or collapse. Let
> her conceive her children . . . Let her travel to the moon, write the
> great American novel, and allow her husband to send her off to
> work with her lunch pail and a cigar."

Confronted with the task of reconciling what he has just asserted with the concept of women's liberation, Mailer's argument simply trails off, and the writer seemingly bails out.

The Prisoner of Sex contains a lot of bad writing of a sort Mailer had never produced before. There is no organization beyond his arbitrarily named sections; there is no one coherent argument; he indulges in flights of fantasy, like imagining a city drawn up according to sexual preferences, an idea that the reader fails to grasp; there has been, it seems, no editorial reining in of Mailer's tendency toward long, turgid sentences of complex clauses piled atop one another (sentences that cry out for pruning or, at the very least, punctuation). No single idea emerges as terribly interesting in *The Prisoner of Sex,* an essay about one of the most pressing issues of the day — surely a first for this culturally prescient writer.

The reader is left with an unfortunate impression of Mailer belittling and condescending to those women who have put a lot of hard work into theorizing their liberation. Feminists in the early 1970s weren't really talking about X and Y chromosomes and biological difference; difference too often precludes equality. Although an integral part of their project was sexual liberation, Mailer had missed the point; feminists were less focused on sex than on the social construction of gender and the inequities to which it subjected women in the home, the workplace, and other spheres — a thoroughly practical task almost entirely unrelated to a subject like the mysteries of gender difference. Mailer and the feminists of his day simply were not talking about the same thing.

Of course, he had taken up the challenge of responding to the women's movement at a time when no other male writer of prominence felt the need to do so. It is to Mailer's credit that he tried to open a dialogue with the feminists; on the other hand, his effort failed because he did not make it in good faith. *The Prisoner of Sex* reveals what was reactionary in his worldview, the corner in which women are biologically different from men and therefore less than equals.

This is not to say that Mailer is the run-of-the-mill sexist he has sometimes been mistaken for. He takes individual women on their own terms — though in Mailer's universe, that means that he may challenge them to a fight. He is suspicious of what he calls "lady writers," as his pointed exclusion of them from his periodic evaluations of "the talent in the room" makes clear. But he did encourage all his wives in their search for a career (if only to undermine them in their efforts at the same time), and he clearly favored independent, strong-minded women as mates.

Yet Norman's instincts are those of a sexual conservative. For all that he advocates sexual liberation and the orgasm, he still believes that the purpose of sex is reproduction, that woman's most important role is as a wife and mother. This is not an unusual view; the existence of a woman's movement shows just how common it is. But Mailer is drawn again and again to the concept of sexual identity, and his meditations on the subject partake of a strange mysticism. The metaphor in the title of *The Prisoner of Sex* can refer as well to the prison that those who believe in biological essentialism make for themselves: if we are bound to our sexual identities, which do not allow us room to grow or change (because we are limited by our biology), we are truly imprisoned. In this way, investing sex with extraordinary meaning — positing sex as a mystical union and reproduction as a sacred rite — truly does make us prisoners of sex. It is not an idea that sits very well with Mailer's bastardized existentialism: prisoners of sex, we are never really free.

In his insistence on the centrality of sex in our lives — even in his conservative mysticism about sex — Mailer aims to upset and agitate his readers, reminding them of the need to challenge authority and break rules. He is at once a progressive — he favors sexual liberation and places sex at the center of our lives — and a sexual conservative — masturbation, contraception, and homosexuality are suspect because the true goal of sex is conception. In *The Prisoner of Sex,* Mailer's progressive side, the source of his best work, is subjugated, while the conservative and the sexual conservative in particular take center stage.

On the other hand, *The Prisoner of Sex* found any number of responsive readers, as the reviews indicated when the book version appeared in May 1971. Anatole Broyard, in the daily *New York Times,* thought the book was Mailer's best so far. (The Sunday *Times* review, by Brigid Brophy, was not as kind.) The *Newsweek* reviewer called it a "brilliant broadside"; Joyce Carol Oates, in a review essay in the *Atlantic Monthly,* saluted Mailer's "heroic mysticism," while V. S. Pritchett, in a companion essay, spoke of him as "a brilliant writer with sharp insights." Many reviewers took the occasion to air some of their own quarrels with the feminist movement.

For the message of the women's liberationists was a direct challenge to the existing hegemony, and, as such, it constituted a threat to a whole way of life and to a whole way of looking at the world. Many feared that feminism would shut off an entire area of moral inquiry because it rendered so many old certainties questionable. For Mailer, the movement ruled out musings about essential womanhood and essential manhood, both preoccupations of his work, and raised the question of whether such characters as Sergius O'Shaugnessy and Steven Rojack were based on reality or the author's fantasies and dreams of power. Mailer could be skeptical about concepts like virility or heroism — or even satirize them, as he did in *Why Are We in Vietnam?* — but he could not bear for them to be dismissed as pre-enlightenment relics or nonsense. For all his progressive nature, Mailer had to draw the line somewhere. If the line was well back in the rear guard, so be it.

THE ISSUE OF *Harper's* containing "The Prisoner of Sex" sold more copies than the magazine had ever sold before. Treatments of the women's movement — often dismissive or distorting — dominated the media in 1970, and a piece by Norman Mailer on the subject was a must-read. Four-letter words were not then the media commonplace that they are now, and the essay was perceived as daring. The editor of *Harper's* at the time, Willie Morris, was forced to resign at the end of February, just as the issue hit the streets, and a rumor started that he resigned because the management did not approve of the Mailer piece. The rumor was untrue (Morris was having arguments with management over financial matters), but he made a self-serving statement to the press that Norman's piece had "deeply disturbed the magazine's owners." In the tumult that followed — six editors left when Morris did — Mailer went to see Morris and even called the chairman of the board in Minneapolis, but there was little left to do. News of the editorial shakeup only heightened the interest in Mailer's essay.

The hardcover book would not be released until May. In the meantime, an opportunity presented itself to Mailer: the Theater of Ideas proposed a debate between him and selected feminists, to be held at the Town Hall on West Forty-third Street in Manhattan on March 31, when prepublication copies of *The Prisoner of Sex* were reaching the bookstores. Norman happily plunged into the arrangements, which were being handled by Shirley Broughton, Elizabeth Hardwick, and Bob Silvers.

The first difficulty was lining up any women for him to argue with. The idea of holding a debate about women's rights annoyed many feminists: rights were not something to be debated. Kate Millett, Ti-Grace Atkinson, Gloria Steinem, and Robin Morgan all refused the offer and stayed away from the event altogether. (Robin Morgan, according to a participant, "said she would come if she could shoot Mailer, citing the particulars of her license to possess a firearm.") As it turned out, the event would not be structured as a debate but rather as a series of presentations by women, with Norman moderating the evening.

Other women were willing to appear, among them Jackie Ceballos, the president of NOW, and Jill Johnston, *Village Voice* writer, dance critic, and militant lesbian. Diana Trilling, Mailer's old friend, also agreed to deliver a speech. The real draw, however, was Germaine Greer, the Australian feminist whose book *The Female Eunuch,* recently published in England, was about to appear in the United States. A striking woman who knew how to work the media, Greer contributed to the hype surrounding the Town Hall event, telling reporters that she planned to seduce Mailer or, alternatively, that she would "carry him like a wounded child across the wasted world."

On March 31, most of New York's intellectuals, literary workers, and feminists seemed to fill the hall; seats in the orchestra were a steep twenty-five dollars, while balcony berths cost ten dollars. Among the audience were Stephen Spender, Arthur Schlesinger, Jr., Jules Feiffer, Betty Friedan, Cynthia Ozick, Elizabeth Hardwick, John Hollander, Jack Newfield, and Anatole Broyard. Donn Pennebaker and his crew were there to film the event. Mailer clearly expected a big show: not only had he arranged for the event to be filmed, but he had also claimed literary rights to the evening through his agent, Scott Meredith. What was to follow was surely one of the most singular intellectual events of the time, and a landmark in the emergence of feminism as a major force. And, oddly enough, given the controversy around *The Prisoner of Sex,* Norman played a highly effective role as facilitator.

Greer and Mailer met in the greenroom, Norman looking paunchy in a dark suit and Germaine gorgeous — if somewhat outrageous — in a black dress and feather throw. She flirted openly with Norman; it seems she was genuinely attracted to him and he to her. "You look much better than I thought you would," Norman told her. (In the weeks to come, she saw Mailer at one of Marion Javits's dinner parties, and he told her, "You're not as good-looking as you were before.")

The debate began sedately enough with Jackie Ceballos of NOW speaking first. Members of the audience interrupted her several times, however — Gregory Corso claimed that men needed liberation too, and another heckler protested the high price of the tickets. Mailer heckled back, but he was on the whole well behaved. After Ceballos's speech, Norman spoke for several minutes about how positive the women's movement was and what a good job NOW was doing, then closed by posing a typically Mailerian question to the panelists about the movement: "Is there anything in your program that would give men the notion that life would not be as profoundly boring as it is today?"

Germaine Greer took the podium. She delivered a speech that made vague allusions to Mailer, commenting on the ego of the masculine artist in society. In return, Mailer criticized her speech: she had not provided a reason why a woman "can be a goddess and a slob at different times." The audience loved Greer, but they also loved Mailer. Though radical and militant lesbian feminists attended the event, they were outnumbered by the intellectuals and the literati, who clearly were indulging Norman. In Pennebaker's 1972 film *Town Bloody Hall,* he is at his most charming; even when he quiets hecklers with a putdown he seems benign. He was performing, and the audience was his.

Jill Johnston appeared next. She didn't seem to have a prepared speech, prompting Mailer to say, "You may use your time like the flight of birds, but I'll have to call you in ten minutes." Johnston went on to speak of the role of lesbians in the women's movement, claiming, "All women are lesbians except those who don't know it yet." She went on beyond her time limit, and Mailer's protests didn't stop her. Finally he interrupted to ask the audience to vote on whether Johnston should continue or get off the stage. He asked for a voice vote, but the voting was interrupted by the appearance of two of Johnston's women friends on stage. The three, in blue jeans and overalls, locked in an embrace, kissed, and then fell to the floor and started rolling around, still groping each other. Mailer, unfazed, told them to stop, and then said if anyone in the audience wanted to see this sort of thing they could go around the corner to Times Square. "Come on, Jill," he finally said, "be a lady." He then turned to the audience and asked for a show of hands on whether the spectacle should continue, and at last the three women left the stage.

Finally Diana Trilling took the podium, somewhat shaken by the way the evening was taking shape. She was aghast that the event was being filmed and that Mailer was followed by a retinue of photographers. She read her prepared speech, which cautioned Mailer that he was attributing far too many traits, like passivity, to women, and that he was moving beyond biology in a dangerous way. ("Biology is all very well, Norman," she said. "All these women have biology and they might be happy to celebrate it with you. But they have, as well, a repressive, life-diminishing culture to contend with.") She referred to Mailer's statement earlier that evening that the *Harper's* essay — which none of the others had mentioned — was "probably the most important single intellectual event of the last four years," which drew an indulgent laugh from the audience. Mailer tried to cut her off at ten minutes, which angered her, but Trilling summarized the rest of her speech and left the podium. She would later complain that Greer and Mailer were passing notes back and forth during her speech; Pennebaker's film does not bear this out, but neither Greer nor Mailer appears to have been listening while Trilling spoke.

After the speakers finished, Mailer opened the floor for questions. Most were directed at him. Betty Friedan read a written statement, and Elizabeth Hardwick asked if he ever actually did the housework. Cynthia Ozick called him a "transcendent sacerdotal priest," while Susan Sontag got up and scolded him for calling Jill Johnston a lady. Mailer's responses were facile, and he played for the laugh. It seems that nobody took the "debate" very seriously, and the air of the whole evening — wonderfully evoked in *Town Bloody Hall* — was festive, not confrontational. The audience liked Norman, and they encouraged him.

After the event, Greer went with Mailer to a party given by Jacob and Marion Javits in the Village, where Greer met Mailer's parents. The two writers were clearly generating a lot of nervous energy, which would continue over the next few weeks, but Greer, on the whole, was resistant to Norman's charms. He suggested to her that they continue the debate on the David Susskind show; she agreed, but then learned that he held literary rights to the debate. It took her publisher's corporate lawyers to extricate her from further involvement, and she was left suspicious of Mailer. He treated her meanly, she later complained, unless she, in effect, babied him: "He rallied [me] with minor kindnesses til [I] reverted to speaking loving words to him."

A few days after the Javits party, Greer, at a luncheon at the National Press Club, was asked, "If you, Norman Mailer, and Edward Kennedy were the last three people on earth, who would you choose to be the father of your child?" Greer was later surprised by the bitterness of her answer: "It would be better that the race should perish than that either of these men should be its father."

Greer's later dissatisfaction aside, the Town Hall event was, by and large, successful. Mailer showed again that it was as a provocateur, a controversialist — *not* as a philosopher mulling over a difficult issue — that he was most effective. While the participants and the audience ignored his opening question — how feminism could make the world less boring for men — they were egged on by his provocative remarks ("be a lady") to show just how intelligent and entertaining — and liberating — feminism could be. In this light, even his mild flirtation with Greer was absolutely to the point. His pugnacious presence, together with the outrageousness of a writer obsessed with masculinity moderating a "debate" about women's rights, defused the hostility in the air. *The Prisoner of Sex* had performed a similar function: it brought the issue of women's liberation into the center of discussion, spotlighting a subject that ran the risk of being marginalized. Few feminists would thank him for it, but, by commenting on the subject — however outrageously — he served notice that it was perhaps the single most important issue of the day.

TWENTY-ONE

"THE TERROR OF THE
TV TALK SHOW"

During the writing of *The Prisoner of Sex,* Norman had been moving forward on a number of fronts; he burned up tremendous energy in 1970, 1971, and 1972. *Of a Fire on the Moon,* he told a *Village Voice* interviewer in 1971, had been his first appearance as a "professional writer"; the press had been responsible for his "turning professional" by reporting that he had sold the moon shot project for a million dollars. He compared his career to that of a boxer: starting out as a streetfighter, the aspiring boxer chooses his opponents out of passion; once he acquires a manager and is fighting for money, his opponents are chosen for him, and something is lost. The writer becomes professional when he no longer chooses his own subject, and again something is lost. This development had not sat well with him: "It was a woe that I had to work twenty times harder than I wanted to work, and it wasn't the particular year of my life I wanted to work." The experience taught him that it might be best to follow his own intellectual instincts rather than write to order. Accordingly, *The Prisoner of Sex* represented an intellectual pursuit, an opportunity to try out his views about the relations between the sexes. It missed the mark. But feminism was an opponent that stimulated him, and he tackled the succession of projects that followed with energy.

Things were relatively quiet on the domestic front. At the beginning of 1971 Norman and Carol Stevens rented a big farmhouse in South Londonderry, Vermont — close enough to the city for him to visit for events like the Town Hall debate and various TV appearances, as well as to see his parents. Barney Mailer was undergoing treatment for the cancer that would kill him in the fall of 1972. Norman was shaken to see his father so reduced and to contemplate his mother's life alone. Buzz Farbar's father died a year after Barney Mailer did, and in his grief Buzz turned to Norman. The counsel

Norman offered reflected the grief he himself had felt, and continued to feel. "It's like having a hole in your tooth," Norman told him. Other people said the memory of a loved one faded over time, but Norman contradicted that. The hole would always remain, he said. It was no use hoping it would be filled again.

At the end of the summer of 1970 — the summer when Norman was alone with the children in Maine — Norman told Beverly that Carol was pregnant. For Beverly, that was the closure she needed. She offered to give Norman a divorce so that he could marry Carol, but Norman refused, citing the case of Ezra Pound, who, he believed, "didn't marry his mistress." On March 21, 1971, Carol delivered a baby girl, whom she and Norman named Maggie Alexandra. She was Norman's seventh child and his fifth daughter.

That spring, New York was buzzing over Mailer's articles on feminism in *Harper's;* in contrast, Norman was enjoying a quiet life in Vermont, planting a garden and enjoying Carol and Maggie. But rural life never appealed to him for long. Just as he had during his exile with Adele in Connecticut in the 1950s, he soon grew restless and began seeking new projects. He took up boxing once again, now in earnest. He invited José Torres, who had retired from the ring in 1969, to join him in South Londonderry. José and his wife rented a nearby house, and soon he and Norman established a daily routine. With the help of Bert Sugar, the publisher of *Boxing Illustrated,* Torres was composing a book on Cassius Clay, now Muhammad Ali, called *Sting Like a Bee,* and he asked his friend to write the introduction. Norman agreed but cautioned the boxer that he would have to read the book first. After he did, he called Torres's publisher and asked him to give José more money and time to write the book as it should be written. Thus it happened that Norman gave José daily lessons in writing, going over the draft mercilessly. Torres found the work incredibly hard going; English was not his first language, and the words came very slowly.

In return, Torres offered to give Mailer boxing lessons. Norman was still in fair shape, though at forty-seven he was developing a paunch, and he pitched himself headlong into the lessons. Torres of course held back, knowing he could hurt his friend, but Mailer urged him not to. At one point Torres asked Cus D'Amato to visit to give his opinion on how the lessons were going. D'Amato, who had seen Hemingway box, thought Mailer was, in comparison, a serious fighter, determined to become a good boxer, while Hemingway's boxing was really a bluff. Torres's and Mailer's joint work culminated in an appearance together on Dick Cavett's TV show to promote Torres's book. They sparred on camera in a makeshift ring, giving the impression of a fair, hard-fought match.

By far the most compelling figure in the boxing world in the early 1970s was Muhammad Ali, the world heavyweight champion; and like almost everyone who followed the sport — and even many who didn't — Norman was fascinated by him. He would follow the boxer's career with interest until the three-time title holder retired in 1981. Ali had been stripped of his title in 1967 when he refused to fight in the Vietnam War out of religious conviction. Eventually the Supreme Court upheld his appeal, and he returned to boxing in 1970.

If anything, Ali's absence from the ring had increased his stature as the most vivid personality in professional sports and perhaps the most visible black man of the day. Before his banishment, Ali had been a flamboyant champion. After he returned, his articulate defense of his refusal to fight the unpopular "white man's war" and his nonstop promotion of his own prowess over such rivals as Joe Frazier and George Foreman — a whole new generation of fighters had appeared during his absence — only increased his prominence.

He had natural appeal for Norman. Here was exactly the kind of personality who made public life so interesting to him, an existential hero who devoted himself to making his own life a work of art as much as he did to his boxing career, and who was prompting responses and possibilities in his public that were absolutely new. People loved him and people hated him, but everybody noticed him.

To Norman, Ali seemed the very embodiment of ego. Yet Ali was at the same time remarkably in touch with his age, and was a potent black leader. Obviously charged with admiration, Mailer would write that Ali was "the swiftest embodiment of human intelligence we have had yet, he is the very spirit of the twentieth century, he is the prince of mass man and the media." *Life* assigned him to write about the first Ali-Frazier fight, billed as "The Fight of the Century," in 1971; the article would appear in the March 19, 1971, issue, titled "Ego," later collected as "King of the Hill" in *Existential Errands* (1972).

In the essay, Mailer explores Ali's character and reviews his two previous fights since his release from jail. He describes the two boxers training for the match and the great stake he and many others had in Ali's winning back the world heavyweight title from Joe Frazier:

> He was coming to claim his victory on the confluence of two mighty tides — he was the mightiest victim of injustice in America and he was also . . . the mightiest narcissist in the land. Every beard, dropout, homosexual, junkie, freak, swinger, and plain simple individualist adored him. Every pedantic liberal soul who had once loved Patterson now paid homage to Ali. The mightiest of the Black psyches and the most filigreed of the white psyches were

ready to roar him home, as well as every hardworking square American who genuinely hated the war in Vietnam. What a tangle of ribbons he carried on his lance.

He goes on to detail at great length the fight itself, which, to the eternal regret of his fans, including Mailer, Ali lost. Like many boxing aficionados, Mailer called for a rematch, and his essay ends effectively there.

"Ego," or "King of the Hill," is a passionate and enjoyable excursion, something the writer obviously enjoyed a great deal; it is a small classic in boxing literature. It was written under tremendous pressure: the fight, held at Madison Square Garden, was on Monday and *Life* closed on Wednesday, so Mailer wrote the article in one marathon sitting, messengering over his text to editor Ralph Graves in installments. It is remarkable that Mailer, caught up in the prefight frenzy and then experiencing the thrill of the fight itself — it lived up to its hype — should have been able to settle in so quickly to write with considerable concentration and stamina. Graves thought the piece contained "some of the best sports reporting ever written. It's in a league with William Hazlitt, or John Updike on Ted Williams." When Mailer turned in the last installment, he told Graves, referring to the Apollo articles, "Ralph, I owed you something good."

Norman would return soon to the subject of Ali. But another project that preoccupied him in 1971 was the ongoing promotion of *Maidstone*, a film that, when the editing was finished in 1970, seemed to him another small masterpiece. Unfortunately, audiences were, for the most part, not in agreement. Norman and Carol flew to London in October 1970 for the film's premiere there; after the film, Norman, glass in hand, took the stage and asked audience members for feedback. "We appreciate Mailer, the writer and author, and God knows why he started making these films," shouted one young man. Another asked, "With all this money to throw around, couldn't you make a film with some content?" Norman demanded to be taken seriously, announcing, "If you have any respect for my writing, you must believe I am up to something." Later he told an interviewer that the film showed "new modes of perceiving reality." Clearly, he had not given up on *Maidstone*: "If you keep seeing it," he claimed, "you see much more order. My bet on the film is that it's capable of being seen over and over." From London Norman and Carol went on to Venice: he introduced the film to the Venice Film Festival, where it got a similar reception.

But what mattered most to Norman was the film's reception in New York. He was unable to find a commercial distributor and thus arranged any showings himself, which accounts for the long intervals between them. In October 1971 the film began a two-week run at the Whitney Museum as part of a fall series devoted to American filmmakers. For opening night,

Supreme Mix, the production company headed by Buzz Farbar and Mailer, threw a big party in the adjacent permanent collection space. Although the invitation promised that Mayor Lindsay, Ultra Violet, Mary Hemingway, and Arthur Schlesinger, Jr., among many others, would attend, no celebrities of any note were present that evening. Still, the theater was packed, and Mailer claimed the film broke the Whitney's attendance record. Some seven thousand saw it over the course of its run, he estimated. Encouraged, he showed the film in a commercial theater one night, but almost no one came. A friend explained it to him: "It's very simple, Norman. There are 7,000 people in New York who wanted to see *Maidstone* and that's it." It received little critical notice: Vincent Canby, reviewing it for the *New York Times*, felt that as a film, it represented "an abrupt decline" from *Beyond the Law*, but, "seen as part of a Mailer continuum, *Maidstone* is a sometimes hilarious, often boring but always adventurous ego trip." *The New Yorker* chose not to review it and instead ran a "Talk of the Town" piece about the invitation and the celebrities the opening failed to deliver.

Over the years, Norman contented himself by saying people had two reactions to the film: they either loved it or hated it. But he had put a great deal into the project; financially, the film crippled him for several years (he had sunk three hundred thousand dollars into it). Later he would say, "I would have done better to have bought a yacht and sunk it." But in 1971 he was still enthusiastic and hopeful. In the same year, NAL put out a paperback called *Maidstone: A Mystery*, which contained a transcript of the film, accounts of the film by journalists Sally Beauman and James Toback, stills from the movie, and a selection showing the cuts that were made in a particular segment of the film. Most notably, it contained Mailer's "A Course in Filmmaking" (which he would include in *Existential Errands*), an essay in which he explains the conception of the film, makes observations about film in general, describes the making of the film, and assesses what he had come to see as Rip Torn's essential contribution to the film (in "attempting assassination" on Mailer/Norman Kingsley).

Reminders of *The Prisoner of Sex* and the Town Hall event reached him at his Vermont retreat. In July, Norman picked up a copy of the *New York Review of Books* and turned to a review by Gore Vidal of Eva Figes's *Patriarchal Attitudes,* a contribution to the growing field of feminist theory. There he read, "There has been from Henry Miller and Norman Mailer to Charles Manson a logical progression. The Miller-Mailer-Manson man (or M3 for short) has been conditioned to think of women as, at best, breeders of sons; at worst, objects to be poked, humiliated, killed. Needless to say, M3's reaction to Women's Liberation has been one of panic." Of course, Mailer's response to feminism was far more complicated than this, and his reaction to Vidal's observation was one of blind rage.

The relationship between these two very public writers had long been strained, despite a long association that at times could be described as a friendship. The trouble had begun at least one decade before, if not two. Both had been hailed for their first novels, both war stories, though Vidal's *Williwaw* did not command quite the kind of attention that *The Naked and the Dead* had. For his part, Vidal revealed, in a 1960 review of *Advertisements for Myself* in *The Nation* that occasioned a retrospective of Mailer's career, that his first reaction to *The Naked and the Dead* had been, "It's a fake. A clever, talented, admirably executed fake." He had not changed his opinion of the book since, he wrote, though his general opinion of Mailer had improved. "Sourly" he remembered the year their respective books had come out, and how Mailer's star had risen as his had not. (Vidal had temporarily abandoned writing fiction for more lucrative screen and play writing.) He related how he'd met Mailer in 1954 — they were introduced by Marc Brandel, a fellow writer — and confessed that his first impression had been somewhat guarded: "I am suspicious of people who make speeches at me." Vidal criticized Mailer's career in the *Nation* piece at length — Mailer is "a Bolingbroke, a born usurper," "a public writer, not a private artist" — but closed the essay with the following: "Mailer in all that he does, whether he does it well or ill, is honorable, and that is the highest praise I can give any writer in this piping time."

Vidal had been very kind to Mailer in the immediate aftermath of his stabbing of Adele. Generally, however, the two kept each other at arm's length and seldom commented on each other's writing. Mailer had accused Vidal of "narcissism" in *Advertisements,* which Vidal took to be a code word for homosexuality — which Mailer in turn denied.

According to Vidal's biographer, Fred Kaplan, the simmering disagreements between the two writers came to a head, at least as far as Vidal was concerned, when both were covering the 1968 political conventions. Vidal, William F. Buckley, and TV journalist Howard K. Smith formed a kind of traveling panel of commentators that met on television during both conventions. The right-wing Buckley established a pattern of baiting Vidal as "a Commie pinko fag," according to Kaplan, while Vidal took to responding by calling Buckley a fascist (or words to that effect). Then Vidal saw Buckley and Mailer rubbing elbows at a bar in Chicago during the Democratic Convention, and something snapped: Norman was brownnosing a fascist, and Vidal had no sympathy whatsoever.

Both writers had sharp wits and sharper tongues, and many a cutting remark reached the other through third parties after this incident. Then came Vidal's comments in his review of the Figes book, and what journalists refer to as a "pissing match" was on. What bothered Mailer most was the absolute conviction and lack of irony with which Vidal — himself not "a suitable valet for Henry Miller," Mailer would later say — posited the connection between himself and Miller and Manson. "Mailer could hardly wait to catch up with Gore Vidal," Norman wrote six years later. He would catch up with him in one of his favorite — if not always felicitous — public arenas, the television talk show.

NORMAN HAD MUCH the same love-hate relationship with television that millions of viewers have. He had begun watching heavily in 1954, the same year in which he discovered pot, and he often watched into the small hours of the morning — first Steve Allen, then Ernie Kovacs, then the national anthem, and finally just gray static — making all manner of cosmic connections between the commercials and the content of the shows. He and Adele had a TV routine: after dinner, the Sid Caesar show, *Playhouse 90,* and *Night Beat,* Mike Wallace's talk show. The Elaine May and Mike Nichols act, aired on some of these shows, was one of Adele and Norman's favorite TV events. Like many parents, they discovered TV's narcotic effect on their children and guiltily exploited it as a babysitter. Over the early years of television, Norman came to see it as a social evil on the order of public housing architecture, plastic, and napalm — but he did not stop watching.

Appearing on television was an entirely different matter, however. As a celebrity author who was unofficially running for the presidency of the literary universe — and who, on and off, harbored desires for earthly political office as well — he was quite aware of television's power. For any budding candidate, and for any artist whose economic value was ultimately dependent on sales to a mass public, TV was of course a tremendous publicity generator; moreover, in spite of his suspicions, Norman could see television in some lights as a creative medium in itself. It is not an accident that Steven Rojack, the hero of *An American Dream,* is a talk show host — or, as Mailer calls him, "a personality on television."

For the longest time Norman had believed that he was a natural on television, that he was good-looking and had enough charisma and personality to impress his host and his viewers. It was not so simple, however. Norman's timing in conversation was not that of a natural wit; his mind was often too subtle for the give-and-take of the television talk show; and he was given to gratuitous insults that alienated the studio audience and disgusted viewers at home. He often appeared paunchy and wrinkled, and his appearance wasn't helped by the several drinks he almost always consumed before appearing on camera.

In an amusing and perceptive article about television written for *Esquire* in 1977, Mailer would review the high (and low) points of his television career. His first appearance was on *Night Beat* in 1957 with the notoriously aggressive Mike Wallace: Norman managed to say that *Life* was a dirty magazine, as well as to call President Eisenhower "a bit of a woman." In 1959 he appeared on David Susskind's *Open End* with two more finely honed wits, Dorothy Parker and Truman Capote, and despite Mailer's attempts to make an impact — he accused all politicians of being whores — Capote stole the show with the remark that what Jack Kerouac did was not writing but typing. (Mulling over Capote's success, Norman asked the program for a kinescope. Viewing it, he decided to shave off his goatee.)

He had a few successes in those early years. He was particularly pleased with himself for telling Irv Kupcinet, host of a Chicago talk show called *At Random*, that J. Edgar Hoover had done more harm to America than had Joseph Stalin; no matter that the show aired at four o'clock on Sunday morning. With such spontaneous verbal hand grenades, he felt, he could make a change in people's lives and in society — as well as imprint his personality on the public's consciousness.

Yet as the years went on, and live shows were phased out in favor of pretaped programs, and as he began to do the talk show circuit for each book that he produced, his enthusiasm dimmed. ("Of course," he wrote, "TV did not cause his books to sell — not with his personality — but still he went on!") Before long he'd been on all the networks and many of their affiliates all over the country; he had appeared with all manner of guests — once, even, with Malcolm Muggeridge and the not yet famous Mother Teresa; he had triumphed on some occasions, and he had lost on many others. He sparred verbally with his old foe William F. Buckley on the Les Crane show and the David Susskind show; finally, on *Firing Line* he enjoyed telling Buckley that Charles de Gaulle and Castro were the only two heroes in the modern world. But in all his appearances he had only a couple of (to his mind) truly shining moments: the Eisenhower remark, and the time when, upon being grilled by David Frost on the connection between murder and sex, he said, "David, do you want me to unzip and lay it on the table and show you the welts and the warts?" Such exchanges had, by 1971, prompted *Time* magazine to dub him "the terror of the TV talk show."

Yet television always wanted him back, not least because his outrageousness drew audiences. The talk shows depended on him because he was right about the times, times that were characterized by huge social upheavals that seemed to demand interpreters who would subvert assumptions and provoke audiences. At a time when many events left commentators either mouthing platitudes or just refusing to comment — about the Vietnam War and the attendant protests, for example — it made sense to book a guest whose point, above everything else, was to recognize these events and the changes they brought with them. And Norman could always be counted on to do this.

Mailer's first showdown with Gore Vidal took place on the Dick Cavett show, broadcast live on December 2, 1971. Primed by three or four drinks at a cocktail party earlier, Norman was in the greenroom trying to compose himself when he felt a caressing hand on the back of his neck. Confronting Vidal, Mailer gave him a stiff "tap" on the cheek. Vidal gave him one back. Then Mailer lowered his head and headbutted Vidal — almost, but not quite, with full force. "You're absolutely mad. You *are* violent," said Vidal, who then went on to take the stage. After some back-and-forth with Cavett, Vidal was joined by *New Yorker* Paris correspondent Janet Flanner, a formidable presence who made it clear her sympathies were with Vidal. Vidal won over the audience with some witty insider's anecdotes about Eleanor Roosevelt, and Flanner's interesting, crusty personality won audience sympathy. "The only answer," thought Norman, still offstage in the greenroom, "was attack. Shatter all prepared positions." "Go out," he said to himself, "and smash that fucking teahouse."

Mailer took the stage, pointedly not shaking hands with Vidal. When Cavett asked why he hadn't done so, Mailer responded with an attack on Vidal's "weak" and "shameless" intellect. Very quickly, Mailer lost his audience; when he described the contents of Vidal's stomach as "no more interesting than the contents of the stomach of an intellectual cow," the studio rang with boos. Realizing that the audience had no knowledge of Vidal's attack on him in the *New York Review of Books* as "M3," Mailer pulled the clipping from his pocket during a commercial break and asked Cavett to give it to Vidal to read aloud. Cavett was decidedly not on Mailer's side — Mailer remembered a show on which he had explained to Cavett what a superior host David Frost was. But he gave the clipping to Vidal, who put it in his pocket and proceeded to spar with Mailer without mentioning it.

More trading of insults followed. Vidal offered to apologize for the Manson comparison if it hurt Mailer's feelings.

> Mailer: No, it hurts my sense of intellectual pollution.
> Vidal: Well, I must say, as an expert, you should know about such things. [*laughter*]
> Mailer: Yes, well, I've had to smell your works from time to time, and that has helped me to become an expert on intellectual pollution, yes.

And so it went. At one point, irritated, Mailer asked Cavett, "Why don't you look at your question sheet and ask a question?" Cavett had his opening: "Why don't you fold it five ways and put it where the moon don't shine?"

Mailer managed to get off one speech about his main complaint, that Vidal had misrepresented him. It had happened many times over the years, he said, and it happened because "I've been so bold as to pretend to be the presumptive literary champ, whether I deserve to be or not." Hemingway had taken the same stance, he argued. Here he was, setting himself up as a champ and therefore willing to let others have their chance to knock him off, but instead "they're simply too damned yellow, and they kick me in the nuts, and I don't like it." He got a round of applause.

But the evening deteriorated, and the audience began to heckle him. Vidal tried to resphrase his M3 statement in a more generous fashion, but Mailer remained stony. Vidal tried to engage him in a discussion about the sexual nature of murder. Here matters took a curious turn indeed, as Mailer accused Vidal, sensationally, of having indirectly committed murder: "You bragged about what you did to Jack Kerouac, after all." Vidal replied, "He didn't die," and Mailer corrected him: "Well, he did." (This exchange, which must have mystified the audience, referred to a long-held and most irrational belief of Mailer's that through having anal sex with Kerouac, Vidal had been responsible for Kerouac's drinking himself to death.)

Mailer's descent to this level — bringing up an irrational argument before people who had no idea to what he was referring — indicates just how completely the discussion had gotten away from him. He was genuinely hurt by the dismissal with which the others on stage — and in the audience — treated him, and he communicated it clumsily. While Cavett, Vidal, and Flanner came across as swift and urbane, Mailer was reduced to pleading with those present in this fashion: "Can I reach you, can I talk to any of you, or is it hopeless? I do have a thing to say, believe it or not."

In the main, Mailer's pugnaciousness and his total lack of perspective were his undoing. Given one remaining minute, he took the time to straighten out a remark of Vidal's: that the hero of *An American Dream* kills his wife and then buggers the maid. In fact, Mailer began, he didn't just "bugger" her; actually his hero entered her "another way." Here Flanner cut him off by saying, "Oh, goodness's sake." Mailer persisted: "I know you've lived in France for many years, but believe me, Janet, it's possible to enter a woman another way as well." Flanner answered coolly, "So I've heard." Cavett then announced that "on that classy note" they would go to a commercial, and the evening was effectively over.

So was the truce with Vidal. Six years later there would be an incident at a party given by New York socialite Lally Weymouth in which a drink was thrown (Mailer's) and a thumb was bitten (also Mailer's). A rematch on the Cavett show followed in 1978. The same year, at a party following the National Book Awards, Norman, drunk, and getting angry watching Vidal socialize, suddenly and without any warning blindsided him, pitching Vidal onto the buffet table. But Vidal got off a good line: "Well, Norman, once again words failed you." In fact, it would be close to fifteen years before the two writers who had so much in common — not least a real talent for feuding — effected a rapprochement.

When it came to television, Mailer never really learned. As someone who viewed performance as an art form, he was strangely unable to understand that a television talk show was not an occasion for a serious exchange of ideas but an occasion for performance. When his attempts to make serious conversation fell flat, he would often respond with unplanned, clumsy, and pugnacious behavior. One so skilled at attack had no talent for the concise, subtle one-upmanship demanded by the television exchange. He simply blundered onstage with a few set ideas in his head and just could not respond if the conversation took an unexpected turn. If he was allowed to lead without any interruption he could usually make his point, but more times than not his point was elusive, overly idiosyncratic, or just odd, so imperfect was his understanding of how to reach a television audience.

IN THE SPRING OF 1972 Norman tried to get himself prepared to cover his seventh and eighth national conventions, both, this time around, held in Miami. Because the magazine he was most closely allied with at this moment was *Life,* he turned to that magazine's editors for an assignment. But the *Life* editors felt that the Republican Convention, where Nixon was to be routinely nominated for reelection, offered no surprises — Nixon had even named his running mate, Spiro Agnew, in advance — and therefore did not merit a magazine piece. *Life* gladly agreed to send Norman to Miami for the Democratic Convention, however. While George McGovern was confidently expected to win the nomination, other interesting candidates were also in the race: Edmund Muskie, Scoop Jackson, Hubert Humphrey, George Wallace (in a wheelchair after an attempt on his life), and Shirley Chisholm. There was a possibility that Teddy Kennedy might be nominated. The Yippies were rumored to be planning an appearance, so unrest was possible.

Norman decided to go to both gatherings anyway; later, he would get the *New York Review of Books* to run his piece about the Republican Convention, and New American Library would publish both pieces as a paperback with the title *St. George and the Godfather.* But *Life*'s instincts proved accurate: the Republican Convention bored him thoroughly, and the protesting Yippies and other left-wing groups in Miami's Flamingo Park were too disorganized and too polarized to get much of a protest going. The left, Mailer wrote, had "headed into the worst trap of all, which is to attack the Godfather in a Media war." It didn't really matter, he concluded, for disrupting the program would only have reinforced Nixon's consensus. As for the Republican break-in at the Watergate office complex and the ensuing coverup, a scandal that would involve abuses of power by officials in the Nixon White House — and the president himself — and that transfixed the nation, he alluded to it only briefly; describing an interview with Henry Kissinger, he did not say whether he even brought up the scandal. Of course, by the summer of 1972 the puzzle was still in pieces. Yet it seems strangely out of character for Norman, so attuned to conspiracies, to have shown so little curiosity about the Watergate break-in and the discovery of the burglars' connections to the Committee to Re-Elect the President.

But then, his coverage of the two conventions was overall a little tired. He called himself Aquarius again — albeit "comfortable middle-aged Aquarius" — and even quoted his own earlier writing on the subject of Miami. While he was impressed by the McGovern campaign's successes, he wrote, "Yet there is no excitement. It is as if a fine and upstanding minister had moved into the empty house up the street: isn't it nice to have Reverend and the lovely Mrs. McGovern for neighbors?" Finally, though he came to like McGovern and would be able to vote for him in the election, Mailer, whose piece in *Life* would be titled, misleadingly, "The Evil in the Room," confessed to profound boredom:

> One had to be partial to a man whose delegates had the fair and average and open faces of an army of citizenry, instead of an army of the pols, and Aquarius knew then why the convention was obliged to be boring. There was insufficient evil in the room. With all the evil he had seen, all the lies and deals and evasions and cracks of the open door, with the betrayals of planks and the voids of promises, still there had been so little of real evil in the room.

He longed for the "old convention," he wrote, at which "a study of faces was equal to a study of American corporations and crime."

The liveliest moments in *St. George and the Godfather* describe something that happened not during the Democratic Convention but ten days afterward: McGovern's request that Thomas Eagleton withdraw from the ticket after his history of electric shock treatment was revealed. In an interview, McGovern supporter and actor Warren Beatty hinted to Mailer that the news about Eagleton came from an anonymous phone call — and thus quite possibly from the Republican camp. This suggestion would animate Mailer's thinking over the months to come.

But the bulk of *St. George and the Godfather* is not inspired. It was not even published in hardcover; instead, NAL issued a paperback in October 1972. It received almost no critical notice and found few readers. Those who did review it complained that Mailer was covering old ground. Garry

Wills, in the *New York Times,* wrote, "Mailer is our literary Rojack; he can get away with murder. And it seems on the face of it, a journalistic crime for him to circle back, doing Miami-and-Miami after his *Miami and the Siege of Chicago.*"

St. George and the Godfather contains some fine writing, but Mailer could not find the political pulse of the conventions. In the case of the Democratic Convention, this represented a real failing. For that convention was historic: organized labor and the old clubhouse politicians had lost their stranglehold on the party, and a whole new generation of younger Democrats (including Bill Clinton and Gary Hart), who had come of age in the 1960s, was coming to the fore. The impact of this shift would be even more noticeable in 1974, with the Democratic landslide in Congress, but the convention marked the end of the old Democratic coalition. Mailer seems to have utterly missed this; moreover, he adopts a strangely crotchety tone toward the new young Democrats to the extent that he notices them at all.

ANOTHER 1972 publication was much more successful. Mailer's *Existential Errands* was the latest in a series of collections that included *Advertisements, The Presidential Papers,* and *Cannibals and Christians.* It is a compendium of essays, reviews, letters to the editor, interviews, his speech accepting the National Book Award, a long essay defending *Maidstone* that attempts to define his aesthetic as a filmmaker, and an open letter to President Nixon. He explains in a preface that the Establishment is not in itself good or evil but is instead a put-on, a species of camp, with no real meaning. Thus, this selection of writing is on "existential" themes. It is no wonder, he writes,

> for in our world of gesture, role, costume, supposition, and borrowed manner which is all of the air that is left to the graces of our city, in that perpetual transformation of moral axes which is the inner life of the drug, there is except for attrition no way out but by way of the moment which proves deeper than any of our pretenses, that stricken existential moment in which Camp is stripped of its marks of quotation, and put-ons shrivel in the livid air.

It is not the most coherent organizing principle, and in fact the collection is diverse and uneven.

Reviewers noted the collection's incoherence but admired individual pieces very much. The *New York Review of Books* found "plenty of strong writing, which in [Mailer's] case also means strong thinking." Cynthia Buchanan, writing for the *New York Times Book Review,* thought the absence of an organizing principle harmed an otherwise interesting book: "With the essays in general, he does not organize quite enough to be persuasive. Simply to flip open the top of his head to expose his frontal lobes throbbing with 'existential' 'entropy' like some misguided gent flashing open his rain coat is not enough. Yet even as he is combing over the bald spots in his theories, his conclusions intrigue."

But *Existential Errands* contains some fascinating performances: Mailer's essay on the Ali-Frazier fight is here, as is his devastating 1968 review of Norman Podhoretz's *Making It*. A fragment from a stage version of *Why Are We in Vietnam?* is a verbal tour de force, even if its dramatic possibilities are unclear. And the last section of the book forms a fairly coherent political statement, with his open letter to the president (in which he calls for "the artful balance of old dialogues and new, of revolutionary approaches to particular problems and the delicate restoration of tradition"), a *New York Times Magazine* article setting forth his vision for the city of New York, and two speeches from his mayoral race. One, before the staff of *Time/Life,* was thought by his campaign manager to be one of the best speeches of the campaign. The other is a curious choice: his disastrous speech before his student volunteers at the Village Gate, when he drunkenly harassed them in the foulest possible language. Perhaps Mailer included it here because he saw it as an existential moment; given his earlier definition of the term — that such a moment be a "pure" activity, free of the put-on and the artificial — perhaps he was right. But most likely he included it because he wanted to remind his readers of one of his most memorable stunts, actions that kept him in the headlines and reinforced his celebrity — if at a price. Certainly the speech, placed alongside more thoughtful political reflections, casts doubt on the seriousness of the pieces it is grouped with; on the other hand, it is delicious reading, and reminds the reader of the man's complexity. Moreover, it saves him from appearing pompous — a very real concern for a writer prone to making pronouncements on weighty matters. If he came off as a bit of a fool, the Village Gate performance served its purpose: it got him the attention he thrived on.

Or he might have included the text of the Village Gate speech for another reason: out of the frustration of a man who just could not seem to get through to people — as in his appearance on the Cavett show. Norman wanted badly to be a communicator and an existential hero, and the mayoral race was particularly frustrating to him: the people simply weren't going to rise up and follow him! He may have concluded by 1972 that politics had failed him, that it hadn't given him a proper stage. Including his awful speech in *Existential Errands* may have represented Norman's final raspberry to the political game. In future, he would turn to more symbolic, iconic subjects, like Muhammad Ali and Marilyn Monroe. He was not alone in this: many 1960s radicals were making a spiritual turn in the beginning of the 1970s. Mailer, who experienced the 1960s as an older man, relatively speaking, turned not to the spiritual but rather to the existential, searching for icons in whom he could believe.

IN 1972, just before he turned fifty, Norman was reluctant to install his mistress, Carol, and new baby, Maggie, in the Brooklyn Heights brownstone; perhaps he thought it might make his mother uncomfortable, something he was especially reluctant to see in the aftermath of his father's death. The lease was up on the Vermont house, so Norman and Carol started looking for a place to buy. Though staying in the city would have made vastly more sense for Carol's singing career, Norman was adamant that he could get more work done outside the city, and in September he bought a large, shingle-style mansion on Yale Hill Road in Stockbridge, Massachusetts, paying seventy-five thousand dollars.

Carol threw herself into decorating, and by the new year the house was completely furnished, largely in Victorian antiques. But Norman was spending little time there. He had a new mistress, his brunette assistant Suzanne Nye, and he spent a lot of time with her down in New York. Carol began to chafe at her isolation and seemed to visitors "sad — not self-pitying, just sad." She befriended Anne Edwards, a nearby innkeeper, who arranged for Carol to sing on Friday evenings at Orpheus Ascending, the inn's cabaret, a place frequented by visiting New Yorkers.

Norman was present at Carol's first performance at Orpheus Ascending and made sure it wouldn't be easily forgotten. Carol was magnificent in a bright green chiffon dress, with yards of fabric held at her shoulder with a rhinestone clip; Edwards thought her "one of the most beautiful women I have ever known, with fine-chiseled bones." Carol went onstage, and immediately two couples sitting near Norman began to make noise, offering drunken comments on her cleavage. Norman went over to the principal offender and butted him in the head. He then asked the heckler to step outside, saying, "I'll challenge you to a re-butt." Carol, who had flown to Norman's side, seethed, saying, "If you do this, Norman, I will never forgive you." Things settled down, and Norman and his opponent retired to the bar, complimenting each other on the hardness of their heads, while Carol sang.

The Stockbridge house was too big for the Mailer ménage, winter version — Maggie, Carol's grown son David, and Norman and Carol — so Norman extended invitations to his New York and Provincetown friends. José Torres came up on weekends, as did Buzz Farbar, sometimes with his wife and three daughters. Fan and Barbara, now married to Al Wasserman, were frequent guests. The writer Selden Rodman, visiting from New Jersey, found Norman's mother in residence, reading from a book called *Fasting Can Save Your Life*. Norman revealed that he had recently completed a two-week fast. Also in attendance, doing odd chores around the rambling house, was Richard Stratton, a fairly recent acquaintance who would become an important friend.

Mailer had met Stratton in November 1970, in Provincetown. Scion of an old Wellesley family, Stratton had won a wrestling scholarship to Arizona State University but had abandoned academia for a peripatetic life as a drug smuggler and striving writer. After taking a writing course at Harvard, he won a fellowship to the Provincetown Fine Arts Work Center in 1970. He was living in an apartment there with his wife, Gabrielle, and stepdaughter, Tanya, supporting himself by doing carpentry. Long a Mailer admirer, Stratton had written to Mailer some time before about his essay on the Patterson fight, especially his description of the Benny Paret fight, and Mailer had responded warmly. Sharing Stratton's Provincetown building was Norman's housekeeper, Bobbie Swafford, who kept insisting that the two men get together. One night Stratton came home to a ringing phone; it was Norman, asking him to come over to watch *Monday Night Football*. That night, over a bottle of whiskey and then a bottle of cognac, the friendship was cemented.

"We had a fine friendship," Norman would later say of himself and Stratton. Though half his age — twenty-four, to Norman's forty-eight — Stratton shared Norman's interests in boxing, headbutting, and wrestling, and in literature and philosophy. In a repeated pattern, Stratton tried to interest Norman in rock music, but Norman, never very musical and out of touch since his 1950s fascination with modern jazz, couldn't respond with much enthusiasm.

When Norman bought the Stockbridge house, Stratton and his wife were put to work on another piece of property that Norman bought around the same time: a farmhouse in Phillips, Maine, a small town in the western part of the state, near Rangeley, a good spot for hunting, fishing, and skiing. Nearby in Kingsfield was another relatively new friend of Norman's, Dick Goodwin. Once a speechwriter for Kennedy and Johnson, Goodwin wrote books and articles on political and social issues and was spending a lot of time in Maine recovering from his wife's recent suicide. Norman was acquainted with Goodwin through his journalistic activities, but it was not until they spent time together in Maine that they became friends. In fact, Goodwin was part owner with Norman of the Phillips farmhouse. Stratton went up to do some work around the house and soon moved there with his family. Though Norman never contemplated living there permanently, Phillips became a real retreat for him.

TWENTY-TWO

MAILER AND MONROE

In the fall of 1972, just before Mailer turned fifty, his career seemed at a turning point. So far as the progress of his reputation was concerned, *Of a Fire on the Moon* and *The Prisoner of Sex* represented holding patterns, although *The Prisoner of Sex* helped fortify his bad boy reputation. Norman knew the public was waiting for his long overdue novel, but he couldn't get anywhere with that. He tried lots of approaches, at one point situating the Mailer clan's origins in ancient Egypt, at another projecting a volume that would take place in outer space. But he could fasten on no single, workable story line. It seemed that no one ever suggested that either of these ideas represented a departure from his previous work; he always maintained that his subject was Time, and presumably thought the work would have to cover a lot of it. As it was, he wrote some in each vein, never very successfully. Moreover, at fifty, he had a distinct awareness of the passage of time. Musing about his tangle with Vidal on the Cavett show, he wrote, "he knew that he had wasted another fierce piece of Time."

It was at this critical juncture that the redoubtable Larry Schiller entered Norman's life. An information entrepreneur, Schiller had a project in need of a name writer: a book of photographs of Marilyn Monroe. The collection of photos had a long history. Schiller himself had taken the last of the (relatively rare) nude photographs of the star. When a fellow Monroe photographer, John Bryson, called Schiller to suggest that they show their Monroe shots at an art gallery running an exhibit of pictures of her, Schiller decided to contact all the photographers who had taken pictures of Monroe and make some money for himself and for them, by exhibiting first in galleries and later assembling a book. He was currently "producing" Albert Goldman's biography of Lenny Bruce for Random House, so he approached Jim Silberman there with his idea of a Monroe book. Silberman liked the idea but thought it needed some prestigious text to go with the photos: the names of *Life* writer Loudon Wainwright and film critics Pauline Kael and Rex Reed were tossed around. But Silberman wasn't convinced, and Schiller wanted fifty thousand dollars for the photographers, more than Random House was prepared to pay.

Schiller approached another publisher, Grosset & Dunlap, with the idea, using Random House as a less than fully legitimate bargaining chip. Harold Roth, Grosset's president, discussed the idea with one of his editors, Bob Markel. Though it is not clear exactly who came up with the idea to have Mailer write the introduction, before long Markel called Norman's agent, Scott Meredith, and offered fifty thousand dollars for a twenty-five-thousand-word introduction. Meredith reported back quickly that Norman had accepted. In November contracts were signed, with Norman to receive fifty thousand and the photographers an equal amount, and with royalties to be divided equally among Schiller, Mailer, and the photographers.

Norman had no idea of Schiller's history; he simply needed the money, and he was promised that it would arrive when he needed it — fast. But his suspicions must have been aroused when he met the garrulous, gaudily dressed, outsized thirty-seven-year-old man. Called by an *Esquire* writer the "agent of death" and by a *Playboy* interviewer a "carrion bird," Larry Schiller bought rights. He bought rights to people's lives: he bought the rights to the life of Lenny Bruce's ex-wife, Honey, and those of the comedian's mother and daughter (Albert Goldman's biography, *Ladies and Gentlemen, Lenny Bruce!*, bore the cover credit, "Based on the journalism of Larry Schiller"); he bought the rights to the story of Manson family member and convicted killer Susan Atkins, and sold her confession to publications around the world; he bought the rights to Jack Ruby's deathbed interview and to the photograph of Ruby shooting Lee Harvey Oswald. He was a man of enormous energy and considerable achievements; in addition to his more ghoulish activities he was a talented photographer, a record producer, a book packager, and a film director. He was really an "idea man" who cooked up projects he thought might sell and then put the rest of the elements together to produce them. Any area of the media was fair game to Schiller, who kept both ears tuned to what an audience might respond to.

Marilyn Monroe had been indirectly responsible for his first big break. In 1962, just months before she died, Schiller was taking poolside pictures of Monroe for a French magazine when she slipped out of her bathing suit. Monroe was not at first willing to release the photographs that resulted, asking Schiller why she should. "You're already famous," Schiller replied. "Now you can make me famous." Schiller was able to sell the most decorous of the photos to *Life* for ten thousand dollars and the rest to publications all around the world, and his career took off. Posthumously, Monroe would give his career a lift again — with the Mailer book and with a company he founded called The Legend and the Truth Marketing (the name comes from the title of his Monroe photography exhibit), which produced a line of Monroe posters, calendars, datebooks, and decks of playing cards with Monroe's picture on the back.

Norman was put off by the odor of opportunism in Schiller's résumé, but he was intrigued as well: Schiller was a kind of operator he had not seen before. It was partly Schiller's West Coast arrogance and partly his eye for the headlines that impressed Norman. For he came away from their initial meetings impressed. As a person Schiller was abrasive, but he got things done, and he knew how to cut a deal. With this hard-driving promoter's involvement, the Monroe project, Norman thought, was sure to attract notice.

A week after the contracts were signed, Schiller sent the Monroe photographs to Grosset & Dunlap from Los Angeles, where they had been on exhibit. Markel called Norman in to see them, and Norman was enormously impressed, particularly by the actress's changing moods. He had a brief chat with Markel, asking him how they were going to handle Bobby Kennedy, a reference to the dead senator's supposed affair with Monroe and his rumored role in her death. Markel knew then that his author was deeply interested in his subject.

Before beginning the project, Norman and Carol went on a nine-day cruise in the Caribbean; he, Isaac Asimov, and Katherine Anne Porter had all been hired to watch the launch of a satellite from Cape Kennedy and lecture on it for the cruise-goers. While on the voyage, Norman read Fred Guiles's biography *Norma Jean* (1969) and realized he wanted to write not just an introduction but Marilyn's life story. As he later told *Time* magazine, "Part of the reason I wrote this book is that I wanted to say to everyone that I know how to write about a woman. When I read the other biographies of Marilyn, I said, 'I've found her; I know who I want to write about.'"

But of course the spark of any Mailer project only catches when he can project himself into it, either as the actual or the secret protagonist. So too with the preeminent 1950s screen goddess. "I felt some existential similarities with Marilyn Monroe," Mailer said in the same interview. Her celebrity was the female equivalent of his, as he saw it: just as he was the epitome of the macho man, so Monroe was some kind of supersymbol of womanhood. Both had their vociferous critics as well as their effusive fans. Both were larger-than-life symbols. In one of the book's most self-indulgent passages, Norman would observe that "the letters in Marilyn Monroe (if the 'a' were used twice and the 'o' but once) would spell his own name, leaving only the 'y' for excess." Nevertheless, he responded to Monroe in what seemed to him meaningful ways. Norman had just missed meeting Marilyn so many times. In fact, they had actually met once, in 1949 in Hollywood, though Norman wasn't aware of it at the time. Norman also remembered his nodding acquaintance with playwright Arthur Miller, who would be Monroe's third husband, in the halls of the Brooklyn rooming house where he wrote *The Naked and the Dead.* And while Norman and Adele were living in Connecticut, Monroe and Miller were neighbors, although the Mailers never met them. Arthur Miller's success was to become a preoccupation of Mailer's in *Marilyn.*

Norman had no intention of writing a "real" biography; that would take years and would require skills he did not possess, as he knew. Rather, he would read through the secondary literature, assemble and watch as many of Monroe's movies as he could, and muse at photographs of her while coming to some conclusions about her sad life. As preparation, he admits in the finished work, he bought a bottle of Chanel No. 5, Monroe's favorite perfume, "and thought it was the operative definition of a dime-store stink." But he would never know, he went on to say, how it smelled on her skin. (Norman hated all perfume, actually, and did not allow his wives to wear it.) Thus he would produce what he calls in *Marilyn* "a novel . . . written in the form of a biography . . . a *species* of novel ready to play by the rules of biography."

Mailer quickly exceeded the twenty-five-thousand-word limit. Schiller was initially delighted. He had the book's designer, Allen Hurlburt, make up a new dummy in a double-column format to accommodate sixty-five to seventy thousand words. By late February 1973, when Mailer turned the book in — less than three months after he had begun — it was a hundred and five thousand words, from which Markel would recommend cuts amounting to some ten thousand words. Markel called Schiller with the news — and Schiller hit the roof. He flew in to New York and drove up to Stockbridge to confront Norman, asking him how many words the text was going to be. After Schiller got his answer, he brought his version of the cover to Markel at Grosset & Dunlap (he called it "his" cover, but surely Hurlburt had a hand in the design). The cover was just a photograph, no title or author. Markel knew that Mailer would have objections, but Schiller was adamant — the author's name and the title would appear only on the spine of the book. The contest was on: would *Marilyn* be a collection of photographs accompanied by some words from Norman Mailer, or would it be Mailer's biography of Monroe, illustrated with some photos gathered by Schiller?

Grosset & Dunlap needed to go to press, and thus had to get Mailer's approval on the layout and cover. He and Schiller fought over these matters, patching things up in a series of emergency meetings and teleconferences.

Grosset & Dunlap scheduled the book for late August, hoping it would be their big fall title. Both the Literary Guild and the Book-of-the-Month Club were considering it for their summer or fall collections. The BOMC said it would make *Marilyn* its "A" selection if Grosset could move the publication date up, as it had already slotted its main selections for the fall. Markel agreed, increasing the pressure on all concerned.

Schiller, unwilling to entrust prepublication publicity to Grosset & Dunlap, was busy selling foreign rights, making his voice heard in all design matters, and alerting the press to this major publishing event. "I knew from the very beginning we were going to have a *Time* cover," he later told an *Esquire* reporter. And Schiller delivered: the newsmagazine planned a cover featuring Marilyn and Norman. Schiller insisted on designing it himself, and came up with a large color photo of Monroe with a smaller black-and-white photo of Mailer superimposed on it; it looked as if Monroe were caressing the author's bushy silver hair. The prospect of the cover worried Markel, for the issue was scheduled for July 16, and he thought Grosset couldn't have enough books in the stores by then. But with the Watergate story breaking so fast, *Time* could not guarantee a later cover. Markel put Grosset's warehouse employees on overtime and managed to get a fair number of copies in the stores on time.

The rushed nature of these proceedings made it impossible for Mailer to remain in control of his text. Both he and the Grosset editors held back for a long time on okaying the Bobby Kennedy part of the story. Mailer wanted to address the possibility that Kennedy was Monroe's lover; more riskily, he wanted to raise the question of Kennedy's possible involvement in her death, which he suggested strongly might not have been a suicide. It was his theory that the CIA or FBI would have been very interested in the rumors that Monroe, the ex-wife of a suspiciously radical playwright, was sleeping with the president's brother, and might therefore have been involved in her death, either to protect the Kennedy reputation or to besmirch it.

The trouble was, he had little to back up his vague musings, and his publishers were understandably wary. He was too busy polishing up his manuscript to fly out to California himself, so he asked Richard Stratton, who shared his interest in conspiracies, to go out and investigate. Stratton did turn up one source who said that the FBI went into the Santa Monica telephone company's office and removed the paper tape listing all of Monroe's phone calls the day she killed herself (it was thought that calls to the White House might show up), and who confirmed other information as well. Mailer could report to Grosset & Dunlap that he was confident there were enough suspicious details surrounding Monroe's death to make his speculations worth putting into print.

Then another, extremely serious obstacle presented itself. On June 22, Mailer's British publisher, Hodder and Stoughton, announced that it was postponing the scheduled October release of *Marilyn*. Mark Goulden, the chair of W. H. Allen, another British house, alleged that two of his firm's authors, Maurice Zolotow, author of *Marilyn Monroe*, and Fred Guiles, *Norma Jean*'s author, had found many instances of plagiarism in Mailer's book. Although they had granted permission to Mailer and Grosset & Dunlap to reprint certain passages, Mailer had gone far beyond the bounds of accepted practice. Zolotow had granted permission for thirty-five hundred words to be excerpted for a fee of two hundred dollars; he found a hundred and fifty additional passages taken verbatim or with only minor changes, which amounted to twenty thousand words. He also noted that he had given permission only for the Grosset and BOMC editions — no foreign rights. Guiles, meanwhile, found that Norman had taken 255 passages from *Norma Jean,* a few of which he had granted permission for, the bulk of them reprinted without permission. Zolotow also announced that he would sue Norman for libel: *Marilyn* included several sharp ad hominem criticisms of Zolotow's book.

After several phone calls, Hodder and Stoughton and Grosset & Dunlap announced that they would go ahead with publication, confident of the written permissions obtained from Zolotow and Guiles. Guiles backed down quickly; on July 17, Scott Meredith announced that "no dispute exists" between Mailer and Guiles or between Grosset & Dunlap and McGraw-Hill, Guiles's publisher. Mailer added a fulsome acknowledgment of Guiles to his text.

Zolotow proved more difficult. He was openly calling Mailer a plagiarist. On July 18, Mailer held a press conference and announced that he would sue Zolotow for libel unless he retracted his statement and apologized. Zolotow, from Los Angeles, announced that he would be filing a $6 million suit for libel and that his publisher, Harcourt Brace Jovanovich, was considering suing Norman as well. On August 4, Zolotow filed suit in U.S. District Court in Los Angeles, claiming libel, invasion of privacy, interference with contractual relationships, intentional infliction of emotional distress, and negligent infliction of emotional distress — but not plagiarism.

Mailer issued another statement on August 6, again announcing his intention to sue for libel. First addressing Zolotow's claim that *Marilyn* defamed him, Norman allowed that he had indeed been hard on Zolotow's book in *Marilyn,* saying, "His material is reamed with overstuffed and hollow anecdotes untrustworthy by the very style of their prose, a feature writer heating up the old dishes of other feature writers, and so a book which has fewer facts than factoids." Mailer discussed that accusation and Zolotow's reaction at some length at his press conference, concluding, "Mr. Zolotow must never have received a bad review until I came along." He also addressed the accusation of plagiarism: "Zolotow has also charged that I have plagiarized his work, and that is a dishonest charge. He knows it . . . If he does not apologize I will be obliged to sue him (even though I detest the working time that must be lost to litigation)." Not until November did Zolotow make an apology for calling *Marilyn* "the literary heist of the century"; he chalked it up to the fact that he had been "hurt, and emotionally upset" at the time because of Mailer's attacks on his book, and acknowledged he had spoken "in the heat of the moment." The suit evidently came to nothing. "No one is going to call me a plagiarist and get away with it," Mailer told *Time* later that year. "If I had to steal from other authors, let me use Shakespeare or Melville. I don't have to steal from Guiles."

And there is no real reason to take Mailer to task for the amount of research he did or did not do. As he states several times in *Marilyn,* he did not have the time for a real biography. Instead, he suggested, he intended a novel, which would more appropriately capture Monroe's elusive quality: "Set a thief to catch a thief, and put an artist on an artist." Indeed, considering that he was asked only for a twenty-five-thousand-word introduction, he may well have been concerned to limit the amount of work he did on the project, however engaged he became with it.

The issue of the extent of Mailer's research came back to haunt him when Mike Wallace interviewed him for *60 Minutes,* in a segment appearing on June 13, 1973, called "Mailer, Monroe, and the Fast Buck." The focus was on the book's allegations about Bobby Kennedy; Norman clarified here that he suspected the attorney general and the movie star were not having an affair but that many believed otherwise, and that if she had been murdered in such a way as to appear a suicide, presumably because of her obsession with Bobby, it would be a huge blow to the Kennedys.

Wallace, announcing to the camera that somebody might have been there that night "who could invalidate all of Mailer's tortured theorizing," cut to an interview with Eunice Murray, Monroe's housekeeper, who said she was alone with the actress all night and that murder was out of the question. "I hate telephone interviews," Norman said when Wallace asked why he had never tried to get in touch with Murray. "I hate that way of getting the facts." He explained the time constraints he had been under, and then said something extraordinary: "I was doing something you don't normally do with a book, which I was getting into the end of the book with a half-finished explanation, and I decided it was important enough to get out there half finished rather than not to get into it at all." Wallace knew a great line when he heard one and closed the segment with the withering conclusion "The best criticism of the book we've heard so far is Norman Mailer's own: it got out there half finished." It was against every journalist's rule: if you aren't sure about something, you have to leave it out.

But in this case Norman was telling the truth, at least in one sense. First, he really had been working under tremendous pressure; Schiller and his publisher had held him to an impossible deadline — which they then moved up at least once. "I'm probably one of the better fast writers in the world now," he told *Time* magazine, which ran its cover story on July 16. "But you never feel good writing a book that fast. I was driving under such march orders that I forgot to dedicate the book." He really did intend to conduct a major inquiry into Monroe's death, he said. At a press conference at Manhattan's Algonquin Hotel on July 18, he told reporters that since the book had gone to press he had conducted more interviews, and that he might rewrite the last chapter for the paperback edition. He confessed that he had relied on his "well-developed instinct" rather than hard facts in setting forth his theory. Finally, he passed out a press release with the coroner's reports, which indicated that Monroe's stomach and intestines were empty, yet that no stomach pump had been used, and he challenged the press to investigate further.

All this controversy, Markel and Schiller believed, had hurt the book's sales; on the other hand, sales to the BOMC, the Playboy Book Club, and the London *Sunday Times* (for $75,000) were all locked up. And the controversy helped sales as much as it hurt them. The arresting if silly *Time* cover, with head shots of subject and author and the tag "Monroe Meets Mailer," had a great impact. Another source of controversy regarding the book was its price ($19.95, a hefty price when most hardbacks still sold for under $10), its size (9 by 11 inches), and its weight (3 pounds, 3 ounces). Major writers were not expected to produce coffee-table books. Then too the book was arresting in appearance: the cover was a giant, larger-than-life closeup of Monroe's face, her red lips breathily parted. The title and the author's name, as Schiller wished, appeared only on the book's spine. It was a book people would remember seeing even if they did not buy. It could be argued that no mainstream book has had as indelible a look since, with the possible exception of Madonna's *Sex* (1992).

The controversy surrounding *Marilyn* just wouldn't quit. Four days after the press conference at the Algonquin, a front-page review appeared in the Sunday, July 22, 1973, *New York Times Book Review.* The reviewer was Pauline Kael, and while she was a longtime admirer of the author and had said so in print, he had recently done something that might have changed her opinion of him. In one of her occasional over-the-top reviews, in the October 28, 1972, *New Yorker,* Kael had declared the screening of Bernardo Bertolucci's *Last Tango in Paris* at the New York Film Festival to be a landmark in film history, comparable in importance to the 1913 opening of Igor Stravinsky's *Le Sacre du Printemps* in the history of music. *Last Tango* was simply "the most powerfully erotic film ever made," she wrote. For some reason Norman, who was a great admirer of the film himself, took issue with this; perhaps it bothered him that a woman would find the movie erotic, or that Kael had beaten him to the punch in praising it in such strong terms. (Her review preceded almost any other write-up of the movie, which annoyed a lot of other critics, in fact.)

Norman got the *New York Review of Books* to allow him to review the film, and opened his review, on May 17, 1973, with an attack on Kael. He quoted from her piece and wondered how she could "pop open for a film." He called her "Lady Vinegar, our quintessential cruet," and then, most damningly, "the first frigid of the film critics."

Kael, who had previously taken Norman on his own terms, was understandably wounded, and that may have colored her reaction to *Marilyn* on the *New York Times Book Review*'s front page. Convinced of his talents for so long, she could not totally dismiss the book: "Though it's easy — in fact, natural — to speak of Mailer as crazy (and only half in admiration), nobody says dumb. *Marilyn* is a rip-off all right, but a rip-off with genius." She gracefully acknowledged the fine points of Mailer's writing:

> About half of "Marilyn" is great as only a great writer, using his brains and feelers could make it. Just when you get fed up with his flab and slop, he'll come through with a runaway string of perceptions and you have to recognize that, though it's a bumpy ride, the book still goes like a streak . . . You read him with a heightened consciousness because his performance has zing. It's the star system in literature; you can feel him bucking up for the big time, and when he starts flying it's so exhilarating you want to applaud.

Yet, she wrote, it's a "good-bad book."

First, as a professional film critic, Kael took issue with Mailer's assessment of Monroe's career, which he believes was that of a potentially great but thwarted dramatic actress. No, Kael stated, her most fitting vehicles in the 1960s would have been *Candy, Sweet Charity, Born Yesterday,* or *Breakfast at Tiffany's.* Other critics would echo Kael's primary criticisms, which point to the book's most serious flaws. One issue she raised that would strike almost any reader of the book, and that would rightly be held against Mailer with some passion, was that he is simply a bully when it comes to the question of the man he obviously considers his rival, Arthur Miller. He acknowledges his envy somewhat cutely and dismissively, but then makes it very clear just how limited a candidate he feels Miller is for Monroe's hand. *Middle-class* is his favorite adjective here, though what he means by that is not clear — probably Jewish. Mailer gives *Death of a Salesman* its due, but then makes much of the fact that Miller's output since had been a letdown — his creative life is "cramped" and "constipated" — and that Miller is stingy and lived off Monroe's money.

Moreover, Mailer implies at every possible juncture that Miller is somehow unmanly. Nowhere is this more evident than in his discussion of *The Misfits,* the novella that the playwright adapted as a screen vehicle for his wife. The story revolves around an aging cowboy (Clark Gable) who lives with Rosalyn Tabor (Monroe) in the desert outside Reno. Two other cowboys, played by Eli Wallach and Montgomery Clift, work with Gable but begin to show an interest in Monroe. What is Miller's role in this? As presented by Mailer, he is the intellectual sitting on the sidelines, doling out sleeping pills to his charge like a nurse. He is also, Mailer implies most damningly, the nice Jewish boy from Brooklyn — the fate Mailer has directed all his actions toward avoiding — a "tall and timid hero of middle-class life." Mailer leaves the clear impression that if *he* had been on the set of *The Misfits,* he would have been roping horses, getting dragged by runaway mustangs, brawling and drinking right alongside three macho-seeming actors, directed by the crusty embodiment of masculinity, John Huston.

But Kael also complained about *Marilyn* on a point that resonated through other reviews, was echoed on television talk shows, and reverberated in the public imagination. She attacked it as physical object: "It's a rich and creamy book, an offensive physical object, perhaps even a little sordid." The cover photograph shows a "fleshy but pasty" Marilyn: "The cover-girl face . . . is disintegrating; and the astuteness of the entrepreneurs in exploiting even her disintegration, using it as a Pop icon, gets to one. Who knows what to think about Marilyn Monroe or about those who turn her sickness to metaphor? I wish they'd let her die."

Monroe was exploited, many believed, and all to the end of making a buck. A publishing industry journal wrote gravely, "[*Marilyn*] permits factoidal gulch . . . to be changed into luxurious, fertile fields to be plowed with the novelist's imagination, sown with questionable psychological seed, and reaped in ripe, green dollars." The *Time* cover story, Schiller's great publicity coup, was itself full of ambivalence about Mailer's achievement. It also drew attention to issues of financial exploitation. The writer asked Mailer why he was attracted to the idea for such a book. "As a way of making money," he responded candidly. "I had some debts. Let me tell the truth. I was seriously behind. I called Scott Meredith, my agent, and said, 'Before I start work on my novel again, I think I need to take a short job that pays well.'"

The criticisms these statements elicited, though they are not without validity, somehow miss the point. As for Mailer's writing the book to make

money, why shouldn't he? It attests to his sense of marketing, his understanding of the public, his recognition of the huge appeal of Monroe — and
of Mailer on Monroe — that he did not turn Larry Schiller away as a
huckster but instead worked with him on what he came to feel was a most
interesting subject, and what turned out to be an enormously profitable
one.

Monroe drew him in ways beyond those he admitted to in the book. He
told *Time* that he wanted to be known as a man who could write about a
woman, and the reader of *Marilyn* gets the impression that what interests
Mailer most is Monroe's femaleness. He describes her personal grooming
habits lovingly — we hear more than once that she sleeps wearing a bra —
and dwells rather more than is necessary on her periods.

Even back in the early 1950s, Mailer wrote,

> she was already promising a time was coming when sex would
> be easy and sweet, democratic provender for all. Her stomach,
> untrammeled by girdles and sheaths, popped forward in a full
> woman's belly, inelegant as hell, an avowal of a womb fairly sali-
> vating in seed — that belly which was never to have a child — and
> her breasts popped buds and burgeons of flesh over many a quest-
> ing moviegoer's face.

The Mailer female protagonist is all sex — and thus a tragic human being.
He invents an adjective for her — *fucky* — and we are told that she will
never seem so "fucky" again as when married to the consummate athlete,
Joe DiMaggio. But Monroe doesn't behave as Mailer has told us women
should, in *The Prisoner of Sex*. She does not bear children but rather seems
quite regularly to undergo abortions. In this guise, she must be punished:

> Yes, she is physically resplendent [when married to DiMaggio], and
> yet her face in those years shows more of vacuity and low cunning
> than it is likely to show again — she is in part the face DiMaggio
> has been leaving in her womb. "Take the money," he says to her on
> one occasion when she is talking about her publicity, and some-
> thing as hard and blank as a New York Yankee out for a share of
> the spoils is now in her expression.

The subject of Monroe and her womanhood fascinated him so much that
he would return to it in 1980, in a little-known book called *Of Women and
Their Elegance,* which is an "autobiography" of Marilyn Monroe written
"in her own voice" by Norman Mailer, in a curious exercise in gender-bend-
ing. If Marilyn is an existential heroine, Norman the existential hero is
determined to know what it is like to be her. One could speculate further,

but it is quite clear that writing about Marilyn Monroe's life was a serious matter for Norman, much more than a get-rich-quick scheme. As a "fucky" woman who kills her own babies, Monroe is a study in contradictions. Possessed of "animal rage," according to Norman, she must yet summon up the sweetness and goofiness of Sugar Kane in *Some Like It Hot.* As an actress, she is better equipped for the existential battle of her life: resisting male attempts to define her. If Norman's "novel biography" is any indication, it is clear that she did not win the battle.

Marilyn was every bit the book-packaging success Schiller predicted. But mostly for Grosset & Dunlap. Scott Meredith allowed Grosset to retain the world rights back when he believed Mailer would be writing a short introduction for a book of photographs. The world rights brought in a great deal of money. Ten different foreign language editions were negotiated, and the publisher sold serial rights abroad as well. All told, the foreign sales brought in about half a million dollars, of which Schiller and Mailer got only half — still a considerable sum, but not what it might have been.

The attention Norman got from *Marilyn* was an embellishment to the notoriety he too often received in the United States. He ran with his celebrity as far as he could. Six months after the book's publication, he went to Markel and proposed a two-page advertisement like the one he had designed for *The Deer Park,* setting the most negative and most positive critical remarks about the book side by side. Though Markel and Grosset's president, Harold Roth, grumbled, Norman insisted that he knew the book-reading public and got his publishers to agree to the ad he had designed. On the left, the page lists the attacks: "Supercolossal exploitation," "Abysmal," "Warmed-over trivia," "This travesty," "Shamefully rehashed potboiler." On the right were listed the encomiums: "Exceptional," "One reads avidly," "A unique and fascinating biography," "Compulsively readable," "Phosphorescent writing."

Marilyn put Norman's name before the public, where it had not been since, possibly, *The Armies of the Night.* The appearance of the book was unforgettable: the term *pop icon* was thrown around often in reviews about the book, but it is fair to say that in establishing Marilyn Monroe as a pop icon, it established Norman Mailer as one too. Perhaps Norman recognized, with Andy Warhol, that it was appropriate and necessary for an artist to aspire to be a pop icon in the current day and age.

But the book's impact was not based entirely on hype. Mailer wrote a text to be reckoned with, whatever elements of exploitation it might contain, a text that replays favorite themes, like the duality of the soul, and rehearses new ones: the notions of karma and reincarnation. "Marilyn had to be alive, not dead," Schiller told an *Esquire* reporter. "I didn't want a book about just another dead movie star. You follow what I'm saying?"

And he and Mailer succeeded in bringing her to life again. There had been books about Monroe, to be sure, but they had been, like the familiar Fred Guiles and Maurice Zolotow volumes, celebrity biographies. *Marilyn* was an event, and it stoked the considerable Monroe cult, which in coming years would attract a feminist interpreter in Gloria Steinem and conspiracy theorists who fastened on the Kennedy, FBI, and CIA involvement in her death (they would be partially vindicated nine years later, when the coroner's report was publicly challenged). Mailer approached Monroe as a phenomenon and made her a phenomenon; along the way, for good or ill, he became a phenomenon himself.

TWENTY-THREE

RUMBLE IN THE JUNGLE

Reporters seeking Norman out in the aftermath of *Marilyn* found him in fine physical shape, better than he had looked for the past five years. Beneath his full, wiry wreath of hair, now mostly gray, his blue eyes were still as piercing as Paul Newman's. A twenty-day liquid fast — which included a ban on alcohol — had dropped his weight to 165 pounds from 188. His torso was still bulky, and this, combined with his relative shortness, made his shape like that of a small barrel. Like many Americans, he had taken up jogging — though he would never enjoy it very much, and would drop the practice before too long. A detached retina (the result of a sparring match in Provincetown) made it advisable for him to give up boxing — a stricture he would as often as not forget after a few drinks.

Norman was still living with Carol Stevens in the Stockbridge house, though he spent a good deal of time at the Brooklyn brownstone with Suzanne Nye. A petite brunette, Nye came across as a tough customer: she was trained in karate and drove a Harley-Davidson. Norman invented another name for her, Elizabeth Cromwell, perhaps remembering how angry he had been at Beverly's taking a stage name all by herself.

He and Nye had spent the early part of the summer in the house at 565 Commercial Street in Provincetown, vacant because Beverly was in North Carolina playing the lead in the prizewinning play *Shay*. But Beverly had returned and was there with the boys on one mid-July day in 1974 when Norman called her to arrange a picnic on the dunes with the boys and maybe a pickup game of baseball. Beverly roasted a couple of chickens in anticipation, but then Norman called a second time and said he had Suzanne with him. Beverly implored him not to bring her into the house, especially with the boys in their rooms upstairs, but an hour later she heard their voices downstairs. She went down and asked Suzanne to leave. Norman said, "No, you leave. It's *my* house. *You* get out of this house." A physical altercation ensued, and Beverly wound up with a black eye and a swollen face. She called the police, who said they could not eject Norman from his own house. Eventually Norman and Suzanne left, Norman hissing to Beverly, "Wouldn't it be funny if Suzanne wound up with this house?"

Beverly, frightened by the escalation in violence, obtained a restraining order against Norman and filed for divorce not long after. She asked for custody of the boys and thirty thousand dollars a year in alimony, telling the judge that as soon as she resumed her acting career she would not need alimony payments. The divorce wars that followed would take up the remainder of the decade, depleting Beverly's financial and emotional resources.

In general, money problems weighed heavily on Norman in the mid-seventies, despite the modest windfall of *Marilyn*. He was downright defensive about the matter, telling *Time*, "I've really gotten to the point where I'm like an old prizefighter, and if my manager comes up to me and says, 'I've got you a tough fight with a good purse,' I go into the ring. Nothing makes an old fighter any madder than to do a charity benefit." With Beverly and Adele, seven children, and a live-in mistress (whom he commonly described as his wife), he needed, he claimed, in a conservative estimate, $200,000 or $250,000 a year to get by. To ease his expenses, or to protect his assets during the divorce, he turned 142 Columbia Heights into a condominium and sold the lower three apartments. He owed considerable money, mostly to Scott Meredith and to the IRS. Cy Rembar had long ago distanced himself from Norman's finances, and the people who handled them now were too fond of taking extensions on the taxes, ignoring all the resulting late fees and penalties. And Scott Meredith lent him money against future earnings, to the tune of $175,000 or $200,000.

Even Larry Schiller took pity on Norman when he heard him bewail his financial situation to Mike Wallace on *60 Minutes*. Schiller knew that Norman was still angry at him because of production issues like the placement of photos in *Marilyn*, but he had recently seen an assortment of photographs of New York City subway graffiti, soon to be published in a book in England (that edition never appeared). With the right text, Schiller thought, they might make an attractive volume in the United States, so he phoned Norman and arranged for the photographs to be sent to him. Norman agreed, a little grudgingly, when Schiller promised he could get him thirty-five thousand dollars. Scott Meredith eventually closed the deal, selling the serial rights to what would be a twelve-thousand-word essay to *Esquire* and landing Norman a fifty-thousand-dollar advance from Praeger Books for the Schiller-packaged essay and photos.

The Faith of Graffiti aroused controversy, for Norman wrote in praise of graffiti, claiming that it was an indigenous art form that ought to be celebrated rather than suppressed. Naming himself Aesthetic Investigator (which would make his graffiti tag A-I, he wrote), Norman interviewed scores of graffiti artists, visited the Museum of Modern Art and the mayor, and dithered a lot about whether graffiti was art or not. But his admiration for the graffiti artists was unmistakable: what he admired about them was their bravery — "there was real fear of being caught" — a quality that always drew him. "What a quintessential marriage of cool and style," he wrote, "to write your name in giant separate living letters, large as animals, lithe as snakes, mysterious as Arabic and Chinese curls of alphabet, and do it in the heat of a winter night when the hands are frozen and only the heart is hot with fear." It is impossible to miss echoes of "The White Negro" in Norman's paean to these young hipsters.

But Scott Meredith was at work on other fronts, trying to put together a deal that could keep Norman comfortable over a fairly extended period. Preliminary negotiations began in November 1973, and on February 21, 1974, the *New York Times* announced the deal. Little, Brown had contracted to pay Norman Mailer $1 million for his next novel, the highest known payment agreed to for a single unpublished work of fiction. Mailer was said to have already completed one hundred thousand words of the novel, which was to be "about the whole human experience." More specifically, it would follow a family "from ancient history to future history," ending on a spaceship, and the parts already written were said to be set in ancient history and modern-day New York. Norman would claim time and again that the million dollars was to be paid out in installments for a total of five to seven hundred thousand words — the equivalent of five novels — but the word was out: he was a million-dollar writer.

The *Times* story reporting this coup carried two unlikely and atypical sounding claims: first, that Mailer "wanted to forestall the temptation" to write magazine articles "and other, lesser projects" along the way (he was now constitutionally incapable of saying no to any reasonable money-making project), and second, that he "plans now to retire from public life to devote himself exclusively to the novel for the next few years." Norman may have intended or "planned" such a retreat, but he was simply too needful of the public gaze to carry it out. Also, though he was a remarkably disciplined writer, he was too gregarious and dependent on the presence of other people to write in any kind of seclusion.

In fact, almost the first thing he did after signing the contract and receiving the first two-hundred-thousand-dollar installment was to accept a commission from *Playboy*. To be fair, this was a hard assignment to turn down: covering the upcoming world heavyweight championship bout between defending champion George Foreman and Muhammad Ali — the much-anticipated "Rumble in the Jungle," promoted as the most spectacular boxing match ever, a billing the fight would live up to, if not precisely for the reasons first projected. His report, from Kinshasa, Zaire, was to appear in the May 1974 issue of *Playboy* and was published in book form as *The Fight* by Little, Brown in June 1975.

The Fight is a small masterpiece in the Mailer oeuvre. The author is an active character in the book, but his persona is not one his readers have met before. This character is called simply Norman. Mailer acknowledges at the beginning of *The Fight* that his brand of participatory journalism now had its critics, who spoke of ego trips and narcissism. In fact, he was inclined to agree. He was tired of his own persona: "His daily reactions bored him. They were becoming like everyone else's. His mind, he noticed, was beginning to spin its wheels, sometimes seeming to repeat itself for the sheer slavishness of supporting mediocre habits. If he was now wondering what name he ought to use for his piece about the fight, it was out of no excess of ego. More, indeed, from concern for the reader's attention."

Eventually he decided just to use his first name — "everybody in the fight game did." They certainly did. "No'min" is a familiar character to the fighters and their entourages — because No'min got a million dollars for writing a book. Much of the book's charm is in how Norman interacts with the fighters: when he extends a hand to Foreman, the fighter explains that he cannot shake because he is keeping his hands in his pockets to prevent any harm from coming to them. Ali wants criticism of his poetry.

It would be an understatement to say that the atmosphere in Kinshasa was charged, all the more so because the fight was delayed a month for Foreman to recover from a cut over his eye. The flamboyant boxing promoter Don King, a former nightclub owner and numbers racketeer who had spent four years in jail after killing a man in a street fight, had encouraged a media circus that generated all sorts of ballyhoo about the upcoming fight. The fight was thought to be a classic match: the gregarious, rhyming, charismatic Ali taking on the solid, impassive, powerhouse Foreman. Bets were on Foreman to win; even some of Ali's handlers thought he might lose. Ali had lost his title in 1973 to Joe Frazier; at a rematch in the beginning of 1974, he beat him, but it was a nontitle fight. Foreman, in contrast, was undefeated. But Ali was a favorite in the journalists' camp; he was always ready to talk to them, and they were impressed by the respect he commanded from the Zaireans, who took to chanting "Ali bom ye!" (Ali, kill him!) during practice. All eyes were on Kinshasa, not just because of the fight but because the world was transfixed by the idea of two American blacks fighting in the heart of Africa. It was the first official boxing match ever to be held on the continent.

Norman's apprehension of the city of Kinshasa and the Zaireans, and the absurdity of Mobutuism, the cult surrounding the dictator who hosted the fight, is a fascinating thread woven into the larger drama of the fight. One of the high points of the personal side of his experience in Zaire is Norman's description of the time he asked to join Ali on his early morning run, partly to find out what kind of condition the fighter was really in, and partly to subject himself to a very severe test. Ali agreed, and told Norman to be ready at three in the morning. Thinking it impossible to sleep between nine and midnight, Norman had a full meal with several drinks and afterward played blackjack at the casino hotel with journalist buddies Hunter Thompson, Budd Schulberg, and George Plimpton. (Plimpton would later write his own very funny version of this incident.) Norman was increasingly uneasy about running, and fretful because he had not moved his bowels. He returned to his room and put on a running suit; leaving his room, he ran into Plimpton, who was returning from the casino, and Plimpton thought the outfit looked like a union suit.

Norman surprised himself by holding his own with Ali. He intended to run only a mile and then drop off, but he found he was able to keep up, though when Ali tried to start a conversation Norman could answer him only in gasps. He peeled off and headed back to Nsele, Ali's camp. Walking alone in the dark African night, he suddenly heard the roar of a lion, which seemed to come at him from all directions. As he broke into a trot he reflected on how fitting it would be for a lion to kill him in Hemingway's Africa.

On his return, he breathlessly told the people crowded in Ali's villa of his close call, and they laughed explosively. One of Ali's handlers explained: the lion could be heard every morning; it was in a zoo at the presidential compound. There were no lions in West Africa anyway. As Plimpton later reported in *Shadow Box,* "the thought of Norman's eyes staring into the darkness, and his legs pumping in their union-suit track clothes to get himself out of there ('Feets, do your stuff!') was so rich that [Ali's manager] asked him to tell them about it all over again. 'Nawmin, tell us 'bout the big lion.'"

Norman sets just the right tone: he sees the humor in his actions, but records the event without making direct fun of himself and at the same time without losing the comedy. (Plimpton, on the other hand, couldn't resist making fun of Norman.) He takes the same approach to a very delicate subject: his presence in an Afrocentric state, surrounded by Africans. He separates out his feelings about American blacks, which were complicated enough, and tries to take the Zaireans on their own terms, reading up on Bantu philosophy and educating himself — fairly seriously, it seems — in West African culture. The most important of his readings was a volume called *Bantu Philosophy,* written by Placide Temples, a priest who had been a missionary in the Congo. As Norman understood it, the Bantus held that men and women are forces rather than beings and that as such they are an organic part of the universe, with all the karma of past and future generations contained within them; their highest calling is to find the force, or *muntu*, in themselves.

Norman had a good time in Kinshasa, making his way about the city, trying to decipher the hopelessly corrupt political system, watching such flamboyant characters as Don King hold press conferences (while King expounded on all the philosophy he had read in jail, Hunter Thompson kept muttering "bad Genet"), making bets on the fight. He most definitely wanted Ali to win, but he worked himself into a superstitious lather about his own possible effect on the outcome of the fight.

Norman often feared that his actions might upset something in the universe and cause the fighter or the team he had picked to lose. This time the stakes were especially high. "A Heavyweight Championship is as charged as a magnetic field," he wrote. *Féticheurs* were common in Zaire; he and Plimpton thought of consulting one. But Norman had his own rituals. Coming home drunk at four in the morning, he finally looked at something he had been avoiding: a very narrow, railingless balcony. At either end were walls separating it from the other balconies. Like Rojack in *American Dream*, he convinced himself that he must walk this parapet if he wanted Ali to win. So he clambered out, groped his way around each wall, returned to his room, and fell into bed, thinking, he tells us, "It was so fucking easy."

But in another frenzy of magical thinking, he worried that such stunts might actually hurt Ali, that he was bringing his man bad luck. Yet he also recognized his "comic relation to magic," and chided himself for such thoughts: "That is a frightful idea for a man to have of himself. It is inverse vanity more poisonous than vanity itself." In many ways *The Fight* is a very personal book, and one of the aspects of Mailer's personality it documents is his recognition of his vanities, his ability to see how comic they are, and his weighing the possibility of leaving them behind him.

Mailer captures the mixed moods of fighters in training, the excitement or dread in their camps, the charged atmosphere surrounding a championship fight. Ali and Foreman become real and complex human beings, and Mailer makes us like and respect each of them. His introduction to Foreman conveys his respect for the boxer's stature: he found the fighter an expression of "vital force." He emerged from the elevator in embroidered denim overalls and denim jacket. "Flanked by a Black on either side, he did not look like a man so much as a lion standing just as erectly as a man. He appeared sleepy but in the way of a lion digesting a carcass." He captures brilliantly Ali's unique brand of braggadocio, boasting coupled with panic: on seeing Foreman hit the heavy bag in training, Ali would gather the press for one more tirade. "The voice of the tirade was, however, growing hollow, and there were occasions at Nsele when the hollow seemed to reverberate back, as if he sent out a call, 'Hear, O walls, the sound of my greatness,' and the walls did not hear him."

As this observation makes clear, Mailer, for all his admiration for Ali, did not present him as a one-dimensional hero. Though Ali became a bona fide superstar because of the fight, Mailer portrays him as a complicated human being. He remembers Ali as Cassius Clay in 1963, a slight, if tall, nervous undefeated boxer terrified of his impending fight with Sonny Liston. Contemplating Ali now, after the Foreman fight, he marvels at how the black fighter handles the black and the Third World press, realizing he has the potential to become a leader of his people. This is a prospect that Mailer, who has come to know the boxer very well, realizes is uncomfortable for Ali: "With what an immensity of anxiety must Ali live at the size of his world rule and his intimate knowledge of his own ignorance." In *The Fight*, Ali's story is in part about the responsibilities of celebrity and the limitations of a skilled but human boxer.

On the fight itself Mailer is superb, describing every blow, every nuance in the fighters' body movements; that he got it all down is a wonder, a testament to his journalistic skills and his long years of attention to the sport. Though Foreman was heavily favored to win, he actually had not fought a fight longer than two rounds in four years. And, in fact, staying power proved to be his weak point. He looked fairly strong in the early rounds. Ali, however, fought from the ropes for most of the match. Foreman couldn't hit him with any consistency; his punches either missed or were blocked by Ali. In the eighth round Ali landed a couple of hard straight rights on the exhausted Foreman, then a quick four-punch combination ending with a right hook that connected solidly with Foreman's jaw. Foreman went down and could not get up by the end of the count. Or, as Mailer writes, "He went over like a six-foot sixty-year-old butler who has just heard tragic news, yes, fell over all of a long collapsing two seconds, down came the champion in sections and Ali revolved with him in a close circle, hand primed to hit him one more time, and never the need, a wholly intimate escort to the floor."

Reviewers of *The Fight* — with the exception of *Time,* which complained that no one was interested in boxing — were genuinely surprised by the seemingly new Mailer. Dorothy Rabinowitz wrote in the *Saturday Review* that his experience at this all-time great sporting event "appears to have opened up in him some long-untouched reserve of charity and ease . . . this book recalls one to a sense of how delicate an ironist, and how serious a reporter, Mailer is."

What readers and reviewers found in *The Fight* is a man who has lost his compulsion for combat, who has accepted and recognized his faults and even seen the humor in them. It was an entirely new Mailer, who hadn't been seen before. It was not, however, a change that came easily to Norman, at age fifty-one, as he had to leave behind much of what had previously defined him.

AS NORMAN FLEW back to New York from Kinshasa in early November 1974, the kind reviews of *The Fight* were a year in the future. He was still feeling the fallout from *Marilyn,* and the book's critical drubbing prompted him to take stock of himself and his career. He had written a book that could not please his serious readers — one cannot imagine the New York intellectuals, the few that remained, even looking at his coffee-table account of a movie star's life, and it did little to enhance his reputation as a serious writer. He had gone a long way toward increasing his celebrity, to be sure, but he was criticized for that even by those who made him a celebrity and those who eagerly ran out and bought his book. He saw his book criticized as a commodity, what Pauline Kael called "a sordid, creamy object." With the announcement of his million-dollar contract with Little, Brown, it seemed to many that he had sold out, that he was writing merely for money.

Mailer explored his thoughts on this shift in the public's comprehension of him in a two-part interview conducted by Richard Stratton for *Rolling Stone* in the fall of 1974. No, he hadn't sold out, he told Stratton:

> I don't think I'm ever going to — well, I have enough respect for the powers of corruption not to say that I know I'm never going to sell out, but I don't think I'd sell out so easily, for so little. What I fear, far more than selling out, is wearing out. And I felt I was entitled, at the time I wrote *Marilyn.* I was entitled to my way of doing things.

Stratton really disapproved of *Marilyn.* He commented on seeing it in stores displayed next to a datebook with pictures from the book and quotes from Mailer's text on each page — the kind of merchandising no one had ever associated with Mailer's work. Yet Mailer refused to apologize for it. "I'm not going to sit here and bleed for the American public when the book was conceived by all in the first place as a project which would ideally make money for all concerned," he said. And he couldn't comprehend what was wrong with that:

> I mean, why does a writer not have the same right to make money that a capitalist does? or an entrepreneur or a corporation? I mean, I'm worried about it because maybe a writer doesn't have the same

right. But when I think of all the cheap hustlers like Mike Wallace who carried on that I was doing it for the bucks . . .

Stratton reminded him of his statement in *Advertisements for Myself:* "The ambition of a writer like myself is to become consecutively more disruptive, more dangerous, and more powerful." Norman couldn't really comment on that except to say that he made the statement in the very repressive 1950s, when disruption was almost a mandate for the American writer, and that today "there is no ground on which to rally." He and Stratton did talk about the "existentialism" of writing for money — that is, if you take it as an action for its own sake and do it well or do it badly. "If you're doing something for money the only way you can get through it alive is to give more than was requested," Norman commented. "If you sit down and say there is such a thing as a literary gift and God gave me one, then the only absolution is to fall in love with the object of my fee."

It might not sit well — as it clearly did not for Stratton — for Mailer to compare himself to a corporation and say that as an individual he has every bit as much right to make money as a commercial enterprise does. But unlike other successful writers, he was forced to defend himself through the press, which found good copy in his financial situation. Norman was absolutely right when he complained that writers like Updike are thought to write out of some pure love for the calling; obviously they make enough to support themselves and then some. But Norman was a creature of a new age: like professional sports, the art world, and the movies, the publishing industry was moving into an era when large amounts of cash — in publishing, in the form of advances — would become common and contracts would leapfrog each other in size, and the press would treat reports of the latest deals made by media stars as news. To be sure, Norman drew attention to himself by writing *Marilyn* expressly to make money, but he was right to sniff out a certain hypocrisy in the press and in his public.

On the other hand, this discussion with Stratton in many ways missed the point. Mailer had done some of his liveliest and best writing in the 1960s for hire, mostly for magazines. It wasn't really writing "for hire" that was the issue here — though the press certainly tried to make it one — but the *kind* of assignment Norman was accepting. It is one thing to cover a political campaign for *Esquire,* and another to produce copy for a decorative book. It is useful to remember that the "copy" Mailer produced for Schiller was quite remarkable. If you "hired" Norman Mailer, you were guaranteed to receive genuine Norman Mailer product — which was completely unpredictable.

Finding the kind of project that would spark him was a more difficult proposition than it had been in the 1960s, when politics was a continual, always changing, but unified narrative that kept him engaged. In the 1970s he had to look elsewhere, and while he found some successful projects, there would inevitably be misfires. To complain that Mailer had sold out was to misunderstand the way he had been operating for some time.

His defensiveness about making money aside, what is remarkable in the Stratton interview is how at peace with himself Mailer seems. What the press wrote and believed had heretofore been extremely important to him; this time, he acts like a man who doesn't care what reporters say. He needed a lot of money to support his extended family, so he had to exert himself especially, at times taking on assignments simply to make some quick bucks. Temperamentally, he brought to such assignments a lively curiosity that ensured the resulting product would be at least interesting if not inspired. *The Fight*, which grew out of an assignment for *Playboy*, turned into a lively book that, among other things, conveys the author's genuine pleasure at being in Zaire to see such a celebrated match. Plimpton remarked that Norman had seemed a changed man in Kinshasa: "I had never seen Mailer in such a relaxed mood and at ease with himself, which always meant he was splendid company."

Perhaps too this sense of a changed man, comfortable with his position in the writing world, was the result of his regained financial security: a million dollars bought him several years to produce his next big book, especially if he could continue to supplement it with such small projects as *The Faith of Graffiti* and *The Fight*. Of course, a big novel was expected of him — *the* big novel — but he had enough confidence in his literary powers that he believed it would come.

IN THE SPRING OF 1975, Norman, at fifty-two now decidedly paunchy, met the woman who was to be his next wife. He was on a grueling lecture tour in the South when he wrote the Gwaltneys, asking to visit them in Russellville, Arkansas. He told them to lay in a supply of light Bacardi rum and Schweppes tonic (rum and tonic had replaced bourbon, for the time, as his drink of choice). Fig Gwaltney wrote back enthusiastically, warning him that there might be a little gathering for him, composed mostly of students from Fig's creative writing course at Arkansas Technical College. It was at this gathering that Norman met Barbara Norris. Here is her account: "I walked in and had on blue jeans and a shirt tied at the waist and tall wedgie shoes, and I was about 6 feet 2. Well, Norman is 5 feet 8. I walked up and said, 'How are you, Mr. Mailer?' and he turned around and walked out of the room." Fig later told her that Norman walked away because he had been overcome by her beauty. Barbara, by all accounts, was stunning. She had a regal head of auburn hair, warm, almost reddish brown eyes, alabaster skin, and a statuesque figure; she moved with style and grace.

Barbara Davis was born in Washington State in 1949 — on January 31, Norman's birthday, as it turned out — where her father, James Davis, was working on a heavy equipment job. But her forebears were from Arkansas, and she was reared in Atkins, a tiny place with a population of fewer than two thousand, twelve miles from Russellville, the nearest real town. Her mother, Gaynell, worked in her own beauty shop in the family's converted garage. During a brief stay in Little Rock, the Davises entered their two-year-old daughter in a beauty pageant and she won, becoming Little Miss Little Rock.

An only child, Barbara excelled in school, joining all the usual clubs and holding offices in most of them. She was raised a Free Will Baptist and went to church three times a week. She was one of only a few classmates who went on to college, all to Arkansas Technical College in Russellville. Barbara declared an English major but switched to art. She worked summers picking beans and packing pickles, a detail that would fascinate Norman. At twenty, she married her first boyfriend, Larry Norris, and dropped out to work to put her husband through college. Larry was off in Vietnam when their son, Matthew, was born; the marriage ended soon after. At the time she met Norman, she was divorced and teaching art at Russellville High School.

She had called Fig and asked if she could come to the Gwaltneys' party because her curiosity was piqued; besides, there wasn't much to do in Russellville. Barbara had dated almost every available single man between Russellville and Little Rock, sixty miles away — including aspiring lawyer Bill Clinton — and was beginning to give up on Arkansas. She was passionate about art. She painted large oils; she also had an extensive doll collection, including more than a hundred Barbies. Her favorite painters were Andrew Wyeth and Edward Hopper; she later told a reporter that she had piled in the car with her friends to drive to Little Rock to see "*an* Andrew Wyeth painting." She had few real intellectual aspirations, but she did have ambition, and she respected culture. She belonged, for instance, to the Book-of-the-Month Club; that was how she came to read part of *Marilyn*, the only book of Mailer's with which she was familiar. Friends knew that Barbara wanted to get out of her rural corner of Arkansas: there wasn't much for a single woman to do there but teach or be a secretary.

Eventually Norman overcame his atypical shyness and introduced himself properly to her. With the Gwaltneys, they went to dinner at the home of Van Allen and Ginny Tyson, where they continued talking. Later they picked up five-year-old Matthew at Barbara's ex-husband's house and took him home. Late in the evening, Norman left, and he left Arkansas the next day. A few days later, a crate arrived from New York containing hardbound copies of every one of his books; Barbara sat down and read them one after another and was overwhelmed.

Barbara had promised to write, and Norman gave her a post office box address so her letters wouldn't come to the house in Stockbridge to be seen by Carol. Several weeks later he came back, bearing a thick silver ring with a pale blue stone, and Barbara met him in Little Rock, where they spent a long weekend, mostly in bed. In June she flew to Chicago, where he was promoting *The Fight*, and a few weeks later to New York, where he stayed with her in the Heights brownstone. Here they discussed their future. Barbara had vague plans to sell her house and use the money to get an M.F.A., perhaps at the Rhode Island School of Design, but Norman said he'd prefer that she stay in New York. She had sent him some pictures of herself from local modeling assignments, and he suggested that she try this in New York. Norman's friends, photographer Milton Greene and his wife, Amy, who owned a chain of spas, thought she might do well as a model — if she lost twenty pounds. So Barbara went back to Arkansas and put herself on a crash diet, which reduced her dress size from thirteen to nine. The lure of New York was very great, and she genuinely adored Norman. To the dismay of her family (who didn't yet know that there was a man in the picture), she announced that she was quitting her job at the high school and moving to the big city, leaving her son with her parents for the time being.

All, of course, did not go smoothly, as Norman was hardly unencumbered. Carol, up in Stockbridge, grew suspicious of his frequent and prolonged trips to the city, and Barbara often felt lost when Norman broke away to spend time with Carol. Fan Mailer decided she liked Barbara — Fan liked and accepted Fig Gwaltney, and associated Barbara with Fig — and got her an apartment in her own Willow Street building, a few blocks from Norman's brownstone. According to Barbara, they spent their days together, going to museums, shopping, and learning the subway. Barbara wrote often to the Gwaltneys, and closed each letter by asking what the people of Russellville were saying about her — not that she cared, she added.

That fall Barbara began modeling for the Wilhelmina agency. Her employers thought the name Barbara Norris too small-town, so she began calling herself Norris. Later, after consulting with Norman, she would choose a new last name, Church; Norman liked few things as much as the prerogative of renaming a woman himself. Norris's face soon started appearing in magazines; clients who used her included Clairol, Ben Kahn furriers, and Gloria Vanderbilt. She was supporting herself fairly well and seeing Norman frequently, but only at New Year's in 1976 did he sever his ties with Carol and move in with Norris at the Heights brownstone for good.

There is no question that Norris brought stability to Norman's life. She was strong-willed, confident, and complex enough to hold his interest. She could be very funny. Friends noted that she didn't seem to compete with Norman: not only was she secure in pursuit of her own ambitions, modeling and painting, but she didn't crave the attention Norman was getting. She could be truly supportive of him and of his work because of her confidence in her own pursuits. Though her edges were rough — she had some endearing "hick" mannerisms that she quickly shed — she was easy to be around, agreeable and gracious. And it swelled Norman's vanity, of course, to have a beautiful woman half his age on his arm. With his own new security in his work, it must have seemed as if the pieces of a puzzle were falling into place.

INTO THE HEARTLAND

Norman and Norris made a trip to Los Angeles to see the writer Henry Miller in the fall of 1975; Norman wanted to put out a collection of Miller's writings, which were famous for their depictions of raw sexuality frankly rendered, with Norman's own running commentary. Although Miller was then eighty-four years old and shuffled about his Pacific Palisades mansion in a blue terrycloth robe and pajamas, aided by a walker, his mind was still sharp, and he received Norman and Norris with enthusiasm. Miller and Mailer came from similar backgrounds — both were Brooklynites — and Mailer's books attracted almost as much attention as Miller's did because of their preoccupation with sex — and, more recently, what was perceived as their male chauvinism. However, the two writers never really connected personally. Miller distrusted Easterners and especially New Yorkers; he was by temperament gentle and suspicious of celebrity. Running for public office, for instance, was absolutely unthinkable for a man of his disposition. But Miller did agree to let Norman excerpt his works.

Miller had been important to Mailer since his time at Harvard, when he read someone's smuggled copy of *Tropic of Cancer*. The older writer's frank bravura about sexuality and life as lived by the down-and-out in expatriate Paris impressed him, and Miller's idiosyncratic, often baroque style affected him so greatly that he put the writer's works aside for a while. Mailer well knew the Miller legend — the Brooklyn boy who at his lowest ebb became an employment manager for Western Union, suffered mightily at the hands of his enigmatic wife June and her lesbian lover, and emerged reborn, writing colossal epics about sexuality and America on the streets of Paris. Mailer knew he owed a great debt to Miller, for they shared similar concerns, and each believed in the power of obscenity and explicit sexuality. But Mailer had never immersed himself in Miller's work, as he would do now. Thereafter he would confidently vow that Hemingway and Miller were his literary betters.

The result of this exploration was *Genius and Lust: A Journey through the Major Writings of Henry Miller,* seemingly an odd book for Mailer to have taken on. It certainly wasn't a book that anyone thought would make a lot of money, although Mailer hoped that young people who were unfamiliar with Miller's work would discover it through this collection. But the main reason that Mailer and Miller's publisher Barney Rosset conceived of the book was the intense admiration they both felt for Henry Miller. Rosset's Grove Press, which published Miller's major works, agreed to bring out *Genius and Lust* to eliminate any issue of permissions.

Mailer had one other consideration in mind when planning the project: he wanted to find work for his good friend Buzz Farbar. At this point Buzz was between editing jobs, and Norman thought he could do a lot of the legwork involved in putting together the book. The contract reflected this: out of a total of $75,000, Norman was to receive a $50,000 advance, Buzz $15,000, and Miller about $10,000 — whatever was left over after expenses. (Miller at the time was receiving so much money in royalties after his best books had cleared the censor that he was forever trying to improve his income tax situation; he did not need more.)

The collection, which in its early stages was to be called *Cosmic Demon,* included excerpts from *Tropic of Cancer* and *Tropic of Capricorn, The Rosy Crucifixion, Black Spring,* and five or six less well known books. As well as a preface, interspersed were seven commentaries by Mailer. These commentaries represent some of the best critical thinking that has been brought to bear on Miller's work: as Mailer pointed out, they help to create a "critical space" around Miller that otherwise does not exist, since critics usually write briefly either to adulate or dismiss him. Mailer, on the other hand, though he was sometimes overcome in his admiration of the man — at one point he wondered whether Miller might be America's Shakespeare — managed to distill the essence of Miller's work and discuss it as would a familiar and practiced guide, showing the reader why each selection does or does not work. He also explored the many Millers: the one who could set up as a pure and immensely talented pornographer; the Miller who could write surrealistic poetry for New Directions; a great travel writer; "a species of Beat Mencken"; the greatest writer the *New York Times Magazine* would ever find. He contrasted Miller with Hemingway in an abstract yet telling vision: Hemingway, he explains, always writes about a camp by the river, he never writes about the river itself; Miller, however, writes as if he *is* the river, unafraid, rushing forward.

Not that Mailer was uncritical of Miller's work. He thought *The Rosy Crucifixion* a failure, though on a mighty scale. He disliked the book of which Miller was most proud, and which many readers cite as their favorite Miller title: *The Colossus of Maroussi*. Mailer called it "his private paean to respectability," saying it was "the first of Miller's works which could be given to the eighty-year-old mother of the minister of the First Episcopalian Church in you-name-the-suburb of Philadelphia." Miller disagreed, but Mailer stood firm. He thought the book, which contained no obscenities and no sex, calculatedly "too nice," and he suspected Miller wrote it to provoke the American literary establishment into recognizing him.

Genius and Lust was, moreover, a distraction from what Mailer was supposed to be doing: writing the first of the big novels Little, Brown had contracted for. He gave an interview to the *New York Times* in December 1976 in which he acknowledged that he was writing with all eyes upon him: "This is a tricky business," he said. "The trick is to go beyond one's reach." And he announced his subject, a most unlikely one: Egypt in the Twentieth Dynasty, 1130 B.C. "Why?" he asked. "Because I fell through a novelistic hole. I thought I would dip into the period and then it began to absorb me." Actually, he clarified, the first third was to be set in Egypt, the second third on a spaceship, while the last third was to be contemporary. "I want the novel to be a consistent explanation of time," he told the reporter. To Henry Miller, in May, he wrote that he had written 130,000 words and had about 350,000 to 400,000 to go. In explaining his choice of the setting, Norman pointed out that Egyptian religious ideas were much like many he had entertained over the years. He didn't further specify, but it seems likely he was referring to his belief in reincarnation.

Yet he was so easily distracted. He had chosen not to cover the 1976 presidential conventions in order to devote himself to his book, but in the late summer he accepted an assignment from the *New York Times Magazine* to interview the Democratic candidate, Jimmy Carter. Though the resulting article, which ran for almost the entire magazine, painted a fascinating picture of the candidate's home town, Plains, Georgia, Mailer botched the main interview by talking too much and focusing on Carter's (or, more often it seems, his own) religious and philosophical beliefs. Carter's religiosity fascinated him so much it threw him off the rails.

Another distraction: in December he gave what was billed as a poetry reading at the Ninety-second Street Y. While he suffered no repeat of his 1961 experience, when the curtain was rung down on him, his reading was obscene enough that many audience members left quietly. When Mailer warned that even raunchier language was yet to come, others left. But he had few poems on hand to read, so he turned to reading from his prose: a section from *The Fight,* the scene from *An American Dream* in which Rojack has sex with the maid, and an obscenity-laden passage from *Why Are We in Vietnam?* He seemed to enjoy the audience's objections at the end: that what he was describing was not sex but violence, and that he was nothing more than a male chauvinist. Mailer argued in return that a true male chauvinist couldn't distance himself enough to write about chauvinism. The evening ended quietly, but the impression was left that he seemed to have some real need to misbehave in public, especially at the "Jewish Y."

The auspices just did not seem to be there for a long, solitary stint of writing. And in fact Norman and Norris were entering a long period that would find them spending considerable time and energy in the social life of New York City's Upper East Side. With former wives Adele and Beverly, Norman had been an inveterate partygoer, but mostly at literary gatherings. Now Norman was entering an elevated social stratosphere. He and Norris, who overcame her initial shyness and was now making friends easily, attended dinners with such columnists' favorites as Kennedy sister Pat Lawford, hostess Jan Cushing Olympitis, film and stage director Peter Glenville, city planner Marietta Tree, real estate mavens Jerry Zipkin and Alice Mason, and socialite Slim Keith. Few intellectuals or writers were counted among this group, and the usual Mailer cronies or even good friends like Torres or Farbar had no place in it. Norman did know George Plimpton and Bill Buckley, and became even closer to them around 1976 and 1977. Increasingly, Norman and Norris appeared at fashion shows, Norman explaining to friends that he did it "for Norris."

Norman and Norris entertained as well, hosting either large bashes for around two hundred or small dinners for six or eight, at which Norris would serve Southern fare like fried chicken and cornbread and pies baked with pecans from a tree in her parents' yard. One typical party, in December 1976, celebrated the anniversary of Dick Goodwin's marriage to LBJ biographer Doris Kearns. Jackie Onassis was in attendance, perhaps accounting for the presence of New York Times columnist Charlotte Curtis, and Curtis mentioned some of the guests she could identify in the dimly lit fray: José Torres; the writer Arthur Schlesinger, Jr., and his wife, Alexandra; Marion Javits, wife of Senator Jacob Javits; Marietta Tree; TV host Dick Cavett and his wife, Carrie Nye; photographer Milt Greene and his wife, Amy; the lawyer and Carter adviser William vanden Heuvel; and Lady Jeanne Campbell, Mailer's third wife. Curtis was able only to glimpse Onassis, but she spotted Fanny Mailer, beaming and exchanging hugs with guests. Norman was jovial and Norris striking in dark lipstick and a white satin outfit. It wasn't a terribly remarkable party compared with others Norman had given, but it was a milestone of sorts for him because it was written up purely as a social evening rather than as a drunken brawl.

On balance, then, Norman was generally happy with his life since Marilyn. He had at last begun his novel, even if its Egyptian setting and his propensity to take on other, smaller subjects were making progress difficult. Norris had, it seemed, brought a measure of stability to their alliance, though old obsessions still plagued Norman, sometimes causing him to pursue lines of thinking that were far from productive. But he felt far less pressure — less pressure to succeed, less pressure to win attention.

IN APRIL 1977, packages began to arrive at Norman's Brooklyn brownstone from Larry Schiller. The packages contained pages and pages of interviews with Gary Gilmore, the Utah murderer who had refused to appeal when sentenced to death, and copies of letters he had written to his girlfriend, Nicole Baker, who had made at least one suicide attempt at Gary's request. Mailer read the material and bought Schiller's proposition: here was a story he could not pass up.

Gilmore had been executed by a firing squad in January 1977; it was the first execution in the United States in more than ten years. The case attracted attention for that alone, but also because Gilmore had refused to participate in appeals and instead asked to be executed. The media camped out in Provo waiting for the execution, and the publicity the case drew spun out of control. When Gary and Nicole entered into a suicide pact and eventually attempted suicide, many observers thought the story was degenerating into tabloid trash, while others were drawn to this story of human suffering and waste. The ACLU stepped in, arguing that to kill Gilmore would be to deny his civil liberties. The case focused national attention on the issue of the death penalty, opening a larger debate on crime and punishment. Many people admired what they saw as Gary's courage, while others thought that his resolution to die represented cowardice.

Schiller had immediately sensed a major story and was one of the first to arrive in Provo. He acquired rights to several stories, working first on a deal with CBS and pursuing other deals when that one fell through. He saw that Nicole's story gave the Gilmore tale a broader, more tragic dimension, and began a series of interviews with Nicole, members of her family, and Gary's relatives. He flew in Barry Farrell, a writer for *True West* magazine, and joined him in interviewing Gary for *Playboy*. While Schiller had many plans for the story — he imagined a Broadway musical, among many other things — the idea nagged at him that this was a story in need of a really good writer, someone like Mailer. He was reluctant to approach Mailer at first, because they had had so many disagreements over *Marilyn*. But finally he followed his instincts and began to send Mailer the material.

Convinced that Nicole was the magic ingredient in the story — she had immense appeal, and was a complicated person for all her lack of sophistication — Schiller brought her to New York to meet Mailer. It was her first time in a big city, and Schiller and his wife, Stephie, showed her around. She met Norman over lunch with the Schillers at Trader Vic's, and they had a good conversation; after lunch, Norman asked her to play chess. After a half-hour alone with her, he was convinced she added a compelling element to the story.

Satisfied that Schiller could be trusted with the deal-making, Mailer flew out to Utah for the first of six or seven trips to conduct interviews and soak up the local atmosphere. He carried with him some nine thousand pages of Schiller's interviews; eventually he would have a total of sixteen thousand, a figure that doesn't include transcripts of the interviews he himself conducted. He rented an apartment in Provo, making two trips to Portland, Oregon, to see Gary's mother, and one to Marion, Illinois, to see the prison where Gary spent much of his adult life.

To Schiller, Mailer seemed relaxed; he attributed it to freedom from pressure to gather facts. Schiller was taking care of all the details, gathering news stories and film footage, and Mailer eventually had his wonderful new secretary, Judith McNally, and another researcher fly out to organize the material; on the New York end was Mailer's assistant Martha Thomases, among others.

When he was not in the field with Mailer conducting interviews, Schiller was trying to put together deals in New York City. Little, Brown, because of Mailer's contractual obligations to them for a novel, could not afford to tie up any more money in one writer, offering only a token advance of twenty-five thousand dollars for the book. Schiller went to Howard Kaminsky, the president of Warner Books, who had bought the paperback rights to *Marilyn* for one hundred thousand dollars in 1973. Kaminsky was not convinced of the story's potential until Mailer came in and talked about it, and he then offered half a million dollars for the paperback rights, a very large sum by 1970s standards. Presumably Schiller was given a percentage of these amounts, but he also had money coming in from other media deals.

Mailer established the time frame of the book — which he would call a "true life novel" — around several key points in Gary's story. First was the time period when he was released, at age thirty-six, from the penal system, which had held him for the last twenty-two years of his life. The stormy romance between Gary and Nicole developed in this period. The second involved the two successive nights in July when Gary robbed and shot first Max Jensen, a gas station owner in Orem, and the following night motel attendant Ben Bushnell in Provo. The third part covered the period when Gary was in prison, the romantic separation of Gary and Nicole, the media coverage, and the events leading up to his execution. A final, closing section chronicled the events after Gary's execution, including Schiller's first interviews with Nicole. The action of the book ended around Christmastime in 1977, seven months after Mailer began work on it.

One aspect of the story cried out for inclusion: its packaging, the media frenzy, and Schiller's role in the story of the story. Schiller reasoned that word would get out that Mailer had been able to tell Gilmore's tale only with his assistance. Schiller had become close to Gary over the course of the long wait for the execution and was the only person who knew about much of the killer's story. He was present at the execution — it was one part of the story Mailer wouldn't have an exclusive on, for Schiller had given interviews without charge afterward. In fact, Schiller's funny nobility throughout the affair would emerge compellingly from Mailer's narrative, and Mailer's feelings toward Schiller would come to be characterized by a grudging respect. Mailer once asked Mikal Gilmore, Gary's brother and the author of a fine memoir of his family and his brother's death, *Shot in the Heart* (1994), why he hadn't wanted to be involved in *The Executioner's Song*. "Because of Larry Schiller," Mikal said. Norman said he knew what Mikal meant and went on to say, "You know, Larry and I have had our disagreements over the years. But I have to say, I think there was something about this experience that deepened Larry."

The interviewing, gathering of material, and writing of the book would continue until the summer of 1978, when Norman turned the manuscript in to Little, Brown. He remained relaxed and easy during the process, unperturbed by urgent interruptions from Schiller, saying he must talk to this or that principal in the story. Norris was partly responsible, of course. She ran a tight ship, and she didn't show the strain it must have caused her, looking regal and beautiful throughout it all. She saw to it that the children were shuffled around their various homes with a minimum of stress. She painted portraits of anyone who would sit still long enough to be photographed (she worked roughly from photos), and she sold a lot of portraits to their wealthier friends. She taught art at St. Ann's, the local Episcopal private school, to defray Matthew's tuition costs.

But a new domestic crisis came into play: Norman and Beverly's divorce case finally came to court. Relations between them had been strained but civil in the years since 1974, when Beverly first brought the case. In the summer of 1977, Beverly had a summer gig in Hartford, Connecticut, playing in *Twelfth Night* and in Preston Jones's *The Oldest Living Graduate,* and Norman and Norris, the boys with them, came to see her perform. But at the end of the summer Norman told Beverly that Norris was pregnant (their son, John Buffalo, would be born on April 16, 1978); Beverly now recognized that the marriage was over.

In court, Beverly's lawyers renewed her initial request for custody of the boys, the house, and thirty thousand dollars a year in alimony — the latter only until she could resume her acting career. Monroe Inker, Norman's Boston lawyer, told the press that his client could not give Beverly what she wanted if he was to care for his other children. Norman was facing a lien on the Provincetown house for filing returns but not paying taxes of one hundred thousand dollars in 1976 and 1977, complaining that he was simply too strapped to pay. For the time being, he was sending four hundred dollars a week to Beverly, four hundred dollars a week to Carol, claiming that she was his "musical director" on future movies, and six hundred dollars a week to Norris, who functioned as his "social secretary" and "troubleshooter": sometimes she was named in the papers as his "research assistant." Norman explained to the court, "I have always been famous for my poor relations, diplomatic relations with friends and enemies in New York. I needed someone who would present a more agreeable side of myself to the public." It should be noted that what he called his "pay" to Carol Stevens and to Norris was probably a deductible expense.

But Beverly dismissed his poverty claims outright, telling *People* magazine, "Listen, he said he was broke when I met him, and it's the same story now. Norman is a corporation." She pointed out that one of his claims was demonstrably false: he paid no alimony to Bea, a token one hundred dollars to Lady Jeanne, and two hundred a week in alimony to Adele, now that the girls were of age — hardly a fortune.

For Beverly, the process was a nightmare, as Norman's legal team rolled out its big guns and brought in the press. She had initially consulted Monroe Inker herself before Norman retained him, divulging many personal details to the lawyer about their marriage, and she was shocked to learn in the courtroom that the judge was allowing Inker to represent her husband, clapping her hand over her mouth in horror. After bringing out her résumés, programs for plays she had been in, reviews she'd received, and head shots, Inker said, "This woman has no career." He held up a picture of Beverly under a movie marquee showing her name and repeated several times, "This isn't you," so many times that Beverly began to believe he was right. He said that his client suggested Beverly go to a community college — a gratuitous insult — to prepare for a new, nonacting career. Then Inker presented her with a piece of paper on which were written the names of married men she had worked with in the theater and some others, including Miles Davis, suggesting that she had earned her living prior to her marriage to Norman not as an actress but as a mistress.

In retrospect, Beverly believes that her lawyers (who were paid by her husband, as is common in divorce cases) believed the nasty characterizations made by Inker and his client. She says she urged them to bring in tax returns, witnesses like her agent, proof of her union memberships to show that she had supported herself as an actress before her marriage, but to no avail. She believes they did not sufficiently investigate Norman's finances. To Beverly, it seemed a chilling demonstration of just how powerful Norman was and how helpless she was.

In 1980, Beverly would be awarded $575 a week in alimony and $200 in child support for the next seven years; Norman's lawyers, according to Beverly, would specify that the alimony should run for seven years because the marriage had been a "brief" one. But she would eventually lose the house at 565 Commercial Street, which Norman allowed to fall into the hands of the IRS, says Beverly, rather than giving it to her or simply settling his tax bill and allowing her to stay there. Beverly hired a new lawyer immediately to appeal the decision, arguing that Monroe Inker's representation of Norman after he had consulted with Beverly was wrong and perhaps unlawful, and that Norman's finances should have been investigated. The Massachusetts Supreme Judicial Court ruled that while it was "close" whether Inker's meeting with Beverly disqualified him from representing Norman, it did not do so, though the court said, "The facts in this case bring us as close to the outer limits as we shall want to go." Beverly lost the appeal. In 1985 she went to family court over cost-of-living increases that Norman had not paid and was granted them.

But by then the damage would be done. In 1985, Beverly underwent the first of several nervous breakdowns. Three more hospitalizations ensued, but Beverly gradually found her way back and is today a working actress and a much-valued member of the Cape community — a recent magazine article spoke of "the brilliance of her career" and called her the "premier actress" of Provincetown — where she and Norman guardedly coexist.

MAILER'S DIVORCE from Beverly gave Norman and Norris an incentive to make some sense of their finances, to which they applied themselves around Christmas 1977. They saw the mistakes Norman's financial advisers had made in the past: paying late fees and penalties, not taking all possible deductions. By the fall of 1977 Norman was about three hundred thousand dollars in debt, mostly to Scott Meredith, who was giving him monthly loans. He owed the IRS, whose penalties got higher every month. The monthly money from Little, Brown was going mostly to pay the loan to Scott, and they needed about a thousand dollars a day to pay the mortgage and taxes, a secretary's salary (and often those of part-time secretaries), the housekeeper's wages, tuition for seven children, and alimony to Adele and Beverly and a token sum to Lady Jeanne. It got so bad that Norman's checks from Warner Books were being attached. (Of course, this was Norman's version of his accounts; he had an interest in protecting his assets and inflating his debts because he still feared action from Beverly's lawyers.)

At the beginning of 1978, Norman was ready to turn the manuscript in, and he wanted to do it then, he needed the money so badly. He told Schiller, who asked how long he needed to get the manuscript absolutely right. Three months, said Norman. Schiller went back to Kaminsky at Warner and asked for another one hundred thousand dollars and a three-month extension. The additional money bought Mailer three months. Schiller even found a way to get his typing done for nothing: he gave it to the script typist at CBS at night, sneaking the cost into a movie budget.

Schiller went to these lengths because he was very excited by what he read. The book was written in an entirely new voice — an uncadenced, sparse prose, what *Playboy*'s Arthur Kretchmer called Norman's "Plains voice." Mailer was not there in the book — not as "Aquarius," not as "the Reporter," not in his usual, baroque, adjective-studded sentences. Paragraphs were kept short, and white spaces separated them — a nice typographical effect that made the reader slow down and pay attention. Mailer's description of Gary's murder of the gas station operator, for instance, is typically laconic:

> Gilmore brought the Automatic to Jensen's head. "This one is for me," he said, and fired.
> "This one is for Nicole," he said and fired again. The body reacted each time.
> He stood up. There was a lot of blood. It spread across the floor at a surprising rate. Some of it got onto the bottom of his pants.

This technique slowed down the pace, giving equal emphasis to each detail of the story.

Mailer had pared the story down to its essentials: Gary's release from prison in Illinois, his arrival in Provo, Gary's relationship with Nicole, and the killings. He had conducted some painful but productive interviews with the widows of the victims. He rehearsed their last moments with their husbands, and in the retelling, the smallest detail seemed at once ominous, unbearably poignant, and yet still mundane, as seen in this description of Debbie Bushnell, who, with her husband, Ben, ran a motel that they also lived in. At this point, Ben was just minutes away from his death:

> In the middle of washing the couch cushions, Debbie Bushnell went out to the front office and asked Ben to go to the store and get some low-fat milk. She was also hoping he would bring back some ice cream and candy bars, and began to giggle at the thought she must

be pregnant again. She had certainly felt telltale cravings. Ben, however, didn't want to go. He was interested in the Olympics.

In Book Two, "Eastern Voices," Mailer shifts his point of view to Schiller in order to convey the story of the condemned man's imprisonment and execution. Though some would find this the weaker part of the book, Mailer widens his focus to take in the media frenzy without losing sight of Gary's trajectory. Schiller's involvement was well known, and rather than attempt to keep his collaboration in the story's background, Mailer decided to make the journalist a full-fledged character. One of the book's strongest features, in fact, is Mailer's portrayal of Schiller's misgivings and doubts surrounding his role in Gary's execution. At the execution itself, Schiller lost his sense of color, describing for reporters Gary's black hood, the line on the floor that spectators stood behind as yellow. "He realized that during the execution something had altered his perception of color." The hood was in fact blue and the painted line white.

Because Mailer included many letters from Gary to Nicole — he cleaned up Gary's grammar and his spelling, but not Nicole's — readers get a good sense of Gary's complexity. Gary reflected at length on karma and reincarnation, though he seemed not to connect these directly to what he had done. He understood that a cosmic reckoning might come: "I know that dying is just changing form," he wrote Nicole. "I don't expect to escape any of my debts, I'll meet them and pay them." He is no hero. But in Gary Gilmore Mailer found an embodiment of existential hipsterism; he recalls the character Sergius O'Shaugnessy from *The Deer Park,* except that Gary lived his life for higher stakes. Only in some ways Gary was guilty of the worst kind of bad faith and thus not an existentialist at all, for what could be more nihilistic than choosing to die? Still, the plane on which such choices are made is classically existential terrain.

Mailer's depiction of Gary's brooding, baroque sexuality, as revealed in his graphic sexual talk to Nicole, adds another layer to one of his most fascinating literary portraits. Gary called Nicole his "elf," reminisced about her "bootie," and imagined bathtub sex scenes. But the deep love he feels for her is undeniable: "I love you more than God," he wrote to her. Yet he also discussed at length whether he should ask her to commit suicide and thus, after a fashion, die with him; eventually they would make a suicide pact together, and Nicole would almost die in the attempt. Still, Gary's humor and Nicole's personality made the relationship resonate. In one of the book's most powerfully rendered scenes, Nicole, thwarted from seeing Gary after she has hitchhiked to the jail, only to find it isn't visitors' day, stands outside the wire fence surrounding the jail and yells, "Gary Gilmore, can you hear me?" She hears a "Yeah, babe," and shouts, "YEAH! Gary Gilmore, I love you!" Gary is delighted to hear his "magic elf's voice." Still, Mailer detailed as well Nicole's continued sexual liaisons with other men; sleeping with strangers seems to have been a compulsion with her.

Mailer's unadorned portrayals of these two flawed and puzzling human beings rescues the story from becoming a stark morality tale; instead, it is a richly Gothic nightmare, rendered in the sparsest, most dispassionate terms. The second half of the book is crowded indeed, with such figures as David Susskind and Bill Moyers putting in appearances, along with a whole new cast of characters, from Schiller's secretaries to Utah death penalty activists. But they enrich and expand the drama's sweeping breadth without shifting the focus from Gary's tragedy. Nicole disappears from the story — she was institutionalized after her suicide attempt. But her voice is still there in her letters to Gary, which become incredibly poignant as the execution date approaches. Indeed, the suspense builds almost unbearably, as time slows down toward the end of the long wait; the course of Gary's last day and night is presented in agonizing detail. After the execution, as the reporters disperse and Gary's intimates go back to their bleak lives, the effect is of a majestic denouement to an epic tragedy.

Little, Brown was no less excited than Schiller by the manuscript. Mailer's editor, Ned Bradford, died while the book was in production; Roger Donald took over from him, coming in at the time the jacket art was being chosen. Expectations ran high. In the meantime, Schiller was busy selling foreign rights. He also let *Playboy* excerpt the book, but only after much argument between Mailer and the magazine editors over what passages to publish.

Copies were in the stores in October 1979, and the reviews began appearing soon after. A handful of negative reviews complained that a guide was needed to this material, that Mailer's voice was missed. For instance, Earl Sovit of the *Nation* wrote, "The reader is left at the end of this exhaustive exploration of the character and destiny of Gary Gilmore unguided by the author and unconfronted with a meaningful shape of experience." *The New Yorker* decried "its inordinate length . . . its longwindedness, its uncertain credibility, and maybe even the portentousness of its title."

But there were more good reviews than bad — and they were extraordinarily good. The quality that each of them noted approvingly, in fact, was Mailer's absence from the book. It was as if he had revealed another facet of his talent. Walter Karp wrote in *Esquire,* "At long last, Mailer has used his immense narrative powers, a true gift of the gods, the way they are meant to be used: to tell a story that is not about himself." In *Newsweek,* Walter Clemons wrote, "Norman Mailer's thousand-page chronicle of the [Gilmore] case is an extraordinary demonstration of his novelistic skill . . . By

God, the book is good, a phenomenal feat of narrative." Frank McConnell reviewed the book for the *New Republic:* "If the novel is a mythology constructed to catch the moral ambiguity of its age, then *The Executioner's Song* is a brilliant, maybe a great novel." Joan Didion, a long-time admirer of Mailer's work, reviewed the book for the front page of the *New York Times Book Review;* the essay is thought to be a small classic itself. "'The Executioner's Song' is ambitious to the point of vertigo," she wrote.

> I think no one but Mailer could have dared this book. The authentic Western voice . . . is heard often enough in life but only rarely in literature. The very subject of "The Executioner's Song" is that vast emptiness at the center of the Western experience, a nihilism antithetical not only to literature but to most other forms of human endeavor, a dread so close to zero that human voices fade out, trail off, like skywriting . . . This is an absolutely astonishing book.

A lot of critical ink was spilled about Mailer's decision to call the book "a true life novel." Debates over designations like this had kept the literary world busy ever since the 1966 publication of Truman Capote's *In Cold Blood.* Mailer had entered the debate with his description of *Armies of the Night* as "history as a novel, the novel as history." What these writers — and others, like E. L. Doctorow, who had taken to the new "genre" — meant must have been that their work rested on historical fact but that they had brought novelistic skills to shaping and telling it. Practical considerations may have entered into the process as well, as a publisher might prefer classification as a novel for sales purposes. Or the writer might prefer such a designation as a kind of truth-in-advertising gesture.

In any event, on April 15, 1980, *The Executioner's Song* won the Pulitzer Prize for fiction, thus temporarily shelving the debate on the book's genre. Norman, explaining that when he won the 1968 Pulitzer for *Armies of the Night* he was too busy with his mayoral campaign to give it much thought, said that this time around he was "kind of pleased." It gave him the opportunity, he told a *New York Times* reporter, to go around quoting his favorite line from Voltaire — "Once a philosopher, twice a pervert." He confessed, "I don't even want to be interrupted for good news," saying he was in the midst of his long Egyptian novel. For once, no snide references to his unwritten "big novel" appeared in the press; *The Executioner's Song* was a mighty achievement. Mailer had delivered again.

TWENTY-FIVE

A RECKONING

As Mailer recounts in *The Executioner's Song,* in the fateful moment when Gary Gilmore faced the firing squad in Utah, just as guards were about to cover his head with a hood, the condemned man uttered his last words: a laconic "Let's do it."

These words, with all their fatalism, their refusal of emotion, and their strange bravery, reverberated long after the media crowds left Provo and Gilmore's remains were incinerated and scattered over the desolate Utah landscape. They had special resonance in the punk community in New York City, a milieu Norman came to know well in 1979 and 1980. LET'S DO IT appeared on the torn T-shirts punk musicians and their followers favored. Another, similar slogan appeared on a T-shirt worn by musician Richard Hell: PLEASE KILL ME, placed over a shooting target.

Mailer's introduction to the punk scene came from the redoubtable Legs McNeil, the nineteen-year-old editor who gave the movement its name with his magazine *Punk.* Legs had considerable charm, was the original chronicler of the punk scene, and enjoyed close friendships with many punk musicians and members of the music press. Norman met him in 1979 at a Village party given by Norman's assistant, Martha Thomases. Legs, recovering from a massive headache, emerged from a dark room to introduce himself to Norman, saying, "I haven't read any of your stuff and you probably haven't read any of mine." Mailer laughed, clearly won over. By the end of the evening, the two had made an appointment for an interview to appear in *Punk.*

Legs was managing a band called Shrapnel, which affected military gear like grenades and sandbags onstage. He knew *The Naked and the Dead* was about World War II and asked Norman about his war experiences. Norman didn't respond with the enthusiasm Legs would have liked, but later he met the members of Shrapnel and, learning they were from Red Bank, New Jersey — not far from Long Branch, Mailer territory — took a liking to them. The interview itself was not very successful: Legs complained that Norman had no beer in the house, and when Norman dared him to walk the catwalks in his aerie, Legs declined, saying, "I haven't got anything to prove."

Not long after, Legs and Martha Thomases escorted Norman to the downtown club CBGB to see the Ramones, the cartoonish band from Queens who became the first New York punks to achieve widespread popularity with such bouncy, two-minute classics as "Blitzkreig Boy" and "I Wanna Be Sedated." The evening was dubbed "A Benefit for Policemen's Bulletproof Vests"; Legs and his friends were quite serious about it, hoping "to piss off the liberals." Before and after the band's sets, the retinue passed the time at the Second Street loft of Arturo Vega, lighting designer for the Ramones. Legs thinks Norman enjoyed the fact that most of those present were "criminals," "psychopaths," while Martha Thomases remembers him holding forth to the Ramones about how much they reminded him of young boxers.

Norman did genuinely like the music — its energy, precision, and violence. And his stance did in fact have something in common with punk; ever since "The White Negro" he had shown an interest in any group of people who lived on the edge, and the punk rockers were legitimate cousins to the hipsters of the 1950s. He asked Legs to hire Shrapnel to play at a party he was giving to celebrate the engagement of his oldest daughter, Susie, to the Chilean economics student Marco Colodro, and Shrapnel played at several more of Norman's parties. Usually these parties were uneventful, though at one, according to Legs, Norman was forced to headbutt Glen Buxton, a former guitarist with Alice Cooper's band, when Buxton attempted to make off with a whole ham under his shirt. On another occasion Norman and Legs wrestled, and Legs opened a cut on Norman's ear, spilling blood everywhere.

Shrapnel and Legs McNeil were big hits with fourteen-year-old Michael and twelve-year-old Stephen Mailer. When Legs told them to watch *Gilligan's Island,* a show he much admired, they did, over and over. The two boys began talking like Legs and parroting his enthusiasms. But Norman, already frustrated with television's looming presence in the lives of his children, could see nothing redeeming in reruns of old sitcoms. "Norman blamed me for destroying his kids," says Legs.

Despite their affinities, Legs, his punk musicians, and Norman were never really on the same wavelength. Legs finally did read *The Executioner's Song* and told Norman that it was a "white trash Bible" and that he loved it, but he also thought, "What we were doing was just more exciting."

Legs was more impressed by Norman's friend Harold Conrad, who regaled the punks with stories about promoting fights in the 1940s and drinking at the Copacabana, and seemed the epitome of cool. Norman, in turn, was suspicious of any movement whose aesthetic was as harsh as punk's.

Yet, according to Legs, "Norman liked the action of punk, the fact that it was new" — which would be difficult to say of any other major writer of his generation, save Allen Ginsberg.

THE SUMMER OF 1980 Norman, Norris, and the children spent in a rented contemporary house on Mount Desert Island. The northern coastal Maine community's social scene was quite different from Provincetown's: it was populated with WASPs, and the favored activity was sailing. Norman was friends with two Harvard classmates who summered there, David Place and Lou Cabot; with Cabot he would often make the two- or three-day run down the Maine coast to Boston. Eileen Finletter, a longtime friend of Norman's, remarked that the old, WASPy families on Mount Desert expected orgies and worse from Norman, but instead they got a big happy family; Norman won over the men by playing chess with them. It came to be said, "That Norman Mailer's wonderful — but he's so normal!"

His divorce from Beverly was final that fall, on September 24. They still couldn't agree on terms. He had let the Commercial Street house be seized by the IRS, which was preparing to auction it off. Norman proposed to buy it back and resell it, splitting the proceeds with Beverly and putting his half in trust for the children, but Beverly did not want the house to be taken from her. She still occupied it; to her mind, it was hers. (She would finally be evicted in October 1981, after a California-based company bought it from the IRS for sixty thousand dollars, the same sum Mailer had paid for it in 1966.) In fact, Beverly's lawyers claimed the divorce was not final because she was appealing the financial settlement ruled on by the court; the judge ordered that everything was stayed pending the appeal. Beverly had always been willing to grant Norman a divorce, for instance when Maggie was born, but Norman chose instead this long battle of attrition.

A great believer in marriage, a newly single Norman then proposed a decidedly strange idea: he would marry Carol Stevens, to honor the relationship and give Maggie legitimacy, then immediately divorce her and marry Norris. Liz Smith broke this odd story, quoting Norris as saying she found it all "a bit disconcerting." But, Norris added, "I am behind Norman's decision, and I understand why he feels he has to do this." Carol, reached by the columnist in Stockbridge, said only, "It's a private affair; there will be no formal announcement." Norman said that he wanted to legitimize the kids, "every last one of the little buggers," overlooking the fact that a child is considered legitimate if the father's name is on the birth certificate. Beverly said, "We're not divorced. It's still in litigation. So how can he get married even once?"

In an extensive 1980 interview with *Puritan* magazine, Norman was asked whether there was a spiritual obligation to sexual relationships. "Well, it's always a spiritual obligation . . . There's a spiritual demand in love, . . . more a demand than an obligation. Love asks that we be a little braver than is comfortable for us, a little more generous, a little more flexible. It means living on the edge more than we care to." To each of his wives Norman brought an emotional intensity that practically guaranteed that the marriage would pass through moments of the greatest ecstasy and content as well as moments of terrible, often sordid despair. As might be expected, the ends of these relationships were extremely painful to all parties. To literary journalist James Atlas, Norman likened divorce to "getting thrown out of a baggage car." For the past five years he had been bemoaning the financial consequences of multiple divorces as well, though his alimony payments were actually rather modest.

Yet he seemed compelled to marry, and while the brief union with Carol took place in a blaze of publicity, he certainly could not have hoped to avoid this. Indeed, his marriage to and divorce from Carol seem to have been born from an old-fashioned gallantry. Perhaps his recent success with *The Executioner's Song* contributed to his decision, making him feel more expansive and pasha-like. He knew full well that legal ties meant financial ties, yet he seemed to believe his obligation to Carol and Maggie was absolute and included financial support. In fact, Carol's alimony and child support were exactly the same as what Beverly received. It is not clear whether Norman would have chosen to marry her had their relationship not produced a child, and it is probably even beside the point: Norman associated marriage with children, so much so that marrying the mother of his child was axiomatic. Clearly, Norman also enjoyed his expanding family; he relished the role of the patriarch, and he discharged his duties with real pleasure, despite the financial burden.

Norman and Carol were married by a justice of the peace, Shirley Fingerhood, at five on a Friday evening; at seven, he flew off to secure his Haitian divorce. He returned the next day, and two days later, on Tuesday, November 11, 1980, Norman and Norris were married by a Brooklyn rabbi. They flew to London, leaving a party in full swing in the Heights brownstone; they had small parts in Milos Forman's film *Ragtime,* then shooting in London, Norman playing Stanford White.

The Mailer household on Columbia Heights was now relatively small, the only children in regular residence being the two-year-old John Buffalo (sometimes called Buffy) and the ten-year-old Matthew, Norris's son, whom Norman had informally adopted; Matthew stayed up in the tower, in the small crow's nest that had once been Norman's office. (Norman now worked in a nearby studio with no telephone or other distractions.) The other children dropped in constantly, and many were weekend and school vacation guests. Fanny came to dinner several nights a week, whether or not guests were present, and soon would come to live with them. Norman now proudly hung Norris's colorful portraits on the walls, just as he once had hung Adele's paintings. Norris developed a specialty: making portraits of friends and family members by taking 35mm photos of them and then projecting the image onto the canvas and painting it in.

Norris was showing her paintings at Central Falls, a SoHo gallery-restaurant, and was writing a novel set in Arkansas in 1969; together, she and Norman were working on a children's book, tentatively called *The Enchanted Circus*. The couple welcomed journalists to their apartment and posed for countless photographs. Norris, with her titian hair and topaz eyes, looked regal and sexy at the same time. Norman, at fifty-seven, looked like a gentleman with his short silver ringlets, his fierce blue eyes, and his Brooks Brothers clothes. Their social circle had expanded to include people like Bill Paley, Gloria Vanderbilt, and Oscar de la Renta; because of his relationship to Pat Lawford, a close friend of Norris's, Teddy Kennedy also became one of the Mailers' circle. Norman looked on his new phase as a socialite as a newly discovered talent. Going to dinner parties, he told a *New York* magazine interviewer in 1983, is "sort of the last of my very small gifts to be developed. It's sort of like finding a new sport, the kind of sport you could never play when you were young." But they kept their socializing down to three nights a week for the sake of the children. "The look on the kid's face is starting to get to us," he told the interviewer. In spite of his new activities, Norman remained loyal to old friends like José Torres, Buzz Farbar, and Roger Donoghue. He usually had his hand in some kind of political activity as well; currently, he was organizing Abbie Hoffman's defense committee.

Most of Mailer's time was devoted to the Egyptian novel. He was still projecting a novel to follow, set in space, which he was calling *The Boat of Ra*, Ra being the sun god who drives his golden boat through the sky, and a third novel, set in the present, to be called *Modern Times*. The writing on the first book was going well, he told journalists.

In June 1982 Little, Brown would bring out yet another collection, *Pieces and Pontifications*. As Mailer wrote in the preface, the "pieces" in the first part "show my shell-shocked despair of the Seventies"; they include his wonderful *Esquire* article on his love/hate relationship with television, the text of his book on graffiti, a review of *Last Tango in Paris* (he felt Marlon Brando had let his fans down in many ways, not least in refusing to bare his genitals), and an essay on his old mentor Jean Malaquais, among other essays.

"Pontifications," the second half of the book, introduces several of the metaphysical concerns that were preoccupying him as he began his next novel. In almost every interview included in this section, he manages to turn the subject to his philosophical and mystical preoccupations. It is as if he had come to a certain watershed in his beliefs and wished to articulate them clearly here. He believes in God, absolutely — yet his abiding preoccupation is whether God is all-powerful. And what of the Devil? Must he exist as well? Are we on the side of the Devil or God, God's creations or the Devil's? Again and again he returns to karma, a concept he was exploring in all its varieties in his Egyptian novel.

PIECES AND PONTIFICATIONS didn't make much of a splash, but the tragic events of the summer of 1981 thrust Mailer back into the limelight. Jack Henry Abbott, a thirty-seven-year-old half-Irish, half-Chinese convict confined in federal prison in Marion, Illinois, had been corresponding with Mailer since 1978, when he learned about Mailer's involvement with the Gilmore case. He told Norman that he thought he could describe for him the life of the "state-reared," long-term convict. Abbott had been raised in a succession of foster homes and juvenile institutions; he had been in jail for his entire adult life but for nine and a half months. At present, he was serving a twenty-year sentence for murdering a fellow inmate. Before long he and Norman were corresponding intensely, with scores of pages from Abbott arriving every week.

From the initial contact Norman knew that Abbott was a powerful writer, and he was transfixed by what he read: descriptions of solitary confinement, the brutality of guards, the violence among prisoners, the horrible isolation of jail, the routine drugging of prisoners. Where Abbott was most brilliant was on the effects of long-term incarceration: the convict can only imagine emotions but not feel any — beyond fear and rage. State-raised convicts, he told Mailer, "emulate . . . a fanatically defiant and alienated individual who cannot imagine what forgiveness is, or mercy or tolerance, because he has no *experience* of such values."

Norman valued these letters not only because they helped him understand Gary Gilmore better — the two men had vast differences as well as similarities — but because of Abbott's depiction of the long-term prisoner's mentality. Though it is not fair to hold Mailer to the standards he promoted more than twenty years earlier, it's hard to distinguish the long-term convict from the hipster of "The White Negro" taken to extremes. The long-term prisoner, with no goals or aspirations, even experiences time in a different way — Abbott is wonderful on the passage of time — and is in a sense the ultimate existentialist, reduced to pure being.

Abbott was also an intellectual, an entirely self-taught individual who made his way, unbidden and without encouragement from anyone, through the most formidable tracts of philosophy, especially Marx. Most of his vocabulary consisted, he told Norman, of words he had never heard spoken. He was drawn to Marx first, he said, because the Communist press was the only place where the truth was told about prisons, and then because Marxism was an elegant theory that he believed explained everything, and because he believed in violent conflict in the future.

Mailer visited Abbott in 1979, taking him a copy of *The Executioner's Song,* and the correspondence continued. In early 1980, Norman showed some of it to his agent, Scott Meredith, and then to Bob Silvers, editor of the *New York Review of Books.* Silvers was impressed, and offered to print a selection in a June issue of his magazine. When Erroll McDonald, a young editor at Random House, saw the letters, he called Norman's secretary, Judith McNally, who had typed and edited the *New York Review of Books* selections. She arranged for Meredith's agency to send him some of the material she'd worked on, and McDonald offered Abbott an advance of $12,500. McDonald visited Abbott in prison in August 1980; in December, he presented the convict with manuscript for his approval. The book was scheduled for publication in June 1981.

Nobody ever thought that Abbott would be released, though he was, in fact, up for parole. In his letters, published as *In the Belly of the Beast,* Abbott made clear that while he obviously longed for freedom, he had grave doubts about the wisdom of releasing him. He said outright, "I cannot imagine how I can be happy in American society." Other passages can be read as explanations for why he should not be released, or even warnings as to what might happen if he were. Explaining that the concepts of judgment and reason exist only insofar as they are expressed in a code of pride and integrity that prizes violence and force above all, Abbott wrote, "Dangerous killers who act alone and *without* emotion, who act with calculation and principles, to avenge themselves, establish and defend their principles with acts of murder that usually evade prosecution by law: this is the state-raised conception of manhood, in the highest sense." Nonetheless, he came up for parole in the late spring of 1981, and one of the documents that members of the parole board had before them was a letter from Norman Mailer offering Abbott a job as his research assistant for $150 a week. Presumably parole was granted in part because of this job offer.

On his release date, June 5, Abbott flew to Kennedy airport, where he was met by Mailer at one o'clock in the morning. The two went back to

Mailer's darkened brownstone and moved out to the terrace to talk so they would not wake Norris and the children. Soon Abbott was settled in his assigned halfway house, a Salvation Army–run establishment on East Third Street.

But *settled* is hardly the word. Abbott hated New York and especially the Lower East Side, which seemed to him as dangerous as prison; he quickly bought a knife, which he carried everywhere. He had been given considerable amounts of Prolixin and other antipsychotic drugs in prison, and he described his temperament in a letter to Norman: "I'm tenuous, shy, introspective, and suspicious of everyone. A loud noise or a false movement registers like a four-alarm fire in me." Everywhere Abbott perceived dangers and threats; if a store owner was surly in giving change, the ex-con feared that this was an affront to be punished by murder. He simply could not function, either: he had no decent clothes until McDonald took him to Macy's, and he was bewildered by such matters as where to buy toothpaste and how to use a subway turnstile. The theft of his three-piece suit — the only thing he owned of any value — totally undid him. Norman and Norris had him as their guest in Provincetown for a few days and urged him to hold on until August, when he could come with them to Maine, but Abbott's fuse was very short.

In the Belly of the Beast was published in early July. Norman later commented on how terrible it had been that publication of a first book and its author's release from prison had happened at the same time; taken together, the events were too much for any individual. What's more, the book was hailed, and Abbott was feted at a literary lunch with Mailer, McDonald, Jason Epstein, Jerzy Kosinski, and other literati, his picture taken for *People* magazine. *Time* thought the book "belong[s] with the best prison literature," and Terrence Des Pres, in a prominent review in the *New York Times Book Review,* found Abbott "an exceptional man with an exceptional literary gift. His voice is like no other, his language is sharp-edged and hurling with rage."

Early Saturday morning, the day before the Sunday *Times* review appeared and scarcely a month after his release, Abbott visited the BiniBon, a restaurant on the corner of East Fifth Street and Second Avenue. There he had a misunderstanding with a young waiter, aspiring actor Richard Adan, over the use of the restaurant's bathroom. Abbott asked him to step outside, and there, in the alley, he stabbed Adan through the heart with his knife. Later that day Abbott fled the city, eventually winding up in New Orleans, where he was arrested as a fugitive in September and brought to New York to stand trial for murder.

For the rest of the summer, as Abbott was being sought, the media was in an uproar. Reporters found that the Cuban-born Adan had a young wife —

the BiniBon was his father-in-law's restaurant — and ran stories next to pictures of Adan's handsome face. Abbott was demonized in editorials across the country. The Sunday *New York Times Book Review* ran a front-page piece by Michiko Kakutani on Mailer's romanticization of violence and the public's fascination with the criminal; she quoted Jerzy Kosinski — who had also had a long correspondence with Abbott — on the public's eagerness for what seemed to be a success story — "from Leavenworth to Random House."

Norman made no public statements; he did not join the fray. He and Norris were badly shaken, Norris in particular. From a letter written by a convict to Bob Silvers at the *New York Review of Books,* Norman had learned in the weeks preceding the killing that Abbott had given names to prison authorities as part of his parole deal, and he confronted his protégé with being a "snitch"; Abbott had replied that Norman obviously knew nothing about the harsh realities of prison. And Abbott was probably right. Norman mistook the intellectual ground he and Abbott shared for real understanding, mismeasuring the vast gulf that separated his world from that of — Abbott's term is useful here — the state-raised convict. As his letters suggest, Abbott simply had no comprehension of the very different rules governing the world outside the prison walls. He literally did not know how to act — and tragically, no one intervened.

Still at issue was Mailer's role in getting the murderer out of prison. That would be the media focus in the tense, emotional trial of Jack Abbott, held in January 1982. High-profile criminal lawyer Ivan Fisher was conducting Abbott's defense; he held that Abbott believed that Adan had a knife and so acted in self-defense. Norman and Norris, who would become good friends with Fisher, were horrified that he, like any good defense lawyer, wanted his client back out on the streets. Norris freely told him and anyone else who would listen that she hoped Abbott would be put away for life. Norman was more cautious; he definitely did not want Abbott at large again, but he thought a maximum sentence would destroy Abbott's talent. What he regretted most about his own behavior in the matter, he told an interviewer later, was his "tunnel vision." He knew that anyone coming out of prison would have problems and might be headed for trouble, but "it had never occurred to me it might be trouble for someone else, so that part of the responsibility I feel, looking back at it now, is that I was so egocentric about it. I saw it as a test for myself rather than a test for strangers. Part of the shock of it afterwards was to have looked at it so narrowly."

The trial itself was stormy. Norman and Norris were usually present, as was Jean Malaquais, who had an uneasy friendship with Abbott based on political sympathies. Actors Christopher Walken and Susan Sarandon were there, prompting speculation about a possible movie. Abbott was often teary and emotional on the stand, or sitting at the defense table as excerpts from *In the Belly of the Beast* were read. At one point Adan's father-in-law, Henry Howard, jumped to his feet and pointed at Abbott. "You scum!" he shouted. "You useless scum! You too, Mailer, and the rest of you freaks." After that outbreak, a juror had to be replaced. Meanwhile, Abbott was claiming that the killing had been the result of a "tragic misunderstanding."

On January 18, Mailer took the stand briefly for the defense and described the history of his friendship with Abbott. After the court session was over, reporters besieged him and he decided to hold a press conference on the spot. The press was out for blood, and Mailer suddenly found himself less than willing to stand there and contritely accept blame in the form of questions. This was going to turn into something more familiar, a Mailerian provocation. He assumed his usual combative stance, shifting from foot to foot, holding his hands high and jabbing them in the air. "What will happen if Jack Abbott gets out of jail and kills again?" asked one reporter. "I will take that gamble," answered Mailer. "I am willing to gamble with certain elements in society to save this man's talent." He didn't sympathize with the family's wish for the death penalty, he said; he didn't believe in "blood atonement." "All I have to offer is my psychic blood," he concluded, before settling into a tirade against this "fascist" country, where "the rich are getting richer and the poor are getting poorer." One female *Post* reporter claimed he called her "a scumbag"; Mailer would the next day announce a $2 million suit against the *Post,* claiming he had called the paper, not the reporter, a scumbag.

It was a sight few reporters present would forget. Photos exist showing Mailer seemingly snarling with rage, and many felt violence was imminent. None of them could know that Norman had been under enormous pressure during the trial, and not just because of the media spotlight. He hadn't known until the last minute whether Fisher would call him as a witness or not, or how the prosecutor might treat him. And the press was very hard on him, particularly the *Post* reporters. Mike Pearl confronted him with an earlier statement, "Culture is worth a little risk," and asked, "Specifically, what elements of society are you willing to risk? Cubans? Waiters?" He followed this by implying Mailer was a racist. At one point Mailer turned on him and said, "What did you do today to make yourself so self-righteous?" *Daily News* reporter Thomas Hanrahan at this point walked out of the press room, saying, "Mailer, you're full of shit."

Norman, and a shaken Norris, fled the courthouse in a cab. Norris had vociferously disagreed with Norman over taking the stand, and now she withdrew, even considering taking the children down to her parents' home in Arkansas. Norman was not exactly overwhelmed by supporters, though some friends did call to say that they understood what he was going through. Two days later, he held another press conference, this time back-pedaling. "I have blood on my hands," he admitted. Adan's family, he said, "has an absolute right to hate and revile me." When, a month later, the flak still had not abated — though Abbott was convicted of second-degree murder and sent back to prison — he arranged to go on Dick Cavett's television show, where he repeated his statement about blood being on his hands.

Once again Norman had collided unsuccessfully with the press. In this reading, he was the victim of a New York tabloid moment. The press, inflamed by sympathy for the innocent Adan, wanted a bigger villain than the second-rate hoodlum who was Abbott, and they found it in the prominent Mailer. He had sought foremost to get published some writing that he and a lot of other people thought was excellent. Norman and Norris did their best to help Abbott, but they could not be with him twenty-four hours a day. Tragedy intervened, and Norman became the scapegoat.

It is also true that Norman had taken a very interesting, highly debatable question — what risks it was worth taking in the name of art — and hung it on a tragic case whose specifics could not bear the weight of the question. A whole series of officials and others had made mistakes, from the parole board on down. Nobody but extremists thought it was wrong to have published Abbott or to have encouraged his talent. Yet critics would differ on the point at which the support the New York intelligentsia and Norman himself had given to Abbott became responsibility, and finally culpability. Though events forced Mailer to assume some measure of responsibility, it is not really clear whether he, in any meaningful way, really had blood on his hands, or believed that he did. It remains a debatable point, but the small bit of history was already written.

NORMAN WAS NOT the first writer to have become involved with a prisoner in a way that ended badly. William F. Buckley had helped win the release of Edgar Smith, a convicted murderer — also a powerful writer — only to see the man arrested soon after for attempted murder. Jerzy Kosinski told the press that he too had been taken in by Abbott, and related his and Norman's sympathy for Abbott to "the '6os, when we embraced the Black Panthers in that moment of radical chic without understanding their experience."

In fact, the Abbott affair had a strange coda in the rebuilding of bridges between Norman and the writer William Styron, from whom he had been estranged since the late 1950s. A longtime opponent of the death penalty, Styron had helped to save Benjamin Reid, a convicted murderer, from execution in 1962. In 1970 Reid's parole was imminent, and Styron was making arrangements for Reid to live with his family and take classes at Trinity College in Hartford. But Reid escaped from prison and abducted a woman and two children, later raping the woman, before he was arrested. Styron was deeply remorseful, and during the Abbott affair he made statements before a PEN conference and at a symposium sponsored by the Fortune Society, a prisoner advocacy group, in defense of Mailer. "My heart goes out to him," Styron said. "I have an Abbott in my life."

News of Styron's statements reached Norman, who was initially suspicious. But before long he wrote Styron, "I thought I'd wait a month before writing to see if I still feel the same, and I do. So I just wanted to say that it was gracious of you and generous and kind of gutty [sic] to speak up the way you did about the Abbott business." Though he and Styron would never be close friends, for the time being it was a great comfort to have a writer of Styron's stature defending his position before the literary community.

TWENTY-SIX

EGYPT, AND A BRUSH
WITH THE LAW

As 1983 approached, Norman put the finishing touches on the Egyptian novel, which had taken him eleven years to write. But as it made its way through Little, Brown's editorial process in the early months of the new year, his confidence in what was a long labor of love wavered. He knew he had taken a big step in trying to mold material so foreign to both him and his readers in conventional novel form. Most unusually for him, he began to downscale his claims for the book, to urge his public not to judge it according to the standards they normally applied to his work. He knew, he told an interviewer for *Writer's Digest,* that "one hurdle" he had to overcome was that people would read the first fifty pages and wonder, "What the hell does this have to do with Norman Mailer?" "This isn't the big book I promised," he cautioned. But he was still ambitious for his new creation. "It is a big book. I think in a literary sense it's the most innovative," he said. "I think this is far and away the most ambitious novel I've ever written."

He had poured an enormous amount of energy into the book, which would be titled *Ancient Evenings.* He read more than a hundred books, he estimated, beginning with *The Book of the Dead,* which took him nearly a year to digest. In the New York Public Library's Main Reading Room, he repeatedly called up from the stacks a ten-volume set of Egyptian drawings. Dating from around 1850, these drawings, depicting temples and tombs, were painted on a very thick paper that reminded Norman of papyrus; when he turned one of the thick, heavy pages he thought of a sail flapping in a lull. He was tempted to learn hieroglyphics but decided against it, taking instead as his bible E. A. Wallis Budge's two-volume hieroglyphic dictionary. There he was fascinated to find that the word for "oil" was the same as the word for "helplessness," or, more meaningfully for him, that the word for "think" was closely related to the word for "anus," which in turn was the same word as that meaning "the moral of the tale." The Egyptians enjoyed completely different psychologies, he came to understand; their emotions were not the same as our own.

The going had been difficult. A trip to Egypt in 1974 didn't help: in the wake of the Israeli-Egyptian war, Cairo was still a war zone and barges were not allowed on the Nile; when Norman climbed a pyramid illegally after bribing a guard, he could see only smoke and car exhaust. Modern Egypt, he found, bore more resemblance to a Third World country than to the ancient Pharaonic empire. Yet in his reading he discovered two central tenets of ancient Egyptian thought that meshed quite promisingly with his own preoccupations. The ancient civilization believed in reincarnation; after death, one's *ka,* or double, could either continue on, being reborn, or perish. Furthermore, Egypt, often called in ancient texts the Two Lands, had an extremely dialectical intellectual culture, inclining toward paired opposites, which temperamentally suited Norman. But he was frustrated by the arcane and uneven quality of Egyptological research. Further, twentieth-century experts did not agree with those from the century before in many key matters, and while some events he wished to describe, like the Battle of Kadesh, were fairly well documented by temple and tomb illustrations to which he had access, others, like a long section he wanted to set in a pharaoh's harem, he had to reimagine almost completely.

As *Ancient Evenings* took shape, Mailer fell into a creative process that resembled nothing he had attempted before. The book opens with a long, lyrical sequence that describes Egyptian methods for the burial of the dead and then retells the myth of Isis and Osiris; from here Mailer passes into the story proper. Young Menenhetet, with two people he believes to be his parents, visits the pharaoh, Ptnah-nem-hokp, or Ramses IX. During days of feasting, pageants, and sleep, the elderly Menenhetet I describes his previous incarnations as a charioteer for Ramses II (also called Usermare-Set-penere), especially in the battle against the Hittites at Kadesh, scenes Mailer describes with great relish and in fine detail. In a later incarnation he is the overseer of the harem, witness to much courtly intrigue set against beautifully drawn backdrops, and still later he is a high priest, initiated into the ways of magic by Honey-ball, a member of the harem. Honey-ball is but one of Menenhetet's lovers; others include Nefertiti and, most notably, Usermare himself, whose sexual acts are rendered in epic phrase.

Throughout Menenhetet's tales, we return to six-year-old Meni II, whom Mailer described in an interview as "having the consciousness of Marcel Proust, but Proust at age fifteen." Meni, who enjoys dalliances with his nurse along with a kind of astral sex with the woman he imagines to be his mother, experiences a form of telepathy with Menenhetet II, which is not surprising when we learn that he is the son of the current pharaoh and the reincarnation of Menenhetet I. If that is indeed what we do learn. Toward the end of the book, the number of stories told and retold — the book consists almost exclusively of the narrations of others — and the aspects of Egyptian psychology that allow such phenomena as telepathy and great feats of memory make it impossible to decipher just how many Menenhetets have passed through just how many incarnations. Mailer might have intended this kind of narrative confusion, but it is difficult for the traditional reader, who expects to engage with a fairly clearly delineated hero with a discrete identity.

The writing in *Ancient Evenings* is at times stunning, marked by an erotic indulgence of the senses. Mailer gives his evocative powers free rein, as when he describes the progress of a state barge making its way down the Nile:

> [The] mast stood alone, its great red mainsail furled, . . . but covered with gold: there was not anything on the boat that did not shine of gold or silver but for the straw matting on the decks, and the carved purple bulwarks of the oarlocks and the rail. In pace with its progress, a troop of charioteers guarded the treasures of the barge by marching down the road that led along the higher back of the river, and an infantry of archers jogged with them in a trot to keep even with the pace of the oarsmen, their equipment jiggling, then a squadron of lances with colored flags and plumed Babylonian horses I saw, and two-man chariots. Purple, orange, red, and a yellow as saffron as the color of my own robes, were on the plumes and ribbons of the horses, and the painted medallions of the chariots. Naked children ran after them for as long as they could keep up — naked but for a bracelet or an armband . . . Red as the mud of the banks were the dates ripening on the trees, and I thought the state barge looked like the golden bark of Ra being rowed across the sky even as it went by the bend in the glare of the sun.

Other passages offer linguistic extravagances, as Mailer must resort to windy abstractions to describe customs and myths of the ancients ("As Ra had His godly boat for travel through the dark river of the Duad, so were a wife and children one's own golden vessel on such a trip"). He invents a whole range of sayings: a man is possessed of the "thighbone of all wisdom"; Meni II's penis is his "Sweet Finger," while Menenhetet's is usually his "sword" or his "battering ram." Much of the novel's excesses, in fact, derive from the sheer number of graphic sexual scenes and their originality. Sodomy is rife, and we are to believe that a mystical exchange accompanies this particular act: Menenhetet's buggery by Ramses II is absolutely central to the plot and the novel's sensibility. In lovemaking with Nefertiti, which Mailer describes as "his obelisk . . . floating on her river," she responds by crying out, "My little *cemetery, unite* with Me, *copulate* with Me." We are given mummified toes, people with tails, scenes of cannibalism, all rendered in exacting detail with Mailer's usual attention to smell. Excrement is at once copiously repulsive and sacred.

For most of Mailer's readers, the result was overwhelming — and puzzling. While the obsessions — with anal sex, smells, homosexuality — were familiar, everything else was unrecognizable. Mailer's fears about puzzling his readers were entirely borne out. Nobody expected a novel so removed from his usual concerns, so bereft of a clear protagonist with whom they could identify, such a flight of the imagination.

Most critics were simply baffled, when they were not outright dismissive. George Stade, for instance, writing for the *New Republic*, suggested hopefully, "Mailer's somber excavation of our aboriginal and buried human nature, I believe, is a new and permanent contribution to the possibilities of fiction and our communal efforts at self-discovery." Yet he wrote in the same review, "If you do not buy his notions of magic and the unconscious, of course, you will simply feel that Mailer and his novel are full of shit."

In the most damning review of all, on the front page of the Sunday *New York Times Book Review*, Benjamin DeMott noted his extreme discomfort in reading the book ("The farther one proceeds in *Ancient Evenings*, the longer one lingers over any page or passage bare of embarrassment") and concluded that it is, "speaking bluntly, a disaster." He ventured that Mailer's standing in the literary community and the public imagination was at stake: "It's possible that 'the Egypt book' is a darker hour than any preceding it in his career; surely the author's hold on the title that's been his for a full decade and a half — the title of America's most consistently entertaining writer — has been weakened."

Other reviewers, more productively, puzzled over what Mailer had been trying to do with this vast historical romance, as did James Wolcott in *Harper's*, who was genuinely mystified but on the right track as to what had gone wrong:

> Nothing Norman Mailer knows of life seems to have leaked into the pages of *Ancient Evenings* . . . What went awry? Norman Mailer walled himself in with *Ancient Evenings* by building up so large a brickwork of mystique, by making us feel that everything else in his career was foreplay for this, The Big One. And by far the saddest feeling one gets from this novel is that [he] had so little fun in writing it; each paragraph seems fitted into place with the dead

weight of obligation, as Mailer struggles to deliver the long-promised, long-anticipated goods.

Good reviews came in as well, of course, but for the most part from out-of-town papers and library journals; time and time again reviewers excoriated its length (709 pages), its emphasis on scatology and excrement, its incoherent worldview. Sales, however, reflected this only in part: two months before publication, bookstores had ordered one hundred thousand copies. On publication, the book reached the bestseller list, where it remained for over three months. Though the book would come to have its fans, most of the reading public heard the reviewers telling them that *Ancient Evenings* was a difficult, not very good book that they could skip.

WHAT EXACTLY DID go wrong with *Ancient Evenings?* Mailer knew, as he was writing it, that it was his riskiest book. "Everyone would be happier if some unknown author had written it," he acknowledged. "There would be an incredible curiosity about who the author was. People would have read the book more easily." Maybe so. But because this was a Mailer product, readers expected to find Mailer somewhere in it, so they could talk, as he said, about "what Mailer had done." Even *The Executioner's Song,* with his voice so strikingly absent, was a Mailer product: readers knew he had gone to Utah, interviewed many of the principals, crafted the narrative. But they were not prepared for *Ancient Evenings,* an imaginative flight from an unexpected quarter, and set in a time almost three thousand years in the past at that.

Wolcott and others were right in blaming the book's shortcomings on the pressure brought to bear on Mailer to write the big novel he had so long promised. And he indeed appears to have planned to write a masterpiece before he even had his subject firmly in mind. He had ruled out a panoramic novel about the United States at the outset. "One of the reasons I went back to Egypt," he told an interviewer, "was knowing that you can no longer write an all-encompassing novel about America. It can't be done." It couldn't be done for technical reasons, he explained. The writer would have to learn about too many different occupations, each with its own technical language, and would have to handle extraordinary detail of place and dialogue. Mailer felt he simply could not write the epic novel he projected if he set it in modern-day America.

Thus the decision to place this magnum opus in a different realm imaginatively. The writer of historical novels can research his or her subject — something Mailer is very good at — and either create a new plot or dramatize a historical situation. This was too modest a genre for Mailer, however.

He was attracted to ancient Egypt precisely because its idea of the human was totally different from that of the modern West. Mailer's attempt, he told *People* magazine, "was to create a new psychology, a new consciousness." The Egyptians, he explained, had a psychology "that existed long before Freud." He wished to recreate that psychology, finding elements in it that corresponded to many of his ideas about sex, evil, death, and reincarnation.

This was an ambitious step indeed. To create a whole new consciousness and render it in a novel readable by a contemporary audience is a tall order; Norman thought the result would be a work of art that challenged such modernist classics as *Ulysses* or the *Cantos*, and even older, more hallowed literary classics. He was probably wrong here, as the idea of recreating an ancient consciousness had been tried successfully by such writers as Robert Graves and Mary Renault. But Norman was after something more.

He succeeds in this respect: *Ancient Evenings* does in fact propose a new consciousness. It illuminates that consciousness's belief system and its gods and goddesses, and it shows how time worked in a way almost incomprehensible to moderns, creating a pace unfamiliar to contemporary readers and explicating a worldview. This worldview believes there is no death and at the same time there are many deaths, it values dung as gold, and it views sexuality as a mystical rite. The careful reader of *Ancient Evenings* can work out the time schemes, can in fact "count" — or, better yet, realize the uselessness of counting — the number of times Menenhetet dies and is reborn. *Ancient Evenings* works as a meticulously realized modernist text, as a fully realized imaginative construct.

Yet it remains inaccessible to almost all of its readers. There are no points of contact that the reader can identify, no guideposts, no points of reference. Historical novels set in, for instance, ancient Greece are at least recognizable, for most readers who select such books either know enough of the history or trust the writer's knowledge to follow the story comfortably. But Mailer chose a historical realm about which very little is known; more than that, most readers aren't aware of what is known or not known about ancient Egypt. Did Egyptians really believe Isis and Osiris were lovers and siblings? Did the Battle of Kadesh — if it happened — end in massive bloodletting, rape, and cannibalism? There is no terra firma for the modern reader.

Mailer wanted this effect. He thought often of Thomas Mann as he wrote — Mann, whom he venerated for his "immense international reputation," and who in his *Joseph* books turned to ancient Egypt for his subject. But Mann inserted himself in the narrative, using a voice that grounded the reader and stopped to explain certain beliefs and historical events with which the reader might be unfamiliar. Mailer consciously decided not to do that. "The reader . . . was comfortable because Thomas Mann was there," he told an interviewer.

> I felt that one doesn't *want* to be comfortable with Egypt; therefore I kept thinking of Mann . . . [as] the model to avoid. What I hoped to do was capture a culture in a way that would make the reader feel right in the middle of it, and so look up in shock and say, "My God, where am I? I'm not here; I'm in Egypt." Such total disorientation would be quite an aesthetic experience.

But not, as those readers who persevered with *Ancient Evenings* discovered, a rewarding or enjoyable aesthetic experience.

Few readers did persevere with *Ancient Evenings*. As the bad reviews came in, Norman was at first shocked and then grew philosophical. He reasoned, probably quite rightly, that reviewers who had only a day or two to read the book could not possibly take it in or connect with it in the way he might have hoped. He suspected that a few didn't even finish it. Over the years he would become more convinced of this.

In fact, Norman would always maintain that *Ancient Evenings* was his best book, a position that would baffle or irritate many of his critics and readers. It is not hard to understand why he valued it so. He had spent eleven years imagining an alternative culture, a culture whose belief systems and preoccupations resonated with his own. He had meticulously researched and thought out this universe, and to his mind, he had imaginatively brought it to life with a suitably complicated and demanding plot. It was an achievement of which any writer would be enormously proud.

His own good feelings about the book, in the summer of 1983, kept him from being devastated by the negative criticism, as he had been before — most notably in the wake of *The Deer Park,* whose hostile reception had triggered a near breakdown. Though he had invested a great deal in *Ancient Evenings* and had harbored great hopes for the boost it might give his reputation, when those hopes were dashed he was unshaken in his conviction of the novel's worth. This was an important milestone in Mailer's literary career, if not the one he had hoped. He, at least, was secure in his accomplishment.

AT THE SAME time that Norman was completing the most difficult and, to him, the most important book of his career, he was in very real danger of going to prison. Sometime in the late 1970s and early 1980s, federal law enforcement officials had pegged Norman as a participant in a large international drug-smuggling ring. The events of 1982 through 1984 would make it all too easy to believe that, as in the Abbott affair, Norman's glorification of the criminal, the outsider, the hipster, had led him out of his depth and into serious trouble.

Norman's acquaintance with the drug world developed slowly, sparked by his old friendship with the ex-wrestler and writer Richard Stratton. Stratton was a part-owner of the Phillips, Maine, farmhouse that Norman and Dick Goodwin had bought in the summer of 1971; eventually, Stratton bought Goodwin out. By 1975, as a freelance journalist on assignment from *Rolling Stone*, Stratton was working on a story about Rochdale College, an experimental school set up under the aegis of the University of Toronto. A large drug underground had grown up around the school, and the ring-leader was the so-called hippie godfather, twenty-three-year-old Robert "Rosie" Rowbotham, who told hair-raising stories about his adventures in the soft drug trade. An enormously appealing young man, Rowbotham came down to the farm in Phillips several times in the mid-1970s and met Norman and Dick Goodwin. When Norman asked what books he liked, Rosie said the only book he'd read in his whole life was *Last of the Mohicans*. "There are people like you who write books," he told Norman. "And there are people who buy books and live through them vicariously. Then there are people like me, who other people write books about." Not surprisingly, Norman was charmed. The stories Rosie told him teemed with drug-sniffing dogs, shipments coming into warehouses in Toronto, staying one step ahead of the cops and the competitors. "You remind me of Errol Flynn playing Captain Blood," he told Rosie, reaching back into his childhood and finding one of his earliest heroes.

The international scale of the drug trade caught his interest as well. He predicted that the FBI and CIA would turn their attention to drug smuggling: "Drugs and foreign policy are going to create endless possibilities for intelligence. I think the drug dealer will replace the KGB agent as the figure of attention — drugs, terrorism, and foreign-policy manipulation form a pretty potent triad."

Stratton, in 1966, had dropped out of Arizona State University at the end of his freshman year to go to Europe, where he set up an operation smuggling hashish out of Lebanon. Now, however, having taken a writing course at Harvard and having held down a writing fellowship at the Provincetown Fine Arts Work Center in the winter of 1970–71, the year he met Mailer, Stratton listened when Rowbotham described himself as the kind of guy other people wrote books about. He began laying plans for a book about Rowbotham and about the drug trade, and he even called on a lawyer to formalize Rowbotham's commissioning him to write such a book. He gradually became involved in Rowbotham's business himself, ultimately setting up his own operation. Stratton was attracted by the romance of the drug-smuggling life; he was a risk-taker and a natural leader. One of his most closely held beliefs was that so-called soft drugs — marijuana, hashish, and the hallucinogens — should be legalized; until they were, he believed in distributing them.

In 1976 Rowbotham was arrested and charged with conspiracy to import and distribute hashish and was brought to trial. Alerted by Stratton, Norman offered to appear as a character witness at Rowbotham's 1977 trial in Brampton, Ontario. According to Rowbotham, Norman told the jury it would be "bad karma" and "bad for the cosmos" for them to convict his friend. Nevertheless, Rowbotham was found guilty and given an especially harsh sentence for his seeming lack of remorse.

From the Phillips farmhouse, Stratton was by now running a major pot-and hash-smuggling operation, and was living it up like a hippie maharajah. He had a ranch in Texas, another farm in Maine, and property in New York, Colorado, Bermuda, and Hawaii. Along the way, in 1978 in New York, he was busted, charged with conspiracy to import hashish. The indictment was thrown out, says Stratton, because there was no evidence — the DEA had sold the impounded drugs. But the arrest drew the government's attention to him and his friends and associates, and a five-year IRS investigation began. From that point on, Stratton would be harassed at entry points on his numerous trips in and out of the country.

The IRS had long been interested in Mailer because of his complicated tax situation, and the FBI had kept a file on him dating back to his appearance at the Waldorf Conference in 1949. But the war on drugs was heating up, and his friendship with Rowbotham and Stratton made him a prime target. "It was DeLorean time," says Stratton, alluding to the automobile entrepreneur and former General Motors executive who had been dramatically convicted on cocaine charges in 1982. "The feds were into star-fucking." Attention focused on Norman, who they seem to have pegged as a behind-the-scenes but pivotal figure in Stratton's drug ring. The feds were zeroing in on Stratton's Maine operation, the farmhouse they knew to be co-owned by Mailer.

Soon after his testimony at Rowbotham's trial, Norman's Brooklyn apartment was broken into and ransacked, according to Stratton. A bag of Mailer's pot, routinely hidden, was pointedly placed in the middle of his bed. This kind of harassment — it's hard to imagine its being anything else, such as an attempted robbery, since nothing was reported stolen — suggested to Norman that the government had an eye on him.

Matters grew more complicated when Buzz Farbar, attracted to the glamour of the drug trade and the promise of a quick buck, became involved with Stratton's operation. Buzz was without a job, though he sometimes worked as a bookie and also did some editing projects and research for Norman, but he seemed to have no idea of how high the stakes were at the level of drug smuggling Stratton had entered. Stratton protested to Norman that Buzz was just a nice Jewish boy from Brooklyn who was going to get in over his head and should be talked out of it. Norman, perhaps noting the "nice Jewish boy" phrase, seems not to have intervened, however, and Buzz became more deeply involved in the drug scene.

In fact, Stratton's smuggling operation was very complicated, and it had built up slowly over time. He brought his hash in from Lebanon, where his main intermediary was a highly placed customs official. Stratton saw that Buzz, with his clean-cut good looks and considerable social skills, would be ideal as a money courier, and also as someone to wine and dine his Lebanese friends when they were in New York. Norman, in fact, went to a cocktail party held for the customs official with Buzz, where he was surrounded by Muslims in headcloths.

The scale was immense and risks abounded. Stratton can remember standing on the Brooklyn Heights Promenade with its panoramic view of the New York Harbor after a particularly large shipment had come in to the very docks below him, and saying to Norman, "Right down there, the shipment came in right down there, and we moved it right over there."

In New York City, the deal that would eventually bring down the operation involved seven-and-a-half metric tons of hash hidden in barrels also containing seventy-five tons of dates imported from Lebanon. At the Jersey City warehouse where they were stored, a customs officer appeared on the scene with a brace of drug-sniffing dogs. Stratton walked in and noticed the smell of hash immediately. But the dogs were perplexed, and Stratton concluded they were trained to sniff heroin, not hash or marijuana. Incredibly, the customs officials chose to believe the dogs rather than trust their own noses, illustrating, according to Stratton, the basic ineptitude of law enforcement. In fact, the authorities never found this particular shipment. But it would come up in the taped conversations that would bring down Stratton and his cohorts.

The operation was too big and involved too many people. It was inevitable that it would topple. In 1982 the feds struck in Springvale, Maine, where they arrested fifteen people, including Stratton, and seized $1.5 million worth of pot and hash, some of it from the Phillips farmhouse that Mailer owned with Stratton. Stratton was arrested on a federal charge of conspiracy to import and distribute marijuana and hashish.

He stood trial on these charges in March 1983 in Portland, Maine, with Norman, Dick Goodwin, and his wife, Doris Kearns Goodwin, in attendance for much of the proceedings. The defense was novel: Stratton's lawyer, a Brooklyn Heights resident named Ira London, said that his client was not smuggling drugs but doing research for a novel about drug smuggling to be called *Drug Wars*. Rosie Rowbotham's life story had been transformed into Stratton's first novel, which, he told reporters, would reveal "the use of funds generated by drugs to finance covert intelligence gathering and paramilitary operations by U.S. agents." London argued that his client was working in the tradition of investigative journalism as practiced by Gay Talese, Hunter Thompson, and Bob Woodward and Carl Bernstein — and Norman Mailer. When Mailer took the stand, he described meeting Stratton in Provincetown in 1970, their boxing together and drinking and talking of writing. "He had a lot of moxie," he told the court, "and great spirit."

But there was ample testimony against Norman's friend, including that of an undercover agent who said that Stratton had identified himself as the boss of a drug operation, and that of the pilot of a private plane that Stratton used to smuggle drugs. Stratton was found guilty of conspiracy to smuggle marijuana and hashish and given the maximum sentence, fifteen years.

Stratton's operation in New York had been collapsing even as he stood trial and went to jail. Several key Lebanese had been arrested, and then were turned loose by the DEA to bring in other operatives. The major New York City law enforcement campaign involved Buzz Farbar — and by extension Mailer, who the feds were convinced was involved in Stratton's operation. Even before Stratton's Maine trial, this investigation had put Norman in very real danger.

In September 1982, Sobhi Hammoud, a Lebanese cabdriver who had been arrested for his part in the smuggling operation, wore a wire during three long rides he took with Buzz Farbar; on two of these trips they were accompanied by DEA agent Marty Maguire, posing as a smuggler. Word reached Stratton in prison that some key Lebanese had been arrested, and he sent news of this to Buzz. But Buzz was still trying to make deals for part of the seven-ton shipment of hash, as he clearly indicated on the tapes. He referred to himself as "the lieutenant of the whole thing," and made some remarks that suggested that Norman had invested in the operation. In a conversation between Hammoud and Farbar about who had been paid by Stratton, Hammoud said, "Richard didn't pay him yet? Didn't pay, ah, Norman yet? . . . No?" Buzz answered no. Later Buzz said that he "grabbed" some of Richard's money "to pay, ah, some people back . . . my friends back. I tried to pay him back and he went crazy and, ah, he got back his investment . . . but nothing more." Hammoud: "Hm, hm. Mailer got back his investment too?" Farbar: "But nothing more."

On the tape made on September 23, Buzz indicated that he wanted to buy some cocaine Maguire described to him. On the final tape, made on November 2, Farbar discussed with Hammoud the news that had reached them that one of the Lebanese, Abu Nassif, had been arrested and was telling all. In spite of this risk, and in spite of the fact that Buzz suspected Maguire was a narcotics agent — he asked Hammoud this directly — he continued to try to set up deals. At a meeting later that month, in the back of Hammoud's cab, parked right outside Buzz's Riverside Drive apartment building, Buzz bought a bag of white powder from Maguire, who promptly arrested him; the fact that the white powder was not cocaine was irrelevant. He handcuffed Buzz and took him upstairs to the Farbar apartment and pointed to the phone, saying, "Call Norman Mailer."

In the days to come Farbar tried to cooperate with the DEA. He had a family to consider and most definitely did not want to go to prison. The problem was that in going along with the DEA, he would also have to go along with the DEA's efforts to implicate Mailer. Ivan Fisher, Buzz's lawyer at this late date (who had also defended Jack Abbott), filed an affidavit stating that the government wanted to use Buzz, whom they believed to be Norman's "lieutenant," to get Norman. To this end, the DEA had Buzz make a date for lunch with Norman, and wired him in advance. Over lunch at Armando's, a Brooklyn Heights restaurant, Buzz tried to bring up the Stratton case. Norman, who by this point probably knew that the DEA would try to get him by way of Buzz, and thus was unlikely to say anything incriminating, later told a reporter that he replied, "Look, I don't have anything to do with any of those guys, and I don't want to hear nothing about it." The feds did not get anything from this tape, which infuriated them further. Mailer was infuriated as well, though at the feds rather than at Buzz; he knew the pressure his friend was under. What is really outrageous, he told a reporter, "is when the government tries to get a man to entrap his friend."

Stratton was being transported to a federal prison in Terre Haute, Indiana, when DEA agents took him off the bus in New York City, charging him, in the case Buzz Farbar was involved in, with conspiracy to distribute marijuana and hashish (he was later also charged with conducting a "continuing criminal enterprise," the so-called kingpin statute). The agents pressured him to name names. They named a few themselves: they wanted him to implicate not only Mailer but Dick Goodwin, Hunter Thompson, and several organized crime figures. Stratton did not comply. Without Stratton's implicating Mailer, the feds didn't have a case against Norman; the references on the tapes Buzz made weren't enough, as it was possible that Buzz only wanted to impress the Lebanese with his connection to a famous writer.

Stratton went on trial with Farbar and three other men in November 1984. From the start, Judge Constance Motley made clear that this was a major case; she effectively sealed the trial from press coverage. Yet the case was straightforward: Buzz had implicated all of them on the tapes. There was no actual evidence: the seven-and-a-half metric tons of hash were never seized. But the prosecution didn't need it. Sobhi Hammoud also implicated all the defendants, and four out of five were found guilty as charged.

The sentencing phase made clear the government's priorities. Judge Motley singled out Farbar and Stratton — Mailer's good friends — telling them that she was giving them the harshest sentences possible because they "refused to cooperate." "To convince you that cooperation is in your best interest," she told them, she was awarding these sentences — clearly holding out the possibility that they might cooperate in the future. All of this was on the record, which would become important later. Buzz was sentenced to jail for six years and Stratton for ten, making his total sentence twenty-five years.

But the government appeared to be using this case as part of a larger agenda — first, to implicate Mailer, and second, to implicate other figures closer to the center of the drug world. Stratton was convinced that trying him in New York was a kind of double jeopardy: he was doing time for essentially the same charges he had been convicted of in Maine, and the only reason the government involved him in the New York trial was to implicate Norman Mailer. Certainly Stratton's sentences could have run concurrently, as is traditional in such instances, and not consecutively, as the judge had ordered. Stratton managed to educate himself in criminal law while in prison, successfully appealed, and won an appeals court ruling that the ten-year sentence was unjust; a person can't be punished for refusing to cooperate. Stratton got out in eight years, Farbar in four. According to Fisher, Norman was "relieved" when Richard's sentence was reduced.

Some observers of the case believed then, and still do, that Norman was involved in the drug operation, probably as an investor. But there is no real evidence for this. "Mailer wasn't involved," Stratton later said flatly. Mailer's name was spoken on the surveillance tapes, and he seems to have had knowledge of illegal activity. But as Ivan Fisher points out, "You can't go to jail for guilty knowledge." Fisher also points out that "among drug smugglers, Norman's name came up like a credit rating. Drop the name Norman Mailer and it was assumed you had money behind you and were important."

Norman attended the trial faithfully. Once he took José Torres with him, and the judge reprimanded him for "threatening the jury" (presumably for bringing a prizefighter into court), which suggests how much the trial was really about Norman. Publicly, he said that he was devastated to see his friends paying such a high price for what they did, particularly in Stratton's case. Throughout, Norman was living with the daily fear that he might be

Above: Campaigning for mayor of New York City in 1969, with early supporter Peter Maas, running mate Jimmy Breslin, and campaign manager Joe Flaherty.
(*Copyright © Fred W. McDarrah*)

Left: At a Village Gate party for his campaign workers, the drunken candidate harangued the crowd, lapsing into his Southern sheriff's accent — a major blunder.
(*Copyright © Jack Banning*)

Below: Mailer was a tireless campaigner and enjoyed being with the people. Unfortunately, most New Yorkers did not know who he was.
(*Copyright © Jack Banning, Everett Collection*)

Above: "Debating" feminism with Germaine Greer and others at New York City's Town Hall on March 31, 1971.
(*Copyright © Fred W. McDarrah*)

Below: Relaxing at a rented house in Maine with Carol Stevens, the woman who became — for one day — Norman's fifth wife.
(*People Weekly © 1975 Arthur Schatz*)

With Fanny at the disastrous fiftieth birthday party at the Four Seasons,
February 5, 1973.
(*AP/Wide World Photos*)

Left: Norman with Norris
Church, whom he met in
March 1975 and married
in 1980.
(*AP/Wide World Photos*)

Below: Norman and Norris
at a screening at Radio City
Music Hall.
(*Copyright © Fred W. McDarrah*)

Above: Norman with three of his brood: from left to right, Matthew, Norris's son from a previous marriage, and Stephen and Michael, his sons with Beverly.
(*Copyright © Fred W. McDarrah*)

Right: With Jacqueline Kennedy Onassis at a 1978 book party.
(*AP/Wide World Photos*)

Above: Outside the New York courtroom where Jack Henry Abbott, the ex-convict whom Mailer had championed, was being tried for the July 1981 murder of a waiter. The headline reads "I'D HELP KILLER AGAIN," referring to a statement of Mailer's. (*AP/Wide World Photos*)

Below: As president of PEN, Mailer invited Secretary of State George Shultz to give the keynote speech at the January 1986 International Writers' Conference — a very unpopular choice. (*UPI/Corbis-Bettmann*)

Right: Carole Mallory, Mailer's mistress from 1983 to 1990.
(*Copyright © Scavullo*)

Center: During Carole's interview with Mailer and Gore Vidal, Mailer left the room in a huff, claiming that Carole was flirting with Vidal.
(*Copyright © Bettina Cerone*)

Bottom: Mailer at a protest defending writer Salman Rushdie.
(*Copyright © Fred W. McDarrah*)

Striking a characteristic pose in a boxing ring at the Gramercy Park gym.
(*Copyright © Michael Brennan/Corbis-Bettmann*)

indicted, which, as Fisher points out dryly, "is a concern you'd rather not have."

Moreover, his relationships with two of his closest friends were changed inalterably. While Stratton would make the best possible use of his jail time, educating himself in criminal law and eventually finishing the novel that he had started back in 1978, *Smack Goddess,* prison proved devastating to Buzz Farbar. He was frustrated that no one on the outside was making any efforts to mount an appeal for him, and he was undergoing a painful divorce suit that had begun just before his trial, making him feel cut off from his family. He had a lifelong history of and a genetic predisposition toward depression. A year after his release in 1990, Buzz would take his own life.

Norman remains close friends with Richard Stratton, but he has said nothing publicly about Buzz. Beyond making an appearance at the memorial service, he has made no overture to the Farbars, the family whose children grew up with his children, since before the trial. Several things that one of Farbar's daughters says Norman said to her indicate that he simply has no understanding of depression and could not comprehend what his old friend was going through. Yet there is little indication that he tried very hard.

Had Norman learned nothing from the Abbott case, or from covering Gary Gilmore's trial? He still glorified the criminal, and seems to have enjoyed associating with Stratton at the height of the smuggling days; Stratton's outfit was like a little Mafia, an association that had always intrigued him and that he — and Buzz — had saluted in the 1968 film *Wild 90.* Drug smuggling abounded in conspiracies, especially drug smuggling on this order, and he loved conspiracy. Buzz shared these leanings, and that was his undoing. Norman, however, saw this little skirmish in the war against drugs as a fantastic adventure.

TWENTY-SEVEN

A MISTRESS, A PATRON,
AND A THRILLER

In the wake of *Ancient Evenings,* at sixty, Norman tried to get comfortable with the idea of old age. His children were mostly grown; his oldest son, Michael, was about to enter Harvard, and his youngest, John Buffalo, was about to start first grade. Susan, his daughter by Bea (now a psychiatrist living in South America), had made him a grandfather with the birth of her daughter, Valentina, in February 1981. His was a handsome and talented brood, and Norman was a proud patriarch. Fan Mailer, now eighty-five, was a frail but somehow commanding presence still.

Perhaps because of this familial stability, Norman strayed, and entered into a serious affair. Carole Mallory walked into Norman's life in December 1983, when Buzz Farbar brought her over to a table at Elaine's at which were seated Norman and Norris and lawyer Ivan Fisher and his wife. Carole, newly sober, assumed that Norman had stopped drinking after stabbing his wife in 1960, and was dismayed to see a whiskey sour at his place. A few days later, she saw in the newspaper that Norman would be present at a retrospective of his films at the Thalia Theater on Ninety-fifth Street and Broadway. She went to the theater and sat through an "interminable" question-and-answer period, during which she composed a note asking him to meet her at the Lenox Hill Coffee Shop for a cheeseburger at 11:00 A.M. She gave the note to him afterward, and they chatted briefly. Carole had a manuscript of an autobiography she was writing for a course at UCLA, called "Picasso Loves Me," the title referring to her five-year affair with Claude, Pablo Picasso's son, to whom she had been engaged. She asked Norman if he would read it.

Norman met her the next day at the coffee shop, telling her he had just come from boxing at the Fourteenth Street gym. He read silently from her manuscript, chuckling and pounding the table with his fist when he came across something he liked. Outside the coffee shop they exchanged a kiss. It was a snowy day, and Carole remembers how he looked with lipstick on his face. She gave Norman her phone number and returned to Los Angeles. Weeks later he flew to L.A. to promote *Tough Guys Don't Dance,* and they consummated the romance in Bungalow Five at the Bel Air Hotel.

Carole was a beautiful brunette actress who had played a Stepford wife in the movie of that name and appeared in *Looking for Mr. Goodbar,* as well as in countless commercials and advertisements. Columbia Pictures had flown her out to Hollywood after seeing her on the covers of *Newsweek, Cosmopolitan,* and *New York.* She was commuting between Hollywood and New York when she met Norman. She came from a German family in Pennsylvania Dutch country; the greatest tragedy in her life thus far had been her father's nervous breakdown when she was thirteen and his subsequent lobotomy — it was discovered, too late, that he had Parkinson's disease, not treatable by lobotomy. Carole put herself through Pennsylvania State University on a partial scholarship and went on to a career first as an art teacher, then an airline stewardess, and then a model and actress. Her manuscript, which Norman enjoyed enormously (though he told her to lose the title), documented her affairs with such celebrities as Warren Beatty, Robert DeNiro, Richard Gere, Matt Dillon, Peter Sellers, and Rip Torn, among others; the Warren Beatty chapter was particularly infamous. Norman liked to hear all the details about each man's performance, and asked Carole to repeat them over and over.

Carole's childhood heroine was Katy Keen the Pinup Queen of Archie Comics, whom she admired for her independence and courage as much as her beauty. Though she had once lacked sexual confidence, she was now sexually accomplished, and she had become a legendary bed companion. Norman enjoyed all this hugely, and gave his imagination free rein in their sexual relationship. He loved role-playing, playing doctor, masseur, or Hollywood director (this last "a favorite," as Carole writes in her manuscript). Carole tried to surprise him every time with new lingerie or new scenarios for them to act out.

Carole honed her writing skills with Norman's help; at their meetings he would typically edit her work, then make love, and then go out to lunch. She saw Norman infrequently in the beginning because he could not often get to L.A., though he made sure he talked on the phone to her every week; when in Los Angeles he took her out on the town. In 1987 she moved back to New York and saw him fairly regularly, often accompanying him on book-promotion tours. Carole was very upset by Norman's drinking and refused to sleep with him if he had been doing so. She asked him to accompany her to meetings for alcoholics, and he grudgingly went a couple of times. He did not believe he had a drinking problem, but Carole saw that even when sober he exhibited the personal traits of an alcoholic: he was grandiose, with an enormous ego and at the same time low self-esteem, and he had a need to control others. Norman's marriage was not at issue; Carole was fairly sure Norris knew about her and accepted the situation. "He was a baby with a rattle," says Carole, "and the rattle was women."

Norman in turn felt that Carole understood him. She especially noted that his supreme egotism belied considerable self-loathing: "You don't know how bad I am," he would commonly tell her. He admired her resilience. "The worst things happen to you," he said to her, "and you bounce right back." He was especially touched by the story of her father, who had only been half available to her; he even took to signing his letters "Herbert," her father's name. Of course, he too was only half available to Carole.

Carole stayed in the relationship as long as she did because she loved and respected Norman despite his flaws. He was not particularly generous; he promised Carole he would pay her rent, but his support was erratic. Money was his other favorite subject, she says. He was often cheap, refusing to let her order a side dish of green beans at China Regency because it was "too expensive." His presents to her were usually copies of his books, wittily inscribed; he once gave her not a mink but three hundred dollars to buy a winter coat.

But he was generous when it came to Carole's writing, encouraging her and providing critiques of her work. In 1988 she published *Flash,* a novel about a female flasher and recovering alcoholic who falls in love with an older man loosely modeled on Norman. Though Norman never did any of the crazy things Sasha does, the character's looks, his mannerisms, and his conversational style are Norman's. The book was a hit, garnering praise from Terry Southern, Gloria Steinem, and Dominick Dunne, among others; sexually explicit, it invited comparisons not only to Jackie Collins and Jacqueline Susann but also to Nabokov's *Lolita* and Southern's *Candy.*

The relationship would continue until 1991, yet through it all Norman projected an image of himself as a happily married man, no longer given to stunts and bad behavior, when in fact he was indulging in plenty of the same in the company of his mistress. He had learned his lesson about compartmentalizing, about keeping such things under wraps, so that to outsiders it seemed that Norman and Norris were enjoying domestic bliss. Like every aspect of his life, it was not that simple.

DURING THE EARLY 1980s Norman's other concern was real estate. The house at 565 Commercial Street had been lost definitively to the IRS back in 1981, and since then the Mailers had been renting in Provincetown. The Brooklyn Heights apartment barely housed Norman, Norris, Matthew, and

John Buffalo. Arranging family gatherings was difficult. The time had obviously come to buy property.

But Norman was, as ever, financially strapped. He was still under contract to write a short novel for Little, Brown. But in the aftermath of the only marginally successful "big book," relations with his publisher were tense. Roger Donald, in Little, Brown's New York office, was his main ally, but Mailer had few friends in the Boston office, where the important decisions were made. It was at this point that Random House, which had been bought by Si Newhouse's Advance Publications in 1980, began its long courtship of Norman Mailer.

A whole series of events had helped bring these parties together, in fact, and perhaps the most important figure in the process was also the unlikeliest — the infamous lawyer Roy Cohn. It was an unholy alliance indeed, and Mailer would strive to keep his relationship with Cohn hidden at all costs.

Although Cohn and Mailer had no doubt met socially over the years, especially given the hours Norman had logged on the Upper East Side social circuit, they were hardly on the same wavelength politically or temperamentally. Cohn, at fifty-six, former chief counsel for Senator Joe McCarthy, was a master power broker, numbering underworld figures, the owners of the notorious Manhattan disco Studio 54, and many of the rich and powerful among his clients. As a lawyer, he was subject to an array of indictments for unprofessional tactics and would eventually be disbarred. His name appeared in all the gossip columns, but he kept his private life secret: he was a not very closeted homosexual who surrounded himself with pretty young men, and he would die of AIDS in 1986, refusing to admit he had contracted the disease.

Casting about for a playground where he could indulge his private whims among tolerant-minded folks, Cohn turned up in Provincetown in the late 1970s, staying at a place called the Boatslip. There he got to know a longtime Provincetowner, Mailer's old friend Peter Manso, who had worked in Mailer's 1969 mayoral campaign and was putting together an oral biography of the writer. Manso profiled Cohn in the August 1981 issue of *Penthouse,* and they remained on good, if distant, terms. Manso and his companion, Ellen Hawkes, were very close to Norman and Norris in those days.

Cohn, sensing that Mailer was a big fish in this part of the world and recognizing him as a celebrity, eventually got to know him. Norman was suspicious of Cohn, of course, but Cohn knew how to win someone like him over: do him a favor. One of Cohn's most prized friendships was with the media mogul Si Newhouse; it dated back to their years together at the exclusive New York boys' prep school Horace Mann. To someone like Cohn, whose stock in trade was favors, the connection to Newhouse was invaluable. As Robert Blecker, a law professor and sometime associate of Cohn's, told Cohn's biographer, the twenty-two Newhouse-owned newspapers were a valuable commodity: "If anyone ever got into trouble in any city in which there was a Newhouse newspaper, Roy could go to Si and Si could go to the editor and there you have a leading member in town who could do a favor."

Cohn was of course happy to do Newhouse favors in turn. On buying Random House, Newhouse had announced to Cohn that he wanted to sign two writers to his new house: Norman Mailer and Robert Ludlum. He wanted Mailer for another reason as well: he had recently bought *Parade* magazine, the ubiquitous Sunday newspaper supplement, and he wanted Mailer to write for it — specifically, a piece on capital punishment, which *Parade* editor Walter Anderson thought was a natural for the chronicler of Gary Gilmore's life and death. Cohn had no connection with Ludlum, but he did have one with Norman. He told Peter Manso that Newhouse would pay seven thousand in cash for the piece. Manso said that was a bit low, and suggested that Cohn call Norman's agent, Scott Meredith. "Well, how much will it take?" pressed Cohn. Manso said that Cohn's figure was unrealistic and suggested that he multiply it by a factor of ten. In the end, a lunch was arranged, with Cohn, Newhouse, and Mailer. It was set up to be held at Le Cirque, but at the last minute Mailer insisted that they not meet uptown (where gossip columnists might record their meeting), but on turf a little closer to Norman's own, a little Italian restaurant in the Village.

The arrangement between Norman and Newhouse, facilitated by Cohn, would continue until Cohn's death. Eventually Newhouse offered seventy-five thousand dollars — in cash, according to Manso — for the *Parade* piece, and Norman's lusterless essay "Until Dead: Thoughts on Capital Punishment" appeared in the February 8, 1981, issue. The connection held; Mailer would write on Clint Eastwood in October 1983, and in May 1984 about a recent trip to Russia. Walter Anderson maintains that Si Newhouse did not urge Mailer on him, but he said, "I consider Norman the quality writer of our time, and Si shares that opinion absolutely." Norman would become a contributor, and later a contributing editor, to another Condé Nast magazine, *Vanity Fair*, in the 1980s, but the magazine's editors, first Leo Lerman and later Tina Brown, have said that Newhouse had nothing to do with this.

By 1982 Cohn was fully apprised of Norman's financial picture: his tax situation, his alimony and child support bills, and his contractual obligations to Little, Brown. He knew as well that Norman and Norris wanted to buy some property in Provincetown and that there was no way that Norman, with all of his debts and responsibilities, would qualify for a mortgage. Norman had a specific property in mind: a brick house with bay frontage at 627 Commercial Street, at the east end of town, a house he later described, somewhat cryptically, as "the richest house in town." It was a house he had rented before, when it was owned by real estate magnate and writer Bob Friedman and his wife, Abby. Norman wanted to buy the house, in fact, with Manso; they intended to split it down the middle, and to raise the roof of its one-car garage (actually a boathouse) and make it a guest-house. (Manso remembers Mailer drawing elaborate plans for the structure, complete with Coptic domes.) When Cohn got wind of Norman's intention, he immediately told Manso that he wanted to be in on the deal; in Manso's words, he "shoehorned his way in."

A Wellfleet lawyer named Charlie Frazier set up the 627 Commercial Realty Trust in October 1983, designed to protect Manso and the property from suits from Beverly Mailer and Norman's creditors. Manso put $32,000 down on the property, which was priced at $302,000. Then a call came from Cohn in New York. "I heard you're buying the house," he said. "I want the garage." Not to worry about money, he told Manso; "I'll get a loan from Si interest-free. We'll each get fifty thousand dollars." The loan would be offered interest-free for seven years, with no payment at all due the first year.

After the phone call, Manso immediately called Mailer, and confided his doubts about the wisdom of consorting so closely with Cohn. Mailer brought him up short, saying tersely, "It's about time I had a patron." Before long, an envelope arrived in Manso's mail with a $150,000 check enclosed, made out to Norman Mailer and drawn on the account of New-house's company, Advance Publications.

The lawyers at Advance balked at some point in the negotiations and asked for the deed on Norman's Brooklyn Heights property as collateral. Norman's response, according to Manso, was "*Fuck* them," and he never gave up the deed. Clearly his refusal did not become a stumbling block, however, as Norman and Norris took occupancy of one half of the Provincetown house in the spring of 1984, with Peter Manso and Ellen Hawkes in the other, and, at a cost of thirty thousand dollars, raised the roof on the garage and converted it into a guesthouse. In early 1985, a moving van arrived with Cohn's furniture — a king-size black Plexiglas bed, Italian-made furniture, and strobe lights. Norman's new friend moved in; for tax reasons he never became an actual owner of the property, but he paid some rent.

Norman and Norris were relieved that he was only a tenant. Norman was afraid of being connected publicly with him. The reasons were partly political: Cohn was avidly conservative, and Mailer, though he called him-self a "left conservative," did not see eye to eye with him on most issues.

Norman also worried about his image: what would it mean to his friends and associates — not to mention the media — this friendship with an unsavory lawyer with Mob connections? He may personally have admired or at least appreciated Cohn's shadier dealings, but he did not want to be publicly associated with the man. At a 1986 party marking Cohn's fifty-ninth (and last) birthday, *60 Minutes* cameras recorded the event, and an anxious Norman spent the evening dodging them.

Moreover, the incongruity of the situation was not lost on him. Once America's most macho novelist, Norman now had for a "tenant" (and secret benefactor) a floridly gay pasha with an entourage of young men. Somewhat comically — though with distinctly homophobic overtones — he was, according to Cohn's biographer and Manso, afraid of Cohn's proximity to his family, especially Michael, twenty, and Stephen, eighteen. "He's going to try to seduce my boys," Ellen Hawkes remembers Norman saying. At dinner one night, with Manso and Hawkes present, Norman and Norris discussed putting a line of lime between his house and Cohn's cottage to stop the spread of AIDS.

Norman grew alarmed when he found Norris painting a portrait of Cohn as he lay on the deck of his cottage. "What are you doing to me?" he ranted. "I don't want to be publicly identified with this man." "But look," Norris reasoned, "I've painted other society people." Eventually Norman consented, and Norris accepted three thousand dollars in cash for the painting. After Cohn's death, plenty of ink would be spilled in the gossip columns about the painting's future.

As uncomfortable as his new friend made him, however, Norman had put himself squarely on Cohn's vaguely defined client list, the network of grateful friends for whom Cohn facilitated deals, both professional and personal. Cohn saw to it that Norman was continually reminded of their friendship, providing free rides on his private plane to the Mailer children on trips back and forth from New York. And he watched as Norman began talks, and later negotiations, with Random House's editors.

Bob Bernstein, then chairman of Random House, told Si Newhouse's biographer that his boss "wanted Mailer and we put together a deal for Mailer. Si was very instrumental in getting him." On August 2, 1983, the *New York Times* announced what it called "the most important switch by a major American literary figure since Saul Bellow went to Harper & Row . . . after thirty years at the Viking Press": Norman Mailer had signed a four-book deal for $4 million with Random House.

Mailer was gentlemanly in commenting on his switch after thirteen years with his previous publisher: "I have had a long relationship with Little, Brown, and for the most part an agreeable one." Scott Meredith added that he did not conduct an auction or bidding because Norman had got on so well with Bernstein. Jason Epstein, Random House's editorial director and Norman's future editor, thinks that the prospect of working with him — someone who knew Mailer well and admired his work — may have been part of the draw as well.

The $4 million deal called for four novels, the first to be delivered in thirty-six months. It was a so-called hard-soft contract, which meant that Random House would publish the hardback edition and would also publish the paperback edition under the Ballantine or Fawcett imprint, though it reserved the right to sell reprint rights to another publisher if it so chose. What Mailer would receive as an advance and when is not known, but the general picture suggests that he would receive $250,000 a year for the next sixteen years — essentially, for what seemed then to be the rest of his writing life. Random House would also consider any nonfiction he wrote for publication, but it would be subject to separate negotiations and, it seems, additional money.

This new arrangement had a certain logic; Random House could ensure its investment by paying him incrementally. In turn, Norman could enjoy the considerable benefits of a corporate employee. Publishers are loath to discuss financial details, and Random House is no exception. However the money was doled out, Norman had the promise that he would live well and enjoy the freedom to write for the next sixteen years — until he was seventy-six. Planning beyond that was impossible.

By the mid-1980s, thanks to his new friends, Norman had secured his foreseeable financial future. With the help of Roy Cohn and Si Newhouse, he owned his own home. The Newhouse empire was his publisher and his source of steady income. He was unlikely to have seen the irony of the situation. He had despised and denounced the corporation throughout the 1950s and 1960s, and now he had in effect joined the corporate world.

NORMAN HAD BECOME a property owner in Provincetown under strange conditions indeed. He and Norris took occupancy of the house in the spring of 1984; Peter Manso and Ellen Hawkes moved in soon after, Manso as a joint owner of the property. The two couples planned to divide the house physically in the future, but for the time being they made a rough division. They shared the kitchen on the first floor, while Manso and Hawkes took the master bedroom suite on the second floor. The attic was divided in two, one half going to Norman for writing space and the other to Manso and Hawkes; Hawkes usually occupied the attic space, for she was finishing her manuscript, "Feminism on Trial," about the case of Ginny Foat, an abused wife who killed her husband, and its meanings for the future of feminism.

Ellen Hawkes says she was worried about the living arrangements; Peter Manso characterizes the household as a "lunatic arrangement." It was an odd setup indeed. Manso, the son of artists who divided their time between Provincetown and New York, had idolized Norman since he was a teenager. He wrote his doctoral thesis at Berkeley on Mailer's work, had spent time cataloguing Mailer's papers, and had compiled and edited documents from Mailer's electoral campaign that were published as *Running Against the Machine*. It was inevitable that certain factors, not the least living in such close proximity as mature adults and sharing a financial commitment, would make the situation an uneasy one. The two couples argued over who could use the dryer and the materials on which Manso's Wüsthof knives could be used. Manso, who had also written a book on racecar driver Jackie Stewart, was completing his oral biography of Mailer, which would appear two years later, and this did not help matters any. Mailer reviewed the manuscript and questioned certain passages; he asked that a reference to artist and Provincetown neighbor Robert Motherwell be taken out, because, he said, according to Manso, "I don't know when Motherwell might be useful to me." Some remarks, he said, were "too expensive." He explained, "At this stage in my life, I know what I can't afford."

Tensions mounted in the summer of 1984, when Norman's children descended en masse. Norman held his sons Michael and Stephen to especially high standards, expecting them to excel academically and athletically. They were subjected to their father's tirades about the use of Peter's chainsaw and Michael's taking out the black BMW 333i. It seemed to Manso and Hawkes that Michael desperately wanted to please Norman and often fell short. As it was, being the oldest son, a lot of patriarchal aspirations fell to Michael: he was expected since birth to become both a prizewinning boxer and a Harvard graduate, ambitions that would seem to most parents mutually exclusive for any child but a son of Norman Mailer. Over his mother's objections, Michael took boxing lessons from an early age. He would be on the boxing team at Harvard, and after his graduation Norman saw to it that he joined the Golden Gloves, where he would be fighting against would-be pros.

Norman's health was another complicating factor in the new domestic arrangements. In the fall of 1984 he made two visits to the emergency room in Brooklyn because of chest pain. He was diagnosed with angina and given nitroglycerin pills to put under his tongue at any sign of pain. Early in the spring of 1985 he announced to Manso and Hawkes that because of his ailments he would not be able to make mortgage payments for a few months. Fanny's health was also a problem; feeble and incontinent, Norman's mother needed full-time care, and eventually he hired an attendant for her. Barbara, who had bought a condo just across the street in Provincetown, pitched in when she could with Fanny's care and in watching after her brother's children. Manso and Hawkes resented sharing their home with the extended Mailer family.

By July 1985, 627 Commercial Street was a hive of resentments, grudges, and quarrels. One night, when Peter was off at an auto race in the Midwest, Hawkes found that Stephen had let her cats out of the house. Her temper flared: it was the one thing she had asked household members to be careful about, as she explained to Stephen in what was at first a very angry discussion. Norman evidently overheard her and launched into a tirade, calling her vile names. She realized then how deep his contempt for her was and fled the house. Relations between the two couples were completely broken off, yet new causes for resentment on Manso's part surfaced immediately: he lost out financially on the real estate deal, and he would come to believe, in 1986, that he was cut out of a movie contract. In the wake of the falling-out, Manso felt that scales had dropped from his eyes, as he later told a Provincetown interviewer: "Norman is no progressive. Norman is no rebel. He's a student of fashion, which in better times was commonly known as an opportunist." In the same interview, he criticized Norman bitterly for spending his time "playing 'house nigger' to wealthy East Side reactionaries."

August was a difficult month, as Manso and Hawkes moved their belongings out. Manso had a confrontation with Mailer, which he described as an "insane macho thing," the two of them staring at each other "balefully." Meanwhile, Fanny's health was declining rapidly; she died on August 28. Norman and Norris packed up Matthew and John Buffalo and flew back to New York to make funeral arrangements. It's impossible to imagine what Mailer made of the death of his mother, the woman who had loved and supported him unconditionally for all of his life. It is clear, however, that it marked the end of a very bad summer.

NORMAN'S MOST IMMEDIATE concern in Brooklyn that fall was his writing life, which was then in a curious holding pattern. The new deal with Random House would not take effect until he produced the short novel his expiring Little, Brown contract still required. His deadline with his outgoing publisher was imminent: "If I didn't write a book in two months, I owed my . . . publisher a large sum of money," he later explained to the *Times*. He was naturally eager to have the Random House contract in effect.

Norman went back to an old story, a local crime that had horrified the outer Cape in the 1960s. Tony Costa, a local Portuguese man from a fishing family, had bedded four young women and then killed and dismembered them, distributing their remains in rural Truro. Norman had actually started such a book in 1967, as he told readers in *Pieces and Pontifications:*

> Living in Provincetown on the edge of those rare, towering and
> windy dunes which give the tip of Cape Cod a fair resemblance to
> the desert of the Sahara, I had begun to think of a novel so odd and
> horrid that I hesitated for years to begin it. I did not like the story; it
> came to me with fear. I imagined a group of seven or eight bikers,
> hippies and studs plus a girl or two living in the scrub thickets that
> sat in some of the valleys between the dunes.

Instead, he took two of his characters and sent them on a bear hunt in
Alaska, and the book became *Why Are We in Vietnam?*

In the new novel, Mailer fashioned a half-Irish and part-Jewish hero,
Tim Madden, a writer who has done three years' time for smuggling cocaine. The novel begins with Madden awakening, twenty-four days after
the lovely but infuriating Patty Lareine — modeled, Norman later said, on
Roxanne Pulitzer, but also certainly on Beverly — has left him. Madden has
a terrible hangover; a vague memory of an evening with a blond woman,
Jessica Pond, and her escort, Lonnie Pangborn; a tattoo on his shoulder
with an unfamiliar woman's name; vast quantities of blood in the passenger
seat of his Porsche; and, in the hole where he stashes his pot in the Truro
woods, a blond woman's severed head. The plot hinges on Madden's search
to find out who has been killed — soon, another blond woman's head
appears in his stash — and whether he did it. Also trying to get to the
bottom of things is a sinister chief of police, Alvin Luther Regency, who
would turn out to be married to the enigmatic Madeleine, Madden's first
wife; Madden's father, an ex-bartender with terminal cancer; and the degen-
erate and rich Meeks Wardley. Thrown into the mix are some local thugs, a
séance, a real estate scam, and some marvelous evocations of Provincetown
in winter, when the vast hordes of tourists and summer people have disappeared.

Tough Guys Don't Dance is very much a book of the moment, informed
by the events in the author's life of 1983 and 1984: the coming trial of
Stratton and Farbar on drug charges and the feds' dogged pursuit of Norman; the terms of his contract with Little, Brown; and the long stretches
of time he spent in Provincetown waiting to move into his new house.
The novel is a love song to the resort town that had become his home. The
local hoods — Spider Nissen, Stoodie — evoke such old P-town locals and
Mailer sidekicks as Eddie Bonetti, Bill Walker, Lester Blackiston; Madden
watches a football game with them, highly charged because each of
them has bets placed on it, just as Norman did countless times with local
P-towners.

Much of the novel was drawn from recent events and from specific locals and their activities. Harpo, for instance, who has a loft over a dry goods store in Wellfleet, was modeled on local painter David X. Young, who had a loft over a dry goods store in Orleans, a town down the Cape from Wellfleet. Years before, Young and Mailer, with some other locals, had conducted a séance to summon up the spirit of jazz musician Dave Lambert, who had recently died in a car accident. According to Young, the séance appears verbatim in the novel, with Harpo and Madden calling up the spirit of a recently dead friend, Fred.

There were other echoes. Madden climbs partway up the Pilgrim Memorial, a tall tower in the heart of the village that boasted an extremely sheer surface, just as Jonathan Thomas, whose wife was Mailer's secretary, Sandy Charlebois, did in the early 1960s. Madden's pot patch and his stash in the Truro woods were true to the custom among local potheads, and the bar culture Madden describes reflects Provincetown's drinking scene very accurately. Mailer ties these elements together with descriptive prose that eschews the usual "land's end" imagery most writers use for such places, and instead puts the Cape at the beginning of time — ready for the sort of elemental contests between good and evil that Mailer favored:

> Conceived at night (for one would swear it was created in the course of one dark storm) [Provincetown's] sand flats glistened in the dawn with the moist primeval innocence of land exposing itself to the sun for the first time. Decade after decade, artists came to paint the light of Provincetown, and comparisons were made to the lagoons of Venice and the marshes of Holland, but then the summer ended and most of the painters left, and the long dingy undergarment of the gray New England winter, gray as the spirit of my mood, came down to visit. One remembered then that the land was only ten thousand years old, and one's ghosts had no roots.

The plot of *Tough Guys Don't Dance* is impossibly convoluted and filled with implausibles — a ridiculous number of corpses pile up — but it moves along; the book is a satisfying read. It touches on virtually all of Mailer's obsessions, from machismo and homosexuality to prizefighting. Madden is given to pompous, windy theorizing of the hard-boiled variety, expressed in language that sounds nice but doesn't really convey anything at all. "Let no one say that a century-old New England whore does not snicker on a cold November dawn," Madden intones at one point, and "Blood, like any force of nature, insists on speaking" at another. Yet many of Mailer's conceits — like Hell-Town, an extinct encampment of brothels that sends dark spirits into Provincetown — are happy ones. For readers impatient with macho preoccupations, Madden is an annoying character, but he is an interesting, complex hero, as is his father. This is a book that the author clearly enjoyed writing.

Completed at the end of September 1983, *Tough Guys* went directly to Little, Brown; Mailer expected to be released from his contract with its publication. But things did not go as planned. Little, Brown had been more offended than expected by Scott Meredith's complaint when he announced the Random House deal that Little, Brown had bungled the paperback sale of *Ancient Evenings* and that Meredith and Mailer "were furious" about this. On October 5, 1983, Roger Donald announced that Little, Brown would not be publishing *Tough Guys* because it was "more appropriate" for Mailer to change publishers now. Meredith was able to announce the same day that Little, Brown rejected the novel that the manuscript of *Tough Guys* had been shown to Random House "out of friendship," and that "they loved it and are most anxious to publish it."

Indeed, Random House gave the book a handsome sendoff in August 1984. It had a first printing of 150,000 copies, and was a dual main selection of the Literary Guild for August. Leo Lerman serialized the novel in the May and June issues of *Vanity Fair* (for fifty thousand dollars). Just before publication, Norman fielded a forty-minute question-and-answer session after a Washington dinner hosted by Random House. He compared himself to an old gambler who says, "I've made a good bet tonight."

Not all the reviewers agreed, however. *Tough Guys Don't Dance* received only mixed notices. Denis Donoghue, in a front-page review in the *New York Times Book Review,* found Tim Madden to be "preposterous[ly] unequal to the work he is supposed to do. He is hardly imagined at all." Though Donoghue found some virtues in the novel, he concluded, "No diversion is created, this time, in the fields of dread, no sanctuary in any of the arenas of magic." In the *New Republic,* Jack Beatty wrote that *Tough Guys* was "an embarrassment," a "successful experiment in literary humiliation." Other reviewers, however, liked the book as readable, light fiction, and seemed to understand that it should not be held to quite as rigorous a standard as other Mailer works. *Time*'s reviewer thought the book was "an engaging murder mystery" and more, a mystery that raised all kinds of questions about American identity and the nature of good and evil.

Generally, reviewers pointed to the novel's implausibility and Mailer's by now familiar attitudinizing about his pet obsessions, while noting a Mailerian energy that carried the reader along. It is, indeed, a difficult book to evaluate. It invites comparison to another book written on short order, *An American Dream,* also about a woman's murder, in which the hero's very manhood is at stake. Madden is another Rojack, a kept man who is suddenly plunged into a criminal investigation and must find his way out of it.

Yet their trajectories are completely different. Rojack, his masculinity tested but intact, "lights out for the territory" like Huck Finn, last seen in a phone booth in the desert outside Las Vegas. Madden, on the other hand, retreats into domesticity, settling down with his first wife, who is pointedly infertile. The sexual obsession of *An American Dream* is sodomy; in *Tough Guys* it is fertility, or the lack of it: what does a union between a woman and a man mean if a child cannot result from it? What does that say about the man's sexual identity? *Tough Guys Don't Dance* is a confused but desperate search for essential answers about what it means to be a man — and, as the title implies, a tough man — while *An American Dream* imagines male identity, tests it, and finally celebrates it. It is hardly strange that Rojack is a believable hero while Madden is an emotional wreck trying to gather the remnants of his male sexuality, or that *An American Dream* is a far more successful book for that.

IN THE SAME month as the release of *Tough Guys Don't Dance,* Mailer made a third appearance in *Parade,* the Newhouses' ubiquitous Sunday newspaper supplement. Titled "A Country, Not a Scenario," the piece described Mailer's visit to Russia that spring. It is not clear who financed the trip, but Mailer's expenses were probably paid by Advance Publications, Random House, or both. Certainly Jason Epstein at Random House urged Norman to go, hoping, perhaps, for that epic novel with its beginnings in Russia that Norman once hinted would be part of the trilogy begun with *Ancient Evenings.* The trip would in fact indirectly lead to a work of nonfiction set in the Soviet Union, the 1995 *Oswald's Tale.* But for the time being Norman went very much as a tourist, and as a solitary one.

He spoke no Russian, and he had no guide. Americans might find it hard to believe, he wrote in the *Parade* piece, but he was allowed to roam the streets freely. Staying at the Hotel Leningrad in Moscow — which he compared to a Holiday Inn in Norman, Oklahoma — he behaved like a typical American traveler abroad, noting the cost of everything, particularly his meals, and, it appears, not taking the trouble to look beyond the surface of what he saw. Bread was almost free, he found, and daily needs were easy to satisfy fairly cheaply. Anyone who wanted a job could get a job, it seemed. Like the United States, the Soviet Union had a beautiful countryside, which was pocked by ugly sites featuring the same "totalitarian" architecture Mailer so decried at home. In Lithuania, he went into a Catholic church in Vilnius and found a service in progress. No one stopped him, so he stayed — and found the service beautiful and moving. He did not understand, he wrote in *Parade,* how the United States lives with the "scenario" that the Soviet Union is an evil force. "We do business with Germany," he observed, "but yet we cannot forgive Russia the gulags." The essay was finally superficial, Norman remaining content with comparing surface aspects of the Soviet Union — the food, the buildings — with their American counterparts, taking the occasion to criticize the United States for not being superior.

Walter Anderson published Mailer's enthusiastic report without hesitation — but Roy Cohn, for one, took great offense, according to Peter Manso. Cohn, a staunch anti-Communist, was on his Provincetown deck with Manso soon after the piece appeared, and said, "Have you seen this? This is outrageous. You know I love Norman, and we all know that Norman is a genius, but this is" — Manso couldn't remember whether he said "stupid" or "naive." Cohn had seen the piece first a few days before. "I was having dinner with Walter and Si," Cohn said. "I told Walter that I'd have to write a reply. Norman has just got to grow up. Those Commies'll drop a bomb on his house and he'll still be praising them. Si convinced me not to do it, though." This was one of the few times Cohn distanced himself from Norman.

Cohn's fears were perhaps ill-founded. If Norman was still reluctant to be anti-Soviet, his views on other traditional flashpoints of liberalism were beginning to change. In fact, the compromise Norman made in aligning himself with Cohn was one of the first of many he would make in the years to come, as in his work as well as in his life he took a more conservative direction.

TWENTY-EIGHT

THE HALLS OF POWER:
THE CIA AND PEN

The Fifth Estate, the organization formed to police the CIA that Mailer had announced at his disastrous fiftieth birthday party at the Four Seasons in 1973, was by 1986 long defunct. Norman's hand in its demise is an interesting story, especially because shortly thereafter he would undertake a massive, possibly multipart novel about the CIA.

The Fifth Estate was actually the fundraising arm of a group called CARIC (Committee for Action/Research on the Intelligence Community); they shared offices at a location off Dupont Circle in Washington, D.C. CARIC had grown out of the antiwar movement and was led by two men with backgrounds in military intelligence, Tim Butz and Winslow Peck (Peck's real name was Perry Fellwock; why he used an alias is not known). Much was planned regarding how the Fifth Estate might interact with CARIC's activities; at one point, for instance, it was proposed that Richard Stratton would begin an investigation of the murder of Martin Luther King, Jr.

The CIA in the mid-seventies was facing pressure from several directions, including Norman's group. In Congress, the Church Committee was conducting a sweeping investigation of the agency, but despite some shocking facts it revealed, this was still a one-time inquiry. The Fifth Estate proposed an ongoing effort to open up an agency that was secretive by definition, and the intelligence establishment that made up the CIA was engaged in the fight of its life. How the Fifth Estate conducted itself, and how the CIA reponded to its efforts, would play a crucial role in determining the direction public opinion would take toward the CIA and the conduct of Cold War foreign policy in general over the next few years.

Early on, CARIC and Mailer's Fifth Estate saw as their mission the identification of intelligence officers in the United States and overseas. This was done very easily, and without access to classified documents, because agents at the time operated under light, shoddily constructed cover. In 1974 former State Department intelligence officer John Marks published "How to Spot a Spook" in *Washington Monthly*. The following year, *Inside the Company*, by former CIA agent Philip Agee, who was closely associated with the Fifth Estate, outlined techniques for spotting agents using such practical devices as lists of embassy employees. The Fifth Estate put out a magazine called *CounterSpy*, which listed in every issue the names of CIA agents around the world. Of course, nothing so infuriated the CIA as publication of agents' names, and it accused the Fifth Estate of endangering national security.

The battle was joined on December 23, 1975, when the Athens station chief for the CIA, Richard Welch, was murdered outside his home in a suburb of the city. The killers were never caught, although a terrorist group called November 9 would claim responsibility. But the identity of the killers was not the big issue in the press. Welch's name had appeared on a list published recently by *CounterSpy*, which named him, incorrectly, as the agency's Peru station chief. The CIA announced to the Associated Press, "We've had an American gunned down by other Americans fingering him — rightly or wrongly — as a CIA agent."

On December 24, the Fifth Estate released a statement saying, "If anyone is to blame for Mr. Welch's death it is the CIA that sent him there." Four days later, the group issued another, longer statement called "The Fifth Estate Responds," which repeated the charge that the CIA was responsible. The *Athens News* had publicly identified Welch as a CIA agent after *CounterSpy* named him, and in the weeks prior to his death, the statement went on, reiterating, "The blood of Mr. Welch is on the hands of the CIA and its supporters and not on the pages of *CounterSpy*."

The Fifth Estate would later contend that Welch made no effort to hide his identity as a CIA man and that he had moved into the house of the previous Athens station chief, making his position common knowledge, even after the CIA warned him not to. In incorrectly naming Welch as the station chief in Peru, in fact, the group had effectively proved that it was not privy to the CIA's inside secrets. But it should also be noted that the Welch murder seemed to have prompted a new direction in the Church Committee hearings, from how to stop the CIA to how to protect CIA agents in foreign countries. "The CIA quickly disseminated the *CounterSpy* 'connection' and in a short-term victory managed to turn Welch into a martyr," wrote Philip Agee and Louis Wolf in *Dirty Work: The CIA in Western Europe* (1978). The agency used his death "to frighten many of its would-be reformers in Congress and in the press. The killings gave Congress an excuse to back down [from investigating the CIA] and the press . . . a pretext to lose interest." Members of the Fifth Estate and CARIC began receiving death threats calling them "Cuban agents" and "communist conspirators" and had to call the police several times for protection. The group's tax-exempt status was withdrawn by the IRS, which put a fifty-thousand-dollar lien on Norman's Brooklyn Heights property, presumably because he was taking deductions relating to the Fifth Estate's tax-exempt status. Rumors that a grand jury was being convened to investigate the Fifth Estate began to surface.

The CIA seemed to be winning the war of words, and the press quickly began to change its tune. Very early in 1976, Norman, who had been briefed daily on these developments, withdrew his support for the Fifth Estate, distancing himself from its activities. He was horrified when he heard that his name had been read out in Congress as one of those responsible for Welch's death. He later told the writer Natalie Robins, somewhat disingenuously — he also told her he had dropped out "after six months" — that the Fifth Estate had become "a little ultra, shall we say? I hadn't intended a citizen's group to go around fingering CIA men to get knocked off — that wasn't my idea how you do it."

Whether Mailer truly believed that the Fifth Estate was responsible for Welch's death — and he would have to have been very naive to think so — it is clear that he was frightened. He did not like being connected to a group that was getting bad press and being discussed in Congress. In fact, Mailer's distancing himself from a group dedicated to critiquing the intelligence community signaled a change in his view toward the CIA and, indeed, toward many aspects of government that had once repelled him. He once thought the agency needed policing; now he believed the CIA was a noble institution. In the space of one year, 1975, he changed his views, electing to dissociate himself from his radical past and choosing instead a safer stance. In fact, this was the prevailing American attitude at the time: "Let's Stop Undermining the CIA" read the title of a May 1976 *Reader's Digest* article. Overall, Norman was inclined to agree. Over the years his defense of the agency would metamorphose into his championing of it.

Why the change of heart? Certainly he had good reason to be frightened. The IRS lien on his property was perhaps the least of it. Around the same time Norman contacted Carl Oglesby, the former SDS head now working on a book about conspiracies, *The Yankee and Cowboy War* (1976), and asked him to remove his name from the masthead of his Assassination Information Bureau, a group investigating JFK's assassination, for which Norman had been serving in an advisory capacity. Oglesby thought of chewing Norman out for backing down, but realized that his friend was under a great deal of pressure — he knew about the IRS lien, and the embattled position of the Fifth Estate — and accepted his resignation without protest.

Mailer was in touch with the writer Natalie Robins in the mid-seventies because she was writing a book about the FBI's dossiers on famous authors and needed their permission to request their dossiers under the Freedom of Information Act. The FBI released 364 pages of Mailer's file to Robins in 1975, shortly before he denounced the Fifth Estate. In it, Norman read this description of his work with the group:

> OCFE [Organizing Committee of the Fifth Estate] was formed in January 1974 by Norman Mailer, a well-known writer who lives in New York City and Massachusetts, to link CARIC with his idea of a Fifth Estate. His idea of the Fifth Estate means groups of citizens who have banded together to research, watch and prevent the type of Orwellian, 1984 concept of Big Brother Is Watching! The group would work against such things as computer dossiers on individuals, police conspiracies against individuals, police conspiracies against individuals and groups, and general attacks by business and police against the citizenry.

The FBI file was not a recent creation: it had been opened in 1949 and detailed Mailer's appearance that year at the Waldorf Conference.

Many, many pages in the dossier were given over to a curious incident that happened around 1952. Barney Mailer, who was working for the U.S. Army as a medium-level (GS-13) accountant, was called by the Civil Service Commission to appear before its loyalty board "because of your continuing close association with your son, Norman Mailer, who is reported to be a concealed Communist." Norman and Cy Rembar drafted an affidavit and submitted it to the commission, and Barney was cleared without a hearing. But it was a troubling development, especially when set against the Red-baiting of the 1950s.

Norman told Robins that "for a long period, maybe a year or two, I just took it for granted my phone was being tapped. There were all sorts of odd noises on it." Later, he corrected himself: "My feeling is that it's been off and on for thirty years." Against this certainty should be put Norman's predisposition toward paranoia. Also, he had had several brushes with the law, and his experience had led him to view any policing authority with apprehension. Norman "is absolutely paranoid on the subject of the FBI," said Diana Trilling in that anxious year.

Such was the state of affairs in 1975. A decade later, Norman had even more reason to be concerned. If, as Richard Stratton says, his Brooklyn apartment was ransacked and a bag of marijuana was left pointedly on his bed, the police or the DEA wanted to arrest him so badly that they had played a cat-and-mouse game with him. The conduct of the justice system and the DEA in the trials of Stratton and Buzz Farbar again showed the government's determination to implicate Norman; he had good cause to be worried.

But Norman seems to have compartmentalized his authority figures quite neatly. The FBI, the police, the DEA, and the justice system were all corrupt to his mind. In his typically Manichaean way, however, this could only mean that some other faction within the government had to be the good guys. The Central Intelligence Agency, he was coming to see, was good and necessary — though it had agents who were classically "bad," which also appealed to Norman's Manichaeism. But this romanticization, coming on the heels of his involvement in policing it, suggests a growing conservatism — and a new yearning for acceptance by the Establishment. (It was at about this time that he made an unsuccessful bid to be elected to the Board of Overseers at Harvard.)

In general, Norman found that he loved the drama of spying and relished any news about the intelligence community. Just after he withdrew his support of the Fifth Estate in 1976, he wrote the essay "A Harlot High and Low" for *New York* magazine, which he would include in his 1982 collection *Pieces and Pontifications*. Ten years later, in the wake of *Tough Guys Don't Dance*, in 1985, he found himself drawn to the subject again. He had at last abandoned the idea of completing the trilogy of which *Ancient Evenings* was supposed to be the first volume. But the CIA seemed to him a great subject for a sprawling novel, taking as its backdrop the history of the agency during the Cold War. He did not intend what he was writing to be a typical piece of spy fiction, à la John le Carré. Rather, he saw it as a bildungsroman, the coming of age of Harry Hubbard, a young CIA operative of his invention, and, through him, the story of Hugh Montague, Hubbard's mentor, an agency leader loosely based on the disgraced CIA counterespionage chief James Jesus Angleton, who had been duped by British traitor Kim Philby.

The book that was to become *Harlot's Ghost* began to take shape as early as 1983, during Norman's short visit to the Soviet Union, which furnished him with a few details for his narrator's stay in Moscow. By 1984 and 1985 Norman was doing serious research for the book, reading everything from E. Howard Hunt's spy novels to Allen Dulles's *The Craft of Intelligence* (1963), taking in along the way "insider" books such as Agee's *Inside the Company* (1975) and the works of conspiracy theorists. His interviewees included Lucian Conein, a.k.a. Black Luigi, the DEA/Special Operations Group head who had served with the CIA, the OSS, and the

French Foreign Legion. With Jim Hougan and Edward Jay Epstein, journalists specializing in the CIA, he formed the Dynamite Club, a group of conspiracy buffs and spy novelists who for a time met weekly.

Mailer's manuscript, as it took shape, blended fact and fiction, mixing real characters with fictional creations. He devised a fictional relationship among Mob boss Sam Giancana, Frank Sinatra, John F. Kennedy, and Modene Murphy, a character loosely based on alleged JFK mistress Judith Campbell Exner. Montague's — and later Hubbard's — wife, Kittredge, the beautiful Radcliffe-educated daughter of a Shakespeare scholar, voices the novel's central idea of Alpha and Omega, representing male and female character traits within the individual. Hubbard writes two manuscripts, the Omega and the Alpha, corresponding respectively to the two parts of the novel — the first, his account of the stormy night at his northern Maine home, the Keep, when he learns of Montague's highly suspicious death, and the second, much longer part given over to Hubbard's account of his history with the agency.

By December 1985 Mailer was able to report that he had four hundred pages of completed manuscript. But he wouldn't really throw himself into the project for another three years. Other matters vied for his attention.

IMMEDIATELY ON NORMAN'S return from Russia in the summer of 1984, he went to a meeting of PEN (Poets, Editors, Essayists, and Novelists), the international writers' association of which he had been a member since 1951, and on whose executive board he had served from 1968 to 1973. Though it would not be announced for a month, on July 25, 1984, Norman had been tapped to become president of the American Center of PEN, the largest of the more than 130 centers of the international PEN. Over the next year and a half, he would be intimately involved in fundraising and planning for the Forty-eighth International Writers' Congress, to be held in New York City in January 1986, the first such gathering to be held in the United States for twenty years. Speaking of the congress, Norman told the press, "It is perfectly possible that there will be no bigger story that week." It was clearly a possibility he relished. "People will have to learn all those foreign names," he went on, "and begin taking writers as seriously as generals."

In *Advertisements for Myself,* in 1959, Mailer had informed his readers that he had been running for president for the past ten years in the privacy of his mind. In 1984, 1985, and 1986 he *was* president — president of all writers in the country, presiding over a congress that brought together writers from all over the world. It would not be his finest hour.

When Mailer had first been proposed to succeed Galway Kinnell as president of the American branch of PEN in 1984, some members felt dubious about the energy and commitment he could bring to an unpaid position. But they quickly stopped worrying, as Mailer realized that his greatest contribution to the group would be in fundraising. "Norman almost solely spearheaded the fund-raising effort" for the writers' congress, Karen Kennerly, executive director of PEN, told a *New York Times* reporter. He garnered individual, foundation, and corporate sponsorships with ease. He put his mistress, Carole Mallory, to work writing fifty or more letters to Hollywood celebrities she knew, asking them to contribute. Beyond that, he convinced many New York City consulates to play host to their nations' writers at parties and dinners, Lincoln Center to donate tickets for guests to its performances, the Metropolitan Museum of Art to pay for an evening reception, and Mayor Ed Koch to host foreign guests at a Gracie Mansion reception. Norman's efforts were so generous and productive that by the time the congress opened on January 13, 1986, *Time* magazine was calling the spectacle "the Rehabilitation of Norman Mailer" or "Norman Goes Legit." (Norman put his money where his mouth was; when his mother died, he set up a Fanny Schneider Memorial with PEN, contributions to which went to the Writers' Fund.)

A particularly noteworthy feature of the fundraising was Norman's proposal for the PEN celebrations, a series of thousand-dollar-a-head dinners — at the time, an outrageously high price — hosted by two writers apiece over eight different evenings in the fall of 1985. Held first at the Booth and later at the Royale Theater on Broadway — donated by the Shubert Organization — the series included Joan Didion, Woody Allen, Susan Sontag, Alice Walker, Tom Wolfe, William Styron, and John Updike; at one of the events, Mailer appeared opposite Gore Vidal — a meeting of "two toothless tigers," as Norman put it. They put aside their longstanding quarrel and discussed literature.

Though the PEN American Center's annual budget was around $500,000, Norman raised approximately $800,000 more to pay for the congress. As the opening day neared, he persuaded Donald Trump to donate two hundred rooms and six suites at the St. Moritz Hotel (which would otherwise have cost $175,000), assembled interpreters to provide simultaneous translation of all events into French, and organized PEN staff to meet the more than fifty guests of honor at JFK Airport. Though many feared that some of the most outspokenly political foreign writers would not be allowed entry into the country under the McCarran-Walter Immigration Act, which barred subversives, the authorities appeared to be in a tolerant mood, as such activists as Günter Grass, Nadine Gordimer, Octavio Paz, and Kobo Abe joined Heberto Padilla, Czeslaw Milosz, and Joseph

Brodsky, who were then in voluntary or forced exile from, respectively, Cuba, Poland, and the Soviet Union. Serving on the program committee with Mailer were William Styron and Kurt Vonnegut.

Also working with Norman was Gay Talese as vice president of American PEN. "He has been the most effective president in my memory," Talese said before the congress opened. "It's been a new and wonderful experience to see an old familiar face with a public persona so different from what I believed to be the case." Donald Barthelme, the novelist, and Richard Howard, the poet, came up with a theme for the congress: "The Writer's Imagination and the Imagination of the State."

The theme was to prove highly controversial, as Mailer himself acknowledged in his opening speech: "The notion . . . that the state may be possessed of imagination is anathema to many of us." However, he noted that states are made up of individuals who, acting in concert, share and actualize plans and programs for the future; sending a man to the moon can, in this light, be understood as an act of imagination on the part of the state. It is the imagination of the state that is the subject of history — not a poetic imagination, certainly, but the spirit that animates an age. Nadine Gordimer, addressing the congress the next day, would counter that it was absurd to imagine that a collective could ever possess an imagination. Though Mailer made a sound argument, the very wording of the theme offended many, broadcasting a combative tone for the congress.

Far more controversial was the choice of an opening speaker, President Reagan's secretary of state, George Shultz, a choice Norman would later try to attribute to John Kenneth Galbraith, president of the American Academy of Arts and Letters, a body that had welcomed Norman among its members in December 1984. Norman would later admit that he did not bring the matter before the board, but added that board members had agreed to the invitation after Shultz had accepted. Nevertheless, the invitation angered many PEN members, including E. L. Doctorow, who wrote in a *New York Times* op-ed piece the day before the conference that PEN had put itself "at the feet of the most ideologically right-wing administration this country has yet seen."

When Shultz arrived at the New York Public Library steps on Sunday, January 12, 1986, to give his opening speech, he was greeted by a public letter signed by sixty-six PEN members calling his appearance "inappropriate" and "distressing," citing the administration's "support . . . [of] governments that silence, imprison, even torture their citizens for their beliefs." On the third floor of the library, in the south reading room, demands came from the back of the room from Grace Paley, among others, that Norman read the protesting letter. Norman responded by apologizing to Shultz for the "silly bad manners" of the hecklers, whom he dismissed as "puritanical leftists."

Two people walked out as Shultz took the podium, and others booed and hissed when the secretary of state told them, "We have more in common than you think." The Reagan administration, he continued, "more than any in this century is committed in philosophy and in fact to reducing the intrusion of government into the lives, minds, and livelihood of the individual. Don't be surprised," he warned, "by the fact that Ronald Reagan and I are on your side."

The following morning Norman appeared before a panel and announced that the protest letter had been brought to him only five minutes before the program opened the previous day. He hadn't heard the writers who asked him to read it, but even if he had, he said, he probably would not have read it because it was bound to get so much publicity anyway. He clung to propriety for his excuse: "I just felt that since I'm conducting the meeting, which has a certain form to it, I didn't like the way that form was being overturned. You can call me a nice Nelly about manners if you want!" In the afternoon he appeared again, this time giving Galbraith credit for inviting Shultz and commenting on Shultz's "astonishingly liberal" speech.

Propriety preoccupied Norman that week. He was "baffled by the disturbance" on the floor when Shultz spoke, he said. He hadn't read the letter because he "didn't invite Secretary Shultz here to be, uh, pussywhipped." He had been delighted at Shultz's acceptance of the invitation to speak, he told the press, because he thought it would "give our organization credibility with the media."

Things never really quieted down. Saul Bellow and Günter Grass locked horns over the question of political action; John Updike waxed poetical over the country mailbox as a symbol of the American pastoral; Bob Bernstein, the president of Random House, led a panel on censorship; and exiled writers gave testimony. Many of the speeches brought fertile discussion, but the combative air of the celebration infected many exchanges.

Controversy erupted again on Thursday, when the women writers at the congress convened and drew up a petition protesting their underrepresentation in the conference's activities. Only 17 women were included among the 140 panelists, they pointed out. Betty Friedan gave an interview later that day saying she had asked Norman why so few women had been included and that he had responded, laughing, "Oh, who's counting?" She and other women demanded that PEN provide an apology that was "not perfunctory," and that it redress the wrongs immediately.

Norman responded disastrously, first by denying the claim. PEN had invited many women, he claimed, naming Mavis Gallant, Nathalie Sar-

raute, Iris Murdoch, Mary McCarthy, Eudora Welty, and Marguerite Your-
cenar, but they had declined to attend. He then tried to explain the reason
for women's underrepresentation, but, attempting to set the record straight,
he merely revealed his own prejudices: "Since the formulation of the panels
is reasonably intellectual, there are not that many women, like Susan Sontag, who are intellectuals first, poets and novelists second. More men are
intellectuals first, so there was a certain natural tendency to pick more men
than women."

The following day, the close of the congress, he put his foot even more
deeply into it. He apologized for not seeking more women participants after
those PEN had approached declined to attend. "We invited the best writers
that we could get," he explained. "We did not want a congress that would
establish a political point at the cost of considerable mediocrity." Hisses
greeted this remark, and several women walked out. Norman apologized
for upsetting them. "We are not upset," a woman called back, "we are insulted." "Those women who would like to leave may do so with the sur-
rogate literary pope's blessing," he called after them, adding disgustedly,
"Thank you for your courtesy."

When he tried to change the subject back to his summary of the theme of
the meeting, one woman called out, "You cut us off for this boring speech of
yours." Mailer replied that as chairman he had the right to do so. But then
— in a move reminiscent of that night in 1960 when, before stabbing Adele,
he asked his party guests to line up for or against him — he called for a vote
on whether he should be removed as chairman. The writers voted not to,
which prompted Norman to deliver a little lecture, complaining, "One of
the ways in which everything is deteriorating is that manners in the world
are getting a lot worse." Following this with more remarks about the rise of
the right in the face of the left's "entropy," he closed the congress.

More than a week later Norman looked back on the congress, marking
his superiority to the average PEN member as an intellectual, a philosopher, and a politico. The theme of the congress, "The Writer's Imagination
and the Imagination of the State," would have "been better for a philosophers' congress or an existentialists' congress," he told the New York Times.
"I lost sight of the fact that most writers are not interested in themes that are
as intellectual and philosophical as that." Speaking as "a leftist for forty
years," he criticized other leftists: "Most of the leftists around today
wouldn't even know how to spell the word 'dialectic.' They're full of stric-
tures. They are as tight in their mental habits as right-wing reactionaries."
Addressing the issue of women's underrepresentation at the congress, he
said, "The reason it happened is that we don't pay attention to that sort of
thing in PEN. We literally don't. We have so many women in positions of
such power." Evidently he had returned to the PEN offices and added up

some numbers of his own, telling the *Times* reporter that women headed six of the eight permanent committees, and that three of American PEN's vice presidents were women.

These were decent numbers, to be sure, but they do not speak to the issue of why women were so ignored in the planning of the forty-eighth congress, nor do they account for Mailer's rudeness — in the name of propriety — not only to the protesting women but to the entire community of writers, whose assembly he disrupted with his attitudes and behavior. "New York never looked so good," he said defiantly to a reporter. "It was damn exciting." If a feud or two had broken out — he acknowledged quarreling with Sontag and with Doctorow — that went with the territory: "How can you have a literary conference without friendships and feuds being formed out of it?"

In fact, the Forty-eighth International Congress had been, thanks to Norman Mailer, little more than a literary brawl. He left behind him an organization whose fiscal strength had grown at the price of its loftier ambitions. Many would credit his fundraising efforts on behalf of PEN, all of which left it a more viable institution. But he also left it the legacy of an international embarrassment; PEN, when he left the presidency, had a sorry reputation as a cause more popular among New York City's glitterati than among writers or readers.

For Norman, his term at PEN seems to have marked a general rightward turn in his thinking. He wanted to get to know and understand people like George Shultz better, perhaps even to see them as protagonists. The PEN presidency was the kind of position he needed to make contact with such potent figures. As head of an important international cultural group, why should he not be able to interact with the secretary of state? The left, with its quotidian causes and concerns — like the women's complaint about representation at the congress — seemed to him to act as an impediment, preventing him from mingling with statesmen like Shultz, whom he increasingly saw not as villains but as complicated players in a Mailerian battle between good and evil. He could not admit, however, perhaps not even to himself, that he had changed. In the postmortem on the congress that he offered to the press, he maintained that he was "far to the left" of PEN, a group he characterized as committed to battling the oppression of writers. "The more clout we have with the State Department," he rationalized, "the more effective we are." The truly "left" vision of the state, he seems to have been saying, was to acknowledge the state's power and try to share in it.

IN THE WAKE of the PEN debacle, Norman turned his attention to a decidedly strange project: writing a script for director Jean-Luc Godard in which he would also star. The filmmaker had imagined a modern version of

King Lear via the Mafia: Norman would play Don Learo, an aged Mafioso raging in the storm; Woody Allen, the Fool; and Molly Ringwald, Cordelia. It was not a film Norman wanted to see made, exactly, but writing a script was part of a deal he had struck with Menahem Golan, chairman of Cannon Films.

The deal had its beginnings in a Cannes restaurant in May 1985, when Golan wrote out the terms on a paper napkin and handed it to Godard. Godard then approached Tom Luddy of Francis Ford Coppola's Zoetrope films, who knew Mailer and contacted him. Mailer was reluctant to write the screenplay, knowing Godard's penchant for ignoring scripts in favor of improvisation.

But Luddy knew that Norman wanted to make a movie of his thriller *Tough Guys Don't Dance.* He told Golan at Cannon that if they agreed to make *Tough Guys,* Norman would agree to write the Godard script. The deal was made, and Norman began meeting with Godard as he wrote his version of *King Lear.* A condition was that Luddy and Coppola would oversee both projects. "I knew that writing a screenplay for Godard is like putting a message in a bottle and sending it out to sea," Norman told movie critic Roger Ebert in November 1986. Indeed, he had finished the script and early that year handed it over to the director, who barely read it. After Labor Day Godard summoned him to Switzerland, where the film was being shot. By this time Godard simply wanted Norman to play himself, and he provided dialogue Norman hated. "I'll make up a new name, or if you want me to play me, I'll decide what I say," Norman told him. They had a terrible fight the next morning over breakfast, and Godard called Golan and Luddy to say Norman wanted to quit. A four-way shouting match ensued, which culminated in Norman's accusing Godard of never having read Shakespeare's play. "I have no need to read it," Godard replied. At that point Golan saw that Godard and Mailer could never work together. Godard's *King Lear* was released in 1987, and in the finished film Norman makes only the briefest of appearances as Don Learo; Burgess Meredith and Godard himself also played Lear. The film itself was judged one of the strangest of Godard's career — and one of the least distinguished.

But Golan did not renege on the deal for *Tough Guys Don't Dance.* He and his partner, Yoram Globus, a pair of flamboyantly ambitious Israeli émigré producers, were trying to remake Cannon Films, a producer of low-grade action movies, into a purveyor of serious films. They allotted Norman a modest budget — $5 million — to make *Tough Guys,* and he was able to hire Ryan O'Neal for the part of Tim Madden and Isabella Rossellini to play Madeleine. (Carole Mallory read for all the female roles in the film, but Norman didn't end up using her.) Norman wrote the script in six months — a long, careful job, considering it had taken him two months to write the novel.

Shooting began in October 1986 and continued for forty-one days. The film was made on Cape Cod, mostly in Provincetown. Mailer's Commercial Street house was used for the home Madden shares with his wife, Patty Lareine (played by a newcomer, Debra Sandlund). The house was redecorated to reflect what Norman and set designer Armin Ganz believed would have been Patty Lareine's plushly cheesy tastes: bleached floors, white couches and a white grand piano, pastels, equine sculptures, and light, plush Persian rugs. (Norman and Norris would have to live with this redecoration, removing some of the tackier *objets* and paintings.) A crew of ninety-seven virtually took over the house for the shooting; scenes to be shot included six interior sets and fifty-nine nearby outdoor locales.

Gaiety and intensity marked the film's shooting. Mailer and O'Neal formed a special bond; Norman had met the actor before in the boxing gym on Fourteenth Street that both men frequented, and they boxed informally on the set. "Ryan hit me," Norman told a reporter for *American Film,* displaying a cracked tooth that he had actually broken when eating an apple. O'Neal went along with the distinctly Maileresque scenario, holding forth on "the kind of homosexual thing — the fight and embrace" that boxing evokes.

Norman, predictably, regarded his filming of his own novel as a milestone in his career, his bid to revive the directorial career he had envisioned in the 1960s. "This is my Africa," he told Dinitia Smith of *New York* magazine. "You know, Hemingway had to go to Africa." He explained how frustrated he had been when his earlier movies didn't succeed, a feeling intensified by his passion for making movies. He loved the process — even the long days and the nighttime shoots. "*Anything's* easier than writing," he told Smith. Despite the fun on the set, he took the movie very seriously. "For one thing," Mailer told a Boston reporter, "it's my vision of the Reagan years. There's a bunch of handsome, strong and ambitious people in the film, and they're all greedy as hell. They're chasing impossible goals, they're drug-ridden — they're a mess." He quoted Günther Grass, who at the PEN congress had said the only response to the bad aspects of the century was "hellish laughter." That, Norman said, could be the title of his film.

The result is one of the strangest commercial films ever made. Many critics rank it on their ten-worst list. Ryan O'Neal is simply not a natural for the corrupt and complicated Tim Madden; the image of the wholesome and innocent O'Neal, familiar to audiences from *Love Story* and seemingly not much older, mouthing such lines as "I feel demented tonight" is decidedly off the mark. In a much-criticized beach scene, the camera spirals up around O'Neal, undone by finding that his wife is dead, as he spirals around with his arms spread, howling, "Oh God! Oh man! Oh God!" Mailer also gave O'Neal a fine assortment of trademark philosophical pronouncements, including, for instance, "Cancer's probably the cure for schizophrenia."

Tough Guys is an overwritten movie, symptomatic of a director who never really found a visual equivalent for what he had done with words. Norman couldn't contain his desire to inject the kind of overripe dialogue that worked well enough in his books into a movie, where less is generally more (especially if it's a thriller). The only visually compelling part of the film is the opening, with its views of morning on Cape Cod, which Norman obviously had a feel for. Also, Norman seems not to have learned that part of his job was to direct the actors, whose performances range all over the stylistic map.

But a vivid energy carries the movie along, as many critics observed. "*Tough Guys Don't Dance* . . . is an easy movie to laugh at," Vincent Canby, the *New York Times* film critic, commented, "but that is to deny how much genuine if loopy fun it is to watch." The actors, he observed, "seem to be having a ball." Pauline Kael, with whom Mailer had sparred over the years, wrote a thoughtful review in *The New Yorker*. The film "is screwed up in a different way from *Wild 90, Beyond the Law,* and *Maidstone,*" she observed. Norman doesn't direct, she complained: "For Mailer, shooting a movie is a vacation . . . He may be having a good time, but does he expect us to get off on his taking a vacation?" Still, she acknowledged, "the tawdriness of Mailer's self-exposure has a low-level fascination. What Mailer provides is an intellectual's idea of a pulp thriller."

By this stage of his career, however, no one around Mailer would criticize him. The actors in *Tough Guys* seem to have gone along with his weightiest interpretations, however ridiculous. Just as *Maidstone* was to have been an event, a happening that encapsulated the 1960s but instead devolved into, in Michael McClure's words, a "psychotic pigout," *Tough Guys* was, as Kael observed, a "vacation" for all involved in it. Yet like *Maidstone, Tough Guys Don't Dance* is marked all over with Mailer's obsessions and ego. No one familiar with the man or his work would ever mistake *Tough Guys* as the product of any other writer or director. It is a Mailer product, instantly recognizable, and interesting for all its flaws.

TWENTY-NINE

AMONG THE SPOOKS

Norman did not shine in the 1980s. He had begun the decade at a high crest with the publication of *The Executioner's Song,* but he followed this with his poorly received Egyptian novel, a quickie thriller, and a very bad movie. He had secured his financial future, to be sure, but the friendship with Roy Cohn on which this future was built severely compromised his integrity. He was beset with ailments, adding arthritis to his angina and gout, and was fitted for one and later two hearing aids. His mother died a long and slow death, and his grown children, though well loved, did not always live up to his expectations, and he sometimes showed himself a bullying and demanding father. He had a major falling-out with a longtime good friend, Peter Manso, and had revealed a vindictive and petty streak in himself. He kept a mistress for most of the decade, whom he did not always treat very well. In one episode that might be said to be typical of the 1980s, the heyday of the yuppie, Norman appeared in a Trump Air commercial with boxing promoter Don King, for which he received fifty thousand dollars, leaving him admittedly "feeling absolutely corrupt, I tell you."

Yet media reports and observers constantly said of Norman that he had "mellowed." Certainly in the 1980s, save for the PEN debacle, he avoided the public scrapes and contretemps that had always punctuated his life as a public writer. This was partly due to Norris's influence. She encouraged him to eat healthier meals and to keep to regular habits — he even cut out drinking entirely from 1984 to 1986 (or so he claimed — Carole Mallory denies it), and when he resumed, seldom did so to excess. (He told one interviewer that "the alternative" was impossible: "You can't get drunk. The thought of getting drunk on a Sunday afternoon on a boat is . . . less supportable.") Norris encouraged him as well to see himself as a dignified man of letters whose days of stunts and scenes were over, and he grew into the image of himself as an aging patriarch. Though he appeared occasionally on the social scene, his social life increasingly consisted of his children and their families. His Random House editor, Jason Epstein, has said, "There are two sides to Norman Mailer, and the good side has won."

The 1990s opened with the completion and publication of *Harlot's Ghost,* which coincided with his decision to end his nine-year affair with Carole. After her sensationalistic novel *Flash* appeared in 1988, she had become increasingly active as a journalist. She conducted nine interviews with Norman himself, placed them all in good magazines, and made sure that squibs about them appeared in the gossip columns. She also published interviews of such celebrities as Mikhail Baryshnikov, Milos Forman, and Julian Lennon. She was developing a specialty: bringing two public figures together for conversation. This series had included one between Kurt Vonnegut and Joseph Heller, another, on literacy, between Jesse Jackson and Brooke Astor, and another that had Erica Jong discussing sex with Jay McInerney.

In 1990 Carole "conducted" another conversation, between Mailer and Gore Vidal, which would appear in *Esquire* the following year. Norman was impossible from the start and left the interview in a huff because he believed Carole was flirting with Vidal. Carole gave each writer a transcript for his review, but when Norman demanded to see the transcripts a second time, she refused. Next, *Esquire* asked Carole to write a brief history of the Vidal-Mailer feud. She researched it and wrote it up, and when Norman saw her draft he became unaccountably furious. Then, when the interview was published, a cartoon of Gore and Norman kissing was included, which he managed somehow to blame on Carole.

Carole believes that Norman broke off their affair when he could no longer control her. His ostensible reason, communicated over the phone, was that Norris had found out about the affair — which was hardly convincing, as Norris had, it seems, known about it all along. In 1995 all of this would be aired on "Page Six," the gossip column of the *New York Post,* which also noted that Carole was circulating a four-hundred-page memoir about her affair with Norman. (She had Norman's written permission to write such a book, she claims.) Norman admitted the charge of adultery, adding that he loved his wife at the time and so viewed his lapse with "regret." He continued, using odd grammar: "Infidelity, once it becomes the confirmed habit of one's youth and middle age, does not go gently into the long, dark night of finding oneself a senior citizen." In the meantime, Carole, since her time with Norman, has devoted herself to the care of her elderly mother and continues to write.

*

"I THINK THIS is far and away the most ambitious book I've written, and the best," Norman told a reporter from the *Philadelphia Inquirer* during the thirty-five-city book tour Random House organized following the September 1991 release of *Harlot's Ghost*. (Elsewhere he would temporize, calling it one of the two best books he'd written, the other being *Ancient Evenings*.)

The book's subject, and Mailer's stance toward it, came as a surprise to both his readers and the reviewers. *Harlot's Ghost* portrays the Cold War–era CIA in loving detail, seemingly uncritical of its history of deception, murder, and worse. The agency presented here is the gentleman's version, strictly Eastern and WASP (although Harry Hubbard is described as one-eighth Jewish). Rising through the ranks at the CIA entailed a lot of grunt work, to be sure, but Mailer makes it out to be an elect calling. As Hubbard realizes, "The CIA was not merely long, shedlike buildings, or the dead-tank smells of people crowded into impossibly small office spaces, nor leering inquisitors who strapped belts and instruments to your body; no, CIA was also a company of the elegant, secretly gathered to fight a war so noble that one could and must be ready to trudge for years through the mud and the pits." To Hubbard, America is a country that "had God's sanction," and he is privileged and honored to serve it. If he is frankly a snob (in one scene he condescends to a Midwesterner, reflecting, "Midwesterners can have their share of virtues, but the fine ladies are all accounted for by the time western Massachusetts reaches New York State"), that's what his upbringing has prepared him to be: a stint with the Knickerbocker Greys, four years at "St. Matthew's," and Yale, along with a summer of rock climbing with the redoubtable Hugh Montague, Harlot of the book's title.

Norman's admiration for the CIA, and his approval of what he takes to be its patrician ways, is obvious in *Harlot's Ghost,* and he professed his partisanship freely elsewhere. In interview after interview, he declared his respect for the agency and its agents. He found Allen Dulles "a very cultured man in style and intelligence"; about the discredited past director Richard Helms, he said, "I respect him without hating him." He knew the agency had to use underhanded and often illegal methods, but as Hubbard realizes, "that was the allure of tradecraft. Is there any state more agreeable than living and working like a wicked angel?" That was his challenge in writing the book, Norman told an interviewer: "I mean, here you have these extraordinarily respectable people in the CIA, many of them good Harvard men of the sort I knew reasonably well when I was there. Now, fifteen, twenty years later they're out trying to murder Castro. Well, how do you get to that point? What's the reasoning?" He even added — and he would repeat this to other interviewers — "I could have been [a spy]. If I'd had a totally different background and came from another kind of family, and had a different set of politics when I was a young man. I could have been in the CIA. And I probably would have been pretty good at it." When asked about his earlier feelings about covert instruments of government and his attempt to create the Fifth Estate — a People's CIA — he said, "I cringe when I think of the name now."

Harlot's Ghost, then, was his big offering. He insisted that it was not the Great Book he had long promised — the novel was too specific to be that — but he maintained that with its sequel (*Harlot's Ghost* ends with the words "To be continued") it would become a "mega-novel" that would crown his reputation. As it stood, the novel was far too long, and by following Epstein's suggestions he was able to bring himself to reduce it from 2,656 manuscript pages to 2,450. Beyond that the novel was barely edited. One of the infelicitous results was that several ungrammatical constructions dot its pages, including a dangling modifier in the first sentence (even when it was pointed out, Norman refused to change it, saying, "I like the rhythm as it stands"). The volume, 1,282 pages long, was priced at thirty dollars, a very high price for the time.

The year 1991 saw a spate of articles on Norman, the result of a massive book tour in support of *Harlot's Ghost.* Their titles indicate something of the way the press had elected to fold his new interest in the CIA into the established elements of his public image: "Stormin' Norman," "His Punch Is Better than Ever," "Mailer Weighs In with a Weighty Ghost," and "Mailer: He's Not Finished Yet." The consensus was that Norman Mailer was very much with us, having produced a major book that demanded to be taken seriously. The reviews, however, were another story. Christopher Lehmann-Haupt, writing in the daily *New York Times,* liked the book, though he allowed, "There is much to fault in the novel," especially its length. Still, he wrote, Mailer "has created a fiction as real and as possible as actual history — even more real, perhaps, because it is more coherent and animated than an actual history of the CIA could ever be."

But that was about as good as it got. More than a few reviewers joked about the effect of coming to the last page and reading "To be continued." "The thought is enough to send a reader in search of a drink," commented *Newsweek*'s critic. Many applauded the opening section — the scene on the island, the Keep, in which Hubbard and Kittredge learn of Harlot's death, a naturalistic tour de force replete with suspense and a ghost, and far and away the best part of the book. Paul Gray, writing for *Time,* admired the early section as "fine and engaging, comparable to the best passages . . . that Mailer has ever written." But "the joyride turns into a forced march . . . Something has clearly gone wrong here. Mailer finally does not use history but succumbs to it . . . Those eager to read Norman Mailer, his unique imagination and intellect reshaping the known world, should read the opening pages of *Harlot's Ghost* and hope, someday, for more of the same." Louis Menand, in a long review essay in *The New Yorker,* was especially damning. *Harlot's Ghost* is "not only the most unsatisfying book Mailer has ever written, it is also the most undistinguished," he declared.

But the notice that meant the most to Norman was that of the Sunday *New York Times Book Review.* He learned in advance that the reviewer was to be John Simon, known for his theater and film criticism, and that it would get the front page. Simon's review was not entirely negative, but he had fun with his subject and along the way got in a number of good jabs. He allowed that some readers might find the book "such a spellbinding re-creation of momentous events that the length of the first installment is well earned," but that others might find it "an arbitrary, lopsided, lumpy novel that outstays its welcome. And keeps outstaying it." Overall, Simon felt that the author's obsessions got in the way of his narrative: "Mailer pursues, manicly or maniacally, power and sex, i.e., achieving supremacy in some profession such as politics or the military, and possessing the most beautiful women in the world. A Stendhal could make some magisterial fiction even out of this, but in Mailer the hang-ups are too naked, puerile, perverse." Simon ended by comparing Mailer to Thomas Wolfe, a gratuitous comparison contrived to set up a parting jab. Mailer was like Wolfe, another Harvard man, he said. But "what he lacks is his editor."

Norman immediately went on the counterattack, but rather than take on Simon's criticisms directly, he zeroed in on the critic's qualifications. The *Times Book Review* critic was primarily a theater critic, he noted disdainfully. "The mark of Simon's incapacity to be a literary reviewer — as a theater reviewer he's vicious but very often interesting — is that he knows very little about the novel," Norman told the *New York Post* the day after the review appeared. In some ways, he said, Simon did owe him one — at a recent literary luncheon he had said that Simon's snobbishness reminded him of "one of the best Balkan headwaiters in hell." Simon, in turn, told the same reporter that Norman's insult had been no more than "a fleabite," and went on to defend his qualifications as a literary critic. In the same interview, Simon charged that Lehmann-Haupt's positive review in the daily *Times* was "a typical, miserable, toadying, cowardly review."

The feud was on. Mailer's shock troops included his old friend Barbara Probst Solomon, who, in an October 27 letter to the *New York Times Book Review* editor, declaimed, "Norman Mailer is part of our cultural patrimony," and questioned the assignment of the review to a theater critic. On November 17, almost two months after the review was published, Norman's "official" response to Simon's review appeared; he was given a full page in the letters section. He imagined the scenario in which editor Rebecca Sinkler assigned the book to Simon, consciously (so he said) ignoring the fact that Simon had savaged *Marilyn* more than a decade before. He described a visit to Sinkler in which he produced evidence of Simon's prejudice against him. Near the end, he pointed out Simon's scathing review of his daughter Kate Mailer's performance in Peter Brook's 1988 production of *The Cherry Orchard.* He went on to describe a bizarre meeting with Simon the previous June at the annual *Paris Review* party, when he challenged the critic with the question "Are you a man of honor?" After Simon answered yes, Norman (in a distinct anticlimax) asked for his phone number, and Simon, who had recently moved, gave it to him. A guest at the table pointed out, however, that Simon had given Norman his old phone number, and Simon corrected the mistake, but Norman was left with the suspicion that Simon was trying to evade him. He closed the letter by listing some of the vicious things Simon had written about such actresses as Mia Farrow, Diane Keaton, and Liza Minnelli, presumably to emphasize that Simon could not be fair.

Simon, in his own response, published with Norman's letter, pointed out that Norman had admitted that the review was only "half unfavorable," and dismissed the notion that Kate's acting was any reflection on his view of her father's writing. (He got in a sly dig here, though. Knowing full well Norman's rivalry with the playwright Arthur Miller, in part over Marilyn Monroe, he wrote of his "favorable notice, in the same production, of Rebecca Miller, daughter of Arthur, whose work I have often criticized severely.") Finally, Rebecca Sinkler answered, claiming that the *Book Review*'s editors knew only of Simon's negative review of *Marilyn* and of his review of Kate Mailer's performance, "which they judged to be irrelevant."

This level of pettiness spoke ill of both Simon and Mailer. One wonders too about Norman's lack of tact in dredging up mean things said about his daughter back in 1988 and in quoting them — surely Kate Mailer would just as soon have forgotten Simon's harsh words. Readers of the *Book Review* who were not driven to go out and buy *Harlot's Ghost* would forever remember the book only in connection with a bitchy, trivial quarrel.

It is all the more unfortunate that Mailer should have chosen to pull discussion of his book down to this level, because he truly believed that *Harlot's Ghost,* with its prospective sequel, which would carry Hubbard to Hollywood and then to Nixon's White House and from there to the Iran-Contra affair, would constitute his magnum opus.

Without the sequel, judging whether he makes good on that claim is of course impossible. But *Harlot's Ghost,* it is eminently clear, is an important novel, containing some of Mailer's best — and worst — writing. Hubbard, for all his snobbishness and patrician background, is an immensely likable hero; the reader sympathizes with his love for Kittredge, tortured though it is because of his reverence for Harlot, her husband. Harlot himself, modeled loosely on James Jesus Angleton, is wonderfully drawn: he is an implacable foe of Communism, and the combination of his zealotry with his high intelligence makes his vision of the Cold War landscape as complex and fascinating as is General Cummings's vision of the political future in *The Naked and the Dead*. With Kittredge, Mailer finally succeeds in creating a fully rendered heroine, with a mean intelligence; her theory of the Alpha and the Omega, the two warring forces in the universe and the human psyche, dazzles Allen Dulles. The drama of her unfolding relationship with Hubbard, expressed in the letters they exchange through the long course of Hubbard's beginnings in the agency, and in the unforgettable depictions of their relationship in the novel's first section, is the strong narrative thread on which hangs the long chronology of Hubbard's experiences as an operative. The oedipal drama of replacing the father is chillingly played out along the way, as Harlot is paralyzed in the same rock-climbing accident that kills his son, enabling Hubbard to marry Kittredge, who divorces Harlot in the wake of the accident.

Reviewers rightly singled out the first section of the book for praise, the taut narrative of a stormy evening at the Keep. Many felt that what followed — the bulk of the novel — was a distinct falling-off. Mailer follows Hubbard's history: his training in Washington, where he learns "tradecraft"; his service in Berlin under the redoubtable Berlin chief of base, William Harvey, a nonfictional figure Mailer breathes into full, frightening life when Hubbard and the evilly handsome Dix Butler explore Berlin's sadomasochistic homosexual bars; his experience in Montevideo, Uruguay, where he works with E. Howard Hunt and has a rather loveless affair with a colleague's wife; and finally his time in Miami, for the Bay of Pigs affair, the Cuban missile crisis, and Operation Mongoose (a plan to assassinate Castro), as well as an affair with a woman modeled on Judith Campbell Exner, allegedly the lover of John Kennedy, Frank Sinatra, and Sam Giancana. All this is rendered in fairly compelling fashion. Over the novel's course, the ins and outs of "tradecraft" and the agency's blunders in its dealings with Castro believably flesh out the narrative.

True, Mailer does try to frame the narrative in a larger, mystical-psychological concept, Kittredge's theory of the Alpha and the Omega. It is a fairly straightforward dualistic conception: the Alpha part of the personality (derived from the sperm cell) is male, concerned with force, pessimism, day, routine, and so forth; the Omega (derived from the ovum) is female, concerned with the moon, optimism, conception, the spontaneous, and so on.

The two "go through life like Siamese twins inside one person." One's Alpha or Omega can be in ascendancy at different times, which adds greatly (how is not made clear) to our understanding of human nature. Though Mailer portentously broadcasts that this system underlies everything in his novel — by, for instance, naming one of Hubbard's manuscripts Omega and the other Alpha — he is unconvincing on the subject, and Kittredge's theory remains a somewhat pretty conceit that the reader can ignore.

Though the Alpha-Omega framework does not work in the way the novelist seems to have hoped, the theory does help to articulate the central features of Mailer's CIA: the agency as essentially a force of good, but in reality made up of flawed ideas and flawed people. For all Mailer's admiration of the agency's undertaking, he recognized this moral trauma in the Cold War landscape. The potentialities of the CIA as a moral battlefield had escaped America's other novelists, with the single exception of conservative William F. Buckley, in whose series of Blackford Oakes spy thrillers the agency operatives appear as a kind of sexy Knights Templars. Mailer saw the subject in a far more complex light, perceiving no clear villains and fewer true heroes. It is an interesting novel to use as a bookend with *The Naked and the Dead,* for in both books he explores such issues as courage under pressure, the morality of a large bureaucracy, service to one's country, and personal integrity threatened by the enticements of power. In the earlier novel, however, the moral landscape is bleak but not hopeless, while in *Harlot's Ghost* the terrain is always shifting beneath one's feet. A lifetime's experience separates the two fictions.

The "why" of Mailer's fascination with his subject and his insistence on glamorizing it remains a vexing question. He was personally invested in his vision of the CIA as a kind of gentleman's club, as his repeated comment to interviewers that he too could have been a CIA man, given a different background, makes clear. Just six months after *Harlot's Ghost* appeared in 1991, Norman paid a day-long visit to CIA headquarters in Langley, Virginia. He gave a speech before five hundred agents in a standing-room-only auditorium and received standing ovations several times. Even with the Cold War over, he told them, the CIA had an important mission, citing especially the need to combat nuclear proliferation and terrorism. With the Soviet rivalry ended, he said, "the CIA can get out of the beartrap of ideology and begin to provide serious and needed intelligence on the rest of the world." The former godfather to the Fifth Estate also surprised his audience by saying he was in fact not opposed to "wet jobs" — the KGB term for covert assassinations — and that he spoke for the American people in saying they would approve, in fact, a wet job on Iraqi dictator Saddam Hussein. After this meeting, Norman met privately with three dozen senior officials in director Robert Gates's conference room.

The *New York Times* reporter who wrote up this story spoke to many CIA figures after the visit, as well as to Mailer himself. The reference to wet jobs shocked many; one agent said, "We've been so conditioned to the fact that such operations are wrong, that they're illegal. Then you hear this and you gasp." Other analysts and officials noted that the agency was never involved in the kind of riotous excess and sex Norman described, not even in the days of William J. "Wild Bill" Donovan, the creator of the OSS, the CIA's predecessor. "Anyone who worked for Bill Donovan knew perfectly well that you didn't run riot," said one veteran officer. Another said that Mailer's characters "would never have passed the polygraph." Norman, in turn, commented on the politeness and normalcy of the crowd. Said an agent in response, "What did he expect? Guys with guns?"

This proved to be yet another indication of how out of step Norman was with the cultural temperature of post–Cold War America. The CIA, under its new director, was trying to move beyond some embarrassing revelations about its doings. The agents who commented to the *Times* reporter weren't so much protesting their innocence as pleading for Mailer to leave the "old" CIA of wet jobs and more where they had tried to bury it. But Norman was never anybody's good soldier, not the CIA's any more than the left's. Instead of helping the agency present a sanitized image of itself, he undermined it by bringing up exactly the kinds of matters it was trying to put squarely in its past.

The same was true of Norman's response — or lack of it — to the culture at large: increasingly, bipartisanship has colored recent politics; there has been a dramatic decrease in voter turnout, almost no interest in foreign policy, and a general disinclination for the moral choices that characterized the decades before. A representative book of the decade was Francis Fukuyama's *The End of History* (1992), which argued that with the end of the Cold War and Communism, there remains only one valid political system, democracy, and one economic system, capitalism, and this will spell the end of ideological division as we have known it in the twentieth century. In this increasingly bland climate, Mailer repeatedly tried to revive the ideological clashes that had drawn him so compellingly in the decades before — for example, in seeking to imbue the reformed and much toned-down bureaucracy that the CIA has become with a measure of the high moral drama for which it once stood.

Norman's involvement with the CIA had a strange coda at this juncture. After the *New York Times* article covering his day at the CIA appeared, his old Fifth Estate friends Philip Agee and Ellen Ray called on him. Saying there was something important they must discuss, Agee proposed meeting for drinks at the Algonquin Hotel. There, the two protested urgently against Mailer's aligning himself with the agency. It was one thing to write a book glorifying the CIA, they said, and quite another to meet with its top brass, uncritically and even enthusiastically. They cited instances of continued CIA illegalities, but to no avail. Mailer placidly but forcefully affirmed that he thought the CIA was absolutely necessary in a time like this, with so many nations possessing nuclear capability and with international terrorism a constant menace. Ray and Agee saw that there was no point in arguing with him, and the three parted. The left and the left conservative had nothing more to say to each other.

EPILOGUE

On one level, *Harlot's Ghost* and Mailer's subsequent statements about the CIA revealed that the writer who wanted a place in the halls of power had triumphed over the provocateur whose favorite sport had been to encourage his audience to regard political institutions in questioning and creative ways. But something else had changed: Mailer was getting old, and a new serenity, or at least a more appropriately predictable, settled regime of work and relaxation was beginning to color his days. Over the course of the 1990s, Norman withdrew to Provincetown, spending ten months out of twelve with Norris in his big brick house on the bay. Supporting himself first on one cane and later on two, because of his arthritis, he took a daily walk along Commercial Street; when the weather was warm, he tried to swim something close to the half-mile he had once managed daily in the bay. By 1998 his last child, John Buffalo, was in college, at Wesleyan, and he was a grandfather several times over. His 1997 *The Gospel According to the Son* was dedicated to all nine of his progeny (including Norris's son Matthew). "I'm tough on the kids," he had told an interviewer years before. "I honor my children most when they do well — and find a limit to my compassion when I have to wonder whether they're trying hard." His bond with his sixth wife remained solid, his nine-year affair with Carole Mallory receding in the distance. Norris had been his companion during the writing of eleven of the thirty-one books published by 1999.

If in the 1990s Mailer has been less caught up in American culture, less responsive to it and alert to its turnings, it should be remembered that these times have had less to offer a writer whose ambition has been to encapsulate, sum up, and shape the Zeitgeist. So, in response, he turned to people from other eras who mattered: Picasso, Oswald, Jesus. He rarely found anything in the current scene that drew him; more problematically, he increasingly became a commentator, not a participant-observer.

Harlot's Ghost turned out to be Norman's most important work of the decade. As the 1990s wore on, his book tours became shorter, his TV appearances less frequent, and his interviews more carefully chosen. Yet his literary output did not diminish. He still worked at least eight hours a day, finishing up at eight or nine at night, although increasingly he did not begin work until after lunch.

Mailer followed *Harlot's Ghost* with *Oswald's Tale,* a second Mailerian meditation on the now-ended Cold War, a period, after all, that had taken up most of his adult life. On the heels of *Harlot's Ghost*'s publication, Larry Schiller had reappeared, telling Norman that he could get access to newly opened KGB files on Lee Harvey Oswald. Despite having publicly distanced himself as early as 1975 from Kennedy assassination theories, Norman had been a conspiracy buff for years, and he could sense a challenging project in the telling of Oswald's story. He spent five and a half months in Minsk, where Oswald had lived while in the Soviet Union, transcribing the KGB's surreptitiously made tapes from the Oswald apartment and interviewing KGB agents. He later estimated that it had been sunny only about ten days of the time, and complained that he had lived on sweet bread and cabbage. He met with Marina Oswald, the assassin's widow, five times in Dallas, Texas, and compiled the manuscript of *Oswald's Tale* in 1994.

The book was published early the following year to almost uniformly negative reviews. Many critics commented on Mailer's success in depicting the marriage of Lee and Marina in the book's engaging first half, but what was revealed for the most part came from the KGB tapes, which Mailer quoted verbatim and could thus take little credit for. Only slightly more newsworthy was his contention that he was "seventy-five percent" sure Lee Harvey Oswald acted alone in killing Kennedy. *Oswald's Tale: An American Mystery* recorded the interesting if overlooked life of a rather hapless outsider and his entry into history, but, unlike *The Executioner's Song* or *Harlot's Ghost,* it afforded Mailer no new chances to transcend his tale and comment on American cultural or political history.

Another 1995 project met a similar fate: Mailer's *Picasso: Portrait of an Artist as a Young Man.* Thirty years before, Norman had signed a contract with Emile Capouya at Macmillan to write a biography of Picasso. He had spent two months at the time looking at the reproductions in Christian Zervos's *Pablo Picasso,* poring over the then twenty-odd volumes in the library of the Museum of Modern Art. He had put the project aside, but his interest in the artist persisted and was piqued anew when he read Arianna Stassinopoulos Huffington's 1988 debunking account, *Picasso: Creator and Destroyer.* Although he had never written, critically or biographically, about an artist before, and his only aesthetic writing had been on film, Mailer at this point in his life suddenly felt he had something to say about the early life of this complicated man.

When he took the completed manuscript of *Picasso* to Jason Epstein at Random House in 1994, Epstein thought it best to show the text to another Random House writer, John Richardson, whose authoritative biography of the painter began with a volume published by the firm in 1991. Richardson objected strongly to aspects of Mailer's interpretations and to the extensive quotations from his own work, calling the manuscript a "scissors-and-paste job." Eventually Mailer withdrew the manuscript and signed it up with Doubleday, with Nan Talese as his editor. But it was not there long and was ultimately published, in 1995, by Atlantic Monthly Press. Reviewers noted the similarities between Picasso's life and Mailer's own, but few were impressed with his interpretation of the artist's work or his biographical technique. Norman would have to defend himself against those who saw the book as a hasty piece of work that heavily quoted the views of other Picasso biographers, memoirists, and critics.

Two years later he made headlines once again with perhaps his oddest project yet: *The Gospel According to the Son,* a retelling of the Gospels in the first person, the narrator Jesus Christ. The press made the inevitable jokes (especially about his use of a first-person narrator), and disbelief at his hubris abounded. Norman didn't help matters by calling the Gospel writers "untalented" and bad reporters: "There are probably a hundred writers who could write a fine narrative [of the Gospels story]," he told the *New York Post* in reassuringly brash fashion, "and I'm one of them." Many critics questioned why he had not talked to biblical scholars before undertaking the project; such a book could have raised larger, very interesting questions about biblical history and interpretation, but Mailer's simple text begged them all.

Although Norman had considerable knowledge about early Christianity and the controversies surrounding biblical and other early Christian texts, he questioned no orthodoxies and demanded no rethinkings in a curiously flat, even boring (incredibly so, given the subject) narrative. Reviews, with the exceptions of thoughtful pieces by Frank Kermode and John Updike and a few others, were almost uniformly dismissive. The *New Republic* featured a cover with a cartoon of Norman on a cross wearing a crown of thorns, with the caption "He Is Finished"; for this Norman later took a swing at editor Marty Peretz. But other responses were extreme indeed, and on some level Mailer must have found them satisfying: televangelist Jack Van Impe, in a 1998 broadcast, waved a copy of the book and then picked up a Bible, intoning, "Mr. Mailer, for your sins all the plagues in this book will be visited on you tenfold!"

Perhaps wisely, Norman closed out the decade and the millennium by turning away from others' lives and returning to his own. In May 1998, on the fiftieth anniversary of the publication of *The Naked and the Dead,* Random House brought out *The Time of Our Times,* a twelve-hundred-page collection of Mailer's writing, arranged chronologically to tell the story of American society from World War II to the present. Compiled and arranged with the help of Robert Lucid, Norman's old friend and a retired academic who had thirty-odd years earlier commenced an authorized biography (now projected as three volumes), and his official bibliographer, J. Michael Lennon (the book is dedicated to both men), the collection provided an occasion for critics to weigh in with observations and reflections on Mailer's long career, most notably David Denby in *The New Yorker* and Louis Menand in the *New York Review of Books.*

Very little that was previously uncollected appeared in *The Time of Our Times,* but those few pieces included Mailer's first plunge into presidential campaign reportage since 1972. Norman covered the 1996 Democratic and Republican campaigns for *George,* the Washington-based political affairs magazine published by John F. Kennedy, Jr., the son of the man Norman had written about so perceptively thirty-six years earlier, while covering his first presidential election. In these lively, insightful, and well-written pieces — perhaps his best work, after *Harlot's Ghost,* of the decade — Norman discovered a strange (perhaps generational) affinity for GOP candidate Robert Dole, finding him basically very upright and often very funny. But his vote went to Bill Clinton, and most of his political energies in the years to follow were reserved for criticizing Clinton for his constant vacillations and lack of real political principles. He still hoped for a politician who was progressive and creative, and Clinton did not fit the bill. He also sought out, in 1996, the populist conservative candidate Pat Buchanan, with whom he thought he might find common ground, but an interview published in *Esquire* in August of that year revealed no real connection; Buchanan came across as another not very imaginative Republican.

On the cultural side, an attempt to interview and interpret the pop singer and icon Madonna, published in *Esquire* in 1994, also fell short. Incredibly, Mailer failed to ask her anything at all about her music, instead using the occasion to denounce the use of condoms, promulgate his strange sexual conservatism, and unsuccessfully try to get a rise out of her by repeatedly returning to the subject of what he called "porny" films. Somewhat more successfully, he commented on the O. J. Simpson case for *New York* magazine in the October 16, 1995, issue, describing it as a dire watershed for American race relations; similarly, he had interesting things to say, in National Public Radio broadcasts and interviews with television host Charlie Rose, about the rise of the militia movement in the 1990s, provocatively suggesting that their real enemy was not the government but that old Mailer bugaboo the corporation.

Moments such as these indicate that Mailer's old instinct to look for new directions in American public life have not completely evaporated. But sadly, at other times he seems to tell us that he is enjoying his protected and relatively prosperous old age and sees no need to engage with pressing and difficult issues in any way. Interviewed for the Manhattan magazine *File* by his son Michael in January 1999, Mailer confessed that he was a keen supporter of New York City's controversial Republican mayor Rudy Giuliani:

> Giuliani . . . made it his business to give us a city where the streets would be safer. He would relieve us of this sense of the poor encroaching on us. After all, what if the poor decide to become violent? Whereas, if we don't see them, we're reminded less of them. . . . People want to be able to go to sleep at night without feeling guilty. Every time a beggar approaches you, if you give him money, you can never know for certain if the act derives from the goodness of your heart or you are just slightly afraid of him. Giuliani delivered us from much of that.

Certainly many affluent New Yorkers and many other Americans at similar vantage points can recognize this feeling. But coming from a writer whose forte has always been confrontation, this relief at not having to wrestle with a matter of conscience suggests that Mailer is no longer interested in exercising one of the key elements in his thinking and his art.

Mailer's expectations for the future of the novel grew even bleaker over the decade. But while the feeling of being cut off from public life might be one reason for this, he blamed an easier target: television. In the early 1990s, he bribed John Buffalo to read ten novels, promising the boy two hours of television per day if he complied. "Serious novelists," Mailer would proclaim to a Smithsonian audience in 1994, "may be as rare as serious poets in another fifty years . . . If the novel dies, a great deal is going to die with it. It's as if there is a brutalization of the art forms going on." Many women in the audience detected grandiosity in this statement, as if he were saying the novel would die with him.

But perhaps Mailer's frustration with the novel form was an understandable gesture from a novelist who had been hurling himself into big projects for twenty years — first *Ancient Evenings,* then *Harlot's Ghost* — in hopes of capping his career with a magisterial magnum opus. He had failed in that, and even lesser efforts like *Tough Guys Don't Dance* and *The Gospel According to the Son* had not hit the mark. Perhaps it is not entirely

surprising that as this contentious, presumptuous writer has become less so
— as comfort and contentment have taken over — his work has fallen off,
his connection with his readers becoming more tenuous.

IF HARLOT'S GHOST is Norman Mailer's most important book of the
1990s, *Portrait of Picasso as a Young Man* is, biographically speaking, the
most interesting, because it is the one occasion on which he would attempt
to reconcile his oft-stated beliefs about masculinity with the changing cultural politics of the current decade. It is also, perhaps not unintentionally, a
close approximation of Norman's self-portrait toward the end of his era,
and a fine vantage point from which to observe his evaluation of the literary
themes that have obsessed him for so long. However indebted his text may
be to others' work, no one questions that Norman's *Picasso* fairly accurately recreates the artist's young life. And while some critics questioned the
work as a piece of amateur art criticism, generally it is an enjoyably jargon-
free, fresh if idiosyncratic response to Picasso's work and personality. (At
first, for instance, it strikes the reader that Mailer sees vaginas everywhere
— but of course, so did Picasso.)

The two men share many superficial resemblances: both short, they
developed barrel-like torsos as they aged. Both had somewhat ineffectual
fathers who were said to be ladies' men, and as children, both were surrounded by doting mothers and aunts. (Like Fan Mailer, Picasso's mother's
"admiration for her son and his genius increased all the time whether she
comprehended his work or not.") Both men showed great talent at a young
age. And while Norman's account stops short of comparing their artistic
achievements, except by inference, both took similar approaches to their
art, shifting styles and genres or media so as to develop new ways to
apprehend reality. Both produced extremely controversial work. Both were
often misunderstood artistically.

Norman detects other resemblances, at once more fleeting and more
important, and his recognition of them suggests a new self-knowledge, or at
least a willingness to consider his quirks as personality traits, rather than to
trumpet them and defend them intellectually. He speculates that Picasso
tended toward the same magical thinking that so plagued him, for example.
He also recognizes the homoeroticism implicit in sleeping with a woman in
full knowledge that she has previously been the lover of a male friend.

Picasso's friend Casagemas — with whom the artist may or may not
have had homosexual relations — killed himself in 1901. Picasso sank
deeply into depression, in the depths of which he started an affair with Casagemas's lover, Germaine, who had refused to marry his dead friend. "[Pi-
casso] was immersed now in homosexual preoccupations," writes Mailer.
"He had to have carnal knowledge at no matter what emotional costs, of

the nominal *widow* of Casagemas. Even as he would copy other painters
. . . as one more means of entering into their mentality, so did he absorb the
loss of his friend by searching for Casagemas's presence in the body of the
woman he had chosen for marriage." So too did Mailer seek communion
with men he looked up to in entering the bodies of Adele, Beverly, and
Carole.

Making the distinction that "there is probably more evidence that [Picasso] was not macho so much as an acolyte of machismo," Mailer goes on
to offer a defense of the concept:

> Today, in a world of prevailing feminism, machismo is scorned.
> Yet, few men are able to sneer at it with absolute confidence. The
> case for machismo, if we can put its extravagances and violence to
> the side, is that it is not an easy way to live. When one puts a large
> investment in personal honor, day-to-day security is mortgaged.

Is he talking about himself here? Norman has called on his own physical
bravery only in situations he deliberately devised for that end — in boxing,
headbutting, or similar contests of strength and will. In tracing Picasso's
life, the homoerotic nature of typically macho exploits seems at last to have
become clear to Norman, though he valued such exploits no less, before and
after his study of Picasso, for that.

But he had always valued the pursuit of machismo as a positive good,
and even now stood ready to defend it. Here is how he carries this familiar
subject into the 1990s:

> If, even in the face of contemporary ridicule, men still strive for
> machismo, that is because it speaks to a primitive certainty in male
> gender — even as a similar claim might be presented for elegance in
> women. Yuppies and wonks may scorn the first, and liberated
> women repudiate the second, but their ridicule remains subtly uneasy. Not many have a conscience so comfortable or so blind that
> they can condemn either without a backward look.

To be sure, from the champion of headbutting, the father who raised his
first-born son to be a boxer, the swaggerer who once said that all women
should be kept in cages, the writer whose greatest hero was Hemingway, the
patriarch who sired eight children, this is a rather remarkable statement. It's
a diminished and qualified plea that essential differences between the sexes
be acknowledged. Mailer cannot give up the essentialist belief that to strive
to be macho is admirable — even if he can now admit that it is almost by
definition an unattainable goal.

In reconstructing Picasso's early life and detailing its points of contact with his own, Mailer does not so much suggest that their work and influence be compared, but he stands fast on another point: that the way an artist, especially a towering figure like Picasso, chose to live his life is equally appropriate for a man of Mailer's time — even in the 1990s, when "yuppies and wonks" and "liberated women" rule the day. *Picasso: A Portrait of the Artist as a Young Man* is nothing less than an apologia for Mailer's own life, an argument that Picasso's approach to the world and his art was, like Mailer's, that of an existential man living in the moment, taking risks and striking out boldly into new artistic realms, and that the way Picasso lived his life was still appropriate, even admirable, at the end of the century. *Picasso* is Mailer's indirect plea that he be remembered as being as important to his time as Picasso was to his. No matter the monster he may have been, Picasso left an indelible mark on the twentieth century; however flawed Mailer is as an artist and a man, he is part of what is distinctive about the second half of this century.

Mailer's assertion that the way an artist lives is tied up inextricably with his work is a double-edged sword when his own life is in question. Many of his flaws as a man derive from the aspect of his life he was able to put to such good use in his work: his celebrity. Like other "stars" of the postwar world — like Frank Sinatra, perhaps, or Ali — he has always been surrounded by an entourage, a group of yea-sayers who encourage his every whim and provide no checks on his often questionable behavior. Celebrity always exacts a toll from those who surround it, and Mailer has often treated those around him in petty or even mean fashion — particularly the women. From his very earliest years, when he was surrounded by a tribe of adoring women — Fan and her sisters, and later Barbara — Norman was told he was a genius who could do no wrong. Often this was to the good, protecting him from feelings of inferiority or inadequacy. At Harvard, a strange mixture of naiveté and arrogance held him aloof from the realization that he was essentially an outsider among his classmates; later, with no awareness of this handicap, he effortlessly joined the elite Signet. Very soon after, with *The Naked and the Dead,* he became famous seemingly overnight, and his stature ensured that he was shielded from reality by a tight band of supporters and family. When he tragically stumbled, stabbing Adele in 1960, his inner circle made sure that he would pay no price for the deed. Over the years, despite setbacks and failures, the situation has not really changed, and Norman has been able to do pretty much what he has wanted, unchecked in any way except perhaps by occasional financial troubles. He has indulged himself with any number of grandiose projects and ideas over the years, and he has been self-serving and self-centered to an embarrassing degree. Those who do not adore him unconditionally he finds some way to control. No one checks him; anyone who tries is ejected from his circle summarily, and sometimes forced to pay for his or her presumption.

On the other hand, Mailer has turned his celebrity — however much of a curse it has been in his life — to excellent account. In at least this one sense, in fact, he has far outshone his idol Hemingway. Perhaps America's greatest literary celebrity of the first half of this century, "Papa" never found a way to turn his swaggering persona to good use in his writing. If anything, it eventually damaged his work. Mailer, in contrast, discovered that celebrity could open up doors to a new kind of cultural expression in which the artist's personal and creative lives inform each other in beneficial ways. Perhaps his finest single demonstration of this is *The Armies of the Night,* in which his notoriety and bad behavior, and his personal preoccupations in general, illuminate many of the issues raised by the March on the Pentagon. But his efforts in this direction actually began with *Advertisements for Myself,* in retrospect one of the key cultural texts of the postwar era. A performative act as much as a literary work, *Advertisements* demonstrated to an Eisenhower-era audience that public life and private life, artistic life and the gossip columns, could not be separated from each other in this media-saturated time, and that the bravest course might just be to embrace all of them. He would continue to operate in this space, whatever the cost, in the personal faith that an "American public" existed for him to speak to, until, in the late 1970s, that public began to fragment and parochialize.

Mailer did not create the space he came to occupy — media like television, popular music, pop art, and even politics in the Kennedy era were creating it around him. But in *Advertisements* (and throughout his work in the 1960s and 1970s) he articulated how an artist could use these new forums to demand a change of thinking and a more creative approach to everything from politics to literature to racial and sexual relations.

In these years, Mailer yearned to blur the lines between the personal, the political, and the creative in any medium he could: essay, novel (*An American Dream*), film, the TV interview, even political campaigning. His 1969 mayoral race, for example, was yet another front in his effort to articulate a sense of possibility in American life, an attempt to arouse an "existential" sense of being in the voting public, using both his imagination and his celebrity. His role in the larger sense was to articulate possibility, not to get elected or spawn a political movement. The space he opened up appeared many times in the course of his life, often in the unlikeliest of places. Speaking at the Town Hall debate on women's rights, could Germaine Greer not have known that without Norman Mailer she would perhaps not have been able to cut the figure she did, flamboyant in feathers, and as the author of *The Female Eunuch,* a feminist text that brilliantly mixed the personal and the political? It was oddly appropriate, given his stubborn lack of understanding of feminism, that Mailer should have emceed that night, because he was instrumental in opening the space in which feminism flourished in the 1960s and 1970s. Over the years, Mailer has still sought to keep open the option of imaginative action in our culture.

What he helped unleash he could not always comprehend. With the rise of "identity politics" in the post-Vietnam era — the advent of feminism and gay rights most notably — Mailer struggled to find a footing. As the culture has become more and more balkanized, Mailer indeed has lost touch with the unified public with which he had interacted so successfully in the first decades of his career. The best our culture had to offer him in the 1990s was the likes of O. J. Simpson. Yet the imaginative space Mailer invoked and has tried to keep open continues to echo. He and his old friend Muhammad Ali gave America a vivid reminder in 1996, in Leon Gast's powerful and aptly titled *When We Were Kings,* an Oscar-winning documentary about the 1974 "Rumble in the Jungle" between Ali and George Foreman, which Mailer covered so vividly in *The Fight.* The great spectacle of Ali — just a boxer, but one who, for reasons both personal and political, *mattered* — is juxtaposed with Norman's animated, dead-on, and insightful running commentary, punctuated by a bravura shot of the aging reporter jumping out of his seat in wonder as Ali's final, unexpected blizzard of blows knocked Foreman out. (One critic said Mailer's performance should have earned him an Oscar.) Perhaps *When We Were Kings* indicates that we are in a transitional period, that our culture may yet be open to the kind of creative, imaginative, political, and cultural experience that Norman believed made American culture so distinctive, the kind of experience that is his cultural legacy.

MAILER MARKED *The Time of Our Times,* the culmination of a fifty-year career, with another party, held some twenty-five years after his raucous fiftieth birthday party at the Four Seasons. But this was a much calmer, more sedate affair. On May 6, 1998, Mailer welcomed an array of guests at the Rainbow Room, giving them each a copy of that outsized book. The spread put on by Random House was lavish: champagne as well as a full bar, chicken satay, coconut shrimp, roast beef. With him were Norris and most of his children, ranging from Susan, his oldest, to John, his youngest, along with Bob Lucid and Michael Lennon and an assortment of distinguished guests as well as long-time Mailer cronies.

Strangely enough, the center of attention was Muhammad Ali, sadly diminished by Parkinson's disease, accompanied by his wife, Lonnie. Mailer made sure all his guests were brought over to Ali, who simply smiled as guest after guest reminisced about his fights and assured him he was still "the greatest." Mailer tried to engage the boxer in conversation, and the two wound up sparring in kidding fashion. A picture taken by *New York Times* photographer Bill Cunningham suggests that there was an edge to the fun: Ali can be seen unsmilingly advancing his left toward Mailer's chin, though Norman is wriggling out of his hold. The sparring gave way to a prolonged photo session. George Plimpton went over and clowned around with Mailer and Ali, the three making rabbit ears over one another's heads. Guests — and Rainbow Room waiters — clamored to be photographed with Ali.

New Yorker writer Lillian Ross, reporting on the event for "Talk of the Town," used the words "gracious," "generous," and even "joyful" to describe Norman's demeanor. A *New York Times* reporter asked, "The boxer, the braggart, the king of all authors, the radical with a prankster's love of debate — where has he gone?" He was still there, Norman said, conceding, "As one gets older, the anger softens. . . . To use Bob Dole's favorite word: Whatever." In an accompanying interview, he told the same reporter that it was tempting to see his latest work as a kind of epitaph, though he labored against it: "It's either my living memorial or else it's a chance to take a large part of my life and look at it before getting on with all I have to do. . . . For certain I'll opt for the second option, but that doesn't mean it's accurate. We'll find out."

Notes

The following abbreviations are used in the notes.

BB — Beverly Bentley
CM — Carole Mallory
F & E Gwaltney — Francis Irby (Fig) Gwaltney and Emma Clara (Ecey) Gwaltney
    Gwaltney Collection — Francis Irby Gwaltney Collection, Special Collections
    Division, University of Arkansas, Fayetteville
NM — Norman Mailer
NYHTBR — *New York Herald Tribune Book Review*
NYRB — *New York Review of Books*
NYT — *New York Times*
NYTBR — *New York Times Book Review*

PROLOGUE: COCK OF THE WALK

Sources include interviews with David Amram and Ellen Ray; Sally Quinn, "NM Turns 50," *Washington Post*, Feb. 7, 1973; Jan Hodenfield, "A Party Scripted by NM, Age 50," *New York Post*, Feb. 6, 1973; Lucian Truscott IV, "Mailer's Birthday," *Village Voice*, Feb. 8, 1973; "The Birthday Party," *New York Post*, Feb. 7, 1973; Robins, *Alien Ink;* Mills, 388–94; Rollyson 250-51; Manso, interviews with Jules Feiffer, John Leonard.

page

    1 "In Manhattan, nobody": Sally Quinn, "NM Turns 50," *Washington Post,*
        Feb. 7, 1973, B1.
    2 "Tell Norman": Stern, *Gloria Steinem,* 176.
    2 "This is his answer": Jan Hodenfield, "A Party Scripted by NM, Age 50,"
        New York Post, Feb. 6, 1973, 2.
    3 "Hey, what is this?": Lucian Truscott IV, "Mailer's Birthday," *Village Voice,*
        Feb. 8, 1973, 24.
    4 The gist of it: Ibid., 25.

4 "You're about to see": Interview with David Amram, May 30, 1998.

5 "Mailer looked confused": Hamill, *Drinking Life,* 263.

5 "I didn't know a thing": Linda Franke, "A Half Century of Mailer," *Newsweek,* Feb. 19, 1973, 78.

5 "Well, there goes": Patricia Bosworth, "Fifth Estate at the Four Seasons," *Saturday Review of the Arts* (March 1973), 7.

6 "best literary, scholarly": Mel Gussow, "Mailer Clarifies His Fifth Estate," *NYT,* Feb. 7, 1973, 45. See also John Leonard, "The Morning After," *NYTBR,* Feb. 18, 1973, 35.

6 "There was an organization": Quoted in Robins, *Alien Ink,* 334. Interview with Ellen Ray, Sept. 30, 1998.

6 "the party part": Quinn, "NM Turns 50," B7.

8 "He is our best": Pete Hamill, "The Birthday Party," *New York Post,* Feb. 7, 1973, 33.

10 "I'm older": Quinn, "NM Turns 50," B7.

10 "I didn't know what": Hodenfield, "A Party Scripted," 74.

10 "I think it's all": Quinn, "NM Turns 50," B7.

CHAPTER I: THE KING

Sources include C. Gershater, "From Lithuania to South Africa," in Gustav Sharon and Louis Holtz, eds., *The Jews in South Africa* (New York: Oxford Univ. Press, 1955); Dan Jacobson, "The Jews of South Africa: Portrait of a Flourishing Community," *Commentary* (Jan. 1963); Barbara Probst Solomon, "A Conversation with NM," *Culturefront* (Winter 1997–98); NM, "Responses and Reactions," *Commentary* (Dec. 1962); Raymond A. Sokolov, "Flying High with Mailer," *Newsweek,* Dec. 9, 1968; Brock Bower, "Never the Champion, Always the Challenger," *Life,* Sept. 24, 1965; Carole Wagner Mallory, "NM," *Elle,* Jan. 1986; Robert Begiebing, "Twelfth Round: An Interview with NM," in Lennon, *Conversations;* Marie Brenner, "Mailer Goes Egyptian," *New York,* Mar. 28, 1983; Mills, 55–57; Rollyson, 2-11; Manso, interviews with Fanny Schneider Mailer, Margaret "Osie" Radin, Arnold "Eppie" Epstein, Rhoda Lazare Wolf, Cy Rembar, Barbara Mailer Wasserman; NM, *Miami, Advertisements.*

11 Drawn by the booming economy of South Africa: For Jews in South America, see C. Gershater, "From Lithuania to South Africa," in Gustav Sharon and Louis Holtz, eds., *The Jews in South Africa* (New York: Oxford Univ. Press, 1955); Dan Jacobson, "The Jews of South Africa: Portrait of a Flourishing Community," *Commentary* (Jan. 1963), 39–44.

12 "Barney was very fond": Manso, *Mailer,* 14.

12 "My grandfather": Ibid., 13.

12 Fanny would reminisce: NM, *Miami,* 30.

14 "Fanny also told stories": Barbara Probst Solomon, "A Conversation with NM," *Culturefront* (Winter 1997–98), 40.

14 "I was a Jew": NM, "Responses and Reactions," *Commentary* (Dec. 1962), 505.

14 "He always had the highest marks": Raymond A. Sokolov, "Flying High with Mailer," *Newsweek,* Dec. 9, 1968, 86.

15 Fan gave him a little: Brock Bower, "Never the Champion, Always the Challenger," *Life*, Sept. 24, 1965, 105.

15 "He was one": NM, *Existential Errands,* 212.

15 "He was the only": Ibid., 213.

16 "the motor in the family": Carole Wagner Mallory, "NM," *Elle*, Jan. 1986, 38.

16 "My father was a terribly": Robert Begiebing, "Twelfth Round: An Interview with NM," in Lennon, *Conversations,* 316–17.

16 "They adored him": Mallory, "NM," 39.

16 "My father was an elegant": Marie Brenner, "Mailer Goes Egyptian," *New York,* Mar. 28, 1983, 35.

17 "Our father is an unusual man": Manso, *Mailer,* 64.

17 "Norman Mailer, IQ of 165": Ibid., 32.

17 "I was a physical": NM, *Advertisements,* 22.

17 "I hate going through": Manso, *Mailer,* 25.

17 Finally, Norman said: Sokolov, "Flying High," 86.

18 Later, Norman was struck: Steven Marcus, "NM: An Interview," in Lennon, *Conversations,* 28.

19 "High school went by": Begiebing, "Twelfth Round," 309.

19 "I left what part": NM, "Responses and Reactions," 505.

20 "he hated this": NM, *Armies,* 93.

20 "a fatal taint": Ibid., 153.

20 "These kids": NM, *St. George,* 33.

20 "[Lawrence's] mind": NM, *Prisoner,* 153.

CHAPTER 2: HARVARD

Sources include interviews with Myron Kaufmann (June 10, 1996), Phil Davis (July 8, 1996), Eileen Finletter (Dec. 14, 1995), Ormonde de Kaye (Apr. 3, 1996), Martin Lubin (May 8, 1996), and Fritz Jacobi (Apr. 26, 1996); Begiebing, "Twelfth Round"; 1943 Harvard *Album;* Dan Oren, *Joining the Club: A History of Jews at Yale* (New Haven: Yale, 1985); NM, "Our Man at Harvard," *Esquire,* Apr. 1977; Jeffrey L. Lant, ed., *Our Harvard: Reflections on College Life by Twenty-Two Distinguished Graduates* (New York: Taplinger, 1982); "On the Shelf," *Crimson,* Apr. 21, 1941; Bowden Broadwater, letter to the author, Mar. 11, 1996; David Thomson, "Mailer by the Bay," *California Magazine,* Aug. 1987; Mills, 38–72; Rollyson, 10–28; Manso, interviews with Richard Weinberg, Alice Adams, Norman Mailer, Seymour Breslow, George Washington Goethals, John "Jack" Maher, Fanny Schneider Mailer; NM, *Advertisements.*

22 Tuition was: Interview with Myron Kaufmann, June 10, 1996.

22 To her consternation: Begiebing, "Twelfth Round," 311.

23 It proved harder: 1943 Harvard *Album.*

23 Although in 1922: See Dan Oren, *Joining the Club: A History of Jews at Yale* (New Haven: Yale Univ. Press, 1985).

24 When classmate Myron: Begiebing, "Twelfth Round," 310.

24 The final club types: Interview with Phil Davis, July 8, 1996.

24 As Norman would discover: Interview with Ormonde de Kay, Jr., Apr. 3, 1996.

25 The boys gossiped: Ibid.

25 Beyond Phyllis Bradman: Interview with Martin Lubin, May 8, 1996.

25 "That experience": Begiebing, "Twelfth Round," 314.

25 In Brooklyn: Ibid., 311.

26 "they *were* the novel": NM, *Advertisements,* 27.

27 A classmate remembers: Interview with Fritz Jacobi, Apr. 26, 1996.

27 He chain-smoked: Interview with Phil Davis, July 8, 1996.

28 "They were beautiful": NM, "Our Man at Harvard," Esquire, Apr. 1977, 111.

28 "the *Advocate* had to be saved": Quoted in Lant, *Our Harvard,* 129.

28 "it reads like": NM, *Advertisements,* 70.

28 "Reaction is the law": "On the Shelf," *Crimson,* Apr. 21, 1941, 2.

29 "utterly refreshing": Bowden Broadwater, letter to the author, Mar. 11, 1996.

29 "Here's a kid": Interview with Fritz Jacobi, Apr. 26, 1996.

29 Ormonde de Kay remembers: Interview with Ormonde de Kay, Jr., Apr. 3, 1996.

29 "You believed him": Interview with George Richardson, Oct. 2, 1996.

30 "I wanted very much": David Thomson, "Mailer by the Bay," *California Magazine,* Aug. 1987, 66–67.

30 "He was the quintessential": Interview with Marvin Barrett, Apr. 10, 1996.

31 In the *Esquire* piece: The Pete Barton story and the Maugham story are described in NM, "Our Man at Harvard," 111–12.

34 "Do you girls fuck?": Interview with Myron Kaufmann, June 10, 1996.

34 "to a bastard": Quoted in Lant, *Our Harvard,* 145–46.

35 "He remembered the burnt body": NM, *Advertisements,* 59.

CHAPTER 3: THE ARMY

Sources include interview with Phil Davis, July 8, 1996; Brock Bower, "Never the Champion, Always the Challenger," *Life,* Sept. 24, 1965; Walter Mitgang, "Book Ends," *NYTBR,* July 1979; NM, *NYTBR,* Dec. 4, 1977; letters in Gwaltney Collection; Steven Marcus, "Interview with NM," in Lennon, *Conversations;* NM, 25th Annual Class Report, Class of '43; Mills, 75–81; Rollyson, 35–38; Manso, interviews with Clifford Makovsky, Sidney Teitell, Isadore Feldman, Emma Clara "Ecey" Gwaltney, Barbara Mailer Wasserman, NM; NM, "Introduction" to *Transit, Naked.*

36 "a young, fairly good mind": NM, *Advertisements,* 28.

36 "Malraux says": Ibid., 42.

37 "I was a little frightened": NM, *NYTBR,* Dec. 4, 1977.

38 Norman managed: Walter Mitgang, "Book Ends," *NYTBR,* July 1, 1979, 27.

38 The warmest reception: NM, "Introduction," *Transit,* ix.

38 "top banana": Manso, *Mailer,* 73.

38 "Getting married": NM to Phil Davis, Feb. 21, 1945; interview with Phil Davis, July 8, 1996.

40 "Here they are, dammit": Manso, *Mailer,* 76.

41 "muted terror": NM to Fig Gwaltney, Jan. 2, 1947; Francis Irby Gwaltney Collection, Special Collections Division, Univ. of Arkansas, Fayetteville.

42 "a hermaphrodite": NM to Phil Davis, Feb. 21, 1945; interview with Phil Davis, July 8, 1996.

42 "Going out on patrol": Brock Bower, "Never the Champion, Always the Challenger," *Life*, Sept. 24, 1965, 109.

43 One of the men: Steven Marcus, "Interview with NM," in Lennon, *Conversations*, 88.

44 "This was the happiest": NM, *Advertisements*, 125.

44 "The occupation filled me": NM, 25th Annual Class Report, Class of '43.

44 "For almost an hour": NM, *Naked*, 326–27.

45 "Whose ass did you kiss": Manso, *Mailer*, 94.

46 "To make an Army": NM, *Naked*, 176.

47 "He had been the pet": Ibid., 313.

48 "compassion for the bird": Ibid., 530.

49 "For the past century": Ibid., 321–22.

50 "atmosphere": Manso, interview with NM, 101.

CHAPTER 4: PARIS

Sources include interview with Eileen Finletter, Dec. 14, 1995; letters in Gwaltney Collection; Gay Talese, "Looking for Hemingway," in Harold Hayes, *Smiling*; Karnow, *Paris in the Fifties*; book reviews cited below; Mills, 94–102; Rollyson, 46-53; Manso, interviews with Adeline Lubell Naiman, Norman Rosten, NM, Alice Adams, Mark Linenthal, Jean Malaquais, Barbara Mailer Wasserman, Cy Rembar; NM, *Barbary Shore*.

54 "In everything he did": NM, *Barbary Shore*, 26.

56 He complained to Fig: NM to F & E Gwaltney, Jan. 5, 1948, and NM to FG, Nov. 11, 1947, Gwaltney Collection.

56 "But they were not Sad": Gay Talese, "Looking for Hemingway," in Hayes, *Smiling*, 863–64.

58 Sartre, except in early childhood: Hayman, *Sartre*, 245.

59 Mark Linenthal has told: Manso, *Mailer*, 118.

60 The forty-year-old Malaquais: Interview with Eileen Finletter, Dec. 14, 1995.

60 "In Western Europe": Quoted in Mills, *Mailer*, 98.

62 Jean's wife, Galy: NM to FG, Feb. 15 [1949].

62 "*le tout* Manhattan": Karnow, *Paris in the Fifties*, 20–21.

62 "Gee, I'm number one": See Mills, 102; Manso, interview with Barbara Mailer Wasserman, 118.

63 "With this astonishing book": Richard Match, *NYHTBR*, May 9, 1948, 3.

63 "Undoubtedly the most ambitious": David Dempsey, *NYT*, May 9, 1948, 6.

63 "I must have done something wrong": Interview with Eileen Finletter, Dec.14, 1995.

CHAPTER 5: POLITICS AND HOLLYWOOD

Sources include William A. Raidy, "Mixed Reaction to Play Doesn't Bother Author," *Staten Island Advance*, Feb. 2, 1967; letters in Gwaltney Collection; Louise Levitas, "*The Naked* Are Fanatics *and the Dead* Don't Care," in Lennon, *Conversations*; Karnow, *Paris in the Fifties*; Brightman, *Writing Dangerously*; Mills, 103–23; Rollyson, 54–64; Manso, interviews with NM, Lillian Hellman, Jean

Malaquais, Mickey Knox, Shelley Winters, Gene Kelly, Harold Hecht; NM, *Pieces and Pontifications.*

65 At Harvard, Norman: William A. Raidy, "Mixed Reaction to Play Doesn't Bother Author," *Staten Island Advance,* Feb. 2, 1967.

67 "'Go to your room'": Bea Mailer to F & E Gwaltney, Oct. 3, 1948, Gwaltney Collection.

67 More tellingly: Louise Levitas, "*The Naked* Are Fanatics *and the Dead* Don't Care," in Lennon, *Conversations,* 6.

68 "When it reaches me": Karnow, *Paris in the Fifties,* 21.

71 "I have come here": *NYT,* Mar. 27, 1949; see Brightman, *Writing Dangerously,* 324.

71 "It has to be just perfect": Manso, *Mailer,* 145.

73 In May 1949: NM to F & E Gwaltney, n.d., Tuesday [May 1949], Gwaltney Collection.

75 "What the fuck": Brando quoted in Manso, interview with Shelley Winters, 149.

75 "my pore flabby wife": Manso, *Mailer,* 146.

76 "a book which in effect": NM, *Pieces and Pontifications,* 12.

76 Love had not totally flown: NM to F & E Gwaltney, n.d. [fall 1960], Gwaltney Collection.

CHAPTER 6: ENTER ADELE

Sources include interviews with Ed Fancher, May 9, 1998 and Alfred Leslie, June 2, 1997; letters in Gwaltney Collection; April Kingsley, *The Turning Point: Abstract Expressionists and the Transformation of American Art* (New York: Simon and Schuster, 1992); Shelley Winters, *Shelley: Also Known as Shirley* (New York: William Morrow, 1980); Adele Mailer, *Last Party*; transcript, *Beverly Rentz Mailer v. Norman K. Mailer,* Barnstable Probate Court; Pete Hamill, "Kindred Spirits: Mailer and Picasso," *Art News,* Nov. 1995; Aldridge, *Lost Generation;* Macshane, *Into Eternity;* Wakefield, *New York;* Calisher, *Herself;* book reviews cited below; Mills, 127–40; Rollyson, 64–80; Manso, interviews with Norman Rosten, John Leonard, Rhoda Lazare Wolf, Ed Fancher, Adele Morales Mailer, Mickey Knox, Emma Clara "Ecey" Gwaltney, Jean Malaquais; NM, *Advertisements, Pieces and Pontifications.*

77 "Greenwich Village with clam sauce": Kingsley, *The Turning Point,* 196.

77 To friends, Norman: NM to F & E Gwaltney, n.d., Friday [1950], Gwaltney Collection.

78 They even bought a puppy: NM to F & E Gwaltney, n.d. [1950], Gwaltney Collection.

78 "Witness the problem": NM, *Barbary Shore,* 198–99.

78 It was the most: Manso, *Mailer,* 155–56.

79 "The truth is": Anthony West, *The New Yorker,* June 9, 1951.

79 "Dull, in execution": *New York Herald Tribune,* May 27, 1951, 6.

79 "At best, the result": Harry Sylvester, *NYTBR,* May 27, 1951, 5.

80 "I suppose I might": NM, *Advertisements,* 106.

80 A rather charming vignette: Winters, *Shelley,* 250–51; see Manso, *Mailer,* 141.

81 "[Bea] was a very strong": NM, *Pieces and Pontifications,* 123.

82 Norman wrote Fig: NM to F & E Gwaltney, n.d. [1951], Gwaltney Collection.

82 Later he would remark: Transcript, *Beverly Rentz Bentley Mailer v. Norman K. Mailer,* Barnstable Probate Court, No. 10942, Oct. 25, 1978, vol. 4, 84.

82 "about adventure and getting up": Manso, *Mailer,* 164.

83 Following their middle-of-the-night: NM to Fig Gwaltney, Sept. 2 [1951], Gwaltney Collection.

83 At a holiday gathering: NM to F & E Gwaltney, Jan. 5, 1954, Gwaltney Collection.

83 The Gwaltneys chose: See NM to F & E Gwaltney, Thursday, May 17 [1951], Gwaltney Collection. Bea apparently made a dramatic entrance at one of Norman and Adele's parties.

84 "I don't need this": Manso, *Mailer,* 171.

84 "It was the postwar world": Winters, *Shelley,* 195.

85 At one rather dull gathering: Adele Mailer, *Last Party,* 89–92, 136–37.

85 Adele knew best: Pete Hamill, "Kindred Spirits: Mailer and Picasso," *Art News,* Nov. 1995, 209; see also Kingsley, *Turning Point.*

86 "the social changes": Aldridge, *Lost Generation,* 239.

87 "I remember when I read": Macshane, *Into Eternity,* 146.

87 "Here we are, the three best writers": Ibid., 122.

88 Norman recalls the group: Wakefield, *New York,* 129.

88 "Word had been passed": Calisher, *Herself,* 93–94.

89 "I decided I was going": Adele Mailer, *Last Party,* 135.

89 Jealousy carried things: Ibid., 327.

90 There had been an altercation: Interview with Alfred Leslie, June 2, 1997.

CHAPTER 7: THE DEER PARK

Sources include interviews with Norman Podhoretz (Apr. 17, 1996) and Michael C. D. Macdonald (May 1, 1998); letters in Gwaltney Collection; Bloom, *Prodigal Sons;* Adele Mailer, *Last Party;* Leslie Fiedler, "The Novel in the Post-Political World," *Partisan Review* (Summer 1956); "Our Country and Our Culture: A Symposium," *Partisan Review* (May–June 1952); Podhoretz, *Making It;* book reviews cited below; Mills, 141–53; Rollyson, 80–98; Manso, interviews with Edith Begner, John Aldridge, Adele Morales Mailer, William Phillips, Mickey Knox; NM, *Advertisements, Existential Errands.*

91 "the deadest winter": NM, *Advertisements,* 186, 154.

91 "one would have to win": Ibid., 154.

92 "a sadness": Ibid., 108.

93 In a fall 1951 letter: NM to F & E Gwaltney, n.d. [fall 1951], Gwaltney Collection.

93 Much later, in the 1960s: See Bloom, *Prodigal Son,* 263–64.

94 One of the few comments: Interview with Norman Podhoretz, Apr. 17, 1996.

94 "We grew up": Leslie Fiedler, "The Novel in the Post-Political World," *Partisan Review* (Summer 1956), 358.

95 "Until little more": "Our Country and Our Culture: A Symposium," *Partisan Review* (May-June 1952), 282–84.

95 "I think I ought": NM, *Advertisements,* 188–90.

96   "I cannot understand why": Sidney Hook, "Our Country and Our Culture," *Partisan Review* (Sept.-Oct. 1952), 569, 574.

97   "What a dreary compromise": NM, *Advertisements,* 185.

97   "At least I was out": Ibid., 154–55.

98   "sex was time": NM, *Deer Park,* 319.

98   "were brought the most beautiful": NM, *Advertisements,* 176.

98   By the end of the summer: NM to F & E Gwaltney, Sept. 2 [1953], Gwaltney Collection.

99   "There was nothing": Podhoretz, *Making It,* 146–47.

100 Macdonald, who never swore: Interview with Michael C. D. Macdonald, May 1, 1998.

101 "Mary-Jane, at least": NM, *Advertisements,* 278.

102 "Most of the time": Ibid., 228.

102 His sister, Barbara: NM to F & E Gwaltney, n.d. [July 1953], Gwaltney Collection.

103 "the finality of the ritual": NM, *Existential Errands,* 40.

103 "In Mexico, pot gave me": NM, *Advertisements,* 232.

104 "I realized in some bottom": Ibid., 232–33.

104 "I don't like": Ibid., 230.

104 "I had never had any sense": Ibid., 232.

105 "I could at last": Ibid., 235.

106 "I was forced": Ibid., 238.

106 "In this book Mailer": Malcolm Cowley, *NYHTBR,* Oct. 23, 1955, 5.

106 "It is studded": John Brooks, *NYTBR,* Oct. 16, 1955, 5.

106 "Norman Mailer has established": William Hogan, *San Francisco Chronicle,* Oct. 13, 1955, 23.

107 "something broke in me": NM, *Advertisements,* 234.

CHAPTER 8: HIP

Sources include interviews with Michael C. D. Macdonald (May 1, 1998), Jerry Tallmer (June 10, 1998), and Ed Fancher (May 9 and June 10, 1998); McAuliffe, *Great American Newspaper;* Wakefield, *New York;* Adele Mailer, *Last Party;* Hendrick, *To Reach Eternity;* Rodman, *Tongues;* James Baldwin, "The Black Boy Looks at the White Boy," in *Nobody Knows;* Mills, 163–78; Rollyson, 99–107, 105–7; Manso, interviews with Mickey Knox, Dr. Jack Begner, Ed Fancher, Jerry Tallmer, Rhoda Lazare Wolf; NM, *Advertisements.*

108 The furniture took: NM to F & E Gwaltney, Feb. 4, 1955, Gwaltney Collection.

109 Dwight Macdonald asked him: Interview with Michael C. D. Macdonald, May 1, 1998.

109 "It occurs to me now": NM, *Advertisements,* 266–67.

110 "At heart, I wanted": Ibid., 277.

111 Aside from the *Villager:* McAuliffe, *Great American Newspaper,* 11. For the early days of the *Voice,* I have relied in part on interviews with Ed Fancher, May 9 and June 10, 1998, and an interview with Jerry Tallmer, June 10, 1998.

111 "I had the feeling": NM, *Advertisements,* 278.

112 "With marijuana for analyst": Ibid., 283.

112 "frustrated in your ambitions": Ibid., 279.

113 "The artist [is] a rebel": Ibid., 302, 313.

114 "the act of rape": Ibid., 314.

114 "a fine novelistic education": Ibid., 319.

115 "Norman, you're acting": Interview with Jerry Tallmer, June 10, 1998.

115 Norman would hold on: Transcript, *Beverly Rentz Bentley Mailer v. Norman K. Mailer*, Barnstable Probate Court, No. 10942, Oct. 25, 1978, vol. 4, 74.

115 "Nobody's gonna": Manso, *Mailer*, 221.

117 "I mean, Shago's a *stud*": NM, *American Dream*, 120–21.

118 He and Adele were guests: Wakefield, *New York*, 112.

118 "opens up new sexual ground": James Jones to Robert Cantwell, Sept. 3, 1955, quoted in Hendrick, *To Reach Eternity*, 227.

119 "As far as I'm concerned": James Jones to NM, Mar. 31, 1956, quoted in Hendrik, *To Reach Eternity*, 242–43.

120 "My answer to my Women's": Rodman, *Tongues*, 177.

121 "It is still true": James Baldwin, "The Black Boy Looks at the White Boy," in *Nobody Knows My Name*, 217–18.

122 "Negro jazz musicians": Ibid., 221.

122 "confident, boastful": Ibid., 220.

CHAPTER 9: "THE WHITE NEGRO"

Sources include interview with Ned Polsky, Apr. 17, 1996; Norman Podhoretz, "The Know-Nothing Bohemians," *Partisan Review* (Spring 1958); Michael C. D. Macdonald, "My Father, Dwight"; Adele Mailer, *Last Party;* Tim Page, ed., *The Diaries of Dawn Powell, 1931–1965* (South Royalton, Vt.: Steerforth, 1995); West, *William Styron;* Mills, 179–92; Rollyson, 99–105; Manso, interviews with Adele Morales Mailer, Maria Irene Fornes, John Aldridge, Chandler Brossard, Nat Halper, Sol Stein, Frank Corsaro, Allen Ginsberg, Michael McClure, Diana Trilling, Irving Howe; NM, *Advertisements*.

123 "the city was not alive": NM, *Advertisements*, 331.

124 Instead, they installed: Adele Mailer, *Last Party*, 240.

125 The critic Ned Halper: See Manso, *Mailer*, 247.

125 "At times it would": NM, *Advertisements*, 332.

126 "Everybody . . . knows": Ibid., 332–33.

126 "I'm a bit surprised": Ibid., 333.

127 "Like a latent image": Ibid., 335.

127 "other people's habits": Ibid., 339.

128 "So there was a new breed": Ibid., 341.

129 "It can of course": Ibid., 347.

130 "the only Hip morality": Ibid., 354.

131 "one of the most morally gruesome": Norman Podhoretz, "The Know-Nothing Bohemians," *Partisan Review* (Spring 1958), 318.

132 "You must be crazy!": Michael C. D. Macdonald, "My Father, Dwight," unpublished ms., 27.

133 "Now, what about": Manso, *Mailer*, 262.

133 "Norman Mailer (in Bridgewater)": Tim Page, ed., *The Diaries of Dawn Powell, 1931–1965* (South Royalton, Vt.: Steerforth Press, 1995).

134 Jones wasn't amused: See Manso, *Mailer*, 239.

134 "So I tell you this": Quoted in West, *William Styron*, 293.

CHAPTER 10: LITERARY POLITICIAN

Sources include Adele Mailer, *Last Party;* Howe, *Margin of Hope;* Plimpton, *Shadow Box;* Vidal, *Palimpsest;* Baldwin, "The Black Boy Looks at the White Boy," in *Nobody Knows;* Macshane, *Into Eternity;* Gingrich, *Nothing But People;* Merrill, *Esky;* Polsgrove, *It Wasn't Pretty;* NM interview with Brian Lamb; Mills, 193–211; Rollyson, 127–28, 131–35; Manso, interviews with Allen Ginsberg, Tuli Kupferberg, Maria Irene Fornes, Gloria Jones, Mickey Knox, Roger Donoghue, Clay Felker, NM; NM, *Advertisements, Presidential Papers.*

137 Adele thought the new apartment: Adele Mailer, *Last Party,* 286.
137 "He had a certain gallantry": Howe, *Margin of Hope,* 316–17.
138 "At cocktail parties": Plimpton, *Shadow Box,* 261–62.
138 Once, when Norman was driving: Vidal, *Palimpsest,* 262; see also 232–33.
140 The older writer: See Manso, *Mailer,* 276–77.
142 "The way to save": NM, *Advertisements,* 21, 17.
142 "he knew in advance": Ibid., 20, 22.
144 "too charming a writer": Ibid., 471–72.
145 "the prettiest novel": Ibid., 464–65.
145 "in a kind of drunken": Baldwin, "The Black Boy Looks at the White Boy," in *Nobody Knows My Name,* 185.
145 "the authority of print": Macshane, *Into Eternity,* 208.
145 Baldwin's first reaction: Baldwin, "Black Boy," 186.
147 "Mailer is forever shouting": Vidal, review, *The Nation,* Jan. 2, 1960, 13.
147 "I wanted to declare myself": Manso, *Mailer,* 274.
147 "a record of an artistic crackup": unsigned review, *Time,* Dec. 5, 1960, 16.
147 "frittering away his time": Granville Hicks, *Saturday Review of Literature,* Nov. 7, 1959, 18.
147 "considerable literary talent": Charles Rolo, *Atlantic Monthly,* Dec. 1959, 166.
147 "Norman Mailer shows": Harry T. Moore, *NYT,* Nov. 1, 1959, 4.
149 "Mailer's earnestness": Gingrich, *Nothing but People,* 302.
149 "hottest magazine": Merrill, *Esky,* 147–48.
150 "the deep orange-brown": NM, *Presidential Papers,* 38.
150 "were not trifling": Ibid., 26.
150 Norman prepared himself: NM, interview with Brian Lamb, n.d. [1995].
151 "the life of bad banquet": NM, *Presidential Papers,* 28–49 passim.
152 "This isn't writing": Quoted in Polsgrove, *It Wasn't Pretty,* 46.
153 "It went through journalism": Ibid., 47.
153 "had more effect": NM, *Presidential Papers,* 60.
153 "At bottom I had": Ibid., 89.

CHAPTER 11: BEYOND THE LAW

Sources include interviews with Barney Rosset (Oct. 18, 1995), Alfred Leslie (June 2, 1997), Harriet Sohmers Zwerdling (June 20, 1998), Bill Ward (June 26, 1998), Lina Delano (Oct. 9, 1997), Lenny Green (Mar. 19, 1998), Eileen Finletter (Dec. 14, 1995), and Michael C. D. Macdonald (May 1, 1998); Wrezin, *Rebel;* Michael C. D. Macdonald, "My Father, Dwight"; Adele Mailer, *Last Party;* Dwight Macdonald,

"Massachusetts vs. Mailer," *New Yorker,* Oct. 8, 1960; Libby Newsom Mohr, letter to the editor, *Brown Alumni Monthly,* Dec. 1995; Atlas, *Delmore Schwartz;* Brock Bower, "Never the Champion, Always the Challenger," *Life,* Sept. 24, 1965; Vidal, *Palimpsest;* letters in Gwaltney Collection; Marie Brenner, "Mailer Goes Egyptian," *New York,* Mar. 28, 1983; Ruas, "NM" in *Conversations;* James Atlas, "Life with Mailer," *NYT Magazine,* Sept. 9, 1979; newspaper stories cited below; Mills, 215–32; Rollyson, 135–44; Manso, interviews with Art d'Lugoff, H. L. "Doc" Humes, George Plimpton, Allen Ginsberg, Larry Alson, Fay Donoghue, Mickey Knox, Midge Decter, Norman Podhoretz, Seymour Krim, Diana Trilling; NM, *Presidential Papers, Deaths.*

155 "a gang of post-Beat": Quoted in Mills, *Mailer,* 196.

155 Participants remember: Interview with Alfred Leslie, June 2, 1997; interview with Harriet Sohmers Zwerdling, June 20, 1998; interview with Bill Ward, June 26, 1998; interview with Lina Delano, Oct. 9, 1997; interview with Lenny Green, Mar. 19, 1998.

156 The Cape tradition: Wrezin, *Rebel,* 181; Michael C. D. Macdonald, "My Father, Dwight," unpublished ms., 34.

156 One was that the Macdonalds: Adele Mailer, *Last Party,* 130–31.

156 Dwight Macdonald's son: Interview with Michael C. D. Macdonald, May 1, 1998.

156 Adele was then dancing: Adele Mailer, *Last Party,* 318.

157 On June 9: Dwight Macdonald, "Massachusetts vs. Mailer," *New Yorker,* Oct. 8, 1960, 154–66.

158 "Nineteen fifty-nine–sixty": Manso, *Mailer,* 281.

159 After a few drinks: "NM in Tiff," *NYT,* Nov. 15, 1960, 28.

160 "for sending the wind": NM, *Presidential Papers,* 69.

161 One afternoon his adored: Adele Mailer, *Last Party,* 340–41.

161 In mid-November: Libby Newsom Mohr, letter to the editor, *Brown Alumni Monthly,* Dec. 1995.

162 "It's been quite apparent": Leonard Lyons, "The Lyons Den," *New York Post,* Nov. 23, 1960, 27. Delmore Schwartz believed Mailer was trying to embarrass him by inviting him to a party at which he stabbed his wife. See Atlas, *Delmore Schwartz,* 336.

163 Adele was holed up: Interview with Harriet Sohmers Zwerdling, June 20, 1998. Adele Mailer maintains she was closeted with a woman named Louise; *Last Party,* 348.

163 "Aja, toro, aja!": Ibid., 349.

165 Fay offered: See Manso, *Mailer,* 321.

165 Amazingly enough, Norman appeared: "NM Sent to Bellevue over His Protest in Wife Killing," *NYT,* Nov. 23, 1960, 26.

165 "You see, the sword's": See Fern Marja Echman, "Mailer's Day in Court," *New York Post,* Nov. 23, 1960, 5.

165 "for personal reasons": Manso, *Mailer,* 322.

166 "In my opinion": Quoted in Manso, *Mailer,* 316.

166 "Naturally I have been": "NM Sent to Bellevue over Protest in Wife Killing," *NYT,* Nov. 23, 1960, 26.

166 "If you put me": Quoted in Manso, *Mailer,* 327.

166 "The awful thing": Brock Bower, "Never the Champion, Always the Challenger," *Life,* Sept. 24, 1965, 95.

166 "I was really in danger": Vidal, *Palimpsest*, 262.

167 "I gamble on human beings": Jerry Tallmer, "NM, Playwright," *New York Post Magazine*, Feb. 11, 1967, 26.

167 "He came at me": "Cocktail Party: The Savage Ending," *Newsweek*, Dec. 5, 1960, 33.

167 "I have no complaint": "No Mailer Complaint," *NYT*, Dec. 22, 1960, 12.

167 "were perfectly happy": "Grand Jury Gets Mailer Stabbing," *NYT*, Jan. 13, 1961, 58.

167 Later, Adele would say: Adele Mailer, *Last Party*, 368.

167 "After various continuances": "NM Goes Free in Knifing Case," *NYT*, Nov. 14, 1961, 45.

168 "Letter written in psycho": Manso, *Mailer*, 329; see NM to F & E Gwaltney, n.d. [Dec. 1960], Gwaltney Collection.

168 "What a tragedy!": Interview with Eileen Finletter, Dec. 14, 1995.

168 "A week or two after": Marie Brenner, "Mailer Goes Egyptian," *New York*, Mar. 28, 1983, 32–33.

169 "to relieve her": Larry Alson, quoted in Manso, *Mailer*, 319.

169 "So long": NM, *Deaths*, n.p.

170 Much later, he would tell: Ruas, "NM," 27.

170 "The man wasn't good": NM, *Presidential Papers*, 64.

170 "A decade's anger": James Atlas, "Life with Mailer, " *NYT Magazine*, Sept. 9, 1979, 94.

CHAPTER 12: THE NEW JOURNALIST

Sources include interview with Bill Ward, June 26, 1998; Adele Mailer, *Last Party*; Schumacher, *Dharma Lion*; Anne Chisholm and Michael Davie, *Lord Beaverbook: A Life* (New York: Knopf, 1993); letters in Gwaltney Collection; Polsgrove, *It Wasn't Pretty*; Brightman, *Writing Dangerously*; Hayes, *Smiling*; "Mailer Debates William Buckley; Chicago Political Bout a Draw," *NYT*, Sept. 24, 1962; Conrad, *Dear Muffo*; Weatherby, *Baldwin*; Robins, *Alien Ink*; Liebling, *Neutral Corner*; Mills, 233–61; Rollyson, 144–52; Manso, interviews with Fay Donoghue, Midge Decter, Anne Barry, Harold Hayes, Harold Conrad, Pete Hamill, Cus D'Amato, NM; NM, *Prisoner, Fire on the Moon, Presidential Papers, Existential Errands*.

171 "I told myself": Adele Mailer, *Last Party*, 366–67.

171 Gore Vidal, then living: Vidal, *Palimpsest*, 262.

171 "It was . . . a period": NM, *Existential Errands*, 200.

172 "The world's worst": Quoted in Schumacher, *Dharma Lion*, 935.

172 "For all the awful things": Anne Chisholm and Michael Davie, *Lord Beaverbook: A Life* (New York: Knopf, 1993), 316.

173 "There had been a period": NM, *Prisoner*, 13.

174 "She wouldn't take shit": Interview with Bill Ward, June 26, 1998.

174 "dear pudding": NM, *Prisoner*, 14.

175 "I have been brave": NM, *Deaths*, n.p.

175 "Hemingway constituted": NM, *Fire on the Moon*, 3–4.

176 Norman, writing to Fig: NM to Fig Gwaltney, July 30, 1962, Gwaltney Collection.

176 "As I was saying good-bye": Chisholm and Davie, *Beaverbrook*, 488–89.

177 Perhaps the stabbing: Adele Mailer, *Last Party*, 371.

177 "the magazine should kiss": Polsgrove, *It Wasn't Pretty*, 66.

178 "What we needed": NM, *Presidential Papers*, 95.

179 "The ultimate direction": Ibid., 141, 261.

179 "out of a reaction": Hayes, *Smiling*, xviii.

180 "so much of one man's": Polsgrove, *It Wasn't Pretty*, 67.

181 "the number of lunatics": Brightman, *Writing Dangerously*, 476.

181 "When people are effectively": Morgan, *Literary Outlaw*, 337.

181 "is all of a piece": NM, *Existential Errands*, 262.

182 "One has to enter": Morgan, *Literary Outlaw*, 339.

182 "You're the regent": Brightman, *Writing Dangerously*, 478.

183 "between a conservative and a hipster": "Mailer Debates William Buckley; Chicago Political Bout a Draw," *NYT*, Sept. 24; 1962, 31.

183 "I had honed": NM, *Presidential Papers*, 257.

184 "Mister Buckley": Conrad, *Dear Muffo*, 157.

184 "one of the last great": Manso, *Mailer*, 356.

184 "a pretty definitive fight": Weatherby, *Baldwin*, 222.

185 "Liston was Faust": NM, *Presidential Papers*, 242.

185 "I had noticed": Ibid., 238, 237.

185 "At one moment, I did get": Robins, *Alien Ink*, 331.

186 "had rooted for Floyd": NM, *Presidential Papers*, 258.

187 "I'm not a newspaper writer": Liebling, "The Morest," in *A Neutral Corner*, 190.

188 "is like the odor": NM, *Presidential Papers*, 217.

CHAPTER 13: CHANGING PARTNERS

Sources include interviews with BB (Dec. 3, 5, and 7, 1998 and Jan. 9, 1999) and Norman Podhoretz (Apr. 17, 1996); NM interview with Oriana Fallaci, *Writers Digest*, Dec. 1969; Stern, *Steinem*; Krassner, *Confessions*, Mary Hemingway, *How It Was*; Jennifer Hagar, "BB: A Life in the Theater of Our Times," *P'Town Women*, 1998; letters in Gwaltney Collection; Adele Mailer, *Last Party*; book reviews cited below; Mills, 261–62; Rollyson, 153–61; Manso, interviews with Anne Barry, Norman Podhoretz, Paul Krassner, Sandy Charlebois Thomas, Alice Adams; NM, *Existential Errands, Cannibals*.

190 "I like to marry": Interview with Oriana Fallaci, *Writers Digest*, Dec. 1969, 47.

190 Anne Barry wrote: Manso, *Mailer*, 364.

190 "Great," Norman said: Stern, *Steinem*, 173–74.

191 With obvious enjoyment: See Krassner, *Confessions*, 87–89; he leaves the legality of their marriage ambiguous.

192 He pestered Podhoretz: Interview with Norman Podhoretz, Apr. 17, 1996.

192 "a bunch of crazy": Ibid.

193 Born in Atlanta: For Beverly's history, see Hagar, "BB: A Life in the Theater of Our Times," *P'town Women*, 40–46; interviews with BB, Dec. 3, 5, and 7, 1998.

194 Mary Hemingway: Mary Hemingway, *How It Was,* 472.

195 The first time she tried: Interview with BB, Dec. 3, 1998.

195 While at the Gwaltneys': FG to NM and BB, July 16, 1963, Gwaltney Collection.

196 "Because I changed": Interview with BB, Dec. 3, 1998.

197 Adele believes: Adele Mailer, *Last Party,* 290. Adele claims they saw Bruce arrested, but Max Gordon, owner of the Vanguard, says Bruce was taped by the police there and otherwise harassed; see Max Gordon, *Live at the Village Vanguard,* 78.

197 "Gore, admit it": NM, *Existential Errands,* 104–5.

198 "the mystical side": NM, *Cannibals,* 113.

198 "a bad novel": Ibid., 110, 111–12.

200 "The President suffers": NM, *Presidential Papers,* 1, 7.

200 "juvenile delinquents": Ibid., 15, 22.

201 "I have dealt": John Kenneth Galbraith, review, *NYTBR,* Nov. 17, 1963, 6.

201 "Half the time": Emile Capouya, *Saturday Review,* Nov. 16, 1963, 37.

202 "What Norman Mailer is doing": Richard Kluger, *Book Week,* Nov. 10, 1963, 4.

CHAPTER 14: A GAMBLE AND A NEW DIRECTION

Sources include interviews with Nick Proferes (Jan. 26, 1996) and Carl Oglesby (Oct. 26, 1998); letters in Gwaltney Collection; Brock Bower, "Never the Champion, Always the Challenger," *Life,* Sept. 24, 1965; book reviews cited below; Mills, 275–87; Rollyson, 161–80; Manso, interviews with Anne Barry, Richard Baron, NM, E. L. Doctorow, José Torres; NM, *American Dream, Cannibals.*

204 He compared the process: NM to Fig Gwaltney, Dec. 20, 1963, Gwaltney Collection.

207 "like he'd been painted": NM, *American Dream,* 165, 97.

208 "that corporate rubbery obstruction": Ibid., 122.

209 "One thing was certain": NM, *Cannibals,* 40–41.

209 "You get *this,* baby": Ibid., 41.

210 "Dad, you're too much": Ibid., 45.

210 Norman was unabashedly proud: Bower, "Never the Champion," 96.

211 "Everyone admired him": Interview with Nick Proferes, Jan. 26, 1996.

211 "totalitarian": NM, *Cannibals,* 51.

212 Carl Oglesby, then president: Interview with Carl Oglesby, Oct. 26, 1998.

213 "our present situation": NM, *Cannibals,* 71, 77–78, 80, 81–82.

214 "If one believes": Granville Hicks, review, *Saturday Review,* Mar. 20, 1965, 23.

214 "Mailer wanted to make money": *Best Sellers,* Mar. 16, 1965, 481.

214 Tom Wolfe, writing: Tom Wolfe, *NYHTBR,* Mar. 14, 1965, 1.

214 "false consciousness": Philip Rahv, *NYRB,* Mar. 25, 1965.

215 "alone . . . in having created": Richard Poirier, review, *Commentary,* June 1965, 91.

215 "This sounds like a ride": review, *Time,* Mar. 19, 1965, 112.

CHAPTER 15: PROJECTS

Sources include interviews with BB, Dec. 3 and 7, 1998; Diana Maychick, "Mailer's 'Deer Park' To Be Film," *New York Post*, Oct. 16, 1984; letters in Gwaltney Collection; Plimpton, *Truman Capote*; Burroughs, preface to *Naked Lunch*; play and book reviews cited below; Mills, 294–307; Rollyson, 190–98; Manso, interviews with Charlie Brown, Sandy Charlebois Thomas, Midge Decter, Diana Trilling, Bernard "Buzz" Farbar, Rip Torn, Walter Minton; NM, *Cannibals, Existential Errands, Vietnam, Armies.*

216 "Edwardian": Manso, *Mailer,* 422.
217 "rebuild the entire urban": NM, *Cannibals,* 233, 235.
217 At the quotidian: See Manso, *Mailer,* 418–19.
218 "It was a bitch": Interview with BB, Dec. 3, 1998.
218 "We do not think": NM, *Cannibals,* 83.
219 "Three cheers, lads": Ibid., 84, 87.
219 "Unless Vietnam": Ibid., 90.
220 "pretentious": Michael Smith, "Theatre Journal," *Village Voice,* Feb. 9, 1967.
221 "Mr. Mailer may have": Edith Oliver, review, *New Yorker,* Feb. 11, 1967, 116.
221 he would attempt to revive it: Diana Maychick, "Mailer's 'Deer Park' to Be Film," *New York Post,* Oct. 16, 1984, 51.
221 "We were a hit": NM, *Existential Errands,* 69.
221 The play remained a favorite: Maychick, 51.
221 "It was by now": NM, *Existential Errands,* 65.
222 "I don't tell you": Interview with BB, Dec. 7, 1998.
222 Norman tried to get: NM to Fig Gwaltney, July 11, 1964, Gwaltney Collection.
222 Fan would send: Interview with BB, Dec. 3, 1998.
223 Beverly's stepbrother has spoken: Manso, *Mailer,* 423.
223 "dirty gabardine raincoat": Plimpton, *Capote,* 276–78.
224 "contains happenings": NM, *Cannibals,* 2, 1.
226 "There are sure to be": J. H. Aldridge, review, *Commentary,* Oct. 1966, 131.
226 "It takes a strong stomach": review, *Newsweek,* Aug. 29, 1966, 63.
226 "[*Naked Lunch*] has great importance": Burroughs, *Naked Lunch,* xv. The Grove Black Cat paperback edition includes testimony from the Massachusetts trial.
227 "Sometimes I think": *NYTBR,* Sept. 17, 1967, 4.
227 "Go out and kill": NM, *Vietnam,* 219, 224.
228 "By gum, man": Ibid., 6–7.
228 "he had kicked": NM, *Armies,* 62.
229 Mailer attributed it: Ibid.
229 "as American as cherry pie": Eliot Fremont-Smith, review, *NYT,* Aug. 4, 1967, 37.

CHAPTER 16: THE ARMIES OF THE NIGHT

Sources include interviews with Nick Proferes (Jan. 26, 1996), Donn Pennebaker (Jan. 10, 1996), Barney Rosset (Oct. 18, 1995), and Lenny Green (Mar. 19, 1998); Leticia Kent, "NM Speaks: Films vs. Plays," *Vogue,* Sept. 1, 1972; NM, "Some Dirt in the Talk: A Candid History of an Experimental Film Called *Wild 90*," *Esquire,*

Dec. 1967; Michael C. D. Macdonald, "My Father, Dwight"; Joseph Gelmis, "NM," in Lennon, *Conversations;* "Mailer of the Movies," *NY Post,* Jan. 9, 1989; "When Irish Eyes Are Smiling, It's Norman Mailer," *NYT,* Oct. 27, 1968; Miller, *Democracy;* Suzanne Fields, "Guess Who Came to the 1967 Vietnam War Protest Dinner?" *Insight on the News,* May 15, 1995; Hamilton, *Robert Lowell;* film reviews cited below; Mills, 301–2, 307–25; Rollyson, 198–206; Manso, interviews with D. A. Pennebaker, Jonas Mekas, Jerry Rubin, Edward deGrazia, Tuli Kupferberg, Midge Decter; NM, *Armies.*

230 Scott Meredith went to Dick Baron: Details of contract supplied by Mills, *Mailer,* 301–2.

231 "Jesus, isn't it a shame": Interview with Nick Proferes, Jan. 26, 1996.

232 "that an uncut piece": Leticia Kent, "NM Speaks: Films vs. Plays," *Vogue,* Sept. 1, 1972, 200.

232 "He thought [the films]": Interview with Donn Pennebaker, Jan. 10, 1996.

232 The film was to be shot: NM, "Some Dirt in the Talk: A Candid History of an Experimental Film called *Wild 90,*" *Esquire,* Dec. 1967.

233 A German shepherd: Macdonald, "My Father, Dwight," 176.

233 "You got three guys": Vincent Canby, "When Irish Eyes Are Smiling, It's Norman Mailer," *NYT,* Oct. 27, 1968, II, 15.

234 Some unidentified women: Interview with Nick Proferes, Jan. 26, 1996.

234 Eventually Norman sold: Interview with Barney Rosset, Oct. 18, 1995.

234 "so much better": R. A., "Beyond the Law," *NYT,* Oct. 24, 1968, 55.

234 "the self-styled Prince of Bourbon": Vincent Canby, "NM Offers Beyond the Law," *NYT,* Sept. 30, 1968, 60.

234 "a real course in filmmaking": Interview with Donn Pennebaker, Jan. 10, 1996.

235 "But making a film": Joseph Gelmis, "NM," in Lennon, *Conversations,* 161.

236 "There was no leadership": See Miller, "Democracy," 282.

237 Government assembled its powers: See ibid., 281–82, and NM, *Armies,* 246–73, for descriptions of the planning of the march.

237 Later that evening: See Suzanne Fields, "Guess Who Came to the 1967 Vietnam War Protest Dinner?" *Insight on the News,* May 15, 1995, 40; see Hamilton, *Lowell,* 363–68, for details of Lowell's involvement in the march.

238 "Now we may leave": NM, *Armies,* 13–14.

238 "He had piped up": Ibid., 72.

238 "No dean at Harvard": Ibid., 83.

241 "Today is Sunday": Ibid., 238–39.

241 "there was a sweet": Ibid., 237, 240.

243 "his habit of living": Ibid., 183, 193.

244 "They would never have looked": Ibid., 110.

245 "enmeshed in these unmanageable": Ibid., 217.

245 "felt a liberation": Ibid., 238.

CHAPTER 17: 1968

Sources include interviews with Norman Podhoretz (Apr. 17, 1996), Donn Pennebaker (Jan. 10, 1996), and Nick Proferes (Jan. 26, 1996); book reviews cited below; "National Book Awards: The Winners," *NYT,* Apr. 11, 1969; Podhoretz, *Making It;*

Nobile, *Intellectual Skywriting;* Mills, 313–36; Rollyson, 207–16; Manso, interviews with Norman Podhoretz, NM, D. A. Pennebaker, Barney Rosset, Michael McClure, Sandy Charlebois Thomas, Tom Quinn, Eugene McCarthy; NM, *Maidstone, Miami.*

247 "I believe that it": Alfred Kazin, review, *NYTBR,* May 5, 1968, 1.

247 "a permanent contribution": Alan Trachtenberg, review, *Nation,* May 27, 1968, 601.

247 "Mr. Mailer's autobiography": Conor Cruise O'Brien, review, *NYRB,* June 29, 1968, 16.

248 The entire public: Richard Gilman, review, *New Republic,* June 8, 1968, 27.

248 "There's something about": "National Book Awards: The Winners," *NYT,* Apr. 11, 1969.

248 "a frank, Mailer-like bid": Podhoretz, *Making It,* 356.

249 "change his mind": Interview with Norman Podhoretz, Apr. 17, 1996.

250 the *NYRB,* in August 1967, put a Molotov cocktail: See Nobile, *Intellectual Skywriting,* 50.

250 "then my dire rival": Manso, *Mailer,* 475.

251 "some kind of psychotic pigout": Ibid., 484.

252 As Norman was strolling: NM, *Maidstone,* 121, 124.

252 "a fight to give him": NM, "A Course in Filmmaking," in *Maidstone,* 140.

252 "[The film] was just": Interview with Donn Pennebaker, Jan. 10, 1996.

253 "obliged, but treated it": Interview with Nick Proferes, Jan. 26, 1996.

253 "The whole old boy": Interview with Donn Pennebaker, Jan. 10, 1996.

254 "The air had been better": NM, *Miami,* 18, 42.

254 "He had no idea": Ibid., 82.

254 "the great American city": Ibid., 85.

255 "the Yippies might yet": Ibid., 187, 188.

255 "write good, baby": Ibid., 190.

256 "total failure": Ibid., 197, 199.

256 "Perhaps he was too old": Ibid., 214.

256 "curious double-bust": Ibid., 222.

257 "Eldridge at least": Ibid., 223.

257 "[did] not seek any resolution": C. T. Samuels, *Book World,* Nov. 3, 1968, 3.

257 "a far more thoughtful book": Peter Shaw, review, *Commentary,* Dec. 1968, 93.

257 "[Mailer] was out there": Wilfred Sheed, review, *NYTBR,* Dec. 8, 1968, 3.

CHAPTER 18: THE CANDIDATE

Sources include interviews with Dave Oates (Nov. 5, 1997), BB (Dec. 5, 1998); and Michael C. D. Macdonald (May 1, 1998); Michael C. D. Macdonald, "Lord of the Flies"; "Mailer — Eastern Seaboard Exotic": *Time,* Oct. 11, 1968; Flaherty, *Managing Mailer;* Michael C.D. Macdonald, "My Father, Dwight"; Manso, ed., *Running Against the Machine;* Gloria Steinem, "The Making and Unmaking of a Controller," *New York,* May 5, 1969; Jimmy Breslin, "I Run to Win," *New York,* May 5, 1969; Gloria Steinem, "The Kafka Effect," *New York,* May 19, 1968; newspaper stories cited below; Mills, 337–45; Rollyson, 221–30; Manso, interviews with Clay Felker, Joe Flaherty, Tom Quinn, Gloria Steinem; NM, *Prisoner, Fire on the Moon.*

259 "Mailer — Eastern seaboard exotic": *Time,* Oct. 11, 1968, 81.

260 The idea of running: Macdonald, "Casting Flies," unpublished ms., 169.

260 "Hitler/Stalin pact": Flaherty, *Managing Mailer,* 11, 16.

261 "reason with Achilles": Macdonald, "My Father, Dwight," unpublished ms., 169.

262 "not an option": Manso, *Running,* 175. This compendium, together with Flaherty's book, is the best source for Mailer's campaign. See also Gloria Steinem, "The Making and Unmaking of a Controller," *New York,* May 5, 1969, 8–9; Jimmy Breslin, "I Run to Win" in the same issue, 42–44; and Gloria Steinem, "The Kafka Effect," *New York,* May 19, 1968, 8–9.

262 "New York City is today": Manso, *Running,* 9.

263 "on the first hot day": Flaherty, *Managing Mailer,* 45.

264 "You conservatives are right": Manso, *Running,* 45.

264 "At least the novelist": "Mailer vs. Breslin," *NYT,* May 3, 1969, 39.

264 "I think I've finally": Manso, *Running,* 55.

265 "Their platform": Interview with Dave Oates, Nov. 5, 1997.

265 "Mailer took the stage": Manso, *Running,* 109.

265 "young, obscene": Flaherty, *Managing Mailer,* 63, 56.

266 "the hottest May": NM, *Fire on the Moon,* 5.

266 "performed a Stanislavskian miracle": Flaherty, *Managing Mailer,* 97–98.

266 "Now look, look": The speech is reprinted in full in Flaherty, *Managing Mailer,* 98–104, and Manso, *Running,* 59–64.

267 "The next day everything": Flaherty, *Managing Mailer,* 105.

267 "I walked out": Interview with Dave Oates, Nov. 5, 1997.

267 A reporter noted: William E. Farrell, "Mailer Touts 'Mayoral Handicap' at Aqueduct," *NYT,* May 31, 1969, 28.

268 "relentless — almost inexhaustible": Bernard Weinraub, "Mailer's Style: An Orthodox Campaign Waged with Some Unorthodox Ideas," *NYT,* June 8, 1969, 73.

268 Scott Meredith announced: See Henry Raymont, "Million Advance for Mailer Seen," *NYT,* May 13, 1969, 44. For the *Post* account, see Manso, *Running,* 117.

268 "I'm devoting all my time to my candidacy": Raymont, "Million Advance," 44.

268 "Their attempt was unsuccessful": Stern, *Steinem,* 176.

269 "fucking beards and leftists": Flaherty, *Managing Mailer,* 117.

270 "There was a subtle": Ibid., 51.

270 "Who did this?": Interview with Michael C. D. Macdonald, May 1, 1998.

270 "The notion that we're": Flaherty, *Managing Mailer,* 179. The speech is given in full in Manso, *Running,* 65–80, and differs from what Flaherty quotes.

270 "If I'm right": Flaherty, *Managing Mailer,* 188.

271 "Norman was lazy": NM, *Fire on the Moon,* 5.

272 "He had in fact": Ibid., 5–6.

272 She was with him: Interview with BB, Dec. 5, 1998.

272 "the point on which": NM, *Prisoner,* 9.

272 "She was an actress": NM, *Fire on the Moon,* 436.
272 "I began to believe": Interview with BB, Dec. 5, 1998.

CHAPTER 19: THE MOON

Sources include interviews with Thomas Griffith (Jan. 26, 1998), Ralph Graves (Feb. 2, 1998), BB (Dec. 5, 1998, Feb. 5, 1999), and Jennifer Farbar (Nov. 15, 1995); Michiko Kakutani, "NM," in *The Poet;* "The New Canaries," *Time,* Dec. 9, 1957; Lukas, *Barnyard Epithet;* Schulz, *Motion;* Mills, 346–55; Rollyson, 230–34; Manso, interviews with Jack Kearney, Charlie Brown, Sandy Charlebois Thomas, Jerry Rubin; NM, *Fire on the Moon.*

273 "Born January 31": NM, *Fire on the Moon,* 4, 435, 141.
274 "We were doing too many": Interview with Thomas Griffith, Jan. 26, 1998.
274 "Not so bad": NM, *Fire on the Moon,* 6.
275 "The first and most unhappy": Ibid., 7–8, 382.
275 "He who had once": Ibid., 107.
275 "But in NASA-land": Ibid., 105.
276 "it was as if": Ibid., 108.
276 "like covering an assignment": Ibid., 89.
276 "There's too much text": Interview with Ralph Graves, Feb. 2, 1998.
277 "To write was to judge": NM, *Fire on the Moon,* 436, 386.
277 "I liked the book": Kakutani, "NM," 48.
278 "his wife and he": NM, *Fire on the Moon,* 436.
278 "He had women": Interview with BB, Feb. 5, 1999.
278 "It took forty-five": NM, *Fire on the Moon,* 437.
278 "hated his beloved Provincetown": Ibid.
279 "a massive Yorick": Ibid., 464.
279 Beverly left the house: Interview with BB, Dec. 5, 1998.
279 "wicked black sheaths": "The New Canaries," *Time,* Dec. 9, 1957, 66.
280 "like a typical earth mother": Interview with Jennifer Farbar, Nov. 15, 1995.
280 "a combination of the Scopes trial": Lukas, *Barnyard Epithet,* 1.
280 "Norman Mailer absolutely magnetized": Schulz, *Motion,* 244.
281 "It was his idea": Clavir and Spitzer, *Conspiracy Trial,* 492–94.
282 "It was plain": Lukas, *Barnyard Epithet,* 76.

CHAPTER 20: THE PRISONER OF SEX

Sources include Sara Evans, *Personal Politics;* Germaine Greer, "My Mailer Problem," *Esquire,* Sept. 1971; *Town Bloody Hall,* dir. Donn Pennebaker, 1972; Isabel Shenker, "Norman Mailer vs. Women's Lib," *NYT,* May 1, 1971; Diana Trilling, *We Must March;* book reviews cited below; Mills, 356–79; Rollyson, 234–43; Manso, interviews with Midge Decter, Diana Trilling; NM, *Prisoner, Presidential Papers.*

284 Sometimes as a result: See, for example, Evans, *Personal Politics.*
286 "Most men who understand": NM, *Presidential Papers,* 131.
286 "they should be kept": NM, *Prisoner,* 29.
286 "Revolution, tradition": Ibid., 30.
287 "as a lady kicking": Ibid., 26.

287 "Some of the writers": Ibid., 40.

289 "speak of women": Ibid., 59.

289 "treat these ladies": Ibid., 80, 90.

289 "Kate-baby": Ibid., 97, 123, 124, 119.

290 "If one gives": Ibid., 213, 233.

292 Anatole Broyard: Anatole Broyard, "Norman Writes a Dithyramb," *NYT,* May 27, 1971, 37.

292 The Sunday *Times* review: Brigid Brophy, *NYT,* May 23, 1971, VII, 1.

292 "brilliant broadside": S. K. Oberbeck, "The Mailer Mystique," *Newsweek,* Feb. 22, 1971, 56.

292 "heroic mysticism": Joyce Carol Oates, "Out of the Machine," *Atlantic Monthly,* July 1971, 45.

292 "a brilliant writer": V. S. Pritchett, "With NM at the Sex Circus," *Atlantic Monthly,* July 1971, 40.

293 "said she would come": Germaine Greer, "My Mailer Problem," *Esquire,* Sept. 1971, 92.

294 "You look much better": Ibid.

294 "Is there anything": All quotations are from *Town Bloody Hall,* dir. Donn Pennebaker, 1972, and Isabel Shenker, "Norman Mailer vs. Women's Lib," *NYT,* May 1, 1971, 19.

295 "Biology is all very well": Diana Trilling, *We Must March,* 209.

295 "If you, Norman": Greer, "My Mailer Problem," 216.

CHAPTER 21: "THE TERROR OF THE TV TALK SHOW"

Sources include interviews with Richard Stratton (Mar. 26, 1998), Paul Jenkins (June 16, 1998), Fred Kaplan (Apr. 11, 1996), BB (Dec. 5, 1998), and Ralph Graves (Feb. 2, 1998); Rosenbaum in Lennon, *Conversations;* John M. Lee, "Mailer, in London, Trades Jabs with Audience over New Film," *NYT,* Oct. 17, 1970; Vincent Canby, "Mailer's 'Maidstone' Opens Whitney Series," *NYT,* Sept. 24, 1971; "Mailer Opening," *New Yorker,* Oct. 2, 1971; Nan Robertson, "Mailer Will Star with his Movies," *NYT,* Jan. 19, 1984; *The Dick Cavett Show,* Dec. 2, 1971; Gore Vidal, "In Another Country," *NYRB,* July 2, 1971; Gore Vidal, "The NM Syndrome," *Nation,* Jan. 2, 1960; Janet Winn, "Capote, Mailer, and Miss Parker," *New Republic,* Feb. 9, 1959; "Women's Lib: Mailer vs. Millett," *Time,* Feb. 22, 1971; Edwards and Citron, *Inn;* Rodman, *Tongues;* book reviews cited below; Mills, 380-88, Rollyson, 241-45; Manso, interviews with José Torres, Cus D'Amato, Anne Barry, Bernard "Buzz" Farbar; NM, *Existential Errands, Pieces, St. George.*

297 "It was a woe": Ron Rosenbaum, in Lennon, *Conversations,* 181.

298 "It's like having a hole": Manso, *Mailer,* 532.

298 "didn't marry his mistress": Interview with BB, Dec. 5, 1998.

299 "the swiftest embodiment": NM, *Existential Errands,* 4.

300 "He was coming to claim": Ibid., 28.

300 "some of the best": Interview with Ralph Graves, Feb. 2, 1998.

300 "We appreciate Mailer": John M. Lee, "Mailer, in London, Trades Jabs with Audience over New Film," *NYT,* Oct. 17, 1970, 21.

301 "It's very simple": Nan Robertson, "Mailer Will Star with His Movies," *NYT,* Jan. 19, 1984, C17.

301 "an abrupt decline": Vincent Canby, "Mailer's 'Maidstone' Opens Whitney Series," *NYT*, Sept. 24, 1971, 31.

301 *The New Yorker* chose: "Mailer Opening," *New Yorker*, Oct. 2, 1971, 33.

301 "I would have done better": Robertson, "Mailer Will Star," C17.

301 "There has been from Henry": Gore Vidal, "In Another Country," *NYRB*, July 2, 1971, 8.

302 "It's a fake": Gore Vidal, "The NM Syndrome," *Nation*, Jan. 2, 1960, 13–16.

302 Mailer had accused Vidal: See Myrick Land, *The Fine Art of Literary Mayhem: A Lively Account of Famous Writers and Their Feuds*, rev. ed. (San Francisco: Lexikos, 1983), 228–44.

302 Vidal, William F. Buckley: Interview with Fred Kaplan, Apr. 11, 1996.

303 "a suitable valet": NM, *Pieces*, 57.

303 He and Adele had a TV: Adele Mailer, *Last Party*, 273.

303 "a personality": NM, *American Dream*, 15.

304 In 1959 he appeared: See Janet Winn, "Capote, Mailer, and Miss Parker," *New Republic*, Feb. 9, 1959, 27–28.

304 "Of course, TV did not": NM, *Pieces*, 49, 52.

304 "the terror of the TV": "Women's Lib: Mailer vs. Millett," *Time*, Feb. 22, 1971, 70.

305 Mailer's first showdown: For details of this conversation, see NM, "Of a Small and Modest Malignancy, Bristling with Dots," in *Pieces*, 13–81; see also *The Dick Cavett Show*, Dec. 2, 1971.

306 Six years later: See Mills, *Mailer*, 419.

307 The same year, at a party: Interview with Paul Jenkins, June 16, 1998.

307 "headed into the worst": NM, *St. George*, 219.

308 "comfortable middle-aged": Ibid., 4, 22, 86.

309 "Mailer is our literary": Gary Wills, *NYT*, Oct. 15, 1972.

309 "for in our world": NM, *Existential Errands*, xi.

309 "plenty of strong writing": *NYRB*, June 15, 1972, 21.

310 "With the essays": Cynthia Buchanan, *NYTBR*, Apr. 16, 1972, 27.

310 "the artful balance": NM, *Existential Errands*, 321.

311 "sad — not self-pitying": Interview with Richard Stratton, Mar. 26, 1998.

311 "one of the most beautiful": Edwards and Citron, *Inn*, 76–79.

312 The writer Selden Rodman: Rodman, *Tongues*, 172.

312 "We had a fine": Dudley Clendenin, "Mailer Takes the Stand for Writer in Drug Case," *NYT*, Mar. 25, 1983, 14.

CHAPTER 22: MAILER AND MONROE

Sources include Robert Friedman, "Hell's Agent," *Esquire*, Oct. 1977; "Two Myths Converge: NM Discovers MM," *Time*, July 16, 1973; newspaper stories and book reviews cited below; Mills, 395-410; Rollyson, 246–61; Manso, interviews with Lawrence Schiller, Robert Markel; NM, *Pieces, Marilyn*.

313 "he knew that he had wasted": NM, *Pieces*, 74.

314 "You're already famous": Robert Friedman, "Hell's Agent," *Esquire*, Oct. 1977, 136.

315 "Part of the reason": "Two Myths Converge: NM Discovers MM," *Time*, July 16, 1973, 65.

315 "the letters in Marilyn": NM, *Marilyn,* 20.

316 "and thought it was": Ibid., 19, 20.

316 By late February 1973: For details, see Manso, *Mailer,* 541.

318 Guiles backed down: "Mailer and Guiles Deny Any Dispute," *NYT,* July 17, 1973, 31.

318 On July 18, Mailer: Lesley Oelsner, "The Mailer Case: Authors and Law," *NYT,* July 19, 1973, 30.

318 On August 4, Zolotow: "Zolotow Files $6-Million Suit Over Mailer's Book 'Marilyn,'" *NYT,* Aug. 4, 1973, 19.

318 "His material is reamed": NM, *Marilyn,* 18.

318 "Mr. Zolotow must never": Eric Pace, "Mailer Threatens 'Marilyn' Suit; Calls for Apology from Zolotow," *NYT,* Aug. 7, 1973, 28.

319 "the literary heist": "Notes on People," *NYT,* Nov. 30, 1973, 27.

319 "No one is going": "Two Myths Converge," 65.

319 "Set a thief": NM, *Marilyn,* 20.

320 "the most powerfully erotic": Pauline Kael, review, *New Yorker,* Oct. 28, 1972, 130.

321 "pop open": NM, *Pieces,* 115.

321 "Though it's easy": Pauline Kael, "A Rip-Off with Genius," *NYTBR,* July 22, 1973.

322 "a tall and timid": NM, *Marilyn,* 143.

322 "It's a rich and creamy book": Kael, "Rip-Off"

322 "[*Marilyn*] permits": F. L. Ryan, *Best Seller,* Aug. 15, 1973, 222.

322 "As a way of making money": "Two Myths Converge," 64.

323 "she was already promising": NM, *Marilyn,* 16, 102, 104.

324 "animal rage": Ibid., 175.

324 "Marilyn had to be alive": Friedman, "Hell's Agent," 136.

CHAPTER 23: RUMBLE IN THE JUNGLE

Sources include interviews with BB, Dec. 3 and 5, 1998; "Two Myths Converge: NM Discovers MM," *Time,* July 16, 1973; Plimpton, *Shadow Box; Mailer* v. *Mailer,* III; Richard Stratton, "Norman Mailer: The Rolling Stone Interview, Part I," *Rolling Stone,* Jan. 2, 1975; "Barbara Davis Mailer," *Arkansas Democrat Gazette,* Aug. 11, 1996; Cathleen Medwick, "Mailer & Mailer," *Vogue,* July 1980; newspaper stories and book reviews cited below; letters in Gwaltney Collection; Mills, 411-17; Rollyson, 362–78; Manso, interviews with Barbara Norris Church Mailer, Jan Cushing Olympitis; NM, *Graffiti, The Fight.*

326 Norman was still living: Interviews with BB, Dec. 3 and Dec. 5, 1998.

326 Beverly roasted: See *Mailer* v. *Mailer,* III, 28–44.

327 "I've really gotten to the point": "Two Myths Converge," 64.

328 "there was real fear": NM, *Graffiti,* n.p.

328 Little, Brown had contracted: Eric Pace, "Mailer Getting $1-Million for Next Novel," *NYT,* Feb. 21, 1974, 24.

329 "His daily reactions": NM, *The Fight,* 25.

330 "the thought of Norman's eyes": Plimpton, *Shadow Box,* 277.

331 "A Heavyweight Championship": NM, *The Fight,* 102.

331 "Flanked by a Black": Ibid., 36, 52.

332 "With what an immensity": Ibid., 183.

332 "he went over": Ibid., 169.

332 "appears to have opened up": Dorothy Rabinowitz, review, *Saturday Review,* Aug. 23, 1975, 46.

333 "I don't think I'm ever": Richard Stratton, "NM: The Rolling Stone Interview, Part 1," *Rolling Stone,* Jan. 2, 1975.

333 "I'm not going to sit": Ibid.

334 "If you're doing something": Ibid.

335 "I had never seen Mailer": Plimpton, *Shadow Box,* 259.

335 "I walked in": Judy Klemesrud, "Life with Mailer: After Four Years, So Far, So Good," *NYT,* Apr. 16, 1979, B16. See also "Barbara Davis Mailer," *Arkansas Democrat Gazette,* Aug. 11, 1996, D1.

336 "*an* Andrew Wyeth": Cathleen Medwick, "Mailer & Mailer," *Vogue,* July 1980, 277.

337 According to Barbara: Barbara Norris to F & E Gwaltney, n.d. [1979].

CHAPTER 24: INTO THE HEARTLAND

Sources include interviews with Barney Rosset (Oct. 18, 1995) and BB (Dec. 3, 5, and 7, 1998 and Jan. 9, 1999); letters from NM to Henry Miller, Apr. 13, May 8, May 25, 1976; NM, "The Search for Carter," *NYT Magazine,* Sept. 26, 1976; Marie Brenner, "Social Stamina," *New York,* June 22, 1981; Marie Brenner, "Mailer Goes Egyptian," *New York,* Mar. 28, 1983; John McLaughlin, "Good Talk," *Harper's Bazaar,* Feb. 1990; Jennifer Hagar, "BB: A Life in the Theater of Our Times," *P'Town Women,* 1998; *Mailer v. Mailer,* V, X; Martha Smilgis, "Once Norman's Conquest: The Fourth Mrs. Mailer Fights the Final Marital Battle," *People,* Feb. 26, 1979; newspaper stories and book reviews cited below; Mills, 417–32; Rollyson, 278–300; Manso, interviews with Lawrence Schiller, Arthur Kretchmer, Barbara Norris Church Mailer, Roger Donald, Alice Mason, Jan Cushing Olympitis; NM, *Genius, Executioner.*

340 The contract reflected this: Interview with Barney Rosset, Oct. 18, 1995.

341 "his private paean": NM, *Genius,* 399.

341 "This is a tricky business": Herbert Mitgang, "Mailer Takes on the Heavyweight Novel," *NYT,* Dec. 19, 1976.

341 To Henry Miller, in May: NM to Henry Miller, May 25, 1976.

341 Though the resulting article: NM, "The Search for Carter," *NYT Magazine,* Sept. 26, 1976, 19.

342 "for Norris": See Marie Brenner, "Social Stamina," *New York,* June 22, 1981, 28.

342 Norman and Norris entertained: John McLaughlin, "Good Talk," *Harper's Bazaar,* Feb. 1990, 194.

342 One typical party: Charlotte Curtis, "New Yorkers, etc.," *NYT,* Dec. 20, 1976, C14.

345 "Because of Larry Schiller": Gilmore, *Shot,* 518.

345 But a new domestic crisis: "Mailer Sued for Divorce," *NYT,* Nov. 30, 1978, C16.

345 In the summer of 1977: Interviews with BB, Dec. 3, 5, and 7, 1998, Jan. 9, 1999.

346 For the time being: *Mailer* v. *Mailer,* V, 66, 105.

346 "Listen, he said": Martha Smilgis, "Once Norman's Conquest: The Fourth Mrs. Mailer Fights the Final Marital Battle," *People,* Feb. 26, 1979, 24–26.

346 "This woman has no career": Interviews with BB, Dec. 3, 1998, Jan. 9, 1999. See *Mailer* v. *Mailer,* X, 2.

347 "the facts in this case": "Court Says Mailer Divorce Lawyer Acted Ethically," *Boston Globe,* Nov. 9, 1983, 12.

347 Peter Manso's 1985 *Mailer*: Interview with Peter Manso, Feb. 19, 1999.

347 "Provincetown's premier actress": Jennifer Hagar, "BB: A Life in the Theater of Our Times," *P'town Women,* 1998, 41.

347 By fall 1977: See Manso, *Mailer,* 590.

348 "Gilmore brought the Automatic": NM, *Executioner,* 224.

348 "In the middle of washing": Ibid., 249.

349 "He realized that during": Ibid., 992.

349 "I know that dying": Ibid., 403.

349 "I love you more": Ibid., 486, 344.

350 "The reader is left": Earl Sovit, review, *Nation,* Oct. 20, 1979, 376.

350 "its inordinate length": *New Yorker,* Jan. 4, 1980, 102.

350 "At long last, Mailer": Walter Karp, review, *Esquire,* Dec. 1979, 25.

350 "Norman Mailer's thousand-page": Walter Clemons, review, *Newsweek,* Oct. 1, 1979, 72.

350 "If the novel is a mythology": Frank McConnell, *New Republic,* Oct. 27, 1979, 28.

351 "'The Executioner's Song' is ambitious": Joan Didion, *NYTBR,* Oct. 20, 1979, 1.

351 "kind of pleased": Herbert Mitgang, "Mailer Book Was 2nd Choice of Fiction Advisory Panel," *NYT,* Apr. 15, 1980, B8.

CHAPTER 25: A RECKONING

Sources include interviews with Legs McNeil (Apr. 21, 1998), Martha Thomases (Mar. 11 and Apr. 24, 1998), Eileen Finletter (Dec. 14, 1995), Peter Manso (June 3, 1998), and Steve Fishman (Mar. 3, 1996); "In a Merry Marriage-Go-Round, Norman Mailer Plans a Double Wedding, to Wives Five and Six," *People,* Nov. 3, 1980; James Atlas, "Life with Mailer," *NYT Magazine,* Nov. 9, 1979; *Norman Mailer by Norman Mailer,* dir. by Jans-Wörg Wehyhmüller, Profile of a Writer, Vol. IV, 1979; Marie Brenner, "Mailer Goes Egyptian," *New York,* Mar. 28, 1983; Cathleen Medwick, "Norman Mailer and Love, Sex, and the Devil," *Vogue,* Dec. 1980; Cathleen Medwick, "Mailer & Mailer," *Vogue,* July 1980; Abbott, *In the Belly;* Mary Vespa, "A Lifelong Con Springs Himself with a Book," *People,* July 30, 1981; Michiko Kakutani, "The Strange Case of the Writer and the Criminal," *NYTBR,* Sept. 20, 1981; Walter Goodman, "Literary Criminals," *NYTBR,* July 24, 1983; Claudia Walls, "In the Belly of the Beast," *Time,* Aug. 3, 1981; West, *William Styron;* newspaper stories and book reviews cited below; Mills, 13–19, 428–30; Rollyson, 302–18; Manso, interviews with Monroe Inker, Jack Henry Abbott, Erroll McDonald, Barbara Norris Church Mailer, Ivan Fisher, Thomas Hanrahan; NM, *Pieces.*

353 usually these parties: Interview with Legs McNeil, Apr. 21, 1998.

354 "Norman liked the action": Ibid. Also on Norman and punk, interviews with Martha Thomases, Mar. 11 and Apr. 24, 1998.

354 "That Norman Mailer's wonderful": Interview with Eileen Finletter, Dec. 14, 1995.

354 His divorce from Beverly: "The Amours of Norman, Chapters 5 and 6," *NYT*, Oct. 14, 1980; interviews with BB, Dec. 3, 5, and 7, 1998.

354 She would finally be evicted: "After a Long Fight, Mrs. Mailer Is Evicted," *NYT*, Oct. 2, 1981, 30.

354 "a bit disconcerting": "In a Merry Marriage-Go-Round, Norman Mailer Plans a Double Wedding, to Wives Five and Six," *People*, Nov. 3, 1980, 34–35.

355 "We're not divorced": "Mailer's Last Two Trips to Altar May Be Double Bigamy," *New York Post*, Nov. 18, 1980, 7.

355 "Well, it's always": NM, *Pieces*, 116.

355 "getting thrown out": James Atlas, "Life with Mailer," *NYT Magazine*, Nov. 9, 1979, 96.

356 Norris developed: Interview with Peter Manso, June 3, 1998.

356 Norris was showing: *Norman Mailer by Norman Mailer*, directed by Jans-Wörg Wehyhmüller, Profile of a Writer, vol. 4, 1979.

356 "sort of the last": Marie Brenner, "Mailer Goes Egyptian," *New York*, Mar. 28, 1983, 34.

356 He was still projecting: Cathleen Medwick, "Mailer & Mailer," *Vogue*, July 1980, 343.

357 "show my shell-shocked": NM, *Pieces*, x.

357 Again and again he returns: Mailer remembered James Jones telling him about karma in the 1950s, on a visit to the writer in Illinois. "You believe that?" he asked Jones. "Oh sure," Jones replied. "That's the only thing that makes sense." In the last four years, Mailer told the interviewer, he'd come to understand that Jones was right: "Yes, that does make sense. Jones was right." See *Pieces*, 89.

357 "emulate . . . a fanatically": Abbott, *In the Belly*, 13.

358 "I cannot imagine": Ibid., 165, 13.

359 "I'm tenuous, shy": Ibid., 42. For Abbott's confusion, see Mary Vespa, "A Lifelong Con Springs Himself with a Book," *People*, July 30, 1981, 62–65.

359 "belong[s] with the best": *Time*, July 20, 1981, 74.

359 "an exceptional man": Terrence Des Pres, *NYTBR*, July 19, 1981, 3.

360 "from Leavenworth": Michiko Kakutani, "The Strange Case of the Writer and the Criminal," *NYTBR*, Sept. 20, 1981, 39.

360 "tunnel vision": Charles Ruas, "NM," 21.

361 "What will happen": Mike Pearl and Cynthia R. Fagen, "Mailer: I Would Risk Freeing Killer," *New York Post*, Jan. 18, 1982, 13. See also Paul L. Montgomery, "Abbott Rejects Account of Him as Violent Man," *NYT*, Jan. 19, 1982, B3.

361 It was a sight: Interview with Steve Fishman, Mar. 3, 1996.

362 "I have blood": "Mailer Admits: Blood on My Hands," *New York Post*, Jan. 22, 1982, 3.

362 William F. Buckley: See Walter Goodman, "Literary Criminals," *NYTBR*, July 24, 1983, 27.

362 "the 60s, when we embraced": Claudia Wallis, "In the Belly of the Beast," *Time*, Aug. 3, 1981, 19.

363 "My heart goes out": West, *Styron*, 429.

363 "I thought I'd wait": Ibid.

CHAPTER 26: EGYPT, AND A BRUSH WITH THE LAW

Sources include interviews with Rosie Rowbotham (June 10, 1998), Richard Stratton (Feb. 15, 1996 and Mar. 26 and June 25, 1998), Ivan Fisher (Mar. 31, 1996 and Apr. 12, 1999), and Jennifer Farbar (Nov. 15, 1995); Michael Schumacher, "Modern Evenings: An Interview with NM," *Writer's Digest*, Oct. 1983; Marie Brenner, "Mailer Goes Egyptian," *New York*, Mar. 28, 1983; "Unbloodied by the Critical Pounding, NM Defends the Egyptian Novel That Took a Decade to Write," *People*, May 30, 1983; Robins, *Alien Ink;* Barbara Amiel, "Johnny Reeferseed," *Maclean's*, June 13, 1977; Andrea Chambers, "Crime and Puzzlement: The Real-Life Mystery Behind NM's New Thriller," *People*, Sept. 10, 1984; Steve Fishman, "NM's Prison Protégé," *GQ*, June 1992; U.S. District Court, Southern District of New York, *U.S. v. Richard Lowell Stratton et al.*, 83 Cr. 482 (CBM); Jennifer Farbar, "Hush of Suicide," *NYT Magazine*, Mar. 5, 1995; book reviews and newspaper stories cited below; Mills, 432–33; Rollyson, 318–23, 330–32; Manso, interview with Roger Donald; NM, *Ancient Evenings*.

364 "one hurdle": Michael Schumacher, "Modern Evenings: An Interview with NM," *Writer's Digest*, Oct. 1983, 32.

364 "This isn't the big": Marie Brenner, "Mailer Goes Egyptian," *New York*, Mar. 28, 1983, 30.

364 He read more than: "Unbloodied by the Critical Pounding, NM Defends the Egyptian Novel That Took a Decade to Write," *People*, May 30, 1983, 59.

365 "having the consciousness": Brenner, "Mailer Goes Egyptian," 34.

366 "[The] mast stood": NM, *Ancient Evenings*, 113–14.

366 "As Ra had His godly": Ibid., 455, 381, 529–30.

367 "Mailer's somber": George Stade, review, *New Republic*, May 2, 1983.

367 "The further one progresses": Benjamin DeMott, review, *NYTBR*, Apr. 10, 1983, 35–36.

367 "Nothing Norman Mailer": James Wolcott, review, *Harper's Magazine*, May 1983, 81.

368 "One of the reasons": Schumacher, *Dharma Lion*, 33.

370 "The reader . . . was": "Unbloodied," 53–54.

371 When Norman asked what books: Interview with Rosie Rowbotham, June 10, 1998. On Rowbotham and Stratton, see Barbara Amiel, "Johnny Reeferseed," *Maclean's*, June 13, 1977, 26–40.

371 "Drugs and foreign policy": Robins, *Alien Ink*, 408.

372 The indictment was thrown out: Interviews with Richard Stratton, Feb. 15, 1996; Mar. 26, 1998; June 25, 1998.

374 The defense was novel: Dudley Clendinen, "Writer of Book on Drugs on Trial for Smuggling," *NYT*, Mar. 14, 1983, 12.

374 "He had a lot of moxie": Dudley Clendinen, "Mailer Takes the Stand for Writer in Drug Case," *NYT*, Mar. 25, 1983, 14.

374 "the lieutenant of the whole thing": Transcript of "Conversation among Sobhi Hammoud, Special Agent Martin Maguire, and Bernard Farbar, a/k/a 'Buzz,' a/k/a 'Dr. Bernard,'" U.S. District Court, Southern District of New York, *U.S.*

v. *Richard Lowell Stratton et al.* 83 Cr. 482 (CBM), Government Exhibit 132 and 132a, Sept. 23, 1982, 5.

374 "Richard didn't pay him": Transcript of "Conversation among Sobhi Hammoud, Bernard Farbar, a/k/a 'Buzz,' a/k/a 'Dr. Bernard,' and 'Tony,'" *U.S. v. Richard Stratton et al.*, Government Exhibit 131 and 131a, Sept. 20, 1982, 8.

375 "Call Norman Mailer": See *U.S. v. Richard Stratton et al.*, Feb. 22 and 23, 1984, 7–8.

375 Ivan Fisher, Buzz's lawyer: Interview with Ivan Fisher, Apr. 12, 1999; see "Affidavit of Ivan S. Fisher," *U.S. v. Bernard Farbar* 83 Cr. 482 (CBM), Dec. 2, 1983, in which he calls Mailer "the government's celebrity target."

375 To this end, the DEA: Andrea Chambers, "Crime and Puzzlement: The Real-Life Mystery behind NM's New Thriller," *People,* Sept. 10, 1984, 42.

376 According to Fisher: Interview with Ivan Fisher, Mar. 31, 1996.

376 "Mailer wasn't involved": Quoted in Steve Fishman, "NM's Prison Protégé," *GQ,* June 1992, 168.

376 "you can't go to jail": Interview with Ivan Fisher, Mar. 31, 1996.

377 "is a concern": Ibid.

377 Several things that one: Interview with Jennifer Farbar, Nov. 15, 1995. See also Jennifer Farbar, "Hush of Suicide," *NYT Magazine,* Mar. 5, 1995, 27.

CHAPTER 27: A MISTRESS, A PATRON, AND A THRILLER

Sources include interviews with Carole Mallory (Dec. 9, 10, and 11, 1998), Peter Manso (June 3 and Oct. 8, 1998 and Feb. 9, 1999), Jason Epstein (May 15, 1996), Ellen Hawkes (June 4, 1998), and David X. Young (Sept. 2, 1998); von Hoffman, *Citizen Cohn;* Maier, *Newhouse;* Alan Richman, "No Longer Such a Tough Guy, NM Frets Over His Shaky Career as a Filmmaker," *People,* Oct. 5, 1987; Edwin McDowell, "Mailer and Random House Sign a $4 Million Contract," *NYT,* Aug. 2, 1983; Raymond Elman, "Tough Talk: an Interview with Peter Manso," *Province-town Arts,* Summer 1987; Edwin McDowell, "Publishing: Mailer Talks about His New Thriller," *NYT,* June 8, 1984; Wilson, *Near the Magician;* Gerald Peary, "He's Doing His Own Dance for the Camera Again," *Chicago Tribune,* Jan. 25, 1987; Edwin McDowell, "Little, Brown Rejects New NM Novel," *NYT,* Oct. 6, 1983; NM, "A Country, Not a Scenario," *Parade,* Aug. 19, 1984; book reviews cited below; Rollyson, 332-38; Manso, interviews with Jason Epstein, Walter Anderson; NM, *Pieces, Tough Guys.*

378 Carole Mallory walked into: Interviews with CM, Dec. 9, 10, and 11, 1998.

382 "If anyone ever got": von Hoffman, *Citizen Cohn,* 420.

382 "Well, how much": Ibid., 446.

382 "I consider Norman": Maier, *Newhouse,* 107, 259.

383 "the richest house": Alan Richman, "No Longer Such a Tough Guy, NM Frets over His Shaky Career as a Filmmaker," *People,* Oct. 5, 1987, 42.

383 "shoehorned his way in": Interview with Peter Manso, June 3, 1998.

383 "I heard you're buying": Ibid.

383 "It's about time": von Hoffman, *Citizen Cohn,* 447.

383 "*Fuck* them": Interview with Peter Manso, June 3, 1998.

384 "He's going to try ": Quoted in von Hoffman, *Citizen Cohn,* 448.

384 At dinner one night: Interview with Peter Manso, June 3, 1998.

385 "wanted Mailer": Quoted in Maier, *Newhouse,* 191.

384 "the most important switch": Edwin McDowell, "Mailer and Random House Sign a $4 Million Contract," *NYT,* Aug. 2, 1983, C14.

385 Jason Epstein, Random: Interview with Jason Epstein, May 15, 1996.

385 "lunatic arrangement": Interview with Peter Manso, June 3, 1998.

387 By July 1985: Interview with Ellen Hawkes, June 4, 1998.

387 "Norman is no progressive": Raymond Elman, "Tough Talk: An Interview with Peter Manso," *Provincetown Arts,* Summer 1987, 25.

387 "insane macho thing": Interview with Peter Manso, Oct. 8, 1998.

387 Meanwhile, Fanny's health: "Mailer's Mother, 87, Is Dead," *NYT,* Aug. 30, 1985, D15.

387 "If I didn't write": Edwin McDowell, "Publishing: Mailer Talks about His New Thriller," *NYT,* June 8, 1984.

387 Tony Costa, a local Portuguese: For a description of the murders and their impact on the community, see Wilson, *Near the Magician,* 235–40.

388 "Living in Provincetown": NM, *Pieces,* 9.

388 The novel begins: Gerald Peary, "He's Doing His Own Dance for the Camera Again," *Chicago Tribune,* Jan. 25, 1987.

389 Harpo, for instance: Interview with David X. Young, Sept. 2, 1998.

389 Madden climbs partway: Interview with Peter Manso, June 3, 1998.

389 "Conceived at night": NM, *Tough Guys,* 7.

389 "Let no one say": Ibid., 41, 29.

390 Meredith announced: Edwin McDowell, "Little, Brown Rejects New Norman Mailer Novel," *NYT,* Oct. 6, 1983.

390 "preposterous[ly] unequal": Denis Donoghue, "Death on the Windy Dunes," *NYTBR,* July 29, 1984, 1.

390 "an embarrassment": Jack Beatty, *New Republic,* Aug. 27, 1984, 40.

390 "engaging murder mystery": Paul Gray, review, *Time,* Aug. 6, 1984, 66.

391 Americans might find: NM, "A Country, Not a Scenario," *Parade,* Aug. 19, 1984, 6–9.

392 Walter Anderson published: von Hoffman, *Citizen Cohn,* 448; interviews with Peter Manso, June 3, 1998; Feb. 19, 1999.

CHAPTER 28: THE HALLS OF POWER: THE CIA AND PEN

Sources include interviews with Ellen Ray (Sept. 30, 1998), Carl Oglesby (Oct. 26, 1998), and Carole Mallory (Dec. 9, 1998); Agee and Wolf, *Dirty Work;* Agee, *On the Run;* Natalie Robins, "The Secret War Against American Writers," *Esquire,* Mar. 1992; Amy Wilentz, "A Rampancy of Writers," *Time,* Jan. 13, 1986; Robins, *Alien Ink;* NM, "The Writer's Imagination and the Imagination of the State," *NYRB,* Feb. 13, 1986; Rhoda Koenig, "At Play in the Fields of the Word," *New York,* Feb. 3, 1986; Maria Margaronis and Elizabeth Pochoda, "Bad Manners and Bad Faith," *Nation,* Feb. 1, 1986; Miriam Schneir, "The Prisoner of Sexism," *Ms.,* Apr. 1986; Edward Rothstein, "Lead Me Not into Pen Station," *New Republic,* Feb. 24, 1986; Roger Ebert, "'Tough Guy' Mailer Shows He Can Dance with the Big Boys," in Lennon, *Conversations;* David Thomson, "Mailer by the Bay," *California,* Aug. 1987; Daphne Merkin, "His Brilliant (New?) Career," *American Film,*

Oct. 1987; Dinitia Smith, "Tough Guys Make Movie," *New York,* Jan. 12, 1987; newspaper stories and film reviews cited below; Rollyson, 338–49, 352–57.

394 "We've had an American": Quoted in Agee and Wolf, *Dirty Work,* p. 79.

394 "If anyone is to blame": Quoted in "CIA Blamed for Death," *NYT,* Dec. 25, 1975.

394 "The blood of Mr. Welch": Quoted in Agee and Wolf, *Dirty Work,* 91.

394 "The CIA quickly disseminated": Ibid., 79.

395 Members of the Fifth Estate: Interview with Ellen Ray, Sept. 30, 1998.

395 The IRS withdrew: See Agee, *On the Run,* 120.

395 "after six months": Robins, *Alien Ink,* 334.

395 Around the same time: Interview with Carl Oglesby, Oct. 26, 1998.

396 "OCFE was formed": Quoted in Natalie Robins, "The Secret War Against American Writers," *Esquire,* Mar. 1992, 106–9.

396 "because of your continuing": Robins, *Alien Ink,* 331.

396 "for a long period": Ibid.

396 "Norman is really paranoid": Quoted in ibid., 399.

398 By December 1985: Edwin McDowell, "Mailer Earns Praise for PEN Efforts," *NYT,* Dec. 23, 1985.

398 "It is perfectly possible": "International Writers' Congress Set," *NYT,* Mar. 7, 1985.

399 "Norman almost solely": McDowell, "Mailer Earns Praise."

399 He put his mistress: Interview with CM, Dec. 9, 1998.

399 "two toothless tigers": Amy Wilentz, "A Rampancy of Writers," *Time,* Jan. 13, 1986, 22.

400 "He has been": McDowell, "Mailer Earns Praise."

400 "The notion that the state": Reprinted in NM, "The Writer's Imagination and the Imagination of the State," *NYRB,* Feb. 13, 1986, 23.

400 "inappropriate" and "distressing": Reprinted in *Nation,* Feb. 1, 1986, 117.

401 "We have more": Walter Goodman, "Shultz Faces Critics in Speech Opening 48th PEN Assembly," *NYT,* Jan. 13, 1986, C11.

401 "I just felt": Rhoda Koenig, "At Play in the Fields of the Word," *New York,* Feb. 3, 1986, 44.

401 "astonishingly liberal": Edwin McDowell, "Shultz Issue Dominates PEN Congress Sessions," *NYT,* Jan. 14, 1986.

401 "baffled by the disturbance": Koenig, "At Play," 41.

401 "give our organization": Maria Margaronis and Elizabeth Pochoda, "Bad Manners and Bad Faith," *Nation,* Feb. 1, 1986, 116–19.

402 "Since the formulation": Edwin McDowell, "Women at PEN Demand a Greater Role," *NYT,* Jan. 17, 1986, C26.

402 "We invited the best": Koenig, "At Play," 47.

402 "You cut us off": Edwin McDowell, "PEN Congress Ends with a Protest," *NYT,* Jan. 18, 1986, 11. See also Miriam Schneir, "The Prisoner of Sexism," *Ms.,* Apr. 1986, 82–83.

402 "been better for a philosophers'": Walter Goodman, "Norman Mailer Offers a PEN Post-mortem," *NYT,* Jan. 27, 1986. For an otherwise good analysis of the congress that overlooks the women's issue, see Edward Rothstein, "Lead Me Not into Pen Station," *New Republic,* Feb. 24, 1986, 20–23.

404 "I knew that writing": Roger Ebert, "'Tough Guy' Mailer Shows He Can Dance with the Big Boys," in Lennon, *Conversations,* 353.

404 "I'll make up": David Thomson, "Mailer by the Bay," *California*, Aug. 1987, 124.

405 "the kind of homosexual": Daphne Merkin, "His Brilliant (New?) Career," *American Film*, Oct. 1987, 48–49.

405 "This is my Africa": Dinitia Smith, "Tough Guys Make Movie," *New York*, Jan. 12, 1987, 32–37.

405 "For one thing": James Verniere, "Mailer, 64, Stays Tough," *Boston Herald*, Sept. 20, 1987.

406 "*Tough Guys Don't Dance* is an easy": Vincent Canby, *NYT*, Sept. 18, 1987, C14.

406 "is screwed up": Pauline Kael, *New Yorker*, Sept. 27, 1987, 103–7.

CHAPTER 29: AMONG THE SPOOKS

Sources include interviews with Jason Epstein (May 15, 1996), Carole Mallory (Dec. 19, 1998), and Ellen Ray (Sept. 30, 1998); Samuel M. Hughes, "Toward a Concept of NM," *Pennsylvania Gazette*, May 1995; Michael Skerker, "A Pulitzer-Prize Winning Author Speaks above the 'Norm,'" *Brown Daily Herald*, Apr. 19, 1995; Richard Johnson, "Mailer's Ex-Lover Writes It Down," *NY Post*, Sept. 15, 1995; NM on Charlie Rose television show, Apr. 22, 1997; Toby Thompson, "Mailer's Alpha and Omega," *Vanity Fair*, Oct. 1991; Matthew Flamm, "Mailer Goes the Distance," *New York Post*, Sept. 30, 1991; "A Critic with Balance: A Letter from NM," *NYTBR*, Nov. 17, 1991; Elaine Sciolino, "Mailer Visits CIA and Finds He's in Friendly Territory. Really," *NYT*, Feb. 3, 1992; Rollyson, 358–68; NM, *Harlot's Ghost*.

407 "feeling absolutely corrupt": Samuel M. Hughes, "Toward a Concept of NM," *Pennsylvania Gazette*, May 1995, 25.

407 "You can't get drunk": Michael Skerker, "A Pulitzer-Prize Winning Author Speaks above the 'Norm,'" *Brown Daily Herald*, Apr. 19, 1995.

408 "There are two sides": Interview with Jason Epstein, May 15, 1996.

408 The 1990s opened: Interview with Carole Mallory, Dec. 19, 1998.

409 "regret": Richard Johnson, "Mailer's Ex-Lover Writes It Down," *New York Post*, Sept. 15, 1995.

409 Elsewhere he would: NM on Charlie Rose television show, Apr. 22, 1997.

409 "The CIA was not merely": NM, *Harlot's Ghost*, 186, 205, 267.

409 "a very cultured man": Frank Green, "Testosterone Aside, He's as Testy as Ever," *San Diego Union Tribune*, Oct. 19, 1991.

409 "that was the allure": NM, *Harlot's Ghost*, 192.

410 "I mean, here": Toby Thompson, "Mailer's Alpha and Omega," *Vanity Fair*, Oct. 1991, 152.

410 "I like the rhythm": "Newsmakers," *Time*, Oct. 29, 1991.

410 "There is much to fault": Christopher Lehmann-Haupt, *NYT*, Sept. 26, 1991, C15.

410 "The thought is enough": Peter S. Prescott, review, *Newsweek*, Sept. 30, 1991, 59.

410 "fine and engaging": Paul Gray, review, *Time*, Sept. 30, 1991, 70.

411 "not only the most": Louis Menand, review, *New Yorker*, Nov. 4, 1991, 113.

411 "such a spell-binding": John Simon, review, *NYTBR*, Sept. 29, 1991, 26.

411 "The mark of Simon's": Matthew Flamm, "Mailer Goes the Distance," *New York Post,* Sept. 30, 1991.

412 On November 17: "A Critic with Balance: A Letter from NM," *NYTBR,* Nov. 17, 1991, 7.

414 "go through life": NM, *Harlot's Ghost,* 174.

415 "We've been so conditioned": All quotes from Elaine Sciolino, "Mailer Visits CIA and Finds He's in Friendly Territory. Really," *NYT,* Feb. 3, 1992.

415 strange coda: Interview with Ellen Ray, Sept. 30, 1998.

EPILOGUE

Sources include Wil Haygood, "Mailer Obsessed: The Author Travels to Minsk and Texas to Bring Oswald Out of Shadows," *Boston Globe,* May 2, 1995; Sarah Lyall, "One Passion, Two Writers and an Editor on the Spot," *NYT,* July 7, 1993; Charles W. Bell, "Gospel According to Mailer," *New York Post,* Apr. 13, 1997; NM, "NM on Women, Love, Sex, Politics, and All That," *Cosmopolitan,* May 1976; David Streitfield, "Mailer's Lament," *Washington Post Book World,* May 8, 1994; NM, *Picasso.*

417 "I'm tough": NM, "NM on Women, Love, Sex, Politics, and All That," *Cosmopolitan,* May 1976, 182.

418 "seventy-five percent": See, for instance, Wil Haygood, "Mailer Obsessed: The Author Travels to Minsk and Texas to Bring Oswald Out of Shadow," *Boston Globe,* May 2, 1995.

419 "scissors-and-paste job": Sarah Lyall, "One Picasso, Two Writers and an Editor on the Spot," *NYT,* July 7, 1993, C13.

419 "There are probably": Charles W. Bell, "Gospel According to Mailer," *New York Post,* Apr. 13, 1997.

421 "Serious novelists": David Streitfeld, "Mailer's Lament," *Washington Post Book World,* May 8, 1994, 15.

422 "admiration for her son": NM, *Picasso,* 222.

422 "[Picasso] was now immersed": Ibid., 53.

423 "there is probably more": Ibid., 217–18.

423 "If, even in the face": Ibid., 218.

Bibliography

SELECTED WORKS BY NORMAN MAILER

Advertisements for Myself. New York: Putnam's, 1959.
An American Dream. 1965. Reprint, New York: Dell, 1970.
Ancient Evenings. Boston: Little, Brown, 1982.
The Armies of the Night: The Novel as History/History as a Novel. 1968. Reprint, New York: New American Library, 1968.
Barbary Shore. 1951. Reprint, New York: Signet, 1951.
Cannibals and Christians. New York: Dial, 1966.
Deaths for the Ladies (and other disasters). New York: Putnam's, 1962.
The Deer Park. 1955. Reprint, New York: Berkley, 1967.
The Deer Park: A Play. New York: Dial, 1967.
The Executioner's Song. Boston: Little, Brown, 1979.
Existential Errands. Boston: Little, Brown, 1972.
The Faith of Graffiti. New York: Praeger/Alskog, 1974.
The Fight. 1975. Reprint, New York: Bantam, 1976.
Genius and Lust: A Journey Through the Major Writings of Henry Miller. New York: Grove, 1976.
Harlot's Ghost. New York: Random House, 1991.
Marilyn: A Novel Biography. New York: Grosset & Dunlap, 1973.
Miami and the Siege of Chicago. 1968. Reprint, New York: Signet, 1968.
The Naked and the Dead. New York: Rinehart, 1948.
Of a Fire on the Moon. Boston: Little, Brown, 1970.
Portrait of Picasso as a Young Man: An Interpretive Biography. New York: Atlantic Monthly, 1995.
Pieces and Pontifications. Boston: Little, Brown, 1982.
The Presidential Papers. New York: Putnam's, 1963.
The Prisoner of Sex. Boston: Little, Brown, 1971.
Tough Guys Don't Dance. New York: Random House, 1984.
Why Are We in Vietnam? New York: Putnam's, 1967.

SELECTED BIBLIOGRAPHY

Aaron, Daniel. *Writers on the Left.* New York: Harcourt, Brace, 1961.

Abbott, Jack Henry. *In the Belly of the Beast.* New York: Random House, 1981.

Abel, Lionel. *The Intellectual Follies: A Memoir of the Literary Venture in New York and Paris.* New York: William Morrow, 1987.

Adams, Laura. "Existential Aesthetics: An Interview with Norman Mailer." *Partisan Review* 42 (1975), 197.

———. *Existential Battles: The Growth of Norman Mailer.* Athens: Ohio State University Press, 1976.

———. *Will the Real Norman Mailer Please Stand Up?* Port Washington, N.Y.: Kennikat, 1974.

———, comp. *Norman Mailer: A Comprehensive Bibliography.* Metuchen, N.J.: Scarecrow, 1974.

Agee, Philip. *On the Run.* Secaucus, N.J.: Lyle Stuart, 1987.

———, and Louis Wolf, eds. *Dirty Work: The CIA in Western Europe.* Secaucus, N.J.: Lyle Stuart, 1978.

Aldridge, John. *After the Long Generation: A Critical Study of the Writers of Two Wars.* New York: Noonday, 1951.

———. "From Vietnam to Obscurity." *Harper's Magazine* (Feb. 1968), 183.

Atlas, James. *Delmore Schwartz: The Life of an American Poet.* New York: Farrar, Straus & Giroux, 1977.

Bailey, Jennifer. *Norman Mailer, Quick-Change Artist.* New York: Barnes and Noble, 1979.

Baldwin, James. "The Black Boy Looks at the White Boy." In *Nobody Knows My Name.* 1961. Reprint, New York: Vintage, 1993.

Bloom, Alexander. *Prodigal Sons: The New York Intellectuals and Their World.* New York: Oxford University Press, 1986.

Bosworth, Patricia. *Montgomery Clift: A Biography.* New York: Harcourt Brace Jovanovich, 1978.

Bower, Brock. "Never the Champion, Always the Challenger." *Life,* Sept. 24, 1965, 94.

Braudy, Leo, ed. *Norman Mailer: A Collection of Critical Essays.* Englewood Cliffs, N.J.: Prentice-Hall, 1972.

Brightman, Carol. *Writing Dangerously: Mary McCarthy and Her World.* New York: Clarkson Potter, 1992.

Calisher, Hortense. *Herself.* New York: Arbor House, 1972.

Campbell, James. *Talking at the Gates: A Life of James Baldwin.* New York: Penguin, 1991.

Cheney, Anne. *Lorraine Hansberry.* Boston: Twayne, 1984.

Clavir, Judy, and John Spitzer, eds. *The Conspiracy Trial.* Indianapolis: Bobbs-Merrill, 1970.

Conrad, Harold. *Dear Muffo: 35 Years in the Fast Lane.* Introduction by Budd Schulberg. Foreword by Norman Mailer. New York: Stein and Day, 1982.

Cooney, Terry A. *The Rise of the New York Intellectuals: "Partisan Review" and Its Circle.* Madison: University of Wisconsin Press, 1986.

Crouse, Timothy. *The Boys on the Bus.* New York: Random House, 1973.

Dickstein, Morris. *The Gates of Eden: American Culture in the Sixties.* New York: Basic Books, 1977.

Edwards, Anne, and Stephen Citron. *The Inn and Us*. New York: Random House, 1976.

Elman, Raymond. "Tough Talk: A Conversation with Peter Manso." *Provincetown Arts* (Summer 1987), 23–25.

Epstein, Jason. *The Great Conspiracy Trial: An Essay on Law, Liberty, and the Constitution*. New York: Random House, 1970.

Farbar, Buzz. "*Viva* Interview: Mailer on Marriage and Women." *Viva* 1 (Oct. 1973), 75.

Flaherty, Joe. *Managing Mailer*. New York: Coward-McCann, 1969.

Gerson, Jessica. "An American Dream: Mailer's Walpurgisnacht." In Daniel Walden, ed., *Studies in American Jewish Literature*, vol. 2. Albany: State University of New York Press, 1982, 126–31.

———. "Norman Mailer: The Mystical Vision." Ph.D. dissertation, New York University, 1977.

———. "Norman Mailer: Sex, Creativity, and God." *Mosaic* (June 1982), 1–16.

Gilbert, James. *Writers and Partisans*. New York: Wiley, 1968.

Gilman, Richard. *The Confusion of Realms*. New York: Random House, 1969.

Gilmore, Mikal. *Shot in the Heart*. New York: Doubleday, 1994.

Gingrich, Arnold. *Nothing But People: The Early Days at "Esquire," A Personal History*. New York: Crown, 1971.

Goodman, Paul. *New Reformation*. New York: Random House, 1970.

Gordon, Max. *Live at the Village Vanguard*. New York: Da Capo, 1980.

Gutman, Stanley T. *Mankind in Barbary: The Individual and Society in Norman Mailer*. Hanover, N.H.: University Press of New England, 1975.

Hagar, Jennifer. "Beverly Bentley: A Life in the Theater of Our Times." *P'town Women* (1998), 40–46.

Hamill, Pete. *A Drinking Life: A Memoir*. Boston: Little, Brown, 1994.

Hamilton, Ian. *Robert Lowell: A Biography*. New York: Random House, 1982.

Hayes, Harold, ed. *Smiling Through the Apocalypse: Esquire's History of the Sixties*. New York: McCall, 1969.

Hayman, Ronald. *Sartre: A Life*. New York: Simon and Schuster, 1987.

Hemingway, Mary. *How It Was*. New York: Knopf, 1976.

Hirschhorn, Clive. *Gene Kelly: A Biography*. London: W. H. Allen, 1974.

Howe, Irving. *A Margin of Hope: An Intellectual Autobiography*. New York: Harcourt Brace Jovanovich, 1982.

Jacobson, Dan. "The Jews of South Africa: Portrait of a Flourishing Community." *Commentary* (Jan. 1963), 39–44.

Jumonville, Neil. *Critical Crossings: The New York Intellectuals in Postwar America*. Berkeley: University of California Press, 1991.

Kakutani, Michiko. "Norman Mailer." In *The Poet at the Piano: Portraits of Writers, Filmmakers, Playwrights and Other Artists at Work*. New York: Times Books, 1988, 45–51.

Karnow, Stanley. *Paris in the Fifties*. New York: Times Books, 1997.

Kazin, Alfred. "The Writer as Sexual Show-Off." *New York*, June 9, 1975, 36.

Kingsley, April. *The Turning Point: The Abstract Expressionists and the Transformation of American Art*. New York: Simon and Schuster, 1992.

Kostelanetz, Richard, ed. *On Contemporary Literature*. New York: Avon, 1968.

Krassner, Paul. *Confessions of a Raving Unconfined Nut: Misadventures in the Counterculture*. New York: Simon and Schuster, 1993.

Lant, Jeffrey, ed. *Our Harvard: Reflections on College Life by Twenty-Two Distinguished Graduates.* New York: Taplinger, 1982.

Lasch, Christopher. *The Agony of the American Left.* New York: Vintage, 1969.

Leeds, Barry H. *The Structured Vision of Norman Mailer.* New York: New York University Press, 1969.

Leeming, David. *James Baldwin: A Biography.* New York: Knopf, 1994.

Lennon, J. Michael, ed. *Conversations with Norman Mailer.* Jackson: University Press of Mississippi, 1988.

Liebling, A. J. "The Morest." In *A Neutral Corner: Boxing Essays.* New York: Simon and Schuster, 1990, 181–90.

Lucid, Robert F., ed. *Norman Mailer: The Man and His Work.* Boston: Little, Brown, 1971.

Lukas, J. Anthony. *The Barnyard Epithet and Other Obscenities. Notes on the Chicago Conspiracy Trial.* New York: Harper and Row, 1970.

Macshane, Frank. *Into Eternity: The Life of James Jones, American Writer.* Boston: Houghton Mifflin, 1985.

Maier, Thomas. *Newhouse.* New York: St. Martin's, 1994.

Mailer, Adele. *The Last Party: Scenes from My Life with Norman Mailer.* New York: Barricade, 1997.

Manso, Peter. *Mailer: His Life and Times.* New York: Simon and Schuster, 1985.

———, ed. *Running Against the Machine.* Garden City, N.Y.: Doubleday, 1969.

McAuliffe, Kevin. *The Great American Newspaper: The Rise and Fall of the "Village Voice."* New York: Scribner's, 1978.

Meredith, Robert. "The Forty-Five-Second Piss: A Left Critique of Norman Mailer and *Armies.*" *Modern Fiction Studies* 17 (Autumn 1971), 433–49.

Merrill, Hugh. *Esky: The Early Years of "Esquire."* New Brunswick, N.J.: Rutgers University Press, 1995.

Miller, James. *"Democracy Is in the Streets": From Port Huron to the Siege of Chicago.* New York: Simon and Schuster, 1987.

Millett, Kate. *Sexual Politics.* Garden City, N.Y.: Doubleday, 1970.

Mills, Hilary. *Mailer: A Biography.* New York: Empire, 1982.

Nobile, Philip. *Intellectual Skywriting: Literary Politics and "The New York Review of Books."* New York: Charterhouse, 1974.

Page, Tim, ed. *The Diaries of Dawn Powell.* South Royalston, Vt.: Steerforth, 1995.

Plimpton, George. *Shadow Box.* New York: Putnam's, 1977.

———. *Truman Capote.* New York: Doubleday, 1997.

Podhoretz, Norman. *Breaking Ranks: A Political Memoir.* New York: Harper and Row, 1979.

———. *Doings and Undoings.* New York: Farrar, Straus, & Giroux, 1964.

———. *Ex-Friends: Falling Out with Allen Ginsburg, Lionel and Diana Trilling, Lillian Hellman, Hannah Arendt, and Norman Mailer.* New York: Free Press, 1999.

———. *Making It.* New York: Random House, 1967.

Poirier, Richard. *Norman Mailer.* New York: Viking, 1972.

———. *The Performing Self.* New York: Oxford University Press, 1971.

Polsgrove, Carol. *It Wasn't Pretty, Folks, But Didn't We Have Fun: "Esquire" in the Sixties.* New York: Norton, 1995.

Preston, Charles, and Edward A. Hamilton, eds. *Mike Wallace Asks: Highlights from 46 Controversial Interviews.* New York: Simon and Schuster, 1958.

Ramsey, Roger. "Current and Recurrent: The Vietnam Novel." *Modern Fiction Studies* 17 (Autumn 1971), 415–31.

Robins, Natalie. *Alien Ink: The FBI's War on Freedom of Expression.* New York: William Morrow, 1992.

Rodman, Selden. *Tongues of Fallen Angels.* New York: New Directions, 1974.

Rollyson, Carl. *Lillian Hellman: Her Legend and Her Legacy.* New York: St. Martin's, 1988.

———. *The Lives of Norman Mailer.* New York: Paragon House, 1991.

Ruas, Charles. "Norman Mailer." In *Conversations with American Writers.* New York: Knopf, 1984, 18–36.

Schultz, John. *Motion Will Be Denied: A New Report on the Chicago Conspiracy Trial.* New York: William Morrow, 1972.

Schumacher, Michael. *Dharma Lion: A Biography of Allen Ginsberg.* New York: St. Martin's, 1992.

Sloan, James Park. *Jerzy Kosinski: A Biography.* New York: Dutton, 1996.

Solotaroff, Robert. *Down Mailer's Way.* Urbana: University of Illinois Press, 1974.

Stern, Sydney Ladensohn. *Gloria Steinem: Her Passion, Politics, and Mystique.* New York: Birch Lane, 1997.

Stratton, Richard. "Norman Mailer: The Rolling Stone Interview." *Rolling Stone,* Jan. 2 and Jan. 16, 1975.

Sukenick, Ronald. *Down and In: Life in the Underground.* New York: William Morrow, 1987.

Torres, José, with Bert Sugar. . . . *Sting Like a Bee: The Muhammad Ali Story.* New York: Abelard Schuman, 1971.

Thompson, Hunter S. *The Proud Highway: Saga of a Desperate Southern Gentleman, 1955–1967.* Edited by Douglas Brinkley. New York: Villard, 1997.

Trilling, Diana. *The Beginning of the Journey: The Marriage of Lionel and Diana Trilling.* New York: Harcourt Brace, 1993.

———. *Claremont Essays.* New York: Harcourt Brace, 1964.

———. *We Must March, My Darlings: A Critical Decade.* New York: Harcourt Brace Jovanovich, 1978.

Vidal, Gore. *Palimpsest: A Memoir.* New York: Random House, 1995.

———. *Rocking the Boat.* Boston: Little, Brown, 1962.

von Hoffman, Nicholas. *Citizen Cohn.* New York: Doubleday, 1988.

Wakefield, Dan. *New York in the Fifties.* Boston: Houghton Mifflin, 1992.

Wald, Alan M. *The New York Intellectuals: The Rise and Decline of the Anti-Stalinist Left from the 1930s to the 1980s.* Chapel Hill: University of North Carolina Press, 1987.

Weatherby, W. J. *James Baldwin: Artist on Fire.* New York: Dell, 1990.

West, James L. W. *William Styron: A Life.* New York: Random House, 1998.

Wilson, Rosalind Baker. *Near the Magician: A Memoir of My Father, Edmund Wilson.* New York: Grove Weidenfeld, 1989.

Winters, Shelley. *Shelley, Also Known as Shirley.* New York: Ballantine Books, 1980.

Wright, William. *Lillian Hellman: The Image, the Woman.* New York: Simon and Schuster, 1986.

Wreszin, Michael. *A Rebel in Defense of Tradition: The Life and Politics of Dwight Macdonald.* New York: Basic Books, 1994.

Index